Comparative Politics of the "Third World"

THIRD EDITION

Comparative Politics of the "Third World"

LINKING CONCEPTS & CASES

December Green
Laura Luehrmann

LYNNE
RIENNER
PUBLISHERS

BOULDER
LONDON

Published in the United States of America in 2011 by
Lynne Rienner Publishers, Inc.
1800 30th Street, Boulder, Colorado 80301
www.rienner.com

and in the United Kingdom by
Lynne Rienner Publishers, Inc.
3 Henrietta Street, Covent Garden, London WC2E 8LU

Library of Congress Cataloging-in-Publication Data
Green, December.
Comparative politics of the "Third World" : linking concepts and cases /
    December Green, Laura Luehrmann. — 3rd ed.
        p.   cm.
    Includes bibliographical references and index.
    ISBN 978-1-58826-792-4 (pbk. : alk. paper)
    1. Developing countries—Politics and government—Case studies. 2. Developing
countries—Economic policy—Case studies. I. Luehrmann, Laura, 1969–   II. Title.
JF60.G74   2011
320.309172'4—dc22

                                                            2011011376

British Cataloguing in Publication Data
A Cataloguing in Publication record for this book
is available from the British Library.

Printed and bound in the United States of America

The paper used in this publication meets the requirements
of the American National Standard for Permanence of
Paper for Printed Library Materials Z39.48-1992.

    5 4 3 2 1

To our sons
Luke, Jakob, and Andrew
We watch as you grow with this book . . .

Contents

List of Illustrations   ix
Preface   xi

1   Comparing and Defining Worlds   1

Part 1 Historical Legacies

2   Precolonial History (Or, What Your "World Civ"
    Class Might Have Left Out)   29
3   Colonialism: Gold, God, Glory   43
4   Independence or In Dependence?   55
5   Linking Concepts and Cases   69

Part 2 The International Economic System

6   Growth and Development: A Progress Report   103
7   A New and Improved Structural Adjustment?   141
8   Alternative Approaches to Development   163
9   Linking Concepts and Cases   173

Part 3 Politics and Political Change

10   From Ideas to Action: The Power of Civil Society   193
11   Linking Concepts and Cases   231
12   The Call to Arms: Violent Paths to Change   249
13   Linking Concepts and Cases   285
14   Ballots, Not Bullets: Seeking Democratic Change   303
15   Political Transitions: Real or Virtual?   335
16   Linking Concepts and Cases   349

Part 4 Beyond the Nation-State

17 Sovereignty and the Role of International Organizations   369
18 Global Challenges—and Responses   401
19 Linking Concepts and Cases   421
20 Dealing with a Superpower:
    "Third World" Views of the United States   439
21 Linking Concepts and Cases   447

Part 5 Conclusion

22 Are We Living in a New Era?   467

List of Acronyms   471
Glossary   475
Notes   497
Selected Bibliography   543
Index   553
About the Book   567

Illustrations

Photographs

Peruvian armed forces employees call for higher wages	131
Nigerian workers join May Day (International Workers' Day) celebrations	146
A silent protest against sanctions in Zimbabwe	165
Young and old in Indonesia at a campaign rally for President Susilo Bambang Yudhoyono	219
Pro-Kurdish demonstrators join a sit-in in Turkey	256
A woman casts her ballot in a shantytown in Peru	304
Women voting in the 2009 elections in Iran	338
A woman carries her sick child to a clinic for internally displaced people in Darfur, Sudan	395
A banner protesting Obama's visit reads, "Beware the evil agenda of the United States in Indonesia"	443
An Afghan girl watches a US soldier on patrol in Kandahar	445

Figures

1.1	Global Village of 1,000 People	7
1.2	Mexico: Profile and Map	18
1.3	Peru: Profile and Map	19
1.4	Nigeria: Profile and Map	20
1.5	Zimbabwe: Profile and Map	21
1.6	Iran: Profile and Map	22
1.7	Turkey: Profile and Map	23
1.8	China: Profile and Map	24
1.9	Indonesia: Profile and Map	25
2.1	Early Non-Western Empires	33
2.2	Why Wasn't It China That Conquered the World?	35
2.3	The Transatlantic Slave Trade	41
2.4	The Opium Wars	41
3.1	How Did Europe Conquer the World?	44
3.2	Did Colonialism Benefit Women?	49
3.3	Israel	52

4.1	The Spanish American Experience	56
4.2	Subversion and Other "Weapons of the Weak"	57
4.3	Spiritualism and Nationalist Resistance	58
4.4	Wars of Liberation	59
4.5	Attempts at Industrialization	66
6.1	GNI per Capita for Rich, Middle-Income, and Poor Countries	105
6.2	Human Development Index, 2010 World Rankings	106
6.3	Life Expectancy	107
6.4	Infant Mortality	108
6.5	Literacy	109
6.6	Share of People Living on Less Than One Dollar a Day, by Region	110
6.7	Development with a Deadline: The Millennium Development Goals	111
6.8	Child Labor: A Benefit to the Child?	129
6.9	Total External Debt	135
6.10	Total External Debt as a Share of Gross National Income	136
7.1	Military Budgets and Adjustment	142
7.2	Dollar vs. Yuan: (Why) Do Exchange Rates Matter?	144
7.3	China's Development Refugees Along the Three Gorges Dam	153
7.4	A Zero-Sum Game?	157
7.5	A Small Investment with a Huge Payoff	157
10.1	Do All Muslims Agree?	196
10.2	"Antisocial" Media	204
10.3	Tibet and the Tibetan People	208
10.4	Are All Arabs Muslim? Are All Muslims Arab?	210
10.5	LGBT Rights in the "Third World"	215
10.6	Iran's "Green Movement"	222
12.1	The Kurds	255
12.2	Taiwan: Renegade Province or Independent State?	258
12.3	Something Has Gone Terribly Wrong	260
12.4	Legality as a Tool of State Terror	263
12.5	Militaries in the "Third World"	267
12.6	The Israeli-Palestinian Conflict	275
14.1	Respect for Political and Civil Rights: How Our Cases Rate	307
14.2	Is Democracy Universally Desirable?	309
14.3	When Islamists Win Elections	310
14.4	Elections in China	319
14.5	Shattering Stereotypes	331
14.6	Measuring Gender Empowerment	332
17.1	Genocide in Rwanda . . . and Darfur?	383
17.2	The Timorese Referendum for Independence	385
17.3	NGOs: When Politics and Sports Mix	398
20.1	Could the Next Superpower Come from the "Third World"?	446

Preface

If you were to go back and watch it on YouTube, we bet you'd agree that at the October 2000 presidential debate held at Wake Forest University, the Republican candidate for president of the United States, George W. Bush, sounded unabashedly isolationist. However, less than one year later, as the leader of arguably the most powerful country in the world, he was almost unrecognizable in his views, leading a global war on terrorism. Fast forward ten more years and the United States had another president, Barack Obama. Always more of an internationalist, he had campaigned promising to reach across the divide, to repair damaged relationships and change the world's view of the United States. Yet, he would find this task far more difficult than he had anticipated and was perhaps just as changed as his predecessor by the experience of his first years in office. Although several other issues vied for this president's attention (including the continuing war on terror), his focus turned more inward, as a massive economic crisis posed the paramount challenge for his administration.

Two presidents marked by one period. What is the lesson of this era? Whether it is about saving us from the next 9/11 or pulling us back from the brink of economic depression, even if motivated primarily by self-interest, it is crucial that Americans attempt to understand the world that we are a part of and with which we are inextricably bound—now more than ever. Why? Because, whether we like it or not, a rebalancing of global power is in progress. Political and economic tectonic plates are shifting. If the pundits are correct, what we are witnessing is possibly the biggest shift in wealth, power, and prestige since the industrial revolution, as North America and Europe increasingly are bypassed by fast-growing, emerging economies such as China, India, and Brazil. We need to sit up and pay attention. Because historians tell us that the periods associated with such shifts have been fraught with rising levels of conflict and instability.[1]

These predictions may be overblown for now, of course. As of mid-2011, however, anyone watching must acknowledge the sense of great anxiety in rich industrialized countries (largely due to a burst economic bubble), whereas there is a sense of expanding opportunity, even buoyancy, in much of the rest of the world. Suddenly, it appears that there has been a change. In many countries real progress has been made in reducing debt and deforestation, as well as child and maternal mortality rates. More boys and girls are in school, more people who need anti-AIDS drugs are getting them, the spread of HIV/AIDS and measles has slowed significantly, and there is a new, effective, and affordable vaccine against meningitis. Fewer people are living in absolute poverty, as the world's average gross domestic product (GDP) per capita is 25 percent higher than it was ten years ago. Even sub-Saharan African economies are forecast to have 6 percent growth rates over the next five years—a figure the United States and most of Europe envy.[2] The list goes on.

The point is that the United States is finding itself in an increasingly interconnected and multipolar world, one in which several actors share the stage. This is a new reality: the United States certainly has leverage, but not as much as we had (or thought we had) before. There are limits to US power, and others who have been demanding a share appear on the cusp of taking it. If we are to avoid some of the mistakes of the past, it is crucial that we recognize the importance of perspective—that there are at least two sides to every story (and usually more). If we are to be adequately prepared to respond to the challenges of the future, our understanding of the world must change to include attention to the ostensibly "powerless." We are finding that the so-called powerless aren't simply one-dimensional victims. They have agency. These are the people living in the countries that compose much of what we term the "third world" or the "non-Western world." They are the majority of the world's inhabitants, but they are too often forgotten.

We prepared this book in order to provide a context in which students can begin to analyze such events and develop a greater appreciation not only of the substantive issues under study, but also of the larger issues behind the headlines. We approach the issues with a perspective explicitly designed to foster critical-thinking and decisionmaking skills. Our overarching goal is to increase students' exposure to dynamics in the third world. We explore issues and controversies in these countries, employing an interdisciplinary perspective. We believe that in order to be informed members of modern society, we all need a solid basis in the history, society, politics, and economics of a range of countries, while being reminded that no single case study is representative of such enormous and diverse regions. The complexities of our world demand it.

Throughout the book, we make a conscious attempt to show students why they should care about what happens in the third world, and how they are affected by it. We also attempt to provoke and engage students by offering them a view of the world they don't often see, including one that is often critical of the West. We strongly believe that, all too often, the voices of leaders and citizens in non-Western countries are sorely neglected even in case studies devoted to such countries. In addition, we work to avoid the marginalization of groups such as women, youth, and indigenous peoples. By integrating these groups into discussions of general theory, we hope that students will begin to appreciate the competing perspectives and their bases—and will walk away with a more accurate view of the world around them.

* * *

We received much assistance throughout the duration of this project, and we owe gratitude to many. Special thanks to Dean Charles Taylor of the College of Liberal Arts at Wright State University for his support of this project. We feel fortunate to be part of an institution that truly supports the integration of scholarship and teaching. Our colleagues in the Department of Political Science have been particularly helpful in the formulation and completion of this book. We give special thanks to our chairperson, Donna Schlagheck, and to Charlie Funderburk for their advice and encouragement during its preparation, as well as Joanne Ballmann and Renée Harber for their assistance and moral support. We are grateful to the students who assisted us by providing critical feedback, research assistance, and help with preparing figures throughout the text, especially Ashley Kitchen, Matthew Conaway, and Jacquelyn Schroeder. Sarah Cassidy was also tremendously helpful with the preparation of footnotes throughout the text.

We want to convey our profound debt to our students, whose questions motivated much of the shape of the book. Their insights, curiosities, and frustrations helped clarify what we believe we needed to include in an introductory text.

We are also grateful to all the wonderful people at Lynne Rienner Publishers, but particularly to Lynne Rienner herself, for understanding the need for this book and for going above and beyond, using her experience and expertise, to refine it. Special thanks to Claire Vlcek, Karen Williams, and our excellent copyeditor, Jason Cook, whose diligence has helped us present a clearer, more accurate narrative. What a joy it has been to work with such a professional and courteous staff.

Finally—once again—our families have endured much during the preparation of this book, from truncated holidays, to late-night writing sessions, to the ups and downs of the publishing process. To them, especially David and Joe, we express our deep gratitude and appreciation. You are our rock.

—*December Green*
Laura Luehrmann

1

Comparing and Defining Worlds

No human culture is inaccessible to someone who makes the effort to understand, to learn, to inhabit another world. —*Henry Louis Gates, historian*[1]

In this book we take a comparative approach to the study of Africa, Asia, Latin America, and the Middle East. How should we refer to this immense collection of territories, comprising approximately 80 percent of the world's population? As you'll see,
we are not the first to struggle with what's in a name. Out of all the possibilities, the
most provocative of these must surely be "third world." Why? The term "third world"
(tiers monde) was coined by French demographer Alfred Sauvy. In a 1952 article,
Sauvy borrowed from eighteenth-century writer Emmanuel Joseph Sieyes to compare relatively poor countries of the world to the "third estate" (the people) at the time
of the French Revolution. Sieyes characterized the third estate as ignored, exploited,
and scorned. Sauvy characterized the third world similarly, but pointed out that it,
like the third estate, has the power to overcome its status.[2]

So what's so off-putting, then, about the term "third world"? First and foremost, it
is objectionable for both logical and emotional reasons. WORLD BANK* director Robert
Zoellick has declared that there is no longer a third world.[3] Not only do critics of the term
disdain the concept as unwieldy and obsolete, but they also fault it as distorting reality
in attempting to geopolitically and economically classify a diverse group of countries.

And let's face it, the term "third world" can be fighting words. The phrase carries a lot of negative baggage. Many people cringe at hearing the term and avoid
using it because, at the very least, it sounds condescending and quaintly racist. It is
not unusual for "third world" to be flung as an insult. For some, the term suggests
backwardness. Third world countries are often thought to play a peripheral role in
the world, having no voice and little weight or relevance.

That is certainly not the case, as this book will demonstrate. We acknowledge
the problems with the designation "third world," but gingerly proceed to use the

---

*Terms appearing in small capital letters are defined in the Glossary, which begins on p. 475.

1

phrase (in quotation marks) because there is no clear, clean, perfectly fitting term that doesn't validate one worldview or another. We employ the term "third world" and its synonyms throughout this text, and use it in the title of the book, precisely because it is so politicized, so loaded. But we seek to avoid using it according to its usual meaning. In this book we propose a variation: we use the term "third world" to remind the reader to be cognizant of the oppressive representations associated with it. At the same time, though, we also believe that it is time to recontextualize the concept in the way that Sauvy suggested: his definition of the *tiers monde* is as much about what it can become, as what it currently is.

The geopolitical use of the term dates back to the COLD WAR, the period of US-Soviet rivalry from approximately 1947 to 1989, reflecting the ideological conflict that dominated international relations. For decades following World War II the rich, economically advanced, industrialized countries, also known as the "first world," were pitted against the Soviet-led, communist "second world." In this rivalry, each side described what it was doing as self-defense, and both the first and second worlds claimed to be fighting to "save" the planet from the treachery of the other. Much of this battle was over who would control the nonaligned "third world," which served as the theater for many Cold War conflicts and whose countries were treated as pawns in this chess game. Defined simply as the remainder of the planet—being neither first nor second—the concept of the third world has always been unwieldy, often bringing to mind countries that are poor, agricultural, and overpopulated. Yet consider the stunning diversity that exists among the countries of every region of the world: surely they cannot all be lumped into a single category and characterized as such today. For example, how do we categorize China? It is clearly led by a communist regime (and therefore is second world), but during the Cold War it viewed itself as the leader of the third world. What about Israel or South Africa? Because of the dramatic disparities within these countries, they can be categorized as third world or first, depending on where we look. The same can be said for the United States. Visit parts of its inner cities, the rural South, or Appalachia, and you will find the third world. And now, with the Cold War long over, why aren't the former republics of the Soviet Union included in most studies of the third world? Certainly the poorest of them are more third world than first.

The fact is, many countries fall between the cracks when we use the first world–third world typology. Some of the countries labeled "third world" are oil-rich, while others have been industrializing for so long that even the term "NEWLY INDUSTRIAL-IZING COUNTRIES" (NICs) is dated (it is still used, but has largely been replaced by "emerging economies"). Therefore, in appreciation of the diversity contained within the third world, perhaps it is useful to subdivide it, to allow for specificity by adding more categories. Under this schema, the emerging countries and a few others that are most appropriately termed "developing countries" are labeled "third world" (e.g., China, India, South Korea, Brazil, Mexico). "Fourth world" countries become those that are not industrializing, but have some resources to sell on the world market (e.g., Ghana, Bolivia, Egypt), or some strategic value that wins them a bit of foreign assistance. The label "less developed country" (LDC) is the best fit in most of these cases, since it simply describes their situation and implies little in terms of their prospects for DEVELOPMENT. And finally, we have the "fifth world," which Henry Kissinger once callously characterized as "the basket cases of the world." These are the world's poorest countries. Sometimes known as "least–less developed countries" (LLDCs), they are very clearly underdeveloping. With little to sell on the world market, they are eclipsed by it. The poorest in the world, with the worst ratings for virtually every marker of human development, these countries are marginalized and utterly dependent on what little foreign assistance they receive.

Today it is more common to hear the STATES of these regions variously referred to as "developing countries," "less developed countries," or "underdeveloped countries." Currently in vogue are also the stripped-down, minimalist terms "low-income countries" (LICs) and "high-income countries" (HICs). These are just a few of the labels used to refer to a huge expanse of territories and peoples, and none are entirely satisfactory. First, our subject—comprising four major world regions—is so vast and so heterogeneous that it is difficult to speak of it as a single entity. Second, each name has its own political implications and each insinuates a political message. For example, although some countries contained within these regions are better off than others, only an optimist would label all of them as "developing countries." Some of the countries we'll be looking at are simply not developing. They are *underdeveloping*— losing ground, becoming worse-off.[4]

Those who prefer the term "developing countries" tend to support the idea that the capitalist path of free markets will eventually lead to peace and prosperity for all. Capitalism is associated with rising prosperity in some countries such as South Korea and Mexico, but even in these countries the majority of people have yet to share in many of its benefits. However, the relative term "less developed countries" prompts the question: Less developed than whom—or what? The answer, inevitably, is what we arbitrarily label "developed countries": the rich, industrialized states of Western Europe, Canada, and the United States, also known as the West (a term that, interestingly enough, includes Japan but excludes most of the countries of the Western Hemisphere).

Although the people who talk about such things often throw about the terms "developed" or "less developed" as a shorthand measure of economic advancement, often such names are resented because they imply that "less developed" countries are somehow lacking in other, broader measures of political, social, or cultural development. Use of the term "developing," or any of these terms for that matter, suggests that countries can be ranked along a continuum. Such terms can be used to imply that the West is best, that the rest of the world is comparatively "backward," and that the most the citizens of the rest of the world can hope for is to "develop" using the West as model.

At the other end of the spectrum are those who argue that the West developed only at the expense of the rest of the world. For these analysts, underdevelopment is no natural event or coincidence. Rather, it is the outcome of hundreds of years of active underdevelopment by today's developed countries. The majority's resistance to such treatment, its efforts to change its situation, is sometimes referred to as the North-South conflict, or the war between the haves and the have-nots of the world. The names "North" and "South" are useful because they are stripped of the value judgments contained within most of the terms already described. However, they are as imprecise as the term "West," since "North" refers to developed countries, which mostly fall north of the equator, and "South" is another name for less developed countries, which mostly fall south of the equator.

Another name signifying location, the all-inclusive "non-Western world," invites still more controversy. As others have demonstrated, it is probably more honest to speak of "the West and the rest" if we are to use this kind of term, since there are many non-Wests rather than a single non-Western world.[5] At least "the West and the rest" is blatantly straightforward in its Eurocentric center of reference, dismissing 75 percent of the world's population and treating "the rest" as "other." In the same manner that the term "nonwhite" is demeaning, "non-Western" implies that something is missing. Our subject becomes defined only through its relationship to a more central "West."

Clearly none of the names we use to describe the countries of Africa, Asia, Latin America, and the Middle East are satisfactory. Even the terms "Latin America" and "Middle East" are problematic. Not all of Latin America is "Latin" in the sense of being Spanish- or Portuguese-speaking. Yet we will use this term as shorthand for the entire region south of the US border, including the Caribbean. And the idea of a region being "Middle East" only makes sense if one's perspective is distinctly European—otherwise, what is it "middle" to? The point is that most of our labels reflect some bias, and none of them are fully satisfactory. These names are all ideologically loaded in one way or another. Because there is no simple, clearly most appropriate identifier available, we will use each and all of them as markers of the varying worldviews presented in this text. Ultimately, we leave it to the reader to sift through the material presented here, consider the debates, and decide which arguments—and therefore which terminologies—are most representative of the world and therefore most useful.

What's to Compare?

In this introduction to the COMPARATIVE STUDIES of Africa, Asia, Latin America, and the Middle East, we take a different spin on the traditional approach in order to discuss much more than politics as it is often narrowly defined. As one of the social sciences, political science has traditionally focused on the study of formal political institutions and behavior. In this book, we choose not to put the spotlight on governments and voting patterns, party politics, and so on. Rather, we turn our attention to all manner of political behavior, which we consider to include just about any aspect of life. Of interest to us is not only how people are governed, but also how they live, how they govern themselves, and what they see as their most urgent concerns.

We employ a political interaction approach. It is an eclectic method that presents ideas from a variety of contemporary thinkers and theories. We characterize this as a comparative studies rather than a comparative politics textbook because our approach is multidisciplinary. We divide our attention among history, politics, society, and economics in order to convey more fully the complexity of human experience.[6] Instead of artificially confining ourselves to one narrow discipline, we recognize that each discipline offers another layer or dimension, which adds immeasurably to our understanding of the "essence" of politics.[7]

Comparative studies, then, is much more than simply a subject of study—it is also a means of study. It employs what is known as the comparative method. Through the use of the comparative method we seek to describe, identify, and explain trends—in some cases, even predict human behavior. Those who adopt this approach, known as comparativists, are interested in identifying relationships and patterns of behavior and interactions between individuals and groups. Focusing on one or more countries, comparativists examine CASE STUDIES alongside one another. They search for similarities and differences between and among the elements selected for comparison. For example, one might compare patterns of female employment and fertility rates in one country in relation to those patterns in other countries. Using the comparative method, analysts make explicit or implicit comparisons, searching for common and contrasting features. Some do a "most similar systems" analysis, looking for differences between cases that appear to have a great deal in common (e.g., Canada and the United States). Others prefer a "most different" approach, looking for commonalities between cases that appear diametrically opposed in experience (e.g., Bolivia and India).[8] What is particularly exciting about this type of analysis is stumbling upon unexpected parallels between ostensibly different cases. Just as satisfying is beginning to understand the significance and consequences of the differences that exist between cases assumed to have much in common.

Most comparative studies textbooks take one of two roads. Either they offer case studies, which provide loads of intricate detail on a handful of states (often the classics: Mexico, Nigeria, China, and India; curiously, the Middle East is frequently ignored), or they provide a CROSS-NATIONAL ANALYSIS that purports to generalize about much larger expanses of territory. Those who take the cross-national approach are interested in getting at the big picture. Texts that employ it focus on theory and concepts to broaden our scope of understanding beyond a handful of cases. They often end up making fairly sweeping generalizations. The authors of these books may reference any number of countries as illustration, but at the loss of detail and context that comes only through the use of case studies.

We provide both cross-national analysis and case studies, because we don't want to lose the strengths of either approach. We present broad themes and concepts, while including attention to the variations that exist in reality. In adopting this hybrid approach, we have set for ourselves a more ambitious task. However, as teachers, we recognize the need for both approaches to be presented. We have worked hard to show how cross-national analysis and case studies can work in tandem, how each complements the other. By looking at similar phenomena in several contexts (i.e., histories, politics, societies, economics, and international relations of the third world, more generally), we can apply our cases and compare them, illustrating the similarities and differences experienced in different settings.

Therefore, in addition to the cross-national analysis that composes the bulk of each chapter, we offer eight case studies, two from each of the major regions of the third world. For each region we include the "classics" offered in virtually every text that applies the case method to the non-Western experience: Mexico, Nigeria, China, and Iran. We offer these cases for the same reasons that so many others see fit to include them. However, we go further. To temper the tendency to view these cases as somehow representative of their regions, and to enhance the basis for comparison, we submit alongside the classics other, less predictable case studies from each region. These additional cases are equally interesting and important in their own regard; they are countries that are rarely (if ever) included as case studies in introductory textbooks: Peru, Zimbabwe, Turkey, and Indonesia. (See the maps and country profiles in Figures 1.2 to 1.9 at the end of this chapter.)

Through detailed case studies, we learn what is distinctive about the many peoples of the world, and get a chance to begin to see the world from a perspective other than our own. We can begin doing comparative analysis by thinking about what makes the people of the world alike and what makes us different. We should ask ourselves how and why such differences exist, and consider the various constraints under which we all operate. We study comparative politics not only to understand the way other people view the world, but also to make better sense of our own understanding of it. We have much to learn from how similar problems are approached by different groups of people. To do this we must consider the variety of factors that serve as context, to get a better idea of why things happen and why events unfold as they do.[9] The better we get at this, the better idea we will have of what to expect in the future. And we will get a better sense of what works and what doesn't work so well—in the cases under examination, but also in other countries. You may be tempted to compare the cases under review with the situation in your country. And that's to be encouraged, since the study of how others approach problems may offer us ideas on how to improve our own lives. Comparativists argue that drawing from the experience of others is really the only way to understand our own systems. Seeing beyond the experience of developed countries and what is immediately familiar to us expands our minds, allows us to see the wider range of alternatives, and offers new insights into the challenges we face at the local, national, and international levels.

The greatest insight, however, comes with the inclusion of a larger circle of voices—beyond those of the leaders and policymakers. Although you will certainly hear the arguments of leaders in the chapters that follow, you will also hear the voices of those who are not often represented in texts such as this. You will hear stories of domination and the struggle against it. You will hear not only how people have been oppressed, but also how they have liberated themselves.[10] Throughout the following chapters we have worked to include the standpoints and perspectives of the ostensibly "powerless": the poor, youth, and women. Although they are often ignored by their governments, including the US government, hearing their voices is a necessity if we are to fully comprehend the complexity of the challenges all of us face. Until these populations are included and encouraged to participate to their fullest potential, development will be distorted and delayed. Throughout this book, in a variety of ways, we will give attention to these groups and their interests within our discussions of history, economics, society, politics, and international relations.

Cross-National Comparison: Recurrent Themes

As mentioned earlier, we believe that any introductory study of the third world should include both the specificity of case study as well as the breadth of the cross-national approach. Throughout the chapters that follow you will find several recurring themes (GLOBALIZATION, human rights, the environment, and AIDS), which will be approached from a number of angles and will serve as a basis for cross-national comparison. For example, not only is it interesting and important to understand the difference in the experience of AIDS in Zimbabwe as opposed to Iran, it is just as important to understand how religion, poverty, and war may contribute to the spread of the disease. In addition, in trying to understand AIDS, we should be aware of its

Figure 1.1 Global Village of 1,000 People

Imagine that the world is a village of 1,000 people. Who are its residents?

585 Asians
123 Africans
95 East and West Europeans
84 Latin Americans
55 Russians and citizens of the former Soviet republics
52 North Americans
6 people of the Pacific

The people of the village have considerable difficulty in communicating:

165 speak Mandarin
86 speak English
83 speak Hindu/Urdu
64 speak Spanish
58 speak Russian
37 speak Arabic

This list accounts for the native tongues of only half the villagers. The other half speak, in descending order of frequency, Bengali, Portuguese, Indonesian, Japanese, German, French, and over 200 other languages.

In this village of 1,000 there are:

329 Christians (among them 187 Catholics, 84 Protestants, 31 Orthodox)
178 Muslims
132 Hindus
60 Buddhists
3 Jews
298 people belonging to other religions, as well as people who describe themselves as atheist or nonreligious.

One-third of these 1,000 people in the world village are children, and only 60 are over the age of sixty-five. Half the children are immunized against preventable infectious diseases such as measles and polio. Just under half of the married women in the village have access to and use modern contraceptives.

This year 28 babies will be born; 10 people will die, 3 of them from lack of food, 1 from cancer, and 2 of them babies; and 1 person will be infected with the HIV virus. With 28 births and 10 deaths, the population of the village next year will be 1,018.

In this 1,000-person community, 200 people receive 80 percent of the income; another 200 receive only 2 percent of the income. Only 70 people own an automobile (although some of them own more than one car). About one-third have access to clean, safe drinking water. Of the 670 adults in the village, half are illiterate.

The village has 6 acres of land per person:

700 acres are cropland
1,400 acres are pasture
1,900 acres are woodland
2,000 acres are desert, tundra, pavement, and wasteland

Of this land, the woodland is declining rapidly; the wasteland is increasing. The other land categories are roughly stable. The village allocates 83 percent of its fertilizer to 40 percent of its cropland—that owned by the richest and best-fed 270 people. Excess fertilizer running off this land causes pollution in lakes and wells. The remaining 60 percent of the land, with its 17 percent of the fertilizer, produces 28 percent of the food grains and feeds 73 percent of the people. The average grain yield of that land is one-third the harvest achieved by the richer villagers.

In this village of 1,000 people there are

5 soldiers
7 teachers
1 doctor
3 refugees driven from their homes by war or drought

The village has a total yearly budget, public and private, of over $3 million—$3,000 per person if it were distributed evenly. Of this total:

Figure 1.1 *continues*

Figure 1.1 continued

$181,000 goes to weapons and warfare
$159,000 goes to education
$132,000 goes to healthcare

The village has buried beneath it enough explosive power in nuclear weapons to blow itself up many times over. These weapons are under the control of just 100 of the people. The other 900 people are watching them with deep anxiety, wondering whether they can learn to get along together; and if they do, whether they might set off the weapons anyway through inattention or technical bungling; and if they ever decide to dismantle the weapons, where in the world village they would dispose of the radioactive materials of which the weapons are made.

Sources: Adapted from Donella H. Meadows, "If the World Were a Village of One Thousand People," Sustainability Institute, 2000; and North-South Centre of the Council of Europe, "If the World Were a Village of One Thousand People," www.nscentre.org.

impact on development, how ordinary people are attempting to cope with it, and what they (with or without world leaders) are prepared to do to fight it.

In a variety of ways and to varying degrees, globalization, human rights abuse, environmental degradation, the emergence of new and deadly diseases, international migration, and the drug trade are all indicative of a growing world INTERDEPENDENCE. By interdependence we are referring to a relationship of mutual (although not equal) vulnerability and sensitivity that exists between the world's peoples. This shared dependence has grown out of a rapidly expanding web of interactions that tie us closer together. Most Americans understand that what we do as a nation often affects others—for better or worse. On the other hand, it is more of a stretch to get the average American to understand why we should care and why we need to understand what is happening in the world around us—even in far-off "powerless" countries. However, whether we choose to recognize it or not, it is becoming more and more difficult to escape the fact that our relationship with the world is a reciprocal one. What happens on the other side of the planet, even in small, seemingly "powerless" countries, does affect us—whether we like it or not.

Globalization

The end of the Cold War opened a window of opportunity that has resulted not only in some dramatic political changes, but also in a closer INTEGRATION of the world's economies than ever before. As a result, the world is becoming increasingly interconnected by a single, global economy. This transformative process is commonly described as *globalization,* and it is supported and driven by the full force of capitalism, unimpeded now because of the absence of virtually any competing economic IDEOLOGY. The world has experienced periods of corporate globalization before (the last was associated with European imperialism). What is unique about the current cycle is the unprecedented speed with which globalization is tearing down barriers to trade. It is also increasing mobility, or cross-border flows of not only trade, but also capital, technology, information—and people. As it has before, technology is driving this wave. The Internet is as symbolic of this era as the Berlin Wall was of the Cold

War. Because of their mobility and global reach, MULTINATIONAL CORPORATIONS (MNCs) are key actors (but hardly the only actors) in this globalization. This is a process that is rapidly unfolding and under no one's control. In fact, even some of its advocates maintain that globalization may be out of control.[11]

For those who embrace globalization, its dynamism and power are part of its appeal. They consider globalization to be a largely benevolent process. They see it as the surest route to development and prosperity—it is even credited with sowing the seeds of DEMOCRACY worldwide. Because of globalization, no corner of the world remains isolated; new values are being spread that challenge traditional belief systems such as fatalism, elitism, and AUTHORITARIANISM. Poverty is alleviated as trade is increased and jobs are created; as the lines of communication are opened, we learn from and begin to accept one another. Ideally, globalization will help to make us more aware of our common interests, our mutual dependence. Among other things, it has brought people together to form the basis of the international environmental movement; it has enhanced scientific cooperation and raised human rights as a universal concern (which some refer to as "moral globalization" or "the globalization of dissent").[12]

According to its admirers, globalization is spilling over into a variety of areas, creating a "world village" based in cultural and political globalization. As it works to overcome the barriers between us, globalization enhances interdependence. It tightens the web of interrelationships that link the world's peoples. Social media no doubt facilitated the wave of protests that swept much of North Africa and the Middle East in 2011. Thanks to globalization, this deepening interdependence is fostering a sense of community and sharing over the identity politics that once divided us by religion, ethnicity, language, and so on. (Although interestingly, some analysts who generally favor globalization argue that being wired for a free flow of information can actually produce hostility and anger. Much of this "shared" information promotes stereotyping and reinforces divisions.[13])

Some analysts go even so far as to suggest that we are moving toward a "post-cultural" world, increasingly blurring the boundaries marking where one culture ends and another begins. They contend that globalization is not promoting homogenization and that it is not the same thing as Westernization; rather, globalization is promoting eclecticism and advancing our recognition of the world's diversity. So-called traditional cultures aren't so traditional. None of the world's cultures have developed in a vacuum, unaffected by outside forces. Even those concerned about globalization's impact acknowledge that cultures aren't static. They are always changing—globalization is just hurrying the process along.

In this sense, perhaps it can be said that globalization is producing a more homogeneous world.[14] Then again, antiglobalists maintain that a more homogeneous world means cultural devastation for the majority. Globalization is a cultural bulldozer. Already the dollar has become the de facto global currency, and English has become the de facto global language. One of the most visible signs of this is the spread of Western consumer culture. While this is something proglobalists generally celebrate, critics despise it as "coca-colonization."[15]

Critics argue that globalization isn't so much about interdependence as it is about furthering dependence. Dependence is a form of international interdependence—except that dependence is marked by an extreme power imbalance. Antiglobalists point out that economic globalization is capitalist globalization, which means that corporations and the rich are being privileged over other social actors. The result isn't anything new. Poverty, the exploitation of the underdog, the erosion of labor and environmental standards, and the abuse of human rights all predate globalization. The difference is that globalization has accelerated and intensified these trends.

Even the proponents of corporate globalization acknowledge that it does create winners and losers; globalization brings profits but also problems. They also recognize that globalization is not a uniform process, and that its effects are more evident in some places than in others. Certainly, aspects of globalization such as deregulation or disappearing trade barriers are more obvious in some places than in others (e.g., the creation of trading blocs within Europe and North America). Thus far, globalization is uneven: it appears to have hardly touched the most economically underdeveloped countries in the world, such as those in the Sahel.[16] Yet this is increasingly the exception, and the rapid economic, sociocultural, and political change associated with globalization is the rule worldwide.

Its boosters argue that for better or worse, globalization is inexorable and inevitable; the INTEGRATION of the world's peoples has gone so far that we can never go back. However, history shows us that even this massive force could be reversed by international events. NATIONALISM and economic downturns have in the past contributed to the end of previous cycles of globalization.[17] The current global financial crisis, which most economists believe began in the United States in 2007, has definitely affected the rest of the world. If it continues for long, or if we enter into a dreaded "double-dip" recession, it could also mean a return to economic nationalism and protectionist policies that could very quickly shred this interdependent web.

Human Rights

The idea that humans share certain natural, universal, and inherent rights—simply because they are human—dates at least as far back as John Locke's *Two Treatises of Civil Government* (1690). The view that abusers should be held accountable for their wrongs, or that others should interfere with how a government treats its own citizens, has more recent origins. It was not until the systematic murder of millions under Adolf Hitler's Third Reich that the world became willing to challenge two dominant principles of international relations: NONINTERVENTION, or the legal obligation to refrain from involvement in the internal affairs of other states, and SOVEREIGNTY, the widely shared belief that STATES are the principal actors in international relations and as such they are subject to no higher political authority.[18]

However, the Holocaust served as a catalyst to the development of what is now recognized as an international human rights movement. The Holocaust ostensibly taught us that in some cases the world must intervene against abusers and that state sovereignty must not always be held as sacrosanct. How a government treats its own people does affect the rest of us—and it is being increasingly recognized across the POLITICAL SPECTRUM that the persistent denial of human rights around the world must be reconceptualized as a security issue. If nothing else, respect for human rights is widely recognized as essential to international peace and stability. At least in theory, the international community accepts that it has a moral mandate to prevent the kinds of abuses associated with the genocide in Europe.

Over the fifty years following the Holocaust, the world community set out to develop a variety of international norms to promote human rights and to institutionalize safeguards against the recurrence of atrocities. Prominent in this effort was the creation of the UNIVERSAL DECLARATION OF HUMAN RIGHTS (UDHR) in 1948, which is widely recognized as the most authoritative and comprehensive of all international statements on human rights. Composed of thirty articles addressing a broad range of issues, the UDHR is accepted as setting the standards to which all states should aspire. The UDHR includes attention to what are sometimes known as "first-generation" or "blue" rights: civil and political rights, such as freedom of speech, freedom of religion, freedom from torture or cruel and unusual punishment, the right to DUE PROCESS, the right to SELF-DETERMINATION, and so on. These rights are based on the assumption that the individual should be protected against state actions that are unusual, arbitrary, or excessive. As long as the right to challenge the government's misuse of authority is permitted, other rights (such as freedom from torture) will be safeguarded. First-generation rights are considered by many people to be key to the enjoyment of all other rights. Yet the UDHR also recognizes the importance of "second-generation" or "red" rights: economic, social, and cultural rights, such as access to food, shelter, work, education, and healthcare. This conception of human rights, sometimes known as the "human-needs" approach, considers the aspects of existence necessary to secure the basic development of the person as primary. Proponents of second-generation rights maintain that a government's denial of basic needs is as much a violation of human rights as torture of dissidents.[19]

Although the governments of virtually every country in the world use the language of human rights and claim to believe in the inherent dignity of human beings, for many years the world has been divided over how most appropriately to define human rights. The governments of most developed countries, especially the United States, have traditionally argued that political and civil rights should be prioritized. They contend that these rights, which place an emphasis on liberty, should come first, because the enjoyment of such freedoms will enable the individual to ensure for him- or herself the provision of subsistence or red rights. Yet who cares about freedom of expression and the other blue rights when one's children are dying of hunger? As the former president of Senegal, Leopold Senghor, put it, "Human rights begin with breakfast." He and others argue that those who seek to exclude red rights have it all wrong, since until people's basic rights, or certain minimal physical needs, are met, there can be no development—let alone enjoyment of more ambitious rights, such as liberties. (Others point out that for low-income countries, government guarantees of food and housing are actually much more ambitious than the relatively "cost-free" guarantees of freedoms, such as expression and assembly. Nobel laureate Amartya Sen maintains that the right to freedom of speech is a precondition for all other rights, since famine, torture, and other abuses rarely occur in countries with democratic governments and a relatively free press.[20])

The UDHR, whose drafters included Westerners and non-Westerners, attempts to get around this debate by proclaiming that human rights are indivisible, interdependent, and interrelated, and that all are necessary for the full realization of human potential. Not everyone agrees. According to the proponents of CULTURAL RELATIVISM, including those who support the "Asian values" argument, human rights (or moral claims) should be defined as the product of a particular society's cultural and historical experience. Therefore, according to the cultural relativists, the proponents of UNIVERSALISM are imposing their conception of human rights on others. For cultural relativists, political and civil rights are based in Western Enlightenment values, which have little appeal or relevance in Confucian cultures, wherein higher value is placed on order and discipline. Blue rights also uphold the rights of the individual over those of the community. This idea is unacceptable in many non-Western cultures, which often hold that the rights of the individual should be subordinated to those of the group, since the individual has no meaning apart from the community to which he or she belongs.[21]

Critics of the "Asian values" argument point to the complexity not only of Confucianism, which is not as conservative as many think, but also of Asian cultures themselves, of which there are a great variety and diversity. Asian cultures draw from many different influences, including Buddhism, which emphasizes individual freedoms and tolerance. Millions of non-Westerners, led by people such as Aung San Suu Kyi and Shirin Ebadi, reject arguments that political and civil rights or freedoms (such as freedom from torture) are uniquely Western. Many non-Western traditions view the individual and community as inseparable, and the relationship between the rights of the individual and the rights of the community as one of mutual obligation. While group rights can be used to restrict individuals, they can also exist to protect individual rights.[22]

As you might imagine, this and other debates over how best to define human rights have hamstrung international efforts to promote such rights. However, there is new momentum behind the human rights movement. Just as the Holocaust once spurred a concern with human rights, perhaps it was the specter of ethnic cleansing, its mass killing and systematic rapes, and the "too little, too late" responses in Bosnia and Rwanda that have propelled this renewed interest. Once again, the human rights movement is developing—and not only toward finding other ways of holding accountable those responsible for such atrocities. The challenges associated with globalization have led to calls for expanding and refining the scope of human rights and including a third generation of "new" human rights. Debate has begun over whether other important values, such as rights to peace, development, and a safe and healthy environment (or "green" rights), qualify as human rights. Are rights to clean drinking water and to live in safety legally enforceable claims, or merely "wishes"? The third generation of rights remains the subject of heated debate. Yet even for the older generations of rights, there remain enormous differences among the governments of the world over how to define human rights, how and when human rights law should apply, and what priority should be given to different categories of rights. While this highly politicized debate continues, it is increasingly common for analysts to return to the argument that is at the core of the Universal Declaration of Human Rights: that the distinction between human rights and human needs is an artificial one. Rather, civil, political, economic, social, and cultural rights are best understood as part of a "seamless web"—indivisible and interdependent.[23] In other words, all the rights discussed here are important because it is difficult to fully enjoy one category of rights without the security offered by the others.

The Environment

Along with globalization and human rights, the health of the planet is another issue of interdependence (and also one that is arguably everyone's business). Environmental issues will turn up in nearly all of the following chapters because the growing body of scientific evidence is becoming more difficult to refute. Development as it is currently being pursued, in both developed and less developed countries, is contributing to a morass of environmental problems that transcend national borders and whose management will require global cooperation. Climate change, deforestation, desertification, loss of biodiversity, depletion of fisheries and destruction of coral reefs, toxic dumping, water shortages—these are just a few of the problems that will require international solutions.[24]

Take, for example, the issue of deforestation. Between 2000 and 2010, the world's remaining rainforests suffered a net loss of 13 million hectares (an area about the size of Costa Rica) each year. However, thanks to local and international efforts, the rate of deforestation has actually decreased (from 16 million hectares destroyed annually in the 1990s). Indonesia and Brazil (which had the highest rates of loss a few years ago) have made particularly impressive efforts to slow the destruction of their forests. But deforestation is still a problem and it is most extensive in South America and Africa, where forests are hot spots for biodiversity (they contain hundreds of species within a single hectare, whereas the average hectare of forest typically contains a handful of species). With a loss of 70 percent of the natural cover protecting them in the past several decades, many of these species have become endangered or extinct. According to the United Nations Environment Programme (UNEP), species are becoming extinct at the fastest rate known in geological history, and this is directly tied to human activities.[25]

Related to deforestation and of similar cataclysmic impact is the threat posed by climate change. According to UN Secretary-General Ban Ki-moon, it is the major, overriding environmental issue of our time, a growing crisis that will have economic repercussions but also consequences for human health, safety, food production, and security.[26] Of central concern is the GREENHOUSE EFFECT, which is produced by the emission of what have come to be known as greenhouse gases: carbon dioxide released by the burning of fossil fuels, as well as naturally occurring methane and nitrogen. Industrialization and economic GROWTH fueled by hydrocarbon-based energy systems (coal, oil, and natural gas) have contributed to the release of these gases, which have reached record highs. These greenhouse gases collect in the upper atmosphere, covering the planet in a blanket of sorts. Incoming heat from the sun penetrates this blanket but is then trapped by it. The effect is likened to a greenhouse, which traps heat indoors. In this sense, the growth of economies based on the consumption of fossil fuels has contributed substantially to global warming over the past fifty years.

While some scientists and politicians argue that global warming is not a human-made event, but naturally occurring and inevitable—part of a long cycle of alternating ice ages and periods of extreme heat—this is the minority view. The majority of the world's scientists agree that we are experiencing a global warming; the main issue under debate is how severe it will be—and how soon it will come. The Intergovernmental Panel on Climate Change (IPCC), the Nobel Peace Prize–winning group of more than 2,000 scientists from a hundred countries, claims to have amassed convincing evidence that climate change is already happening. The past ten years (2000–2010) have been the hottest since records have been kept, and concentrations of greenhouse gases have reached unprecedented levels. According to these scientists, there is overwhelming evidence that the Earth's climate is undergoing dramatic transformation because of human activities. They call this "anthropogenic warming" and warn that it may continue for decades even if human-made emissions can be curbed.[27] If fossil fuel combustion continues even at twentieth-century levels, virtually every natural system and human economy will be at risk. Higher temperatures will mean rising seas from melting glaciers and ice sheets, more frequent and severe storms, and more intense droughts. These changes will alter every ecosystem on the planet, as pests and diseases will spread to areas where they were previously unknown. There is alarming evidence that we may have reached or surpassed tipping points that could lead to irreversible changes in major ecosystems. Climate change is already exacerbating the misery of already poor areas, creating a vicious cycle in which poverty and environmental degradation coexist and accelerate through globalization.[28]

In a variety of ways, the globalization of the past few decades is just hastening processes that were already well under way. However, because of its speed, globalization is putting unprecedented pressure on the planet's capacities. Displaced rural populations are migrating into cities in search of livelihood, or into forests in search of new resources. This only contributes to the greenhouse effect, not just because the burning of forests releases more carbon dioxide into the atmosphere, but also because the loss of these forests means the loss of "pollution sponges," since forests absorb carbon dioxide and slow global warming. As low-income countries embrace the developed-country model, pursuing growth at any cost, they will add to these problems. However, as it currently stands, the 20 percent of the world's population living in developed countries consumes 80 percent of the world's resources. In 2006 China surpassed the United States as the largest emitter of greenhouse gases (producing 22 percent of the world's total), but the United States is close behind, producing just under 20 percent of the emissions associated with global warming (India and Russia each contribute about 5 percent).[29] It is less developed countries (those who contribute the lowest levels of carbon dioxide and other gases) that are likely to feel the most severe impact of environmental devastation. Not only are they more vulnerable to many of its effects, but these low- and middle-income countries also are likely to lack access to the technologies that might ameliorate its impact. Over the past few years, a number of creative solutions based on cooperative efforts have been proposed for dealing with the environmental problems that we share. Unfortunately, finger-pointing and recriminations between advanced and emerging economies, and efforts by each to shift the burden of responsibility to the other, suggest that the international leadership (and funding) so desperately needed to address these problems will remain sorely lacking.

Disease

Just as environmental degradation is taking an increasing toll on all of us, so is disease. Again, it will be the poorest who are hit hardest and have the least capacity to cope with the challenge. Not only is there an income gap between developed and less developed countries, but there is also a health gap. A variety of threats come together to explain why infant and maternal mortality rates remain higher in low-income countries and why life expectancy is still relatively short in so many of them: undernutrition, infectious diseases, and chronic debilitating diseases—are all associated with poverty. These problems contribute to much of the misery and hardship found in the regions we will study. Although cardiovascular diseases are the biggest killers of adults worldwide, infectious diseases, such as tuberculosis, malaria, and HIV/AIDS, kill millions every year. For example, HIV/AIDS is the leading cause of death of women aged fifteen to forty-nine. The good news is that after four decades of fighting the disease, it appears that the epidemic peaked in 1999 and the world has since begun to halt and reverse its spread. Globally the rate of new infections is down by 19 percent. More people than ever are getting tested (although only about 40 percent of us know our status). Of those needing treatment, more people than ever are receiving the medicines that can dramatically prolong and improve quality of life. And it is now possible to virtually eliminate mother-to-child transmission of HIV/AIDS. In many ways, our global investment in prevention and treatment is working. However, approximately 33 million people worldwide are living with HIV/AIDS, and 10 million of them, living in middle- and low-income countries, are denied access to these medicines because of their cost. In 2009, for the first time, global funding for programs to treat and prevent HIV/AIDS flattened. If this trend continues and money dries up, clinics will close, people who need testing and treatment will be turned away, and the fragile progress that the world has made in dealing with this disease will be undermined.[30]

HIV/AIDS is by no means a problem unique to the third world, and within the third world it varies by region. However, most people living with HIV/AIDS reside in low-income countries (68 percent of AIDS patients are African, though it is important to note that some regions of Africa, such as western Africa in general, are not as seriously affected as others, such as southern Africa).[31] Throughout the world, this viral infection is spread through sexual contact and other activities involving the exchange of body fluids. In rich and poor countries alike, people become infected with HIV in a variety of ways, including blood transfusions, intravenous drug use, and both heterosexual and homosexual sex. Each country and region has its own particular mix of circumstances reflected by patterns of transmission. As we will see in Chapter 7, poverty is a major factor contributing to the spread of the disease.

In most countries, squeamishness about addressing sensitive social norms plays a role in the spread of HIV.[32] Many leaders refuse to recognize that especially vulnerable groups, such as drug addicts, gay men, and sex workers, exist. In addition, because of social taboos, there is still a striking lack of awareness about how HIV is spread. Fearing punitive laws, stigma, and discrimination, people are ignorant about how to protect themselves or to know their status. Worldwide, men who have sex with men may be imprisoned or lynched. People living with AIDS are reluctant to obtain access to the medical care that can dramatically improve their quality of life (and reduce the chances of spreading the disease).[33] Multiple heterosexual relationships (for men) may be socially tolerated or even encouraged. Other practices considered traditional, such as early marriage, female genital cutting, and wife inheritance, also contribute to the spread of the disease. Related to this are imbalances of power that often put females at risk of HIV infection. Given their unequal access to economic resources, women or girls may take part in transactional sex (exchanging sex for money, goods, accommodations, or other basic needs) as a survival strategy. Females of all ages, especially young women (and married women), often have a difficult time rejecting a man's sexual advances or insisting he wear a condom, since many cultures—Western and non-Western—teach females to be subordinate to male authority.

In the long term, changing how males and females relate to each other and how men treat women and girls will amount to a fundamental advance not only against this disease, but also against many other barriers to development. In the near term, however, smaller, more mundane efforts must be made. For example, the Ugandan, Brazilian, and Thai governments were all early adopters, taking proactive measures to promote health education and safer sex before the leaders of many developed countries had even broached the subject. But in the communities of many high- and low-income countries, there is still a great deal of ignorance about the disease. Condoms are not regularly used (when available) and are stigmatized for a number of reasons. Women who request that their partners wear them are often treated with suspicion. Where fertility is celebrated and child mortality rates are high, condoms are rejected because they are a form of birth control.

However, male and female condoms, vaginal microbicides, and other tools are a crucial means of helping women to take their lives (and the lives of their children) into their own hands. Without access to information and services to protect themselves, more women are infected with HIV every day. What was once thought to be a "gay male disease" has shifted, and worldwide, half of all people living with AIDS are female. In the past few years the number of new infections among females has grown in every region; the rates are highest in eastern Europe, Asia, and Latin America. There is said to be a feminization of the epidemic; for political and physiological reasons, females are more vulnerable to infection than males. In sub-Saharan Africa, the rate of infection in young women is three to six times higher than in young men.[34] What's more, all of these estimates on death rates associated with the disease are conservative; it is likely that many people who are HIV-positive have no idea that they are dying. They can't afford the tests, and given the stigma that people with AIDS face worldwide, many feel they shouldn't bother. There is currently little recourse for millions of those who would test positive, since they lack access to the medicines that could prolong their lives. Put yourself in their shoes: Why worry about something that might kill you ten years down the line when you're struggling with a host of other life-threatening problems on a day-to-day basis? Such questions provoke a variety of reactions. In the meantime, the world is facing a pandemic that has been likened to the Black Death of the fourteenth century. If it continues to go uncontained, its long-term impact may be unlike any the world has ever known.

Conclusions: It Depends on Who You Ask

Let's put it flatly: There will be no simple answers to many of the questions we have raised here or will raise throughout the chapters that follow. The best we can do is to present you with a wide range of thinking and alternative perspectives on many of the challenges faced to some degree by all of us—but most directly by people living in low-income countries. In this book we will be looking at a series of issues of interdependence, such as the drug trade, migration, and arms transfers, from a number of angles. Before you make up your mind about any of the contending theories we present here, we ask that you judge each on its merits. We firmly believe that reflecting on another's point of view and considering more than one side of any story is the only way to begin to understand the complex social phenomena we now set out to discuss.

Linking Concepts and Cases

The information in this section is provided as a primer for the case studies we will be discussing throughout the rest of the book. Figures 1.2 through 1.9 should serve as a point of reference as you read about the histories, economies, and politics of the eight case studies introduced here. Throughout the book, we will return to the same countries, applying the ideas introduced in the conceptual chapters to the reality of their experiences.

Now It's Your Turn

From a simple examination of the statistical information that follows, what would you expect to be the key issue, or the most pressing problem each country faces? What can a sketch such as this tell you about life in each of these eight countries? Which ones appear most similar, and in what ways? What are some of the most striking differences between these countries? What other information not included here do you consider deserving of attention? Why?

Figure 1.2 Mexico: Profile and Map

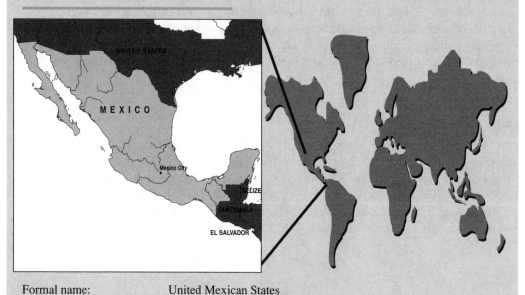

Formal name:	United Mexican States
Area, km²:	1.97 million
Comparative area:	Slightly less than three times the size of Texas
Capital:	Mexico City
Establishment of present state:	September 18, 1810
Population:	112 million
Age under 15 years:	29%
Population growth rate:	1.1%
Fertility rate (children per woman):	2.3
Infant mortality (per 1,000 births):	18
Life expectancy:	76
HIV prevalence (adult):	0.3%
Ethnic groups:	Mestizo 60%, Amerindian 30%, white 9%, other 1%
Literacy rate:	86%
Religions:	Roman Catholic 89%, Protestant 6%, other 5%
GDP per capita (PPP):	$13,200
GDP growth rate:	−6.5% (2009)
Labor, major sectors:	Services 63%, industrial 23%, agriculture 14%
Population in poverty:	47%
Unemployment rate:	5.5% (with extensive underemployment)
Export commodities:	Manufactured goods, petroleum and petroleum products, silver, fruits, vegetables, coffee, cotton
External debt:	$177 billion (2009)

Source: CIA, *World Factbook 2010.*

Figure 1.3 Peru: Profile and Map

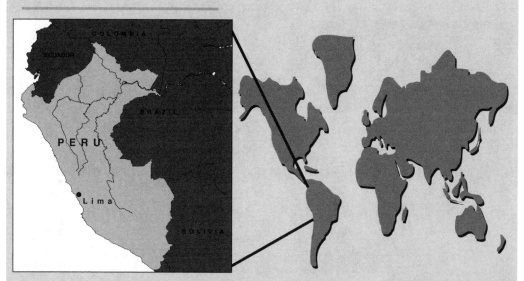

Formal name:	Republic of Peru
Area, km^2:	1.28 million
Comparative area:	Slightly smaller than the size of Alaska
Capital:	Lima
Establishment of present state:	July 28, 1821
Population:	29 million
Age under 15 years:	29%
Population growth rate:	1.1%
Fertility rate (children per woman):	2.3
Infant mortality (per 1,000 births):	27
Life expectancy:	71
HIV prevalence (adult):	0.5%
Ethnic groups:	Amerindian 45%, mestizo 37%, white 15%, other 3%
Literacy rate:	93%
Religions:	Roman Catholic 81%, Evangelical 12%, Protestant 2%, other 5%
GDP per capita (PPP):	$8,500
GDP growth rate:	0.9% (2009)
Labor, major sectors:	Services 75%, industrial 24%, agriculture 0.7%
Population in poverty:	44%
Unemployment rate:	8% (with extensive underemployment)
Export commodities:	Copper, zinc, gold, crude petroleum, and petroleum products
External debt:	$30 billion (2009)

Source: CIA, *World Factbook 2010.*

19

Figure 1.4   Nigeria: Profile and Map

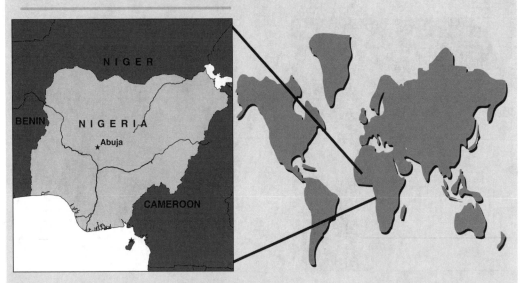

Formal name:	Federal Republic of Nigeria
Area, km^2:	923,768
Comparative area:	Slightly more than twice the size of California
Capital:	Abuja
Establishment of present state:	October 1, 1960
Population:	152 million
Age under 15 years:	42%
Population growth rate:	1.9%
Fertility rate (children per woman):	4.8
Infant mortality (per 1,000 births):	92
Life expectancy:	47
HIV prevalence (adult):	3.1%
Ethnic groups:	(More than 250 groups) Hausa and Fulani 29%, Yoruba 21%, Ibo 18%, Ijaw 10%, Kanuri 4%, Ibibio 3.5%, Tiv 2.5%
Literacy rate:	68%
Religions:	Muslim 50%, Christian 40%, indigenous beliefs 10%
GDP per capita (PPP):	$2,300
GDP growth rate:	6.1% (2009)
Labor, major sectors:	Agriculture 70%, services 20%, industrial 10%
Population in poverty:	70%
Unemployment rate:	5% (with significant underemployment)
Export commodities:	Petroleum and petroleum products, cocoa, rubber
External debt:	$10 billion (2009)

Source: CIA, *World Factbook 2010.*

Figure 1.5 Zimbabwe: Profile and Map

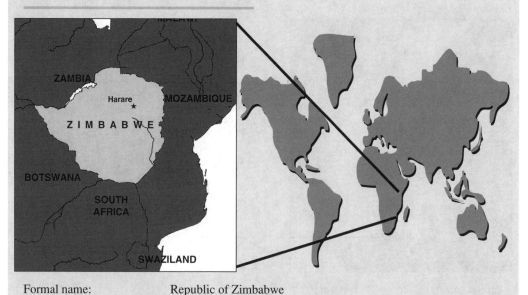

Formal name:	Republic of Zimbabwe
Area, km²:	390,580
Comparative area:	Slightly larger than the size of Montana
Capital:	Harare
Establishment of present state:	April 18, 1980
Population:	11 million
Age under 15 years:	44%
Population growth rate:	2.9%
Fertility rate (children per woman):	3.6
Infant mortality (per 1,000 births):	31
Life expectancy:	47
HIV prevalence (adult):	15%
Ethnic groups:	African 98% (Shona 82%, Ndebele 14%, other 2%), mixed and Asian 1%, white < 1%
Literacy rate:	91%
Religions:	Syncretic 50%, Christian 25%, indigenous beliefs 24%, Muslim and other 1%
GDP per capita (PPP):	–$100
GDP growth rate:	–1.3% (2009)
Labor, major sectors:	Agriculture 66%, services 24%, industrial 10%
Population in poverty:	68%
Unemployment rate:	95%
Export commodities:	Platinum, cotton, tobacco, gold, ferroalloys, textiles
External debt:	$5.8 billion (2009)

Source: CIA, *World Factbook 2010.*

21

Figure 1.6 Iran: Profile and Map

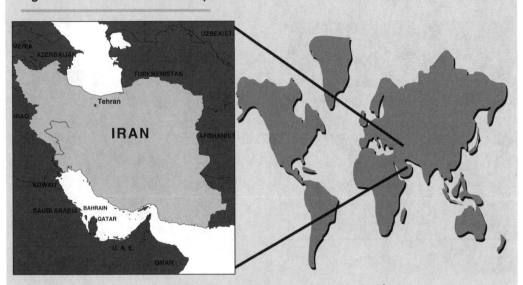

Formal name:	Islamic Republic of Iran
Area, km²:	1.65 million
Comparative area:	Slightly larger than the size of Alaska
Capital:	Tehran
Establishment of present state:	April 1, 1979
Population:	77 million
Age under 15 years:	22%
Population growth rate:	1.2%
Fertility rate (children per woman):	1.8
Infant mortality (per 1,000 births):	43
Life expectancy:	70
HIV prevalence (adult):	0.2%
Ethnic groups:	Persian 51%, Azeri 24%, Gilaki and Mazandarani 8%, Kurd 7%, Arab 3%, Lur 2%, Baloch 2%, Turkmen 2%, other 1%
Literacy rate:	77%
Religions:	Shia Muslim 89%; Sunni Muslim 9%; Zoroastrian, Jewish, Christian, and Bahai 2%
GDP per capita (PPP):	$12,500
GDP growth rate:	1.5% (2009)
Labor, major sectors:	Services 45%, agriculture 25%, industrial 31%
Population in poverty:	18%
Unemployment rate:	11%
Export commodities:	Petroleum, chemical and petrochemical products, fruits, nuts, carpets
External debt:	$18 billion (2009)

Source: CIA, *World Factbook 2010.*

Figure 1.7   Turkey: Profile and Map

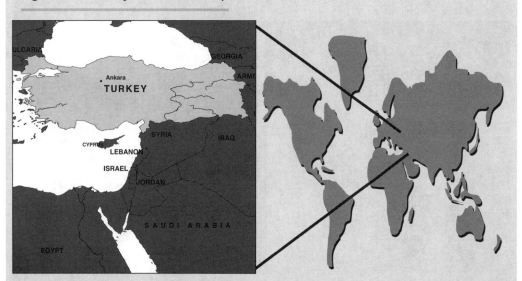

Formal name:	Republic of Turkey
Area, km²:	780,580
Comparative area:	Slightly larger than the size of Texas
Capital:	Ankara
Establishment of present state:	October 29, 1923
Population:	77 million
Age under 15 years:	27%
Population growth rate:	1.2%
Fertility rate (children per woman):	2.1
Infant mortality (per 1,000 births):	25
Life expectancy:	72
HIV prevalence (adult):	less than 0.1%
Ethnic groups:	Turkish 70–75%, Kurdish 18%, others 7–12%
Literacy rate:	87%
Religions:	Muslim (mostly Sunni) 99.8%, other 0.2%
GDP per capita (PPP):	$11,400
GDP growth rate:	–4.7% (2009)
Labor, major sectors:	Services 65%, agriculture 9%, industrial 25%
Population in poverty:	17%
Unemployment rate:	14%
Export commodities:	Apparel, foodstuffs, textiles, metal manufactured products, transportation equipment
External debt:	$274 billion (2009)

Source: CIA, *World Factbook 2010.*

23

Figure 1.8 China: Profile and Map

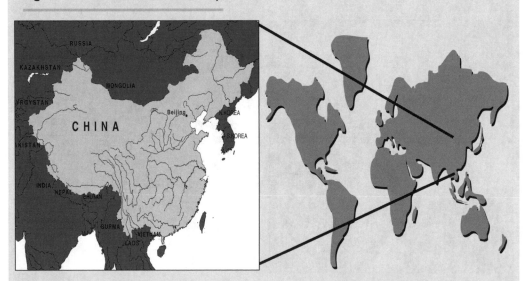

Formal name:	People's Republic of China
Area, km2:	9.60 million
Comparative area:	Slightly smaller than the size of the United States
Capital:	Beijing
Establishment of present state:	October 1, 1949
Population:	1.33 billion
Age under 15 years:	20%
Population growth rate:	0.4%
Fertility rate (children per woman):	1.5
Infant mortality (per 1,000 births):	16
Life expectancy:	74
HIV prevalence (adult):	0.1%
Ethnic groups:	Han Chinese 91%; Zhuang, Uighur, Hui, Yi, Tibetan, Miao, Manchu, Mongol, Buyi, Korean, and others 9%
Literacy rate:	92%
Religions:	(Officially atheist), Taoist, Buddhist, Christian 3–4%, Muslim 1–2%
GDP per capita (PPP):	$6,600
GDP growth rate:	9% (2009)
Labor, major sectors:	Agriculture 39%, services 33%, industrial 27%
Population in poverty:	3%
Unemployment rate:	4% (urban; substantial unemployment and underemployment in rural areas)
Export commodities:	Electrical and other equipment, machinery, textiles and clothing, iron and steel, optical and medical equipment
External debt:	$347 billion (2009)

Source: CIA, *World Factbook 2010.*

Figure 1.9   Indonesia: Profile and Map

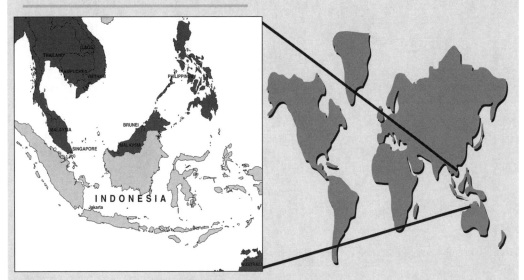

Formal name:	Republic of Indonesia
Area, km²:	1.92 million
Comparative area:	Slightly less than three times the size of Texas
Capital:	Jakarta
Establishment of present state:	August 17, 1945
Population:	243 million
Age under 15 years:	28%
Population growth rate:	1%
Fertility rate (children per woman):	2.2
Infant mortality (per 1,000 births):	29
Life expectancy:	71
HIV prevalence (adult):	0.2%
Ethnic groups:	Javanese 41%, Sundanese 15%, Madurese 3%, Minangkabau 3%, other 38%
Literacy rate:	90%
Religions:	Muslim 86%, Protestant 6%, Roman Catholic 3%, Hindu 2%, other 3%
GDP per capita (PPP):	$4,000
GDP growth rate:	4.5% (2009)
Labor, major sectors:	Agriculture 42%, services 39%, industrial 19%
Population in poverty:	18%
Unemployment rate:	8%
Export commodities:	Oil and gas, electrical appliances, plywood, textiles, rubber
External debt:	$150 billion (2009)

Source: CIA, *World Factbook 2010.*

PART ONE
Historical Legacies

How does one possibly condense thousands of years of the histories of four vast and diverse regions into a few chapters? It is not a simple proposition, but a necessary one. For all their differences, there are some experiences generally shared among these regions, and we will draw your attention to some common patterns. In order to make this broad sweep of time more comprehensible, we'll be speaking in generalities. We will illustrate with some specific examples throughout the chapters. However, as much as possible, we have attempted to avoid a long list of names and dates. At the risk of leaving out some exceptions to the rule, we believe that it is important to develop a general sense of the non-Western world's history. It is only with a sense of the full range of experience that one can go on to understand the complex issues that characterize life in the non-Western world today.

The most renowned historians of our time tell us that there is much still unknown about early human history. Dating back over the last 2 million years or so, much of world history is still incomplete, and (with a few exceptions) this is very much the case for the non-Western world. Unfortunately, this lack of information has provided fertile ground for the development of myths, stereotypes, and distortions—many of which continue to be popular today. As you will see, many of these beliefs—that the peoples of the non-Western world made no contributions, had no achievements, had no history—were used by Westerners to justify enslavement, conquest, and domination. Westerners' denials of the contributions of non-Westerners and portrayals of them as pagan, barbaric, warlike, or even childlike in some cases, are widely denounced today. For years, historians have worked diligently to repair the damage done by colonial apologists. A more balanced representation of the past is important work for its own sake. But it is also crucial that these histories be reconstructed because so often Western colonizers did everything they could to destroy all records of them. A greater understanding of the tremendous variety of human experience may not only help to restore the sense of IDENTITY that was taken from colonized peoples—it may also serve as a source of inspiration for indigenous solutions to some of the problems we must face today.

In their zeal to correct for the wrongs of the past, some historians have overcompensated and ended up providing an equally distorted version of history. Some adopted Western value systems and focused only on the "great civilizations" or EMPIRES of Africa, Asia, Latin America, and the Middle East. They ignored the vast array of smaller (but not lesser) forms of social organization. Yet the regions we are studying were inhabited for thousands of years by many different groups of people, with different ways of life. Some lived in relative isolation and some had long histories of contact with other peoples across great distances—well before these territories were "discovered" by white men. In fact, much of the non-Western world was integrated on some level into larger regional and even transcontinental networks of trade.

However, in their efforts to correct negative distortions, some historians provided overly romantic views of these empires, extolling only their virtues and portraying the world as it was before the arrival of Europeans as some sort of golden age of peace and plenty. Most analysts today agree that neither portrayal is accurate. There is fairly wide agreement that each extreme oversimplifies. Because humans populated these societies, it is fair to assume that they were neither all good nor all bad. Most historians currently embrace a more balanced approach that seeks to understand these societies in all their complexity. And that complexity includes attention to the vast diversity of societies that existed in the long stretch of history we refer to as "precolonial"—not just empires or small bands of hunter-gatherers, but also everything in between.

2

Precolonial History
(Or, What Your "World Civ"
Class Might Have Left Out)

The past reappears because it is a hidden present.
—Octavio Paz, writer[1]

One way of conceptualizing the many different ways in which humans organize themselves into groups is to picture a continuum. Large, hierarchical, centralized societies (or EMPIRES) lie at one end of this continuum, and much smaller, more egalitarian, decentralized societies are located at the other end, with most societies falling somewhere in between, containing elements of the two more extreme types. Without valuing one form of organization over another, anthropologists often make distinctions between STATE SOCIETIES and STATELESS SOCIETIES. Whereas the great empires have drawn most of the attention of archaeologists and historians, increasingly we are learning about somewhat smaller STATES. Anthropologists tell us that our earliest human ancestors lived in stateless societies. This system of organization has largely disappeared, as its members have been pushed into the most inhospitable environments or absorbed by larger groups. Yet both state and stateless societies could be found in Africa, Asia, Latin America, and the Middle East at the time of European conquest. Consequently, all these systems deserve attention, as no single type can be considered representative of these vast regions.

Stateless Societies

It is the democratic character of stateless societies that Westerners frequently find most striking. Relatively speaking, in stateless societies power is shared among the members of the group (often but not always both male and female). Also known as ACEPHALOUS SOCIETIES, they have no full-time political leaders, chiefs, presidents, or monarchs. It is not uncommon for elders to guide the affairs of the group. Or a member of the community known for his or her prowess in war or some other talent might serve on a temporary basis to lead communities in a certain function (military, religious, or economic). However, for these groups there is no tradition of a supreme ruler who governs continuously and beyond their immediate area of settlement. Unlike state systems with their courts, retinues, full-time militaries, and so on, in stateless societies people's day-to-day lives are conducted without interference from "government" as we know it.

Yet no society is truly stateless. Even in these noncentralized societies, there are widely accepted rules that provide a basis for the orderly functioning of the community. Government might appear to be more informal, in that there are no palaces, courthouses, or government buildings of any kind. However, this system is actually highly organized and there are often harsh penalties for violations of the public good. Within stateless societies, a variety of associations (such as all-male or all-female secret societies or age grades) are based on kinship, or family relationships. They exist to settle disputes among members, forge unity, and maintain order. These often-complicated arrangements promote cooperation, and time-honored rules allow families to draw on the labor they need in times of hardship. A web of kinship ties forms the basis for this kind of organization. All members of the extended families who make up the community know that the survival of all is based on this system of mutual aid and obligation.[2]

A strong sense of community pervades stateless societies, which exists among small bands or tribal groups of 20–200 people. Stateless societies are renowned for their egalitarianism. Relatively speaking, there are no divides based on CLASS, no rich and poor. Often working as hunter-gatherers who migrate in seasonal cycles, they rarely establish themselves in one place for long, nor do members produce or accumulate wealth above the bare necessities. Whether primarily composed of hunter-gatherers or small farmers, stateless societies are often associated with subsistence economies. However, the extreme hardship such groups live under today is not traditional—they have been pushed to the most inhospitable environmental margins. Life in such societies was not always tenuous. Many hunter-gatherers preferred what they saw as the good life compared to the hard work and risk involved in food production.

Based on their intimate knowledge of the resources available, the members of stateless societies employed a wide range of techniques to support themselves.[3] Going back at least 3,000 years, statelessness is known to have existed among pastoral populations as well as more settled populations practicing slash-and-burn techniques and shifting cultivation. Some groups, such as the Guarani of Brazil, lived off of some combination of these activities. This sense of communalism and egalitarian sharing of resources based on kinship was central to the early success of wet-rice cultivation in Southeast Asia.[4] Stateless societies were identified in the sierras of northern Mexico and in the pampas of South America, as well as in the Amazon Basin.

Small, highly mobile hunter-gatherer populations often lived alongside pastoralists and larger groups of sedentary farmers in symbiotic relationships. There is a great deal of evidence of the interpenetration and complementarity of hunter-gatherer groups by food producers (and vice versa). At times, relations could be described as cooperative, as hunter-gatherer groups like the San, or the !Kung of southern Africa traded game and other goods such as wild honey for farm products and implements such as nets or other technologies. Trade was also important for forest farmers, such as the Ibo of Nigeria. Through village markets, trading has long been a tradition for women of state and stateless societies in much of western Africa.

However, at other times, relations between these neighbors turned hostile. Conflicts could arise over any number of matters, most notably access to resources. Especially during times of environmental stress, it was not uncommon for settled farmers to come into conflict with pastoralists over land, as herds might destroy a field or farmers might encroach on prime pasture. Like hunter-gatherers, pastoralists did not generally form states, but they did sometimes take them over by conquest. Pastoralists, organized and unified under a strong central regime, were known to raid settled populations. For example, Turkic nomads and other warriors on horses repeatedly swept into India to plunder sedentary societies. Herding populations such as the Masai of eastern Africa had a number of advantages, which enabled them, as well as larger, more centrally organized societies such as the Zulu (southern Africa), to overwhelm their stateless or less centrally organized neighbors. Similarly, the Aztecs started out as a small group of tough nomads who made alliances to conquer sedentary groups. Often, sedentary societies found it necessary to form larger political groupings, to make alliances and take common action in self-defense. They might erect a walled town at the center of their farmlands to serve as a refuge against raids from their neighbors. The need for defense was one of the most common factors behind the DEVELOPMENT of states.

State Societies

Historians continue to disagree about the causal relationship between population booms and increased food production. It is still a chicken-or-egg question: Does GROWTH in the production of cereals such as rice, millet, and maize contribute to a population boom? Or do population booms necessitate an intensification of agricultural production? Either way, the two factors are clearly associated with the development of state societies. Once production is increased to the point of surplus, time is freed up for some people to work in capacities other than food production, including as full-time political leaders. When this happens, we begin to see more social stratification. There are divisions based on wealth, and clear differences between the rulers and ruled. A merchant class of traders emerges, markets grow, and trade becomes more regularized. In state societies in all regions, the craftwork produced by an artisan class of weavers, potters, and metal- and woodworkers was highly prized. For example, the Chibcha of Colombia were known for their magnificent gold work, recognized as perhaps the finest in the ancient Americas.

At this intermediate level of social organization, clearly a state society but not an empire, government is described as comprising relatively simple small states or chiefdoms. As states grow larger we see a more centralized political organization and more complex forms of government supported by bureaucracies with increasingly specialized functions such as ambassadors, harbor masters, special judges, treasurers, tax collectors, and so on. Commercial city-states dominated the trade in the Southeast Asian archipelago. Often state societies were absorbed into larger empires in their efforts to monopolize trade. The Swahili city-states of the eastern coast of Africa, such as Pemba, Mombasa, and Zanzibar, were autonomous and loosely linked through commercial ties (until they were all brought under the Omani Empire). Similarly, the city-states of Mesopotamia were eventually integrated into a single, powerful entity to ensure the security of trade routes.

States of this size existed long before the conquest of Latin America, especially in the circum-Caribbean area (Panama, Costa Rica, northern Colombia, Venezuela, Puerto Rico, Jamaica, and Cuba). A paramount chief or king arose (in some cases chosen by election, in other cases because of some exceptional talent or charisma, magical powers, skills as a protector, etc.) and was assisted by councils drawn from the heads of the lineages composing the village. At this level of organization, the chief's rule was not absolute. He was limited by his advisers and required to consult the council, although the power of the council varied by state. Often in state societies in Africa and Southeast Asia, decisions were reached by consensus between a king and a council. After lengthy deliberations, the king would pronounce a final decision representing a compromise of views.

In some cases kings had veto powers and could disregard the consensus of deliberations. Elsewhere, if the council disagreed with the chief's decisions, it could give counter-orders and seek to unseat him. In the Oyo kingdoms of western Africa, a leading minister could command an extremely unpopular king to commit suicide on the basis that the people, the earth, and the gods rejected his rule. There are examples of tyrants in such societies, but generally speaking, rulers still depended on the support of the population. Kings were respected as long as they fulfilled their responsibilities as protectors and providers. There were usually no standing armies to help kings impose their will, and abuses risked reprisals. Therefore, in some states at least, there were traditional checks on the rulers' powers.

Empires

Historians tell us that the differences between chiefdoms and larger, more complex kingdoms or empires are difficult to draw. Certainly empires are distinguished by size of the territories and populations they control. Beyond this, the difference is mostly a matter of degree, as empires are in the simplest sense an expansion and deepening of tendencies found in chiefdoms.[5] The former empires of what is now called the "third world" greatly resembled those in today's "first world" in terms of size of population or expanse of territory, use of official religions, or conquest of smaller states. Larger kingdoms often developed from these smaller states. Some were very large: historians estimate that the Aztecs controlled a population of nearly 25 million people in the early sixteenth century. Europeans were often surprised at how much the empires they encountered were like the ones at home. In fact, the Aztecs dominated a total area not much smaller than that of Spain. Hernan Cortés wrote that the Aztecs lived much like people in Spain, in terms of harmony and order, and that it was remarkable to see what they had achieved. The Spanish conquerors of Cuzco, the Inca capital, described it as beautiful, with buildings as fine as those in Spain.[6]

The oldest settled communities developed intensive agriculture along rivers, in oases, or in coastal areas. The Nile, the Tigris and Euphrates, the Yellow, and the Niger Rivers were centers of early civilization. The Fertile Crescent of ancient Palestine and Babylon was long accepted as the earliest site for mass cultivation. Yet there are reports of early kingdoms emerging in coastal and delta regions in other regions as well, such as the Niger Bend of western Africa. In several different parts of the world, over thousands of years, people domesticated wild plants or adopted new ones. It is becoming increasingly clear that at various times and places there were also revolutions in food production—and not all of these crops and methods have a Middle Eastern origin. In the Fertile Crescent, as in other food-producing "homelands" such as China, the Andes, along the Nile, in Amazonia, and in Mesoamerica, it was common that once a mainstay of the diet was perfected, agriculture spread swiftly across the region, in some cases to other continents.

Figure 2.1   Early Non-Western Empires

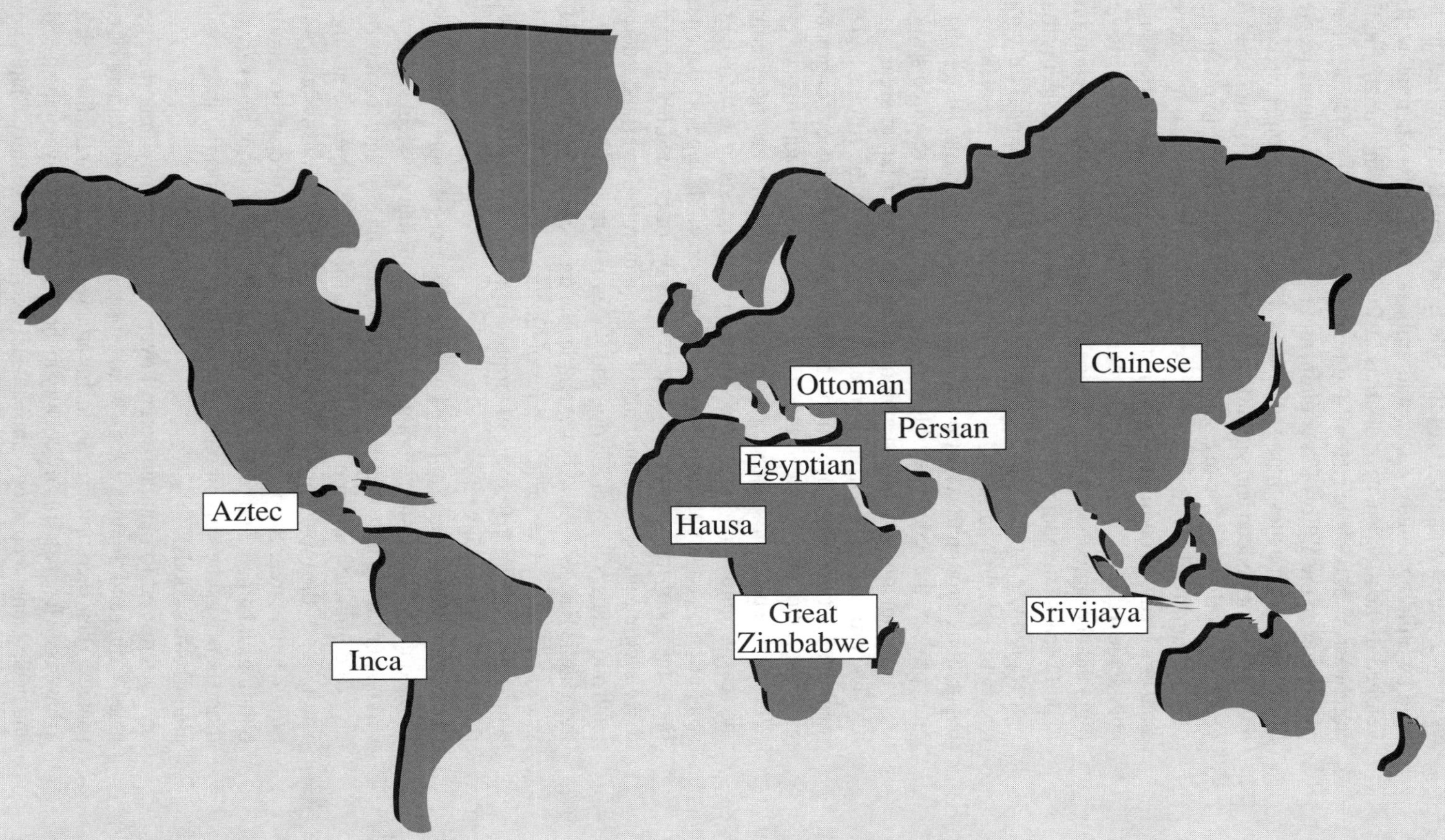

The Egyptian Empire, one of the preeminent powers in the world for over 2,000 years, was based on the soils of the Nile floodplain. It maximized the benefits of the Nile by building canals, dikes, and embankments. Elsewhere as well, empires developed in the most successful areas of food production. Funan, the first empire in Southeast Asia, became rich off the rice from the Mekong Delta. The Chinese Empire began on the Yellow River plain, and is made up of an uninterrupted succession of two dozen dynasties over 4,000 years. Many other empires were also long-lived; although it influenced and was influenced by Egypt, Kush flourished for over 1,000 years as an original African civilization, and many other empires in the four regions of study survived for hundreds of years. In Latin America, Mesoamerica is often cited as a cradle of civilization. There the Olmecs, Maya, and Aztecs attained remarkable achievements in a variety of pursuits. The desert coasts of Peru and later its highlands became the economic base for the Inca. Food production increased there in part because the indigenous peoples developed irrigation systems that allowed for higher productivity. Moreover, centralized states could compel the cooperation necessary to extending farmlands. These large states could harness the energy of larger populations through the creation of public works programs. Historians argue that the huge projects that contributed to a boom in production required strong and centralized governments and the extension of authority over larger areas.

The production of surpluses meant an increase in the volume and types of goods available for trade. Increased trade not only created the need for greater political organization, but also financed the increasingly complex activities of evolving states. Whereas the trade of some states was land-based, other emerging empires turned to the seas. Commercial kingdoms situated on the coasts or at the edges of the desert were often based almost exclusively on commerce. Their power depended upon a reliable means of transport (navigable waterways or beasts of burden) and their ability to secure routes. For hundreds of years a lucrative overland trade was based on cloth and beads, silks, gold, ivory, and slaves as caravan routes linked Europe, Africa, the Middle East, and Asia. For example, the trans-Saharan trade lasted for over 1,000 years and financed the great empires of Ghana, Mali, and Songhay in western Africa, whose wealth was based on monopoly control and taxation of the gold passing through their domains.

Seafaring states also amassed great riches. For example, Srivijaya, considered to be the only maritime state among the Southeast Asian classical states, was a commercial power taking revenues from passing trade. Its strategic location allowed Srivijaya to dominate maritime activity and patrol the archipelago around the Malacca Strait, one of the most significant links in the world trading system. As the dominant power in the area, Srivijaya controlled piracy, provided harbor facilities for shipbuilding and repair, and offered reprovisioning and warehousing services—all in addition to its business in camphor, bird nests, perfumes, pearls, and peppers and spices, among other goods.[7]

Determined to maintain control over this strategically important network of sea-lanes, China and Southeast Asia were pioneers in the development of early naval capacities. Their accomplishments in this area were so substantial that China is considered to have been far ahead of any country in the world in the development of the sailing ship and navigational technology until at least the fifteenth century. Shipbuilding and naval activity were especially common in the Southeast Asian archipelago. Some ships were up to 120 meters long and large enough to carry 500–1,000 people. In the fifteenth century China sent treasure fleets with hundreds of ships across the Indian Ocean—decades before Christopher Columbus's three ships made their way to the Americas.[8] There is evidence that Indonesians and possibly the Chinese traveled as far west as Madagascar. Some historians believe Asian sailors may have traveled to the Cape of Good Hope, or even around it, long before Europeans did.

However, as early as the second century B.C.E., Arab middlemen conducted much of the trade between East Africa and Asia. From the seventh century through the twelfth the Muslim trade network was vast, and various Muslim empires functioned as free trade areas. Their central position between east and west gave them a decisive advantage in the various long-distance trades at the center of the world economy for hundreds of years. Through their commercial activities Muslim traders disseminated technological innovations and greatly advanced the areas of navigation, shipbuilding, astronomy, and geography. These coastal merchants visited the Swahili city-states on a sea trade governed by the monsoon winds. Many stayed on and intermarried with African women, forming an ELITE class of merchants on East Africa's coasts.

While a corps of diplomats or ambassadors was key to maintaining stable relations along this trade, an interest in protecting or expanding trade and the accumulation of wealth also contributed to the development of another institution common to the world's empires: full-time militaries. Some kingdoms did not have standing armies. Most soldiers were actually farmers or herders who provided their own weapons and provisions. Other states, such as China by the fourth century B.C.E., had professional armies. In western Africa, Mali was renowned for its disciplined cavalry. It had horses and coats of chain mail long before its neighbors. Some Indian kingdoms, such as the Mauryan, had a cavalry of elephants and chariots. Ghana was said to have had an army of 200,000 men, including 40,000 archers. And the Ottoman militaries became regarded as a state within a state, so powerful that they could make and unmake rulers. Similar corps, such as the Mameluks, ruled Egypt for over 200 years.

Where warfare was endemic, its frequency changed the relative importance of the military, which became the core of some states, such as those of the Zulu and the Assyrians. With superior weapons and horses, some groups gained the military power to conquer neighboring groups and expand in order to collect tribute from subjugated populations or vassal states. As these states grew, they attained larger

---

Figure 2.2 Why Wasn't It China That Conquered the World?

With all of its advantages, why wasn't it China that conquered the world? Historians cite internal divisions within China in the fourteenth and fifteenth centuries. A power struggle between two factions in the Chinese court ended with the ascendance of a group who sought to turn inward. This marked a turning point in China's history, as the empire stopped sending out fleets and dismantled its shipyards. It also abandoned other technologies, in effect stepping back from the verge of its own industrial revolution—about 400 years ahead of Europe. Because it was so centralized politically, under this system China effectively retreated from technological innovation and halted it, just as Europe was rising.

surpluses by preying on neighboring populations and requiring tribute payments. Warfare between chiefdoms became common, and captives were taken in warfare and enslaved.[9] Stronger groups imposed their wills on weaker groups. The Mongol invasions rearranged politics in India and mainland Southeast Asia. Arab invasions had a similar effect in northern Africa. Tribute could come in the form of material resources or labor. For example, the Akan of western Africa wanted captive labor to mine gold, the basis of the Asante Empire in the eighteenth century. Slaves composed a large class in most empires; only slightly better off were subjugated peoples paying tribute.

Therefore, one important part of understanding empires is to see them as a collection of different communities over which there is a centralized government. These kingdoms routinely ruled over vast, sprawling, and varied areas. The Inca Empire ran north to south for over 3,200 kilometers. Such large states required effective political and military institutions to integrate conquered people into the system, and exercised executive, judicial, and legislative authority. They set about enforcing laws, organizing armies, and collecting taxes. Some were better administrators than others. Centralized states such as Persia (Iran) were broken into provinces and run by elaborate bureaucracies. The Inca divided their empire into four quarters, each with a lord (usually a close relative of the emperor). Besides tribute collection and organization of public works, the Inca sought to assimilate conquered peoples by encouraging their use of Quechua, the language of the empire. The imperial government required all those living under its rule to accept the official state religion, but allowed people also to continue worshipping their own gods. Similarly, the Persian Empire imposed uniform laws and used a single language for administration, but was tolerant of local cultures.

Still, the relative egalitarianism found among stateless societies appears to have been unknown at the state level. Rather little is known about women in most early societies, and what we do know is mostly about elite women. Men dominated most state systems. This was not always the case, however, as women sometimes played key political, economic, and religious roles in their communities. Aztec women worked as doctors, artisans, merchants, and in temple service. Even in studies of the most famously patriarchal empires (such as those of the Aztecs, Inca, and Zulu—which also tended to be the most militarized), the genders are not described as equal, but as serving complementary functions. Inca noblewomen had access to land, herds, water, and other resources through their mothers, and some historians argue that their activities were viewed as of equal importance to those of men. For the Aztecs, death in childbirth for women was considered the equivalent of death in battle for men— and revered with great honor.[10]

Many of the empires of western Africa also reserved an honored place for women. In fact, women's social position and personal liberty often astonished travelers. Women are known to have served as political leaders of Swahili (Zanzibar was once governed by a Muslim Swahili queen) and Mayan city-states. More often, however, women served at lower levels, as the heads of towns and subregions within empires. Among the Yoruba in Nigeria, the *iyalode* was a female official with jurisdiction over all women, who spoke on women's issues in the king's council. Similarly, among the Aztecs there were female officials charged with overseeing the affairs of women. Women also served in some imperial armies, and there are examples of all-female regiments led by women (such as the Amazons of Dahomey and the Sotho of southern Africa).

Although less commonly found in Latin America, there are examples of empresses and warrior queens in the histories of Asia and Africa. In the Hausa state of Zaria, Queen Amina outfitted her armies with iron helmets and chain mail to successfully wage a series of military campaigns. However, in most cases when women held this kind of power, it was treated as a temporary arrangement. Women served as regents, ruling when the successor to the throne was too young to assume (his) full duties. In matrilineal societies, such as the Asante in Ghana, maternal relations were crucial in determining succession, inheritance, and other matters. Here and elsewhere queen mothers and queen sisters were major power brokers, and often had considerable leverage and influence. An Asante queen mother, Ya Asantewaa, is considered a heroine for leading her kingdom in resistance against British rule in 1900.

The Asante had a relatively large empire. One of the most notable differences between empires and smaller states is that the kinship ties that unite chiefs with commoners in states do not exist in empires. Rather, in empires the ruling group claims separate origins from the MASSES and lives apart from them. A variety of sources tell of the spectacle and luxury of life enjoyed by elites in the empires of the non-Western world. Large retinues of ministers, scholars, and courtiers surrounded emperors. Often imperial courts included harems, as royal polygamy was not uncommon. Kings of large states such as Mwene Mutapa (Zimbabwe) distinguished themselves by having 2,000–3,000 royal wives.

Always at the pinnacle of power in this hierarchy was the emperor, who ruled as an absolute monarch. There was little left of the kind of constitutional monarchy described for smaller states, in which a king confers with a council. At the level of empire, the emperor's authority took on a divine status and usually was unquestioned. This far greater centralization of power was supported by a religious IDEOLOGY that had enormous influence over the population. Every empire was linked with a state religion, and based on some mix of THEOCRACY and royal despotism. As the "son of heaven," the Chinese emperor was considered godlike. Egyptian monarchs were regarded as gods on earth. Rulers often claimed special powers of intercession with God or the gods.[11] As chief religions and philosophies of state, Hinduism and Buddhism helped provide the unity necessary for the first kingdoms of India to become larger political entities. Similarly, Islam created a unity among rival Arab clans. It was this unity based in religion that contributed to the rapid growth of the Arab Empire, known as the Caliphate. This empire rivaled Rome at its peak, and controlled an area that stretched from the Mediterranean into Central Asia from the seventh to the eleventh century.

Religious ideologies served the state in other ways as well. In all four regions, emperors were believed necessary for performing important rites. For the Inca, the emperor was responsible for defending the order and existence of the universe. For the Aztecs, the emperor was a renowned warrior, and conquest was necessary to the proper worship of the god Huitzilopochtli—the only assurance that the sun would continue to pass through the sky. Across empires in the non-Western world it was also common to find that kings and emperors lived lives of ritual seclusion apart from the population. They were often separated from the public behind a screen and communicated only through intermediaries—all based on the belief that the emperor was too holy for common gaze. For example, the Alafin of Oyo, considered to be the incarnation of a chief god, could only be seen through a veil and could never be seen eating. It was not unusual for emperors to be thought to possess supernatural powers.[12] They were often the only ones allowed to transgress the ordinary rules of social life, such as the taboo against incest.

In deference to emperors' unquestioned power, life at imperial courts around the world was immersed in elaborate ritual and ceremony. We know from various sources that the capitals of these empires were often lavish. These were true cities, serving not only as economic but also as cultural centers and populated by tens of thousands, even millions, of people. For example, the Aztec capital Tenochtitlan and the valley of Mexico were home to nearly 1 million people in the early sixteenth century. Described by Spaniards as an "Indian Venice," the city sat on an oval island connected to the mainland by three causeways and interlaced with numerous canals. Chang'an, the capital of the Tang Dynasty of China, was described as magnificent, and was once probably the largest city in the world, with an estimated population of 2 million. Timbuktu and the other capitals of western African empires were described as awash in gold, dripping in opulence, and capable of serving thousands at banquets. The generosity and hospitality of these courts was commented on by visitors of the time. In the tenth century, the emperor of Ghana was known as the richest monarch in the world. The annual revenue of the Mongol emperor in the seventeenth century was said to be ten times that of his contemporary, Louis XIV. When the Mansa of Mali made his pilgrimage to Mecca in 1324–1325, he impressed the world with his wealth and munificence.[13]

Besides feats of monumental architecture, many empires were renowned for their buildings of remarkable beauty and distinctiveness. Many empires also invested in enormous public works projects. The most famous of these is China's Great Wall, a continuous fortification built along its northern frontier. On a similar scale in China is its Grand Canal, a 1,600-kilometer waterway linking north to south. The massive engineering of water systems, such as the use of dams and irrigation, helped the Chinese, the Funan, the Inca, and others increase food production on limited arable land. The Inca produced a surplus in the highlands through agricultural terracing and irrigation. They maintained control over the empire through an impressive system of roads and built suspension bridges to render immense gorges passable. For many lowland Asian empires, wet-rice cultivation required sophisticated water management and regulation in order to create the higher volume of production necessary to feed larger populations.[14]

As mentioned earlier, the surplus created by such innovations allowed for state patronage of the arts and religion, which contributed to the development of rich material cultures. Empires were known for their production and vast exchange of goods and services, including luxury items. Various empires had specialists in jewelry making and goldsmithing, feather working, silk weaving, and production of other adornments. Empires from all regions are known for their wall paintings and sculpture, such as the Ajanta caves in India, and the cast-bronze portraits of the kings of Ife and Benin in western Africa. Not only did the Gupta kingdom provide for peace and prosperity by reuniting much of northern India, but its two centuries of rule are also described as a period of cultural brilliance, a creative age for the arts and sciences. In the Middle Ages, Muslim society was the scientific center of the world, and Arabic was synonymous with learning and science for over 500 years.[15]

Arab and other non-Western peoples contributed to the development of technologies in several different fields, such as metallurgy. For example, China used coal as metallurgical fuel and for heating houses 700 years before the West.[16] But such feats were by no means confined to Asia. Although little of the non-Western world is considered industrialized today, a variety of industries once flourished throughout these regions. Weaving, which goes back in Egypt and Nubia for a millennium, was once a primary industry in parts of Africa, Asia, the Middle East, and Latin America. The Chinese are credited with technological achievements such as the invention of water-powered mills, drought-resistant rice strains, gunpowder, and optical lenses. Some historians argue that China was near its own industrial revolution in the thirteenth century, and world history would be much different today if not for the Mongol invasion and later emperors' failures to resume the Song Dynasty's initiatives.[17]

What we today call the "third world" was the site of a series of accomplishments in the field of mathematics as well. Arab scholars introduced algebra and the use of zero to the West. Egyptians were the first to use the decimal system. The Chinese are known for their use of geometric equations and trigonometry. Several empires prioritized the study of the sciences, particularly astronomy, through which the Maya are said to have made observations and calculations of astounding complexity. This includes the development of a calendar that is more accurate than the common Western systems in making adjustments in the exact length of a solar year.[18]

The Maya are also known for their complex glyphic writing, which has still not been decoded but is widely considered to be the most advanced in the ancient Americas. Although Sumer is believed to be the first civilization to have created cuneiform writing (about 5,000 years ago), the Egyptians developed writing (about 3200 B.C.E.) and the Chinese have preserved script that dates back as far as the second millennium B.C.E. Instead of lettering, the Inca used mnemonic devices, knotted quipu strings, which were used in recordkeeping and accounting.[19] Yet there were also highly artistic and prosperous urban civilizations, such as the Ife of Nigeria, who did not have writing. Oral cultures there and around the world have produced a large body of myths, legends, and poetry, as well as theater, prose, and philosophy. Griots and other professional historians have transmitted the genealogies and histories of these peoples by memory.

The Assyrians collected their literature in libraries, filled with thousands of stone tablets. The Gupta in India, the Maya, and the Persians are known for their patronage of scholarly activity, including the recording of official histories. In addition to being the center of trade on the Southeast Asian archipelago, Srivijaya was a center of Hindu and Buddhist learning. Correspondingly, Baghdad was such a gathering place for Muslim scholars during the Umayyad Dynasty. Timbuktu, at the time that it was the major hub for the trans-Saharan trade and one of the most celebrated of savanna cities, was also famous for being a city of universities, attracting scholars of international repute. In the third millennium B.C.E. Egypt achieved high intellectual, social, and material standards that compared favorably with most other parts of the world.[20] The Greeks borrowed heavily from the Egyptians in philosophy and the sciences, transmitting to the West many of their accomplishments. Therefore, it is not only the West that has a rich intellectual history. In fact, the West became what it did because of an infusion of knowledge from the non-Western world.

For all of their strengths, however, we find a common pattern among Western and non-Western empires—authority was inversely related to distance. The larger the area conquered, the more difficult it was to maintain HEGEMONY, or absolute control over the empire. The Songhay Empire in western Africa was almost perpetually engaged against dissidents across its vast frontier, as was the Chinese Empire, which frequently broke down into fiefdoms. Empires tended to overextend themselves and were constantly plagued by problems of administration and succession (one reason Ghana lasted so long is that it stayed relatively small). Whereas smaller groups often unified into larger states under a common cause (such as defense against an external threat), after the shared problem was eliminated these larger units tended to break back down into smaller and more local organizations. This was a cycle that repeated itself in all four regions—Africa, Asia, Latin America, and the Middle East—many times before European conquest.

Yet it is for a variety of reasons (not all of them well understood) that many of the empires described here had long passed from the scene; their capitals were no longer as dazzling and prosperous by the 1500s, when Europeans began arriving in larger numbers. By the time European powers became intent on expansion, many of these empires were showing signs of distress. They were at risk of DISINTEGRATION from infighting and fragmentation.[21] For example, the Mongol Empire was fragmenting when the Europeans arrived. Indian and foreign rivals defeated the Mongols, so that by the time the West began its invasion the empire was vulnerable and divided into many small successor states that were easily played off each other by the French and British. We see this pattern among empires in all four regions. There were the internecine dynastic struggles of China, the civil wars over succession crises of the Inca and Oyo (Nigeria) states, and slave raiding in Africa, which spread firearms throughout the region and contributed to endless wars between various groups. In all of these places, the once-central leadership was weakened, administrative controls broke down, and outlying tributaries attempted to break free of the empire's grasp.

The potential for revolt in these kingdoms was aggravated by heavy taxation and other stresses. These often became more burdensome as empires struggled to survive. For example, just before Spanish conquest, the Aztecs greatly stepped up the pressure on conquered groups. They demanded mass human sacrifices to assuage the gods and prevent a predicted cataclysm. Consequently, tributary and minority groups, long resentful of imperial domination, were eager to ally with the invaders. Europeans benefited enormously from this circumstance and employed a strategy of DIVIDE AND CONQUER.[22]

While it is important to remember that Europeans were not invited guests, there are cases in which people didn't immediately recognize the Europeans as invaders and ended up compromising themselves. There are countless stories of how non-Westerners received the European visitors peacefully—even warmly. Many societies active in the Indian Ocean network of trade accepted the Portuguese enclaves as they had other outsiders for as long as anyone could remember. They gave the Europeans a cautious welcome and sought to profit from their presence. The Aztec emperor Moctezuma at first offered generous gifts to encourage his unearthly-looking visitors to leave. When that didn't work, Moctezuma warily welcomed Cortés and his men to Tenochtitlan and treated them as guests.[23]

Once the emperor recognized his error, it was too late. The Aztecs, like most of the other military empires of Africa, Asia, Latin America, and the Middle East, were unprepared to counter European penetration. In some cases, people quickly adapted to the new reality and worked hard to reclaim the advantage. However, many groups fought pitched battles against the invaders and some succeeded (at least temporarily). The emperor Menelik drove the Italians out of Ethiopia in the late nineteenth century, and as a result it was one of the few territories never formally colonized. Equipped with European arms his forces had built for themselves through reverse engineering, Samori Touré was able to keep the French out of large parts of western Africa for nearly twenty years. The Inca were able to hold off the Spanish for decades, as resistance was not finally put down until 1572.[24] These are just a few of the examples of indigenous peoples' fierce resistance to European conquest. But in most cases it was too late.

Figure 2.3   The Transatlantic Slave Trade

Unique in terms of the enormity of human devastation it caused, the transatlantic slave trade lasted for nearly 500 years. Although it began on a small scale in the 1400s, by the seventeenth century, labor shortages in the Americas had greatly increased the demand for slaves. At its height, thousands of men and women in their most productive years were taken from their communities on an annual basis and sent across the Atlantic on the harrowing trip known as the "Middle Passage." Because so many died along the way, the total number of slaves is still unknown, although most historians estimate that at least 12 million people served as human cargo in this trade.[25]

Figure 2.4   The Opium Wars

Those states that were not so open or that didn't receive Europe so warmly were also forced into the new order—on Europe's terms. As the Middle Kingdom, China believed itself to be at the center of the universe. Largest in size and population, longest in history, untouchable in cultural achievement, the Chinese Empire was in many ways the premier entity when Europeans started arriving in more significant numbers in the sixteenth century. Yet Europe's appetite for Chinese porcelains, silks, and teas was not reciprocated by Chinese interest in European goods.

As a result, the Europeans (and particularly the British) struggled with their trade deficits until they did find one commodity the Chinese found habit-forming: opium. This narcotic proved to be a boon to the British economy. Although the Chinese government had recognized the devastation caused by opium addiction and outlawed its sale, the British sold the drug through a smuggling network along the coast. When China attempted to destroy the contraband trade, the British fought what were known as the Opium Wars to force open the country to foreign trade. In decline at the time, the Chinese Empire was easily overwhelmed by the British military. The resulting Treaty of Nanjing in 1842 was the first of several "unequal treaties" that established European dominance in China. The Chinese coast was carved up into five ports open to Westerners. In effect, the emperor was forced to grant concessions at gunpoint—truly a low point in the empire's history. At the mercy of foreigners, China faced a century of humiliation.[26]

3

Colonialism:
Gold, God, Glory

Whatever happens we have got / The maxim gun and they have not.
—Hilaire Belloc, writer[1]

In most cases, European conquest of what would become the so-called third world did not come overnight. Rather, colonization was the culmination of processes that had begun hundreds of years earlier. The fifteenth and sixteenth centuries represented a turning point for Europe—and for the non-Western world. Most historians agree that until this time, Europe had little on Africa, Asia, the Middle East, or the Americas. It was just another of the world's regions, with its share of accomplishments and failures. In the fifteenth century few could have dreamed that Europe would dominate the world. How did it all change? How did Europe manage to conquer virtually the entire world? One currently popular view is that Europe simply took advantage of a set of fortuitous circumstances. It was willing to build on the achievements of others (such as gunpowder, the compass, and improvements in shipbuilding) and use its military power to take control of the seas and world trade.[2]

What other kinds of generalizations can we make about colonialism? Several, since the main differences between the colonizers were in degree, but not in kind. There are some interesting comparisons to be made in terms of style, but not in terms of substance.[3] Who were the colonizers, who assumed the role of "MOTHER COUNTRY"? The major colonizers in Latin America were the Spanish and the Portuguese, although the British, French, and Dutch took the Guianas and parts of the Caribbean. Spain dominated the Philippines, Puerto Rico, and Cuba until the United States replaced it after the Spanish-American War. The British took much of Asia, including India, Pakistan, Sri Lanka, Burma, and Malaysia. The French claimed Indochina (including Vietnam, Cambodia, and Laos). In Asia the Portuguese had only a few small holdings, and the Dutch controlled the vast archipelago today known as Indonesia.

The British and French were the dominant colonial powers in Africa, with the French taking much of the northern and western regions of the continent, and the British controlling much of the eastern and southern regions. Other colonial powers took pieces of the African cake as well, including the Belgians, Germans, Italians, Portuguese, Spanish, and Dutch.

Figure 3.1 How Did Europe Conquer the World?

How did a relative handful of Europeans succeed in conquering these empires? A variety of advantages served the European cause, but the shortest answer is weaponry. Europeans had enormous advantages in military technology throughout the period of conquest. By the seventeenth century, guns were the main weapons favoring Europeans (an early machine gun, the maxim gun, revolutionized violence). Yet weaponry had made all the difference even hundreds of years earlier.

In Latin America in the early sixteenth century, the Spaniards used steel swords, lances, small firearms, and artillery, as well as steel body armor and helmets against far greater numbers of indigenous soldiers with much less effective weaponry and protection. The Inca and Aztecs were equipped only with clubs and axes of wood or stone, slings, bows and arrows, and quilted armor. Brought in on ships from Europe, horses provided the Spaniards with another tremendous advantage in battle. Horses gave the invaders height in combat (which protected riders by giving them a raised fighting platform) and speed in attack. Foot soldiers could never succeed against a cavalry in the open. In addition, the Spaniards unleashed massive dogs in combat. As vicious killers they terrorized the population. The invaders benefited from other psychological advantages as well. Aztec priests had been predicting the return of the god Quetzalcoatl, as well as the end of the world. The Aztecs had never before seen men with light-colored eyes and hair, let alone horses (which when mounted by Spaniards appeared to be two-headed animals). Combine these advantages with differences in battle tactics (by Aztec standards, the Spanish didn't fight fair; the Spanish fought to kill, the Aztecs to take prisoners). Add to that the death toll from the diseases Europeans brought with them, and the effect was the literal decimation of populations—not only in Latin America, but in Africa and Asia as well.[4]

Although several European powers were interested in the area, the British dominated the waters of the Persian Gulf and influenced surrounding territories from the late nineteenth century until the middle of the twentieth. After the fall of the Ottoman Empire at the end of World War I, much of the Middle East was divided as mandates between the French and British. The Russians continued to dominate Central Asia, and they vied with the British for control of Persia until the two agreed to divide it between themselves into spheres of influence.

Not all of the non-Western world was formally claimed and occupied by Europeans, but even territories that were never formally colonized fell under heavy European influence. Because China's coast was carved up between five different alien powers and its emperor was rendered a puppet, it is said to have been "semicolonized" after the Opium Wars of the mid–nineteenth century. Similarly, because they were not insulated from trends ongoing elsewhere, Turkey, Thailand, Ethiopia, Liberia, and the handful of STATES that were never officially colonized share many of the legacies of colonialism.

Just as the players involved vary by country, so do the length and period of colonialism. The Spanish and Portuguese were the earliest colonizers, and Latin America was the first region to be colonized. Its era of colonial rule was relatively long, beginning in the early sixteenth century and lasting 300 years or more. Yet independence came relatively early to Latin America; with a few notable exceptions in the Caribbean and Brazil, most of the region became independent in the 1810s and 1820s.

Compared to Latin America's experience, colonialism in most of Africa, Asia, and the Middle East was relatively short-lived. After years of encroaching influence, nearly all of Asia was formally colonized after the 1850s but independent less than a hundred years later, in the 1940s and 1950s. Most of Africa was parceled out to the Europeans at the Conference of Berlin in the 1880s and was (formally) self-governing by the end of the 1960s.

The Middle East's experience is somewhat different. Though the Russians had been encroaching on Central Asia since the sixteenth century, most European powers were more cautious about taking on the Ottoman Empire. During the nineteenth century, when Europe was most active in acquiring colonies, most of the Middle East (with the notable exceptions of Persia, Saudi Arabia, and Yemen) was under Ottoman control. Perhaps because of a long history of mutual antagonism between Christians and Muslims, perhaps because Europeans knew relatively little of the land and overestimated the Muslim powers' military strength, or perhaps because at the time they had little economic interest in the region, European penetration of the Middle East was delayed. As a result it was the last major area to fall to the West.

However, by the end of World War I, the Ottoman Empire had bottomed out after a long decline. Despite promises of independence to the Arabs, who had risen up against the Ottomans, Ottoman territories (including former German colonies in Africa and the Pacific) were set aside by the League of Nations as mandates, or wards of the international community. The Western-dominated League granted supervision of the mandates to Britain and France. The French acquired Syria and Lebanon. Control over Iraq, Transjordan, and Palestine passed to Britain. Under this system, the Europeans' primary responsibility was to prepare their wards for eventual self-government. However, many analysts characterize the MANDATORY SYSTEM as a fig leaf for colonialism, as the mandates were treated no differently than colonial possessions elsewhere. Still, the period of mandates was relatively brief. Most of these territories declared their independence in the post–World War II period.

Whether it lasted for one generation or for many generations, most students of the non-Western world agree that colonialism was a formative experience. Although they may disagree about how long-lasting its legacy was, the fact remains that, in one form or another, colonialism is the one experience that virtually every non-Western country has shared. Why did the Europeans conquer the world? What were they after? And what impact did their policies have on the colonized? Analysts disagree in terms of the relative weight they assign the different interests that motivated the Europeans, but most agree that it was based in a mix of what Ali Mazrui characterized as "the three Gs"—gold, God, and glory.[5]

Gold

In many ways, colonialism was the culmination of a process that wrecked indigenous economies, ruined local industries, and replaced traditional networks of trade with a world system in which Europeans dominated and the rest of the world served. Gold, or the economic motive, was a major if not *the* major drive behind colonialism. By the beginning of the age of imperialism in the fifteenth century, an overland long-distance trade had linked Europe and the non-Western world for over a thousand years. However, it was a technological revolution that would dramatically shift the balance of power—the Europeans' ability to dominate world trade by sea.

From the time of Henry the Navigator, Portugal had led Europe in decades of exploration. Early in the fifteenth century, as the Portuguese began making stops along the coast of Africa, they established plantations in Cape Verde and the Canary Islands.

In Africa, the Portuguese were literally seeking gold, but later it was slaving that set in motion a process that would dramatically alter Africa's relationship with Europe. By 1487 the Portuguese had rounded the Cape of Good Hope and entered the bustling Indian Ocean trading network. The newcomers originally sought access to the highly lucrative trade in pepper and spices. They did this by setting up trading posts at strategic bases along the coasts of Africa, Asia, and the Middle East. Over the next hundred years, Portugal practiced a policy of expansionism. Seeking to eliminate the middlemen and gain direct access and control of this trade, Portugal defeated fleets of Egyptians, Arabs, and Persians. Portuguese traders eventually reached as far as China by the early sixteenth century, although the European presence went largely unnoticed by the Chinese emperors until much later.[6]

Meanwhile, seeking another route to the Indies, the Portuguese were joined by the Spanish, who together claimed the Caribbean and much of the Americas as their own. In a papal bull in 1493, Pope Alexander VI randomly determined the line dividing what would become Latin America between the two Iberian powers. This pronouncement formed the basis of the Treaty of Tordesillas in 1494, which formalized their claims. All was decided even before the Portuguese landed in Brazil, but the exclusivity of this relationship would be more or less maintained for another 300 years, until the independence of these territories in the nineteenth century.

The Portuguese weren't as successful at maintaining their interests in Asia. They benefited from a near monopoly in the region for over a hundred years but were later displaced by the Dutch, French, British, and others, who entered the Indian Ocean trade as competitors in the seventeenth century. The employees of chartered companies (such as the Dutch East India Company) were often the first to make contact in these distant territories. Serving as agents of the crown, these companies paved the way for imperialism. Under a royal charter granting him access to much of southern Africa, Cecil Rhodes's British South African Company had the power to conduct warfare and diplomacy and to annex territory on behalf of the British monarch. With enormous resources at their disposal, these companies established EMPIRES in Asia and Africa with a variety of economic interests in mind. They later pushed for concessions and enjoyed monopolies in the Middle Eastern mandates—these profits were also repatriated to Europe. With the exception of the early colonies established by the Spanish and Portuguese, Europeans maintained long relationships in these territories prior to outright colonization.

This was the age of MERCANTILISM, the precapitalist stage marked by the accumulation of capital through trade and plunder on a worldwide scale. Under mercantilism, each power sought commercial expansion in order to achieve a surplus in its balance of trade. Colonies were developed to suit the mother country's interest, as sources of raw materials and guaranteed markets for its manufactured goods. Colonialism was never about free trade. Rather, in the earliest days it was mercantilist, and through to the end it was protectionist. Whether it was the Spanish in the fifteenth century or the French after World War II, this exclusive arrangement served as the umbilical cord linking the mother country to her colonies.

From the earliest days of colonization this arrangement simply meant expropriation without compensation. In Spanish America, mining was the principal source of royal revenue. The crown acquired enormous wealth by hauling treasure off in its galleons, creating monopolies, and taxing all wealth produced in the colonies. Under the *quinto,* one-fifth of all gold, silver, and other precious metals belonged to the crown. Innumerable taxes weighed on the indigenous people, who paid the costs of colonial administration and defense and were expected to produce a surplus for the crown. Such wealth promoted the growth of European industry and subsidized the consolidation of European commercial and military power in Asia and Africa.[7]

With industrialization fully under way in the eighteenth and nineteenth centuries, European economic interests in the non-Western world grew. In order to ensure the quantity and quality of the raw materials they desired, Europeans yearned to eliminate local middlemen and establish their own monopoly control of production and trade. Eager to sell their newly manufactured wares, the colonizers sought guaranteed markets and set about destroying their indigenous competitors. They interfered with preexisting regional and long-distance trades. For example, the Spanish colonies were prohibited from producing any goods produced by Spain. In Africa, Asia, the Middle East, and Latin America, self-sufficient economies were destroyed or transformed and subordinated. India, which once produced the world's finest cotton yarn and textiles, was flooded by cheap, factory-made British fabrics and effectively eliminated as a competitor. Millions of artisans were put out of work, with little choice but to turn to farming. Similarly, the Ottoman Empire's handicrafts manufacturing couldn't compete with industrialized production techniques of the West. Colonized peoples were driven out of the most important sectors of their economies, as industrialists, craftsmen, and merchants.

Europe's industrial revolution also demanded reliable access to cheap raw materials. The colonies were established to serve as feeders to the industrial economies of the colonizer, and the result was the development of economies centered on the export of raw materials. Justified by the principle of COMPARATIVE ADVANTAGE, which holds that efficiency is enhanced by specialization in production, the mother countries decided what their new colonies would produce, based on the colonizer's needs and the particular resources of each territory. Monocultures were created: sugar from Cuba, hides from Argentina, coffee from Kenya, cotton from Egypt. Nigeria and India were unusual in that they exported a handful of different cash crops. The colonies were never to be self-sufficient; instead they were undiversified, vulnerable, and dependent.

To ensure the desired quality and quantity of goods, the mother countries often imposed a system of compulsory crop cultivation. Small farmers were given quotas and obliged by law to produce the assigned cash crops. Those who did not fulfill their quotas could be fined or arrested. In Latin America, Indians were forced to sell their goods at fixed prices usually well below world market value. In addition, they were compelled to buy goods at artificially high prices. Because of the relatively low value of unprocessed goods versus the high cost of imports, colonialism established a fundamental inequality of exchange. The people of the colonies ended up producing what they didn't consume and consuming what they didn't produce.[8] They were in effect marketing raw goods to the West, to repurchase them in finished form.

For all intents and purposes, the resources of one territory were drained to enrich another. The Europeans opened up mines and plantations. Germans and South Africans stripped Namibia of its once-vast diamond wealth. After the Dutch East India Company took Indonesia, all of Java was set aside and parceled into large plantations to grow export crops such as coffee and pepper. Europeans busied themselves obtaining concessions, such as a sixty-year British monopoly to find and develop petroleum and natural gas in most of Persia. Soon foreigners owned the right to control every aspect of this asset, and Persia was the richest known source of petroleum at the time.[9]

Someone had to produce these commodities, and one of the first concerns of every colonial power was how to meet its labor demands in terms of mining, portage, construction, and cultivation. Slavery, tenancy, and debt peonage existed throughout the colonial period. Although King Leopold of Belgium was unrivaled in the barbarism he used to compel labor in Congo, other colonizers used forced labor as well. Under the Spanish system of *repartimiento* (or the *mita*), all adult male Indians had to spend part of their year laboring in Spanish mines, farms, and public works. Barely disguised slavery, the *mita* was an important source of labor for the Spanish until the end of the colonial period.[10] Similar practices, such as land curtailment, or the large-scale appropriation of territory by Europeans, denied the indigenous people an alternative source of cash income. Once-independent farmers and herders were converted to wage labor. In addition, taxes were imposed at such a rate (and to be paid in the colonizer's currency) that people were left little choice but to seek employment in the colonial economy. Perhaps the most oppressive labor regulations were found in southern Africa, where pass laws and labor contracts created a system of migrant labor that gave employers enormous advantages. To some degree it continues to this day.

Wherever colonialism existed, no matter who was doing the colonizing, the effect on the colonized was much the same. The demands of the colonial economy often resulted not only in an intensification of the exploitation of labor, but also in a great disruption of community and family. Often men and women were forced to leave their families behind to work as migrant laborers. Overall health and nutrition deteriorated as demands for labor grew. Although most people continued to work as farmers, colonial agriculture was much more extensive than anything known before, demanding more energy and resources to produce commodities for sale in markets. Most Africans, for example, were so busy in their cash-crop farming that there was little time for the production of staples or to supplement their diets with hunting or fishing as before. Often the result was vulnerability to overwork and disease, which spread rapidly with the dislocations associated with an intensification of production and trade volumes. A variety of colonial policies rendered indigenous populations landless. Under French rule in Vietnam it is estimated that two-thirds of the population were tenant farmers.[11]

In the worst cases, traditional welfare systems were destroyed. The stress and dislocation of colonialism combined with economic hardship to contribute to a rise in social violence and self-destructive behavior, such as opium addiction in southern China and alcoholism in India and southern Africa. In some places populations actually declined, as death rates rose while fertility rates fell. Forced to produce government crops, Indonesians were left dependent on purchasing rice. But the low contract price for the spices they produced meant that entire regions became impoverished. The commercialization of agriculture left peasants vulnerable, and famine occurred with regularity. It is estimated that 15 million people in India died of famine between 1875 and 1900. During the first forty years of colonial rule, overwork and abuse reduced the population of the Belgian Congo by half. Perhaps the most devastating results occurred in the Valley of Mexico, where 90 percent of the population is believed to have died during the first hundred years of colonial rule.[12]

Figure 3.2 Did Colonialism Benefit Women?

Colonialism is sometimes argued to have improved the status of women, since the missionaries sought to destroy indigenous customs and social practices they saw as barbaric, such as female genital cutting, polygamy, and suttee (the practice of burning widows on the funeral pyres of their husbands). However, throughout the precolonial societies of the non-Western world, women's experience varied by race, class, region, age, and other factors. In some communities non-Western women were much more "liberated" than their Western sisters. Where women had shared political authority or enjoyed economic or sexual autonomy before colonialism, European sexism and colonial policy destroyed such systems and marginalized women. Where patriarchy long predated the arrival of Europeans, colonialism laminated it. Western and non-Western patriarchies joined in an attempt to control women's labor and sexuality, deny them access to education and employment, and deprive them of political power. The colonizers sought to win the allegiance of men by granting them increased authority over women. However, women were not passive victims in this process. In Zimbabwe and elsewhere, some women agitated for a return to the relatively favorable status they had held in their societies before colonialism. In a variety of ways, including the use of so-called weapons of the weak, they asserted their interests. Often, colonial women (both colonizer and colonized) enjoyed more independence than is usually assumed—despite rigorous efforts to keep them "in their place."[13]

God

Often alongside the conquistadors in Latin America and the traders in Asia and Africa were the missionaries. "God" would be invoked to justify colonialism, and to varying degrees proselytizing was a large part of the colonial effort. Priests came to Latin America on Columbus's second sailing in 1493. The Catholic Church was joined by Protestant missionaries who served as aggressive agents of cultural imperialism as well, to compete for souls in Asia, Africa, and to a lesser extent in the Middle East. Catholic or Protestant, some missionaries saw themselves as protectors of the colonized and were "pronative" in conflicts with the mother country over their treatment. However, these people of God were colonizers as well, collaborators crucial to the administrative success by helping to bring indigenous peoples under control. In a massive effort, work was fused with conversion. The "heathens" were gathered together so that they could be not only more easily evangelized, but also taught "Christian virtues" of hard work and unquestioning obedience.

More than any other actor, the missionaries were responsible for compelling colonized peoples to recognize their domination by the invading culture. Missionaries assertively challenged all preexisting belief systems. Their churches were often built on holy grounds, on top of razed temples, to drive home their message. The earliest days of conquest and pacification were often times of violence, dramatic social change, and transformation. For many people colonialism meant the destruction of their world, since indigenous religions were assaulted by the persistent imposition of European values. Time and again evangelization was conducted with such zeal, and was so heavy-handed, that it amounted to forced conversion. Christianity was imposed with an intolerance that was new in most regions.

Although there were some significant differences in approach (the Portuguese and Spanish were much more interested in religious conversion than the Dutch, for example), wherever colonialism existed it was based in racism and cultural imperialism.

Propounding social Darwinist theories of evolution and survival of the fittest, the Europeans saw themselves as more civilized, cleaner, smarter, and better educated than the people they colonized, who were variously described as devious, lazy, or immoral. The expression of this chauvinism or racism took different forms, depending on the colonizer. For example, whereas the policy of assimilation was based in the French belief in their own cultural superiority, the British were better known for the use of a color bar, based in their sense of racial superiority. However, institutionalized segregation and discrimination was the rule in every colony. Whereas the French were determined that their civilization should be accepted by all living under French rule, the British stressed the differences between themselves and the colonized, and were contemptuous of indigenous peoples' attempts to adopt the English language and culture.

Yet in British colonies and all the others, "white man's burden" was about more than just saving souls. It provided a rationale for domination: the fruits of Western civilization should be shared with the heathen. Again it was missionaries who took it upon themselves to bear this burden. They were given a virtual monopoly over colonial education. Building schools and clinics was an effective way of evangelizing and advancing the colonial effort. Apologists for colonialism often laud these efforts, which did provide formal education and improved healthcare for some. However, these services were grossly inadequate and unevenly distributed. It is estimated that fewer than 10 percent of Zambian children ever saw the inside of a schoolhouse. Secondary schools were rare in colonial Africa until after World War II. Few universities and technical schools were established; not a single university was built in Brazil during the entire colonial period. There was not one university in Indonesia until 1941. Where schools did exist, often it was only whites or the children of "notable natives" who received these benefits.[14]

In other ways as well, the colonial educational systems existed primarily for the benefit of European settlers and administrators. The schools served as instruments of subjugation. They perpetuated racial inequality by indoctrinating the colonized into permanent subservience and sought to convince indigenous people of their inferiority. A few professionals were trained, but mostly the colonized were prepared to work as soldiers, clerks, and low-level administrators. The curriculum not only was irrelevant to their needs, but also taught colonized people to disown their birthrights, to give up their traditions, dress, customs, religion, language—in some cases even their own names. For example, French language, literature, and history were compulsory in colonial Syrian schools, while Arabic language, literature, and history were ignored. The achievements of non-Westerners were disregarded or denied. European institutions were assumed to be innately superior to anything that might have existed before colonialism. In effect, the children who went through these schools were taught to embrace all that was European. These students, who grew up to be the ELITES of their countries, ended up alienated from their own cultures. They were taught to assimilate and adore European culture and to look down on their own as decadent and worthless. The result was an IDENTITY crisis not easily resolved.[15]

Glory

A third factor commonly observed as motivating European efforts to conquer the world was the search for the glory and prestige that comes with recognition as a great power. Nationalistic rivalries for world dominion, in particular the rivalry between the French and the British, compelled the various European powers to claim a share of the cake. Strategic and economic interests combined to raise the stakes in this rivalry. No one wanted to be left out; the colonizers competed fiercely for markets. They also sought control of sea-lanes, access routes, and strategic locations such as the Suez Canal, Cape Town, Aden, Ceylon, and Hong Kong in order to protect their military, logistical, and economic interests. For example, the Suez Canal was considered by the British to be the "lifeline to India," since cutting through it from the Mediterranean to the Red Sea greatly reduced the long journey from Europe around Africa. Not only did this shortcut mean an enormous increase in the volume of trade, but control of India also greatly facilitated the exploitation of China. Therefore, location made Egypt strategically pivotal and the British insisted on maintaining a strong presence there.[16]

Yet other European powers were just as determined to establish their empires. Out of concern that such intense competition might lead to war, the British, French, Germans, Belgians, and others made agreements for the orderly extension of European influence. Through various meetings, they set out rules for the "legal" appropriation of territories. At the Conference of Berlin in the 1880s, the Europeans divided Africa among themselves. The arbitrary lines they assigned as borders are largely the ones that exist today.

Similarly, the Europeans carved twenty-four nations out of the Ottoman Empire with little knowledge or care as to what they were creating. Often the partitions took place on maps that didn't reflect the interior of the territories. Some of the resulting entities were left landlocked; some were left with little base for economic DEVELOPMENT. Just as devastating in terms of long-term feasibility, the colonizers ignored local factors and drew boundaries between states that cut across religious and ethnic groups.[17] Some groups such as the Kurds became STATELESS NATIONS, spread through Iran, Iraq, and Turkey with no government to call their own. In addition, groups with very different cultures, traditions, and beliefs about government were thrown together to live in MULTINATIONAL STATES. Where divisions are deep, such as in the Sudan, this has meant real problems for the development of national identities. Fearing dominance by larger groups, minorities often maintain their subnational loyalties. Many religious and ethnic groups in Indonesia, Lebanon, and Nigeria, for example, have little sense of national identity. As a result, state SOVEREIGNTY is weak. The existence of multinational states and stateless nations has contributed to innumerable territorial challenges over the years. The result has been attempts at SECESSION (Nigeria, East Timor) as well as IRREDENTIST WARS to redraw boundaries (such as those between Israel, Somalia, Iraq, and their neighbors).

In hindsight it is clear that the borders established by the colonizers would pose long-term problems for the non-Western world. However, in the late nineteenth and early twentieth centuries Europe argued that colonialism was for the indigenous peoples' own good.[18] Perhaps to satisfy public concerns back home, the colonizers took the paternalistic position that those with a "higher civilization" should be entrusted with the responsibility of tutoring their "little brown brothers" in Western political and social institutions. Westernization was assumed to be synonymous with modernization, and modernization was identified with progress. Colonized peoples were described as childlike or nonadult. The League of Nations determined that this period

Figure 3.3 Israel

After the fall of the Ottoman Empire, a variety of interests motivated the West's desire to create a home for the Jewish people. Yet at about the same time that the British had promised to create a Jewish state, they had also committed themselves to the establishment of a Hashimite kingdom—in much the same area, then known as Palestine. Unclear as to its precise borders and without attention to the rights of the majority Arab Muslims living there, the West helped to found the state of Israel in 1948. Though many people celebrated this accomplishment, for others the creation of Israel was symbolic of the triumph of Western imperialism over the entire Arab world. Only hours after its founding, the inhabitants of the area (Muslim, Jewish, and Christian) began fighting for control over this land, and the fighting continues to this day. It has been particularly fierce over specific sites sacred to all of them, such as Jerusalem. Jews claim the land back to the time of King David as their gift from God. Christians refer to the region as the Holy Land, and for Muslims it is sacred as well. While some Arab leaders accept the existence of Israel as a reality, many Muslims regard the very existence of this state as deeply offensive. Consequently, many Israelis consider their incursions into neighboring areas as necessary for their defense, whereas others in the region regard such moves as expansionist.[19]

of guardianship should continue until the peoples of Africa, Asia, and the Middle East were deemed by its largely European members "to be ready" for self-rule.

The role of benevolent father figure was another aspect of the glory Europe was seeking. This self-aggrandizement was clearest in the mandatory system, when the League of Nations authorized France and Britain to govern the territories of the Ottoman Empire. As stewards responsible for the area's welfare, the period of mandate was to be a "sacred trust." While the mandatory system was supposed to prepare the area for independence as soon as possible and be a benefit to its wards, in fact it was foreign occupation.

How much did the guardians do for their wards? How much tutelage in self-rule occurred during colonialism? What kind of lesson in government was colonialism, exactly? Although some historians get caught up in debates over the significance of style and approach, colonial government was overall rigidly hierarchical, lacking democratic forms of ACCOUNTABILITY, autonomy, or decentralization. Although colonialism's reach was concentrated in the cities and dissipated through the hinterland, its rule was authoritarian, and the primary objective of government was the imposition of order.

To this end the mother countries were abusive. They relied on repression to maintain control. Colonialism created a legacy of military privileges by rewarding soldiers as a special caste with their own set of interests, not subject to civil power.[20] The colonizers created full-time standing armies to crack down on dissent, dissolve parties, and force nationalist leaders such as Nelson Mandela underground. Others, such as Sukarno, were sent into exile. Justice was arbitrary; the colonizers imprisoned leaders such as Gandhi and Kenyatta and sometimes used appalling force to put down resistance. It was not uncommon for them to collectively punish entire populations. In one of the worst cases, the Germans fought a war of annihilation against the Herero in South West Africa (Namibia), reducing the population by 85 percent. In many places the colonizers became quasi-military authorities, reduced to imposing martial law to maintain control.

Not only was Europe determined to hold on to power, but administration was to be on the cheap, with little or no costs to the mother country. To do this, the colonizers relied on the cooperation of indigenous peoples, and distorted preexisting political systems whenever possible to administer colonial controls. Although there were differences in how much they relied on them, to some degree the British, French, and the others depended on the assistance of "native elites." Known as caciques in Mexico and the Philippines, curacas in the Andes, and mandarins in Indochina, these were indigenous peoples who either were large landholders or had held traditional power prior to colonization. If no local elites were sufficiently accommodating to colonial interests, the Europeans simply appointed what were called in some areas "warrant chiefs," ambitious men with no traditional claim to power but who had proven themselves loyal to the colonizer.[21] Rewarded with privileges such as exemption from taxes or labor service, they served as brokers for the colonial state, charged with overseeing the enforcement of colonial regulations, collecting taxes, and conscripting labor. Under colonialism, corrupt officials often became quite wealthy, administrators embezzled, and offices were bought and sold. In fact, in all four regions it is said that colonialism created a mentality of CORRUPTION. One of its longest-lasting legacies is the notion that government can be manipulated by money, and that political power is the surest route to wealth. Not only was corruption pervasive, but some colonial systems were particularly notorious for their inefficiency and immense bureaucracies.[22]

In effect, then, colonialism destroyed precolonial political systems and delegitimized traditional leaders without providing a viable alternative to AUTHORITARIANISM. Individual rights and freedoms were subordinated to the mother country's desire to hold on to power. Western ideals such as egalitarianism and SELF-DETERMINATION were seldom applied to non-Westerners. The colonial model of government was a small elite maintained in power through reliance on coercion. Despite all its grandiose claims, the colonial state was no DEMOCRACY. Rather, it was government based on intolerance.

Government based on intolerance, alienation from one's own culture, and the creation of economic dependency—this was what colonialism meant to the colonized. Gold, God, and glory all had a role to play in the push for empire. Rather than attributing colonialism to any single factor, it is perhaps best to understand European motivation as based in a mix of these three motives. Certainly the impact from political, economic, and cultural imperialism is still felt throughout the former colonies. Although it would go too far to blame all of it on colonialism, much of the instability found in so many former colonies should be understood as the logical consequence of this relationship.

4

Independence
or In Dependence?

You have tampered with the women. You have struck a rock. You have dislodged
a boulder. You will be crushed. The weight is heavy. We need our mothers. We
won't give up, even if we're jailed. We are ready for our freedom.
                    —*Women's freedom song from the 1950s, South Africa*[1]

Colonialism was not only a time of dislocation; it was also a time of unrest. There
was always resistance to European domination. However, it grew in intensity and
complexity over the years. Especially in the cities, ostensibly nonpolitical associations such as study groups, prayer groups, and even dance clubs provided people
the opportunity to congregate and discuss grievances. Such associations became nascent political parties advocating various forms of resistance. These groups became
nationalist movements as they came together for larger demands such as SELF-
DETERMINATION.

Groups that usually saw themselves as sharing few interests joined together
against the MOTHER COUNTRY (whether Sunnis and Shiites in Iraq or members of different ethnic groups in Ghana and so on) and were relatively successful in setting
aside their differences for their common goals. Yet multiethnic, multireligious revolts contained the seeds of possible fragmentation, even self-destruction. Nationalist movements in some countries such as Nigeria were always divided by bitter,
regional rivalries. Ideological, ethnic, religious, and other divides simmered just
under the surface of many of these movements, yet for a while at least, the colonized managed to transcend their differences to unite against the colonizer.[2]

A number of factors combined to promote unity against the colonial powers. In
most of Africa, Asia, and the Middle East, the rise and intensification of NATIONAL-
ISM corresponded with the period between World War I and World War II. Not only
were the colonies expected to sacrifice for the war effort, but the Great Depression
hit most of the non-Western world especially hard. An already difficult situation had
become intolerable. Asian and African soldiers returning home from the world wars
(many of them conscripted) had seen colonial doctrines of white supremacy dramatically challenged. Nationalist movements were emboldened by the Japanese defeat of Russia in 1905, and the near defeat of the Allies in the Pacific in World War

Figure 4.1   The Spanish American Experience

Latin America was the first of the four regions under study to be colonized, and the first to win its independence. Nationalism manifested itself there as a sense of "Americanness," which grew rapidly after the 1750s in response to a power vacuum in Spain. Heavily in debt from years of wasteful expenditures, Spain was an absolutist empire decaying from within. When it undertook an assertive program of reforms that had the overall effect of increasing taxes, the colonizer's relationship with its colonies was further strained—and the colonized were already pressed to their limits.[3]

By the end of the eighteenth century, dissatisfaction with the status quo was widespread. Rebellions became more common, and in Mexico, at least, it looked for a while as if self-rule would be won by the masses through social revolution. However, throughout most of Spanish America, Creoles (American-born, of Spanish descent) usurped the more radical nationalist efforts of Indians, mestizos, and people of African descent. An aristocracy with limited access to the highest levels of state and church, they had long resented the favored treatment given to Peninsulars (Spaniards born in Spain), but the Creoles also feared more fundamental social change that might threaten their interests. In the end the American-born elite exploited the crown's weakness and declared their independence. However, Spain didn't give up without a fight. It was only after years of devastating military campaigns that most of the territories colonized by Spain became independent, in the period 1810–1826.[4]

II. Supported by international organizations such as the Pan-African Congress, these servicemen were joined by students, workers, professionals, and others who stridently expressed their revulsion toward occupation. If World War II was a struggle against racism and tyranny, then why should colonized peoples everywhere not be granted self-determination?

Beyond these common questions, nationalist movements varied greatly in terms of IDEOLOGY, membership, goals, and strategy. They disagreed over whether peaceful change was possible, or if violence was necessary. And there were serious divides over how much change was necessary, if reform would suffice or if REVOLUTION was a must, and over what kind of government and economic system was preferred.

Although sometimes the split within and between nationalist movements was a matter of rival personalities and ideologies, frequently it was generational—the old versus the new ELITES. The older generation was composed of a relatively privileged CLASS of teachers, religious leaders, and low-level civil servants who resented the restrictions they faced as "nonwhites." Generally social conservatives, they were very class-conscious and tended to distance themselves from the MASSES. The self-titled "civilized natives" in Africa, for example, were calling for more rights primarily for themselves. These were not radical demands; most old-style elites were not asking for independence. Rather, they were seeking better treatment within the system.

Not only were their requests of the colonial government relatively modest, but their tactics were moderate as well. More trusting of the system, the older generation of nationalists played by the rules. During World War I, for example, the Indian National Congress hoped to win favor for its cause by cooperating with the British. These activists undertook letter-writing campaigns and submitted petitions to the colonial powers asking that they end abuses and do more to provide for the welfare of the colonized. Seeking to spur the mother country to take corrective action, they

Figure 4.2 Subversion and Other "Weapons of the Weak"

Although not usually described as "nationalist" per se, people resisted colonial rule for a variety of reasons and in a variety of ways. Tax evasion, desertion, feigning illness, breaking machinery, and other means of subterfuge are known as weapons of the weak. They are far more common than revolts and wars but have not usually been covered in history books. In part, this is because some means of resistance were never recognized as such. Escape, for example, can be a weapon of the weak, such as when mass waves of people took flight across regions during the period of conquest and "pacification" under colonial rule. People sought escape through a variety of other means as well, including alcohol abuse and suicide. Although we generally hear that populations grew under colonialism, in some places birthrates fell because women refused to bring children into this new world of oppression. Abortions and infanticide are believed to have been common in Peru, the Belgian Congo, and elsewhere during the period of colonialism. It is important to recognize that what may appear to be individual, private actions may be linked to larger issues as a response to an insufferable situation.[5]

wrote editorials. Some, such as the South African National Native Conference (later known as the African National Congress), used diplomatic means. Egyptians sent a delegation to London to present their case for self-rule. Elite and commoner alike even went to the colonial courts for redress of their grievances.

On the other hand, the new elite was primarily composed of a later generation of the educated class. Having mostly attended university abroad, the new elites were mobilized by liberal notions of freedom and self-determination. These new elites formed groups such as the Nigerian Youth Movement, which were often more militant and more radical in their aims than the older generation of leaders, whom they frequently disdained as accomplices of colonialism. Many once-cautious and genteel groups that had been known for their moderation, such as the Indian National Congress and the African National Congress, were radicalized by colonial refusals to budge. As a newer generation assumed leadership of these movements, it adopted a harder line.[6]

Well organized under charismatic leaders such as Castro, Nkrumah, Gandhi, Sukarno, Nasser, Ho Chi Minh, and Mandela, the nationalist movements gained in membership and strength. Instead of simply ameliorating colonialism, these new nationalists sought to completely uproot it. Their strategy was much more GRASSROOTS-BASED, including previously excluded groups such as women, workers, and youth. Like earlier generations the new elites used the press and international congresses to make their causes known. But whereas the resistance offered by earlier generations was marked by its politeness and civility, this generation of nationalists organized mass campaigns and were much more confrontational toward those they viewed as their oppressors. Demonstrations, strikes, boycotts, and other forms of mass resistance proliferated in Africa, Asia, and the Middle East after World War I, but boomed after World War II. Starting in the 1920s and 1930s, Latin Americans joined broadly based mass parties seeking more radical change as well. At times this nationalism took the form of radical mass mobilization. Demonstrations and strikes turned into countless riots and rebellions—and sometimes even revolutions. In the Aba Women's

War, one of the most famous events of this period in Nigeria, market women un-dressed and marched to Governor's Palace to protest taxes and unfair treatment. In response to the threat to their communities, women also led riots in Mexico and Peru, armed with spears, kitchen knives, and rocks. Men and women turned out into the streets under such circumstances, to let the authorities know that they should lis-ten to their complaints.[7] Often these mass strikes and riots were put down with se-vere reprisals. In the protests at Amritsar, for example, the British responded savagely, leaving a thousand Indians dead and many more wounded.

Often these movements did attempt to influence the terms of colonialism (or in the case of Latin America, NEOCOLONIALISM). For example, West African farmers sought to alter wage rates and the prices for their crops through cocoa "holdups" of the sale of their produce, refusing to sell until they got a better price. Throughout this period there were many demonstrations of rural and urban discontent. Colonized people everywhere wanted improvement of health and educational facilities, and equality of economic opportunity. Yet the movements led by the new elite generally had larger goals in mind. More willing to use violence if necessary, and more revo-lutionary in their goals than the old-style elites, these nationalists were seeking some form of national self-determination—autonomy, if not independence.

In terms of their vision for the future, many of these groups stressed the positive aspects of indigenous cultures and the need for a cultural renaissance, to revive the traditional order in the face of the foreign assault. Some favored Western constitu-tional models for change; some advocated peaceful change, practicing techniques of noncooperation such as civil disobedience and passive resistance. Others adopted and adapted Marxist Leninism, in the belief that capitalism would never lead to DE-VELOPMENT and that violent, revolutionary change was the only way independence could be achieved (Algeria, Vietnam, Angola). Others (such as the African National Congress in South Africa) used a mix of methods. Again, they disagreed not only about how independence should be achieved, but also about the best blueprint for the future.

For many years the colonizers were able to use the divide between the old and new elites to their advantage. Infighting within and between nationalist movements

Figure 4.3   Spiritualism and Nationalist Resistance

Just as religion was used to colonize, spirituality was used in resistance. Because of colonial at-tempts to co-opt or destroy traditional sources of authority, spiritual leaders were frequently the only ones left with legitimacy. Often denigrated by the colonizers as "witch doctors," priests and mullahs, prophets, spirit mediums, and healers inspired nationalist movements around the world. Some of these movements were moderate and advocated reconciliation and peaceful change. Others predicted the end of the world and a coming cataclysm for whites. In Southeast Asia, Islamic and Buddhist religious revivals mobi-lized populations. Pan-Islamism fused religion with nationalism, creating a jihad tradition that spurred resistance to imperial penetration. Sep-aratist and millenarian churches in Latin Amer-ica and Africa were often based in ancestral traditions. The common theme across the four regions is that these movements sought to re-cover the identity and defend the cultural dignity of colonized peoples.[8]

Figure 4.4 Wars of Liberation

For many countries, the road to independence was one of intense conflict and violence, marked by insurgencies and revolts. Where peaceful means didn't work, where all efforts were met with ruthless suppression, men and women turned to armed struggle. Particularly where there were large numbers of white settlers (e.g., Zimbabwe, Algeria), these conflicts often developed into revolutions and wars of liberation. Contrary to popular perception, both men and women participated in these wars. Women risked their lives to feed and house guerrillas. They performed crucial services, such as moving weapons and information to fighters. In some cases, women carried the rifles, serving as rebel soldiers in El Salvador, Zimbabwe, Algeria, and elsewhere. These women became important symbols and rallying points for their nations. For example, Hawa Ismen Ali, who became known as Somalia's "Joan of Arc," was killed while protesting Italian colonialism in 1948.[9]

over goals and strategy no doubt delayed independence. Still, despite the Europeans' best efforts, eventually it became clear that the nationalist movements could not be ignored or written off by the colonizers. The anticolonial struggle was greatly assisted by the fact that after the world wars the imperial powers were weakened, impoverished, and exhausted. Public opinion in Europe had turned against unnecessary expenditures, and most of the remaining colonial powers had lost the will to hold on. The colonies were reeling as well; the wars had intensified pressures on them not only for troops, but also for forced labor and supplies. After sacrificing for the war effort, living with shortages, price hikes, and wage freezes for years, the Arabs, Indians, Africans, and others expected rewards for their contribution. They wanted concessions from the mother countries and they expected to be granted more participation in running their own affairs. For example, during World War I in return for their cooperation against the Ottomans, the Allies had made promises to the Arabs for immediate self-government. The Arabs were infuriated when it became clear this was not to be. Why freedom for Czechoslovakia and Yugoslavia and not the peoples of Africa, Asia, and the Middle East?

With some notable exceptions, the United States and the Soviet Union generally supported the nationalists' demands. Whether for altruistic or not-so-altruistic reasons, both new superpowers generally adopted an anticolonial stance and pressured Europe to dismantle its EMPIRES. Moreover, in much of the diplomatic language of the times—from the Atlantic Charter, which upheld the right to self-determination, to the charter of the newly established UNITED NATIONS—colonial powers were finding it much more difficult to maintain their LEGITIMACY. Increasingly, in the international arena, they were being held accountable for their actions. The UN received complaints from the colonies, and required regular progress reports on how well it was preparing its wards for independence. In effect, a constellation of events, both domestic and international, came together to make the hold of empire less and less tenable. Buoyed by the vacuums created by international events, nationalism throughout the non-Western world was the driving force behind this change. This was as true in the early nineteenth century for Latin America (with the decline of the Iberian powers) as it was by the mid–twentieth century for Africa, Asia, and the Middle East.

The end of colonialism came about at different times and in different ways, but it is fair to say that it mostly came about over the objections of the mother countries. In most colonies, there was little power-sharing until the very end. The vast majority of colonized peoples were excluded from the rights of citizenship. In much of the non-Western world, all attempts by indigenous peoples to participate in politics were squelched until after World War II. Although the British and French were more likely than the Belgians, the Dutch, or the Portuguese to allow for an independent press and the right to an associational life, overall the "best" of the colonizers hurt democratization more than they nurtured it. Even those most willing to allow some political opening made often-inadequate and superficial reforms. For every concession granted, there were restrictions that continued to limit political participation.

Yet these were the lucky ones. Where the colonizers recognized independence as inevitable, and the forcible retention of empire as impractical and unprofitable, they acted pragmatically. With foresight, they initiated a gradual devolution of power so as to maintain the close ties established under colonialism after independence. While this might have meant problems for the former colonies in terms of continued dependency, a graceful exit by the mother country meant a far greater likelihood that independence would at least begin with some form of DEMOCRACY.

Others were not so fortunate. For the vast majority of colonized peoples living under Belgian, Dutch, Spanish, or Portuguese rule, there was little preparation for independence or democracy.[10] Even when they left peacefully, as the Belgians and French did from most of their African colonies, they delayed the handover of power until the very end and then left virtually overnight. To punish the colonies for seeking self-determination, the former mother countries cut off aid. There are stories that the French even took the light bulbs with them when they left, and that the Portuguese destroyed water systems. Worse, where strategic interests loomed large or where white settler populations lobbied against independence, the colonizers fought long and bloody wars in a desperate attempt to hold on to power. In countries where class and race conflicts were deepest, independence was achieved with more difficulty and democracy quickly failed. Similarly, where it took a revolution to win liberation, the new government was likely anti-Western, anticapitalist, and based on one-party rule.[11]

Is It "Independence" Only in Name?

However fiercely the colonizers struggled against it, inevitably the period of empire had passed. Although most of Latin America had won its independence more than a hundred years earlier, formal independence in Asia and the Middle East was granted or won in the 1930s, 1940s, and 1950s. The 1960s is the decade most associated with independence in Africa, although several countries were not liberated until later—the last colony to win its freedom was South Africa, in 1994.

For the majority of people living in South Africa and the other former colonies, independence was a time of great optimism and celebration. With the exception of a few elites, most citizens of the non-Western world looked forward to the freedoms associated with self-determination. Freedom was variously defined as everything from the end of forced labor, to political autonomy, self-determination, and individual liberty, to the end of colonial monopolies. Finally, it was time for the non-Westerners to control their resources for their own benefit. People anticipated a restoration of the dignity taken from them by colonialism, and in these heady days people looked forward to a smooth road ahead. However, too soon it became clear that each newly independent STATE would have its own problems to face. Above all, the nationalists who had brought their countries to independence faced formidable challenges of organizing new governments that would provide the political stability necessary for economic GROWTH.

Political Development

The architects of these new systems had very different ideas about the best way of organizing government. Consequently, the first experiments in self-rule resulted in a diversity of governmental forms. While some independence governments were established as monarchies (e.g., Iraq, Morocco, Saudi Arabia), most became republics. In part, the mode of decolonization explains the range of experience after independence. Although those that won their independence through wars of liberation usually turned to more radical experiments, those that achieved their independence in relative peace often adopted in some form the mother-country model. For example, many of the formerly British colonies experimented with a PARLIAMENTARY SYSTEM. Most of Latin America has spent some time under PRESIDENTIAL SYSTEMS like that of the United States, its highly influential neighbor to the north.

Experience with constitutional government in the newly independent states varied widely. In democracies power often swung back and forth between conservatives and liberals. Over the years we have seen other shifts as well; some constitutions granted a degree of state autonomy through federalism, while others provided for greater centralization in decisionmaking. In Latin America and Africa, most constitutions were short-lived; they were written and rewritten several times. In Mexico, Nigeria, Iran, and many other countries, democratic or not, there has been a constant struggle over how religious or secular government should be. Consequently, for many countries the only thing constant has been change.

For many of the people living in these new states it was their first experimentation with democracy. Others attempted to build on democratic traditions that predated colonialism. The experiment worked better in some places than others; some countries created democracies shortly after independence that continue to exist today (e.g., India and Botswana). However, such successes were relatively rare. Instead, democracies floundered in most countries just a few years after independence. In many Arab countries, for example, where the idea of popular participation was said to be an alien concept, democratic traditions grew slowly if at all. There and elsewhere power devolved from civilian to military rule, and many other countries as well soon became mired in a variety of despotisms. In part this was due to a REVOLUTION OF RISING EXPECTATIONS. Governments might be following constitutional and legal procedures, but they were failing to address the needs of their people. Those who had been waiting so long for a decent life soon became disillusioned with the pace of change and frustrated by the inability of their new governments to produce the desired results. As we will see in the following chapters, economic and political instability are closely linked. Across the non-Western world, governments at the helm of countries experiencing economic hardship tend to lose public support. They become weak and vulnerable to upheaval and military takeover. Now as then, people who come to view democracy as only serving the interests of elites frequently end up calling on the military to overthrow constitutional governments to establish stability and carry out speedy reforms.[12]

Whereas the demise of so many of these democratic experiments was disappointing to some, it was widely applauded by large margins in Iraq, Syria, and Egypt. There and elsewhere, dictatorship often had broad appeal, because in many ways "independence" was just a change of masters. These countries' so-called independence did not necessarily mean self-government and did not usually result in radical changes in the lives of the majority. This was most clearly the case in Latin America in the nineteenth century, but was also largely true of Asia, the Middle East, and Africa over a hundred years later. Hierarchies were reproduced, just deracialized (although in Latin America it was mostly a matter of American-born whites replacing the Iberian-born). Democratic constitutions were façades. Political and economic power was concentrated in the hands of a few, linked by class, ethnicity, or religion. When elections were held, they were often blatantly manipulated, and even under civilian rule AUTHORITARIANISM became entrenched.

Nonetheless, more radical models resulting from revolutions were often no more successful in meeting people's expectations. Interestingly, radicals often justified their rule in the same ways conservatives did. Both left- and right-wing authoritarians maintained that their countries were in crisis, and that they could not afford democracy because it was too disruptive. In some cases it was argued that democracy should be rejected because it was not traditional to indigenous cultures. Elsewhere the justification was that the masses only dimly perceived their own interests. Until they knew what was good for them, they needed to be led by the vanguard, a revolutionary elite that could show them the way.

Dictators used any or all of these arguments to rationalize the emergence of single-party states. Many of the nationalists who led their countries to independence refused to share power through democratic means. On paper or in practice, governments were created in which executives were strong, legislatures and judiciaries weak. Government existed to serve as a rubber stamp for the party and the leader (e.g., Mexico under the Institutional Revolutionary Party [PRI], Malawi under Banda, China under the Communist Party). Through the creation of cults of personality, leaders monopolized political and economic power.

In Latin America these strongmen were known as CAUDILLOS, and nearly every country in the region had at least one in the early years after independence—and has had since (as we will see in Chapter 14). In Africa, Asia, and the Middle East, in monarchies, and in civilian- and military-ruled republics, these leaders established themselves as "supreme protectors" or "presidents for life." Based on personal, not constitutional authority, Sukarno ruled Indonesia for two and a half decades. Ferdinand Marcos clung to power in the Philippines and Mobutu Sésé Seko in Zaire for more than twenty years. Despite the fact that they were famously corrupt, these leaders portrayed themselves as all-seeing, all-knowing father figures responsible for the welfare of the nation. Much like the monarchs of long ago, their power was based on their charisma, their ability to co-opt populations by doling out favors—and their willingness to use violence to quell dissent.

With few exceptions, under civilian and military rule, in both left-wing and right-wing governments, the size and influence of militaries expanded. Dictators dependent on the use of repression to maintain power tended to overindulge the military in order to maintain its loyalty. As a result, spending on the military ballooned in most countries, further aggravating economic difficulties. Mexico was one of the countries most generous with its military. Military spending under a series of CAUDILLOS consumed approximately 60 percent of the national budget in the 1820s, and under Antonio López de Santa Anna in 1854–1855 the military share of the budget was 94 percent.[13] Yet Mexico was unique only in the extent of such excess. Governments around the world (including those of developed countries) have routinely put guns before butter, favoring military spending above healthcare, education, and the like. Although there were some revolutionary military governments that sought to overturn the status quo, most often militaries tended to intervene to protect the interests of conservative landowners and urban elites. However, this relationship on occasion became strained. Growing military contempt for civilians often resulted in coups against democratic and less-than-democratic governments. In many countries, the military's political importance grew as that of civilian authority declined.

Why has AUTHORITARIANISM been such a persistent feature of politics in all four regions? At times coups were applauded and authoritarians enjoyed widespread popularity, simply because they provided the order that was so widely viewed as necessary to economic growth and progress.[14] Another factor that motivated populations to put security issues above other needs is that very soon after independence many countries had begun falling apart. With their common enemy gone, nationalists turned on each other. Divisions that had run just under the surface during the nationalist period resurfaced to plague many of the newly independent states. With the end of colonialism, the competition for power was naked and constant. Politics quickly became regarded as a ZERO-SUM GAME, in which whatever power one group won came only at the loss of power by another. Although we hear a lot about "tribal" conflicts in the non-Western world, clashes were frequently based on power politics portrayed as based not only in ethnic but also in regional, linguistic, or religious differences. Across countries in all four regions, these CLEAVAGES have contributed to a process of fragmentation. The result has been civil war, often involving efforts at SECESSION, and international wars, to redraw boundaries and claim resources. In Nigeria, Guatemala, Indonesia, and elsewhere, when politicians have manipulated religious, ethnic, or other communal divides to win power, it has meant chaos.[15]

Old resentments that may have preceded colonialism but were aggravated by policies of divide and rule were rendered even more deadly by the COLD WAR. During the period running from the end of World War II until the demise of the Soviet Union in the early 1990s, non-Western countries often found themselves the targets of superpower influence. In the major ideological battle of the twentieth century, the world was divided between the United States and the Soviet Union into spheres of influence. In this struggle the United States favored conservative governments and rebel movements friendly to capitalism and routinely embraced military dictatorships because they were anticommunist. As President Harry Truman famously put it about his counterpart, Anastacio Somoza of Nicaragua, "He's a bastard, but he's our bastard." No more idealistic in its choices, the Soviet Union supported radical, anti-imperialist forces that had come to power (or were seeking to come to power) through revolution. In its own rivalry with China, the communist powers vied with each other to be recognized as the champion of the third world.

In their effort to divide up the third world, the superpowers made a series of bilateral treaties and regional alliances, often based on the superpowers' promise of military and economic assistance. The people of Africa, Asia, Latin America, and the Middle East were given an ultimatum by the United States and told that they were either with it or against it. They could not sit on the fence (although India and others objected to such treatment by forming the NON-ALIGNED MOVEMENT).

Once the United States and the Soviets had achieved nuclear parity, the fear that direct conflict would result in mutual assured destruction led the superpowers to seek other theaters of war. PROXY WARS were fought in Africa, Asia, Latin America, and the Middle East, with the United States supporting one side and the Soviets the other in various civil and international wars. With both the United States and the Soviets focused on their own battles, the superpowers intervened in domestic politics with little understanding of or interest in local conditions, let alone the issues at stake for their proxies. In Cuba, Afghanistan, and Vietnam, in wars between Somalia and Ethiopia, Israel and its neighbors, and in many other conflicts throughout the non-Western world, the superpowers again and again intervened, hoping to shore up their allies and overthrow governments supported by their adversary. Conflicts in these faraway countries were just a small part of a larger battle that each superpower portrayed as monumental—a war between the forces of good and evil. However, there is an African saying that goes, "When elephants fight, only the grass gets trampled." This was certainly the case for countless civilians caught between the two sides in what were often bloody wars of attrition.

Economic Development

To put it mildly, the political instability exacerbated by the Cold War was hardly conducive to the political or economic development of the non-Western world. Meanwhile, superpower efforts to prop up allies who were doing little or nothing to promote development meant prolonged economic hardship and volatile politics in many non-Western countries. Upon independence these countries had enormous needs but simply not enough resources. New leaders came to power promising to improve standards of living, increase incomes, provide essential services, and build infrastructure. Hopes were very high. However, even after formal independence, the economies of most countries were weak and under the direction of foreigners. Because of discriminatory colonial policies, there was a shortage of trained and experienced indigenous professionals, since nationalist leaders had frequently been relegated to a role in the opposition or as revolutionary fighters.

Just as the way in which independence was achieved had an effect on government forms, it also had an effect on the structure of postindependence economies. Countries that were liberated through revolution were much more likely to argue that the main lesson of colonialism was that capitalism didn't work. From their view, private enterprise had contributed to a distorted development, in which wealth was shared among a few. Thus postrevolutionary governments called for a socialist or communist system that would offer protections to the masses by granting a larger role to the state in production and distribution. Yet for a variety of reasons these experiments largely failed to produce the intended results. Isolated from the capitalist world, communist- or socialist-led countries often became just as dependent on the Soviet Union as they had been on their former mother countries.

On the other hand, the majority of countries had won their independence with relatively little bloodshed. They were more likely to be capitalist and to maintain close economic ties with their former mother countries and the West. Often new leaders didn't attempt to transform the status quo. Rather, they sought to open their countries to foreign trade, incorporate them more fully into the international economy, and replace the colonizers as the primary beneficiaries of the system. Most countries became plutocracies, in which rich families joined together to run regions and nations. With a few exceptions, landownership patterns remained largely unchanged. Indigenous elites sometimes replaced foreigners, but existing economic and social structures were largely kept intact.[16]

To the frustration of many, the colonial economic system essentially went on as if there had been no political change at all. With a few important exceptions, most countries continued as producers of raw materials—often exporting the very same commodities assigned to them under colonialism. The performance of these sectors varied; there were occasionally times of prosperity (e.g., Peru's guano boom in the nineteenth century), but for the most part their exports were more vulnerable than finished goods, subject to periodic and dramatic price changes. Cycles of international boom and bust had devastating consequences, even for those countries that had managed to industrialize.

Meanwhile, unless there was strong state intervention guiding these economies, foreign corporations continued to dominate them. This was especially the case in petroleum-producing countries, but to some degree true of all raw materials producers, since most non-Western countries had little control over production levels, pricing, processing, marketing, or the transportation of their goods. Still largely undiversified monocultures, they were dependent not only on foreign investment, but on foreign imports as well. Since these countries were earning too little from their exports to pay for imports of oil, food, medicine, and other consumer items, they soon fell into a pattern of deficit spending. African, Asian, Latin American, and Middle Eastern states became caught up in a cycle of borrowing to pay their debts and spending revenues on debt service rather than the internal improvements that might promote development. Within a few years of independence, many countries were in default on their debts and vulnerable to the whims of their creditors. Foreign influence, whether through MULTINATIONAL CORPORATIONS (MNCs) or INTERNATIONAL FINANCIAL INSTITUTIONS (IFIs) and other organizations, eventually became so pervasive that the term NEOCOLONIALISM was coined to describe the condition of many non-Western states, which were now independent only in name.[17]

Conclusions: From Interdependence to Dependence?

Although we tend to think of the INTERNATIONAL ECONOMIC SYSTEM as a contemporary phenomenon, it existed long before Europeans colonized the world. Empires in Africa, Asia, and the Middle East had prospered in the world marketplace for over 2,000 years. The Americas were linked in a busy regional trade. Although some areas remained isolated, others played an integral part in the evolving international trade. African, Asian, and Middle Eastern craftsmen and merchants once traded on equal par with Europeans, as equal partners in the world economy.[18] It is important to understand that before the age of European empire, Europe was just one part of the international economy. A world economy and system of interdependence predates colonialism.

Figure 4.5 Attempts at Industrialization

Why not just break out of the raw materials rut? Countries in all four regions have attempted to industrialize, to diversify their economic bases, and to lessen their dependence on foreign trade—in most cases through import substitution industrialization (ISI)—that is, by replacing expensive foreign imports with domestically produced consumer items. Some countries (particularly in Asia) have managed to successfully industrialize, mostly due to strong state intervention and protectionism. However, more often these early attempts at industrialization have failed. State-owned enterprises (SOEs) frequently proved to be inefficient, and the infant industries they were trying to launch simply could not compete against more established enterprises in developed countries.

However, that interdependence was fundamentally changed by European imperial expansion. One major effect of this expansionism was that the economic relationship between the West and much of the world shifted substantially over time—to Europe's favor. Whether it lasted for three decades or three centuries, the mercantilist policies associated with colonialism played a decisive role in Europe's rise to power. Noneconomic interests did play a part in motivating this expansionism. But the accumulation of capital created by the transatlantic slave trade, the pillage of foreign lands, and the creation of European monopolies provided the base for Western industrialization and the development of capitalism.

Whereas this early form of GLOBALIZATION meant unprecedented wealth for Europe, for the people to be conquered the European presence was much like an apocalypse. Yes, the history of the world can be described as a series of conquests, and the rise and fall of empires is a recurrent phenomenon in the histories of all regions. This wasn't the first time outsiders had swept through these territories, but it usually involved a relatively marginal disturbance to the underlying continuity of life. The European colonization of Africa, Asia, Latin America, and to a lesser extent the Middle East marked a fundamental, long-term change in institutional structures as a whole and a modification of the network of social norms and beliefs that constituted entire cultural systems. It radically altered people's lives. The effect was often devastating as indigenous political systems were undermined or destroyed. Social structures were warped, economies were distorted, and cultures disintegrated.[19]

There are analysts who refute such arguments and characterize the effect of European colonialism on the colonized as essentially benign, or even a positive good. They contend that the colonial experience contributed to the overall well-being of indigenous peoples. Many non-Westerners would remind the defenders of European imperialism that by and large, colonial rule was established through conquest—it was not something that the colonized ever asked for. It is undeniable that colonial policies resulted in an opening of more international trade routes and an expansion of the volume of trade—but on what basis? The mother countries did introduce new crops and animals, and transfer new tools and techniques to the colonies, but this in no way compensated for the demographic losses and suffering associated with the slave trade and colonialism. The colonizers did bring new ideas and worldviews with them. There was a valuable interchange of ideas, but at what cost—in return for exploitation, pauperization, and humiliation?[20]

Despite all the fanfare, the formal independence of these territories did not fundamentally change the lives of the majority of people living there. Nor did it create the space for the new states' rapid economic development. Rather, colonialism left behind a number of legacies—political, economic, social, and cultural. The former colonizers had put these countries on an unhealthy course from which it has been very difficult to deviate. Much of the non-Western world continues to suffer from neocolonialism in the sense that, since independence, other developed countries have joined the former colonizers to reap the benefits of colonialism without its costs. During the Cold War the non-Western world was clearly allowed only as much "independence" as the superpowers deemed compatible with their interests.[21]

Now as then, during the various incarnations of globalization, the non-Western world has struggled against its dependent status. The West has regularly intervened to overthrow non-Western governments seeking radical structural changes in class relationships and income distribution. Mohammad Mossadeq in Iran, Jacobo Arbenz Guzmán in Guatemala, Patrice Lumumba in the Republic of Congo—these are just a few of a string of leaders who were eliminated because they dared to challenge the status quo. But it is not just radicals who remember and have hard feelings about these foreign interventions. Ordinary people throughout Africa, Asia, Latin America, and the Middle East resent the fact that they are still not treated as equals. Far less than their counterparts in the West, they control their own destinies, plan their own development, manage their own economies, determine their own strategies and priorities, and generally manage their own affairs. Ironically, non-Westerners are uniquely deprived of a fundamental and inalienable right so lauded by the West— the right to liberty.[22]

Whether it lasted for 60 or 300 years, colonialism was not just a historical blip for many people living in the third world. Rather, it was an extremely important part of their experience, a watershed event they still struggle to overcome. Yet in recent years it has become the fashion (even among some third worlders) to argue that blaming colonialism is an old and tired argument. Those who dwell on its excesses are increasingly accused of beating a dead horse. Is it high time to get over it and move on? Or is it really that simple?

5

Linking
Concepts and Cases

The last three chapters have outlined in broad strokes some of the history of what would later become known as the "third world." To consider some of the legacies of this past, we invite you to explore the patterns described here in greater detail by taking a look at our CASE STUDIES. Too many people believe that the third world was always "third world," that life in the non-Western world began only during the period of colonization or that the only "civilization" is Western civilization. As you read about the specific histories of these eight case studies, consider the following questions.

How are the precolonial and colonial experiences of these countries similar? How do they differ? What countries colonized them and in what manner were they colonized? How were these countries integrated into the world system before and after colonialism?

What factors if any aided the European conquest of these territories? How did these countries attempt to free themselves from Western domination, and why were some struggles less peaceful than others? Did the experiences of those countries that became independent through the use of violence differ dramatically from the experiences of those that became independent through peaceful means? Since independence, what kinds of problems have these countries experienced, and how have they approached these problems? Which experiences since independence have been widely shared, and which have differed?

Case Study: Mexico

Well before it was "discovered" by Europeans, the area once called New Spain had developed a variety of civilizations based on maize surpluses and extensive trade networks. Although archaeologists are still piecing together the region's history, it appears that the Olmecs, dating back to 1200 B.C.E., may be the mother civilization to the EMPIRES of Mesoamerica. With their distinctive cities, monumental buildings, art, and sculpture, the Olmecs, and later the Maya (C.E. 250–900) played an important part in shaping the early history of this region.[1]

The Mexica, relative latecomers to the fertile Valley of Mexico in the thirteenth century, were a minor group who eventually built the Aztec Empire around its city-state, Tenochtitlan. At its height, it is estimated that this powerful, complex civilization ruled a population of 25 million. Much of its wealth was based in conquest, as it subjugated its neighbors and took tribute from them. Built on the belief systems of earlier cultures, the Aztec worldview mixed war and religion. The Aztecs believed that conquest was essential to the proper worship of the Sun God. Perhaps the world's leading practitioners of human sacrifice in terms of volume, the Aztecs saw themselves as staving off the end of the world. To ensure the passage of the sun through the sky, they believed it was necessary to feed the Sun God with life—human blood from ritual killing. To satisfy the Sun God's appetites (in one year just before the Spanish invasion, it is estimated that 20,000 people were sacrificed), they warred on their neighbors, taking captives for sacrifice. As you might imagine, the Aztecs had many enemies.

But when a relatively small expedition of Spaniards arrived in 1519, led by the conquistador Hernan Cortés, the existence of local people willing to ally against the Aztecs was only one factor in favor of the foreign adventurers. Though the stage was already set for a strategy of DIVIDE AND CONQUER, just as crucial to the success of the Spanish invasion was a slow and indecisive response by the Aztecs. In part this was because for ten years prior to the arrival of the Europeans, there had been a series of foreboding omens. The emperor and absolute ruler of the Aztecs, Moctezuma II, had expected a coming cataclysm upon the return of the god-king Quetzalcoatl (the feathered serpent). Quetzalcoatl had been known as a white-skinned deity who took the shape of a man. Understandably, then, the emperor was taken aback by Cortés, with his pale complexion, blue eyes, and red hair. Although still suspicious that the newcomers were men and not gods, Moctezuma initially tried to bribe the mysterious visitors to leave by offering them generous gifts of gold. Yet this only confirmed the Spaniards' resolve to march on Tenochtitlan and confiscate all its wealth. With the help of superior weaponry, the invaders were able to overcome their numerical disadvantage and quickly decapitated the empire by taking Moctezuma hostage. Although the Aztecs did rebound and made a last attempt to fight off their attackers, by 1521 they had been devastated by smallpox and were literally starving to death. The empire was destroyed and the rest of central Mexico fell soon thereafter.[2]

Built atop of the ruined Aztec capital, Mexico City became the center of the Viceroyalty of New Spain. The territory it covered was immense; it would eventually run from Panama to California, and include a few Caribbean islands as well as the Philippines. For 300 years, New Spain was the most productive and most populous of the Spanish colonies. Although it was eventually silver that produced the most fabulous wealth for Spain, the Spanish crown also encouraged the establishment of haciendas with the *encomienda* system, which rewarded the conquistadors with land grants and guarantees of plentiful labor. For the Indians this meant their virtual enslavement, as they were now compelled to provide their colonizers with tribute and free labor, in return for the right to live on their own land. Under their agreement with the crown, the *encomenderos* were supposed to Christianize and assimilate the Indians into a faithful, Spanish-speaking work force. To help them do this, the Franciscans and other Catholic missionaries arrived early in the sixteenth century and succeeded in making widespread and rapid conversions. However, more than protecting the new converts, the *encomienda* system and later colonial policies allowed for their exploitation and abuse.

Eventually it became clear that there simply was not enough labor for the colonial economy to produce the wealth Spain demanded. Living conditions under colonialism were so harsh that the area remained relatively depopulated for some time. To augment the labor force, African slaves were brought in, to share with Indians the lowest rungs of the racist social order. These groups joined mestizos in sporadic rebellions against their mistreatment. However, it was another group—the Creoles, a relatively privileged CLASS—who proved pivotal in Mexico's break from Spain. These second-class citizens within the ELITE, stigmatized simply because they had been born in the colonies, greatly resented the privileges granted to the immigrant Peninsulars. Moreover, the "Americanos," as they were known, chafed at the fact that the colonial economy was being managed for the benefit of Spain. Instead, the Creoles wanted commercial freedom in order to trade with countries other than Spain, and to become rich without the crown's interference.[3]

For these reasons many Creoles initially supported Father Miguel Hidalgo's social REVOLUTION in 1810. However, once it was clear that the changes sought by this movement were so far-reaching as to threaten their interests, the Creoles joined the Peninsulars to put down this and later rebellions seeking radical change. The movement for independence was stalled for nearly a decade until, in 1821, in reaction to liberal reforms in Spain, one elite, led by Agustín de Iturbide, displaced the other. Rallying broader support with talk about popular SOVEREIGNTY, the Creoles claimed power for themselves. Spain was too weak to do much about it, and Mexico became independent with relatively little bloodshed.

In its first fifty years of independence, Mexico continued to suffer from chronic instability. Between 1821 and 1860 the country went through at least fifty different presidencies, each averaging less than one year, and thirty-five of Mexico's presidents during this period were army officers. Government was changed at gunpoint; it was the age of CAUDILLOS, warlords seeking wealth, promising order, and surviving on patronage. Antonio López de Santa Anna was the most notorious of them all—he held the presidency on nine separate occasions. It was also during this period that Mexico suffered its most humiliating experience, enduring several foreign interventions. After a disastrous war with the United States in 1848, Mexico was forced to cede the huge swath of land between Texas and the Pacific (approximately half of Mexico's territory).[4]

For much of the rest of its first hundred years of independence, Mexico was polarized politically, torn apart by the rivalry between liberals and conservatives. In this often-bitter battle, conservatives sought to promote order and defend the Catholic Church, which was by now institutionalized as a wealthy and influential interest group in a firm alliance with elites. On the other hand, liberals were anticlerical and argued that the Church was entirely too powerful—politically and economically— and that reforms were badly needed. The leader of the liberal movement during much of the nineteenth century was Benito Juárez, who as president sought to strip power from both the army and the Church. Conservatives counterattacked and even supported the French, who invaded to collect on Mexico's debt and overthrew the Juárez government in 1864.

The period of French rule under Emperor Maximillian was relatively brief and Juárez was eventually reinstated, but the liberal-conservative divide continued to dominate politics until the rise of the last caudillo, Porfirio Díaz. It can be said that

Díaz, who took the post of president through a coup d'état and remained in power for over thirty years (1876–1911), finally provided Mexico with some stability, if nothing else. Associated with the "modernization" of Mexico, Díaz made generous concessions to foreign investors, sold Indian landholdings to private entrepreneurs, and argued that the repression associated with his rule was for a good cause—to modernize Mexico. Considered a loyal friend of the United States, Díaz ensured that any "progress" for Mexicans made on his watch accrued to himself and his cronies.[5]

One lesson of history is that policies that create such widespread misery tend to invite disorder. Francisco Madero, a liberal seeking democratic change in Mexico, ran for president against Díaz in 1910. However, after his suspicions were confirmed that Díaz would not allow himself to be voted out of power, Madero and his followers resorted to more violent means. From all over the country the people answered his call for the overthrow of Díaz, including Emiliano Zapata from the south and Pancho Villa from the north. This was the beginning of the Mexican Revolution; the movement grew rapidly and Díaz, surprisingly weak, stepped down in 1911.

But it was only the beginning of the first major social revolution of the twentieth century. Madero was now president, but he was more of a parliamentarian than a revolutionary. Because the changes he initiated were deemed too little, too late, he was soon confronted by his former compadres. During the most violent phase of the revolution, the country broke down into a brutal civil war that raged until 1917. It was only after disposing of Zapata and Villa that Venustiano Carranza became president, declaring the revolution a success.

The constitution resulting from this revolution was startlingly radical for the times. It set out a framework for significant changes in Mexico's power relationships. Among other things, the constitution (which remains the foundation of Mexico's government today) places significant restrictions on the Church. Far more progressive than labor laws in the United States at the time, the 1917 constitution established the right to strike, the right to a minimum wage, and the right to a safe workplace. As one might expect after years of foreign domination, the document is intensely nationalistic, and places restrictions on foreign ownership. Most significant, perhaps, the constitution gives the government the right to control Mexico's resources and to redistribute land.

The first years of implementation of the revolution's goals were very slow. In part this was because the government was sidetracked by a civil war in the 1920s when conservative Catholics sought to regain power for the Church. It was also partly due to the fact that the leaders who survived the revolution were not nearly as progressive as its architects. However, by the 1930s, Mexicans had in Lázaro Cárdenas a president determined to reaffirm the revolution's goals. His administration was responsible for distributing 18 million hectares of land, almost twice the amount distributed by all his predecessors combined. Moreover, the Cárdenas government recognized the necessity of providing support services to assist land recipients, whether they lived in the communal system of *ejido,* or on individual family plots.

Although he attempted to steer a middle course, neither too socialist nor too capitalist, Cárdenas was most of all a nationalist, and his attempts to make real the promises of the revolution were perceived by foreign interests—including the United States—as threatening. As late as the 1930s, foreign firms had effectively controlled Mexico's oil reserves. However, invoking the constitutional right of Mexico to control its subsoil resources, Cárdenas expropriated these properties, compensated the companies, and established PEMEX as a state oil monopoly.[6]

Petroleum was only one vital industry in which the state would play a large role. However, the bulk of the Mexican economy continued to be held privately. From the 1940s to the 1960s, Mexico experienced a "miracle" in terms of economic GROWTH, which was nearly unsurpassed, averaging 6 percent per year. Elites were the primary beneficiaries of the so-called miracle. The Mexican middle class grew, but poverty persisted and the gap between rich and poor actually loomed wider. To address this problem and win the support of the poor, the government created a broad system of social assistance. Although it has never amounted to a significant redistribution of income, since the 1940s Mexico has had one of the most progressive social assistance programs in Latin America.[7]

As indicated by its economic policy, Mexican politics since 1917 have been more pragmatic than revolutionary. Soon after the revolution, power was centralized under a single party, which took power in 1928 and controlled the government for seventy years. Known since 1945 as the Institutional Revolutionary Party (PRI), its longevity can be attributed to several, less-than-democratic factors, including its organization. It gradually took control of the military and organized labor, and then welcomed its rivals into the fold. It operated an immense system of patronage, in effect mobilizing the support of the peasantry and buying the loyalty of those who might threaten it.

Under the PRI, Mexico became known as the "perfect dictatorship" because, unlike many of its neighbors to the south, where coups were the norm, Mexico enjoyed remarkable stability. However, it is important to remember that the PRI government was authoritarian; as we will see in later chapters, it was not above relying on electoral fraud or even physical coercion to retain power.

Still, compared to many other countries such as Chile and Argentina, such behavior was uncharacteristic of Mexico. As the primary force guiding Mexican politics since the revolution, the PRI was pragmatic ideologically. Although there have always been differences within this large and heterogeneous party, a "pendulum effect" ensuring a tendency toward the center worked for decades to hold all the different elements of the PRI together. For many years this was the secret of the PRI's success. Until the 1980s, Mexico was effectively a single-party state; the opposition was small and seldom won elections. However, by the early 1980s that had begun to change, as elements within the PRI recognized that the party's survival was incumbent upon its ability to adapt to a variety of changed realities. The split within the PRI became more apparent as Mexico set out on a long road to POLITICAL LIBERALIZATION. The modest political opening continued gradually and the PRI appeared to reverse course on several occasions, such as when it claimed victory in the highly disputed presidential elections of 1988. However, prodded by CIVIL SOCIETY, the PRI managed its internal divisions to allow in 2000 for the freest and fairest elections in Mexico's history.

Case Study: Peru

Although the first Peruvians are believed to have been seminomadic shellfish collectors and fishermen, the earliest known permanent settlements developed with the introduction of maize and the adoption of impressive irrigation systems. The transformation of marginal lands into abundant fields formed the basis of several pre-Inca civilizations, such as the Moche and the Nazca, known for their sophisticated crafts and ceremonial buildings.

However, it is the civilization of the Inca for which Peru is best known. Its empire was immense, running 4,000 kilometers along the spine of the Andes. Heralded for their material well-being and cultural sophistication, the Inca rivaled or even surpassed other great empires in world history. Although there are still debates as to the origins of the Inca, in a relatively short period of a century they were able to subdue and incorporate nearly 12 million people.

At the helm of power was the emperor, who was considered both man and god. Divinely ordained, he enjoyed absolute power and controlled vast material resources. Systems of mutual assistance and expectations of reciprocity were core values of the Inca. Kin groups were allocated shares of land by the state. In return, individuals were expected to work the land, keeping a third of their produce for themselves and turning over a third to support state functions and a third to serve ecclesiastical needs. Subjects were also expected to perform *mita,* or draft labor, through which they helped construct and maintain public works, including a remarkable system of roads and bridges.

Yet this highly sophisticated, militarized state, defended by tens of thousands of warriors, was unable to stand against 168 Spanish adventurers seeking their fortunes. Clearly, the Spanish had an overwhelming military advantage. Just as crucially, the empire was already factionalized and vulnerable when the foreigners arrived, having just been through a civil war, the result of a succession crisis. The Spanish were able to capitalize on this, using a policy of divide and conquer. Led by the seasoned conquistador Francisco Pizarro, the Spanish ambushed the overconfident Inca and took their ruler, Atahualpa, hostage in 1532. The empire fell soon thereafter.[8]

In the early colonial economy of plunder, Peru became Spain's great treasure house. Lima was constructed as the capital of this seat of Spanish colonial administration, and became known as the Viceroyalty of Peru (1543). Mining overwhelmingly dominated the colonial economy. Little else mattered; as one viceroy famously put it, "If there are no mines, there is no Peru."[9] Silver became the engine for colonial DEVELOPMENT in Peru, as the demands of the boomtowns created by mining stimulated agricultural production. In addition, Lima became a vibrant center for merchants active in the Atlantic and Pacific trades.

However, because the prosperity of Spain and its settlers was dependent on a reliable source of cheap labor, the indigenous peoples of Peru were pressed into service. Harassed and humiliated by the Spanish, in the early years of colonial rule many Indians were rendered landless and virtually enslaved under the feudal *encomienda* system. Under a form of extortion known as the *reparto,* Spanish administrators forced Indians to buy European goods at high prices. Distorting the Inca system of *mita,* the Spanish compelled all adult male Indians to spend part of their year laboring in Spanish mines, farms, and public works (without the state providing anything in reciprocity). Because the silver and mercury mines were such notorious death traps and paid little, the *mita* served as a crucial source of labor for the colonial economy.[10]

Such policies had a devastating impact on the indigenous population.[11] The *mita* drained off able-bodied workers, contributing to the social DISINTEGRATION of indigenous communities. Famine became commonplace, and populations already weakened fell easily to disease. People were demoralized. Abortion, infanticide, and suicide became common forms of escape. Because of the depopulation of Indian communities, significant numbers of Africans were brought to Peru as slaves to meet the colonial economy's demand for labor.

Although they were treated as less than human by the colonial system, Africans, Indians, and mestizos were by no means passive in their acceptance of this situation. The eighteenth century was an especially tumultuous time in Peru, as over a hundred popular uprisings occurred, some of them seriously threatening the established order. The most significant of these insurgencies was the Great Rebellion of 1780–1781. Led by a curaca who adopted the name of the last Inca king, Túpac Amaru, this revolt was based in Inca NATIONALISM and spread rapidly throughout the southern Andes. Determined to contain the well-organized mass movement, the Spanish set out to reconquer the area, terrorizing villages. Six months later this short but vicious civil war was over, with more than 100,000 dead (nearly 10 percent of the entire population).[12]

The Great Rebellion had the effect of unifying Creoles and Peninsulars against the threat to their privileges. By the early nineteenth century, compared to the rest of Spanish America, the Viceroyalty of Peru was a royalist stronghold. And because the colonial ruling class didn't fracture in Peru as it did elsewhere in Spanish America, it took an intervention of foreign armies to bring independence to the country. With General José de San Martín pressing into Peru from the south, and General Simón Bolívar coming in from the north, Peruvian Creoles reluctantly declared independence in 1821. However, it was not until Bolívar undertook his final campaign against Spain in 1824 that his troops, assisted by Indian GUERRILLA forces, finally defeated the royalists. The republic was established and Bolívar set about the difficult task of establishing the first political institutions of independent Peru.[13]

However, Peruvians were divided over what type of government to pursue, and no constitution lasted for long. Although its constitutions contained liberal guarantees of DEMOCRACY, equality, and respect for human rights, Peru remained a highly stratified society where race and class determined privilege. Power remained dispersed to the countryside as a semifeudal network of Creole landowners controlled vast areas, free from restraint. The 1890–1930 boom in agro-exports accelerated the problem of landlessness for the majority, while the largest haciendas were owned by a group known in Peru as "the forty families." As a result, landholding in Peru remains grossly unequal, and among the most skewed in all of Latin America. During much of the twentieth century, 0.1 percent of farm families controlled 30 percent of the country's land, and more than half of its best soils.[14] This oligarchy, composed of businessmen and landowners, continued for years to dominate Peru. A COMPRADOR class, these elites manipulated politics to serve their own economic interests. For many years this oligarchy was backed by two of the most powerful institutions in the country, the military and the Catholic Church.

In the early years of independence, civilian and military strongmen fought for political power. The country fell into a long period of caudillism. Coups and countercoups were common, particularly in the first thirty years of independence, when there were twenty-four changes of regime. This initial experience established a pattern for Peruvian politics that has persisted, with use of force widely accepted as a means of resolving political conflict.

Just as Peru's politics have swung back and forth between civilian and military rule, its economic fortunes have alternated between boom and bust. After the wars for independence, Peru was in an economic crisis. Silver production had dropped, military spending was high, and the country suffered from chronic deficits. However, by the mid–nineteenth century, guano, or bird droppings, were to have the same effect on the economy that silver once did. Accumulating over thousands of years on the islands off Peru's coast, guano was rich in nitrogen. Once used by Indians as a fertilizer, guano was rediscovered and exported to Europe in the 1840s. For fifty years the guano boom created great prosperity for the Peruvian oligarchy and the British (who took about half the profits). However, by the 1880s the guano deposits were largely depleted, and Peru was soon unable to pay its bills. Peruvian governments began a tradition of selling off state interests to foreigners, and ended up putting the country's development in the hands of outsiders.

Eventually Peru managed to move away from its dependence on a single export, and began selling a variety of raw materials to Europe such as copper, tin, and rubber.[15] However, because the economy remained focused on production for the international market, not domestic demand, it was more vulnerable to price swings created by forces beyond its control. Adopting a program of export-led growth, Peru continued to experience boom-and-bust cycles. The gap between rich and poor continued to grow. Whenever a government suggested reforms that threatened the interests of traditional elites, the military stepped in.

However, when the military intervened in 1968, "politics as usual" in Peru were dramatically altered. Cuba's Fidel Castro described it "as if a fire had started in the firehouse."[16] The military, which had traditionally repressed all demands for drastic change, initiated a social revolution. At the head of this revolution was General Juan Velasco Alvarado, who as president proclaimed a new economic order that would be based on neither capitalism nor communism. At the heart of this program was a sweeping agrarian reform, to rectify the entrenched imbalance in landownership and severe inequalities intensified by an economic decline and accompanied by a marked growth in population. Military reformers also sought to promote a more autonomous development by nationalizing the assets of the foreign corporations that dominated the Peruvian economy, such as the International Petroleum Corporation.

However ambitious the revolution's goals, very little worked as planned, and by 1975 it was over. The reforms were halted and a new government set out once again to calm the oligarchy's fears, embrace a free market approach, and assure foreign capitalists that they were welcome in Peru. However, the economy did not recover. Rather, world prices continued to decline for the country's exports and its foreign debt ballooned. When Alan García Perez was elected president in 1985, he attempted to turn the country around by rejecting the liberal economic strategies of his predecessors. An economic nationalist, García shocked the international community by announcing he would limit Peru's interest payments on its foreign debt to 10 percent of its export earnings. The INTERNATIONAL MONETARY FUND (IMF) responded by declaring Peru ineligible for new credits. The punishment took its toll; Peru was bankrupt and suddenly the world's basket case.[17]

Meanwhile, Peruvians had become caught up in a brutal civil war provoked by the glaring gap between the affluent coast and the desperately poor sierra. The highly secretive Maoist guerrilla group, Shining Path (Sendero Luminoso), called for the creation of an egalitarian utopia. During the 1980s, both Shining Path and the Peruvian military became known worldwide for their use of terror. As the war grew more intense, the rebels seemed unstoppable, taking large portions of the countryside. Civilian governments declared states of emergency, giving the military a free hand in much of the country, and suspended most civil rights. Secret military trials of those suspected of ties to Shining Path landed thousands of innocents in prison. García and his successor, Alberto Fujimori, were both caught in the unenviable position of having to rely on the army against Shining Path. In 1990, after twelve years of uninterrupted civilian rule, Peru's constitution granted excessive powers to the executive, while its democratic institutions were still alarmingly weak.[18] Elected that year, Fujimori immediately took aggressive steps to deal with the economic and political instability rocking Peru. To jump-start the failing economy, he adopted an extreme policy of NEOLIBERALISM and imposed austerity measures advocated by the IMF. In the war against terror, President Fujimori preferred a similarly draconian approach. In return for cooperation in the US war on drugs, he amassed enough military power to turn loose his security forces on the countryside. When questioned about the iron grip he claimed was a necessity, the democratically elected president of Peru carried out an *autogolpe* (self-coup) in 1992, taking for himself the power to rule by decree. With the help of the military, he closed the congress and the judiciary, suspended the constitution, and proclaimed a state of emergency. Initially the public overwhelmingly supported the *autogolpe,* primarily because they were desperate for a solution.

Peruvians later reelected Fujimori president, since he was able to provide some semblance of order. Although Fujimori was eventually credited with destroying the terrorists and stabilizing the economy, over time his support dwindled as the population began to question the necessity of his continued AUTHORITARIANISM. When Fujimori once again attempted to extend his hold on power, ensuring his reelection through whatever means necessary, Peruvians risked clashing with the military and went out into the streets to demand his resignation. After scandals involving videotapes and a manhunt that now seems almost farcical, Fujimori, one of the few dictators left in the region, did finally step down in 2000, paving the way for Peru to make yet another attempt at democratic government and economic development.[19]

Case Study: Nigeria

The country today known as Nigeria contains hundreds of different ethnic groups, each with its own history. Because of the heterogeneity of these peoples it is impossible to begin to describe all of them here. However, a sketch of the Hausa, Yoruba, and Ibo gives one a sense of the diversity existing in Nigeria. They are the three largest ethnic groups, composing two-thirds of the country's population.

Situated at the edge of the Sahara, the Hausa states of northern Nigeria were kingdoms that rose to prominence based on their location as a major terminus of the trans-Saharan trade. Not only fine craftsmen and rich merchants, their kings taxed goods that traveled through their territory on caravans. A strong cavalry-based military ensured the orderly conduct of business, and offered travelers protection from raiders. From the fourteenth century on, Islamic culture and religion gradually spread through northern Nigeria, primarily through commercial networks. Kano was long a famous center of Islamic learning, although Islam did not become a mass religion among the Hausa until an Islamic revolution in the early nineteenth century. A Fulani preacher, Usman dan Fodio, led devout Muslims displeased with corrupt Hausa kings, excessive taxes, and laxity in the practice of Islam in a JIHAD against their rulers. He brought together the discontented into a powerful revival movement that incorporated the Hausa states into a vast THEOCRACY, the Sokoto Caliphate. Conversion was brought with war, as the jihad spread Islam into central and southwestern Nigeria.[20]

One of the groups affected by this expansionist policy in the south were the Yoruba. This powerful empire was based on a confederation of ancient Yoruba kingdoms and known for its remarkable bronzes and terracottas. The most influential of these kingdoms, Oyo, was at its height between the sixteenth and eighteenth centuries. A large and prosperous megastate, it controlled the trade routes to Hausaland and had a formidable military, with overwhelming numbers of bowmen and cavalry.[21] The power of Yoruba kings was limited by a constitutional monarchy that required that kings confer with a council. However, by the late eighteenth century the Oyo king had become increasingly despotic, violating the traditional rights of the population to participate in decisionmaking. This contributed to a series of devastating civil wars that lasted for the next century.

As opposed to the more centralized Hausa and Yoruba governments with their kings and hierarchies, the Ibo lived in relatively egalitarian ministates in which political power was decentralized. There was no empire, no expansionist military; in fact, there were no kings, presidents, or full-time political leaders of any kind. Rather, the Ibo lived in STATELESS SOCIETIES. If democracy is largely about the right of political participation, then traditional Ibo politics were extremely democratic. Nearly all Ibo were part of the great assemblies that came together to make important decisions for the group. A council of elders and other age- or gender-based associations enforced these decisions. Although the Ibo traditionally lived in the forests of southeastern Nigeria, they were hardly isolated. As forest farmers, the Ibo produced valuable commodities such as kola nuts (important for ceremonial reasons and one of the few stimulants allowed Muslims) to sell in the long-distance trade that crossed the Sahara.

European demand gradually redirected the caravan-based desert trade toward the coast. Nigeria was located in the heart of what became known as the Slave Coast. At the peak of the transatlantic slave trade, 20,000 people each year were taken from this area to be sold as slaves. Throughout much of Nigeria, larger military states such as those of the Hausa and Yoruba raided their neighbors for war captives, who were then passed on to African middlemen and sold to Europeans waiting at trading stations on the coast. Although some Africans became wealthy from this trade, it proved devastating for many others. As the slave trade became less profitable it was replaced by the LEGITIMATE TRADE. A number of European countries were by this time rising industrial powers intent on trading their manufactured goods for cheap raw materials. In Nigeria, British trading houses promoted the production of cash crops such as palm kernel, which could be used as an industrial lubricant and processed into a variety of products, including soap and candles.

French and German merchants were also interested in this territory, which by the late nineteenth century Britain considered to fall within its sphere of influence. In an effort to eliminate foreign competition of all kinds, African leaders were compelled to sign treaties of protection and free trade (in effect bypassing indigenous middlemen and maximizing British profits). The British sent military expeditions to "pacify" those who resisted this encroachment. With conquest still not complete, the British claimed control of the Colony of Lagos and the Protectorate of Southern Nigeria (1900) and the Protectorate of Northern Nigeria (1903). The British conquered these territories separately and they administered them separately, as two very different systems. This policy continued even after the so-called amalgamation of the northern and southern protectorates in 1914.

The architect of this policy was Sir Frederick Lugard, who believed that the north was different from the south and that each should develop autonomously. To overcome shortages of funds and personnel, the British attempted to use a policy known as indirect rule. As opposed to the direct rule associated with the French and which required large numbers of French administrators, indirect rule was much less expensive because it allowed the British to govern through indigenous rulers. It depended on the cooperation of traditional elites, or "native authorities," who served as intermediaries between the British and the indigenous MASSES and enforced colonial policy.

Perhaps not surprisingly, in many parts of Nigeria the native authorities were hated by their own people and viewed as corrupt collaborators of colonialism. Although people from all classes found ways to indicate their displeasure with foreign rule, ironically it was the Western, Christian missionaries who educated a new elite of African nationalists. Urban and predominantly southern Nigerian teachers, clerks, doctors, and other professionals asserted themselves as agents of social change. They urged other Nigerians to join across ethnic and regional divides to form trade unions, independent churches, newspapers, and various movements that would become the country's first political parties in the 1920s. Leaders of these early political movements, such as Herbert Macaulay (considered by many the father of Nigerian nationalism), often sought reform, not independence. They criticized the colonial government and looked forward to self-rule, but expected the transfer of power to be gradual. On the other hand, radical nationalism experienced an upsurge after the 1930s, as the movement for independence spread beyond Lagos. For example, students organizing the Nigerian Youth Movement were more militant in their demands, calling for mass education, equal economic opportunities, and a transfer of power to Nigerians.

The British reacted in a variety of ways to the nationalist demands. In some cases they resorted to repressive measures, firing on or jailing nationalists. Eventually the British offered some concessions, including a series of constitutional proposals for self-government. After years of negotiations, the transfer of power began in 1948. Suddenly Nigerians were to be prepared for the administration and development of their country. The participants agreed that upon independence they would establish a parliamentary democracy and continue with a capitalist economic system. The British left peacefully, assured that their vital economic interests would be protected.

As the date of independence neared, the nationalists abandoned the unified, pan-Nigerian approach they had adopted against colonial rule. The major ethnic groups formed regionally based political parties caught up in a three-way struggle: the Action Group (largely Yoruba), the Northern People's Congress (representing the Hausa), and the National Congress of Nigeria and the Cameroons (which drew mostly Ibo support). With the British effectively out of the way, now the enemy was other Nigerians. Perceiving politics to be a ZERO-SUM GAME, there was a polarization of the political process as each group vied for control of the country's resources.

Yet in 1960, when Nigeria finally became independent, most people were still hopeful about the ability of Nigerians to steer the country toward development. The new government was modeled on British parliamentary democracy. The country was to be administered through a federal system, and was initially divided into three regions: north, west, and east. In the first general elections, in 1964, the Northern People's Congress easily established its dominance, controlling enough seats in parliament to name Tafawa Balewa prime minister of Nigeria's First Republic, its first attempt at civilian rule. When Nigeria became a republic, a Nigerian from the east (Nnamdi Azikiwe) replaced the British queen in the ceremonial role of head of state. Obafemi Awolowo of the Action Group was to lead the loyal opposition.

However, almost immediately, all went wrong. Although technically Nigeria had a multiparty system, in each region one large ethnic group dominated all the smaller ones. Even more problematic, the northern region was given twice the area and population of the other two. Given their long history of distrust, there was little prospect of the eastern and western regions ever joining together effectively against the northern region. Tensions mounted. The 1964 parliamentary elections were widely suspected of fraud, and ethnic minorities complained about their lack of representation. Violence broke out in various parts of the country and the government was too weak to contain it. Politics had become a winner-take-all game in which compromise was extremely difficult. Because the country was in constant crisis during its first six years of independence, no one was surprised by (and many Nigerians welcomed) the country's first coup d'état, led by Ibo officers in 1966.

Yet like the rest of Nigeria the military too has suffered from ethnic, regional, and other divisions. Fear of Ibo dominance contributed to a second coup in 1966, and again northerners controlled the government. The purges and pogrom that followed convinced the Ibo to secede and declare the independent Republic of Biafra. Just seven years after independence, Nigeria was fracturing, consumed by a civil war, the Biafran War, from 1967 to 1970. Determined to maintain the territorial integrity of Nigeria (as well as control over its oil wealth, much of which would have been lost to Biafra), the federal government put up a fierce resistance. The fighting was prolonged, as the federal government could not prevail against the forest fighters. In the end, the government resorted to quarantining eastern Nigeria and cutting off food supplies to the Ibo. By the time the Ibo submitted to such tactics and surrendered, an estimated 1 million people had been starved to death.

Remarkably, the country remained intact, largely because of a government program of reconciliation and reconstruction. Such a policy was greatly facilitated by the sudden windfall produced by the jump in the price of oil in the 1970s. As a member of the Organization of Petroleum Exporting Countries (OPEC), Nigeria enjoyed great prosperity in this period. Overnight it had become one of the wealthiest countries in the world. Unfortunately, since then most of Nigeria's fortune has been stolen or squandered. This was particularly the case during the Second Republic, from 1979 to 1983, when President Shehu Shagari turned politics into a business. The democratic process was subverted as abuse of power occurred on an unprecedented scale. CORRUPTION was so massive and Shagari's government so audacious that fires were set in public buildings to destroy evidence. After a sham vote in which Shagari had himself reelected, the country broke out into open conflict that was only brought to a halt with another coup.

Thus Nigeria settled into a long period of military rule. During most of the 1980s and 1990s, the generals who ruled Nigeria were more authoritarian and kleptocratic than ever, even as the country slipped into a deep economic decline. After years of overspending and misusing funds, it was now a major debtor. The structural adjustment prescribed by the IMF prioritized debt repayment over basic needs. Nigeria's relations with its creditors improved, but the reforms failed to correct the economy's structural ills.[22]

Meanwhile the dictatorship was under foreign and domestic pressure to make political as well as economic reforms. After putting off the transfer of power as long as possible, General Ibrahim Babangida offered up his personal design for a Third Republic. When relatively free and fair elections were finally held in 1993, one of Babangida's handpicked candidates, Moshood Abiola, was elected president. As a Muslim Yoruba, he would be the first civilian president from the predominantly Christian south. However, almost immediately Babangida annulled the result, for reasons that are still unclear. Such actions confirmed Yoruba suspicions that the north would never share power or control over the country's oil revenues. Protests shook the country and Babangida stepped down. Within just a few months, one of Babangida's advisers, General Sani Abacha, had overturned the weak interim government.

Abacha presided over the most predatory dictatorship Nigeria had ever known. Living standards fell to their lowest point in twenty years. Brazenly corrupt and notoriously cruel, Abacha set about crushing all dissent. For asserting himself to be the legitimate president, Abiola was arrested for treason (a capital offense) and imprisoned until his death, of apparently natural causes, in 1998. The government became an international pariah for its use of STATE TERRORISM against its own people. It is sometimes said that Nigeria became as quiet as a graveyard—until, in what is widely considered a "coup by God," Sani Abacha was found dead in his own bed under somewhat scandalous circumstances.[23]

Abacha's death was celebrated with dancing in the streets. His sudden departure paved the way for another attempt at a transition to civilian rule. The Fourth Republic began with elections in 1999, with all the same problems of its predecessors. This time, it was up to a former military dictator, Olusegun Obasanjo, to lead the country in correcting these problems before the cycle began yet again.

Case Study: Zimbabwe

There was great cultural, political, and economic diversity among the early people of Zimbabwe. Hunter-gatherers long preceded the Shona, Zimbabwe's largest ethnic group, who arrived in the area around C.E. 300. Among the Shona were several subgroups, some of whom lived in empires, and others who preferred stateless societies. Although they are known to have mined and worked with a variety of minerals, most notably iron ore and gold, cattle-keeping was a more important activity for most Shona, who also worked as farmers. Perhaps the wealthiest empire of southern Africa, Great Zimbabwe was an ancient city famous for its stone buildings and vast walls. For reasons that are still unclear, Great Zimbabwe declined and was abandoned in the fifteenth century. On its heels a larger Shona empire was founded in the north, known as Mwene Mutapa (Great Plunderer). Like Great Zimbabwe, it too had an expansionist policy and took tribute from subjugated populations. Though without the cultural and technological achievements of Great Zimbabwe, Mwene Mutapa was also rich in resources and favored by its river access to the main trading centers on the coast. Long before the Portuguese established trading posts nearby, the Shona had been involved in a regional network of trade that connected southern central Africa to coastal trading cities and the Indian Ocean trade.

Most of Zimbabwe continued to be dominated by various Shona kingdoms until the early nineteenth century, when events in South Africa changed the balance of power dramatically. Various South African ethnic groups, including the Ndebele, fled, seeking shelter from the Zulu military onslaught known as the Mfecane, or "Great Crushing." By the 1840s the Ndebele had settled in southwestern Zimbabwe, which became known as Matabeleland. Though unable to defend themselves against the overwhelming might of the Zulu, the highly centralized Ndebele kingdom had a professional army and absorbed the resident Shona-speaking inhabitants. The Ndebele also dominated many Shona groups in eastern Zimbabwe, raiding Mashonaland periodically for cattle, grain, and women.

Another raider of sorts, Cecil John Rhodes was one of the biggest empire builders of the nineteenth century. Having come to South Africa from Britain at age seventeen, Rhodes soon became a self-made millionaire as a founder of DeBeers Diamonds. Interested in money for the power it could buy, Rhodes was a British supremacist and advocate of British imperialism. His interest in Zimbabwe was based on rumors of more gold fields to the north of South Africa's enormous Witwatersrand gold reef. Rhodes sent emissaries to Matabeleland to push for concessions. In 1888 the Ndebele king, Lobengula, was deceived into signing an agreement, known as the Rudd Concession, that basically gave the British mineral rights to the entire territory, placing it within the British sphere of influence.[24]

Soon after winning the concession, Rhodes formed the British South Africa Company, and obtained a royal charter to colonize and administer the area north of the Limpopo River on behalf of Britain. Rhodes recruited a "pioneer column" of settlers to invade and occupy Zimbabwe. Upon arrival in Zimbabwe in 1890, the whites first established themselves in the predominantly Shona east.

Conditions were ripe for conflict. Disappointed with its luck at striking gold, the British South African Company began looking beyond Mashonaland for new areas to mine. Yet not only were the Europeans antagonizing the Shona, but the Ndebele considered the east to be their raiding ground and resented the whites' presence. When the British attempted to establish a boundary requiring the Ndebele to confine their raids to the western side of the "border," a clash between the settlers and the Ndebele was inevitable. After a series of provocative incidents, the two parties were at war. Although the company's forces were greatly outnumbered, the British, with their modern firearms against the Ndebele's spears, swept into the west. Lobengula died during his escape, and with the Ndebele demoralized, Matabeleland was opened to white settlers. The British forced the Ndebele onto dry and infertile reserves and gave Lobengula's cattle to whites. The entire territory was placed under colonial rule in 1895 and became known as Rhodesia. By all appearances, the once-powerful Ndebele were now prostrate, utterly defeated.

So when a series of uprisings broke out in 1895–1896 and spread over Zimbabwe, the British were taken by surprise. Yet for the Ndebele and the Shona, colonialism not only meant political oppression and economic exploitation, but also an assault on their way of life. Aggravating their problems were a series of natural disasters. Many Ndebele and Shona believed that these misfortunes were attributable to the presence of whites on their land. Traditional religious authorities blamed the whites for angering God, and warned that Africans must fight to drive out the whites or they would continue to suffer. Consequently, so many of the indigenous people responded to the war cry "Chimurenga!" that the whites, even with their military advantages, found the uprisings difficult to put down.[25]

However, with the help of imperial troops, by 1897 the leaders of what is called the First Chimurenga War had been killed or captured. The British colonial office took over responsibility for Rhodesia, although the white settlers largely administered the country to suit their interests. Africans became second-class citizens in their own land, as racist laws enforced a color bar.[26] Blacks were systematically humiliated and exploited. The country was divided into white areas and black areas. White settlers poured in, taking the best land and establishing large farms. Most blacks were left poor and landless, forced to live in the 31 percent of the territory assigned to them—the wastelands known as reserves. Africans were compelled to work in slavelike conditions. To earn money to pay taxes to the colonial state, young men had little choice but to sign contracts requiring them to leave their families behind on the reserves for a year at a time while they worked in white-owned mines or farms. There discrimination was systematic; the disparity in wages between white and black workers was enormous. As late as the 1960s, white mine workers earned twelve times as much as Africans—and white farm workers earned twenty times as much as blacks.[27]

Moreover, the colonial system did everything it could to ensure that African political participation was kept at a minimum. Theoretically, Africans could vote in elections for a legislative council, but because the property and educational qualifications for the franchise were set so high, blacks were legally denied a political voice in this "democracy." This does not mean, however, that blacks had no political voice. Against the overwhelming force of the colonial military, many Africans turned to WEAPONS OF THE WEAK, adopting postures of noncooperation or "refusal to understand." When possible, workers simply deserted the most abusive bosses and shared "market intelligence," leaving wayside messages such as signs carved on trees that alerted others to avoid those employers.[28]

Some Africans submitted to colonial rule, but this does not mean that they accepted it. Rather, in order to survive, they chose to cooperate and seek some amelioration in their treatment. Still, self-government was a long-term objective for many. By the 1920s, larger numbers of Ndebele had adopted modern forms of political protest. Led by a new elite known for its moderation, they sought change through constitutional means. Black immigrants to Zimbabwe were frequently the initiators of mass-based protest. South Africans founded the Rhodesian Bantu Voters Association, which brought together Zimbabweans from different regions and ethnic backgrounds, and appealed to ordinary people by focusing on the land issue. Churches such as the millenarian Watch Tower movement mobilized grassroots protest.[29] The first African trade union in the colony, the Industrial and Commercial

Workers Union, was formed by a Malawian. In response to desperate conditions, Africans led a number of strikes in the first half of the twentieth century. More often than not, such actions were systematically put down by the state.[30]

In their determination not to give in to African demands, the settlers attempted to tighten their control over Africans. One way of doing this was through repression. Under a state of emergency, government was given power to put people in prison without trial. Parties were banned; activists were rounded up, detained, and imprisoned. Another strategy was to ally with traditional elites. Many of these elites, who had long worked for the colonial government as Native Authorities, were valued for their loyalty and the influence they held in their communities. By co-opting these elites and giving them more power than they traditionally held, including more power over women, whites could in effect buy their allegiance and promote a policy of divide and rule, by encouraging tribal consciousness.[31]

A third way of dealing with African nationalism was promoted by white liberals frightened by the Mau Mau killings of British settlers in Kenya. In the 1950s, whites voted in an administration intent upon making Rhodesia appear to be doing something to placate Africans. This government promised land and other reforms (but not "one man, one vote," and franchise qualifications were actually raised). For these reasons, most blacks rejected these "multiracial" reforms as paternalistic delaying tactics.[32]

Nor did the liberal policy sit too well with whites for long. The 1962 elections were the end of the liberal experiment, as for the next two decades white voters put into office right-wing extremists led by the Rhodesian Front. In 1965, without consulting Britain (which still had ultimate responsibility for the colony), Prime Minister Ian Smith cut ties with the MOTHER COUNTRY. Through the Unilateral Declaration of Independence (UDI), the settlers displayed their disregard of international opinion and declared Rhodesia an independent, white-run state.

Despite African hopes that the British would use force against the UDI government, they were unwilling to intervene. After diplomatic efforts failed, Britain joined the UNITED NATIONS in imposing economic sanctions on Rhodesia. Sanctions were not a complete failure, but they had little effect, primarily because the United States and other Western countries broke them. Some characterize this policy as racist, and in part it was, because the West viewed the struggle in Rhodesia through a COLD WAR lens. For Africans the Second Chimurenga War, which began in 1966, was a war for liberation. Yet the white government was able to portray the African opposition as communist, and the conflict in Rhodesia as part of the larger East-West struggle. The two parties that dominated the anticolonial effort, the Zimbabwe African People's Union (ZAPU), led by Joshua Nkomo, and the Zimbabwe African National Union (ZANU), led by Robert Mugabe, eventually joined forces toward the end of the war in what was called the Patriotic Front. Both called for a socialist transformation of society. Even more damning, from a Western perspective, they each received military assistance from the Soviet Union and China, as well as neighboring African countries.[33]

Pressure was building on the white government, and despite Smith's claims that majority rule would come "not in a thousand years," by the early 1970s it was becoming increasingly clear that the white government was losing the war. Desperate to hold on to power, Smith tried to preempt the guerrilla victory by promoting a political coalition. The Rhodesian Front was eager to end the war with the Internal

Settlement of 1978, based on a sharing of power with noncombatant African "moderates." After years of negotiations, Smith was eventually able to win over Bishop Abel Muzorewa, a conservative who had long been associated with the anticolonial cause. Although elections were held in 1979, ZANU and ZAPU, the two parties with the largest African following, boycotted the polls. Yet Africans had achieved some semblance of political power, as Muzorewa became the titular head of government. However, whites continued to control power. The armed forces, police, civil service, and the economy remained in white hands. Because Muzorewa could not control the guerrillas and because the Patriotic Front was joined by most of the world in denouncing the new government, the internal settlement was not durable. The guerrillas refused to surrender, international sanctions remained in place, and the war intensified and was virtually won by the guerrillas in 1979.

That year the three parties met in London to negotiate a peace settlement brokered by Britain. The resulting Lancaster House Agreement served as the basis for a new constitution based on majority rule, but with protections for minority rights. It established a PARLIAMENTARY SYSTEM with a president acting on the advice of the prime minister and set a date for elections. The parliamentary elections, held in 1980, were an extraordinary exercise in democracy, as the three bitterly hostile armies put down their weapons to campaign against each other. Voting did largely break down along ethnic lines, and though there were some irregularities, international observers found the process to be free and fair. An estimated 94 percent of the electorate voted and Robert Mugabe, because his party, ZANU (now known as the Zimbabwe African National Union–Patriotic Front [ZANU-PF]), had won an overall majority in parliament, became the first prime minister of independent Zimbabwe.

As prime minister, Mugabe recognized that Zimbabwe needed stability if it were to develop, and that there could be no stability without a policy of reconciliation. Although there were some hard feelings on all sides, Mugabe did create a coalition government, inviting Nkomo and even a few whites to serve as ministers in his cabinet. However, strains resurfaced by the end of the first year, and the country soon fell into a civil war. After years of peacemaking efforts, the two Patriotic Front rivals sat down at the bargaining table. The Unity Accord was reached in 1987 and ZAPU was absorbed into ZANU-PF.

As mentioned earlier, the government's policy of national reconciliation also applied to whites, many of whom had panicked after the Lancaster House accords and planned to leave Zimbabwe. Some did go, but Mugabe worked hard to assure whites that their property rights would be respected. Although an avowed socialist, Mugabe abided by the Lancaster House restrictions on the redistribution of wealth and adopted an economic pragmatism that surprised many. In fact, the mixed economy continued on much as it had before, with the tiny white minority controlling a disproportionate share of the country's resources. For more than twenty years the most crucial issue of all, the land issue, has gone unresolved. So far, at least, many Zimbabweans have found freedom to offer few material rewards.[34]

Case Study: Iran

Iran, which was known as Persia until 1935, experienced a dramatic transformation from a vast Persian empire into an Islamic republic. Grandeur, triumph, invasion, and discord color the historical legacy of this land and people. As a major world empire, the Persian civilization and its culture endured nearly twenty-five centuries of dynastic rule. It was named for the ancient province Parsa, where the first Iranians settled, and at its height ruled over much of the area we now call the Middle East. The survival of Persian cultural and linguistic traditions provides Iranians a nearly continuous cultural tradition up to the present day.

Modern Iranians go out of their way to emphasize their non-Arab, Aryan heritage, including distinguishing themselves from Arabs by speaking the Persian language. By the middle of the tenth century, a new Persian language developed that grammatically is not that distinct from Pahlavi, the language of pre-Islamic Iran, with Arab script. Acceptance of Shiism (discussed in Chapter 10) also distinguished Iranians from Turks and Arabs. As evidence of the continuity of some aspects of pre-Islamic culture, the Zoroastrian tradition of celebrating the Nurooz is still celebrated today as the first day of the Iranian calendar as well as the first day of spring (March 21).

Inhabitants occupied the region now known as Iran as early as the middle paleolithic period, approximately 100,000 years ago, with sedentary cultures as far back as 18,000 to 14,000 years ago. The Elamites were the original inhabitants of southern portions of the Iranian plateau. Their language is believed to be unique, with no discernible connection to any other linguistic group.[35] The Elamites created a regional civilization, which was highlighted in both Akkadian and Babylonian texts. Iran's abundance of mineral resources was known as early as 9000 B.C.E. and copper metallurgy became common in 5000 B.C.E.

The first dynasty of Iran's pre-Islamic phase was the Achaemenid Dynasty (546–334 B.C.E.), founded by Cyrus the Great, who was known for freeing the Jews from Babylonian captivity. The Achaemenians spoke an Indo-European language and believed in Zoroastrianism, a monotheistic religion that rose in Persia before Christianity. In fact, it is believed that the biblical Three Wise Men who visited the Baby Jesus in Nazareth were likely Zoroastrian. A ruler who described his empire as "Iran-shahr," meaning "land of Aryans," or people who are of pure, noble, and good birth, used the name "Iran" as early as the third century B.C.E.[36] Achaemenid leaders created a hereditary monarchy and empire, which spread throughout the Middle East.

Contemporaneous with the Roman Empire, the Sassanid kings led one of the Persian Empire's grandest dynasties in Mesopotamia and the region now known as Iran. Leadership continued to be hereditary, with a fusion of spiritual and religious power. Sassanid kings imposed Zoroastrianism as the state religion, granting immense powers to members of the clergy. The gradual embrace of Islam began after Persia's wars with the Roman and Byzantine Empires had drained the country, increasing discontent within the population. The "golden age" of Islam followed, under rulers called the Abbassids. This 400-year period was marked by tremendous amounts of trade both within the large empire and beyond its borders, widespread public education, scientific developments (especially in medicine and healthcare), and mathematical advances. Although this golden age began to collapse from within—torn apart by internal division and schism—its end was hastened by the European Crusades.

The Mongol invasions of 1258 ended Abbassid rule and divided the Islamic world. A succession of dynasties ruled until 1501, when the Safavid Dynasty—later known for its militarism and conquest—was seated. Safavid rulers battled with the Ottomans, eventually settling on frontier lines roughly equivalent to the modern Iranian-Turkish border.[37] This was also the dynasty that imposed Shia Islam as the state religion, in a succession dispute that is discussed in Chapter 10.

A new dynasty of Turkish origin, the Qajars, ruled from 1796 to 1925. Similar to what would follow later in Iran, this dynasty struggled to integrate religious authority with modern rule, all the while attempting to return to the glories of the earlier Persian Empire. It was under the Qajars that Tehran became the capital of Persia. Early-nineteenth-century educational reforms began to create elites who challenged Iran's relations with the West, fomenting local protests and rebellion and ultimately leading to the first limits on royal power. In 1902, Qajar Shah Muzaffar al-Din, facing the demands of reformers, designed a constitution (based on the Belgian constitution of 1831) that combined a national assembly (the Majles) with a constitutional monarchy.[38] The significance of this change was only eclipsed by the discovery of oil in 1908.

The religious-secular debate that colors much of Iran's modern postrevolutionary history is nothing new. In the 1906 constitution, the government officially enshrined religious influence and recognized some rights of religious minorities (especially Zoroastrians, Christians, and Jews) by granting them the right to elect one representative to the Majles. Yet legal protections as well as legal limits on power were ignored, often at the urging and intervention of imperial powers. The young national assembly lost much of its newfound power after England and Russia pressured it to dismiss Morgan Shuster, a US adviser who was quite popular within the Majles.

The Qajar Dynasty gave way to the Pahlavis, who became the last Iranian royal family. In 1921 a former peasant and military soldier of the Persian Cossack Brigade, Reza Khan, staged a coup, dethroned the Qajars, and founded the Pahlavi Dynasty in 1925. In keeping with tradition and alluding to Iran's historical notions of authority, he took the name Reza Shah Pahlavi (Pahlavi was the language of pre-Islamic Iran). He took Turkish leader Mustafa Kemal Atatürk as his model, promoting secularization and limited clerical powers. In 1936 he forced women to unveil, making Iran the first Islamic country to declare veiling illegal (an ironic point to which we will return in Chapter 10). He alienated many groups in Iranian society, but especially the religious clerics. In his modernization plan, Reza Shah attempted to combine retrospective elements of Iran's pre-Islamic civilization with Western technological achievements. He nominally tried to reduce foreign power, but his desire to modernize meant he was dependent on Western technology, especially since Britain controlled the Anglo-Persian Oil Company, which financed many development projects and had fueled the British fleet in wartime.

External interference in Iranian affairs became one of the leading grievances of the population under Pahlavi rule, and ultimately led to the dynasty's downfall. England viewed Iran as a buffer zone to protect its interests in India and competed with Russia to gain prominent spheres of influence. British and Russian troops partitioned the country at the end of World War I. After the Bolshevik Revolution led to the withdrawal of Russian forces, the British attempted to dictate Iran's transformation into a protectorate. The controversial Anglo-Persian Agreement of 1919 provided British "advisers" to Iran—on Iran's bill—as a way to ensure Iran's stability and ultimately its ability to serve as a buffer state protecting India. The agreement was shady at best: Majles deputies never had any opportunity to comment on it, nor was it presented for discussion at the League of Nations.

Iran was again occupied during World War II, even though its leaders had proclaimed neutrality in the conflict. During the war, the Allied powers accused Reza Shah of being pro-German, forcing him to abdicate, board a British ship, and head toward exile in South Africa, where he died in 1944. Even if the Shah himself did not explicitly support the Germans, there was much public sentiment encouraging him to follow the lead of the Ottoman Empire by entering the war on the side of Germany.[39]

The British and the Russians had considered restoring the Qajar monarchy, but decided instead to continue the Pahlavi Dynasty by transferring power to Reza Shah's son, Mohammed Reza Pahlavi, who ruled from 1941 to 1979. He continued the absolute power he inherited from his father, while increasing Iran's controversial ties to the West. During his rule he was significantly challenged by two leaders—both of whom questioned Iran's ties to Western powers. The first was Mohammad Mossadeq, who was considered to be a liberal nationalist. Mossadeq, a Majles deputy educated in Switzerland, became a leading voice in the calls for the nationalization of the oil industry, which England had exclusively controlled. As Mossadeq's popularity increased, the Shah appointed him prime minister in 1953. Yet the West vilified the prime minister for leading the changes in Iran's oil dealings, even though he was one of the country's leading voices for liberalism. London threatened military force, imposed economic sanctions, and even took Iran to the International Court of Justice in The Hague over oil, to no solution. The final nail in the coffin came when a joint mission between the US Central Intelligence Agency and Britain's MI6, in collaboration with the Iranian army, overthrew Mossadeq. As a result of these actions, supported if not encouraged by Pahlavi, the leader lost his domestic LEGITIMACY—already on shaky ground—and was labeled "America's Shah." There was much truth to the charge, as the weakened Shah increasingly relied on Western power games to maintain his own authority as he was vilified at home. Despite objections, the alliance between the Shah and the United States lasted for almost thirty years, as the oil industry was denationalized and the US and British companies raked in the profits.

The second man to challenge the Shah, and ultimately inspire the forces that led to the end of the Pahlavis, was Ayatollah Ruhollah Khomeini, a prominent Shiite fundamentalist cleric. Khomeini's first book, *Secrets Revealed,* published in 1941, defended the Persian constitution. But after police killed theology students in the holy city of Qum, Khomeini declared war on the Shah, which led to Khomeini's arrest and exile. Khomeini was able to capitalize on the festering resentment within Iran as people grew increasingly discontented in the face of prolonged economic crises, humiliating international domination, and attempts to secularize the state. The regime's attempts to marginalize Khomeini—including articles in the official press accusing him of being an anti-Iranian British spy or a homosexual—blew up in its face.[40] Khomeini voiced his criticism of the Shah ever louder, increasing his support. The Shah's response was to increase the power of his repressive secret service, SAVAK, which went to great extremes in arresting perceived enemies of the regime. Increasingly, the Shah lost control over his own government, and in the face of widespread protests and chaos, he and his family left the country for good in January 1979. Khomeini came in on his heels, declaring the establishment of the Islamic Republic of Iran in April of that year. Rejecting SECULARISM, Khomeini established the Council of Guardians, which institutionalized the role of clerics in interpreting Iranian laws, and ratified himself as "Supreme Leader" of the state, answering only to God.

Khomeini ruled during an extremely turbulent decade in Iranian life: the country became increasingly isolated from the international community, was devastated by the ten-year war with Iraq, and fractured along multiple internal divisions that had disappeared during the time of opposition to the corrupt Shah. But people had united around Khomeini, and after his death in June 1989, mourning masses attempting to touch his body caused it to fall from its platform during the funeral march. Defying the Western prediction of the chaos that would follow Khomeini's death, outgoing president Sayyid Ali Khamenei succeeded Khomeini as Supreme Leader in a relatively seamless transition of power. Ali Akbar Hashemi Rafsanjani, the popular speaker of Iran's Majles, was overwhelmingly elected president, and served in this capacity for two four-year terms, from 1989 to 1997. Rafsanjani was succeeded by the surprise victory of long-shot Ayatollah Mohammad Khatami, the former minister of culture known for his advocacy of the relaxation of controls over the press and media. Khatami surprisingly defeated the clear favorite of the religious establishment, Nateq Nouri, to become president. He served two terms and was succeeded by the POPULIST nationalist Mahmoud Ahmadinejad in 2005, marking a shift back toward conservative dominance in the Islamic Republic.

Case Study: Turkey

The Ottoman Empire of Turkey prevailed as one of the world's great civilizations for over 500 years. Because of the empire's overwhelming power, the "Turks" were characterized by some as the "scourge of civilization."[41] This image was memorialized in Shakespeare's play *Othello,* in which a main character warns against the "general enemy Ottoman." Once you understand more about Turkey's historical journey, it may be clearer throughout the rest of the book why some of its leaders proclaimed the importance of secularism for its future, for religious struggle played a tremendous role in the history of this land and its people. Turkey's history is surrounded by religious struggle and domination, including the early conflict between those desiring conversion to Islam and those desiring conversion to Christianity.

Turkish history is rich with a sense of strength, conquest, and creativity that we now understand through archaeological discoveries, including tens of thousands of written tablets that link the ancient residents of the Hattian lands to the biblical people known as the Hittites. It is believed that people began to populate the Anatolian plateau (also known as Asia Minor) during the neolithic period, in approximately 10,000 B.C.E. Some of the earliest evidence of settlements suggests that before 7000 B.C.E., sun-dried mud structures, grain agriculture, and items of luxury, including mirrors, daggers, and jewelry, were prominent.[42]

The Hittite civilization (1600–1200 B.C.E.) has been important to the Turkish sense of national consciousness, even if most awareness of this civilization was scarce prior to the 1920s. The Hittite period conforms approximately to the Late Bronze Age and is known for its creation of the two-wheeled chariot. The regime collapsed around

1200 B.C.E., in spite of its defeats of the Egyptian pharaohs, largely due to its inability to maintain its reach as well as the dramatic income disparity within its rule. The breakdown of this kingdom was followed by other monarchies, marked by uncertainty, warfare, and invasion. Numerous kingdoms were born in its wake, including the Phyrygian state, the Urartian kingdom, and the Lydian state, which is known for its creation of coins for monetary exchange.

The Anatolian interior remained under Persian rule for 150 years, until conquered by Alexander the Great, who ushered in a period of Hellenistic (Greek) influence. The Anatolian lands then became a battleground between Rome and the Parthian Empire. It was under Roman imperial rule that some of the most important early Christian Church councils, including Nicaea, Ephesus, and Chalcedon, took place. The Greeks were followed by the Romans, and later the Arabs, each bringing their own interpretations of religious tradition and opening Anatolia as a battleground of religious conflict.

Arabs began their conquest in the seventh century, although the Taurus Mountains served as a physical barrier between the developing Christian and Muslim bases. Europeans did not begin to refer to the lands of Anatolia as "Turchia" until the end of the twelfth century; the rise was a gradual one, taking nearly two centuries. The Turks were seminomadic tribal peoples who began conversions to Islam in the tenth century. They began to rise to prominence in the region known as the Byzantine Empire (also known as the East Roman Empire) and became consumed in struggle, lessening their presence in Anatolia. This absence allowed the Turks to conquer Armenian regions and push them to the south. The Christian Crusades, which began in 1095 at the calling of Pope Urban II and ended nearly two centuries later, failed to convert the Turks to Christianity, instead reinforcing their image as the people who wanted to destroy Christianity. Martin Luther blasted, "The Turks are the people of the wrath of God."[43]

The Turkish "golden age" took place under the Ottomans, the most successful Turkish clan, which was founded by Sultan Osman. The Ottomans were early converts to Islam, as the simplicity of this faith appealed to them over the complexity of Christian rituals. They conquered the Christian city of Constantinople, renaming it Istanbul. This was followed by rule over Athens, Tabriz, Damascus, Cairo, Belgrade, Baghdad, Tripoli, and Cyprus—the Ottoman Empire included much of the Middle East and northern Africa as well as most of present-day Hungary and southeastern Europe. Eclipsing the Protestant-Catholic divide in Europe, there was concern that the Ottomans would be able to go as far as Paris, for they almost conquered Vienna.[44] Despite the empire's Islamic focus, the Ottomans organized members of the non-Muslim minority into relatively self-governing units known as millets, Turkish for "nations," which were protected by the sultan. The three primary millets were the Christian Armenians, the Greek Orthodox Christians, and the Jews. Although this was recognized as a period of ethnic harmony, cultural diversity, and legal codification, it was also a time of little peace and almost continual warfare.

During the Ottoman era, the Islamic Empire ruled the seas. Ottomans held powerful posts on the Mediterranean Sea and Indian Ocean, and were viewed as leaders of the Islamic world. Ottoman leaders were very successful in their pursuit of land and followers, and adopted the title "sultan" (a leader whose authority is granted by the caliph, the ultimate leader of the Islamic world) as a way to establish authority, both spiritual and temporal, over conquered peoples.

Yet in the eighteenth and nineteenth centuries, the Ottoman Empire declined, especially in the face of the Christian powers of Europe. Despite defeating Napoleon Bonaparte in a triple alliance between Britain, Russia, and the Ottomans, the empire became increasingly drained of resources and became widely known as the "sick man of Europe." The proud people experienced great humiliation as Ottoman sultans were forced to sign treaties with European Christians over whom they had always viewed themselves as superior. The beginning of the end was the empire's alliance with Germany in World War I, pursued in the attempt to avoid isolation and, in the view of some, as a possible way to recolonize the empire's lost areas. The Turkish people suffered immensely throughout the war, and in 1920 the empire was divided into British and French protectorates, with the Greeks occupying western Anatolia. The greatest human tragedy was the Armenian genocide of 1915–1916 by the Ottomans, in retaliation for Armenian loyalties with the Russians (the Christian Armenians had vainly hoped that the Russians would support their independence after the war). While the number of casualties is a matter of great dispute today, most estimate that, at a minimum, 800,000 Armenians were murdered, starved, or died of disease as a result. The government of Turkey, to this day, denies complicity in the affair.

Following the war, the Ottoman territories were partitioned and the remnants of the empire were centered in Anatolia, one of the last regions discussed by the Entente statesmen after the war and whose domination and occupation by these statesmen the citizens of Anatolia increasingly came to resent. Out of the ashes of this semicolonization, the empire eventually gave way to the Turkish Republic, largely through a one-man revolution. Mustafa Kemal Pasha, later known as Atatürk (literally, "Father of the Turks") rose to prominence as the Ottoman monarchy started to rot from within. He founded a subversive group called the Committee of Union and Progress, which outsiders referred to as the Young Turks. But it was a revolution whose gains were costly, as nationalists fought for control over former Ottoman territories occupied by Greece, Italy, Britain, and France.

Atatürk had become the rallying force for a defeated nation after the German monarchy was overthrown and the Allies decreed that the empire be divided between British and French protectorates, with a small region left to the sultan and the granting of power in western Anatolia to the Greeks, the latter of which deeply offended the Turks. Istanbul was placed under international control: all the Turks had left were the mountainous regions of central Anatolia. Some have called this settlement more severe than the Treaty of Versailles was to Germany.[45] Capitalizing on Turk anger over the Greek occupation of Anatolia, Atatürk and his supporters launched the independence movement from the Turkish interior, with Ankara as the new capital. Atatürk's motto, similar to those of other nationalist independence leaders, was "Turkey for the Turks." In the end, though, the Young Turks were able to reverse the most egregious terms of the peace settlement, and gain sovereignty over the Turkish people (Turkey was the only losing power of World War I to avoid reparations). Like many other revolutionary leaders, Atatürk took on an image beyond hero status as the single true patriarch of the people, against whom nothing negative could be said.[46] The new Turkish Republic dramatically restructured social life, especially in its promotion of a secular state unbound to Islam. Women were given the right to vote in 1930 and encouraged to work.

Following Atatürk's death in 1938, the leadership succession was complicated by the absence of competing parties. For much of Turkey's early years as a republic, it operated as a single-party state, ruled by the Republican People's Party (RPP). This legacy of weak political parties continues to mar Turkish politics today. The young republic also struggled with a military that often intervened in the name of protecting the legacy of Atatürk, referred to as Kemalism. Yet unlike other states in the third world, even though the military intervened three times between 1960 and 1980, it returned rule to civilians after each power grab.

As we discuss throughout the book, the Turkish military views itself as the protector of "New Turkey's" founding virtues. Leaders who followed the "Father of the Turks" struggled with his legacy, especially his insistence on the importance of secularism for Turkey's modernization. President Ismet İnönü, who immediately followed Atatürk, attempted to liberalize life in Turkey, increasing his pressure especially after World War II. Other leaders rose to power demanding that the military be removed from the business of settling scores. The leader of the Motherland Party, Prime Minister Turgut Özal (who later became president), challenged the power of the military generals. Following Özal's death in 1993, Tansu Çiller, an economist trained in the United States, became Turkey's first female prime minister—and her years in office were plagued with economic and separatist problems. Perhaps the most controversial leader in recent Turkish history was Prime Minister Necmettin Erbakan, of the Islamist Refah Party, who came to power in 1995. The military demanded his resignation two years later, attempting to bar him from politics for challenging the secular tenets of Kemalism.

As you can see, this combination of many different thorny issues has produced great drama within the Turkish Republic, as leaders and citizens alike face a daunting number of challenges and questions—some that have been around for centuries and others that are products of the modern era. As you will discover throughout the course of this book, the modern Turkish Republic is a crossroads state, standing at the intersection of cultures (Europe and the Middle East), religious traditions (Islam, Christianity, and secularism), and IDENTITY. It is also a state that occupies a less certain role in the power plays of the twenty-first century than it did during the Cold War, when its geographic positioning attracted much superpower attention, especially from the United States. Turkey continues to be a state of great importance, albeit one facing many struggles along the way.

Case Study: China

It is often said that China is at once over five millennia old and five decades young. This contrast, between one of the world's oldest civilizations and its endurance for more than fifty years as a "People's Republic," captures much of the intrigue that is China today. Ancient China had great influence over its Asian neighbors, especially in the secular rituals derived from Confucian traditions. Today, Chinese civilization is viewed as the world's oldest, charting the relatively continuous existence of human communities for approximately 20,000 years. (Isolated human skeletons have been discovered from much earlier times, contemporaneous with Indonesia's "Java Man.") China's literary tradition is over 3,500 years old, and its written words (known as "characters") can be traced to linguistic precedents dating to approximately 1500 B.C.E.

Similar to many others, Chinese civilization was centered on river systems, especially the Yellow River in the north, where China's earliest recorded history is found, and the Yangtze River in the central and southern regions. It was a region ruled by over a dozen imperial dynasties, marked by fluctuating periods of stability, chaos, conquest, and cultural progress. The leader of each dynasty exercised authority based on the belief that they possessed the "Mandate of Heaven," which can best be understood as receiving the favor of one's spiritual ancestors.

China's first documented dynasty, the Shang, began in approximately 1700 B.C.E. Although Chinese records indicate at least one earlier dynasty, the existence of this community through archaeological records is yet to be proven.[47] Evidence of the Shang Dynasty is found in the so-called oracle bones, discovered only in the late 1800s, which were used to receive guidance from the heavens.

China's first unified dynasty, and indeed the source of the Western name "China," was achieved during the Qin Dynasty, which began in 220 B.C.E. Lasting only fifteen years, this was a remarkable dynasty that completed two wonders of the world. The Qin emperor ordered earlier walls used for fortification and defense to be linked literally into one "Long Wall" (known in the West as the "Great Wall"), providing modern Chinese an incredibly important symbol of the endurance of their culture.[48] The second famed creation of this dynasty was the emperor's elaborate tomb, composed of over 8,000 terracotta soldiers and horses buried to protect their identity. This major capital project of the dynasty required extensive resources, including labor power and coercion, and many of the 750,000 workers who planned and constructed the tomb, located in the ancient capital of Xi'an, were killed so they could not reveal its location. China's greatest dynasty, the Han, lasted for four centuries (206 B.C.E.–C.E. 220), and introduced the world's first wheelbarrow, as well as widespread use of paper and porcelain. It was during this dynasty, contemporaneous with the Roman Empire, that the famed Silk Road, a 7,000-mile trade route from Xi'an to Rome, increased China's interaction with the rest of the world. China's interaction with the West grew steadily after this dynasty, and by the Ming Dynasty (1368–1644), contacts with the Spaniards, Russians, and Dutch were extensive. It was during this time that the Jesuit Mission of Matthew Ricci was begun, launching China's extensive yet troubled relationship with Western religions.[49]

It is important to note that in the midst of this exploration and grandeur, ordinary Chinese citizens lived a difficult life filled with TOTALITARIAN leaders, extensive tax payments to finance imperial projects, and little freedom in either their work or their personal lives, which were mired in poverty. Advancement in Chinese society throughout most of its past was based on academic credentials achieved through a complex examination system that was based primarily on Confucian texts, affording luxury to an extremely small minority of the population (from which women were expressly excluded).

China's relative isolation and size encouraged a "Middle Kingdom" philosophy in which rulers and ordinary citizens alike viewed themselves at the center of world civilization. This attitude manifested itself in China's tributary system of trade, in which foreign powers were required to give gifts to the emperor to show respect or gain favor (and sometimes protection). Additionally, the Chinese viewed anyone outside of their cultural civilization to be "barbarians," little deserving of equal contact or negotiation. Part of the measure, in Chinese eyes, of whether one was civilized or barbarian, was one's allegiance to the teachings of a man who lived approximately 2,500 years ago, Kung Fuzi, known in the West as Confucius. His teachings, which may be viewed more as a way of life than a religious tradition, produced a great degree of cultural continuity in Chinese civilization, and even though modern leaders have gone to great pains to eradicate his influence, it continues today. Confucian thought influenced almost all of Asia, well beyond the borders of the Middle Kingdom. Confucius was a traditionalist who reflected, in extremely chaotic times, on solutions to his society's problems. One of his core beliefs centered on the importance of tradition and ritual. He proposed that paternalistic kings who set good examples could govern society best. To him, the virtues of respect and reverence were most important, especially in relation to the elderly and the educated in society. Confucius taught of an inegalitarian, hierarchical system of relationships that required the more powerful person to provide care and guidance, while the less powerful in the relationship was mandated to respect and obey. Confucian thought eventually became required understanding for those who wanted to consider themselves "educated Chinese," and it was officially adopted as the state IDEOLOGY in the second century B.C.E. The Confucian school certainly was not the only worldview during China's past (the Taoists found these teachings restrictive and authoritarian, and the legalists found them too retrospective and lacking in rules), but it certainly was the most important. As a measure of its dominance, the Qing or Manchu Dynasty, China's last, was actually introduced to China by foreigners from the north. The Chinese welcomed them, though, because of their internalization of the Confucian code of conduct and rule.

The Chinese Empire traded extensively with Arabs and Persians for hundreds of years before European contact, under the tributary system discussed above. The Chinese never regarded their trading partners as equals, and indeed, for much of its history China's power was unrivaled, especially on the seas and in its protectorates and colonies throughout Asia, including Vietnam, Burma, and Korea. China's imperial power began to decline, though, in the 1500s, as its leaders turned increasingly inward and encouraged more isolation from the rest of the world. It was the outcome of this turn of events that led, in many ways, to the eventual European conquest of much of China, beginning in the late 1700s. In their desire to increase access to Asia through a Chinese trading point, the British and others established permission for foreign citizens to live in China without being subject to Chinese authority, a system known as EXTRATERRITORIALITY. This was the beginning of the erosion of China's sovereignty, as foreigners began living in the country not bound by Chinese laws, but rather by the laws of their home countries. As its trade deficit with China spiraled higher, England goaded China into a series of battles referred to as the Opium Wars (see Figure 2.4). China's loss of Hong Kong (and other regions, including Taiwan, Macau, and Shandong) symbolized the imposition of foreign rule over a grand imperial land, rule that was not relinquished until the end of the twentieth century. (Taiwan, which was ceded to the Japanese in 1895, remains an example of contested sovereignty—discussed in Chapter 12.) On a larger scale, to most Chinese these events symbolized the loss of the famed Mandate of Heaven and gave birth to a flurry of potential solutions to the crisis. It was a time when many feared that Chinese civilization would fracture endlessly, exacerbated by localized warlord politics or regional military powers.

Shortly after the collapse of the last dynasty in 1911, Beijing University students staged the first mass demonstration in China's history, on May 4, 1919, to protest the status of Shandong, administered as a German colony since 1898. The warlord-dominated government in Beijing had entered into a secret agreement with the Japanese during World War I. During the Versailles Peace Conference at the end of the war, many Chinese placed great hope in Woodrow Wilson's rhetoric about SELF-DETERMINATION, but their hopes were crushed when they learned that Shandong had been granted to Japan as part of the Versailles settlement. Protests erupted throughout China and within Chinese communities abroad, and China never did sign the Versailles agreement. Out of this environment of distrust and disappointment, two dominant groups led the way to China's future: the Nationalist Party (KMT), led by Sun Yat-sen, and the Chinese Communist Party (CCP), eventually led by Mao Zedong (even though he was a minor leader for the first years of the party). Both parties focused on rallying different Chinese groups to their cause, and engaged in bitter battles with each other despite two formal attempts to unite for China's future. The final straw was the Japanese invasion of northern China in 1931, after which the CCP was perceived as the aggressive fighter for Chinese interests and for the needs of ordinary people. Following Japan's defeat in World War II and its expulsion from China, all-out civil war ensued between the KMT and the CCP, with the defeated Nationalists eventually exiling themselves to Taiwan. The People's Republic of China (PRC) was declared on October 1, 1949, although its hold on Chinese territory, and on world opinion, was less than complete, which set the stage for a rough ride especially during its first thirty years.

Mao Zedong, affectionately known as "The Chairman," led China for over two and a half decades, from the beginning of the PRC in 1949 until his death in 1976. His legacy remains a mixed one: he united the country and made the Chinese people proud of their heritage and achievements, while inflicting incredible civil disarray during his attempt to "continue the revolution" from 1966 to 1976, in the period known as the CULTURAL REVOLUTION (discussed in Chapter 13). Mao was followed by another longtime member of the CCP, Deng Xiaoping, who had been a member of the party during its rise to power in the 1930s and 1940s. Deng dramatically changed the face of China by opening it to the outside world, promoting the development of political and economic institutions, and attempting to move away from the charismatic rule of his predecessor. Deng, who died in 1997, has also left a mixed legacy: while the lives of ordinary Chinese citizens improved dramatically under his watch, the blood of the Tiananmen Square demonstrations of 1989 is also on his hands. Leaders who followed in his footsteps, including Jiang Zemin and Hu Jintao, faced the difficult task of trying to preserve the Communist Party's monopoly on power while attempting to carefully manage China's reemergence as a major regional and global player. It is a balancing act that continues to challenge China's leaders today.

Case Study: Indonesia

Modern Indonesia is an identity born of trade routes and colonial experience. Despite regional prominence and rich cultural traditions, there was little sense of commonality among the peoples who lived on the thousands of islands in the South Pacific prior to the early nineteenth century. The tense division that exists in modern Indonesia at the beginning of the twenty-first century has a long history, as the concept of unity was rarely evidenced in the islands of the archipelago.

The region known today as Indonesia was long populated by human beings. You may be familiar with "Java Man," the fossilized bones of a hominid that were discovered in 1891. It is believed that this human, known as *Pithecanthropus erectus,* lived over 750,000 years ago and had the capacity for fire-building and language. Subsequent archaeological discoveries confirmed populations extending 35,000–40,000 years ago, including Solo Man, named after a river in central Java, and the later Wajak Man, who lived 12,000–13,000 years ago.

Despite the presence of human communities almost 1 million years ago, the majority of today's Indonesians descend from two ethnic groups who immigrated to the islands from the north: the Melanesian peoples, who are believed to have inhabited the islands approximately 6,000 years ago, and the Austronesians, who migrated to the Indonesian archipelago from Taiwan at approximately the same time.

The Indonesian archipelago was an active player in the early Malay world, with a handful of states and kingdoms that thrived in trading. Early settlements prospered on the main islands, including Ho-Ling in central Java. Chinese records of this civilization report extensive war exploits, labor surpluses, and entertainment based on shadow plays and drums. By the sixth century, major kingdoms developed on Java and Sumatra, highlighted by the Srivijaya kingdom in southern Sumatra. Considered one of the most powerful kingdoms in Southeast Asia, Srivijaya emerged as the chief state and the only maritime state among the classical states in the region. As a commercial state, it began and ended earlier than others. Srivijaya's rulers controlled the critical Straits of Malacca, the preferred travel route between China and India, and the kingdom's influence reached to southern Vietnam.[50] The exchange of commercial goods was not the only type of trade in Srivijaya: it was also viewed as the center both of Hindu and Buddhist studies.[51]

Not surprisingly, due to its location, Srivijaya was famous for its navy, financed largely by taxes collected on foreign ships traversing its path. It eventually controlled a vast territory, including most of Sumatra, present-day Malaysia, and Singapore, yet the authority of the king expanded farther, to Borneo and Sri Lanka. The wealth of this kingdom was memorialized in the story that each day the king would toss a gold bar into the sea to acknowledge it as the source of Srivijaya's prosperity. At the end of his reign, the number of gold bars retrieved from the waters quantified the king's power.[52] Yet because of its export focus, it was a vulnerable state, dependent on the economic situation in India and China.

Even after Srivijaya's decline, Indonesia's prominence in Asian trade continued, and the city port of Malacca rose to prominence in its absence. Asian states (especially China and India) as well as Arab states provided ideal export markets for products abundant on the archipelago, especially spices. The region's abundance of spices, especially cloves, nutmeg, and pepper, were sought by traders around the world. Early Indonesians had established colonies in Madagascar for the transport of spices abroad (especially to the Romans); today, Austronesian languages can still be found there as remnants of this influence.

Increased trade led to heightened cultural interaction between islanders and their mainland Asian neighbors. By the third century, both Hindu and Buddhist traditions had filtered into the western islands from India. Neither system was adopted writ large; they were both regionally adapted and made to fit earlier customs, especially animism, a tradition based on the reverence for all living things. Islam did not become a major influence until the thirteenth century, and even then it was often combined with native religious traditions, as well as Hinduism and Buddhism. The Portuguese and the Dutch introduced Christianity much later, in the sixteenth and seventeenth centuries. Another cultural artifact of Indonesia's status as the trading center of Southeast Asia was the adoption of the Malay language by dissimilar people: it became the unifying factor facilitating trade between diverse groups. As Islam spread through the archipelago, the use of Malay became even more predominant.

Islamic traditions existed in parts of Indonesia as early as the thirteenth century, primarily through the rise of Malacca as a prominent trade port, and the spice-trading route between Malacca, northern Java, and Maluku was a major avenue for the spread of Islam. Even in its earliest days, though, Islam was interpreted in diverse ways, with *santri* Muslims closely following traditional Islamic rituals, and *abangans* adapting Islamic traditions to their Hindu beliefs. Aceh was one of the first parts of Indonesia to convert to Islam, and to this day the Acehnese are known for their relatively strict interpretations of Islamic traditions and for the strength of their convictions.

European influence in the region began in the fifteenth century. The first Portuguese ships sailed into Malacca in 1509, in search of inexpensive spices to preserve meats. The Portuguese eventually took over Malacca, only to hasten its downfall. Throughout the 1600s, Dutch Protestants established the Dutch East India Company (in search of a monopoly over the spice trade), and gradually increased their territory of control as it fit their economic interests, beginning with the "spice islands" of Maluku and the northwestern coast of Java. They consolidated their rule by expelling other colonial aspirants, including Spain and England (although the English maintained their colonies on Borneo). Even after the collapse of the Dutch East India Company, the Netherlands defeated the English to gain control over their colonies in Southeast Asia by 1816. Despite serious indigenous challenges to their authority, the Dutch prevailed in establishing control.

As Dutch colonial rule over the archipelago increased, and they began to integrate native Indonesians into their administrative structure, the growing sense of discrimination fostered much discontent. As we have observed in revolutionary leaders elsewhere, in the context of rising expectations, those native Indonesians who were afforded the opportunity to pursue higher education and serve in colonial officialdom as physicians, engineers, and other professionals chafed at the rigid subordination they faced compared to their European rulers. Although the nationalist movement was just beginning to form, many voices were calling for change, including that of Javanese princess Raden Adjeng Kartini, who championed the emancipation of Indonesian women.[53] As discussed above, this situation of choosing a select few for opportunities produced extremely difficult identity struggles among those selected.

The nationalist independence movement was launched in the early years of the twentieth century, and was given an added spark by ironic celebrations by the Dutch of their own centennial of liberation from Napoleonic rule—which they commemorated in the midst of occupied Indonesia.[54] It all began to come together under the leadership of a young engineer named Sukarno (following the Javanese custom, he had one name). Sukarno founded the Indonesian Nationalist Party in 1927. In response to their independence rhetoric, the Dutch exiled Sukarno, Mohammed Hatta, and other nationalist leaders. World War II provided them an opportunity to return, reorganize, and lead their country to independence.

Indonesia's formal colonial era ended with the Japanese occupation of 1942–1945, during which the Japanese plundered the region's oil fields to support their imperial navy. Ironic in hindsight, many Indonesians initially welcomed the Japanese, believing they would help in their fight for independence, and that the Japanese would not stay long. Instead, the Japanese sent Indonesians to work as forced laborers in Japan's territories. Those Indonesians who had been recruited and trained by the former Dutch colonial powers were again used as pawns during the Japanese occupation, as they became enforcers of the harshest Japanese policies on their neighbors and compatriots. But it was the Japanese defeat at the end of World War II that spurred Indonesia's independence movement into full gear. Prior to that time, Indonesian nationalists Sukarno and Hatta had begun to campaign for independence. Yet the movement was hindered by disagreement, rectified mostly by Sukarno's *pancasila* proposal, which emphasized the five principles shared by all Indonesians regardless of ethnic, religious, or political beliefs. These beliefs remain today, enshrined in the preamble to the modern Indonesian constitution.

Indonesia declared its independence in Sukarno's garden the morning of August 17, 1945—two days after the Japanese surrendered—but struggled with the Netherlands for over four years before the Dutch recognized its independence, only after bloody battles and intense international pressure. Sukarno embarked on a program euphemistically referred to as "guided democracy" for most of his rule, from 1949 to 1965. As a world traveler, Sukarno eloquently espoused the needs of the third world, especially in the Bandung Conference of Asian and African States in 1955. He was also stridently anti-Western, taking over British and US businesses, expelling Dutch nationals, and withdrawing from the United Nations. A 1965 coup, supposedly masterminded by the Communist Party of Indonesia (PKI), led to much bloodshed—as many as 400,000 were killed in fear of communist insurgency. The Chinese minority in the country suffered devastating losses in the attacks that followed the change of government.

Out of the ashes of the 1965 coup, the military commander Suharto rose to power. Suharto, who himself had attended a Dutch-run military academy and fought against the Dutch in Indonesia's war of independence, knew well the importance of military strength in maintaining his rule, a principle he applied fiercely throughout his "new order" government, from 1966 to 1998. Although dramatic social improvements were achieved in the first years of his leadership, including declining poverty and increasing literacy rates, Indonesia increasingly became a repressive state, complete with a gulag system used to enforce religious and political oppression. He was forced to resign from power in May 1998, in the face of widespread protests against his handling of the Asian economic crisis and international pressure to resolve the country's economic woes. A caretaker government led by interim president B. J. Habibie, a close associate of Suharto's, was in power for thirteen months before the groundbreaking elections of June 1999, the first free and fair elections to take place in four decades. In this election, the Indonesian Democratic Party–Struggle (PDI-P), led by Megawati Sukarnoputri, scored a resounding majority once the voting results were finally ratified in August 1999. The Indonesian legislature, the People's Consultative Assembly, met in October 1999 and chose Abdurrahman Wahid—who was supported by an unprecedented Islamic alliance—as the state's fourth president.[55] Megawati, a critic of Suharto and daughter of Indonesia's founding father, was named vice president. Wahid, a Muslim cleric who was partially blind and in frail health, led the country for approximately twenty months before he was voted out of office by the legislature in July 2001, capping off a six-month impeachment process. Shortly after Wahid had agreed to leave the presidential quarters, Megawati and her vice president, Hamzah Haz, took power in a country dizzied by political upheaval, internal violence, and a reeling economy. The pattern continued as Susilo Bambang Yudhoyono (popularly known as "SBY") became the country's first directly elected president in 2004.

Now It's Your Turn

As you move on to more contemporary considerations of these eight countries, keep in mind their diverse and rich histories. In what ways can you see their contemporary experience being driven by their past? From the brief overviews provided, what traditions or values do you believe should be revitalized or adapted to serve the peoples of these countries? In what ways do you see legacies of Western domination continuing to play out in these countries?

PART TWO

The International Economic System

Next we will look at the economies of the "third world" and consider whether the INTERNATIONAL ECONOMIC SYSTEM is contributing to the development or the underdevelopment of much of this world. The following chapters focus on INTERNATIONAL POLITICAL ECONOMY (IPE), or how economic and political issues interface. As an area of study, IPE's interest in the politics of economics includes a broad array of topics and concerns. In this part of the book we will focus on the gap in wealth and material well-being that exists between high-income countries (HICs) and low-income countries (LICs). The existence of such often-massive inequality is a major source of friction between rich and poor; it is the source of what is sometimes referred to as the North-South conflict. People belonging to two dominant but diametrically opposed schools of thought, NEOLIBERALISM and STRUCTURALISM, have very different ideas about why this gap exists and how to bridge it. Procapitalist neoliberals are highly optimistic about the ability of the market to work its magic. On the other hand, structuralists characterize capitalism as exploitative. To varying degrees, structuralists are pessimistic about the possibility of authentic development happening under the existing system. As you will see in the following chapters, the two schools of thought offer widely divergent answers for the questions we will consider: Why is the gap between rich and poor narrowing so slowly (if at all)? And why do so many of the world's countries continue to suffer from underdevelopment? Is this underdevelopment due to poor decisions made by the countries themselves? Or is it due to the position of these countries in the international economic system, a capitalist system that is dominated by rich countries and the organizations working for them?

6

Growth and Development: A Progress Report

> The combination of extreme poverty and inequality between countries, and often also within them, is an affront to our common humanity.
> —*Kofi Annan, former UN Secretary-General*[1]

As this book went to press, a number of European economies had hit the skids—and it looked like the United States, with a debt of nearly $14 trillion as of December 2010, might be close behind. Everyone was hoping that the turmoil associated with the Great Recession that started in 2007 was over, that there wouldn't be a second round, and that the fragile global economic recovery could be sustained. Although this economic crisis, the worst since the Great Depression of the 1930s, is said to have started in the United States and other high-income countries (HICs), it spread around the world, spilling into rich and poor countries alike.

Just a few years earlier it was a very different story; 2003–2007 is viewed nostalgically by economists as one of the most favorable periods for the world economy in forty years. Many markets were booming, some going gangbusters. Economic GROWTH was up and DEVELOPMENT indicators were actually improving—even in some of the world's poorest countries. However, in a classic boom-and-bust cycle, the period 2007–2010 saw the largest drop in international trade—ever. Many of the gains in human development that low- and middle-income countries had made had vanished. Sixty-four million people who had just managed to struggle their way out of poverty fell back into it (earning less than $1.25 a day), as economies tanked, investment shrank, and hundreds of millions of jobs were lost worldwide. In 2009 nearly 1 billion people were going hungry—the largest number in four decades. There were food emergencies in thirty-one countries, and hardship associated with the global financial crisis is believed to have contributed to as many as 50,000 additional infant deaths in Africa alone in 2009.[2]

Yet some countries managed the recession better than others, some staved it off, and some were relatively unaffected. Interestingly, many emerging economies survived better than advanced economies—and are experiencing faster recoveries. Even many developing countries that were hit hard by the global downturn appear to be coming out of it; according to the WORLD BANK, since 2008 low-income countries

(LICs) on average have experienced better growth rates than HICs. Growth in advanced economies was expected to average 1.9 percent in 2010, whereas 8–9 percent growth was expected in China and India that year. Sure, such growth rates were some of the highest in the world and nothing new for enormous economies such as China and India, but most countries of Africa, Latin America, and the Middle East were expecting more modest but still impressive 4–5 percent growth.[3] Analysts were forecasting that this growth would be sustained through the next few years; on average, developing economies were projected to grow by about 6 percent per year from 2010 to 2012.[4] Although some countries are likely to struggle longer and register lower growth rates, the good news is that it appears that most LICs are now more resilient than they used to be—suggesting that there is much more economic diversity in the "third world" than one might expect.

Yet, before we go any further with this discussion of how we are all doing, it is important to become familiar with two concepts fundamental to any discussion of INTERNATIONAL POLITICAL ECONOMY (IPE): growth and development. Both are generally considered to be desirable, and the terms are often used interchangeably to describe economic progress. However, growth and development are actually two very different things. While proponents of NEOLIBERALISM would argue that one needs growth to fund development, structuralists point out that it is certainly possible to have growth without development, as has been the case in many less developed countries. And, as the case of Cuba has demonstrated, it is possible to have development without growth, although this is not easy.

Growth refers to an expansion in production, output, and perhaps income. Neoliberals argue that maximized economic efficiency produces growth, which is associated with rising profits. A common indicator of growth is gross domestic product (GDP) per capita, which is obtained by dividing GDP by population. GDP per capita (or the newer term, gross national income [GNI] per capita) supposedly gives one an idea of how much income the average citizen earns in a year (see Figure 6.1). However, keep in mind that income is only one, albeit important, measure of economic well-being, and GDP or GNI per capita assumes that income is divided completely equally—a situation that exists nowhere on earth. In fact, one can assume that in most cases, a few people will earn much more than this figure and the majority will earn far less.

Whereas growth describes an increase in volume or output, development is generally understood to mean human development and pertains to issues of distribution. Development is a broad concept that is measured by composite indices such as the Physical Quality of Life Index (PQLI) and the Human Development Index (HDI) (see Figure 6.2). Both indices offer a more detailed picture of the economic well-being of a population. Growth rates alone tell us little about how people are doing. A country's economic growth rate does not reflect how wealthy it is. We often speak of the income gap between countries, but for the past two decades (for forty-eight of seventy-three countries for which data are available) the world has witnessed growing inequity in the distribution of incomes within countries. For example, income inequality has increased in both fast- and slow-growing economies, such as Bangladesh, Cambodia, Nepal, and China.[5] In fact, it is not unusual for citizens of some of the fastest-growing economies to live in some of the worst conditions in the world (e.g., Afghanistan and Niger in 2009). For the past several years China has set a record for sustaining the fastest growth rates on the planet (averaging 10 percent per year). It is true that a significant number of its citizens have seen their standards of living

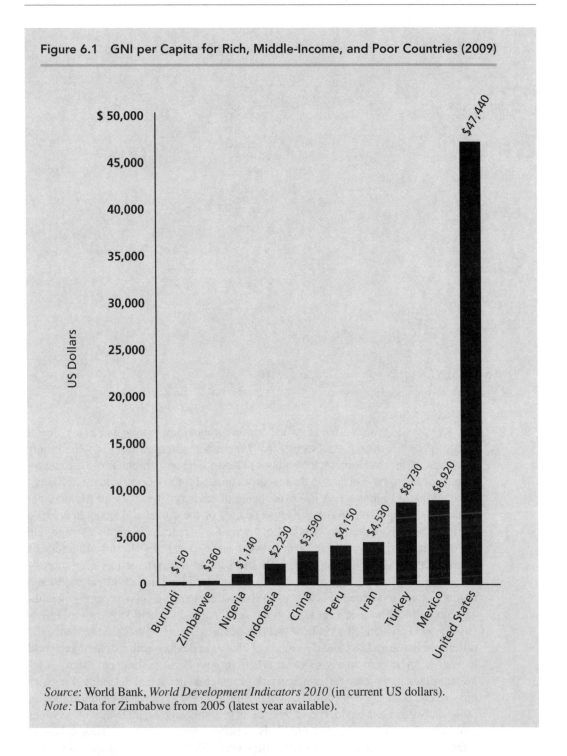

Figure 6.1   GNI per Capita for Rich, Middle-Income, and Poor Countries (2009)

Source: World Bank, *World Development Indicators 2010* (in current US dollars).
Note: Data for Zimbabwe from 2005 (latest year available).

rise. For example, the average starting salary for migrant laborers in China grew by approximately 80 percent between 2003 and 2009. Yet even at these growth rates it would take another forty years of constant growth before average Chinese incomes would reach 2005 income levels in the United States.[6]

Figure 6.2   Human Development Index, 2010 World Rankings, Selected Countries

Norway	1	Turkey	83
Australia	2	China	89
United States	4	Botswana	98
Germany	10	Indonesia	108
Spain	20	Vietnam	113
Hong Kong	21	India	119
United Arab Emirates	32	Nigeria	142
Qatar	38	Haiti	145
Portugal	40	Rwanda	152
Uruguay	52	Niger	167
Saudi Arabia	55	Congo, Democratic Republic of	168
Mexico	56	Zimbabwe	169
Peru	63		
Kazakhstan	66		
Iran	70		

Source: UNDP, *Human Development Report 2010.*

As opposed to measures of growth, development indices give us a much clearer idea of people's overall quality of life. Three essential capabilities are commonly associated with development: the abilities to lead a long and healthy life, to be knowledgeable, and to have access to the resources needed for a decent standard of living.[7] Take a look at Figure 6.3. A life expectancy of seventy-five years for Mexico, because it is comparable to the life expectancies of the citizens of many developed countries, suggests that the standard of living for Mexicans is relatively high. On the other hand, that the average Zimbabwean can expect to live to forty-four tells us that something is very wrong. The HDI and similar indicators tell us even more— not only in regard to life expectancy, but also about infant and child morbidity and mortality rates and maternal health, as well as access to social services such as healthcare and education (see Figures 6.4 and 6.5). Although there is great variability (within and between LICs) in how well people are dealing with these problems, the difference between LICs and developed countries in dealing with maternal and child mortality can be particularly shocking where progress is slow (or nonexistent). Adolescent pregnancies carry an elevated risk of maternal death and disability. Pregnant girls whose bodies are not fully grown are more likely to develop obstetric fistulas (holes between their bladders and vaginas or rectums and vaginas) as well as other problems; their newborns are more likely to suffer from low birth weights and die in infancy. Although from 2000 to 2010 there was a 10 percent drop in the adolescent fertility rate in many countries (such as China, Morocco, and Pakistan), the numbers remain high in Niger, Chad, and Mali.[8] In the 1990s, African children were nineteen times more likely to die before reaching their fifth birthday than children born in

Figure 6.3 Life Expectancy (2008)

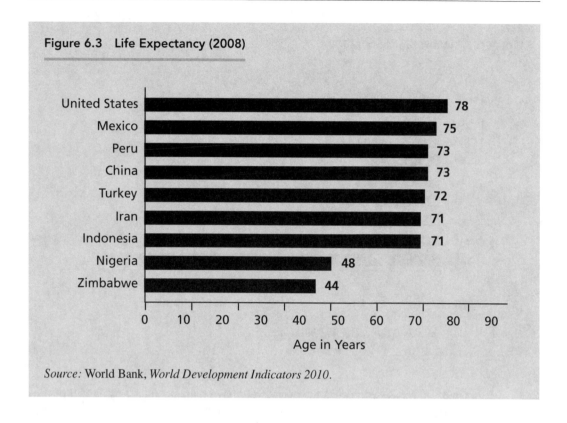

Age in Years

Source: World Bank, *World Development Indicators 2010.*

HICs, and twenty times more likely in 2008. Overall, though, it is heartening that infant and child mortality rates dropped in LICs in the 1990s and 2000s, but in these countries approximately 8.8 million children under five still die each year—two-thirds of them from preventable illnesses.[9]

Development indices also include attention to other aspects of well-being: caloric intake, access to clean water and sanitation—access even to telephones and computers. For example, the digital divide (in terms of access to computers in the North and South) is high but shrinking overall. But the gap in access to high-speed Internet, proven to be so crucial in providing the information necessary to achievement of economic, social, and other goals, remains wide. Australia (with a population of 21 million) has more broadband subscribers than all of Africa (with 900 million people). On average, an Internet user living in an advanced economy is 200 times more likely to have access to high-speed Internet than someone living in a poor or middle-income country. On the other hand, access to cell phones has grown enormously in LICs over the past decade (for example, three out of four Haitians have access to them). Mobile phones are the most equitably distributed of all information and communication technologies. There are over 4 billion cell phone subscribers worldwide, who (besides using them to share information) can also utilize these phones in a variety of other ways as well. For example, people working abroad can use them to access bank accounts and send remittances back home to relatives. Instead of distributing goods or vouchers, aid groups can put money into recipients' cell phone savings accounts. Recipients can then use the account to withdraw cash

Figure 6.4   Infant Mortality (2008)

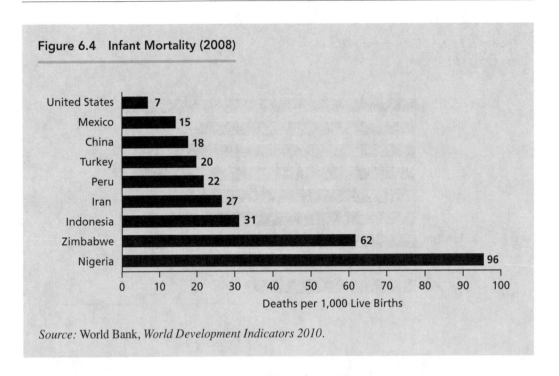

Source: World Bank, *World Development Indicators 2010.*

or make purchases. Because the poor rarely have bank accounts, using cell phones for mobile banking or microsavings is a low-cost, safer way to store their money and it is revolutionizing commerce and the provision of services.[10]

Beyond traditional definitions that emphasize access to goods or services, development has more recently been expanded to include considerations of people's range of choice. This dimension of development includes concerns such as political empowerment and participation, HUMAN SECURITY, protection of the environment, and gender equality. In this sense, human development clearly includes but goes beyond material needs. This understanding of development recognizes people's need to be creative and productive, to live in dignity, and to enjoy the sense of belonging to a community. Increasingly, human development is being conceptualized as a development of the people, for the people, and by the people. It must therefore be understood as a process as well as an end, a process in which those targeted for development are participants in deciding how they will pursue it. In other words, human development is ultimately about freedom. It is as much about the process of enlarging people's choices as it is about providing people access to things valuable to their well-being.[11]

The rate of advancement in every category of human development varies among countries. By some measures, such as a sense of community belonging, it could be argued that, generally speaking, the citizens of less developed countries are far ahead of those living in developed countries. There has been some overall progress in terms of other, more widely recognized aspects of human development across the third world. However, not all have benefited equally from these improvements. Among LICs, some are making faster progress on certain aspects of development (e.g., Peru on infant mortality rates, Mexico on primary-school completion rates). For others, progress is much slower (e.g., in Zimbabwe, where because of HIV/AIDS, life expectancy has actually

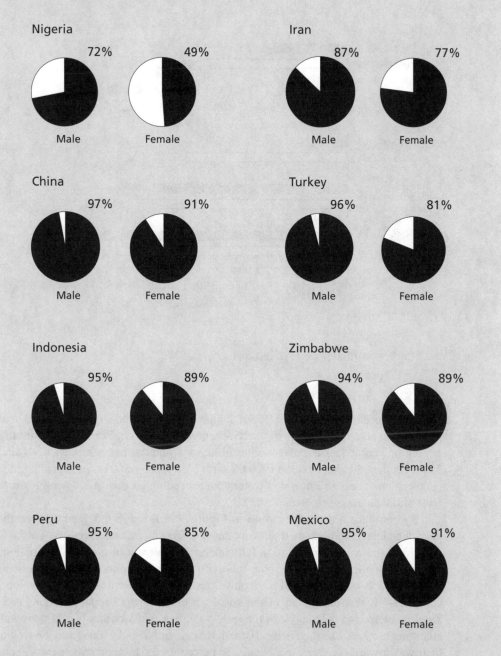

Figure 6.5   Literacy (2005–2008)

Source: World Bank, *World Development Indicators 2010.*
Note: Literacy is defined as the percentage of the population over age fifteen who can read and write.

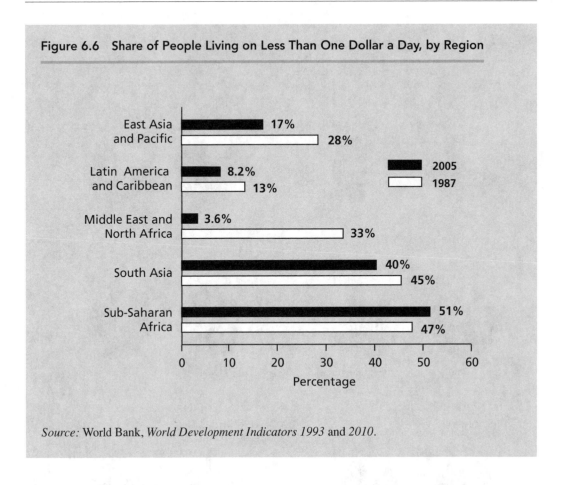

Figure 6.6   Share of People Living on Less Than One Dollar a Day, by Region

Source: World Bank, *World Development Indicators 1993* and *2010.*

regressed since independence in 1980, though it has improved slightly in recent years after hitting an appalling low of thirty-seven years in 2006). Worldwide, more than 1.5 billion people lack access to toilets or latrines, and this has barely changed since 1990. On the other hand, since 1990 the world has made progress in providing more people with access to improved water sources (although one in six people worldwide still lack access to clean water).[12]

By comparing the information in Figures 6.1 through 6.5, you can see that growth and development are often very uneven. Developing countries account for 85 percent of the world's population but generate 20 percent of global gross national product.[13] While we might assume that with time more countries will experience CONVERGENCE—that they will eventually "catch up" economically with developed countries—there is disagreement about whether this will ever happen. In what Fareed Zakaria referred to as "the rise of the rest,"[14] there is evidence that big, fast-growing emerging markets like the BRICs (Brazil, Russia, India, and China) may be well on their way toward convergence. Nearly 30 percent of the total increase in world output in 2000–2008 occurred in the BRICs, which already capture a great deal of attention (and demand more decisionmaking power) at international economic and political forums. Some analysts predict that the BRICs' combined GDPs will exceed that of the Group of Seven (the richest HICs: Canada, France, Germany, Italy, Japan,

Figure 6.7   Development with a Deadline: The Millennium Development Goals

At the start of the new millennium, the leaders of the world's countries and major development organizations agreed on a bold blueprint for action. They set forth an ambitious but feasible development agenda and pledged to work toward eight specific goals, known as the Millennium Development Goals (MDGs), aimed at meeting the basic human needs of all people by 2015:

1. Eradicate extreme poverty and hunger
2. Achieve universal primary education
3. Promote gender equity (in education, employment, and political representation)
4. Reduce child mortality
5. Improve maternal health
6. Combat HIV/AIDS, malaria, and other diseases
7. Ensure environmental sustainability
8. Establish a global partnership for development

The architects of this plan realized that such an undertaking would require unprecedented focus, resources, and effort. Every country and institution would have to do its part to meet its commitments. Five years away from the 2015 deadline, a progress report claimed that the targets were still achievable. Many regions were on the path to reaching at least some of these goals; some countries were doing better on some things than others. As of 2010, overall the world had made significant progress toward poverty reduction, the provision of a safe water supply, interventions against measles and malaria, and the control of HIV/AIDS. However, often progress has been slow and gains have been vulnerable. Many fear that the world recession and slow recovery might mean a major setback. Without a significant push in the last stretch, there was a very real danger that the world will fail to meet its objectives regarding hunger (the number of malnourished has increased as a result of the global financial crisis). Progress in terms of gender equality has been stubbornly slow. Although there have been some great improvements in these areas, it appears that the world will fall short of the targets for providing universal education and reducing child mortality. As the authors of this report card on the MDGs noted, failure in any one of these areas is a problem for all of us, since failure to meet basic human needs anywhere breeds instability. A less just world means a less secure world.[15]

the United Kingdom, and the United States) by 2027, and that they will dominate the global economy by 2050. (Occasionally a few other countries are included with the BRICs—BRICET: BRICs plus East Europe and Turkey; BRICS: BRICs plus South Africa; BRICM: BRICs plus Mexico.) Then there are the CIVETS (Colombia, Indonesia, Vietnam, Egypt, Turkey, South Africa), the countries forecasted to be the next sizable emerging markets. They too may reach convergence, but (if current trends continue) much of the rest of Africa, Asia, the Middle East, and Latin America is likely to be left behind.[16]

But even for those that aren't members of one of these clubs, not all the news is bad. Some non-Western countries, especially those known as emerging economies, have made impressive progress in improving their citizens' standards of living. In 1987 the number of people living in extreme poverty (less than one dollar a day) was 1.2 billion. Over the past two decades the world has witnessed the largest decrease in ABSOLUTE POVERTY in history; it is estimated that 440 million people's incomes grew. This raised them out of the ranks of the extremely poor (the figure was recently adjusted to less than $1.25 a day). It is estimated that the poverty rate worldwide dropped by 25 percent between 1981 and 2005. This is a remarkable accomplishment, but it is important to note that one country—China—accounts for much of this improvement, as its poverty rate declined from 85 to 16 percent. Excluding China, the global poverty rate was reduced by approximately 10 percent.[17]

This is still, without a doubt, a triumph; however, half of these 440 million who have made their way out of extreme poverty are still in poverty. They are living on less than $2 a day (versus $1.25 a day). Nearly one and a half billion remain mired in extreme poverty (most of them in Africa).[18] Although poverty certainly exists in HICs, most residents of these countries cannot fathom the poverty found in much of the third world. In 2008 the average American earned more in three days than the average resident of Niger earned in an entire year.[19] It is clear that poverty remains a long-standing problem.

Yet even within the sweeping category known as the third world, there are major differences in the levels of income and economic development. Taiwan, Singapore, Hong Kong, and Israel, sometimes referred to as advanced economies, are relatively wealthy, on the cusp of being considered economically developed. Of our CASE STUDIES, China, Turkey, Iran, Peru, Mexico, and (to a lesser degree) Indonesia are middle-income countries, while Zimbabwe is low-income. Although Nigeria is a major oil exporter (upwards of 90 percent of exports are petroleum or petroleum-based products), by many measures it is a relatively poor country. Indonesia, Iran, and Mexico are also dependent on petroleum exports, but to varying degrees. For example, Mexico's economy, spread across the agricultural, industrial, and service sectors, is much more diversified than Nigeria's. With the proliferation of *MAQUILADORAS,* or assembly plants, Mexico's economy is increasingly based on the export of manufactured goods, as are the economies of China, Indonesia, and Turkey. At the start of the twenty-first century, the growth of these economies was largely based on the success of this sector.

China is still a low-income country, but it is also the second-largest economy on earth (behind the United States). It enjoys regular trade surpluses (in 2010 its trade surplus was estimated at $28.7 billion) and absorbs the vast majority of foreign investment going to LICs.[20] Of our case studies, China, Mexico, Turkey, Peru, and Indonesia would qualify as emerging economies. Over the next ten years these economies are expected to continue to grow; if trends continue, China will pass the United States and become the world's largest economy by 2030 (by then India will likely be the fourth largest).[21] Based on higher demand (and prices) for their exports, these countries managed to sustain high growth rates for several years—until 2007 and the start of the Great Recession (after which some of these economies slowed more than others). On the other hand, the combination of domestic upheaval and international isolation has meant that until 2009, Zimbabwe missed out on the boom of the mid-2000s. In fact, Zimbabwe had the world's fastest-shrinking economy during most of this period. Peru's economy is heavily dependent on minerals (the prices of which can be quite volatile), and Zimbabwe's foreign exchange is typically earned from the sale of goods such as tobacco and nickel. But the relatively diverse base of their economies makes them the envy of more monocultural economies such as Guinea-Bissau, which earns 95 percent of its foreign exchange from the sale of cashews. The economies of all of our case studies are highly export-oriented. Because they are so dependent on sales abroad, they are vulnerable to economic slowdowns in the United States and other developed countries (their biggest customers).

Another measure offering a closer look at poverty, from a different angle, is the Gender-Related Development Index (GDI). Among other things, it tells us that although no country in the world treats its women as well as its men, gender inequality is strongly correlated with poverty. The rising impoverishment of women and their children is sometimes referred to as the "feminization" of poverty. This poverty is manifested in several different ways. According to economist Amartya Sen, by 1990 the comparative neglect of females worldwide in terms of health and nutrition had contributed to more than 100 million "missing" females—most of them in Asia, where a preference for male children is largely still the norm. While some recent studies have scaled down that estimate to 60 million missing or attributed half of the missing to natural causes (such as Hepatitis B), the numbers have worsened in recent years (in part because of the widespread use of ultrasounds for sex-selective abortions).[22] As a result, the number of boys born (compared to the number of girls) is highly skewed in several countries. The natural sex ratio (in the absence of sex-selective abortion) is 105 boys for every 100 girls. However, some regions of China now have a sex ratio of 120–130 boys to 100 girls, and in Vietnam the ratio is 112 to 100. Such imbalances will eventually mean that these countries will have surpluses of men; it is expected that within the next decade 40 million men in China will be unable to find wives, and demographers predict that such circumstances could lead to social and political instability. The governments of these countries are concerned about a looming crisis and are reportedly adopting policies aimed at normalizing the ratio.[23]

There are certainly differences in the status of females between and within countries, depending on CLASS, regional origin, ethnicity, and other factors. However, in the poorest countries, women and girls are more likely to be illiterate, to earn three-quarters (or less) of a male's wages, to consume fewer calories, to become sick more often, and to die at younger ages than their male counterparts. They are also less likely to own land, despite evidence that women often farm more productively than men.

However, there has been some progress in rectifying these imbalances, largely because development planners now recognize that when women benefit, so do their families and their communities. "Women in development" (WID) has been a catch-phrase since the early 1970s. Prior to this time, development planners largely neglected women. If they were included at all, it was mostly for instruction in home economics and family planning. Although WID projects continue to have their problems, the best ones are designed keeping in mind how women contribute to the overall development of their countries. Research in several countries shows that the money women earn is more likely to be spent on their families, whereas men are often more likely to spend it on themselves.

Since the 1960s, larger numbers of women in developed and less developed countries have entered the paid work force. Female participation in the labor force has grown tenfold in the past sixty years in China, from 7 percent in 1949 to over 70 percent in 2009.[24] Increasingly, employers worldwide are recruiting women because they are desperate enough to accept the work and pay that men reject. Consequently, the feminization of poverty can occur even as more women are entering the FORMAL SECTOR. Women have a higher incidence of poverty than men, and female poverty tends to be more severe than male poverty, despite the fact that around the world, women often work more hours than men. Female poverty is often intergenerational; overworked mothers may find that they must depend on the assistance of their daughters to make ends meet and to help them with childcare responsibilities. If parents are expected to pay school fees, it is less likely that girls will attend school. It is estimated that 72 million children of primary-school age do not attend school, 57 percent of whom are girls. The gaps are largest in low-income and rural areas, and girls from ethnic, religious, or caste minorities are doubly disadvantaged. Thanks to important reforms such as the elimination of school fees, female literacy rates have improved in several regions. Still, in 2010, two-thirds of the world's 759 million people who cannot read or write a simple statement were female.[25] In many Latin American countries, girls' enrollment is surpassing that of boys. Many Caribbean and East Asian countries have also made progress in promoting gender parity at the primary- and secondary-school levels since 2000. But with entrenched gender barriers, girls continue to face hurdles in obtaining their education, particularly in many western Asian, African, and Arab countries. It is important to remove these barriers because development workers have known for years that the investment in education for females pays off in the long run with healthier children and smaller families.[26]

Many of the girls who leave school do so for a variety of reasons, including early marriage and pregnancy, as well as sexual harassment and the discrimination they face in schools. However, one of the most common reasons girls drop out is to help on farms. Although women are crucial agricultural producers in much of the world, producing the food crops that ensure their families' survival, they rarely have equal access to appropriate technologies. Instead, women must rely on manual techniques that are heavily labor-intensive, wasting time and energy. Part of the reason women lack access to tractors, fertilizers, and other inputs is because they lack credit. In Nigeria and elsewhere, women are often unable to obtain credit because they have no independent access to land. Where most of the population is employed in some capacity or another as agriculturists, access to land is the single most important factor in determining well-being. But it is by no means the only one. According to the UNITED NATIONS, women produce 50 percent of the world's food. Female employment rates are consistently lower than those of males (especially in the Middle East, northern Africa, and southern Asia), but women perform 66 percent of the world's work. They are often the first fired when economies contract, but 60–80 percent of export manufacturing work in LICs is performed by females. And despite all this, women earn just 10 percent of the world's income and own only 1 percent of the world's property.[27]

Although the feminization of poverty should be viewed as being rooted in the denial of resources and opportunities to women, it is often associated more than anything else with an increase in the number of female-headed households. It is important to remember that female-headed households are not a new phenomenon, yet their numbers are rising: it is estimated that one-third of households worldwide are female-headed, and 13–24 percent of households in Africa, Asia, and Latin America have female heads.[28] And whether or not there is a male present in the household, around the world women are becoming the main providers for the family. Although female-headed households are overrepresented among the poor, it is now recognized that homes headed by females may face social stigma, but they do not always exist at a material disadvantage. Whereas families headed by women tend to be treated as the poorest of the poor and the most powerless, clearly income and status vary among these households as they do in others. Women become heads of households for a variety of reasons, on a permanent or temporary basis. Their husbands may migrate periodically in search of more lucrative work and leave them behind to farm. Some women head households after they are abandoned or widowed (this is especially common where young women marry much older men). Another reason that women end up as household heads is because the vast majority of the world's refugees are women and their children—often unaccompanied by male relatives. Still, it is important to recognize that in some cases women choose to be household heads. Although women alone were once assumed to be powerless, a growing body of evidence now indicates that female household heads employ a variety of coping mechanisms, and that female-headed households may actually be more resourceful than those headed by males.

However, in general, rural women are the poorest of the poor, and the gap between their quality of life and that of the rest of the world is not narrowing in the way that it should—if what was being promoted in these countries was truly "development." Gender bias is a large part of why development initiatives have so often failed. Even where there has been impressive growth, we now know that economic growth alone will not eliminate inequality: societies must promote women's rights in order to reduce gender disparities.

When faced with these arguments about the underdevelopment of much of the world, the optimists admit that, yes, the gap between rich and poor is growing wider, but argue that the floor under the poor is rising steadily in much of the world. Analysts disagree about whether the gap between the rich and poor, known as RELATIVE POVERTY, is growing. As mentioned earlier, prior to the recession of the late 2000s, growth was up and absolute poverty was falling. But GLOBALIZATION's effect on inequality is ambiguous.[29] Neoliberals are confident that an unequal concentration of wealth will eventually trickle down. They believe that the concentration of wealth serves as a spur to investment, bringing faster economic growth. They maintain that all STATES reap benefits from the international economic exchange of goods and services. International cooperation is facilitated through the development of trading relationships. This is good for everyone, in that it promotes not only economic stability but also political stability. For the neoliberals, who dominate the governments of developed countries, the boardrooms of MULTINATIONAL CORPORATIONS (MNCs), and the international economic organizations and commercial banks known as INTERNATIONAL FINANCIAL INSTITUTIONS (IFIs), growth is everything. Countries cannot reduce poverty and will not develop unless they increase growth rates first.

Globalization

The best way to increase growth rates, according to neoliberals, is to embrace globalization. In other chapters globalization is discussed more broadly, in terms of its sociocultural and political aspects, or how it has spilled over to affect just about everything: social relations (including class, race, and gender relations), culture, politics—even climate. In this chapter, we focus on globalization as an economic phenomenon. Globalization should be understood as the spread of capitalism worldwide. It is an all-embracing, multidimensional force based in ECONOMIC LIBERALIZATION, or the adoption of capitalist, market-based reforms. Neoliberals are proponents of this economic liberalization, arguing for open markets and laissez-faire economics. The French term "laissez-faire" translates as "let it be." By this neoliberals mean that government's proper role is to withdraw from economics as much as possible and to "let economics be"—or allow the "invisible hand" of supply and demand to work. Market forces allowed to operate unimpeded by government interference maximize efficiency, according to these analysts.

Consequently, neoliberals regard globalization as a positive force that helps to further integrate the economies of the world into the international marketplace, often referred to as the INTERNATIONAL ECONOMIC SYSTEM. This system is capitalist, and it is supported by a number of very powerful institutions and organizations, most notably the INTERNATIONAL MONETARY FUND (IMF). Both the IMF and its counterpart, the World Bank, were founded in the years after World War II, initially to assist in the reconstruction of Europe. Each of these multilateral institutions has its own mandate, but over the years their roles have changed and today there is some overlap in their functions. Both organizations are dominated by developed countries, since decisions in the INTERNATIONAL GOVERNMENTAL ORGANIZATIONS (IGOs) are made through weighted voting (that is, based on each member country's financial contribution). Structuralists describe this as a system based on "the golden rule" (whoever has the gold makes the rules). Whereas the World Bank's primary mission is to provide development assistance to the world's poorest countries, the IMF serves in a number of capacities, including the promotion of global economic stability. One way the IMF promotes stability is by serving as the lender of last resort to countries in economic crisis. It distributes loans to countries whose economies are failing.

According to the dominant players in this system, further INTEGRATION into the world economy is exactly what underdeveloped countries need. LICs should embrace globalization and raise growth rates by trading more in the international marketplace and competing to attract foreign capital. The WORLD TRADE ORGANIZATION (WTO), created to update the GENERAL AGREEMENT ON TARIFFS AND TRADE (GATT), works to promote free trade by providing a forum for discussion of the unresolved issues that cause friction between states. Established in 1995, the WTO has significant influence, since its 153 members account for more than 97 percent of the world's trade.[30] Neoliberals contend that because global capitalism is the best hope for the development of the third world, the WTO provides an invaluable service. The free flow of technology, capital, and ideas is raising living standards higher, faster, and for more people than at any other time in history. Economies are becoming more integrated: world exports of goods and services nearly tripled between 1990 and 2007, with LICs' share of this trade growing from 17 to 28 percent.[31] To take greater part in the feast, neoliberals argue that these middle- and low-income countries need only make a few necessary adjustments to further liberalize their economies.

Part of what makes globalization such a fascinating process to study is that it can have positive as well as negative effects. It can contribute to increased cooperation and unity while at the same time creating conditions for fragmentation and conflict. As Thomas Friedman has pointed out, globalization is everything and its opposite. It can be both incredibly empowering and incredibly coercive. Both proponents and critics of globalization agree on its overwhelming force. Neoliberals contend that when it comes to LICs' absorption into the international economy, the question isn't so much "When?" as it is "How?"[32]

Yet structuralists maintain that the majority of LICs already share a common position within the world economy. They are relatively powerless within it. Third world countries as a whole have very little influence in setting the agenda or making decisions for the international economic system. Through its enforcement of the existing rules of trade, the World Trade Organization further marginalizes LICs. Although low-income countries are lining up to join the WTO, in general developed countries are much more enthusiastic about the existence of the WTO than are low-income countries, many of which view the organization as just another way for developed countries to protect their advantageous position within the existing system. For example, the WTO makes it very difficult for LICs to protect infant industries and diversify their economies. Structuralists also accuse the organization of selectively dismantling trade barriers in a lopsided liberalization that is skewed in favor of industrialized countries and multinational corporations. In some cases, WTO rules that promote free trade in manufactured goods force LICs to open up their markets to the products of developed countries, while the products of LICs (especially agricultural goods, such as orange juice) often face the highest trade barriers and are effectively shut out of the developed countries' markets.

Ironically, for all their talk about "free trade," it is the subsidies and various protectionist measures of developed countries that have made it hard for much of the third world to earn an honest living through trade. In the past decade, rich countries have increased poor countries' access to their markets, particularly for agricultural products.[33] However, one way that high-income countries boost their own producers while hurting competition is through subsidies, or payments to domestic producers (sometimes small farmers but often large agribusiness corporations). For example, European Union (EU) countries have a lavish subsidy program, supporting their own domestic producers' sugar exports, boosting (over)production and driving down world prices for sugar by one-third. Similarly, US cotton subsidies for American producers led to a drop in cotton prices on the world market, resulting in Benin's poverty rate jumping from 37 to 59 percent in 2001–2002.[34] The United States and Europe spent $376 billion on agricultural subsidies in 2008 (much more than they spent on aid to poor countries). However, for all the HICs' talk of free trade, because cutting subsidies would be politically unpopular back home, no agreement could be reached, and years of WTO negotiations fell apart in 2008. Attempts to restart the negotiations failed at the GROUP OF 20 (G-20) talks in 2010 due to rising protectionist pressures associated with the global recession. Distrust was high at the talks, and it became clear that the world's leading economic powers (advanced and emerging economies), all eager to cut mounting budget deficits, were more interested in risking trade wars (in competing for market shares and protecting domestic producers) than they were in free trade.[35]

The much needed multilateral rules to enforce compliance with the ideals of free trade were languishing as of late 2010. Yet if developed countries were to practice the free trade they preach—if the governments of the United States and Europe were to cut the billions of dollars per day that they spend on agricultural subsidies—it would dramatically improve the welfare of millions of households (in western Africa alone). If rich countries were to stop dumping cheap cotton onto the market, thereby eliminating the cotton subsidy, it would result in a 5–12 percent increase in the world market price for cotton. Because cotton (also known as "white gold") is so critical to the economies of many of the world's poorest countries, cotton subsidy reforms would amount to a huge boost for third world cotton farmers, raising their incomes by 8–20 percent ($46 to $114 per household per year). As it is, because

HICs' subsidies drive the world market price for cotton so low, farmers in LICs try to scrape together a living by moving into new areas and overworking the land, causing significant ecological damage.[36]

Globalization's critics contend that non-Western governments are effectively immobilized by the combined influence of developed countries' governments, corporations, and international financial institutions. They argue that agents of globalization, such as the International Monetary Fund and the World Trade Organization, wield such power over LICs that these countries are in effect being recolonized. Though LICs can bring their complaints to the WTO, they frequently cannot afford costly legal battles. Poor countries can't afford the lawyers and lobbyists that the MNCs and rich countries hire to find loopholes in trade rules and buy the influence they need. The WTO's decisions are binding on members, and those that fail to comply with its rules risk potentially crippling sanctions. In sum, structuralists argue that the SOVEREIGNTY of LICs is steadily being eroded as governments are forced to give their decisionmaking authority to the IMF, MNCs, and developed countries.

However, one recent turn of events must have given many structuralists pause. Brazil successfully challenged US agricultural subsidies at the WTO in 2009. In a disappointing decision for the United States, the WTO found that the US price support program for cotton violated trade agreements. The United States resisted the ruling, saying that it would cost American businesses hundreds of millions of dollars. In an unusual move, the WTO gave Brazil approval to suspend normal property protections and authorized it to cross-retaliate (not sanction US goods but violate US intellectual property rights). In the end, the United States and Brazil reached an agreement to settle this long-standing dispute (with the United States electing to pay Brazilian farmers $150 million a year rather than end the cotton subsidy). It is hard to overstate the enormity of this WTO decision (which some call a "historic breakthrough" on cotton). However the WTO decision is characterized, it reflected a shift in bargaining power, showed developing countries that they might have a chance at promoting their rights through the enforcement of trade rules—and actually promoted free trade.[37]

Trade

As you may have guessed by now, structuralists argue trenchantly against the economic orthodoxy, while neoliberals accuse structuralists of overstating their case and ask what feasible alternative they offer. This is the case for trade as well. According to neoliberals, the best way to jump-start growth rates is to adopt a strategy of trade liberalization or free trade. They maintain that the wealthiest countries have built their success on trade and (with a few important exceptions) by being open to competition. In fact, neoliberals argue that there is not a single example in modern history of a country successfully developing without trading and integrating with the global economy.[38] On the other hand, they point out, it is no coincidence that the poorest countries in the world are the ones that have been less than friendly to free trade. The countries that are worst-off have adopted a variety of protectionist policies, artificially "protecting" domestic producers by slapping tariffs on imports. This kind of government interference with trade is notoriously inefficient, argue the neoliberals. Developing countries that have adopted market reforms and opened their economies, such as Hong Kong, Singapore, and Chile, have reaped the largest gains in terms of standards of living. Simply put, open economies grow much faster than closed economies. According to neoliberals, the existence of fast-growing economic powerhouses such as China, Brazil, and India proves that it is possible to thrive in the current economic system.[39]

Neoliberalism's critics argue that the rich countries are hypocrites when it comes to openness, and that openness does not guarantee wealth; a country's wealth depends less on ease of trade than it does on what is being traded.[40] Openness involves great risk, and the countries experiencing relative success are few and far between. Not all countries can achieve the success of China, nor should they want to follow the Chinese example, which is hardly the model of an open economy. Structuralists recognize that the impetus toward trade liberalization and embrace of globalization is nothing new. In fact, they argue that the reason why so much of the third world is underdeveloped today is because of the position it was assigned during colonialism or within the NEW INTERNATIONAL DIVISION OF LABOR (NIDL). What is "new" about the international division of labor today (though it is actually not so new) is that a handful of LICs are moving in to fill the voids in manufacturing that are left as developed countries mature into service-based economies. The textile and steel mills that were once so important to the United States, British, and German economies have since moved South, creating the existing division of labor.

One aspect of the NIDL that is actually not so new is the expansion of regional and product specialization, based in the principle of COMPARATIVE ADVANTAGE. Seeking to increase efficiency through specialization in production, the colonizers created monocultural economies throughout the third world. This principle, widely revered by liberals for hundreds of years, is based in the assumption that countries differ in their ability to produce certain goods based on their natural resources, labor, and other factors. In order to maximize wealth, countries should specialize in producing goods for which they have a comparative advantage. Today the vast majority of LICs continue to produce many of the same goods assigned to them during the days of colonialism—unprocessed primary goods for export. This makes good business sense, according to neoliberals. By concentrating on a few goods for export, LIC economies can become more fully integrated into the world economy. With the hard currency they earn from the sale of their raw materials, LICs can pay their debts and import everything else they need (including food, fuel, manufactured goods, etc.). Moreover, if all countries liberalize their economies and open up to trade, it will mean that businesses will have to work harder to be competitive. The result will be improved and less expensive products—a benefit to all.

Neoliberalism's critics argue that it isn't quite that simple. Although many people are giving up and heading for the cities, the majority of the world's population continues to live in rural areas and work as farmers. During colonialism rural communities were disrupted, many subsistence farmers were forced off the land, and small plots were consolidated into large plantations. This is happening again today, as rising world food prices have led to a land rush in which private foreign investors and governments are leasing millions of hectares of arable land owned by African governments and displacing tens of thousands of farmers.[41]

Those so far unaffected by such deals farm plots of various sizes; most are smallholders or are landless. The landless often drift around the countryside looking for seasonal work, and are employed as tenant farmers or as migrant laborers on much larger farms or plantations. Smallholders in developed and less developed countries are rapidly being displaced as they find that they can no longer support themselves through farming and are increasingly forced to sell their land to huge agribusinesses. For example, until recently in Zimbabwe, large commercial farms produced more than 40 percent of the country's exports. What small farmers had in common is that they once practiced subsistence farming. Farmers ate what they produced and sold the surplus. However, today the majority of countries have moved away from food production and can no longer be considered subsistence economies. Rather, these are export-based economies, increasingly centered on the production of commodities known as cash crops. Coffee, flowers, sisal, and bananas are just a few examples of cash crops, which are produced for sale abroad (mostly to consumers in developed countries). Mines producing bauxite, copper, and diamonds, and aquaculture and ranches producing salmon and beef, are also sites for the production of cash crops. What these commodities have in common is that they are raw materials, or unprocessed goods that will most likely be sent elsewhere for manufacture into finished goods.

Critics of this situation argue that as producers of raw materials, LICs are assigned a disadvantageous position in the world economic system, and not only because most raw materials are vulnerable to sometimes dramatic price fluctuations that make it extremely difficult to plan or budget from year to year. It is a rule of economics that labor adds value. Because raw materials are unprocessed, they will always fetch a lower price than they would once processed into a finished good. The prices of exports by developed countries (mostly finished goods) have risen; meanwhile (with the exception of windfall gains for a few producers due to strong demand for a few commodities such as oil, aluminum, and copper) the prices of "soft" commodities (most of Africa's exports) have been falling, suffering a deterioration in the terms of trade.[42]

The "terms of trade," or the overall relationship between the prices of exported and imported goods, are therefore inherently disadvantageous to LICs' economies. Producers of raw materials must struggle to turn out larger volumes just to earn the hard currency to pay for the higher-priced finished goods they must import. The laws of supply and demand simply work against the LICs. For example, Ghanaian farmers can work harder to produce more cocoa for sale on the world market, but the harder they work the less they will earn, since an oversupply of cocoa will drive down its price. Worse, prices are driven down even further as farmers inadvertently add to the problem of oversupply. They produce even more when prices are down, since it takes a bigger crop to scrape by. Meanwhile, because they do not produce the things that they need, these countries are heavily dependent on imports (but without much income to pay for them). The result is that they import more than they export, contributing to a trade imbalance (which they must finance, often by going into debt). Import dependence is a very common problem; according to a recent World Bank study, 80 of 111 LICs had negative trade balances in 2008 (and 67 of them were worse off than they had been in 1990).[43]

There is very little that producers of most raw materials can do about this situation as long as their economies remain centered around the production of cash crops for export. No single country can demand higher prices for its goods, since there are many other producers competing for the sale. And demand for most raw materials is relatively elastic. Even if producers of any single raw material could form a producer's club or cartel to obtain a stronger bargaining position, consumers could turn to substitutes—they could increase their own domestic production of the good, or simply adjust their consumption of it. It is only because demand for oil is relatively inelastic that the oil producers' cartel, the Organization of Petroleum Exporting Countries (OPEC), has been able to raise oil prices by slowing down production and restricting oil supplies.

Therefore, structuralists argue that the world economic system as it currently exists works to reinforce LICs' dependence and leaves them vulnerable to a variety of problems. Having an undiversified economy is like putting all your eggs in one basket. Chinese manufacturers' appetite for commodities such as iron ore, copper, and soybeans helped to raise the price of these goods from 2003 to 2007, but amounted to a "re-primarization" of the economy and made it harder for countries like Peru and Chile to break out of the trap of exporting raw materials and get into the development of value-added manufactured goods and services. As long as commodity prices remain high, it will be hard for these countries to change course.[44] But these economies are also vulnerable to swings in world market prices for their goods—as well as to blight, drought, and other causes of crop failure. For example, Peru, the world's largest exporter of fishmeals (feed sources used in aquaculture and for livestock), saw supplies squeezed in 2010 because of the El Niño weather pattern and warmer ocean temperatures, which reduced its catch by one-third. In a good example of the world's INTERDEPENDENCE, with the supply down, higher prices for fishmeals are likely to translate into higher prices for meat and fish worldwide.[45]

Moreover, overreliance on the export of one raw material (or a few) has left countries that were once self-sufficient in the production of food crops, like Nigeria, now dependent on food imports. Even worse, some countries with hungry populations produce food crops for export. Brazil, for example, although trying to ensure that its own population is fed, is tearing down its forests to grow soybeans (a lucrative cash crop) to satisfy Chinese and European demand. Whereas the IMF and donor agencies encourage LIC economies to focus on export-based production as a means of earning revenue, critics maintain that such a focus is unlikely to produce healthy economies that can support their populations.

Until now, most LICs have had little choice but to accept this advice. And although many countries have attempted to diversify their economies, this is easier said than done. The poorer the country, the more likely its economy is centered on five or fewer products.[46] There may be entrenched ELITES within the country who profit from having the economy structured as it is. Governments that are willing to open up new sectors are limited in the funds available to change things. It takes time and capital to diversify an economy. Moreover, the skills of local inhabitants are likely to be concentrated in the production of what are now traditional cash crops, and the infrastructure may only tie together existing points of production to points of exit.[47]

Even more debilitating than a monocultural economy is no economy at all. Many of the poorest LICs have little or nothing to sell on the world market. Some governments are so desperate to earn hard currency that they have joined the booming business of refuse disposal. As the citizens of developed countries become more aware of the dangers of pollutants to human health and comfort, they have organized into

NIMBY ("not in my backyard") movements. For years, the more affluent communities of developed countries have searched for other places to dispose of their refuse. And for years, poor neighborhoods in these developed countries have become the sites of dumps and landfills. But in response to mounting pressure from NIMBY movements and regulations about waste containment in developed countries, an international trade in refuse removal has emerged. Many LICs that find it difficult making ends meet from the sale of cash crops are now competing to house the garbage and toxic wastes (including e-waste, or electronic waste—such as discarded computers, televisions, and cell phones—which is often hazardous) of developed countries. This practice of wealthy (predominantly white) populations dumping their often-poisonous wastes into poor (predominantly black or brown) communities is known as "environmental racism." In one of the worst examples of this practice in recent times, in 2006 more than sixteen people died and 70,000 sought hospital care after being sickened by the chemical fumes from industrial waste that, after having been rejected at European ports, was dumped in the middle of the city of Abidjan in Côte d'Ivoire. The UN estimates that it will take millions of dollars to clean up the contamination.[48]

Burgeoning industries such as refuse removal are only the latest examples of how LICs have attempted to cope with their weak position within the international economic system. While some initiatives are best understood simply as coping mechanisms, others have been undertaken with the aim of changing the place of LICs within the system. IMPORT SUBSTITUTION INDUSTRIALIZATION is an example of one such effort. In an attempt to follow the developed-country path to development through industrialization, many LICs have sought to break out of the mold as exporters of unfinished goods and lessen their dependence on imports. However, for a variety of reasons, most notably their inability to break into the markets of developed countries or compete with multinational corporations, this experiment has often failed. Turkey adopted this model in the 1930s, but its STATE-OWNED ENTERPRISES (SOEs) were never efficient. As late as the 1970s, Turkey was still overwhelmingly dependent on the export of agricultural products. However, since then its SOEs have been sold off to private interests, which have had more success in building a textile industry. Still, most countries of Africa, Latin America, and the Middle East remain locked in their position as producers of cash crops in export-based economies.

Interestingly, until recently it was East Asia that liberals pointed to as evidence that capitalist development worked. The export-driven economies of the FOUR TIGERS—Hong Kong, Singapore, South Korea, and Taiwan, all highly successful emerging markets—were based on the production of light manufactured goods. For decades, growth rates regularly exceeded 5 percent per year. Per capita income increased more rapidly in these economies than anywhere else in the world. Between 1960 and 2009, for example, GDP per capita in South Korea grew almost fifteenfold, far surpassing that of Brazil, China, and India. There were similar gains in life expectancy and literacy rates, and an overall reduction in poverty, in South Korea and the other industrializing countries. Most impressive, the percentage of South Koreans living under the poverty line during this period was dramatically reduced—from 60 to less than 15 percent.[49]

However, analysts have always disagreed about whether the experience of the Four Tigers could be replicated elsewhere. Since the Asian economic crisis of the late

1990s, more serious questions have been raised about the use of this model. Neo-liberals attributed the success of these emerging economies to their openness, embrace of capitalism, and export-oriented approach as well as their well-educated, disciplined, and hardworking labor force. In addition, emerging economies were credited with having an innovative entrepreneurial class, a high rate of savings, and relatively well-developed infrastructures.

Still, these countries were hardly examples of success based on less state involvement in economies. This was not laissez-faire capitalism at work. Under the Asian model of STATE CAPITALISM adopted in the 1950s, governments were heavily involved in nurturing and protecting industries and businesses until they were globally competitive. Although there is some heterogeneity among the East Asian emerging economies, in most cases these states undertook what is called an export offensive. Throughout the region, governments manipulated nationalist interests to promote economic mobilization. Under this policy, the state became a driving force, directing the economy with the aim of improving international competitiveness. The South Korean and Taiwanese governments, and those of other emerging economies, directed economic growth through their allocation of credit to priority sectors. Scarcely a case of the "invisible hand" at work, these governments played an active, catalytic role in guiding investment strategies. They offered incentives and disincentives to prod the economy toward particular exporting industries. Most of these industries were initially light manufacturing and labor-intensive but gradually became higher-tech. These infant industries were nurtured and protected; the state intervened aggressively and employed protectionist practices to ensure that domestic firms could compete with foreigners.

At the same time that these governments were insulating their infant industries from foreign competition, they avidly sought to attract foreign investment. Decades ago, South Korea and Taiwan successfully lured investors by offering tax incentives, keeping unions weak, and eliminating minimum-wage legislation. For many years, these East Asian governments could only be characterized as dictatorships determined to modernize. These authoritarian regimes manipulated nationalist identities to mobilize the population to work and sacrifice for the good of the nation. Governments provided little in terms of social welfare. Air and water pollution soared. Political and civil rights were forsaken for economic growth, and governments used repressive mechanisms to resist popular pressure for change.

It is important to note that incomes in Taiwan, South Korea, and the other emerging economies of Asia have gradually improved, as have quality-of-life indicators and (with the notable exception of China) respect for political and civil liberties. But it is primarily because of this policy of aggressive government intervention in the economy that the emerging markets were able to capture shares on certain goods. For example, today the East Asian economies make up the world's largest source of electronic components. They base their success on the partnerships that their governments made with businesses to raise productivity and capture an increasing share of the world market. Although this close relationship has been characterized as "crony capitalism" because it is associated with corrupt practices, it has also resulted in the creation of huge economic conglomerates. These economies were so competitive and their performances so strong that in some cases they dominated the market in certain goods. For two decades now, many of these emerging economies have enjoyed trade surpluses with developed countries. The IMF now characterizes Hong Kong, South Korea, and Taiwan as advanced economies. But it is important to remember that, so far, their experience is the exception, not the rule.

Foreign Investment

Although it slowed as global trade took a hit with the recent global financial crisis, foreign direct investment (FDI) by multinational corporations increased ninefold between 1990 and 2008.[50] Yet a global MNC presence is nothing new; since the days of colonialism (and often predating it), multinational corporations have been active throughout the third world. In low-income countries these businesses have dominated the agriculture and mining sectors. Until three decades ago, relatively few of the world's manufactured goods were produced in LICs. However, as mentioned earlier, this has been changing. Some non-Western countries have industrialized, and more and more MNCs are looking to lower the costs of production by creating assembly plants overseas. These corporations are highly influential nongovernmental actors in the process of globalization; their investment decisions often mean the difference between whether a country is increasingly drawn into the global economy, or marginalized by it.

Neoliberals and their critics agree that MNCs are extremely powerful economic entities with an enormous scope and range of activities, including banking, pharmaceuticals, industrial goods, oil, foodstuffs, service—virtually any consumer item or need. Coordinating production on a global scale, they are hardly newcomers to the global economy; their precursors, such as the Dutch East India Company, were at the forefront of colonialism. Now as then, as economic units, the largest MNCs easily dwarf the vast majority of non-Western economies. As of 2009, of the world's 150 largest economic entities, more than half (59 percent) were corporations, not countries. That year the revenue of Wal-Mart, the world's largest retailer, exceeded the GDPs of 174 countries. In addition, Royal Dutch Shell, BP, and Exxon-Mobil were in the top forty on that list—ahead of Portugal, the United Arab Emirates, and Finland.[51] The economic power of MNCs is growing rapidly and although the number of these corporations is estimated at more than 60,000, their power is becoming more concentrated in a few huge firms. J.P. Morgan, for example, has $2 trillion in assets (making it a larger economic entity than Canada). General Electric, with $781 billion in assets, is a larger economic entity than Colombia, Ireland, and Turkey.[52] Analysts have been predicting for years that soon the vast majority of the world's production will be controlled by a handful of MNCs. Such predictions seem to be coming true, as nearly every day one learns of another acquisition, merger, or buyout among these corporate behemoths.

MNCs are headquartered in what we call parent countries. Until recently, the European Union rounded out the top three, but today China has joined the United States (the leading single source of FDI) and Japan as the countries parenting the largest number of Global 500 companies. It is in parent countries where decisions are made, and to which profits return. Yet because of their size, some predict that in the not-too-distant future the power of MNCs may overtake that of the NATION-STATE. For decades sociologists have predicted that our primary IDENTITY may change as we come to view ourselves more as employees of the company for which we work, than as citizens of the country in which we live. In many ways the power of MNCs already rivals that of the nation-state. While MNCs have been accused of being agents of their national governments, the governments of their parent countries are often put to work for the corporation's interests. US interventions to protect MNCs in Chile, Iran, and Guatemala are just a few examples of political meddling, including the overthrow of LIC governments, when MNCs and developed countries have perceived a government's politics as threatening to the economic status quo.

However, today it is increasingly common to hear that the once-cozy relationship between corporations and their parent countries is over. Multinational because of their international operations, MNCs are truly stateless entities, not obligated to any particular country. For years the United States and other countries have bemoaned their inability to force MNCs to comply with their foreign policies (cooperating with sanctions against Iran, for example).

As you may already be sensing, the role that MNCs play in the development of low-income countries is extremely controversial. However, stripped of all the politics, MNCs are simply for-profit corporations with activities abroad stemming from foreign direct investment. Through their investments these businesses establish subsidiaries or branches in what are known as host countries. In the third world, the vast majority of MNC activity is concentrated in the BRICs (Brazil, Russia, India, and China), which received more than half of the foreign direct investment inflows to developing countries in 2009. Leading the pack is China, where capital continues to pour in at twice the rate that it does to India and Brazil.[53] There and elsewhere, these corporations argue that they are just managing the production cycle, cutting costs by subcontracting the work. For example, Apple's iPods are made by smaller enterprises in China and elsewhere.

As for-profit enterprises, MNCs are constantly seeking to improve their profit margins. Two of the easiest ways of accomplishing this are to lower overhead costs and expand markets. That is precisely what these corporations are doing, whether they are investing in LICs or in other developed countries. So much foreign investment goes to China because MNCs want access to the potential spending power of the country's 1.3 billion consumers as much as they want the ultracheap labor. At the turn of the twenty-first century some workers in China labored for as little as 3 cents per hour.[54] Average wages in China have risen over the past few years; Stephen Roach, chair of financial advising firm Morgan Stanley Asia, estimates that in 2006 the average Chinese worker earned about 81 cents per hour. But wages vary widely. Upset about the rising cost of living, more educated, and aware of their rights, Chinese workers in coastal cities have successfully pressed for higher wages (ranging from $132 to $300 a month).[55]

Interestingly, over the past few years employer concerns about labor shortages in China (as well as worker demands for higher wages and improved working and living conditions) have led merchandisers such as H & M, Zara, and Wal-Mart to move production to countries such as Bangladesh, Cambodia, and Vietnam, where wages are even lower and workers are thought to be less restive. For example, Bangladesh's garment exports doubled between 2004 and 2009, but its 3 million (mostly female) garment workers are the lowest-paid in the world. However, Bangladeshi workers have recently demanded (and won) an 80 percent increase in the minimum wage (increased to $43 a month). Investors threatened that if the workers received the raise, companies would pack up and move to Vietnam. Instead, it appears that at least some factory owners are choosing just to ignore the government-mandated pay increase. The result has been labor protests and violent clashes with police.[56]

Although some would argue that until these workers are paid a decent wage, they are unlikely to become the consumer market the MNCs so look forward to, neo-liberals urge us to take the long view and consider the presence of MNCs around the world generally as a positive force. They contend that foreign investment is an important agent for growth, generating wealth through the ability to invest freely around the world and the efficient use of the world's resources. According to the pro-MNC argument, when these corporations invest abroad by opening factories, mines, or plantations, they accelerate the development of the host country in a number of ways. First, MNCs create jobs and, frequently, employees of MNCs earn more than they could elsewhere in the economy. Chinese suppliers to Western multinationals are said to pay more generous wages and offer better conditions because these suppliers are monitored for compliance with labor rules (although this may just be a way for Wal-Mart and Nike to cover themselves, as cheating by their suppliers is said to be pervasive).[57]

But a multinational's presence may mean other benefits for workers. Where Westerners have invested in joint ventures with Chinese firms, workers are said to have more rights, more institutionalized procedures for filing grievances, and so on.[58] Western and non-Western proponents of foreign investment maintain that labor and other activists living in developed countries who call for international standards (such as an international minimum wage) are actually just trying to protect the jobs of workers living in rich countries. Neoliberals argue that activists who are critical of free trade and foreign investment are "the well-intentioned but ill-informed" being led around by "the ill-intentioned but well-informed (protectionist unions and anarchists)."[59] Neoliberals maintain that consumer boycotts of the goods made in these factories are actually hurting workers in LICs, because such boycotts mean a loss of jobs. They offer examples of assembly-line workers in El Salvador, China, and Vietnam who are horrified that Americans would try to "help" them by putting them out of work. The MNCs are the ones "helping" them, by giving them a chance to earn a wage.

And by offering people the opportunity to work for a wage, MNCs may be assisting in the development of the community as well. The creation of jobs has a spin-off effect for the larger economy, as MNC workers will spend their earnings on rent, food, and so forth, in the local economy. In addition, the wages earned will create more demand for imported goods, including goods produced by other subsidiaries of the MNC. Furthermore, MNC employees will become skilled workers, familiar with the new technologies the MNC brings with it when it sets up shop. MNC employees and host countries in general are said to benefit from the corporation's presence, in that by simply being there, MNCs alter "traditional" attitudes. They are said to stimulate the spirit of innovation and entrepreneurship, teach important lessons about competitiveness, and create marketing networks that can extend into and benefit the local economy.[60]

On the other hand, critics of globalization and of MNCs in particular contend with virtually every argument the neoliberals put forward. Instead of being the beacons for change, the structuralists and others maintain that these corporations are actually predatory monopolies that compound an already skewed distribution of wealth. MNC activities widen the growing gap between rich and poor—not only between developed and less developed countries, but also within them. A local elite, known as the COMPRADOR class, dominates LIC economies and political systems, and makes sweetheart deals with these corporations to exploit their own people. In return for kickbacks, a series of Nigerian political leaders and their cronies have nurtured a very special relationship with Royal Dutch Shell and other oil companies in order to join in on the exploitation of the country's riches for the benefit of a few. Theirs is a reciprocal relationship in which compradors work to maintain a climate conducive to MNC interests, and the corporations in turn use their wealth and political clout to help keep local aristocracies in power. If the relationship falls apart, or the population elects a government less compliant and willing to accede to MNC prerogatives, MNCs have been known to "help create" a government more to their liking (as in the 1953 coup that overthrew the democratically elected government of Iran).

Moreover, critics argue that even ordinary citizens of developed countries are at the mercy of these giants, not only as workers to be displaced in the constant quest for ever-cheaper labor, but also as consumers who are overcharged for goods made for a pittance. Over the past couple of decades, MNCs have sought to reduce the costs of overhead even further by setting up shop in EXPORT PROCESSING ZONES (EPZs) around the world, in countries such as Mauritius and Sri Lanka. Corporations are attracted to EPZs because there they pay only minimal taxes and can operate without being held to the environmental standards they would find at home. Developing as well as developed countries have been accused of taking part in a "race to the bottom," diluting environmental regulations and labor laws in order to attract investment. And it is working: corporations are finding it profitable to relocate for all of these reasons—especially for guarantees of cheap and controllable labor.

Much of the work in MNC assembly plants is labor-intensive and low-skilled. In recent years, EPZ employers have become notorious for hiring females and paying them too little to live on, with the rationalization (true or not) that because females are supported by male breadwinners, their wages are mere "lipstick money" and need be only supplemental. In addition, corporations base their preference for female labor on stereotypical ideas about females being "naturally" patient and better suited for the mind-numbing tedious labor demanded by MNCs. Female workers are assumed to be not only more dexterous (important for sewing operations and in microprocessing computer chips, for example) but also more docile than men, more accepting of male (managerial) authority, and less likely to join unions.

However, another class of workers has joined the labor force—one with more nimble fingers who are even more likely to submit to fatherlike authority. Between 2004 and 2008 the total numbers of child laborers worldwide declined (mostly in Asia and Latin America). But it is estimated that one in four children in Africa are working, and the number could rise if the global economic downturn continues. According to the International Labour Organization (ILO), as of 2008 nearly 215 million children aged 5–17 were working full-time worldwide and 126 million in extremely hazardous conditions.[61] Some of the states tolerating the worst child labor practices are India, China, Morocco, and Côte d'Ivoire (in the news in recent years for the slavelike conditions under which children toil for chocolate producers). One of the most dramatic tragedies resulting from the exploitation of children was the 2001 explosion of a Chinese school that was doubling as a fireworks factory. Although the government at first vehemently denied that such a cottage industry existed, more than forty people (most of them children) died in the blast, the result of third-graders mounting fuses on fireworks as part of a "work for study" program.

In Peru, where a former president (Alejandro Toledo) once worked as a shoeshine boy, the legal minimum age for child workers is fourteen. Still, enforcement is lax, and unknown numbers of children work in the country, particularly in rural areas. Child labor is especially common in the gold-mining regions of the Amazon, since their small size enables eight- and nine-year-olds to work deep in the mines in narrow shafts. Children working instead of going to school is a regular occurrence in Nigeria and elsewhere, particularly in agriculture, and it is likely to continue to grow as long as corporations seek to remain competitive while increasing profits— and as long as consumers demand ever-cheaper goods.

In addition to paying wages that can only be described as exploitative, MNCs are criticized for cutting corners and ignoring abuses, exposing their workers to SWEATSHOP conditions. These corporations have long been associated with abusive practices such as forced overtime and corporal punishment, and "sweatshop belts" run through parts of Asia and Latin America. A fire killed twenty-four garment workers in Bangladesh, where it is not uncommon for factory owners to keep the exits locked (to keep the women at their machines). In China and Mexico, workers often live and toil in compounds behind locked gates and high walls surrounded by barbed wire. Not only is the housing often overcrowded and unsanitary, but the work can be dangerous as well. In 2006, tens of thousands of Mexican miners and metal workers led a nationwide strike, complaining of unsafe conditions amounting to "industrial homicide."[62] In 2008, four workers in Turkey producing bed linens for Ikea died due to unsafe working conditions. One died when he fell into the funnel of a coal boiler.[63]

In one region near Hong Kong, factory workers producing goods for Dell and Disney on fast-moving assembly lines lose or break 40,000 fingers on the job every year.[64] Firestone says that it has zero tolerance for child labor, but reportedly places such impossible harvesting quotas on its Liberian rubber workers that they must rely on the assistance of unpaid family members (including small children) to keep their jobs (which paid $3.19 a day in 2008).[65]

In many parts of the world, forced labor and prison labor are routine. Relatively speaking, the lucky ones are those who in effect work as indentured servants, often from 7 A.M. until 11 P.M. seven days a week, with only one day off each month.[66] In factories around the world, workers must stand long hours and handle adhesives and other toxic substances such as lead with their bare hands, in harshly lit, poorly ventilated, and sometimes deafening environments. Though there is variation in practice, it is not uncommon for workers to be subjected to an astonishing array of rules and corporal punishments. There are often strict guidelines limiting bathroom breaks and talking. Punishments for violations can be quite devious. Easily distracted children may be kept at their work by the requirement that they hold a matchbox under their chins (without using their hands)—under threat of being beaten if they drop it to talk or even look around the room. Women have been subjected to sexual harassment and humiliation, such as compulsory pregnancy testing in *maquiladoras* in Mexico and elsewhere. Such abuses have ended only when brought to light and companies squirm under the pressures of bad public relations.

Figure 6.8   Child Labor: A Benefit to the Child?

The issue of child labor may be more complex than it seems. As hard as it may be to believe, some advocates for children argue that it can actually be a good thing. There are many different types of child labor, and the image many of us associate with it—of an estimated 1.2 million children leased out by their parents as indentured servants every year, many working in dangerous conditions (in fishing boats, in the carpet and glass industries, or for silk thread manufacturers) for a pittance—is truly horrific.[67] Any child working under such conditions is one too many, but just 5 percent of the world's child workers are involved in the production of exported goods. Most of the rest are working (as generations of children did before them) for their families on farms, in cottage industries, as domestic workers, or as apprentices to artisans. Some human rights advocates argue that Western indignation and efforts to ban all forms of child labor only throw the poor into greater misery.

Moral outrage can be counterproductive. For example, when it was reported that Wal-Mart was selling clothes made by children in Bangladesh, a boycott forced factories to fire its child workers, who ended up going into more dangerous industries, including prostitution. Moreover, an uproar may close a few factories, but it does precious little to address the root of the problem—poverty. In fact, these well-meaning interventions often wind up increasing families' hardships, without addressing the global inequities that create mass suffering. In some cases, such activism is injurious not only to economic well-being

but to social and cultural rights as well, as traditional art forms handed down through generations are lost. These days, human rights activists are more hesitant to advocate boycotts and instead urge that people invest in a socially responsible way, as an antislavery tool.

Yet traditions are not always benevolent. In many parts of the world, child labor is the last vestige of modern slavery. And there are those who argue that if children are working, they aren't attending school or don't have the freedom to simply be children. Therefore, some advocates of child labor are devising ingenious ways of validating the argument that work in itself can teach important lessons, while creating more opportunities for children to learn in formal settings as well. In Morocco, where some argue that the abolition of child labor would mean the loss of traditional arts and handicrafts, the United Nations Children's Fund (UNICEF) is trying to speak to the concerns of all by bringing teachers into the workhouses. In India, parents are being encouraged to adjust their labor needs so that their children can also attend school. Increasingly, advocates are moving away from an absolutist stance that views all forms of child labor as abuse. While they insist that all children should have the right to a formal education (and many argue that this begins with the abolition of school fees), they are coming to realize that working with the family and community can help to shape children's identities and give them a valuable sense of responsibility and belonging.[68]

Moreover, critics of MNCs dispute the claim that host-country populations benefit from exposure to the technologies the corporations bring. Nor do most workers learn a skill: the vast majority remain unskilled or low-skilled and very few local people ever make it to the ranks of management (a position often reserved for nationals of the parent country). Instead of raising productivity by promoting the use of labor-intensive technologies that are relatively cheap, simple to use, and labor-enhancing, the technologies these companies do introduce are often inappropriate and capital-intensive. Such technologies are not well suited to the needs of low-income countries, since they are acquired at a significant cost. Not only are they expensive and sophisticated (requiring fossil fuels, costly imported spare parts, and highly skilled technicians for maintenance), but worse yet, these machines serve as devices of labor replacement. They replace the need for human labor and add to already high unemployment rates.

Another topic of dispute concerns MNCs' claims about the transmission of values such as modernity and entrepreneurship. Many critics are disturbed by such claims because they smack of ethnocentrism. Too often people say "modernity" when they mean "Westernization." By implication then, whatever is non-Western becomes lumped into the category of "backward." Neoliberals assume that this modernity is a universally desired goal, when in fact what most of the world's people want is an escape from their material poverty. People of the third world may want the comforts and choices many Westerners enjoy; this doesn't necessarily mean that they want to become Western. Furthermore, what MNCs are selling isn't modernity—it is the image of modernity. These firms are actually creating dependence by aggressively marketing their products and seeking to alter consumer tastes and attitudes through glossy and often deceptive advertising campaigns.[69]

The classic example of how MNCs prey on the desperation of the poor is the Nestlé baby-formula scandal of the 1970s. In an attempt to create an even more profitable market for its powdered-milk products, Nestlé undertook a massive advertising campaign of misinformation. Targeting countries with appallingly high infant mortality rates, the company designed slick advertisements that strongly suggested that its infant formula was preferable to breast milk. While such claims were patently false on a number of counts, Nestlé was not satisfied with just taking the money of desperate parents. In some countries, it went even further to guarantee itself a market. Ostensibly offered as a welcoming gift, the company went about providing two weeks' worth of baby-formula "samples" to mothers leaving clinics with newborns—without informing them that if they used the formula for two weeks, their breast milk would dry up. The UNITED NATIONS GENERAL ASSEMBLY condemned Nestlé for these actions, but less dramatic forms of abuse by other companies, such as the sale of adulterated baby food, have continued to occur. For example, in 2008 at least six Chinese infants died and 300,000 were sickened because the company making their baby formula had sought to cut costs by lacing it with melamine, an industrial chemical used in plastic that makes the protein content of the formula appear higher than it is.[70]

Under fire for ethical, environmental, and other lapses, many of today's MNCs are fighting negative publicity and working hard to humanize their image by promoting philanthropy and adopting a posture of corporate responsibility. In recent years, several companies have sought to deflect criticisms by hiring monitors to meet with employees to hear complaints and investigate problems. As mentioned earlier, corporations are increasingly subcontracting parts of the production line to smaller firms that work in greater obscurity. When these abuses are exposed, corporations claim that they have limited power or leverage over these independent contractors or that host governments should be blamed for inadequate labor laws. However, as long as the neoliberals' staunch advocacy of deregulation prevails, the most that can be expected from MNCs is voluntary compliance with ethical norms and self-monitoring.

MNCs and neoliberals argue that voluntary codes are good enough, since it just isn't good business to misbehave anymore. In response to a newly recognized aspect of consumer preference, some companies have changed the way they do business and are treating workers better than required by often-weak regional laws. For example, Shell and BP, though once part of an alliance that lobbied hard against taking the threat of global warming seriously, now advertise with calls for reductions in carbon dioxide emissions. Nike has pressed its suppliers to open their factories to independent inspections, to remove child laborers from its lines, and to provide a better environment for its workers. Wal-Mart says that it has gone "green," not only looking to become the biggest retailer of organic foods, but also promising to become more energy efficient and to reduce solid waste.[71]

In another example of corporations shifting under pressure, although the high price of medicines is still a problem, some pharmaceutical corporations have lowered the prices for some of their drugs in some countries (for example, a common combination of these medicines costs $12,000 per person per year in HICs, whereas the same medicines in some LICs can be had for as little as $100 per person per year).[72] Partly this is a response to the development of cheap generics, but since 2003 there has been a dramatic increase in the number of people receiving HIV/AIDS medicines.

In summary, neoliberals contend that with very few exceptions, foreign direct investment is a boon for economies. With very few exceptions, multinational corporations abide by the laws of their host countries and if anyone should be blamed for a lack of standards, it is the governments of low- and middle-income countries. But often the only COMPARATIVE ADVANTAGE most LICs have is cheap labor and lack of government regulation, including environmental protections—and there are many LICs, vying for investment and jobs. But even if these countries were to upgrade their working conditions to the standards of developed countries, they would lose

Peruvian armed forces employees call for higher wages (Reuters/Mariana Bazo)

business. So the situation facing LICs is a difficult one. Even among those critics and proponents of MNCs who agree that international minimum standards are necessary to keep people (wherever they live) from being exploited, they have a hard time agreeing on what those standards should be, let alone how to enforce them.

Aid and Debt

Although it played a much larger role during the COLD WAR, foreign aid of one form or another is still of critical importance to most non-Western economies. The vast majority of foreign assistance is distributed as bilateral aid, commonly defined as the transfer of concessional resources from one government to another. Multilateral aid is the transfer of resources from a group of donors (such as the United Nations or the Organization for Economic Cooperation and Development [OECD]) to a recipient. In either case, aid is very definitely a tool of diplomacy, employed in such a way as to manipulate the behavior of possible recipients. Aid is used as a carrot to encourage or reward loyalty or desirable behavior. Or the withholding of aid can be a stick used to punish those deemed undeserving. In actuality, the majority of US aid does not go to the world's poorest people. With the current "war on terror," as during the Cold War, US foreign aid is not provided on a needs basis, but rather is based on strategic calculation. Since September 11, 2001, the amount the United States spends on foreign aid has increased—particularly for certain developing countries that have clear strategic value, as aid is increasingly being linked to cooperation with the war on terror. As a result, a handful of countries, including Iraq, Afghanistan, Pakistan, Israel, and Egypt, receive the lion's share of all US bilateral assistance.

For years, aid has been welcomed by low-income countries as a spur to development. For a variety of reasons, many countries have become aid-dependent; foreign aid composed 44 percent of Burundi's GNI in 2008, and 189 percent of Liberia's.[73] However, there have always been concerns that much of this aid is being stolen or wasted and not doing much to help countries actually develop. As a result, by the 1990s, the popular slogan among many donors (and a growing number of recipients) was "trade, not aid." Some, however, such as former French president Jacques Chirac, say that this slogan should be "aid for trade."[74] As with nearly every other topic raised in this chapter, there is a great deal of disagreement about the effectiveness of aid. Both neoliberals and their critics agree that more aid is not necessarily better at promoting development. Nearly everyone, even those who call for increased funding for foreign aid, have problems with the ways in which aid packages have been designed and managed. Neoliberals contend that aid can promote development if it is used as part of a larger package of reforms. Some, such as former UN Secretary-General Kofi Annan, view aid as only one element in a development strategy that can be more effective if it is offered to help recipients run their own economies.[75] Critics on the left argue that aid is too often used to benefit the economic or strategic interests of donor countries, as a tool of capitalism that actually increases dependency and contributes to the further underdevelopment of states. From the right, conservatives argue that foreign aid is too often simply a waste of good money and that development can only come from the efforts of private-sector entrepreneurs and political reformers.

Foreign assistance comes in a variety of forms: loans, cash, food, clothing, medicine, arms, or just about any other commodity. Contrary to popular American belief, the United States is not a major donor of aid. Most Americans believe that the United States is much more generous, even overly generous, with the aid it offers LICs. Consequently, it is highly unlikely that US politicians will campaign for larger aid budgets. Although the United States does give more in total dollars ($28 billion in 2009), it gives less as a share of its GNI (about 0.2 percent) than any other developed country except Greece, Japan, and Italy. In other words, on average, each American pays approximately $4 a year in taxes toward foreign aid. Years ago, in 2002, leaders of the world's rich, industrialized countries agreed that this was not enough and set a goal of contributing 0.7 percent of their GNIs to foreign aid. As of 2009, only Norway, Sweden, the Netherlands, Luxembourg, and Denmark had met (or surpassed) that goal (Sweden, for example, gives 1.01 percent of its GNI in foreign aid).[76]

Although still well short of their commitments, foreign aid flows from high-income to low-income countries increased between 2000 and 2008 (to $120 billion total—the highest level ever, amounting to 0.31 percent of the GNIs of rich countries).[77] Since the Great Recession, the foreign aid budgets of the United States and other HICs have been more constrained; many large donors reduced or postponed their pledges for 2010, with total aid projected to drop to $108 billion. This reduction comes at a bad time for many poor countries that are also struggling to recover. UN Secretary-General Ban Ki-moon has urged HICs not to cut their aid, but donors have instead shifted their attention to find other ways to fund development, such as a new financial tax or green bonds.[78]

With difficult economic times in the United States, perhaps it is easy to understand why President Barack Obama has not made good on his 2008 campaign pledge to double US foreign aid (to $50 billion by 2012).[79] Yet for many years it has been argued that the United States is the principal beneficiary of the vast majority of its foreign aid to other countries, since so much of this aid is "tied" in order to guarantee a market for US goods. For example, the United States might extend a loan to Nigeria to buy tractors. This is a loan that the United States fully expects Nigeria to repay with interest, yet Nigeria has no choice but to use that money to buy US tractors, even if Japanese or French tractors are less expensive, or preferred for some other reason. As a result, tied aid is estimated to reduce the value of development assistance by 15–25 percent.[80] Aid activists point out that such packages should be recognized for what they are: subsidies of donor economies. Low-income countries argue that development should not be a profit-making enterprise for the rich at the expense of the poor. Britain was an early proponent of this argument, and has begun to untie some of the strings attached to the aid it offers. The United States and other HICs have untied some aid, but given hard economic times at home it is increasingly difficult to persuade their constituents of the need for foreign assistance. Most Americans think that the United States already gives too much aid (for years, polls have shown that most Americans believe that 25 percent of the federal budget goes to foreign aid—when it is actually less than 1 percent).[81] Regardless of the reality, politicians find it an easy part of the budget to talk about cutting. Those who seek to sustain or increase aid levels find it politically necessary to show that tied aid offers a reciprocal benefit by creating hundreds of thousands of jobs for the citizens of donor countries.

After the Cold War ended there was enormous pressure on the United States and other developed countries to cut foreign aid, as part of the "peace dividend." Since then, the vast majority of foreign assistance offered (to most countries) has come not in the form of grants or gifts, but as loans. Although most people's definition of "aid" would seem to call for the concessional terms offered by soft loans, with their low interest rates and long repayment periods, a substantial number of these loans are hard loans, bearing high interest rates and short repayment periods. Many of these loans are taken out to service debt (or make the scheduled payment on the debt accrued from past loans).

Therefore, a great deal of the assistance that developed countries offer is in the form of loans meant to pay the interest on an outstanding debt. This only adds to that debt, which may exist for a variety of reasons. In some cases, the monies owed are Cold War debts; the West lent to its anticommunist allies knowing that the resources would wind up in the hands of irresponsible, wasteful, or kleptocratic governments (some consider this to be "odious debt" and argue that creditors should not expect repayment because they made the loans with full knowledge of how the money was to be used). Or LICs lost money in failed (but expensive) attempts at industrialization. In other cases, world recession or unexpected changes in the global economy (such as sudden jumps in the price of oil or food) contributed to deficits that put countries into debt. Most LICs have sunk into debt because they have consistently faced shortfalls in their balance of payments (again, due to their disadvantageous position in the international economy).

Clearly, external factors beyond these countries' control have played a large part in creating the crisis. However, to some extent, each country's debt grows out of its own particular combination of problems. Regardless of the source of the debt, it only became a crisis as far as the IMF and donors were concerned in the early 1980s, when Mexico and other debtors declared their inability to pay and threatened a moratorium (or temporary halt) on servicing their debts. Such threats were widely regarded as amounting to an emergency, since banks had eagerly overextended themselves for years, making loans to LICs without worry as to their creditworthiness. Banks and donors feared that if other countries had joined Mexico in the formation of a debtors' cartel, their collective default could have led to the collapse of the international financial system.

Since the debt crisis of the 1980s, IFIs and donors have recognized how vital it is that the vast majority of debtors be willing and able to pay. Donors are working with international financial institutions and are determined to manage the system to better protect it. There have been a variety of attempts to manage LIC debt over the years. For a variety of reasons, the debt burdens of some LICs have eased, but for others they are still very real. In 1970, total LIC foreign debt was less than $100 billion. It rose to $600 billion by 1980, and to $1.6 trillion by 1990. As of 2008, the total external debt for all low- and middle-income countries was $3.7 trillion (in comparison, the total external debt of the United States in 2010 was $14 trillion).[82] Nearly $4 trillion of debt equals well over $500 of debt for every man, woman, and child living in poor and middle-income countries (remember that the average income in the poorest countries is less than $1.25 per day). Most of the increase in debt in the 1990s was due to the fact that countries had to take out more loans to service (or pay the interest) on their existing debt. For example, in 2000, Argentina's debt service (as a share of its income) was 69 percent, Turkey's was 29 percent, and Mozambique's was 26 percent.[83]

When countries are in this position, scraping by, just making the minimum payments on their bills, there is precious little left over to spend on education, healthcare, or other aspects of development. For years, African countries spent much more on debt repayment than on healthcare.[84] They wound up literally choosing between food and debt, making what has been called "the cruel choice." In 2005, Kenya budgeted as much for its debt payment as it did for water, health, agriculture, roads, and transportation combined.[85] Some analysts contend that the situation amounts to debt slavery, and is as devastating to a population as war. Yet by the mid-2000s, more people (including donors) were beginning to realize that it was time to make the connection between debt relief and development. How could sub-Saharan Africa ever develop when it paid approximately $15 billion each year to HICs and international financial institutions in debt service?[86]

Latin America was the region hit hardest by debt service a decade ago, paying nearly a third of its entire export earnings to the banks. This debt is as debilitating for the countries with the largest total debts (such as Mexico and Brazil) as it is for countries with lower total bills but much smaller economies (such as many countries in Africa) (see Figures 6.9 and 6.10). To put this in some perspective, the World Bank defines countries as "severely indebted" if their debt-to-GNI ratio is over 50 percent. As of 2008, of our cases, only Zimbabwe qualified for this category. Indonesia, Turkey, Mexico, and Peru were "moderately indebted," and Iran, China, and Nigeria ranked as "less indebted."[87] It doesn't take an accountant to see that when the debt burden is heavy, at a certain point payment becomes impossible and

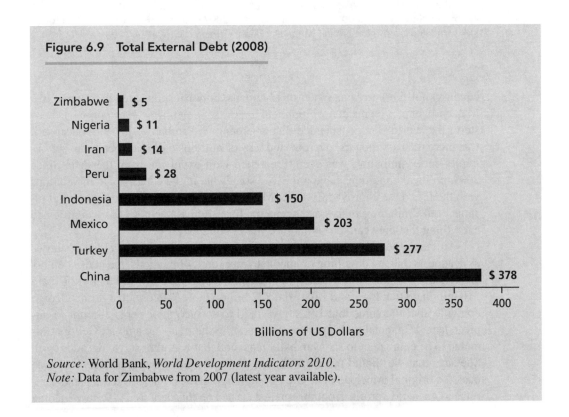

Figure 6.9 Total External Debt (2008)

Source: World Bank, *World Development Indicators 2010.*
Note: Data for Zimbabwe from 2007 (latest year available).

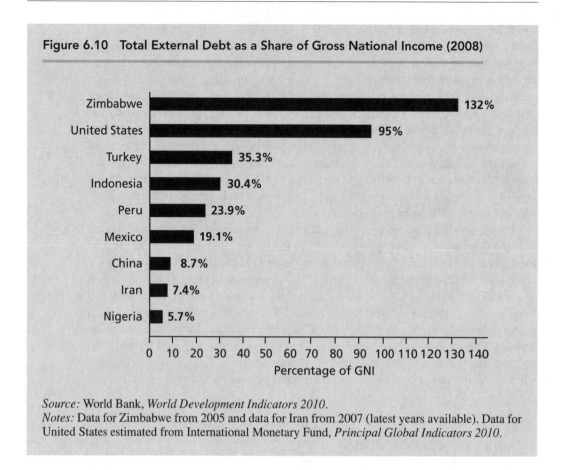

Figure 6.10 Total External Debt as a Share of Gross National Income (2008)

Source: World Bank, *World Development Indicators 2010.*
Notes: Data for Zimbabwe from 2005 and data for Iran from 2007 (latest years available). Data for United States estimated from International Monetary Fund, *Principal Global Indicators 2010.*

countries fall into arrears. When this happens, donor response tends to vary, as it frequently hinges on the donors' political interests. Sometimes the response has been stern: the World Bank suspended disbursements to Zimbabwe in 1999 because it was more than six months' overdue and tens of millions of dollars behind in servicing its debt. Zimbabwe was even threatened with expulsion from the IMF. Since 2009, political conditions have improved somewhat in the country, and its relations with the IFIs have improved. But the IMF has made it clear that lending will not resume until Zimbabwe makes arrangements for its unpaid debt.[88] Most countries do everything that they can to stay in the IMF's good graces.

Although the publics of developed countries largely regard indebted countries as deadbeats that are unwilling or unable to meet their obligations, the major debtors are actually net exporters of capital. For example, Nigeria borrowed $5 billion, paid $16 billion on that loan, and still owed $32 billion more.[89] Economist Susan George contends that the sums that LICs have paid to service their debts amount to unprecedented financial assistance from the poor to the rich—an amount George estimated to be equivalent to six Marshall Plans (and that was almost two decades ago). She says that we should not worry about the banks going hungry—they've made back the original principal and more through high interest rates. And the banks continue to make tidy profits from the interest earned on this debt. In 2007, low-income countries paid $12 billion in debt service ($34 million a day).[90] In Nigeria and elsewhere, many of the governments that accumulated this debt and misappropriated these funds are long gone. However, the citizens of these countries are left holding the bag, responsible for repaying a debt they never asked for, and from which they derived no gain. Eduardo Galeano likens this system to an open artery: LICs are being bled dry. Rather than being healed by the IMF, the veins are kept open for the purpose of drawing more blood—this at a time when the developing world is facing its worst economic crisis since the Great Depression.[91]

Neoliberals maintain that such characterizations are unfair and point to a variety of efforts over the years that the IMF and donors have devised to pull countries out of debt (which we will describe in the next chapter). Yet their critics argue that what IFIs have been doing is developing strategies to protect themselves so that they will be much less vulnerable to the kind of pressure they experienced in the 1980s—a divide-and-rule strategy that results in debtors having a harder time uniting to confront their creditors because each country has to meet with the IFIs to restructure its debt privately and on an individual basis. The terms of each deal are secret, and in the hope of more preferential treatment, countries know they must go it alone. And this is an offer they cannot resist, since most countries must meet the terms of the IMF or risk being deemed uncreditworthy. For most LICs, a bad rating from the IMF can mean economic suicide. Noncompliance risks isolation and severe punishment: the flow of capital in the form of investment, debt relief, or any other type of assistance dries up. After months of economic crisis stemming from IMF shock therapy in 2001 and 2002, Argentina refused further treatment. Few countries are willing to take such risks (or are in the position to get away with it).

On the other hand, countries willing to accept IMF demands are usually offered some form of debt relief, which may involve debt rescheduling or, more rarely, restructuring or forgiveness. Rescheduling of debt defers payment to a later date; it is a temporary reprieve, allowing for an extension of the period of repayment of the loan. Rescheduling is considered crucial for many countries because it makes their debt burden more bearable.[92] As opposed to rescheduling, restructuring is an agreed default on part of a debt, whereas forgiveness means reducing or writing it off. While in the past forgiveness was usually the option of last resort, a global campaign to forgive debt has developed since the late 1990s. This program, put forward by an unusual collection of personalities and religious figures, such as U2's Bono and Reverend Billy Graham, became an international movement, known as Jubilee 2000. It called for forgiveness of debt as part of a biblical mandate (the Book of Leviticus sets down that every fifty years all debts should be canceled, land returned to the dispossessed, and slaves set free). The time of liberation was known as "Jubilee," and its namesake movement pressed during the millennium year for a onetime full debt forgiveness for the world's poorest countries.

The argument for forgiveness goes as follows: in countries where the majority of the population lives on less than one dollar a day, it is not only wrong but also inefficient to require them to spend so much of their revenue paying back their creditors. Perhaps partially in response to such calls, rich countries did promise a record amount of foreign aid in 2005, and some of that aid came in the form of debt relief. However, with a few exceptions (such as tens of billions of dollars of forgiveness for Iraq), the closest the IFIs and donors have come to forgiveness for most countries is a program for HIGHLY INDEBTED POOR COUNTRIES (HIPCs).[93] Highly indebted poor countries were originally defined as having a gross national product (GNP) per capita of less than $675 (as of 2008 the cutoff was $1,100) and "unsustainable" debt (amounting to more than 80 percent of GNP). Under the HIPC program, developed countries promised to expand and accelerate debt relief measures, and to share a token of their prosperity with the poor. This idea was reiterated at the 2005 meeting of the Group of Eight in Gleneagles, Scotland, where the United States, Canada, Japan, and several European countries pledged to cancel the multilateral debt of about two dozen of the poorest countries (mostly African) that fulfilled the HIPC conditions. Relatively speaking, this does not amount to a lot of money, since the HIPC program currently accounts for a small part of the total external debt of LICs. To be considered for the HIPC program, not only must a country be desperately poor, but it also must be willing to divert all the money it would have paid on its debt to programs promoting education, healthcare, and economic development. Where debt relief has been implemented, it has made a real change in people's lives. For example, thanks to the HIPC program, over 1 million Tanzanian children were able to return to school. Zambia was able to hire 4,500 new teachers and abolish school fees as well as offer free healthcare in rural areas. In Niger, the infant mortality rate dropped from 156 to 81 per 1,000 live births, and the percentage of people with access to potable water climbed from 40 to 69 percent.[94] In virtually every country that has received debt relief, social spending has increased by as much as 75 percent and social indicators have begun to improve.[95]

For countries that qualify for the HIPC program, or for the MULTILATERAL DEBT RELIEF INITIATIVE (MDRI), an enhanced relief program, just one more string is attached: applicants must be willing to faithfully accept all the conditions set for them by the IMF. Only countries that successfully complete key structural reforms are said to have reached the completion point, making them eligible for as much as 100 percent debt reduction. As of early 2011, thirty-five countries had been granted reductions of $57 billion on future debt payments; and twenty-eight countries had reached completion and received an additional $25 billion in debt relief under the MDRI.[96] Jubilee 2000 (now called the Jubilee USA Network) has so far failed to win its demand for full debt cancellation without preconditions. There is some good news: the average debt-to-GDP ratios in many low-income countries declined from 2000 to 2008 and most non-Western regions cut the percentage of export revenues that go to service their debt. Latin America made the most progress of any region, cutting its share of export revenues for debt service from 22 to 7 percent over this period. Sub-Saharan African countries on average halved their debt thanks to reduction programs.

On the other hand, since 2008 it is the high-income countries that have accumulated higher levels of debt (Japan's debt in 2009 was more than 150 percent of its GDP, whereas most low- and middle-income-country debt was 30 percent of GDP). As of early 2011, Brazil, China, and India had low debt-to-GDP ratios, and three-fifths of sub-Saharan African countries had what the IMF considers "sustainable" debt positions (thanks largely to debt relief, better debt management, and the expansion of trade during the boom preceding the Great Recession).[97] In 2011, some of the countries with the highest debt-to-GDP ratios were Ireland, Zimbabwe, and Greece. In terms of total dollars, the United States has the world's largest external debt, which has grown significantly since the 2007–2009 financial crisis. The mounting debt for advanced economies is no doubt concerning, but countries like the United States and Japan have traditionally been considered safer bets in that they can more easily manage debt, in part because they have better credit ratings and can therefore pay lower interest rates (although this is not always the case; in 2010, South Africa's credit rating was better than that of Greece).[98]

However, economists are concerned that the recent positive trends regarding debt in low- and medium-income countries may reverse.[99] Analysts point out that the Group of Eight countries have yet to make good on the commitments they made in 2005; as of early 2011 there was a $20 billion gap between what they promised and what they had delivered. This has hurt sub-Saharan African countries in particular, because the HICs had pledged to double the share of foreign assistance directed toward them specifically. It is estimated that Africa will only receive approximately $11 billion of the $25 billion increase agreed upon at the Gleneagles meeting.[100] Since the global financial crisis of the late 2000s, the amounts of relief pledged by donors and IFIs has been small (compared to the need); there is not enough aid for additional countries to have their debt restructured or forgiven, or to help them achieve sustainable debt. Moreover, most of those countries eligible for the HIPC program are, like Niger, dependent on the sale of one or two raw materials (in Niger's case, uranium), the prices of which have fluctuated widely over the past several years. Consequently, some economists argue that among the countries that have had their debt canceled, some will eventually fall back into debt unless their position in the world economy fundamentally changes. The Jubilee movement recognizes that debt cancellation must be combined with other, far-reaching change. Its members emphasize that forgiveness is only a first step, offering debt-burdened countries the new beginning they desperately need.

7

A New and Improved
Structural Adjustment?

The only thing lacking is for us to pull down the Argentine flag and replace it with the IMF's. —*Alfredo Avelin, governor of San Juan, Argentina*[1]

The "wretched of the earth" want to go to Disney World—not to the barricades.
—*Thomas L. Friedman, writer*[2]

As mentioned in Chapter 6, the conditions attached to the program for HIGHLY IN-DEBTED countries (or any debt restructuring, for that matter) are based in NEOLIBER-ALISM, in a set of ideas known as the Washington Consensus. Although two decades old, the Washington Consensus still sums up the position of the INTERNATIONAL FINANCIAL INSTITUTIONS (IFIs) and the donors that dominate them (the United States, Canada, the European Union, and Japan): that underdevelopment is due to the domestic failings of the underdeveloped countries themselves. In other words, it is argued that low-income countries (LICs) need internal structural reforms to stabilize their economies. Just as the diagnosis of the problem is universal, so is the cure. A fairly uniform prescription is proposed for dealing with any economy's ills: an opening up (or liberalization) of the economy to foreign competition, and the adoption of a series of market-based reforms, including privatization and deregulation, as well as an embrace of GLOBALIZATION. According to the Washington Consensus, economic crises (wherever they occur) should be approached in the same way and treated with a consistent dose of ECONOMIC LIBERALIZATION and fiscal austerity, or belt-tightening. The prognosis for LICs is quite optimistic: if countries will only take their medicine, they will experience healthy growth rates. Healthy growth rates will provide for the growth of a middle class, and then more stable, viable democracies are sure to follow.

It is usually the INTERNATIONAL MONETARY FUND (IMF) that administers the cure. The IMF plays several highly influential roles in the world economy, and these roles have shifted over time. Increasingly, the IMF's focus is on the promotion of global economic stability (and the prevention and management of financial crises).[3] The IMF promotes stability by serving as the lender of last resort to countries in economic crisis, distributing loans or lines of credit (ideally, concessional loans or credit)

Figure 7.1 Military Budgets and Adjustment

Until the end of the Cold War, many third world governments (both civilian and military) received much of their foreign aid in the form of military assistance. With the tacit if not outright approval of the West, many of these governments also spent the lion's share of their budgets on the military. In less-than-democratic regimes, the armed services played (and continue to play) a large part in keeping these governments in power. However, many people living under authoritarian rule hoped that with the end of the Cold War and the rise of new democracies around the world, the military's influence would wane. They looked forward to a democracy dividend, in which money would be cut from military budgets and reallocated to long-neglected social services such as education and healthcare.

Unfortunately, this democracy dividend has been slow in coming in many countries, for reasons that are sometimes perplexing. Global military spending grew by 6 percent between 2008 and 2009 to more than $1.5 trillion (it has grown by 49 percent since 2000). The United States is by far the biggest spender, accounting for just under half of all military spending (China is a distant second, spending approximately 7 percent of the world total). However, military spending has also increased elsewhere, in countries such as Algeria, Chad, and Ecuador. As of early 2011, all regions, except the Middle East, were spending more. Only smaller economies that are struggling with deficits due to declines in the prices of their export commodities (such as Iraq, Venezuela, and Chile) have cut military expenditures.[4] Seemingly, for most countries, this is one budget priority that even a global financial meltdown won't affect.

to countries whose economies are facing temporary shortfalls. By shortfalls, we are referring to an imbalance in payments, or a situation in which a country is spending more than it is earning. When this occurs, a country is said to be experiencing a deficit, and must find ways to finance or cover this deficit. This is how many countries go into debt: compared to the unpopular alternatives of raising taxes or cutting spending, governments prefer to take out loans to cover the shortfall. When countries run into serious financial trouble, it is often the IMF to which they turn for RESCUE PACKAGES: emergency loans, bailouts, or possibly even debt relief. Again, countries get "rescued" only after they have agreed to the IMF's cure. Obviously, this makes the IMF an extremely powerful institution, with tremendous influence over the decisions of governments.

So what is the cure, exactly? What are the conditions attached to the provision of new loans that are so necessary for the servicing of old debt? The first thing to understand is that there is a regimen associated with the cure, now known as EXTENDED-CREDIT FACILITIES (ECFs). Also called AUSTERITY PLANS, ECFs are said to allow for more input from the countries they target. According to their proponents, ECFs treat the countries involved more like stakeholders, participating in the design of the plan, and are somewhat less onerous than their predecessor (STRUCTURAL ADJUSTMENT PROGRAMS [SAPs]). ECFs, as opposed to SAPs (which were known as "shock therapy"), are designed to be kinder and gentler. They often include fewer conditions and more emphasis on poverty reduction (as opposed to a singular emphasis on GROWTH). But the IMF's critics contend that the difference between ECFs and SAPs is mostly window-dressing—or public relations for the IMF.[5] Like SAPs, these programs are premised on the neoliberal consensus that the world should be run like a business. The IMF argues that its goal is debt reduction. That means getting countries to follow what neoliberals would characterize as more sensible economic policies. According to this view, countries need to adopt multiyear plans based in pro-growth policies and ensure that their revenues exceed their expenditures—in order to get out of the red. For all the talk about LIC participation, there is little dialogue taking place. At its core, any adjustment program is based in the adoption of market reforms, which are believed by neoliberals to lay the basis for future growth. What countries need most is to keep their eyes on the bottom line. In general, short-term consumption should be curtailed in order to promote long-term investment.

For all of the talk about local ownership and adapting to local conditions, the new ECFs are still remarkably uniform, based in the idea that debtor countries need to undergo a series of reforms to promote growth, get themselves out of debt, reduce poverty, and foster DEVELOPMENT. The first order of business is reducing deficits, or attaining a balance of payments. One way to do this is by cutting spending. Although some argue that the prescribed economic reforms aren't quite as draconian now as they were in the past, the governments of debtor countries, after meeting with the IMF, are to return home and cut the "fat" from their budgets, most commonly spending on social welfare programs. Uncharacteristically for the IMF, at the peak of the global economic crisis in 2008, it actually called for a stimulus (or fiscal boost) to prop up a few of the hardest-hit economies, like Tanzania and Mozambique. Other countries, such as China, Malaysia, Vietnam, Brazil, and Chile, also adopted sizable stimulus packages, investing in "make work" programs, investing in infrastructure, and maintaining social spending on poverty alleviation programs (and in some cases even expanding it).

However, since 2010 the IMF has returned to business as usual.[6] The cuts in social spending associated with deficit reduction are likely to take even more of a toll in LICs than they do in HICs, since in many LICs, private income is so low for so many that public provisioning is crucial. Even the middle classes are hit hard by AUSTERITY PLANS; when Argentina's economy went into a tailspin in December 2001, teachers and other professionals joined the poorer classes in looting to help make ends meet.

Moreover, cuts in social welfare programs mean reduced government funding for education, healthcare, sanitation, provision of clean water, price controls, and subsidies for food, as well as nutritional supplements for young children and nursing mothers. In China, budget cuts have meant the dismantling of the once hugely popular and widely emulated "barefoot doctor" program. One of the greatest successes of the CULTURAL REVOLUTION, the free rural healthcare provided by the Chinese government greatly improved the quality of life for millions of people. However, since the 1990s there has been a huge reversal in social spending, the safety net has been shredded, as now more Chinese citizens must pay for healthcare out of their own pockets. It is estimated that in 2005, the out-of-pocket costs for healthcare in China were a hundred times what they were in 1980.[7] As a result, access to care, quality of care, and health outcomes vary considerably depending on who you are and where you live. For better-off Chinese, health outcomes have improved tremendously over the years. However, in the case of a catastrophic illness, when the bill for a hospital stay adds up to more than the yearly income of most peasants, a lack of barefoot doctors means that families either are pushed further into poverty or simply go without care—often until it is too late.[8] The toll this is taking is already reflected in startling statistics: China has the second largest tuberculosis burden in the world (after India), with more than 4.5

million cases. Another 1.4 million cases are expected in China each year, many involving drug-resistant forms. Tuberculosis in China poses a major public health threat; although the World Health Organization (WHO) recommends free treatment for the disease, in China people are likely to delay treatment, given its cost.[9]

In addition to the revenues saved by cuts in spending, austerity plans often require governments to increase their income by increasing export earnings. The most common means of doing this is export promotion, which for most countries means an intensification of the production of raw materials for sale on the world market. Working in tandem with this effort at export promotion is the devaluation of one's currency, which a government undertakes by changing its official exchange rate. A currency devaluation is prescribed because it promises to accomplish two goals at once. It should spur increased export earnings, since one's goods will be cheaper (and therefore more competitive) on the world market. At the same time, devaluation means that because the currency is worth less, the cost of imports will rise, putting goods out of the reach of most of the population and therefore conserving scarce hard currency. Again, the idea is to achieve a balance of payments (or even a surplus) where there has been a deficit. According to neoliberals, deep cuts in spending com-

---

Figure 7.2   Dollar vs. Yuan: (Why) Do Exchange Rates Matter?

When we consider "free" and "state-run" economies (and the multiple variations in between), one example that illustrates the involvement of government in economic decisions is the value of the country's currency. The relative weight of currencies compared against each other is known as the exchange rate (for example, in March 2011 one US dollar was roughly equivalent to 11.9 Mexican pesos). Although it is certainly not the only one to do so, China is an example of a country that has intervened in the markets to control the value of its currency, known as the yuan or renminbi. For nearly a decade now, the United States has encouraged China (and a few other countries as well) to permit their currencies to be traded at more market-oriented rates. Many economists maintain that the Chinese currency is *under*valued, which makes Chinese exports cheaper and foreign imports (which compete with their products at home) comparatively more expensive. Many in the United States contend that currency manipulation has helped China sell more than it buys abroad, which has ballooned the Chinese trade surplus with the United States by hundreds of billions of dollars.[10]

The United States has pressed China to increase (or appreciate) the value of its currency in order to encourage imports from abroad and decrease exports. The charge is that Beijing is deliberately keeping its currency artificially weak to maintain its competitive edge in trade (not only because this draws more foreign investment, but also to help large Chinese companies, many of which are state-owned, avert job losses and possible social unrest). On the other hand, if the yuan appreciates in value, Chinese products will become more expensive. This should help the United States and other manufacturers not only break into the Chinese market and sell more goods to Chinese consumers, but also compete with Chinese goods in other markets.

In the end, many analysts in China and the United States argue that the real problem lies with the imbalances that exist within both economies. The Chinese economy is dependent on export surpluses to promote growth; the United States is dependent on consumption. Washington contends that the world needs an appreciation in the value of the yuan to rebalance the global economy. Beijing argues that the international pressure for Chinese currency reform is political and amounts to protectionism. One thing that nearly everyone agrees on is that if China's economic growth continues, the renminbi is likely to become a major exchange currency, rivaling the hegemony of the US dollar.

bined with a jump in revenues from export sales will help countries accumulate the hard currency to get out of debt and on the path to prosperity.

The path to prosperity is predicated on the acceptance of some other conditions as well. Here the emphasis is on the adoption of policies that will enhance productivity and encourage capital flows based on foreign investment rather than aid. The way to accomplish these goals, according to the IMF, is to privatize the economy. Privatization means selling off STATE-OWNED ENTERPRISES (SOEs), which are often wasteful and inefficient. Although SOEs were originally created to reduce foreign dominance of LIC economies, neoliberals argue that these government monopolies over the delivery of public services such as water and electricity should be put on the open market and sold to the highest bidder—whether local or foreign. It is not unusual for these state sell-offs to amount to extremely lucrative, high-stakes deals that are less than transparent. Although neoliberals push for privatization because they believe that taking these sectors out of government hands will reduce CORRUPTION, it is commonly said that all that privatization does is to privatize corruption. Another problem is that the privatization of utilities has often meant higher prices for water, electricity, and telephone service, but neoliberals argue that private investors have dramatically improved and expanded services, thereby increasing the poor's access to these services.[11]

Others doubt such claims and are concerned particularly about privatization of resources such as water, access to which many consider to be a human right. In 2000, Bolivians fought a "water war" when the American-owned MULTINATIONAL CORPORATION Bechtel took over the waterworks and nearly doubled the price of water. After days of nationwide, violent protests and a declaration of martial law, the company was forced to leave the country. The community-run waterworks that succeeded it has not been without its problems, and most analysts now agree that when it comes to water, for example, the private sector has not been the solution. Too often the private sector has been accused of price-gouging, and has not achieved better success than the public sector in extending services.[12]

In cooperation with the terms of its IMF reform, Mexico has sold off hundreds of state-owned enterprises, including its control over the seaport, railroad, and telecommunication industries. President Felipe Calderón has had to back off from the idea of privatizing PEMEX, the state-owned oil and gas monopoly, because most Mexicans so strongly reject the idea. In 2010 the Egyptian government reversed a decision to sell state-owned companies to private investors after widespread protests raised concerns about corruption and insider-dealing. India is expecting a huge row over a discussion of just selling shares in (let alone privatizing) its 473 publicly owned companies.[13]

China is feeling some of this pressure, too. Much of its growth has been based on STATE CAPITALISM, or using STATE-owned companies as the basis of its economy. As of 2010, China's state-owned sectors account for approximately 40 percent of GDP. The country's biggest cell phone operator, China Mobile, is a state-owned company.[14] Although it has closed many of its weaker SOEs, China has been slower to sell off these companies, fearing the creation of social unrest due to mass unemployment. The nonpublic sector in China has developed rapidly since 2005, and by 2009 a much smaller proportion of its industrial work force was employed by the state (20 percent, down from 70 percent a few years ago). But full privatization would still result in layoffs of millions of Chinese workers.[15]

Nigerian workers join May Day (International Workers' Day) celebrations
(Reuters/Akintunde Akinleye)

Facing similar hardship on a smaller scale, Peru bit the bullet and went ahead with privatizations in 2002 that resulted in such violent strikes in the south that then-president Alejandro Toledo felt compelled to call for a state of emergency. Such strikes and demonstrations in response to the hardship caused by neoliberal economic reform are known as "IMF riots," and they occur on a regular basis around the globe. Rising food prices (some the result of cuts in government subsidies, required by the IMF) led to demonstrations in more than sixty countries in 2007 and 2008. Violence and arrests were associated with the widely publicized 2010 IMF riots in Greece, but also affected India, where a one-day strike protesting a gasoline price hike of 30 cents per gallon shut down much of the country.[16]

Beyond privatization, neoliberals argue that LIC governments must work harder to attract foreign investment of all kinds. They must make themselves attractive to multinational corporations (MNCs) for all the reasons neoliberals have put forward regarding the benefits associated with the presence of MNCs in host countries. Governments should work aggressively to lure more foreign investment in a variety of ways, including a policy of deregulation (the removal of legal constraints on the operation of businesses, such as eliminating health, safety, and environmental regulations). Advocates of privatization argue that it also helps if the country has a large pool of laborers who are willing and eager to work with little interference from unions or other activists.

Budget cuts, privatization, deregulation, and openness to foreign investment are just a few of the conditions commonly associated with the IMF's economic reform packages. To fully understand the impact of conditionality, take the case of Indonesia. In 1997, in return for $43 billion in emergency funding, Indonesia agreed to an adjustment that had more than a hundred conditions attached. Among them was the requirement that the government close its clove monopoly and eliminate price subsidies on basic foodstuffs. The upheaval caused by such policies led to the downfall of the long-standing Suharto government (more than one analyst has suggested that this amounted to a coup sponsored by the IMF).[17] In Zambia, after the privatization of copper mines, 45 percent of the population in Copperbelt towns had to pay user fees or do without healthcare. In Tanzania, when school fees were introduced as part of an austerity plan, primary- and secondary-school enrollment dropped.[18]

By the early 1990s the IMF and donors had added another condition. With the COLD WAR over, the neoliberals began admonishing LICs to go beyond "getting prices right" and to also work at "getting politics right." Based in the view that DEMOCRACY is a natural complement to capitalism, donors argued that the hardship blamed on austerity and the IFIs' seeming failure to deliver on promises of growth and development was actually due to failures of government, not the model. As we will discuss in more detail in Chapter 14, the West became convinced that a lack of "good governance" was the problem—not the neoliberal model itself. When other East Asian countries, which had for so long been upheld as models for economic development, stumbled in the late 1990s, neoliberals blamed the "Asian flu" on the lack of POLITICAL LIBERALIZATION in these countries. For more than a decade, Western donors had ignored rampant corruption in Asia and elsewhere as long as governments embraced neoliberal reforms. However, by the late 1990s, corruption, cronyism, and the "incestuous" relationship between government and business in Asia were deplored as the cause of the region's ills. These countries had gotten prices right, but they had suffered from a lack of regulation, supervision, and TRANSPARENCY—in effect, they hadn't "gotten politics right."

The problem, as identified by neoliberals, was one endemic not only to East Asia but also to much of the third world: political reform had lagged behind economic reform when, from a neoliberal perspective, the success of either reform would be inextricably linked to progress in the other.[19] As a result, political reforms aimed at fighting corruption and promoting democratization became another condition promoted by the Washington Consensus. Interestingly, in recent years many countries have turned to China as a source of loans, because in what is called the "Beijing Consensus," China makes it a point not to press such conditions. It attaches other strings (access to markets, support for its policy on Taiwan, etc.), but China certainly isn't going to call on other countries to become more democratic.

Neoliberals maintain that in the long run, perseverance in economic and political liberalization will pay off. It just takes time and patience. They point to a number of countries, such as Mexico and South Korea, that have taken this sometimes-harsh medicine in return for emergency loans, and whose growth rates have since indicated a recovery. Moreover, Mexico and South Korea have undergone extensive political reforms at the same time that they have adopted economic reforms. Not that long ago they were authoritarian systems, but both countries today have made substantial progress in their transitions to democracy.

How "Getting Prices Right"
May Be "Getting Development Wrong"

Critics of the neoliberal model don't mince words when they argue that globalization is the new colonialism. Its aims and outcomes are remarkably similar to those of colonialism in that the "development" it promotes is not one that improves the lives of LICs' citizens. Rather, according to the structuralists, free trade and globalization are about ensuring markets for Western goods and retaining the third world as a source of cheap labor and raw materials. Sure, under ECFs, the governments of developing countries are consulted and allowed to have some input in the decisions that affect the lives of their citizens, but the destiny of these non-Westerners is still ultimately left in the hands of their former colonizers. The IMF's economic reforms amount to a financial coup d'état in that ECFs may not be all that different from the SAPs before them; they undermine the SOVEREIGNTY of the state and deny people the right to economic SELF-DETERMINATION. Even if the model one day proves effective in promoting economic development, the IMF has been unwilling to reform itself in any significant way that alters the balance of power between high- and low-income countries (or that reflects the changing reality of the global economy). In 2010 members of the GROUP OF 20 (G-20) called for a redistribution of 5 percent of the IMF's voting power (from rich countries to emerging economies) and for open and meritocratic elections to decide the leaders of the IMF and WORLD BANK. But voting power has so far not shifted to reflect the growing importance of LICs in the world economy, and IMF and World Bank leaders remain American and European, as has been the custom since the bodies were founded in 1944.[20]

Given the existing imbalance of power, the conditions attached by IFIs amount to blackmail, say the structuralists. The restructuring of debt has resulted in a system of international peonage. According to this argument, LICs fell deeply into debt because of their position in the INTERNATIONAL ECONOMIC SYSTEM, and neoliberal economic reforms effectively force them to remain in that position. The donors and the institutions they run appear to be more interested in the business of business than in the business of development. Described as a debt collector for commercial banks, the IMF is so busy making sure LICs continue to service their debts that the promise of development as the outcome is a cruel joke. Critics point out that Ghana has been the poster child for IMF reforms in Africa. It began implementing an austerity plan in 1983, and achieved an economic growth rate averaging 5–6 percent from 2004 to 2008 (though it slowed to 3.5 percent in 2009). Ghana was the first country in Africa that Barack Obama chose to visit as president, in part because it is considered an African success story. It has made progress on a number of development indicators; however, after nearly three decades of economic reforms, gross domestic product (GDP) per capita is $671 and the poverty rate is still 28 percent. The Ghanaian democracy is doing all that the IMF asks, but is still battered by volatile price swings for its exports.[21] Thus the economic reforms imposed on LICs are entrenching the very development model that caused their original problem—overreliance on the export of raw materials.

Whereas neoliberals emphasize the positive benefits of globalization and maintain that adjustments are necessary to promote long-term economic health, critics argue that structural adjustment serves the interests of the powerful. Globalization is contributing to a grotesque and dangerous polarization between those who benefit from the system and those who are passive recipients of its effects.[22] The combined effect of the reforms imposed on LICs is devastating. These economic reforms throw the middle class into poverty, but they take their hardest toll on the poorest of the poor. There are good reasons why adjustment is known as "shock therapy." Shock waves ripple throughout countries, with multiple consequences. Zambia has benefited from debt reduction, but had to meet the IMF's conditions in order to obtain it. As it edged closer to meeting these conditions, life expectancy dropped, the mortality rate for children under five rose sharply, and three-quarters of the population was living on less than one dollar a day.[23] In the following sections we will briefly describe how the millions who are worse off because of the IMF's reforms are seeking to cope with their effects. According to structuralists, globalization is contributing, both directly and indirectly, to a series of interconnected problems that vividly illustrate the downside of INTERDEPENDENCE. Neoliberal reforms have often been promoted by developed countries with little thought to the human and environmental impact on LICs.

Migration

In a variety of ways, globalization and structural adjustment are adding to a series of large and growing human migrations. These migrations occur within countries, from rural to urban areas, and between countries, from underdeveloped to developed countries. For the poorest, globalization has often made what was once a subsistence living increasingly untenable. With lower prices for their cash crops and no food security in rural areas, people have become desperate. Rural dwellers have always been drawn to the cities (in developed as well as less developed countries) for the opportunities they are believed to hold. For example, urban residents in China in 2009 earned on average three times more than rural dwellers.[24] Not only do people come hoping for work, but they also come for the chance to improve their lives, through access to education, healthcare, and other government services. For many years, it has been a common practice for governments to try to keep urban populations satisfied and stable by providing subsidies that ensure that the populations surrounding them are fed and the lights are on. As much as there is a pull factor drawing people to the cities, there is also a push factor: the hardship of rural life.

Although millions of immigrants are estimated to have illegally entered developed countries, the majority of LIC migrants do not cross international boundaries. Rather, they are setting up residence in São Paulo, Mumbai, Shanghai, and Manila. Today, for the first time in history, more than half the world's population lives in urban areas. Africa's cities are expected to triple in size over the next forty years, and by 2030 it is expected that 5 billion people worldwide will be city dwellers.[25] The flight from rural areas has had a number of consequences, among them over-urbanization and the rapid creation of megacities—cities with populations of over 10 million. The fifth largest of these, Mexico City, in 2010 had a population of 17–23 million. The crush of bodies in this and other cities contributes to overcrowding and a number of health problems. It also raises a number of serious political, economic, and social dilemmas.

Hastily erected shantytowns house most of these new residents. It is common for a thick fog from coal-fueled cooking to hang over these cities. Without adequate sanitation or waste disposal, the cities emit poisonous gases that make one's eyes water and make it difficult to breathe. It is estimated that over 1 billion people live in slums, shantytowns, bidonvilles, and squatter settlements worldwide (and this number is expected to double by 2030).[26] Nine million people left the highlands during Peru's civil war to live in such a place, a garbage dump north of Lima. It is filled with rats and gangs, and is unsafe not only because it is far from police control, but also because it is located near a lead factory. As a result, children living in this enormous trash heap have been found to have four times the safe amount of lead in their blood.[27]

Yet newcomers are met with other disappointments as well. Not only are there no places to live and few government services, but there is also no work. The shutdown of state-owned enterprises associated with structural adjustment often means mass layoffs, adding to unemployment and underemployment rates. Where the unemployment rate is high, as in Zimbabwe, where it is estimated that 95 percent of the population is without work, many of the displaced make their living scavenging.[28] In one more way of coping, people survive by picking through the endless filth of the cities for plastic bottles, cardboard boxes, pieces of aluminum and glass, and the like, to sell in junk shops.

In recent years hundreds of Nigerians have died in explosions caused by "scooping," another form of scavenging. When one of the many gasoline pipelines that run unattended for miles throughout the country develops a leak, accidentally or not, the poor scoop up the flowing gasoline into cans and buckets. They then haul it away and sell it on Nigeria's thriving black market. Always a dangerous practice, it has worsened in recent years as organized crime cartels have joined this part of the scavenging business. Now it is believed that gangs recruit children to scoop pipelines that are deliberately punctured. When a lot of people are gathered around a gas leak, all it takes is for someone to light a cigarette, or for a motorbike to backfire, to ignite an inferno. The result is bodies burned beyond recognition, many of them poor women and children eager to earn a bit of money.[29]

Such tragedies create tremendous pressures on governments, which have resorted to increasingly aggressive attempts to reduce urbanization and the press of impoverished populations. Yet even the most stringent policies have failed to contain the growth in urban populations. For example, it is estimated that there are 1 million illegal residents in Shanghai alone (a city with a total population of more than 20 million). In what has been described as perhaps the largest movement of labor in human history, millions of rural Chinese residents have left their home villages to travel from city to city in search of work, sending their earnings home to their families. They have become known as the "floating population," and their ranks have doubled since 1993, from 70 million to 150–211 million people in 2010. Although migration slowed due to layoffs associated with the current global economic crisis, if trends continue it is expected that the floating population in China will crest at 350 million by 2050.[30]

The Informal Sector

With little hope of employment in the FORMAL SECTOR, large numbers of city dwellers turn to the underground economy, also known as the INFORMAL SECTOR. Although it is the single largest employer in many LICs, the informal economy is a shadow economy of sorts. It is composed of semilegal or illegal activities transacted under the table, and therefore not included in the calculation of a country's gross domestic product. Given the characteristics of the work, there are no accurate estimates of the numbers of people involved, although analysts agree that worldwide the number of informal-sector workers runs into the millions and is growing much more rapidly compared to the formal economy. It is estimated that 31 percent of the labor force in South Africa, 47–84 percent in Latin America, and 90 percent in India work in the informal sector.[31] In Peru and many Latin American countries, where underemployment is vast, women who have recently migrated from rural areas compose the backbone of this labor force. Latin America's experience is by no means unique; the informal economy provides an important cushion against austerity. It is a central means for survival in Africa, Asia, and the Middle East for men and women alike.

Although informal-sector work is often viewed as independent self-employment, it is also work performed semilegally or illegally for an employer (such as piece-workers making lace from their homes for subcontractors). In the informal sector there are no explicit, written labor contracts, and no state regulation of wages or working conditions. Much of the informal sector, such as the microenterprises of female petty traders selling the equivalent of fast food along roads and sidewalks, amounts to what are known as male-dependent enterprises: they replicate in the public sphere the work that is often traditionally undertaken within the reproductive realm. This is true of the other major sources of work for women in the informal sector, as domestic labor and as sex workers. As you might imagine, much of this work is highly dependent on disposable income, and during times of austerity these sectors are hit especially hard.

Yet there are benefits to this work as well. As opposed to formal-sector jobs, which rarely provide for childcare, many women working in the informal sector bring small children to work with them, as they find ways of making petty trading, knitting and selling sweaters, hairdressing, and catering compatible with their childcare responsibilities. Petty trading is an important part of informal-sector activity for men and women, and sexual divisions of labor often exist within the market, whether it falls into the formal or informal sector. For example, in the Dominican Republic, women are disproportionately represented as vendors of less lucrative goods such as clothing and food, whereas men tend to be involved in the sale of legal and illegal commodities that generally fetch a higher price. Although the majority of women working in this sector just barely make ends meet, some jobs are more lucrative than others, and some women make relatively impressive incomes.

Violence Against Women

The rapid economic change associated with globalization has created opportunities for some women, but it has exposed them to a rising backlash. This backlash is expressed in a number of ways, including dramatic growth in the range, incidence, and intensity of gender violence. According to the UNITED NATIONS, one in three females worldwide are targeted for attack simply because they are female.[32] Where populations are undergoing rapid change and economic hardship, newly autonomous women become an easily identified threat. Women are often caught between neoliberal policies that propel them into the work force and a traditionalist backlash that seeks to drive them back into their homes. In many parts of the world, men experience what some analysts call status inconsistency, or anxiety associated with changes in gender relations, the structure of the family, and the position of women. As Valentine Moghadam argues, the World Bank wants women to have fewer babies, work outside the home, and earn enough to feed their families, but isn't doing much when things get ugly and women are scapegoated. Globalization is related to a backlash of sorts, one manifested in a rising incidence of violence against females. For example, Peruvian activists recognize close links between rising rates of domestic violence and economic disarray. There the economic reform has contributed to massive unemployment, low wages, and troubling insecurity. People are described as living in a constant state of frustration, and women have often borne the brunt of this frustration.[33]

Where there is mass unemployment, women's entry into the labor force is sometimes viewed with hostility by men, who see women as displacing them. In cases around the world, women are finding themselves more often to be the targets of individual attacks as well as attacks by conservative SOCIAL MOVEMENTS. Women are blamed not only for taking jobs from men, but also for the loss of traditional cultures (another byproduct of globalization). Often considered the keepers of tradition, their growing visibility and perceived competition with men in the labor market angers and terrifies traditional elements, both male and female. The autonomy that comes with work outside the home is often believed to make women immodest, decadent, cultural traitors. Conservatives uphold tradition as providing a secure base in a scary world and argue for a world in which men and women know and accept their proper place. They acclaim virtues of traditional womanhood, and the proper dress and behavior of women become paramount. Those who accept this role as wife and mother are honored and exalted; those who resist are deemed traitors who must be punished. As a result, working women are held morally accountable and subjected to a broad variety of assaults and affronts, both public and private. In Afghanistan in 2009, female candidates for election received death threats, and young Afghan schoolgirls were sprayed in the face with acid for daring to seek an education.[34] As we mention in Chapter 14, around the world (in low- as well as high-income countries) women who are perceived as resisting social norms face retaliation. The result has been a variety of "cleanup campaigns," which include mass arrests of women, punishment for violations of dress codes, a rise in honor killings, as well as sexual harassment and other forms of discrimination against females.[35]

Rape (and the threat of rape) is another way of "putting women back in their place." In many countries, rape and other forms of sexual assault can only be committed against "honest" women—women of "good moral character," whose chastity can be vouched for. Women who work outside the home, who live without a father or husband, are especially suspect and rarely afforded the protections of society.

When rape is used to target particular groups, it is also used to humiliate men and to undermine communities. Although we usually think of mass rape as a weapon of war, it is also utilized in other types of conflict as well. For example, ethnic Chinese women living in Jakarta, because they were identified as prosperous and foreign, were singled out for sexual assault as part of the violence that rocked Indonesia in 1998. The Indonesian government asserts that nothing happened and not one rape was reported. However, human rights activists estimate that more than a hundred sexual assaults occurred. Some speculate that the security forces were directly involved.

And many human rights workers believe that the attacks were not spontaneous, that the government and military encouraged anti-Chinese sentiment to divert hostility over price hikes (directly resulting from the government's devaluation of the rupiah) toward individual retailers.[36] Similar attacks have targeted women in Rwanda, the Democratic Republic of Congo, Sudan, Kosovo, and elsewhere.

The Environment

The assault on the environment is another negative consequence of globalization. Urged on by the IMF, the World Bank, and other donors, NEWLY INDUSTRIALIZING COUNTRIES (NICs) have followed the path of developed countries: for years they placed a higher premium on growth than on environmental protection. The results are staggering: for example, ozone levels exceed World Health Organization standards 300 days a year in Mexico City. Reportedly, some residents' noses are so badly damaged from inhaling toxic particles that they are losing their sense of smell.[37] Yet in other ways as well, the results of a policy of "growth at any price" are long-term and devastating. China's economic boom, based on the use of coal and fuel-inefficient technologies, is rapidly creating pollution problems of unparalleled magnitude. Until recently, HICs were the biggest polluters and consumers of the world's resources, but now China and India are among the top four producers of greenhouse gas emissions (China is the top producer, followed by the United States, Russia, and India). Sixteen of the twenty cities with the worst air pollution are in China, where it is estimated that 750,000 premature deaths each year are caused by diseases related to air pollution. China's situation is unique only because of its extremely rapid growth and large population; most countries, especially developing countries, are pursuing economic growth without much concern for long-term environmental damage.[38]

However, the blind pursuit of growth at all costs is the approach taken by the exporters of raw materials as well. Structural adjustment programs that encourage export promotion result in intensified pressures on the land and other resources. The

Figure 7.3 China's Development Refugees Along the Three Gorges Dam

Leaders of the People's Republic of China (PRC) recently completed a project that has been envisioned by leaders for centuries: controlling the swells of the world's third largest river, the Yangtze, and building the world's largest hydroelectric power plant, named the Three Gorges Dam. This dam, which flooded most of the legendary Three Gorges region in south-central China, was built in an effort to reduce the country's reliance on coal, which currently supplies 70 percent of the PRC's growing energy needs. The dam, which became fully operational in 2008, provides hydroelectric energy (producing an estimated 6 percent of the country's total demand) and increased river transport into China's central regions. But these gains come at a huge cost. Over nineteen cities, and over 46,000 precious hectares of farmland along the banks of the Yangtze, were flooded. Priceless historical landmarks are under water. Additionally, approximately 1.6 million residents have been permanently displaced, forced from their homes due to the construction of this dam, which many deem structurally unsound. Since completion, there have been problems with deadly floods and mudslides. The resettlement process has been anything but smooth: monies set aside to assist in the transition have been siphoned off to well-placed officials, who use the relocation funds to finance trips abroad and lavish homes.[39]

deforestation and desertification associated with the overexploitation of the environment have accelerated with neoliberal economic reforms. Globalization is directly related to environmental devastation in a number of ways. IMF reforms urge countries to increase their growth rates by increasing productivity. Often this is defined as an opening up of untouched areas and exploitation of resources to their fullest extent. What this means is that land is stripped of its resources, and fragile ecosystems such as rainforests are destroyed. In the early 1990s, of the twenty-four largest debtors, eight never had or no longer had significant forest reserves. Of the sixteen major debtors remaining, all of them were recognized as major deforesters. In other words, the top non-Western debtors were all among the top ten deforesters: Brazil, India, Indonesia, and Nigeria, to name just a few. Hardly anyone would argue that debt is the exclusive cause of deforestation and the other problems described here. However, the landless of these countries have few alternatives but to push into the forests for their subsistence needs.[40] In the drive to increase sales on the world market, land is needed and new mines and plantations are opened to satisfy the growing demand for resources. For example, until recently Indonesia was one of the world's largest carbon emitters. It has since moved away from this approach, but for years the country put its economic growth ahead of all else, clearing its forests at a rapid rate to expand production of palm oil and to create jobs.[41]

Poor management of the environment is costly in monetary terms as well. It is estimated that in Nigeria the losses from ruined land and disappearing forests run about $6 billion each year. The British Petroleum oil spill in the Gulf of Mexico is said to be puny compared to what Nigeria has experienced every year without end.[42] Haiti is now almost completely deforested; without trees (or their roots) holding the soil together, hurricanes and earthquakes create landslides, eroding the topsoil and devastating agriculture, which exacerbates the country's already wrenching poverty.[43] As the world begins to recognize the global threat that environmental disasters pose, the IMF, World Bank, and other donor agencies have come under increasing pressure to be more environmentally responsive, and have allocated larger staffs to address the issue. There is more funding for environmental projects, and environmental impact statements for development projects are now mandatory.

Environmentalists welcome this shift, yet some question the sincerity of such concerns, since the overall prescription that results in environmental disasters remains unchanged. China is adopting tougher fuel-economy standards and is now considered to be a leader in clean and renewable energy production. The country's leaders have begun to view climate change as a security issue and are viewing it as threat to stability.[44] Yet China is not alone in this concern; there are significant asymmetries between which countries are most responsible for climate change and which will suffer first (and the most). Experts expect that Africa, Asia, and Latin America will suffer disproportionately, with the most deaths and livelihood disruptions. The United Nations estimates that many of the 40 million people uprooted around the world in 2010 were climate change refugees and that their numbers will reach 200 million by 2050.[45]

But for every important gain in promoting a green initiative, there is another project that appears oblivious to the ecological havoc it causes. The World Bank and similar organizations have made progress in this area but need to do more to support

LICs in transitioning to a low-carbon development path and incentivize a reduced dependence on fossil fuels.[46] Unfortunately, for every commitment to renewable energy, there is a worthwhile project that has not been adequately financed or is small compared to oil, gas, and coal projects. For example, the World Bank is continuing to invest in fossil fuel plants in India and China rather than pursuing the development of renewable forms of energy. Huge and expensive dam projects are built to irrigate plantations owned by agribusiness and to electrify cities. They contribute to 12–16 percent of the world's food production and 19 percent of its electricity. But these projects, such as Sardar Sarovar Dam in India, are controversial because often it is only the urban rich who benefit from them. Moreover, big dams have forced the resettlement of millions, creating what are known as "development refugees." One expert estimates that 472 million people are negatively impacted by the 50,000 large dams around the world. In some cases this form of "development" has resulted in damage to fragile ecosystems and the loss of irreplaceable archaeological treasures.[47]

Similarly, since its green conversion the World Bank has approved several other highly controversial projects, such as construction of a 650-mile oil pipeline running from Chad, a desperately impoverished country, through Cameroon and out to the Atlantic Ocean. This enormous project was backed by a group of oil companies that promised to boost Chad's revenues by 50 percent. To make a long story short, the oil began to flow in 2003, the Chadian government backed out of the deal, and the Bank left in 2008. Instead of being invested in development, the oil money funds the dictatorship. Meanwhile, the pipeline runs through protected areas and poisons ecosystems, and even a small oil spill could wipe out fisheries and ruin local economies.[48]

Structural adjustment is linked to environmental devastation in other ways as well. For example, cuts in fuel subsidies have pushed more people to the forests in search of fuel wood. People are turning to the forests to cushion the blow of shock therapy. In parts of Southeast Asia, Central Africa, and Latin America, commercial hunting in tropical forests has boomed as the hungry have pushed into the forests. There has always been hunting in these areas, but never on this scale. People are eating much more wild meat now, as the cost of meat from cattle and chickens is out of reach. In parts of tropical Africa, as a result of these combined consumer pressures— and the logging industry, which is building roads that make access to the rainforests even faster—hunting for "bush meat" (e.g., gorillas, chimps, rodents, birds, reptiles) is considered out of control. Moreover, the international market for wild meat, desired by some for its novelty, by others as a luxury, is huge and growing (more than 2.2 million tons of bush meat from the Congo Basin are sold each year, and in 2010 some of these proteins were being snapped up for as much as $18 per pound in Paris). At the current rate, in just a decade or two, the world's second largest tropical forest (in the Congo Basin) could be emptied of large mammals. Gorillas and chimpanzees could become extinct. This situation—called "empty-forest syndrome"—is just another example of how economic hardship is forcing the adoption of coping strategies that are detrimental to the environment and human health; the 2003 SARS (severe acute respiratory syndrome) epidemic has been traced to human consumption of bats and civet cats in Asia. Hunters follow logging, and poverty leaves wildlife as a primary source of protein for larger numbers of people. These are all examples of how "development," as it is currently being pursued, can be problematic.[49]

Disease

The massive population movements both back and forth within countries and across international borders have a number of effects, including the spread of disease. Any number of dangers to human health can be aggravated by the changes associated with structural adjustment and globalization. Shifting rainfall patterns linked to global warming, and the movement of populations into previously forested areas, have been linked to an unprecedented increase in the incidence of malaria, with 247 million cases (and more than 1 million deaths) in 2008. Malaria, which can be prevented with inexpensive interventions such as bed nets, is treatable and curable. It disproportionately affects the very poor and is responsible for 20 percent of all childhood deaths in Africa.[50]

As mentioned, economic hardship has added not only to political instability but also to pressures on the environment. In a vicious circle, these are diseases of poverty and causes of poverty.[51] Economic and environmental pressures are contributing to the emergence of resistant strains of malaria, as well as to the surfacing of new diseases such as the West Nile virus and Ebola. Austerity has contributed to rapid urbanization, which means that health workers must deal with a host of public health nightmares—just as the budget cuts often necessitated by austerity have left them profoundly ill-equipped to deal with these problems. Total healthcare spending per capita in Bangladesh in 2007 was $15. In Burundi it was $17. Of our CASE STUDIES, Mexico, at $564 per capita, had the highest healthcare expenditure in 2007, while Turkey spent $465, China spent $108, and Indonesia allotted $42. As of early 2011, due to slow recovery from the global recession, donors were freezing or cutting aid, and healthcare providers had to ration care and make hard choices, turning people away until they could come up with the money to pay for care out of their own pockets.[52] Plus, the meager sanitation systems that may or may not have served city populations a decade or two ago simply cannot handle the massive influx of people now fleeing the poverty of rural areas. Budget cuts mean that the public health sector is drained: it is not uncommon for clinics and hospitals in the poorest countries to lack not only electricity and running water, but also sterile equipment and protective gear. The health delivery system in Zimbabwe, for example, has been described as paralyzed, as vital life-saving equipment at government clinics has broken down and there are no spare parts. The hospitals (which are closed and reopened) are avoided and considered as places one goes only to die. Under such circumstances the healthcare system itself becomes a vehicle for the transmission and spread of disease.

The combination of overcrowding, lack of adequate sanitation, and lack of clean water is adding to the death toll for common killers of children under five, such as dehydration from diarrhea. It is also contributing to a resurgence of old scourges such as tuberculosis and cholera, not to mention more virulent and drug-resistant strains of diseases such as malaria (and tuberculosis). While everyone recognizes that ill health is highly correlated with poverty and a major impediment to development, in a variety of ways it could be argued that structural adjustment is ensuring continued underdevelopment. After two and a half decades of neoliberal economic reform, despite all the promises of science, life expectancy for too many of the world's people has risen slowly or hardly at all. Although the mortality rate for children under five was cut in half between 1960 and 1990, approximately 8 million children, most of them infants and toddlers, die each year of preventable causes.[53]

Figure 7.4 A Zero-Sum Game?

Whether the question is saving the rainforests or the Arctic National Wildlife Refuge, the relationship between growth and the environment is often posed as a winner-take-all, zero-sum game. For purists on both sides, there can be no compromise. On the one hand, there are citizens of non-Western countries who will claim that they want these projects, that they desperately need them—and the income that might trickle down from the construction of roads, dams, pipelines, and other projects. Of the over 1.4 billion people earning less than $1.25 a day, most of them live in rural areas with the most biodiversity.[54] With so many people living in poverty, it is argued that environmental protection is a luxury that they cannot afford. Many non-Westerners point out that the United States and Europe did not adopt environmental protections when they were developing, and that it is hypocritical of rich countries to impede development in low-income countries because of pollution and other environmental concerns.

Some analysts offer the "Environmental Kuznets Curve" in validation of this argument. According to the theory, the environmental quality in a country initially deteriorates as the economy begins to industrialize, but then improves as citizens reach a certain standard of living. Most economists disagree about exactly when it is that countries turn this corner, but contend that by the time a country has a per capita income of $5,000–$15,000, it is likely to have become more environmentally conscious.[55] With so many countries falling far below that mark, we can expect a significant delay before the majority become willing to make this shift in priorities. Perhaps in the meantime we should move away from treating the promotion of development and the protection of the environment as an either-or choice.

Figure 7.5 A Small Investment with a Huge Payoff

The international community recently had a reason to celebrate when it was announced that (after two decades with little good news to share) efforts to reduce maternal mortality were finally paying off. The number of women dying in pregnancy and childbirth declined by 34 percent between 1990 and 2008. This is extremely encouraging because it demonstrates that money invested in simple interventions, if properly directed and focused on the countries with the greatest need, can reap very real rewards. We have learned that different countries require different approaches. For some, reducing pregnancy rates has been the key, while others have succeeded by increasing incomes (associated, among other things, with improved nutrition) or improving female access to education. In nearly all countries, training more midwives, and improving hospitals and clinics so that they can assist pregnant women and provide emergency obstetrical care as well as postnatal care, have all gone a long way in reducing maternal mortality.

However, those working in what is known as the "safe motherhood" movement emphasize that the risk of maternal mortality is still unacceptably high; it is thirty-six times higher for women living in a low-income country than for women in high-income countries (the poorer a woman is, the higher the risk, which is compounded if she is a rural dweller, belongs to an ethnic minority, is HIV-positive, or lives in a conflict zone). Because of their large populations, improvements in China and India explain much of the overall decline in maternal mortality. On the other hand, six countries accounted for more than half of all maternal deaths in 2008: Nigeria, India, Pakistan, Afghanistan, Ethiopia, and the Democratic Republic of Congo. Worldwide, pregnant women and girls continue to die (1,000 a day, 358,000 a year) from four main causes: severe bleeding after childbirth, infections, hypertensive disorders, and unsafe abortions. Yet most life-saving interventions cost very little money. For example, $10 can buy clean birthing kits for six women, And $5 pays the cost of providing one pregnant woman with quality antenatal care. However, as long as those in a position to give continue to consider foreign aid to be a waste of money, even the easiest and least-costly health improvements will remain out of reach.[56]

The infectious diseases that are most devastating throughout much of the third world are preventable, curable illnesses that incapacitate and kill, such as malaria, tuberculosis, and acute lower-respiratory diseases like pneumonia. For example, the World Health Organization estimates that the death rate from measles has been cut dramatically, by 70 percent between 2000 and 2008, with a vaccination campaign.[57]

Although HIV/AIDS kills fewer people every year than malaria, tuberculosis, and diarrheal diseases together, and although scientists now contend that the epidemic has halted (and perhaps even reversed), the disease still has the capacity to make a mark on the world unrivaled since the Black Death of the fourteenth century. In just three decades HIV/AIDS has killed over 25 million people worldwide. Nearly 2 million more die every year, most of them children or young people in the prime of life. Another 33.3 million people worldwide are living with HIV or AIDS—and 2.6 million more people are infected each year. The good news is that these numbers are not nearly as high as they were once projected to be, and the number of deaths each year from AIDS and AIDS-related causes has been declining for the past several years. The number of new infections is down by 19 percent from its peak in 1999. New interventions (such as male circumcision, vaginal microbicides, and drugs that offer preexposure prophylaxis) offer promise in terms of prevention.[58] Antiretroviral drugs can significantly prolong life and improve the quality of life for people living with HIV/AIDS, they can virtually eliminate mother-to-child transmission of HIV, and more people in LICs have access to these drugs than ever before (from 50,000 in 2003 to 5 million in 2010). But 10 million people who need these drugs do not have access to them, the rate of treatment is not keeping up with the rate of infection, and the disease is hitting areas of the world least prepared to deal with it. The incidence of HIV/AIDS is declining in many African countries (including Zimbabwe), but 70 percent of new infections are in Africa.[59]

As it is with other diseases, poverty is intricately connected to the perpetuation of HIV/AIDS as well. AIDS was once most common among male truck drivers and soldiers; incidence ran highest where there were well-developed roads and bridges. Yet women now compose half of all people living with HIV/AIDS, and the disease is found in all occupational groups and classes. The extreme hardship associated with austerity is an aggravating factor, not only promoting male out-migration but also leaving many women little alternative but to enter the informal economy as sex workers. Likewise, people who cannot afford antibiotics and medicines to treat other sexually transmitted diseases live with genital sores that make them more vulnerable to HIV infection.

The rapid transmission of disease (including HIV) in southern Africa and many other LICs is facilitated by a migrant labor system that dates back to colonialism. Unfortunately, the separation of families created by male out-migration in search of work is hardly a historical artifact. This situation, in which men (and some women) leave their families behind to work in the cities, in mines, in factories, and on plantations, is common today in many non-Western countries. Men away from home for months at a time are more likely to form liaisons with local women who may have seen other partners come and go. These men become infected with HIV and when they return home they pass it on to their wives, who then pass it on to their babies.

Despite the development of new tests and improvements in administering them, screening for HIV is still physically and financially inaccessible for many people worldwide. Too often a woman is already pregnant before she becomes aware of her HIV status, since many women are tested only when they come to clinics for prenatal care. Without wider programs, the children born to many of these women will soon become orphans, as even extended families find it difficult to support the rapidly growing burden upon them as AIDS spreads to rural areas. In the meantime, many of the children of weakened and ill parents leave school to assume greater household responsibilities. In 2008, worldwide there were more than 17.5 million children under seventeen who had lost one or both parents to AIDS. What to do with them is yet another problem also unrivaled in human history.[60]

Other Effects on Children

As we have seen, the budgetary cuts imposed by structural adjustment have a variety of direct effects on children in addition to the dislocations felt by their families. The combination of rising food prices and diminishing food subsidies and nutrition programs has taken its toll. Several countries in Latin America have reported sharp increases in infant mortality rates since cuts to social services. In the months after Peru's implementation of its austerity plan in 1988, poor children temporarily stopped growing due to malnutrition. In addition to health concerns, rising school fees have made it is less likely that all children will receive an education. And the quality of education is also eroded by budget cuts, as schools become overcrowded in dilapidated buildings, with classes often taught by overworked and underpaid teachers. As mentioned in Chapter 6, because of the pressures on their families, today children spend more of their time working in a variety of capacities to help make ends meet.[61]

Compounding the problems associated with the growing numbers of orphans created by AIDS in several parts of the world, the stress associated with neoliberal reforms has also been linked to higher rates of child abandonment and abuse, resulting in growing numbers of street children worldwide. No one knows exactly how many children live on the streets on a regular basis. For example, bigger cities in Turkey face a growing population of children, mostly homeless, who make a living on the streets. As many as 7,000 children may live on the streets of Istanbul alone. As families become displaced, children leave home at younger ages to join the paid work force, beg, or steal, either as a source of support to their families or entirely on their own. Often these children exist in utter destitution, living homeless or in packs in abandoned buildings, surviving on very little and spending what money they have on drugs, or paint thinner and glues to dull hunger pains.

Perhaps just as troubling is the fact that around the world, mistreatment of children is becoming more socially accepted. It is not uncommon for street children in Congo's capital, Kinshasa, to be accused of sorcery and "exorcised" through beatings and deprivation. Around the world, street children are often viewed as a threat or an eyesore; in the worst situations they are targeted for attack by "social cleansing squads" composed of vigilantes and police.

Is Globalization Entirely to Blame?

Although the single-minded pursuit of the neoliberal paradigm has unleashed an array of problems, manifested in various forms of social DISINTEGRATION and economic dysfunctionality, there is no one cause for all of the troubles described in this chapter. While the spread of HIV, destruction of rainforests, massive human migrations, and exploitation of labor are based in social and economic institutions and systems of relationships that predate globalization, these processes are argued by some to be accelerated by the adoption of the neoliberal reforms that provide the momentum for globalization. Perhaps it is an overstatement to suggest that such tragedies are due to structural adjustment, but growing evidence suggests that the variety of problems identified here are associated with growing economic hardship. Structuralists assert that in many ways—economically, socially, culturally, politically, ecologically—the neoliberal approach has been a disaster for the world's poor. It is not working, it has cured nothing, and the international financial institutions have had plenty of time to impose their plans.[62]

Neoliberals reject such assertions. When presented with the above arguments, they point out that many LICs now deserve the name "emerging economies." They counter that if their way appears to be failing in some countries, then this failure is due to irrational or inefficient domestic policies, not to the irretrievably inequitable position of these countries in the world economy. The problem is poverty. It isn't globalization that is contributing to disease, emigration, and the like—it is the poverty that results from a *lack* of INTEGRATION into the world economic system. It is the countries that are most integrated into the international system (the BRICs, for example—Brazil, Russia, India, China) that are the fastest-growing and have the best shot at development. It should be pointed out, however, that the BRICs have to varying degrees accepted neoliberal reforms. The Chinese state is still heavily interventionist, for example. Brazil, under former president Luiz Inácio Lula da Silva, has combined some of the macroeconomic reforms of the Washington Consensus with enhanced spending on social services, pursuing what some call the "Brasilia Consensus." This approach, which views social welfare as being just as important as structural reform, has improved the lives of many Brazilians.[63] There is still much work to do in terms of income inequality and poverty reduction in Brazil and in all the BRICs, but impressive numbers of people are entering the middle class in these countries. Per capita income in Brazil, China, and India is still relatively low, but it has grown significantly in just a decade or so, and these countries have made progress in alleviating poverty. In 1981, for example, 84 percent of Chinese lived below the poverty line. By 2005, only 16 percent did. During this same period, Brazil cut its poverty rate from 17 to 8 percent and India from 60 to 42 percent (admittedly, the percentage of the poor in India is still very high, but a nearly 20 percent decline is significant).[64] On the other hand, according to the neoliberals, if other countries aren't achieving these results, it is because they have undertaken needed economic reforms too slowly or halfheartedly. They warn that economic liberalization is like riding a bicycle: you either move forward, or you fall off. It is this hesitancy, or lack of full cooperation, that explains why so few have yet to see improvement in their standards of living.

Neoliberals go on to contend that many of these problems are rooted in individual behaviors: people *choose* to work for the wages they are offered, they make the decision to have unsafe sex, they deplete the forests in search of firewood. Therefore it is individuals and their choices—not structures—that should be blamed. However, others contend that more often than not, each of these so-called choices should be understood as a coping mechanism. For most of the world's population, the behaviors condemned are not so much about choice as they are about survival.

The Neoliberals Make an Adjustment

For all of their arguments, it has been hard for the neoliberals to avoid acknowledging the IMF riots—the dislocation and hardship associated with their economic reforms. The collapse of East Asian economies in the late 1990s and the Great Recession a decade later forced a broader reassessment of the reform model by even its most ardent advocates. Under criticism from the right and left, the IMF and other international financial institutions maintained that they have made some needed reforms of their own. In an effort to salvage the neoliberal approach by softening some of its hardest edges, the World Bank became the leading player charged with helping (some) countries construct safety nets to carry them through the period of adjustment. It and the IMF appeared to have heard their critics, declaring that there was no single recipe for economic success. In an interesting turnabout, the IMF took the position that every country was different and a one-size-fits-all solution would be unlikely to suit the particular needs of each. According to the IMF today, with the shift to extended-credit facilities, countries can now play a greater role in defining the terms of their adjustment and setting their path for reform. Such a modification would mark quite a departure from the old IMF, in which decisions were made by donor countries, for aid recipients.

According to the IMF's defenders, the move from structural adjustment programs to extended-credit facilities signifies the transformation to a "beefier but gentler" approach; today the IMF is all about partnering with countries in order to make the system work better. Does this mean that the nearly seven-decade-old international financial system—and foundation of the Washington Consensus—has truly undergone a conversion? Given more than two decades of IMF reform and relatively few success stories, is there a crisis of LEGITIMACY now for the neoliberal model and its prescription? The answer, according to neoliberals, is a resounding no. The lesson learned is not that the Washington Consensus is wrong, but that it is incomplete. It is probably safe to assume that the Washington Consensus isn't declining; rather it is evolving, adapting, shifting in response to perceived needs.[65] The new, more flexible IMF has retooled its conditionality: conditions continue to be necessary, but countries are allowed more of a voice in helping to identify what those conditions should be. Part of this voice will come through voting reform, or allowing the third world more of a role in decisionmaking in the IMF and World Bank. This idea has been on the table for several years. As of late 2010, the G-20 had only gone so far as to agree to shift 6 percent of the IMF's voting power from high-income countries to emerging economies (most notably China, Turkey, South Korea, and Mexico). According to the IMF, these reforms are historic; these countries were given more voting power in order to reflect their relative size and growing clout in the international economy. Those with the most clout—the United States (which has 17 percent of the IMF vote) and Europe (23 percent)—maintain that they support this reform in the hope that it will restore the institution's legitimacy and encourage these emerging powers to feel more invested in the current system. For now, at least, the poorest countries of the world—those most dependent on the IMF—continue to have a very small role in the discussion.[66]

The IMF's very disparate group of critics have differed over how seriously they take the talk about reform. Some neoliberals have even split with the IMF over the question of its proper role. They insist that the organization is already doing too much, that it needs to get out of the antipoverty business. These more conservative analysts maintain that the IMF's RESCUE PACKAGES are a mistake, because they give countries (and lenders) the idea that they will always be bailed out. As a result, governments and investors are never forced to recognize the consequences of their mistakes. They will continue to be reckless with their lending and this will only mean future crises.

On the other hand, others reject such an analysis. Their issue is that the extended-credit facilities are really nothing new; countries resent the reforms forced onto them as a precondition to assistance, and argue that it still treats them like children. The BRICs have at times taken the lead in facing down Western demands (sometimes using neoliberal institutions such as the WORLD TRADE ORGANIZATION to do so). But there is tremendous diversity between and within the large number of countries comprising the "third world." Those who experienced enormous hardship in association with the IMF's reforms are deeply distrustful of it and other international financial institutions. All states object when IFI intrusion veers toward violations of sovereignty. Three decades of neoliberalism have resulted in increased social inequality and a great deal of frustration in the poorest countries, and there is a great desire to find another way. Although few alternatives appear promising, there is no doubt that those who are left behind very much want change.

Structuralists insist that they see through all this talk about change. They claim that for neoliberals, there is still only one road to development. But some analysts view the neoliberal mea culpa and subsequent reforms as having some potential, particularly if this means that countries might be able to travel the road at different speeds, or even at their own pace. There is some public support for this idea within the third world. In Latin America, for example, public opinion polls suggest that most people favor the market economy and see their countries as progressing. Brazil, Bolivia, and Uruguay, for example, elected leftist governments and have seen poverty decline and social indicators improve in the past few years. Although the recession of 2001–2002 undermined many people's faith in democracy, especially in Central America, most of those polled do not blame their governments for the latest economic downturn.[67] Rather, they appear to support leaders such as Brazil's former president Lula, who demanded that the IMF no longer urge LIC governments to adopt policies promoting trade liberalization that the rich developed countries themselves have yet to undertake. As mentioned earlier in this chapter, it is common for IMF reforms to force LICs to open their economies to foreign trade while developed countries continue to subsidize and protect their domestic producers from LIC competition with subsidies and tariffs. LICs argue that they would have a much better shot at benefiting from free trade if everyone played by its rules. Whatever the case, it appears that in its effort at "getting politics right," the IMF may need to take some of its own medicine. Perhaps it too should have to work harder at good governance—become more democratic, more transparent, and more accountable to the public, as well as to all of its 187 member states.[68]

8

Alternative Approaches to Development

Our movement must continue demanding a change in economic policy, which has demonstrated its failure . . . the model must be changed. You cannot put new wine in old bottles.
—*Andrés Manuel López Obrador, Mexican opposition political leader*[1]

Poverty is not created by poor people. It is produced by our failure to create institutions to support human capabilities.
—*Muhammad Yunus, founder of the Grameen Bank of Bangladesh*[2]

Both proponents and critics of GLOBALIZATION argue that it is faceless, emerging everywhere at once. Like the view that promotes and seeks to perpetuate it, based in NEOLIBERALISM, globalization's overwhelming dominance verges on the HEGEMONIC. By hegemonic, we mean that something is so dominant, so powerful, that there are no apparent rivals. When it comes to globalization and the neoliberal approach to DEVELOPMENT, low-income countries (LICs) are told again and again to remember TINA—"there is no alternative." Yet critics of the orthodoxy struggle to provide other choices; they demand a counterhegemonic approach that includes considerations of justice. These analysts seek to put development on an equal par with GROWTH, if not ahead of it. Instead of "getting prices right" or "getting politics right," they argue for "getting institutions right for development."

Over the years a variety of alternative paths to development have been proposed—some reformist, some more revolutionary—but few of them have met with much success. Many of these proposals urge the creation of indigenous models and self-reliance, such as Tanzania's Afro-socialist *ujamma*. Others, such as China's Great Leap Forward, centered on a rejection of the capitalist world system and instead proposed autarchy. Still others, such as the NEW INTERNATIONAL ECONOMIC ORDER (NIEO), attempted to reform the INTERNATIONAL ECONOMIC SYSTEM to make it fairer. Among other things, they called for developed countries to increase their foreign aid allocations, and to invest in research and development of technologies appropriate to non-Western needs. Proponents of the NIEO asked that more soft loans be made available to developing countries. They called for debts to be renegotiated or forgiven. The NIEO's architects agreed that there should be less conditionality on loans; developed countries should not be so eager to impose adjustments on others that they themselves would be loath to accept. MULTINATIONAL CORPORATIONS (MNCs) should be regulated to create a fairer system that fosters development. LICs should be allowed more of a voice at the INTERNATIONAL GOVERNMENTAL ORGANIZATIONS (IGOs) that dominate their lives, especially the INTERNATIONAL MONETARY FUND (IMF) and the WORLD BANK. In addition, using the Organization of Petroleum Exporting Countries (OPEC) as a model, LICs should create cartels or producer clubs for other raw materials. These cartels could then negotiate on the world market with buyers of their goods, to set a price range acceptable to all—in order to achieve a more stable and fairer price for their products. As you can see, the proposals of the NIEO are wide-ranging and comprehensive. They date back to the 1960s, and various aspects of the NIEO are periodically resurrected for consideration. However, thus far, even the most moderate reforms have failed, mostly because LICs have so little power with which to renegotiate the terms of their incorporation into the world economic system.

Today, a variety of activists concerned about the continued underdevelopment of much of the third world are facing the same fundamental problems that earlier generations did in their calls for a restructured world order or the creation of a counterhegemonic approach. Although there is plenty of disagreement among the critics of corporate-led globalization (or "globalization from above"), they generally agree on the need for "globalization from below," or a GRASSROOTS-BASED APPROACH that prioritizes sustainable human development and security. In short, sustainability considerations (not only SUSTAINABLE DEVELOPMENT but also sustainable consumption) are based in the belief that the welfare of present generations should not be pursued at the expense of future generations. In its broadest sense, even the World Bank and WORLD TRADE ORGANIZATION (WTO) have embraced the term "sustainability," calling it one of their principal objectives. Yet critics argue that sustainability means much more, and that it directly runs counter to neoliberal values that place a premium on greed, the profit motive, and consumerism.

HUMAN SECURITY, on the other hand, is based in an entirely different set of values, such as cooperation, compassion, economic DEMOCRACY, and decentralization. It speaks to individual and collective perceptions of present and potential threats to physical and psychological well-being. "Human security" is a relatively new term that takes understandings of security beyond issues of armaments and territorial security. Analysts who support the counterhegemonic approach maintain that security against direct violence is just one form of human security, and have extended the concept to include the security of people, not just nations. Human security is defined as the absence of structural violence such as poverty and other forms of economic, social, and environmental degradation.[3]

Efforts to promote human security center on the eradication of extreme poverty and take a holistic approach. This definition of development views it as a process and an end, the result of a complex set of interactions between political, economic, social, environmental, and cultural factors.[4] For example, one aspect of human secu-

A silent protest against sanctions in Zimbabwe
(Reuters/Philimon Bulawayo)

rity is the promotion of gender equality, which seeks to end discrimination against females in all areas of life. Such initiatives are proactive as well, focused on creating choices and opportunities for women and ending all forms of violence against them. Human security is also promoted through projects that target investments to benefit low-income groups. One example is agrarian reform, which includes land redistribution, the building of infrastructure such as rural roads and clinics, as well as increasing accessibility to credit and appropriate technologies. In order to get the maximum benefit from such policies, all aspects of the reform (including land titles) need to be made available to women (and men). Other "pro-poor" economic growth policies invest in physical and human capital and expand employment opportunities by upgrading skills in traditional and untraditional occupations, so that businesses and other enterprises can be more competitive.

One area of intense disagreement within the counterhegemonic approach centers on the question of whether it might be possible to promote human security through globalization. Some (such as Dot Keet) call for "deglobalization," a move away from the dominant economic system and toward large-scale change that would require (among other things) reconceptualizing our understanding of progress.[5] On the other hand, reformists like Joseph Stiglitz argue for a "reglobalization" (a re-do, so to speak). They aren't fighting globalization as much as they are resisting its worst features. They believe that (if properly managed) a fairer globalization can be created. Stiglitz advocates Keynesian reforms that allow for more state management of economies (rather than leaving it to the market forces that set off the Great Recession and have left too many mired in poverty for too long). Public management of the economy was the approach that President Franklin Delano Roosevelt used to lead the United States out of the Great Depression. According to this idea, the state stimulates the economy through deficit spending. Investments in infrastructure, industry, and other projects are undertaken to generate employment and create conditions for stability and growth.[6] You may recognize this as the line of attack that the Obama administration credits for keeping our recent recession from becoming a depression.

This approach has been used elsewhere as well. The high-income countries (HICs) that have been the most successful in eradicating poverty (the Scandinavian countries) have not left it to the market to sort out—rather, their governments have actively intervened with antipoverty measures. Similarly, many developing countries, including Brazil and Mexico, have reduced income inequality by promoting pro-poor stimulus programs such as CONDITIONAL CASH TRANSFERS (CCTs). Under CCT programs such as Oportunidades in Mexico, the government invests in human capital by providing stipends to poor families who take their kids for medical checkups and ensure that they stay in school. When designed effectively and implemented transparently, such social assistance programs have proven to be enormously successful at promoting short- and long-term development goals.[7]

According to Stiglitz, these are ideas that can benefit both LICs and HICs.[8] Although they disagree about how to get there, those who promote reglobalization and deglobalization agree that it is time for a post–Washington Consensus. They are joined by labor and human rights activists, environmentalists, consumer advocates, and others who are prioritizing equity and working to replace the corporate view of ECONOMIC LIBERALIZATION with a more democratic, fully participatory model. Such a model would press donors to honor their pledges in regard to aid and hold MNCs accountable for their misdeeds. It would allow countries to escape externally imposed conditionality and redefine their own (homegrown) development directions, tailored to local conditions.[9]

Those who believe the question is not whether we globalize, but how we globalize, are seeking to adapt or manage globalization. Groups such as Oxfam and the Jubilee movement are offering credible alternatives for the way in which we think about debt relief, labor standards, and other issues. As a whole, those who seek to adapt globalization are defining a goal. They want people to have more choices and more control over their own lives, and to expand the possibilities for SELF-DETERMINATION. A one-size-fits-all approach to development is counterproductive. Instead, countries are like patients; they have different ailments and will require different treatments.[10]

Most of these activists generally acknowledge that there are some benefits of globalization, but they want to blunt its negative impacts. The majority agree that integration into the world system is inevitable and possibly even desirable, but they call for stricter labor and environmental regulations to minimize the system's exploitative potential. They may not be able to reduce conditionality, but they can reshape it. In other words, the reformists favor engagement with the global system on terms and conditions carefully selected and coordinated by a state committed to social interests and accountable to its citizens. They seek to rewrite the rules of globalization, to make it work for people and not just profits. Such ideals are summed up by the slogan "Another world is possible."[11]

In addition, the advocates of a post–Washington Consensus argue that local people should be encouraged to evolve development solutions that are self-governing and culturally appropriate, in conformity with their own norms and practices. They contend that projects should begin on a small scale. Community successes can then be scaled up to regional and even national levels, but remain reflective of local ways of life and prioritize social responsibility. They suggest that in some cases the end result may be a hybrid, a fusion of two or more approaches that may even still include aspects of the neoliberal model. For example, they recognize the necessity of a free market, but argue for a more flexible one in which governments set their own path and pace for reform. Some offer China as a model for the flexible approach. Its gradual installation of economic reforms, including the creation of rural industry to employ displaced farmers, hasn't been without hardship (inequality continues to be a major problem), but it has resulted in high, consistent growth for over twenty-five years.[12]

Other initiatives include a variety of successful grassroots-based projects that exist throughout the third world. Whether they come in the form of cooperatives, microenterprises, or the like, grassroots-based projects are the purest expression of the idea of "development of the people, for the people, by the people." Advocates of this approach insist that participation that includes the poor and previously excluded groups is key to human security. Sustainable development is a people-centered development. Examples of success stories in terms of participatory, sustainable development include the not-for-profit, local public water management utility operated with citizen oversight in Porto Alegre, Brazil. Similarly, youth groups in Nepal and Bangladesh have coordinated villagers to install public toilets or latrines that benefit all.[13] This approach values local knowledge and wisdom as the basis for an authentic development. While the government can play an enabling role, providing people with the opportunity and environment for self-development, a just and sustainable development is based in ownership and inclusiveness—it is a people's movement, not a foreign-funded initiative.[14]

Such a line of attack demands a fundamental shift away from the majority of development thinking, which takes a highly centralized TOP-DOWN APPROACH. We shouldn't be treating targeted populations as victims to be "saved." This only winds up patronizing and ultimately alienating the very people whom agencies are trying to assist. Instead, a participatory, grassroots approach is decentralized and bottom-up: it views the targeted population as a rich source of information, as the real experts on the environment in which they live, as conveyors of a culture that has sustained them for thousands of years. Economist Nancy Birdsall is an advocate of this approach, which is based in the idea that donors should trust local people and give them more control over aid spending, because it is the people who live there who know what they need and the best way to deliver results. She calls for COD (cash on delivery) aid, in which aid donors and recipients draw up a contract that recipients design and implement. Together they come up with a solution to an agreed-upon problem and donors pay agreed-upon sums only after specific outcomes are achieved (such as reducing HIV transmission or maternal mortality rates).[15]

Democratically determined development is manifested in a variety of forms. Among other things, it focuses on long-term goals of practical relevance while also setting immediate targets that are achievable in the near term.[16] It may involve land reform, a focus on small farmers and the production of staple foods, enhancement of the role of women as agents of change, satisfaction of critical needs, investment in human capital, or any variety of self-help programs.[17] The Grameen Bank, founded in Bangladesh in 1976 by economist Muhammad Yunus (recipient of the 2006 Nobel Peace Prize), is an example of how powerful a seemingly novel, indigenous-based, BOTTOM-UP APPROACH can effectively alleviate poverty. The opposite of a trickle-down approach, the Grameen Bank offers microcredit, or small, microenterprise loans (the average is $395) to the landless, poor, and others without collateral. The vast majority of the landless and poor targeted for assistance by the Grameen Bank are women (97 percent), whose only other choice would be to turn to moneylenders or loansharks.[18] But these microcreditors do much more than provide credit to those without collateral. They foster entrepreneurship and emphasize self-employment over wage labor. Loans are not extended for immediate consumption needs, but as seed money to encourage the startup of small businesses. For example, a woman might borrow just enough money to buy thread and start an embroidery business, or open a small kiosk or lunch stand. Or, where telephones are a luxury, she might buy a cell phone and charge for its use.[19]

The bank, actually a network of village-based franchises, is self-sustaining. It is run like a club. Members demonstrate their reliability by initially taking out very small loans and repaying them. Gradually they become eligible for larger amounts of credit. In addition, members are educated about the value of credit. They are obliged to follow the bank's code, which among other things calls upon members to grow vegetables to eat and sell the surplus, to look after the health and education of their children, and to be ready to help each other. Peer pressure in these tightly knit groups keeps defaults rare (at about 1 percent—a much lower rate than for commercial banks). Building on the success of the program in Bangladesh, the Grameen Foundation network now partners with thirty-six countries. Since 1976 it has dispersed loans worth $9.8 billion (with a 97 percent recovery rate). It has helped more than 8 million clients make their way out of poverty and is widely considered one of the most successful antipoverty programs in the world.[20] While microlending programs are not a panacea—they are too small alone to effectively address the larger internal and external barriers to development—they are liberating in the sense that they promote social change by focusing on traditionally marginalized groups. Although, like anything else, it can be misused, and even Grameen has been accused of being less than transparent. Microcredit is a practical solution that has made a tremendous difference in the lives of individuals. Its proponents also claim that it is changing the way the world sees the potential of the poor.[21] Donors are coming to realize that when the poor have access to the institutions the rich enjoy, they can become self-reliant and prosper.

Programs such as this can make a real and immediate difference in people's lives. On the other hand, a comprehensive approach that combines grassroots-based programs focusing on individuals with larger-scale efforts aimed at changing the playing field may hold the most promise of all. But the larger-scale efforts have proven to be more problematic. For example, many of the analysts promoting a re-globalization or deglobalization doubt the benefits to LICs of entering into free trade agreements with HICs. Too often such agreements have undermined labor rights, proven environmentally costly, and wound up leaving the developing country more dependent on its rich partner. However, with a view to making change on a larger scale, many countries have attempted to emulate the success of the European Union (EU) and promote regional INTEGRATION. As we discuss in greater depth in Chapter 17, many of the more successful efforts at integration began as initiatives to reduce barriers and promote preferential trade arrangements between partners. Building on their successes, they later developed into political and security alliances as well. Regional trade accords have proliferated since the 1990s (there are more than 400 in force). Every part of the world has undertaken a number of attempts to build strength in numbers and harness its economic energies in order to create economies of scale and to lessen dependency on developed countries. Over one-third of all world trade occurs within regional trade blocs and most countries are members of at least one such group.[22] In this effort to gain strength from numbers, these experiments have varied widely in their ability to create growth or development, let alone produce any leverage within the international economic system for developing countries.

In Asia, one of the most promising exclusively regional efforts at integration is the Association of Southeast Asian Nations (ASEAN). Composed of ten Southeast Asian states (and comprising a market of more than 570 million people), ASEAN was formed in 1967. It is one of the most active regional groupings outside Europe, promoting political and economic cooperation. To encourage regional stability, ASEAN's charter calls for its members not to interfere in each other's domestic affairs (this policy of nonconfrontation has been criticized for propping up authoritarian governments, including Burma's). With a combined gross domestic product (GDP) of $1.5 trillion, ASEAN's members are accelerating their drive to form a single market like the EU and have agreed to deepen the integration of their economies by 2015, but without a common currency. The goal is to allow the free movement of goods, labor, and capital, but one hitch is that because of the disparity in economic power between members, ASEAN countries have often been reluctant to make sacrifices for the common good. Yet they realize the need to form a COMMON MARKET if there is to be any hope of competing with neighbors China and India. These smaller economies know that they'll need to focus on sectors that their neighboring economic giants can't easily replicate, such as palm oil in Malaysia or ornamental fish farming in Singapore. In the meantime, to promote coexistence, ASEAN has entered into a free trade agreement with China. In 2010 the ASEAN-China Free Trade Area (ACFTA) became the world's largest free trade zone by population (1.9 billion) and third largest by GDP ($6 trillion).[23]

Together comprising a membership of 250 million people and over $1.1 trillion in gross national income (GNI), Mercosur (also known as Mercosul, or the Common Market of the South) was established in 1991. Its original members (Brazil, Paraguay, Uruguay, Argentina) came together to harness their economic strength with the goal of one day uniting the economic power of every country on the continent. Since its creation, Bolivia, Chile, Colombia, Ecuador, and Peru have joined as associated members (Venezuela's membership has been in political limbo for years over a requirement that all members be democracies). In many ways, Mercosur is a success of South-South cooperation: trade between members has more than quadrupled, making it the largest trade bloc in the region and the fourth largest in the world.[24] However, in part because its members are so often at odds, Mercosur has so far not lived up to expectations and in recent years several new regional organizations have sought to usurp it.

Although Mercosur has had some success in promoting trade between members, it has not made much progress toward enlarging its membership or functioning effectively as a CUSTOMS UNION. In an apparent shift of strategy, instead of deepening ties with existing members, Mercosur is expanding its reach to include new members—beyond Latin America. Members are seeking to make the organization into a strong regional body and to reduce their traditional dependence on the United States by liberalizing trade with what is now Mercosur's single largest customer, the European Union. Negotiations between South America and Europe to create one of the world's largest bilateral free trade zones (with a population of 750 million and goods valued at $83 billion a year) continue (as of early 2011). But in the past, talks were derailed over Europe's unwillingness to lift protectionist policies and expose its agricultural producers to foreign competition. Such an opening to trade is what Latin America (and many LICs without preferential trade agreements with the EU) has been waiting for, since notorious EU trade barriers have effectively shut it out of the highly lucrative European market. Analysts doubt that the deal will go through, because of vociferous opposition from powerful European lobbies.[25] However, if the marriage of the EU and Mercosur becomes a reality, the European shift will likely be due to its fear of losing markets if the United States manages to pull Latin America ever closer through free trade agreements. If globalization is indeed the only game in town, Latin America—and all LICs—can try to strengthen their position by diversifying their trading relationships.

The rise of giant economies such as China, India, and Brazil has provided many LICs with a way to do just this. As with ASEAN, the BRICs (Brazil, Russia, India, China) have significantly increased their economic linkages to their neighbors in recent years, and are expanding their reach. The most prominent example is again China, whose primary interest in the rest of the third world is as a market for its manufactured goods, as a source of natural resources for its industry, and as a source of lucrative investment. However, China is beginning to disappoint as an alternative to the West. Because of asymmetries in its relationships with other countries, China's activities in Asia and Africa in particular (but also the Middle East and Latin America significantly) are increasingly resented and characterized as a new colonialism.

Such asymmetries are not limited to but have long plagued intraregional trade blocs, leading to tensions, disputes, and (in more than one case) the demise of these unions. Unless special and differential terms are accorded to members to make up for disparities in power, the existence of regional hegemons is likely to mean that the benefits of even South-South integration will not be shared by all.

Conclusions: Must We Accept TINA?

In this chapter we have discussed a range of "post-Consensus" development paradigms and proposed a number of alternatives. Some are radical and others reformist; some focus on individuals as agents of change while others promote international cooperation. Yet repeatedly we are reminded by neoliberals that "there is no alternative." Neoliberalism remains hegemonic. Even critics of globalization agree that it can seem unstoppable. Non-Western economies are expected to conform to the rules and accept the adjustments pressed upon them by donors. With very few exceptions, low- and middle-income countries are operating within the constraints of a global capitalist system. It is important to recognize that while they are not powerless, the political leaders of non-Western countries are limited in their capacity to make decisions. To some degree, of course, this is true for the leaders of relatively rich countries as well. With a total national debt of nearly $14 trillion as of December 2010, the United States has several times the combined debt of all of the third world.[26] However, because of the advantageous position of the United States within the international economic system, and because it is a leading member of the international economic organizations calling the shots, even the world's largest debtor is not held accountable to the rules in the same way that less powerful debtors are.

9

Linking
Concepts and Cases

As we turn now to a discussion of how our eight CASE STUDIES are faring in the INTERNATIONAL ECONOMIC SYSTEM, think about the impact of the Great Recession on each. Identify some of the various ways in which these countries are coping with the economic pressures on them.

How are our cases doing in terms of GROWTH and DEVELOPMENT? Have there been any significant changes in their economic fortunes since this book was published? Which countries do you consider to be better-off? Which are performing the worst? Why have some countries been more successful in their adoption of NEO-LIBERALISM than others? How do you define "success"? How do you see the struggle between growth and development playing out in these countries? How do these countries compare in terms of their progress in achieving the MILLENNIUM DEVELOPMENT GOALS? In which countries has the pursuit of economic growth meant environmental devastation? How dependent is each of these countries on the export of raw materials? How diversified are their economies? Is it appropriate to characterize all (or any) of these countries as "third world"? Why or why not?

Case Study: Mexico

A decade into the twenty-first century, Mexico was in many ways considered by the West to be a model of economic reform. However, twenty years earlier the country was at the epicenter of a debt crisis. Its economic problems can be traced at least as far back as the 1970s, when it was one of the world's largest oil producers. Oil prices had reached an all-time high and governments of the Institutional Revolutionary Party (PRI) borrowed large sums and spent lavishly. Unfortunately for Mexico, oil prices dropped by the early 1980s and the country was left with one of the largest debts in the world—$80 billion. The government had borrowed far beyond its means, was being charged exorbitant interest rates, and could not keep up with its payments.

After Mexico rocked the international financial system by threatening to default on its debt, the country was compelled to adopt a series of AUSTERITY PLANS throughout the 1980s. However, Mexico's economic problems continued and its debt piled up. By late 1994, in order to win US support for Mexico's membership in the North American Free Trade Agreement (NAFTA), Mexico agreed to the terms of another round of economic reforms. Mexico had little choice but to faithfully meet the conditions outlined by the INTERNATIONAL MONETARY FUND (IMF). Then-president Ernesto Zedillo announced a series of measures, including a 40 percent devaluation of the peso, that went into effect literally overnight. The combined effect of the reforms proved a shock to the system. The peso collapsed and the economy took a nose dive. Growth rates plunged into the negative digits. Inflation and interest rates soared. The effect on the middle class and the poor has been compared to that of a financial neutron bomb: it destroyed the population, leaving only the real estate standing. People couldn't afford basic necessities. Instead of milk, some parents had to feed their children coffee just to put something in their stomachs.

The gravity of this crisis spurred the United States to press the IMF to provide Mexico with a $40 billion emergency bailout package—at the time the largest rescue ever. This intervention prevented Mexico from defaulting on its debt and enabled it to continue on with its economic reform. By the late 1990s the country appeared to have made it through its period of austerity and surprised many with the speed of its recovery (it enjoyed healthy growth rates of 6–7 percent from the late 1990s through 2000).

While some of Mexico's economic growth since then has been related to higher oil prices, much of it is due to the country's membership in NAFTA. In 1994, NAFTA established a free trade zone between the United States, Canada, and Mexico. Because goods produced in Mexico can be exported duty-free to either of its NAFTA partners, and because Mexico has low wages and lax enforcement of environmental regulations, MULTINATIONAL CORPORATIONS (MNCs) such as General Motors, Sony, and Goodyear eagerly set up shop in the country. As a result, foreign investment grew rapidly during the 1990s. Since the passage of NAFTA the numbers of *MAQUILADORAS* in Mexico have mushroomed and created jobs, but with devastating results for rivers, which are now rank with industrial byproducts and raw sewage. Millions of Mexicans farming on small plots have had a hard time holding on after NAFTA eliminated tariffs and opened up Mexico to competition against US and Canadian agribusinesses, which could now sell their cheaper foodstuffs in Mexico duty-free. Yet many analysts consider NAFTA to have been a boon for the Mexican economy; trade with the United States and Canada has more than tripled, and Mexico's economy is the second largest in Latin America.[1]

In the years since NAFTA, gross domestic product (GDP) per capita has gradually risen (in 2010 it was about $13,000). Over the past decade, Mexico's Human Development Index ranking has generally improved, partly due to conditional cash-transfer programs such as Oportunidades (which provides nearly a quarter of the population an average of $35 each month). Although there are still problems with the quality of public schools, access to education has improved; approximately 70 percent of Mexican children attend secondary school.[2] However, as of 2010, almost half the population was still living in poverty and some analysts were predicting that Mexico would be unable to achieve some of its Millennium Development Goals (particularly in regard to the provision of water and sanitation, and reducing maternal and child mortality).[3] After more than fifteen years of NAFTA (and three decades of ECONOMIC LIBERALIZATION), income inequality in Mexico has finally begun to decline and the middle class is growing (composing about one-third of the population), but the gap between the rich and poor is still twice that of a country like Denmark.[4]

Because Mexico's market is already one of the most open in Latin America, the country's experience illustrates both the benefits and the risks of GLOBALIZATION: the Great Recession, which began in the United States in 2007, hit Mexico harder than any other Latin American country. Economic contraction in its neighbor to the north dramatically affected demand for Mexican goods. This contributed to plummeting prices for its exports, and Mexico's growth rates nose-dived to its lowest rate since 1932—to negative 6.5 percent in 2009.[5] It should come as no surprise (given that 80 percent of the country's exports go to the United States) that analysts make their forecasts for Mexico based on the status of its major trading partner to the north. Whereas sales to China have helped other economies weather the recession, Mexico is in the unfortunate position of producing many of the same things China does— and selling little that the Chinese are looking to buy. Although Mexico's growth rate rebounded to 5 percent in 2010, its recovery is largely dependent on that of its northern neighbor.[6]

Worse, its recovery is also affected by the perception that Mexico is losing its competitive edge. Mexico has been unable to keep up with its rivals in offering cheap labor. One problem with NAFTA had always been that it created mostly low-wage jobs, but it has since been undercut in this regard by China. Since joining the WORLD TRADE ORGANIZATION (WTO), China can export its goods to the United States on a more favorable basis. As a result, Mexico has been knocked by China from second to third place as an exporter to the United States (Canada is number one).[7]

President Felipe Calderón believes that the answer to these financial woes is a more vigorous application of neoliberal principles. He appointed a former IMF official to lead the budget office and implemented a number of economic reforms, including a continued opening to foreign trade and investment as well as the privatization of STATE-OWNED ENTERPRISES (with the notable exclusion of PEMEX, Mexico's state-run petroleum monopoly).[8] However, Mexico is still in the same rut as the United States. In Mexico, which once prided itself on having the lowest unemployment rates in Latin America, over 25 percent of the population is unemployed or underemployed. Recognizing this problem, Calderón campaigned as the "jobs president." He knows that he must show some progress on this front, since if the economy doesn't reverse its downward slide, it will mean big problems for everyone.[9]

Case Study: Peru

Since independence, Peru has struggled through fifty-year cycles of debt, dependence, and default.[10] In the nineteenth century its economy was based on the export of raw materials such as guano and nitrates, and it has been dependent on the sale of agricultural goods and mineral products for much of the past hundred years. Here is a country where the gap between rich and poor is only recently beginning to show signs of closing. As discussed in Chapter 5, a tiny ELITE of landowners and merchants have long controlled the country's wealth.

In the 1970s, prices for Peru's exports plummeted while its expenditures rose, and the country fell deeply into debt. Peru was in crisis. By the 1980s its creditors were demanding that the country pay half of all the hard currency it earned each year to service its debt of $16 billion. Unable to keep up with its payments, Peru fell $1 billion into arrears. In what has been described as a "brave but dumb" strategy, then-president Alan García declared a moratorium on servicing its debt, limiting payments to 10 percent of its export earnings. The international financial community responded by making Peru ineligible for credit. Peru became a pariah—desperate for cash, forced to dramatically cut imports, and living day to day. Economic trends in Peru in the 1980s were among the worst in Latin America—and the region as a whole was struggling with what is often called the "lost decade."[11]

By the end of García's term many Peruvians were frantic for another approach. Although as a presidential candidate Alberto Fujimori had campaigned against IMF reforms, after his inauguration he promised that he could get results from an ambitious program of neoliberalism. With the backing of business elites, the new president undertook one of the most radical privatizations in Latin America and opened Peru to foreign investment. The displacement of workers associated with the sale of STATE-OWNED ENTERPRISES, combined with drastic cuts in social spending, was likened to a form of shock therapy (so named for the invasive psychiatric procedure in which the patient is nearly killed in order to be saved). This policy became known in Peru as "Fujishock."

In this case the patient reacted by going into a deep recession. The sudden lack of government services, including sanitation and potable water, paved the way for a reappearance of cholera, a poverty-related disease that had been unknown in Peru since the 1800s. Some parts of Peru had never before known such economic distress. Yet because Fujimori was willing to push through the reforms, Peru was able to resuscitate its relationship with the IMF and obtain debt relief. By the mid-1990s foreign investment was up and the country was registering impressive growth rates. Most important for Peruvians, inflation was brought down to the lowest levels in forty years. Despite the hardship associated with Fujishock, the end to hyperinflation bought the president enormous goodwill.[12]

Yet events beyond Fujimori's control soon brought that brief period of recovery to a close. Growth remained stagnant until Fujimori was forced to step down in 2000. The campaign slogan of his successor, Alejandro Toledo, was "More Work," and this made sense, given that Peruvians suffered from extensive underemployment—nearly three-quarters of the population could find only part-time work. Toledo, a former economist for the WORLD BANK moved forward with IMF-sanctioned privatizations (today most mines are foreign-owned) and kept social spending low. Peru has successfully attracted foreign investment, but mostly in sectors such as mining and oil, which do not generate many jobs. While Toledo's fiscal conservatism was applauded in Washington, his policies were met with such violent protests that the new DEMOCRACY experienced its first governability crisis. Peru's highly mobilized citizenry was impatient for results, and the president was forced to call a state of emergency.

Toledo left the presidency in 2006 with his popularity ratings in the single digits. That year the long-discredited Alan García made a comeback. In what amounted to a major shift toward the right, García now embraced neoliberal reforms. He continued with Toledo's market-friendly policy of promoting foreign investment and ardently pursued a free trade agreement with the United States. Under the US-Peru Trade Promotion Act, which entered into force in 2009, trade and investment between the two countries has grown. The United States now buys more Peruvian exports than any other country. Meanwhile, Peru has also entered into trade deals with Canada and China, among others. Reborn a pragmatist, García cultivated a new beginning with the IMF; this made Peru's one of the most centrist of the governments in the region.[13]

The livelihoods of most Peruvians did not improve during Toledo's (or García's) tenure; however, in macroeconomic terms, the Peruvian economy was one of the most vibrant in the region, often characterized as thriving. Growth rates in Peru ranged from 4 to 9 percent per year during the 2000s, based largely on a growing Asian (especially Chinese) demand for its minerals and higher prices for gold, copper, tin, and other exports. The global financial crisis did take a toll (growth slowed to 0.9 percent in 2009), but as of late 2010 the forecasts were predicting growth to rebound to 5.5 percent.[14] The mining sector continued to dominate the economy, accounting for 63 percent of Peru's export revenues in 2007. This is a problem, though, because mining still doesn't produce enough jobs. In addition, any country so dependent on mineral extraction is prone to boom-bust cycles. Still, things were looking up, as Peru had cut its debt to almost half of what it had been ten years earlier. Inflation was down and the country's trade surplus was growing.[15]

Remarkably, growth over the past several years has translated into improvements in the incomes of more Peruvians; it has led to more jobs and Peru has actually cut its poverty rates from 50 percent to about 34 percent over the past decade. But much more still needs to be done to extend the benefits of this growth to a greater proportion of the population and to reduce poverty (Peru has double the poverty rate of its neighbor Chile).

Interestingly, the good economic news has not necessarily translated into an embrace of García's free trade policies.[16] Intent on maintaining Peru's title as one of the region's best economic performers, the government plans to open 70 percent of the Peruvian Amazon to business. Arguing that it is necessary to develop "idle land" in order to develop the country and create jobs, García's administration has begun boldly granting new oil and gas concessions to large (many of them foreign) corporations in territories long claimed by indigenous communities (and thus closed to such production). Although García is well liked abroad for his openness to free trade and friendliness to foreign investors, in Peru it is something of a different story. Toward the end of his first term (second presidency) in 2010, García had come out swinging, attempting to face down those who had criticized his economic policy as not only destructive to the environment, but also racist. The president's neoliberal policies have awakened a perhaps unprecedented wave of indigenous social activism, as we will see in Chapter 11.

Case Study: Nigeria

As the world's eighth largest exporter of oil, Nigeria would seem to be the envy of much of the world. However, Nigeria is one of the world's poorest countries. Seventy percent of the population lives below the official poverty line.[17] Oil didn't guarantee Mexico's development, and is often said to be a curse of sorts for Nigeria.

Part of the problem is that one Nigerian government after another has stolen a large portion of the hundreds of billions of dollars in revenue generated by oil. And what hasn't been stolen has often been misspent. Windfalls from the days when oil prices were high were wasted on white elephants. Initiated in 1979, the Ajaokuta steelworks was one of the biggest industrial projects in Africa. Costing more than $6 billion, it has never come into operation, and although there are now talks of resurrecting the beast, some analysts believe that it will require another $10 billion in investments and can never operate efficiently.[18]

Before all the blame goes to corrupt or incompetent policymakers, however, a word needs to be said about the role of MNCs in Nigeria, especially Shell Oil, the region's biggest operator, which carries on with little or no government oversight. The Niger Delta, site of most of the country's onshore petroleum and natural gas reserves, is an environmental basket case. Although it has received almost no international attention, it is said that the amount of oil spilled every year in Nigeria's wetlands for the past five decades makes the 2010 British Petroleum disaster in the Gulf of Mexico seem puny by comparison. Shell operates in more than a hundred countries, but 40 percent of all of its oil spills have been in Nigeria (and many have never been cleaned up).[19] While oil analysts chat excitedly about the shift of focus to offshore, deepwater development in Nigeria, the Niger Delta remains one of the country's poorest areas. Little of the wealth created by the extraction of approximately 2 million barrels of oil per day has been returned to its residents.[20]

Nigeria's rank on almost any level of human development is especially tragic given the country's tremendous potential. Its vast resources could provide a diversified economic base, its huge population could create an economy of scale. Its resilient small farmers have tenaciously hung on for years—even as the government has doggedly shifted its focus from agriculture to oil. Yet Nigeria is a classic monocultural economy. Approximately 95 percent of its foreign exchange is earned from the sale of petroleum and petroleum-based products, but the industry fails to serve or employ many Nigerians (it is estimated that as many as 60 percent of northern college graduates are unemployed).[21] Ironically, because of the state of disrepair of its refineries, Nigeria imports nearly 85 percent of its fuel needs.[22] Nigerian motorists routinely spend hours of their workdays waiting in some of the longest gas lines in the world.

In 1999 Nigerian citizens turned out at the polls hoping that a civilian-run government might be able to straighten out the country's economic mess. By the time he took office in May of that year, democratically elected president Olusegun Obasanjo found the treasury empty. In arrears in repayment of a nearly $30 billion debt that exceeded 75 percent of the country's GDP, Obasanjo came into office desperate for debt relief. Servicing the debt would account for more than 30 percent of the budget.

To pay it, Obasanjo attempted to raise revenues by quickly increasing Nigeria's output of oil and by attracting foreign investment. For example, Obasanjo pursued "Oil for Infrastructure" agreements with the Chinese, as a result of which Nigeria's trade with China grew from $3 billion (2006) to $7 billion (2008).[23] To please Western partners, he declared himself a neoliberal reformer. Within a year of Obasanjo's inauguration, Nigeria accepted an austerity plan that (among other things) meant cutting government subsidies of food, which resulted in higher prices for basics such as oil, rice, and flour. When fuel subsidies were cut in 2002, labor unions launched a general strike, to which police responded with tear gas and bullets. People could not afford basic necessities.[24] With so little money in pocket, few could pay the user fees introduced for public services, including education and healthcare.

And all of this just as Nigerians were expecting things to get better. Instead of a DEMOCRACY DIVIDEND, Nigerians felt the impact of the IMF adjustment: after more than a decade of democracy, life expectancy is forty-seven years; infant mortality has been reduced only slightly (and is still high), at 92 deaths per 1,000 live births (compared to 6 per 1,000 in the United States). It is estimated that 90 percent of Nigerians earn less than two dollars a day.[25] In 2003, just four years into the new democracy, the pressure Obasanjo was feeling from the IMF was matched by the heat he felt at home, and the president didn't have the stomach for it. Obasanjo went on a binge: the government spent $93 million on a space program and over $330 million on a new soccer stadium—more than it allocated to health or education.[26]

Such excessive spending could have jeopardized Nigeria's line of credit with the IMF. Yet, just in time, the windfall from skyrocketing oil prices enabled the government not only to pay down its debt, but also to negotiate historic programs of debt relief and receive debt write-offs totaling $30 billion.[27] A condition of this assistance was the adoption of more economic reforms recommended by the IMF. Since 2008, Nigerian governments have made many of these reforms, such as deregulating fuel prices and modernizing the banking system.

Although some of the money saved by the debt relief is expected to go toward meeting basic human needs, analysts expect that Nigeria will need a ten-year extension (from 2015 to 2025) in order to make substantial progress toward the Millennium Development Goals. There were hopes that Obasanjo's successors, Umaru Yar'Adua (until his untimely death in 2010) and Yar'Adua's vice president (now president), Goodluck Jonathan, would also move the country more purposefully toward goals such as building infrastructure, providing an adequate power supply, and enhancing agricultural production. But the country was paralyzed by Yar'Adua's long illness and questions regarding the transfer of power. For President Jonathan, the fracas over his candidacy for the April 2011 elections has proved debilitating. From 2007 to 2010, inactivity at all levels of government, a major employer and investor, was striking, having a palpable effect on the economy. During this period economic growth rates remained steady (mostly due to demand for oil), averaging 7 percent. However, the percentage of Nigerians living below the poverty line actually rose by 10 percent (to 70 percent of the population).[28] Meanwhile, ironically, Wall Street and other foreign investors remained bullish on Nigeria. As the first decade of its fourth try at democracy drew to a close, Goldman Sachs claimed that if Nigeria could continue what it started in 1999, within twenty years it could become one of the world's twenty leading economies.[29] Nigeria had a favorable credit rating and (in terms of macroeconomic indicators) was on solid footing. Was the average Nigerian any better off? Not yet, anyway.

Case Study: Zimbabwe

For the past few years Zimbabwe has held the dubious title of "Africa's fastest-shrinking economy." With its comparatively diverse base, Zimbabwe's economy should be better off than that of many other African countries. At independence it was relatively more industrialized than much of Africa, with its sugar refineries and textile industry. Although tobacco long dominated its exports, Zimbabwe also sells gold and other minerals on the world market. Until about a decade ago it was able not only to feed its population, but also to export its surplus foodstuffs. It once enjoyed a healthy tourist industry based around Victoria Falls, truly one of the wonders of the world. Most impressive, under President Robert Mugabe and the government of the

Zimbabwe African National Union–Patriotic Front (ZANU-PF), a liberation movement turned political party, Zimbabwe was making significant strides in human development with an antipoverty campaign as a priority. The new government invested
heavily in schools and healthcare, undoing the years of neglect that had been policy
under white minority rule. Such programs succeeded in attaining for Zimbabweans
one of the highest literacy rates on the continent.

However, deep in debt for many of the reasons mentioned in previous chapters
and needing to attract foreign investment and promote trade, the Mugabe government
had little choice but to accept the terms of a STRUCTURAL ADJUSTMENT PROGRAM
(SAP) in 1991. Because of the budget cuts required by the IMF, the government's
"Growth with Equity" program was reversed and conditions for the majority worsened. Two years in, the country was losing the impressive gains it had made in terms
of infant and child mortality and literacy rates. Per capita spending on public health
plummeted below levels seen in the 1980s—at a time when HIV/AIDS infected
about 20 percent of the adult population.[30] The rate of infection is lower now (approximately 15 percent), but this is largely because so many people have already
succumbed to the disease, what some have called a "die out."

In much of Zimbabwe the SAP came to stand for "Suffering for African People."[31] The government decided to back away from structural reform after 1998.
Growth rates hovered around zero. The annual income of the average Zimbabwean
is estimated to have dropped from $620 in 1998 to $437 in 1999.

Things have only gotten worse since then, although there is plenty of blame to
go around. Growth rates in 2008 were negative 18 percent. The currency was worthless, but the government kept printing money. It is estimated that 80 percent of the
population was living below the poverty line.[32] People found that they could not afford basic necessities such as cornmeal as inflation grew from 22 percent in 1995 to
80 percent in 2000 to 500 billion percent in 2008 (the highest rate on the planet).[33]
The Zimbabwean dollar became worthless (billion- and trillion-dollar notes were
used as confetti for the prime minister's inauguration in 2009). Those who managed
to find the money to pay higher prices routinely waited in long lines for gasoline,
kerosene, cooking oil, and even bread. Most worrisome is that hunger existed even
at harvest time. By 2009, nearly half the population needed food aid. Another quarter of the population had left the country. International aid groups were resorting to
halving rations and many Zimbabweans were eating one meal a day or less.[34] And
famine is something that many Zimbabweans had thought was a thing of the past.

The Mugabe government blames several years of drought and international sanctions for the country's economic shambles. The World Bank and Western donors
blame the Mugabe government's CORRUPTION and mismanagement for the country's
woes. In 1999, faced with upcoming parliamentary elections and sporadic riots over
shortages, Mugabe chose a course that many have described as self-defense. He appealed to the 70 percent of the population who live in rural areas, resurrecting the
long-neglected issue of land reform with his slogan "The Land Is the Economy, the
Economy Is the Land."

For over a century, land has been a central issue in Zimbabwean politics. Because
the vast majority of Zimbabweans earn their living from agriculture, it is also a key economic issue. As of mid-2002, white Zimbabweans composed 1 percent of the population. Yet more than two decades after independence, hundreds of thousands of blacks

were still on waiting lists for land while 4,500 whites still owned 70 percent of the country's best acreage. Make no mistake about it: land reform is an issue the government absolutely must deal with. Rather than confronting the issue of land reform, Mugabe adopted a more radical approach. In what his critics considered a thinly veiled attempt to save his political career, he urged the seizure of white farms without compensation.[35]

The effect on the economy was clear. By 2006, harvests were half of what they were when the 2000 land reform began. The government admitted that much of the land had fallen into disuse because of the new farmers' lack of expertise, capital, and equipment.[36] Not only did the confiscation of large farms mean the loss of jobs for hundreds of thousands of farm laborers, but business confidence was in tatters, investors were scared off, and tourism ground to a halt. Zimbabwe's healthcare system, which had once been one of Africa's best, collapsed. Maternal mortality quadrupled from 1990 to 2007, and whereas in 1994 over 80 percent of Zimbabwe's children were on schedule with their vaccinations, by 2007 only 53 percent were up-to-date with their shots. The government was completely unable to cope with a cholera outbreak that sickened nearly 100,000 and killed over 4,000 in 2008–2009. In sum, the 2000s amounted to a headlong fall into the abyss; Zimbabwe, which was once second only to South Africa in terms of the size of its economy, was at the end of the decade the smallest economy in the region.[37]

In 2007, Zimbabwe's economy was said to be suffering from the worst crisis of any country in peacetime. As a snapshot of how bad it was for the average Zimbabwean, life expectancy had dropped from sixty-one years two decades earlier to thirty-seven—the lowest in the world. In 2009, when a unity government was formed between Mugabe's ZANU-PF and the Movement for Democratic Change (MDC), the economy began to turn around. Life expectancy increased to forty-seven years. For the first time in nearly a decade, economic growth rates crept up to 5.7 percent (and were projected to continue slowly rising in 2010).[38] And inflation finally began to fall (to a much more manageable 3.6 percent by 2010) as the government abandoned the Zimbabwean dollar in favor of the US dollar and other, more stable currencies.[39] Foreign investment began to trickle in, bank deposits tripled, and civil servants once again began to receive their paychecks.[40] By early 2011, most Zimbabweans hadn't yet seen much change in their living conditions—with 95 percent of the adult population unemployed and children dropping out of school because their parents could not afford the $36 in fees—but things appeared to be finally heading in the right direction.

Case Study: Iran

Leaders of the Islamic Republic of Iran have long struggled with many issues related to political economy. The current economic system combines central planning, state ownership of key industries (oil, textile, and automotive companies), village farming, and the rise of small-scale private industries to produce a mixed and challenged result. Since the 1990s the country's financial problems have intensified—impacted by domestic mismanagement and external sanctions. Iran's openings to the West, especially in its attempts to exploit its chief export, oil, remain a tricky balancing act between national interest and international condemnation (Iran has faced sanctions for both human rights abuses and its nuclear program). Leaders have long tried to balance economic well-being, self-sufficiency, and the role of the postrevolutionary government in providing for the Iranian people. The founder of the Islamic state and first Supreme Leader, Ayatollah Ruhollah Khomeini, famously promised, "We will build real estate, make water and power free, and make buses free." This revolutionary pledge, among others, has yet to be realized.[41]

One of the central issues facing Iran is its economic dependence on Western countries, especially through the preeminence of oil in Iran's political economy. Sometimes referred to as "black gold," oil has dominated all aspects of life in Iran since its discovery in the early 1900s—Iran possesses approximately 10 percent of the world's crude oil reserves and is second to Russia in natural gas. For many years, Iran's IDENTITY in the world economic system was as a provider of cheap oil and a consumer of Western goods and services. Economic self-sufficiency was a goal elucidated by the post-1979 leadership, largely in vain. Despite these concerns, which prompted attempts to diversify, Iran continues to be plagued by export dependence and the fluctuations that accompany it. At times this has worked in Iran's favor, such as in the early 1970s and mid-1990s, but at other times, when oil prices are low, this reliance has caused many problems. For example, from 1977 to 1989 the economy hit a downturn and income per capita dropped nearly 45 percent.[42] Profits from oil keep the government afloat—receipts from oil and gas exports constitute 70 percent of the government's fiscal budget.[43] The heightened demand for oil within China and India (China imports approximately 8 percent of its oil from Iran, and India nearly 15 percent of its crude oil) is greasing many areas of the economic picture.

Iran's economy was hobbled by its war with Iraq in the 1980s, and the painful economic reconstruction that followed. Natural disasters (the country is very prone to earthquakes, with small tremors being felt almost daily), combined with the high numbers of refugees fleeing to Iran from Afghanistan and Iraq, have stretched the economy to its limits. Additionally, attempts to produce growth through rapid industrialization and virtually unlimited urbanization have wreaked havoc on the Iranian natural environment, which is only belatedly receiving attention.

As an Islamic state, Iran has attempted to integrate the teachings of the Quran into all aspects of life, including the financial sector. Iran and Sudan have been the most comprehensive in their incorporation of an Islamic banking system, which is interest-free, although other countries, including Turkey, Malaysia, Afghanistan, Pakistan, and Kuwait, offer Islamic banks as an option to conventional, interest-bearing banks. Even though Islamic banks avoid traditional interest calculations because they are viewed to be exploitative, other profit arrangements, based more on future profits of borrowers, are used in many Islamic banks throughout the world.[44] The national currency, the rial, is now fully convertible (even though analysts contend it is grossly overvalued), and the Tehran Stock Exchange, which opened in 1967, trades shares of over 300 companies.

Unemployment is high (officially reported at nearly 12 percent, although it is likely much higher), and the gap between the rich and the poor is growing. Attempts to privatize nationally owned companies and corporations threaten to further increase unemployment, and plans to decrease state subsidies on critical items, including basic foods (flour, sugar, eggs), medical goods, gasoline, and utilities, are met with fear and sometimes violence. Poverty remains endemic for nearly a fifth of the population. While women are increasingly integrated into the work force, they tend to have the strongest presence in fields such as education and healthcare, and their employment can be curtailed by the wishes of their husbands.

Economic woes have played right into POPULIST leader Mahmoud Ahmadine-jad's campaigns for president, and he continues to frame himself as a champion of the poor, presenting even the end of state subsidies as part of his plan for "economic justice" so that the government may provide more financial assistance to assist the poor in the face of steep price increases.[45] The regime has shown a heavy hand in response to any unrest generated by economic malaise—after gasoline rationing was introduced in 2007, gas stations were burned to the ground and the government faced widespread protests. The challenges are even more intense in urban areas, where social services for a growing population are already strained, and where families have incomes too high for state support yet not high enough to weather significant increases. Some view the Iranian economy as "strait-jacketed."[46] Ahmadinejad receives much of the blame—in fact, by June 2006 the president had mismanaged the economy so poorly (despite a boom in world oil prices) that fifty prominent Iranian economists attacked him in an open letter.[47] Nationalist populism, economic mismanagement, and a tense international climate converge to create a complex, yet increasingly bleak, economic picture for the Islamic Republic.

Case Study: Turkey

Turkey is a state rich in natural resources. One of the most productive of these resources is its geography; ancient Anatolia was a main crossroad between East and West on the famed Silk Road between Xi'an (in China) and Rome. Yet its location at this intersection of East and West, and its fragile relations with neighboring countries, pose both challenges and opportunities to the Turkish people today. Demonstrative of the vulnerabilities of many non-Western economies that rely on export-oriented growth, Turkey's economy took a hit during the UNITED NATIONS embargo against Iraq (a major export market for Turkish businesses), the war in Bosnia, and the currency devaluation throughout Asia and in the Russian Federation. Each of these events, occurring outside Turkey's borders, signify some of the more problematic aspects of its attempts at global INTEGRATION, and help explain Ankara's efforts to diversify its economic ties beyond the United States and other major powers.

The Turkish economy, the sixteenth largest in the world, has much dynamism, combining both modern industry and traditional crafts. It also has a history of mingling state control with private enterprise. State intervention in the economy was largely curtailed in the 1980s, except for the industrial sector. Unlike Iran, for example, Turkey's primary export of textiles and clothing remains under private rather than governmental control. Yet this vitality has been weakened, as all types of disasters have hit home in Turkey as well, including natural, political, and economic crises. For example, the devastating earthquake of 1999, which claimed over 17,000 lives, struck the region that accounts for over 35 percent of the state's GDP, just when leaders of the country were negotiating a $5 billion loan from the IMF. Because of the government's delayed response to the crisis—a natural disaster exacerbated by shoddily constructed apartment buildings that were greased with corrupt payoffs—public confidence in the government plunged.

Since the end of World War II, Turkey's leaders have increasingly looked to the West for economic markets and trade. Much of this "glance West" has surrounded Turkey's attempts to become a member of the European Union (EU), a complicated effort that will be discussed in later chapters. Turkey became an associate economic member of the EU's precursor, the European Community, in 1963, and the arduous work toward full membership continues. A combination of domestic human rights concerns (especially related to Turkey's treatment of the restive Kurdish population) and tensions over EU member Cyprus (which Turkey invaded in 1974 and whose northern region Turkey continues to partially occupy) help explain this dichotomy of economic ties without political acceptance. Adding insult to injury, former French president Valéry Giscard d'Estaing publicly stated that, in his opinion, inviting Turkey to join the EU would mean "the end of Europe."[48] He verbalized what many in Turkey have long believed—that the EU is a "Christian club" that is unlikely to welcome them with open arms. France and Germany have even argued that Turkey should not obtain full membership even if it does fulfill all the criteria set forth. As one analyst stated, Turkey's "long journey to the gates of Europe has slowed to a crawl."[49] Formal accession talks began in October 2005, and it is unlikely that Turkey could complete the full accession process before 2020. The lack of certainty about whether Turkey will actually be accepted as a full member of the EU is tremendously curbing any EU enthusiasm within the country, despite a sense of urgency among leading politicians.

As we have seen with other countries in the non-Western world, economic gains are often made while exacting a great toll on the agricultural sector—such is the case in Turkey as well. Roughly 30 percent of the labor force is focused on agriculture, and small farmers face increased competition from transnational corporations and other large conglomerates as they endure increased costs while receiving less return from sales. Struggles with inadequate investment in technology and manufacturing, unceasing unemployment, and widespread income disparity have become the norm rather than the exception. High unemployment rates, hovering around 14 percent, combined with underemployment of approximately 4 percent, present consistent challenges. Youth unemployment, a significant measure given the fact that nearly half of the Turkish population is under the age of thirty, is over 20 percent. Even though inflation has been tamed in recent years, hitting a thirty-four-year low of 6.5 percent in 2009, it remains a concern.

The IMF and the World Bank have been key players in Turkey's economic story, demanding the privatization of telephone, airline, and power services, as well as improvements to the famously corrupt and moribund banking system. In addition to the threat of widespread unemployment from the restructuring of state-owned companies, these painful demands risk endangering already weak political coalitions. Yet a transformation is occurring. Not that long ago, Turkey was listed by these institutions as one of the "world's most perilous developed economies."[50] Once home to the world's highest denomination of currency, the 20 million–lira note, Turkey simply removed six zeros from all its currency bills to more accurately reflect their value (and reduce the millions required to take a taxi across town).[51] Now, Prime Minister Recep Tayyip Erdogan is widely given credit for transforming Turkey "from a financial basket case to a star emerging market."[52] As this emergence deepens, there is the possibility of both great promise and substantial peril as economic issues interface with identity, regional politics, and culture in this dynamic state.

Case Study: China

It is perhaps ironic that a state that once prided itself on autarky and self-sufficiency (in the 1950s and 1960s) is now one of the most rapidly growing and interconnected economies in the world. Yet some say, "All we really know about the Chinese financial system is that it's big and growing and filled with ugly stuff like tons of bad loans in government-owned banks and heavy government ownership of the economy."[53] Bookies would have a hard time determining the odds of China's future economic situation. Part of what makes China's case unique is the dizzy pace of its change. At this juncture, China's economic ties, including very large aid and investment packages to states in the Middle East and Africa, and its huge financial investments in South America, are raising eyebrows and concern. As China has emerged from the global financial crisis arguably better than any other country, some are talking of an emerging "Beijing Consensus" (state-ordained economic progress, propped up by low wages and subsidies and undervalued currency, with restrictions on civil liberties) to rival the neoliberal, laissez-faire orthodoxy of the Washington Consensus.

Because of the glitzy images of China's hyperdeveloped big cities and reports of growing consumer comforts, many students are surprised to hear of China's inclusion in a book on third world affairs. Yet China's economic achievements over the past three decades, as huge as they are, have been uneven, and continued economic prosperity is hardly a certainty. The comfortable existence of many urban Chinese in prosperous industries including real estate, computer technology, and financing is not replicated by the vast majority of Chinese citizens. Even beyond the gap between haves and have-nots is the fundamental question of sustainability: How long can Beijing manage this pace of growth and expansion? As one analyst warned, "An economic slowdown of some sort is close to certain for China."[54]

China's leaders have adopted multiple economic models, some disastrous and some successful. In the late 1950s, Mao Zedong launched the so-called Great Leap Forward as a way to economically modernize the country and catch up with the West. Through intense agricultural and industrial programs that included encouraging farmers to construct "backyard burners" in their fields in order to melt down pots and pans to make steel, Mao proclaimed that the Chinese people could surpass Western production totals in less than fifteen years. The results were disastrous: as many as 20 million people are believed to have died of starvation and terror because of the misguided agricultural and ideological policies of the period—and recent archival research estimates this total could be as high as 45 million.[55] The man to follow Mao, Deng Xiaoping, took economic growth and prosperity as his primary goal. Touting such non-Marxist phrases as "to get rich is glorious" and "it is all right for some to get rich first," Deng launched a new economic revolution of sorts in the 1980s—it is his policies that prepped the People's Republic for its reemergence at the onset of the twenty-first century. Ordinary people could start up their own companies and trade their agricultural products with local governments, and even foreign firms such as Atlanta-based Coca-Cola were invited to produce, market, and sell their products on the mainland.

As we discussed throughout the preceding chapter, compared to the recent performance of other non-Western countries, China is an anomaly. Today, even though hundreds of millions of Chinese have been moved out of poverty since 1978, the stark differences between regions of the country can be astonishing. Although perhaps hyperbolic, a report examining two of China's major cities (Beijing and Tianjin), and the "belt of poverty" that surrounds them, described the picture as "European cities with an African countryside."[56]

The Chinese economic situation today is sprinkled with many contrasts. On the one hand, China is second to the United States in terms of the numbers of billionaires in the country (64 out of approximately 1,000 in the world).[57] This includes half of the world's fourteen self-made female billionaires (noninherited wealth).[58] Chinese banks were once prototypes of the most cumbersome bureaucratic practices around, but today four of the world's ten biggest banks (by market value) are Chinese, even though they remain laden with bad debts.[59] The country is awash with entrepreneurial startups, especially in fields such as consumer goods and real estate. Yet the same middle-class citizens who flocked to the stock market in the 2000s now find that they cannot afford to purchase an apartment, and poorer Chinese pay nearly 50 percent of their family income for food. Inflation presents an enormous hurdle to continued economic growth and development. Medical costs—even for wealthy urbanites—are spiraling, and the healthcare sector remains in a bizarre state of "partial reform" (most prices, including for expensive surgical procedures, are set by the market, while prescription medicines remain government-regulated), and the banking system, laden with poorly performing loans and muddied TRANSPARENCY at best, is in sore need of wholesale repair. Since China became a World Trade Organization member in 2001, its agricultural sector has been exposed to steep global competition. It was not a surprise when, during the 2010 meetings of the Communist Party Congress, leaders endorsed an "inclusive growth" model that highlights the need to balance development across different geographic regions as well as the different sectors of society, even if that means (or requires) taming the country's rapid growth rates.

Perhaps the most concerning impact of these economic difficulties, most certainly from Beijing's view, is the possibility of unrest in response to economic difficulties. The widening gap between rich and poor is producing a possible cauldron for social unrest over increasing food and housing prices. Strikes and work stoppages are increasingly common, even if the state-controlled media are limited in their appetite for covering these events. In what has been dubbed the "wage contagion" by the *New York Times,* workers at Honda plants in the south forced closures in order to negotiate higher wages and better working conditions.[60] As word of the strikes spread, Tianjin plants faced paralyzed production as well. Widely publicized suicides at Taiwanese-owned Foxconn plants (the world's largest manufacturer of electronics) brought attention to abhorrent conditions and worker strife in the enormous gated compounds that have been used to lure rural workers to cities. The "Beijing Consensus" includes limited political engagement, which is increasingly being tested as calls for independent labor unions, officially forbidden in the People's Republic, grow louder.

Pressures to revalue the Chinese currency, as discussed in Chapter 7, continue, and are likely to color China's bilateral relations with major world economies for years to come. Yet most analysts, Chinese and Western alike, argue that in order for China to continue its economic gains of the past two decades, the government will need to stimulate its own domestic consumption of products rather than remaining reliant on exports. The Chinese economy has grown by exporting inexpensive items around the world (exports make up approximately one-third of the country's GDP), but manufacturers are already relocating to Vietnam, Cambodia, and elsewhere in response to the increased wages in China. Demographically, China is facing a dwindling labor supply of sixteen- to twenty-four-year-olds, the age bracket that once packed factories and fueled the country's export-driven success. Beijing is taking efforts to spark domestic consumption, including increasing pensions and unemployment checks and providing subsidies for major investments such as education, homes, and durable goods. There are some signs that the campaigns are working: in 2009 the number of automobiles sold in China surpassed the number sold in the United States for the first time ever. It's unclear how far this trend may go: as a culture, the Chinese remain frugal (credit cards remain a rarity, for example).

No longer can Chinese leaders entertain thoughts of self-sufficiency. In fact, projections of China's future growth patterns fare prominently in World Bank estimates of global economic health.[61] China's economic achievements in the past three decades have been huge, yet the gains may be more tentative than not. A popular saying captures some of the dynamic: "The economists are never right; businessmen have always been right; and the government is sometimes right."[62] As this dynamic continues to unfold among these three sets of players, "getting it right" may become an elusive goal.

Case Study: Indonesia

Beginning in the early 1990s, Indonesia was hailed as one of the successful "Little Tigers" of Southeast Asia. Although there was a period when it seemed the tiger would fall, Indonesia today is once again hailed as a success. Some analysts have even suggested that a second "I" be added to the acronym "BRIC" (Brazil, Russia, India and China) to include the state with the world's largest Islamic population.

Indonesia has long been searching for a viable economic model that fits the needs and resources of its people. Even after its hard-fought political independence from the Dutch, the Indonesian economy continued its dependence on primary crops introduced by the Netherlands (namely pepper, coffee, rubber, and sugar). Under the so-called Guided Economy of 1959–1965, Sukarno nationalized all plantations—a move that led to widespread stagnation and capital flight. The president and his economic cronies concentrated on prestige projects, paying scant attention to day-to-day management of financial matters. Inflation and poverty were widespread after the government defaulted on its foreign debt and foreign assistance ended. Indonesia's second president, Suharto, attempted to turn the economy around, especially by mending ties with other countries. As a staunch anticommunist (who came to power under the guise of overthrowing a communist plot in 1965), Suharto received much aid from Western countries. His model of economic development was a familiar one in Asia: promote industrial and business growth under the tutelage of government sponsorship and support, with political control to limit unionization and dissent.

After Indonesia's oil boom, Suharto began to shy away from the so-called Berkeley Mafia free market advice of the 1960s (Indonesia's own version of the Washington Consensus). Throughout the 1970s the president pursued increasingly restrictive trade and investment policies, favoring the steel, shipbuilding, and aircraft industries. The oil collapse in 1985 and 1986 wreaked havoc throughout the country as prices fell below $10 per barrel; in response, returning to "Mafia" advice, Indonesia increased its exports of textiles, clothing, footwear, and wood. This system was marred with corruption: contracts were traded for regime support, and the families of high-profile politicians did famously well. The Suharto family, believed to have amassed a family fortune totaling $15–35 billion, held a monopoly over the control of some spices, including cloves, and other prosperous domestic industries, such as the processing of citrus fruit. Because of back-scratching financial arrangements, few cautioned against (or even noticed) trends in poor loans, increases in short-term external debt, and other ill-conceived projects, including Suharto's children's scheme to build a "national car," which was later abandoned.[63]

The gains of the 1990s came to a screeching halt as the crisis of 1997 hit—no Asian country fared worse than Indonesia. The economy contracted nearly 14 percent in 1998. Inflation topped 65 percent and the national currency lost 70 percent of its value, producing what the World Bank referred to as one of the most dramatic reversals of fortune ever. In January 1998, Indonesia's rupiah was labeled the world's worst-performing currency. Today, many Indonesians look to the Chinese model of state-supported economic growth, the so-called Beijing Consensus, as an apt replacement for the neoliberal Washington Consensus, which many blame for the extreme economic crises of this period.[64]

After nearly a decade of political instability, President Susilo Bambang Yudhoyono (elected in 2004, reelected to a second five-year term in 2009) has attempted to promote growth and employment while at the same time addressing the challenges of poverty. He has achieved much success, placing Southeast Asia's largest economy in a strong position. Indonesia emerged from the Global Recession in a relatively strong position, thanks to increased domestic consumption, strong investment, and exports. One part of this success can be tied to Indonesia's wealth of natural resources, including oil. A member of the Organization of Petroleum Exporting Countries (OPEC) from 1962 until 2008, the country has been a net importer of oil since 2004. Indonesia withdrew from the cartel after it consistently struggled to meet production quotas. Corruption challenges and local revenue-sharing deals have made the country less attractive to foreign oil giants, curtailing the exploration for untapped petroleum reserves. But Indonesia has cornered the market for palm oil (a major source of revenue during its colonial period as well), which is a common ingredient in many processed foods because it is currently cheaper than other vegetable oils; it is now the world's largest producer and, together with Malaysia, commands 90 percent of the global market for this high-demand oil.[65]

In subsequent chapters we will discuss Indonesia's regional discord. Although much of this strife is highlighted by cultural and religious differences, there are clear economic components to Indonesia's regional battles as well: the restive areas of Aceh and northern Sulawesi have long been economically oriented to the outside world, and when economic constriction hits, these regions tend to fare the worst. The problems aren't always human-made. Aceh was nearly leveled following the 2004 tsunami in the Indian Ocean—some coastal villages were nearly decimated, and the Asian Development Bank estimates that 44 percent of the people in Aceh lost their livelihood. Additionally, disparities in economic well-being between Indonesia's myriad ethnic groups are more pronounced compared to the relatively prosperous ethnic Chinese community—a group that is consistently targeted for attack when the economic situation sours. As we see in so many other situations, a debilitating economic environment tends to exacerbate other conflicts into crisis.

Similar to many of our country CASE STUDIES, Indonesia was rocked by the demands of lending institutions to make dramatic changes. IMF conditions for the $45 million aid package in 1998 included a requirement to redirect funds away from assistance programs and social spending, and sparked a fury of unrest throughout the country. Initial runs on banks led to street riots. Demonstrations against Suharto, who was viewed as impotent in the face of outsider demands, eventually toppled the longtime president. In the post-Suharto period, Indonesia has experienced some debt forgiveness (including a $3 billion restructuring plan following the 2004 tsunami), and a gradual restoration of assistance programs. Indonesia faced tremendous struggles making its debt payments throughout the middle to late 1990s, yet achieved significant progress by 2009, when it became the only country in the GROUP OF 20 (G-20) to reduce its public debt-to-GDP ratio.[66] Corruption and poor governance, though, have curtailed monies from multilateral institutions (especially the World Bank and the Asian Development Bank) as well as from individual governments, and millions of Indonesians remain under the poverty line. Yet in 2010 the IMF characterized the Indonesian economy as "strong with room for improvements."[67] If this course continues, the Sumatran Tiger may once again demonstrate its prowess.

Now It's Your Turn

Perhaps as the neoliberals tell us, the experience of a handful of countries should be a lesson to all the rest. However, after two decades of sacrifice and deteriorating conditions for the majority, is it right for developed countries to continue to insist that the neoliberal model is the only feasible path to development? Are neoliberals correct about TINA—is there really no alternative?

Should the leaders of less developed countries simply press for a more flexible approach to further integration into the INTERNATIONAL ECONOMIC SYSTEM as it currently exists? Will the managers of the system (Western donors and the international organizations they control) allow alternative paths to be forged? Or can a combination of strategies that utilize indigenous experience and culture create a system more beneficial for all? What does "independence" mean in a globalized world economy?

PART THREE

Politics and Political Change

Ideas are among the most powerful forces we possess. All people hold opinions and viewpoints about the world around them. Should income be equally distributed? Should political leaders provide moral and religious guidance? How should citizens respond to perceived CORRUPTION and abuse of power? Thoughts about authority, society, gender relations, economic resources, the environment, and other values help shape the general perspectives that people hold about their role in the world. Ideas about the way things should be often impel people into action, sometimes in violent ways, and this will be the subject of the chapters that follow.

Also in this part of the book we will consider the impact of ideas and their translation into action in terms of the "third wave" of democratization, which hit much of the world toward the end of the COLD WAR. (The "first wave" of DEMOCRATIC TRANSITIONS is commonly identified with the expansion of democracy in the United States and Western Europe [1820s–1926]. The "second wave" [1945–1962] is associated with independence and the experimentation with democracy in much of Asia and Africa.) As we will see, the result for governments around the world has been a crisis of sorts. We will explore the various ways in which different governments have handled this crisis. In doing this we will consider, implicitly at least, the chances for DEMOCRACY in the third world, the odds of which vary by country. While several countries do not appear to be headed in the direction of Western-style democracy at all, there are some well-established democracies in the third world. On the other hand, some fragile democracies have already broken down. Many countries are at varying stages in the process of reform. Others just appear to be making this transition, as their democratization is more "virtual" than real. In more than a few cases POLITICAL LIBERALIZATION has been precluded by instability, due to fundamental problems such as disagreements concerning whether the state should continue to exist intact. In most but not all cases, carefully crafted negotiations, pacts, and other agreements have at least temporarily resolved some problems. But even when contested SOVEREIGNTY is not an issue, both democratic and nondemocratic governments struggle to grapple with other demands. Any new democracy faces a host of challenges. In the chapters that follow, we will discuss these challenges and assess the nature of political transitions in the third world.

191

10

From Ideas to Action:
The Power of Civil Society

Sometimes decades pass and nothing happens; and then sometimes weeks
pass and decades happen. —*attributed to Vladimir Lenin*

In this chapter we explore a range of perspectives held by ordinary citizens, activists,
and leaders. These viewpoints derive from many sources, including history (both
ancient and recent), practical experiences of daily life and policy, and leadership
cues and demands. Additionally, worldviews are framed by a combination of more
seemingly subtle influences, as varied as educational systems, entertainment opportunities and institutions, and basic information sources that are made available to
the public. We examine belief systems that both unite and divide people, and focus
on ideas as sources of conflict and cooperation. Passion is a major part of the story.
Yet our emphasis goes beyond simply the beliefs that people hold: we examine the
forums in which these views are expressed, the ways that other groups attempt to curtail people's ability to express opinions, and how crafty activists subvert limits on expression.

Ideas merge theoretical, often-fuzzy concepts of the way the world "should be"
with the necessarily concrete actions that people take on a day-to-day basis to try to
implement their visions. The sheer multiplicity of ideas invites controversy: When
one person's or group's ideas conflict with those of others, how can these differences be reconciled? Why do some people's ideas seem to count, at least in the public realm, more than those of others, and how is this negotiated (or not)? We often
think of leaders as holding a monopoly on creating the ideas that "count," but this is
certainly not always the case. When groups of people begin to identify with a value
or idea system different from that of their leaders, they may organize and challenge
the status quo. Sometimes they succeed, and sometimes their efforts result in painful
failure.

Ideologies
Ideas that are free-floating, unattached to a more general perspective or value system, are not very likely to have tremendous impact. Yet when connections between

sets of values and perspectives are recognized as interconnected, and when these views impel people to action, they literally have a force that may change the world.

When people share a similar set of ideas linked to programs for action, we refer to this idea set as an IDEOLOGY, literally the "science of ideas," although such beliefs are hardly described with scientific precision. At their most fundamental level, ideologies are sets of ideas that describe the world or current state of affairs, help people understand their role within society, and arouse people to take an action, either to preserve or to change the existing situation. Ideologies consist of loosely connected systems of ideas: few traditions propose a strict laundry list of beliefs one must hold in order to subscribe to a given ideology. Rather, people notice common tendencies in beliefs, and often unite together with others who share similar perspectives.

Ideologies attempt to simplify complex problems and point toward potential solutions. They tend to be the foundation of most policies and actions, even if they are not identified as such. Most of the major systems of ideas that have been at the forefront of the non-Western world were formulated in response to experiences with colonialism and dependence, especially the economic struggle to survive. Leaders and ordinary citizens alike turn to ideologies to help them cope with civil unrest, crushing poverty, and international humiliation. Ideologies often provide deceptively clear-cut answers to complicated realities, especially during times of instability. Frequently, groups of people who share an ideological worldview get together to form a political party as a way to implement the ideas that they feel are important. Yet while political parties appear and disappear, and quite often adopt varying and misleading names, political ideologies endure.

Common in discussions about ideologies are the terms "conservative" and "liberal." These concepts represent two major schools of ideological thought. They are relative terms, meaning that what is seen as conservative in one country or social situation might not be so seen in another. Liberalism, which developed throughout European societies in the early 1800s, is often considered the first coherent political ideology. Liberals emphasize the freedom of the individual, limits on governmental interference, and the equality of all human beings. The idea that all people possess inalienable rights to life, liberty, and the pursuit of property, for example, is a classical liberal idea derived from the writings of John Locke. Liberals hold optimistic beliefs about what individuals and groups can achieve, and they often fight for progressive (forward-moving) changes.

Because of liberalism's high value on freedom, this ideology had a tremendous impact on the wars of liberation discussed in Chapter 4. If all people are created equal, as liberalism contends, then individuals should be able to rule themselves, rather than having decisions made for them by colonial leaders in a faraway land. Liberal beliefs encouraged the fight for self-governing peoples who had been subjugated to foreign rule, some for centuries. This movement was particularly pronounced in the post–World War II environment. The outcome of many of these wars of national liberation, however, was the perpetuation of political control and limits on freedom. Liberalism also has influenced the desire by some ethnic groups to pursue their own homeland, often distinct from the government in which they live. We discuss these ethnonationalists in Chapter 12. Yet the desire for cultural representation and self-expression does not always lead to the fight for a new STATE. Owing to the influence of liberalism, some ethnic groups have staked a claim to greater public expression of their culture and ways of life, achieving rights to use their native language, educate their children about their history and culture in public schools, and demand greater representation in public life.

Liberal ideas have also been responsible for many revolutions throughout the world, especially popular movements to overthrow monarchies, dynasties, and other forms of hereditary rule that precluded individuals from power. Some liberal revolutions attempted to redistribute land and economic resources that had been taken away from people. One example is found in President Benito Juarez's La Reforma program in Mexico in the mid-1800s, which stripped the Catholic Church of much of its property and power and formally granted civil rights to indigenous peoples. Juarez's liberal program was also popular for its staunch resistance to French invaders. Other liberal movements fought to bring voting rights and other participatory freedoms to groups, including women, minorities, and youth. Liberal proponents today in the non-Western world attempt to advance greater respect for human rights and individual freedoms, and they often lead the vocal charge toward democratic institutions. Fundamentally, liberals agree that the power of government needs to be limited, although they disagree over the fine lines of state involvement, especially in the realm of economics.

If liberals agree that governmental power should be limited and that individuals should have a say in decisions that are made about their lives, there is disagreement about matters of degree. Debates about the role of government in people's lives have led to two major types of liberals. One group, often called positive liberals, arguing that government ought to shoulder some level of responsibility for people's lives, calls for diminishing the inequality among groups, fostering greater participation, and in general promoting the well-being of citizens. Positive liberals are often the strongest supporters of welfare-state policies, including childcare, healthcare, education, unemployment insurance, and pensions. People often assume that welfare policies are designed only for the needy in society, but actually many welfare programs, including public education and public pensions, are distributed to all citizens, irrespective of need, and are present in most states of the world. In contrast, negative liberals believe that there should be minimal government involvement in the economy, arguing that the market, regulated only by the forces of supply and demand, should be allowed to operate freely. This group argues that government involvement often has the unintended consequence of limiting individual freedom by creating patterns of dependence and perpetuating cycles of poverty. These debates can become quite heated. Yet in the non-Western world, the degree of governmental assistance is often framed not by ideological but rather by economic concerns.

Ideas rarely exist in a vacuum. They often are formulated, expressed, and modified in response to other views of the world. This explains the development of the other major school of thought, conservatism. Conservatives are known for attempting to preserve the status quo, and sometimes for encouraging a return to values and traditions of the past. As conservatism began to develop, it challenged each of the major premises of the liberal way of viewing the world.

Traditional conservatives emphasize an organic view of society, in which the needs of the whole society, the so-called social fabric, are more important than individual freedom. In contrast to the liberals' emphasis on the equality of all people, conservatives emphasize that every person is born with natural inequalities, thereby contradicting the liberal notion of the fundamental equality of all people. Conserva-

Figure 10.1 Do All Muslims Agree?

At the turn of the twenty-first century, followers of the Muslim faith were second in number only to Christians. While estimates vary, most agree that Muslims compose nearly 25 percent of the world's population—it is the fastest-growing faith tradition in the world.[1] With so many adherents, it is logical to assume that there are varying levels of agreement and disagreement among the Muslim faithful. The biggest source of lasting division originated in a succession struggle launched after the prophet Mohammed's death in 632. Today, the majority of Muslims, approximately 90 percent, characterize themselves as Sunni Muslims. The name "Sunni" derives from Sunna, meaning "the tradition of the prophet Mohammed." The primary schism is Shia Islam, meaning the "Party of Ali."

Upon Mohammed's death in 632, his cousin and son-in-law, Ali, claimed to be the leader of all Muslims. But most believers followed Abu Bakr, who was reputed to be the first outside Mohammed's family to convert to Islam. Abu Bakr became the first of the four caliphs, or successors, in the Sunni tradition. Twenty-three years after Mohammed's death, Ali was named the caliph. His rise to leadership was controversial and not recognized by many. Syria's leader, among others, refused to recognize Ali, who ruled from Kufah, Iraq, facing much dissension.

A series of succession crises, including the murder and torture of disputed leaders, led to the creation of Shia Islam, the first major schism within Islam. Sunnis today continue to outnumber Shiites, although Iran, Iraq, Azerbaijan, and Bahrain are majority-Shiite states. The Shiites replaced the caliphate with imams, claiming that their leadership was hereditary from Mohammed. After the schism, Shiites were persecuted and acted in secret, during which time they devised their own teachings on the implementation of the word of Mohammed. One change was the designation of an authoritative figure to interpret divine will, rather than placing the onus on the community of believers, as Sunnis taught.[2] The Shiites believed that imams, as religious leaders, possessed knowledge of which the masses were incapable. This view complicated the challenges of rival successors, since imams were viewed as infallible leaders. Although most Turks are Sunnis, the Shiite minority in Turkey is known as Alvis.

The major Shia sect is the "Twelvers," named for the twelve imams following Mohammed. Twelver Shia Islam is the state religion in Iran. Developed in the sixteenth century, this sect highlights the twelve legitimate imams, beginning with Ali and ending with the twelfth or "hidden" imam, who went into concealment in 941 but who will reappear some day in the future to finish the triumph of Shia Islam. Between the sixteenth and the eighteenth centuries, Twelver Shia Islam merged with Persian tradition, forging a tight bond with the development of Iranian identity and nationalism.[3]

The Iraq War has had a lasting impact on Shiite communities, even though Shiites, like their Sunni counterparts, remain a greatly diverse and amorphous sect who are not united under a single leader. As Vali Nasr, author of *The Shia Revival,* argues, "The Middle East that will emerge from the crucible of the Iraq war may not be more democratic, but it will definitely be more Shiite."[4] Despite the sectarian bloodshed that marked much of the Iraq War, the two major sects of Muslim believers lived mostly in peace throughout the centuries.

In the eighth century, the mystical movement of Sufism developed, in protest to the formalism of Islam. The title comes from the Arabic word *suf,* meaning "wool." Many Sufis wore coarse woolen clothes, imitating the Christians from Syria. Although both Sunni and Shiite fundamentalists reject it, Sufism has appeal among those who are frustrated with the power-seeking *ulamas,* or clerics, and who view Islam as a religious experience rather than a call to political action.[5]

tives emphasize the talents and skills that some people have at birth that others do not. They advocate a slower approach to change, highlighting the utility of existing institutions and patterns of behavior and reviling the dangerous passions and actions of revolutionaries. They lament the liberals' pace of rapid change, and believe that revolutions tend to bring about more harm than good, because they damage key traditions and hierarchical structures that serve as the basis for social traditions and IDENTITY. Many conservatives prefer familiar patterns of relations, rather than the uncertainty that comes from progressive change. It is from this belief that we tend to associate conservatives with the status quo; in fact, the label "conservativism" derives from the Latin word *conservare,* which means "to save or preserve." Conservative parties and groups today, while they often support democratic institutions, urge caution in the pace of transitions and cast a wary eye toward liberal causes.

One modern manifestation of conservative ideas is found in religious fundamentalism, including Christian and Islamic variants, the adherents of which promote the value of religious institutions and authority, often placing great emphasis on traditional family structures and gender roles. Much of the debate surrounding fundamentalists and their detractors relates to the adaptations of religious institutions to the modern world. Adherents to fundamental traditions often promote a stricter, sometimes-literal interpretation of religious texts, whether they be the Torah, Bible, or Quran. Islamist movements, also discussed in this chapter, have often been motivated by the perceived encroachment of Westernization, concomitant with the rise of individualism and SECULARISM, which are viewed as threatening to traditional lifestyles. After the Soviet withdrawal from Afghanistan in 1989, civil war ensued. One group that emerged from the ashes was the Taliban, an Islamist political group that ruled the country from 1996 until late 2001, and reemerged as an insurgent movement in 2004. This group promotes a rigidly conservative approach to Islamic religious beliefs that includes strict gender segregation based on a belief that men and women are fundamentally unequal. The Taliban's actions are couched in the refutation of Western, secular standards of behavior. The resurgence of the Taliban throughout Afghanistan has been disastrous for all Afghanis, but especially for women. The world has witnessed several grim images that testify to this fact—for example, one Afghani woman was mutilated, her ears and nose sliced off, because she fled an abusive marriage; another, a pregnant widow, received 200 lashes and then was shot to death because she was accused of adultery. When top Taliban spokesmen deny complicity, they hardly convince critics; for example, in the case of the pregnant widow, Taliban spokesman argued that she should not have been shot to death, but stoned instead.[6] Honor killings, public executions, and other forms of punishment are promoted by extremist leaders, with aggrieved citizens watching and even getting in on the action. Multiple concerns remain, including whether or not groups even loosely affiliated with the Taliban may become the face of law in the region.

Christian fundamentalists express hostility toward individualism and secularism, objecting to the liberal separation of church and state that made religious values and practices a private rather than a public matter. Conservative evangelical Christians have been very active in many parts of the non-Western world, including Latin America (especially Guatemala and Brazil), Africa (including South Africa and Zimbabwe), and some Asian states (notably the Philippines). While there is great variation among followers, in general evangelical Christian churches advocate conservative sexual and gender mores, economic discipline, as well as a greater role for some newer church institutions. In Brazil, for example, evangelical leaders in government have publicly contested the role of the Catholic Church in society. In Guatemala, fundamentalist Protestant groups rally in opposition to unions and against LIBERATION THEOLOGY, a left-leaning perspective on Catholicism discussed later in this chapter. Many of the fundamentalist traditions in Africa trace their origins to the anticolonial movement. In Zimbabwe, the Pentecostal Assemblies of God is believed to include approximately 10 percent of the population.[7] Disparate groups of fundamentalist Christians in Africa, believed to number in the tens of millions, have joined together in opposition to abortion, feminism, and the rights of homosexuals.[8]

Conservatism and liberalism are only two of many traditions of like-minded ideas. The other major world ideologies that have affected social, political, and economic life include socialism, communism, fascism, and anarchism. Each of these ideological systems developed in response to liberal views of the world, and promotes its own ideas about the value of individualism, governmental involvement in the economy, and the structure of society. It is important to understand the basic definitions of each of these distinct ideologies. But it is also necessary to keep in mind that the underlying components of any ideological system are manipulated, changed, and adapted by people to fit their particular circumstances and to match their goals. Nonetheless, a fundamental understanding of the common characteristics of these views provides an important starting place for this inquiry of the role of ideology in the non-Western world.

Socialism is an ideological tradition that has had tremendous impact throughout the entire world, either in its application or in its opposition. Because of the centrality of economic matters, socialism, in multiple variants, has been a particularly important ideology in the non-Western world. Historically, socialism was critical of private property and the uneven distribution of wealth. It is an idea that significantly predates one of its most famous adherents, Karl Marx, who adapted early socialist ideals and melded them onto a revolutionary framework. Marxist socialists argued that fundamentally there are two types of people in the world, making up the dominant CLASSES of society. First are the few who own property and therefore exert much influence in economic, political, and social affairs. They are known as the BOURGEOISIE. Yet the bourgeoisie could not exist without the MASSES, who in a Marxist framework are forced to work at the mercy of the powerful, and labor tirelessly without proper compensation or protection against abuse. This second class, which always outnumbers the first, is known as the PROLETARIAT. Writing in the midst of the European industrial revolution of the late 1800s, Marx argued that once the workers of the world were made aware of their uneven plight caused by the powerful property owners, inevitably they would rise up in anger and overthrow their oppressors. Marx predicted that after the revolution, which was likely to be violent, proletarians would rule in their self-interest, attempting to eliminate the bourgeoisie. During this stage of initial socialism, economic inequalities would persist, but they would be eradicated in the final stage of the revolution, when communism would be achieved.

While Marx's ideas may seem particularly appropriate for individuals living and working in the non-Western world, it was really only after the innovations of another revolutionary activist that his ideas were applied in the effort to promote widescale change. In imperial Russia, the activist later known as Vladimir Lenin, hardly a paragon of the industrial battlefield that Marx predicted would bring his revolutions to life, took up the ideas articulated by Marx and his collaborator, Friedrich Engels, and from them crafted a plan to implement a Marxist revolution by a group of ELITES, a highly disciplined VANGUARD PARTY. This Leninist party would not wait around for electoral victories that Lenin believed would never come. Rather, it would seize state power and implement a Marxist revolution from above. Revolutionary hopefuls throughout the non-Western world found a solution in Lenin's model, which ran counter to Marx's initial focus on worker-led mass revolutions. Lenin's ideas on the connection between imperialism and capitalism seemed especially relevant to many at a time when capitalism was rapidly becoming a global movement. Lenin taught that richer capitalist countries used the poorer countries of the world to finance their own GROWTH and prosperity. Capitalism, by definition, would promote uneven DE-VELOPMENT, as the rich countries would get richer on the backs of cheaper labor in the non-Western world, which was becoming increasingly dependent on trade with the imperialist powers. These ideas strongly resonated with citizens in non-Western countries who recognized their exploitation, especially in countries with formal imperialist governing structures. Communist movements, following the Leninist model, were integral in independence movements in Vietnam, Indonesia, Angola, Mozambique, and Guinea-Bissau.

Even though Karl Marx believed that communist revolutions would be conducted in the advanced, industrialized countries of Europe and North America, his ideas were most vigorously applied to countries in the non-Western world. In fact, some would argue that the perceived failures of communism since 1989 were predictable from the beginning: a Marxist revolution simply was not tailored to a non-Western, nonindustrial country. Yet even today, the world's largest communist party, with approximately 70 million members, can be found in the People's Republic of China (PRC), a country that retains a large population of citizens engaged in agriculture. Chairman Mao Zedong's application of Marxist communism in a nonindustrialized setting spawned similar revolutionary movements in other countries, including Peru's Sendero Luminoso (Shining Path). In countries where full-fledged Marxist-Leninist revolutions have been undertaken, however, the leadership has never moved beyond the stage of initial socialism, during which time a single party can rule, theoretically, in the name of achieving final communism. It is because of this connection, some would say deviation, of Marxist socialism that many people associate socialism with one-party rule. This correlation, however, is not wholly accurate.

Democratic forms of socialism have also influenced SOCIAL MOVEMENTS in the countries we are studying. Fabian socialists argue that the original goal of socialists has been distorted by its revolutionary application by Marx and his adherents. They argue that democratic, peaceful means are the only viable way to promote the socialist cause. These democratic socialists attempt to promote greater equality (especially economic equality) among citizens, and advocate a strong role for government in promoting the needs of society. Democratic socialism was especially influential during the African wars of independence of the 1970s, when leaders encouraged governments to be proactive in citizens' lives, especially in the areas of literacy and education. From the mid-1960s until the recession of the 1970s, President Julius Nyerere of Tanzania, for example, promoted a socialist model of economic development under the *ujamma* model, a Kiswahili word that means, roughly, "familyhood" or "pulling together." Nyerere not only collectivized agriculture and factories, but also, under the leadership of a single party, mandated major investments in primary schools and social services. In general, socialist leaders are critical of unbridled capitalism,

pointing to often-disastrous effects of the market on the environment, family and social relations, and culture. They tend to be the people leading the charge against international economic institutions such as the WORLD BANK and the INTERNATIONAL
MONETARY FUND (IMF), although they are certainly not alone in their critiques. Socialism in the non-Western world, though, emphasizes NATIONALISM and local traditions, rather than the international and universal working-class identity promoted by
initial socialist activists.

If liberalism emphasized people as individuals, conservatives urged a focus on
society and its traditions, and socialists viewed the world in the framework of classes.
In response to each of these ideologies, another combination of ideas—fascism—
was formed that found fault with each of the preceding characterizations of the
world. Similar to the other ideologies, its basis was found in historical tradition, including linguistic interpretations of history, so-called scientific understandings of
race and racial identity, and an elitist prescription for political power and governance. Ideas that would form the core of fascism existed long before the ideology
was named. Fascism emphasizes that which unites people as a way of segregating
individuals into homogeneous groups in order to promote unity and strength. Because of its opposition to most of the systems of ideas that developed before it, and
because of its negative proscriptions on life in general, it may be argued that it is
clearer to understand what fascists are against than what they are for.[9]

Fascists believe that the class focus of socialism is too divisive, especially because it emphasizes status as either a worker or an owner over a person's national
heritage. The term "fascism," first coined in Italy, comes from the Latin word *fasces,*
alluding to a set of reeds tightly bound together. Fascist leaders emphasize the importance of race and nationality, promoting in many cases a racially pure community
of individuals who work together without division. Fascism also teaches that it is
necessary to have a strong leader who will provide guidance and direction to the
masses, and that the all-powerful leader understands the needs and the interests of
the people better than they themselves do. In this sense, fascism is clearly an elitist
ideology, which openly concentrates the majority of the power among a small minority of seemingly qualified individuals.

Fascists emphasize the fundamental inequality of humans and have a clear hierarchy, often based on biological conceptions of race, of "superior" and "lesser"
peoples. While fascists are not the only group to deny the universal equality of all
people, they go a step further, openly advocating the use of violence for handling
contradictions that exist between people. While the most destructive fascist dictatorships were promoted in the European countries of Italy (under Benito Mussolini)
and Germany (under Adolf Hitler), fascist authoritarian movements have also been
strong in the non-Western world as well, especially in Chile under Augusto Pinochet.
Fascism is an authoritarian ideology of exclusion, and regimes that adhere to it promote division and hierarchy, violating the fundamental human rights of those deemed
inferior and preventing individual liberties for all except the few deemed worthy of
holding power. Fascists deny the desirability of a multicultural society, arguing to violent extremes that multiple ethnic groups cannot coexist within a single society. This
ideology calls for a strong government that organizes and leads the masses, as well
as a developed propaganda system that educates and motivates them into action.

In recent years, groups adhering to neofascist beliefs have gained prominence in many parts of the world, especially in economically troubled regions where immigrants, refugees, migrant workers, and other groups seen as outsiders can be scapegoated for a wide range of social and economic problems. Contrary to its antecedent, neofascist violence is aimed at particular ethnic communities rather than the state. Neo-Nazi attacks in Germany, for example, have targeted the immigrant Turkish, African, and Vietnamese populations with firebombs and other violent attacks. Similar to their ideological predecessors, these activists condone the use of violence and segregation in order to promote the cause of their own, self-defined group.

Ideologies develop as a way to capture the relationship between leaders in government and ordinary citizens. Anarchists challenge the desirability of hierarchical power structures, emphasizing voluntary cooperation and free association over power and control. Anarchism is difficult to characterize as a single school of thought, as its adherents' beliefs straddle those of almost all groups along the ideological spectrum. Noam Chomsky defines anarchism as a "historical tendency" or a "tendency of thought and action" rather than an ideology per se. Anarchists are often known for their acts of disobedience. They share a concern about the concentration of power, whether governmental power over ordinary citizens, patriarchal power of men over women, or global corporate power exercised by business conglomerates. Most anarchists promote the values of democratic participation, decentralization, and opposition to bureaucracy. While some anarchist groups condone the use of violence to further their cause, this is a point of disagreement among those adhering to this ideological perspective.

Anarchist movements have been especially popular among youth. In major Turkish cities, for example, members of the Anarchist Youth Federation protest against sexism, capitalism, gerontocracy, and nuclear proliferation. Conscientious objectors of required military service have also aligned with antimilitarist anarchist youth groups. Anarchists claim that no one should have authority or control over another. In this they often challenge basic rules of behavior. Puerto Rican feminist and labor activist Luisa Capetillo is perhaps Latin America's best-known anarchist; she gained notoriety by becoming the first woman to wear pants in public in Puerto Rico. Through her work to encourage labor unionization in Puerto Rico, she worked to redefine women's freedom. The 1994 Zapatista uprising in Mexico and student strikes there have been particularly influenced by anarchism, challenging especially the power of government over minority ethnic groups. This movement, which has been viciously repressed by authorities, has awoken indigenous activists across Latin America and in other regions as well.

Because of their disdain for governing structures, anarchist movements tend to reach across borders and geographic limitations to embrace a global audience. The environmental movement Earth First confronts government and corporate behavior, especially its disregard for ecological concerns and its anthropocentric, or human-centered, bias. Additionally, diverse movements against transnational corporations and seemingly supranational organizations such as the WORLD TRADE ORGANIZATION (WTO), the IMF and the GROUP OF 20 (G-20) have mobilized activists of all stripes to challenge the authority and actions of large bureaucracies. Protests organized to disrupt such meetings unite environmentalists, farmers, students, intellectuals, feminists, and union activists. Although not all of the participants are necessarily anarchists, the focus on the negative aspects of global capitalism goes right to the core beliefs of anarchism. Many terrorist groups, discussed in Chapter 12, base their actions in the ideology of anarchism as well.

While it is clear that a variety of often-competing ideological systems exist in our world at the beginning of the twenty-first century, true understanding of the power of these worldviews can only be found in comparison. To examine systems of ideas, it is helpful to visually align beliefs on the POLITICAL SPECTRUM. We commonly use the terminology of "left, right, and center" to place beliefs in comparison with each other. The terminology we use comes from seating arrangements in the National Assembly of France during the revolution of the late 1700s. Moderates sat in the center, those who favored DEMOCRACY and rapid change congregated on the left side (or wing), and those who supported the monarch and the Catholic Church, arguing against change, sat on the right. We continue to use this linear system today to compare belief systems, although it is helpful only as a general guideline. People and groups cannot be placed on the spectrum with clear precision (few of us hold completely consistent views and opinions), and all discussions about the spectrum in a particular country or society must be understood as relative to particular circumstances.

To aid the comparison of beliefs, ideas are placed along the political spectrum according to views on the importance and desired direction of change, the role of government in the economy, and the perceived value of church and religious institutions. To the left of center, beliefs focus on the positive value of change (especially forward-moving developments), a larger role of government in economic matters, including the promotion of greater equality, and a smaller public role for religious institutions in the lives of people. To the right of center, church and religious institutions serve a more important role in both government and society. Advocates of right-wing ideologies are more suspicious of change, and prefer that government be less involved in economic affairs generally. To the right of center, people tend to emphasize the decline of society and advocate a reevaluation of social, political, and economic structures, and often a return to values of an earlier period. Because anarchist beliefs usually complement other ideological traditions, and because of the great variety of perspectives embodied within anarchism, it is difficult to clearly place it on one side of the spectrum or the other. As the language of this explanation suggests, there are few absolutes in the characterization of ideologies, but these general patterns capture the most important ideas. Keep in mind that an understanding of the dominant ideological leanings in a particular society or governing administration will provide only limited information about the policies of the regime. For example, although we have highlighted the role of government and political intervention as a point distinguishing some ideological traditions, state interventionist economic programs have been used both by regimes characterized as rightist (Juan Peron's Argentina) as well as by those characterized as leftist (Salvador Allende's Chile).

How and why do people develop particular opinions and views? We are all products of a lifelong process generally referred to as socialization, through which individuals acquire their beliefs and values. Some of this socialization is accidental. Other aspects of socialization are deliberate attempts to pass on values and belief systems from generation to generation. Beliefs about government, politics, economics, and the role of the military are all influenced by some of our earliest life experiences. Educational and religious institutions, the media, peer groups, and family each influence the development of beliefs. While much of the process of acquiring attitudes about society is implicit and somewhat taken for granted, such as family relationships between women and men, governments and social groups may also explicitly influence people's sense of values, especially as they relate to the governing system. Institutions of the media are often overlooked as sources of socialization, yet newspapers and television programs can be people's sole source of information about civic and political life.

The media both inform and persuade. Recognizing the power implicit in controlling access to information, it is common for governments to exercise some level of control over communications media, often through a monopoly over news and publishing outlets. Sometimes two versions of media are produced, an official version for public consumption, which downplays the tensions existing in society, and a version meant only for viewing by government leaders, which expresses a more accurate account of pressures and hot spots. Government regulation of the media, which makes the expression of unofficial opinions problematic and even dangerous, often forces dissident groups to publish their opposition views underground, in the so-called gray media or second channel.[10] These unofficial communication avenues, which straddle the permissible and the forbidden, have been especially lucrative in environments where entrepreneurship and risk-taking are encouraged. In China, for example, simply stamping a book "for internal consumption only" means that there will be a huge market on the side for bootlegged copies. Arguments over media control also fare prominently in Iran, where, despite the proliferation of media sources, both print and electronic, boundaries are enforced by the powerful Council of Guardians. Editors who challenge the boundary of the permissible have been shut down, jailed, and even flogged.

The proliferation of the Internet, including blogs, social-networking sites, and online petitions, has provided new ways to communicate while at the same time inviting novel means by which a government can spy on its population. China introduced its "Great Firewall" in 2003 to block access to seemingly sensitive sites and information, especially references to dissident movements and views. Iran has some of the most sophisticated means of controlling and censoring information on the Internet, including the ability to monitor individual communication using "deep-packet inspection," which permits central authorities to infiltrate all online traffic.[11] Myanmar essentially turned off the country's Internet network for six weeks during antigovernment protests in 2007.[12] Cyber-duels ensue, and crafty Netizens find ways around limits. In China, users can use a virtual private network (VPN) to circumvent censorship by way of a secure connection through a different country, browsing the Web as if they were in that country. When Tehran blocked text messaging on the day of the 2009 presidential election, people turned to Twitter (and simple word of mouth) instead.[13] Internet censorship is conducted by countries all around the world, Western and non-Western alike, as content is inspected to assist in fighting TERRORISM, child pornography, human trafficking, and other illegal activities. In fact, the NONGOVERN-MENTAL ORGANIZATION Reporters Without Borders reports that in 2009, sixty countries had implemented some form of Web censorship, twice the number as in 2008.[14] The use of information communication technologies does not always lead to positive results.

Figure 10.2   "Antisocial" Media

The Internet provides some novel opportunities for social organization and the expression of citizen voice. Yet many of the same characteristics that make these technologies useful can make them dangerous as well: the forum is quick, ripe with information that its users provide (including sensitive contact information and personal details); it crosses national borders, making the legal terrain more complicated; and the (at least temporary) anonymity it provides makes accountability more difficult to establish. In some societies, "Internet mobbing" and "virtual lynchings" have arisen, sometimes with grim consequences. *The Economist* quipped that "antisocial media" are developing, providing opportunities to target individuals for revenge or retribution.[15] Lists of targeted teenagers appeared on Facebook in southern Colombia, with three of the sixty-nine people named on the hit list killed within less than two weeks (police originally viewed the lists as a hoax, even though just a month earlier, a university student in Bogotá was imprisoned for allegedly creating a Facebook page calling for the assassination of the Colombian president's son, Jeronimo Uribe). In China, a woman was dubbed the "stiletto kitten killer" for crushing a kitten's skull with her high heels, and a nationwide hunt began. She was tracked down five days after her personal contact information was posted on QQ, China's wildly popular, free instant-messaging service.[16] Chinese Internet forums, dubbed "human-flesh search engines," are creating a "cyberposse"[17] of sorts— eager Netizens hunt down presumed violators of an unwritten moral code, forcing individuals to take cover to attempt to evade the branders of local justice. Uncivil society meets the information age.

Looking at the world around us, we observe similarities and differences among groups of people. It is often difficult to put our finger on the source of differences, when they exist. Much of it is related to the processes of socialization. When we compare political attitudes across multiple societies, people commonly speak of a POLITICAL CULTURE that exists among a defined group of people, such as "Mexican political culture" or "Turkish political culture." This concept was developed to capture the commonly shared understandings and basic assumptions that people in a common experience tend to exhibit.

To say that a group of people share a particular political culture does not mean that they agree on all of the important issues of politics and governance. Rather, it means that they are likely to share a common perspective about their public surroundings, including their political leaders, governmental structure, and the enduring symbols and values of public life.[18] Political culture includes citizens' general feelings toward government, including their desire (or lack thereof) to participate in political issues. It also captures a sense of people's understanding of the decision-making process, including attitudes about its merits. Understanding that people have social, political, and economic experiences different from our own helps us avoid assumptions that the way relationships and institutions operate in one setting is the way that they exist elsewhere. The concept of political culture helps us recognize the long-term impact of social, historical, and economic circumstances.

A classic study on political culture attempted to use these ideas to compare cultures throughout the world. The *Civic Culture* study of the 1950s and early 1960s, based on survey research, was conducted by a group of leading US political scientists.[19] It identified three dominant types of political culture. First, Gabriel Almond and Sidney Verba classified a "participant culture," in which most people exhibit pride toward their country's political system, feel that they should participate in it, and have a sense that their participation makes a difference. They also generally understand the way the system works. Second, the study identified a "subject culture," in which people tend to discount their ability to participate in and change politics; rather, they view themselves as obedient subordinates of the government. People in these societies tend to be aware of the operations of the political system, but overall are cautious about participating in it. Finally, the study identified a "parochial culture," in which people tend to identify almost exclusively with their immediate locality, feeling that national political issues have very little to do with them. In such cultures, people tend to speak little about political affairs, because in their viewpoint such matters rarely touch their lives.

What did Almond and Verba conclude about political culture from this study? The only one of our cases that was included in this original study was Mexico, which was characterized as the prototypical parochial culture. While recognizing that each country contains people with a mix of views, the leaders of the study generalized about each society as a whole. This was a pivotal attempt to make broad statements about many countries at once, in a comparative framework.

Yet there are serious limitations to such an approach. For one, it invites the potential for discriminatory assumptions or, at the very least, establishing a hierarchy of favored characteristics. It was clear by the way the findings were presented that a participatory, aware, and active population should be the ultimate goal for each society. Yet there was little recognition that the standards for the study were based on Western traditions and cultures, which promote civic duty and activism as a virtue. The *Civic Culture* study and others that have followed in its footsteps are indicative of the wide-eyed optimism of many Americans in the late 1950s and 1960s. The implicit hope was that Western-style democracies were going to flourish around the world, and that there was a single model of the so-called developed, democratic state. In fact, the guiding assumption of the *Civic Culture* study was that the participant culture is a precondition to stable democracy.

In addition to being ethnocentric, this approach tended to emphasize the changes that were not taking place, presumably because people did not exhibit characteristics found in other Western cultures, rather than the realm of the possible, or what could take place. Also, such an aggregated view of single political cultures oversimplifies complex societies. The assumptions of national culture make grandiose claims that are difficult to substantiate. For example, in a state like Nigeria, with over 250 different ethnic groups, does it really make sense to talk of a singular "Nigerian" political culture? There is also a problem of translation: concepts such as EFFICACY, duty, and participation do not always translate very clearly, and people have differing images in their minds as to the precise meaning of these terms. Political culture is useful to explain differences among groups, but it is less helpful when used to explain so-called national traits, as David Elkins and E. B. Simeon identified.[20] While it is clear that culture is important, it is less clear how to measure it. At best, the concept of political culture is useful for understanding general orientations, but it is important that we not make assumptions much beyond this.

Identities

When individuals make assessments about the world around them, they make decisions based on a self-perception of who they are, or their identity. Increasingly, we understand that people's self-perception influences their behavior and attitudes. It affects whom we define as potential collaborators or competitors, and it impacts the outcome that we seek. The traditional ideologies discussed earlier are largely devoid of an explicit awareness of self-identity: they aim to provide an outlook based on larger issues often irrespective of individual attributes. Yet a growing trend in social thought and action revolves around identity issues that fundamentally get at the question of who we are. They tend to be very personal ideologies that encourage people to fight for recognition of the joint needs and preferences of particular groups, often those that have been denied expression in the past. Identities are extremely complex concepts. For one thing, we each have multiple individual characteristics: one individual embodies the identities of friend, daughter, Asian, worker. We choose to emphasize a particular trait based on the context in which we are involved. For example, at a sporting event, people are usually defined as either athletes or spectators. At an international sporting event, it becomes even more complex, with the characteristic of national identity becoming important. Yet at other gatherings, such as some religious meetings, one's categorization as a female or male, or as a believer or nonbeliever, can be the defining characteristic.

Individual and group identities are quite closely related; in addition to describing themselves individually, people group with others. This involves the development of a collective, or shared, identity. Groups of ordinary people mobilize around a common self-definition, usually as a way to achieve a common goal. Additionally, leaders attempt to rally their citizens around an identity related to their own power. Officials who are defensive about their own ability to maintain power are particularly adept at rallying people around a shared sense of belonging, often making promises to varied groups as a way to lock in their support. Zimbabwe's Robert Mugabe provides a good example, with his promises of land and "Africa for Africans." Such POPULIST attempts can be particularly strong in countries undergoing dislocation or change. The Peronists in Argentina exemplified populism by forming coalitions of the urban poor and parts of the organized working and middle classes, promising greater economic equality and independence (especially economic) from foreign countries. The 1979 Iranian Revolution was a populist movement that rallied the common people against the West, personified in opposition to the Shah. Even long after his election in mid-2005, Iranian president Mahmoud Ahmadinejad seemed to deliver campaign-style speeches across the country, dressing plainly, speaking simply, and promising a better life for his audience while railing against CORRUPTION and the wealthy, including the powerful clerics.[21] Venezuelan president Hugo Chávez exemplifies both the appeal and the challenges of populism. Like other leaders before him, he rose to power in 1999 as a spokesman for the poor, promising to return some of the vast oil wealth of his country to those who were lacking. Following a 2009 referendum on his power, Chávez seems to be eyeing a stay in power even beyond the end of his term in 2012, even as he is increasingly unable to provide evidence of economic improvements across his country. Populist movements are fundamentally about identity and pride: they attempt to rally groups to action in the name of the self-described "people": they may be left or right in orientation, but their motivation is nearly the same. The difficulty with populism on its own, however, is that "the people" rarely fit into one category. Populism is usually combined with other movements. Nationalist movements, for example, have been common bedfellows for populist leaders.

For over 200 years, the idea of nationalism has been used to promote the interests and needs of a particular nation, or group of people. Usually, nations are identified as sharing a common history, culture, language, ethnicity, or religion, although the actual components of national identity can vary widely. Nationalist movements have been a potent uniting (and dividing) force throughout many of the countries that we are studying. The initial struggle faced by many of these countries was to establish a common identity after the colonial period. National identities were therefore defined more in opposition to the colonial rulers than in composition of shared characteristics. The concept of "Indonesia," for example, was an entirely novel identity for the disparate ethnic groups who had operated a vast trading network from the islands of Java and Sumatra for centuries. Yet especially between the two world wars, the notion of a single, independent Indonesia was created and promoted, mostly by students and young professionals, in opposition to Dutch rule. It is an identity still waiting to be wholly crafted and accepted by all who live under the government of the republic.

Throughout the non-Western world, indigenous nationalist movements developed as a way to honor unique local traditions and ethnic identities. After a sense of identity was mobilized against the occupying powers, nationalist movements sometimes turned to violence as a means of expelling foreign influence, as in Vietnam, Algeria, Indonesia, Zimbabwe, Mozambique, and Angola. Some nationalist leaders propelled their movements with socialist ideology, such as Ho Chi Minh in the Vietnamese struggle against France and later the United States. Other nationalist leaders turned to socialist policies to help reconstruct their countries after achieving independence, including Algeria, India, Guinea, Mozambique, and Angola. In its opposition to capitalism, socialism presented a means for national self-sufficiency and economic independence.[22]

Today, nationalist movements of identity are on the rise, but they certainly are not new—as discussed in our study of wars of national liberation in Chapter 4. We identify two types of nationalist mobilization: one calls for independence from larger political units that attempt to incorporate multiple national groups, and the other tries to bring attention to their identity in the face of global homogenization. Most of the countries that we are studying are richly multinational, made up of people with diverse linguistic, religious, historical, and cultural traditions. For some, this has not been an issue of great division, either because the leadership suppresses such discussion (as in the case of Tibetan identity in China), or because the groups themselves fail to see a need to challenge the status quo. For others, the expression of diverse national identities can be dangerous business. For example, the Kurdish people, many of whom identify as a nation with a common language and culture, have increasingly challenged their incorporation within the political entity of Turkey. Turkish leaders have defined the "Kurdish question" as a terrorist threat, and have until recently outlawed any independent expression of Kurdish identity, including their native language. The arrest of Kurdish leader Abdullah Öcalan lessened separatist tensions somewhat, but the potential for aggression, in both separatist action and state response, remains. We will return to the question of the role of violence in irredentist movements in Chapter 12.

In addition, with increasing economic INTERDEPENDENCE and trade, the rise of GLOBALIZATION motivates some national groups to emphasize their unique characteristics in the face of the commercial and cultural homogeneity. While there are many positive aspects of a global economy and the conveniences it brings, many believe that it inhibits indigenous cultures and traditions in the name of modernity. In response to the perceived growth of Western values and goods, many groups increase their expression of microidentities. Some of this has been in response to global corporate developments. For example, there was much resistance in China when Seattle-based Starbucks opened a coffee shop in the cherished Palace Museum, the former residence of the emperors and empresses known outside China as the Forbidden City. Many Islamic groups decry the pervasiveness of Western standards in areas of fashion, gender relations, and entertainment. One scholar, Benjamin Barber, has named the tension "Jihad vs. McWorld."[23] Since September 11, 2001, though, Barber and others have quickly cautioned us not to make the easy and inaccurate assumptions that the world can so neatly be characterized in a binary fashion, grouping people in tight categories as either in favor of Western-style modernization, or not. Rather, the image that Barber attempted to convey in the provocative title of his study is more accurately viewed as a means of capturing the diverse opposition that has formed to the proliferation of mass markets, technology, and Western-dominated popular culture.[24] For many groups on the receiving end of this new culture, it forces a reevaluation of their fundamental identity.

Figure 10.3 Tibet and the Tibetan People

Located in southwestern China, Tibet is a great example of a region in which people exercise multiple identities. Living on the world's highest plateau, the Tibetan people have fought against conquest by many peoples, including the Mongols, the imperial Chinese, and the British. Shortly after the declaration of the People's Republic of China in 1949, troops of the Chinese Communist Party marched into Tibet, attempting to enlarge their rule over the important border region. Their suppression of the Tibetan uprising was fierce: thousands of Tibetans were killed and hundreds of sacred monasteries were destroyed. While the Chinese Communist Party was nominally successful at establishing its rule, many, including the main spiritual leader of the Tibetan people, the Dalai Lama, fled to India in 1959, where the government-in-exile remains today.

Buddhism was declared the official religion of Tibet in the eighth century. Yet Tibetan Buddhists are not all unified in their expression of religious tenets or doctrine—in fact, a fierce rivalry has long existed between two groups, the "Yellow Hat" sect (known as the Gelugpa) and the "Black Hat" sect (the Kagyupa). Until the 1600s the Black Hats, led by the Karmapa Lama, dominated Tibetan affairs, but for the past four centuries the Yellow Hats, under the leadership of the Dalai Lama, have persevered. The current Dalai Lama, believed to be the fourteenth reincarnation of the spiritual leader, received the Nobel Peace Prize in 1989 for his advocacy of peace and environmental concerns. Not all Tibetan Buddhists, though, share his passion for nonviolence.

Residents of Tibet today include native inhabitants of the region, as well as Chinese migrants from other regions of the country—including many of the Han Chinese majority, who moved to Tibet in search of economic opportunities promoted by the government in Beijing. Many native residents of the territory fear they are losing their indigenous culture, religious traditions, and way of life, which are challenged not only by Han migration to the region but also by the modernizing ways of young Tibetan residents. Changes are likely to accelerate now that the world's highest railway route has opened between Beijing and Lhasa (a forty-eight-hour trek).

People also emphasize their class identity, which is based on their status within the economic structure. For example, people who consider themselves "working class" tend to identify with others who receive hourly wages for their labor. Although the origins of class awareness are largely Marxist, people who speak of a class identity are not necessarily Marxist revolutionaries. Income is unevenly distributed in every society. Guillermo O'Donnell and others have argued that a middle class, who are without the extremist tendencies of either wealth or dire poverty, is critical in transitions to democracy, as we discuss in Chapter 14. But especially in societies where there is a sharp divide between the rich and the poor, such as Peru, identity as a member of the working class or the upper class is extremely important, a lesson that feminist mobilizers took some time to learn. Class identity has been an often-cited rallying cry to stand in opposition to the status quo.

Another source of identity that is often masked by the dominance of the government is a regional identity. This shared identity among residents of a particular region, such as a north-south distinction, or the type of region, such as urban or rural, is heightened when governments pursue economic reforms that promote regional disparities. For example, regions in Mexico may be differentiated by the prevalence of export industrialization in the north, leading to relative prosperity as compared to destitution in the south, where the economy is more dependent on domestic sales. Northern Nigeria, which is predominantly Muslim, has since independence dominated political power and decisionmaking, but most of the money is found in the southern, predominantly Christian and animist parts of the country. Indonesia is another country with pronounced regional differences, compounded by linguistic and religious differences that are geographically concentrated. The westernmost province of Aceh, deemed the most "Islamic" of any region in the state, is sometimes called "the front porch of Mecca" because it points toward Saudi Arabia. It also has great natural wealth in its possession of liquefied natural gas, which distinguishes it from other provinces. On the other geographical extreme, easternmost Papua (formerly Irian Jaya) lags behind the rest of Indonesia in infrastructure and economic development, and three-fifths of the population are Protestant.[25]

In many countries of the third world, a majority of the population lives in the countryside, often making their living off of the land. Contrary to popular belief, rural dwellers are not necessarily conservative in their political views, nor are they passive recipients of the status quo. In some cases, peasants may be the forerunners to democratic processes. For example, one scholar counters popular belief by demonstrating that voter turnout in African rural areas tends to be higher than in the cities.[26] Peasants around the world are known as crafty political entrepreneurs who know how to work the system to their maximum advantage. In 2002, villagers outside Mexico City held a long standoff with the government, protesting the loss of their land to the state. At about the same time, Nigerian women staged a takeover of an oil terminal and held hundreds of oil workers hostage (many of them Westerners) until ChevronTexaco agreed to build schools and electrical and water systems. There is also much evidence of mass protests by Chinese peasants against leaders who are perceived to be corrupt. These demonstrations, which tend to leak to the Western media weeks after the fact, can have tens of thousands of participants at a time. But the picture is complex, and clientelism, or the maintenance of PATRON-CLIENT RELATIONSHIPS that reinforce the status quo, can persist in rural areas. Mexico's Institutional Revolutionary

Figure 10.4   Are All Arabs Muslim? Are All Muslims Arab?

Despite the fact that the terms are often used interchangeably, there are important differences in meaning between "Arab" and "Muslim." Generally, Arabs are viewed as a community defined either linguistically (countries in which the dominant language is Arabic, which is a member of the Semitic family of languages), politically (citizens of a country that is a member of the Arab League, an organization of twenty-two states that is headquartered in Cairo, Egypt), or genealogically (families who trace their ancestry to the Arabian Peninsula or Syrian desert). Any categorization has exceptions—Somalia, for example, is a non-Arab country that is a member of the Arab League, and many people who speak Arabic do not consider themselves to be Arab.

Arabs identify with many different religious traditions. The majority of Arabs are Muslim, but there are also Arab Christians (concentrated in Lebanon, Egypt, Palestine, Jordan, Sudan, and Syria), and Arab Jews (in Morocco and Tunisia). Not all Muslim-majority states are Arab. The Islamic Republic of Iran, for example, is Persian, not Arab.

Muslims are adherents of Islam. Muslims come from many different ethnic groups, and are connected by their belief in Islam. Less than a quarter of the world's Muslims are Arab—the world's most populous Muslim countries are in Asia: Indonesia, Pakistan, Bangladesh, and India.

Party (PRI) relied on rural support for years, and rural dwellers fearful of change have been a crucial base of support for the Mugabe regime in Zimbabwe.

Throughout the world, religious affiliations also serve as an important sense of identity. It is not surprising that one's basic values and assumptions about human beings, morality, and justice color opinions on issues of politics, economics, and culture. In the United States, a separation of church and state tends to be promoted, meaning that religion is often viewed as a personal matter, and that religious beliefs should not become too closely involved in matters of politics and governance, although the dividing line is increasingly being challenged. The separation of church and state is a contested concept in many regions and within many spiritual traditions of the world. In fact, in some of the countries that we are studying, a greater fusion of religion and politics is desired not only by the political elites, but by ordinary citizens as well.

When contemplating religious issues and their importance in politics and governance, many think of the Middle East, the birthplace of the world's three major monotheistic religions: Islam, Judaism, and Christianity. While religious issues are indeed important in this region, religious values and beliefs are difficult to separate from events in other parts of the world as well. Our two Middle Eastern cases place religious principles front and center in public affairs. These two predominantly Muslim countries present an interesting paradox. In Turkey, where the population is approximately 98 percent Muslim, the government, supported by the ever-watchful military, fiercely fights to retain its SECULARISM, established at the beginning of the modern republic in 1923. Iran, however, is officially an Islamic republic, established by the revolution in 1979, making it a THEOCRACY. For example, Iran's highest institution of authority, the Council of Guardians, bases its decisions on the sacred Muslim text, the Quran, rather than the country's 1979 constitution. Attempts to develop political and religious pluralism face fierce opposition from religious clerics, who hold much of the power within the country.

As we have discussed, the labeling of any action or group is fraught with difficulty, especially from the perspective of the people being discussed. This controversy has become particularly acute as analysts try to characterize so-called political Islam. Many terms have been coined to capture the ideology and political program that some derive from their Islamic faith, with "Islamism" becoming a commonly used term by both advocates and detractors alike.[27] As we find with almost any label, as much is obscured as is understood—not all politically active Christians see the world through the same lens, for example, so why should it be assumed that all Muslims do? Because of these terminological debates, trying to characterize the numbers is difficult: it may be that a large majority of Muslims cannot even accurately be characterized as Islamists.[28]

Another source of the controversy is related to the connection between those who use Islam as a source for their political ideology and those who undertake violence in the name of Islam. Most Muslims view JIHAD, often translated from the Arabic as "struggle," as an individual struggle to overcome temptations and submit to the will of God, or Allah (the term "Islam" means "submission to God"). It is true that some, a minority within the faith, view jihad as struggle against enemies of Islam. These individuals and the groups they support may accurately be characterized as advocates of militant Islam, just as we have discussed regarding adherents of more aggressive forms of other traditions above. And extremists who claim that their faith inspires violent acts usually lose the support of others in their faith community, as Al-Qaida experienced in most Muslim circles after 9/11.

The intellectual roots of Islamism can be traced to Sayyid Abul Ala Maududi, an Indian journalist who fought in the anti-imperial struggle and then moved to Pakistan to build a more pure Islamic state, later founding the Islamist party Jamaat-e-Islami (JEI) in 1941 to counter the secularism and Westernization of Pakistan. He emphasized personal transformation and the grounding of all human activity in faith. Another source of Islamist views was Sayyid Qutb, an Egyptian civil servant who, after graduate study in the United States, rejected Western values as corrupt and immoral. Returning to Egypt, he vocally criticized what he perceived to be his government's replication of Western decadence. Qutb eventually became a leader of the oldest Islamist party, Egypt's Muslim Brotherhood. As an activist, his outspoken ways landed him in jail (where he refined his ideas), and ultimately he was hanged by the Egyptian government.

More recently, some Islamists have been emboldened by what they perceive as the corrupt, HEGEMONIC ways of Western governments, most notoriously the United States. They took great exception when, following the Gulf War in 1991, Saudi Arabia agreed to the stationing of US troops inside of the land that is home to Mecca and Medina, the two most sacred sites of Islam. Islamists hold views in varying levels and degrees, some arguing that the greatest threat to peace is internal (e.g., believers who are not faithful), and others targeting external threats (e.g., the United States). Just as is found in other belief systems, there are moderate Islamists (members of the Justice and Development Party [AKP] in Turkey advocate for greater democracy instead of greater religiosity), and extremist Islamists (including Al-Qaida and Jemaah Islamiah, a militant Islamist organization active throughout Southeast Asia that was implicated in the Bali bombing of 2002). Danish cartoons depicting the prophet Mohammed as a terrorist insulted Muslims (whether Islamist or not) around the world to varying degrees, and contributed to the sense that, as a faith community, Muslims remain poorly understood by many non-Muslims. Even more insulting to many Muslim faithful around the world has been the connection, made mostly by then–US president George W. Bush and other US conservatives, between Islam and fascism, coining the seemingly catchy phrase "Islamofascism." This has been widely discredited as a simplistic means of casting the war on terror in stark terms and clouding more than it clarifies.[29]

The role of formal Catholic Church institutions has been a keen issue in Mexican politics since as far back as the mid-1800s. Mexicans have fought two civil wars to decide the Church's role. The country is overwhelmingly Roman Catholic but fiercely anticlerical. The 1917 revolution sought to limit the Church's involvement in politics. Religious schools were closed, and church property was seized. Priests were prohibited from voting or wearing the collar in public. But the election of the socially conservative National Action Party (PAN) in 2000 emboldened the Church and reignited a number of controversies.

In some countries, governments construct a specific doctrine to explain the role of religion in politics and society. Political and military leaders in Indonesia, for example, long promoted the importance of the *pancasila,* literally the "five principles." These pillars of Indonesian life are monotheism, national unity, humanitarianism, representative democracy by consensus, and social justice. Sukarno, the first president of Indonesia, created the *pancasila* creed as a way to unite the diverse peoples of Indonesia. Although the meaning of the *pancasila* doctrine is debated today, it remains an important symbol of leaders' aspirations to create unity out of diversity.

Another example of the importance of religious identity in the non-Western world comes from a Christian tradition. Liberation theology is a movement that started within the Catholic Church, and it has had an especially powerful impact in Latin America. In Brazil alone—the world's most populous Roman Catholic state—there are more than 80,000 lay communities organized around this philosophy.[30] It is by definition an action-oriented ideology that calls on its followers to promote social justice, focusing especially on the most economically poor members of society. As a system of thought, it is intriguing because of its combination of Marxist revolutionary ideas (which are explicitly hostile toward organized religions) with Christian teachings. While its origins were within Roman Catholicism, it is increasingly becoming an ecumenical movement, including other Christian churches and institutions. And although many of its leaders received training in European religious institutions, liberation theology is increasingly becoming an indigenous intellectual and ideological movement, with native theologians addressing the social ills plaguing the less developed world.

In 1971, Peruvian theologian Gustavo Gutiérrez published *A Theology of Liberation,* considered by many to be the definitive statement.[31] In it he stressed social praxis (practice), with a commitment to critical reflection and a renewed dedication on the part of the universal church to the disenfranchised poor and destitute. Gutiérrez argued that too many Christians, especially Catholics, focus on the orthodoxy (correct teachings) rather than on the orthopraxis (correct practice) of a Christian life. Liberation theology maintains that people need to move beyond doctrine to focus on the economic, political, and social issues that affect ordinary people on a daily basis. Advocates of this approach contend that poverty is caused by structures (such as the INTERNATIONAL ECONOMIC SYSTEM) rather than individual, idiosyncratic characteristics, including laziness, bad luck, or other sources of blame. Therefore, the "liberation" of the poor is more than an act of individual charity; it is a demand for a new social and economic order in order to promote the universal humanity of all peoples. Second is the idea of collective sin, articulated by Brazilian theologian Leonardo Boff, who argued that people who support unjust regimes, even if they themselves do not personally exploit the poor, are collectively responsible for the result.[32] Boff's statements implicated not only leaders and citizens in the Western, developed world, but citizens of poorer countries as well. Liberation theology has impacted many of the countries we are studying here. A 2000 pastoral letter in Mexico, for example, criticized political and economic systems as "poverty-generating structures," and called on people to fight to build a more just society. The South African Council of Churches applied the principles of liberation theology, through black theology, to end apartheid. Several ecumenical organizations, including the Zimbabwean Catholic Bishops Conference and the Zimbabwe Council of Churches, played important roles in the struggle against white minority rule, and continue to condemn human rights abuses. They argue that poverty is due to oppressive structures and call for activism, primarily through the development of base Christian communities that work to educate, evangelize, and empower the economically poor. Movements inspired by liberation theology have met with harsh repression by governments (backed by military force) and institutional churches as well, especially in El Salvador and Guatemala. This has provoked an increase in violence by adherents.

Mobilization around issues of gender has been particularly strong throughout the non-Western world, especially since 1975, when the UNITED NATIONS held its first international women's conference in Mexico City. Similar to other groups, women have mobilized in response to repression, exclusion, and other crises, both on their own behalf and in the interest of others, especially children. As we discuss below, there is no single brand of feminism, but rather many different viewpoints commonly united around the desire to advance the voice of women in today's world. Some view feminism as a solely Western idea, although many women in the non-Western world disagree.[33]

Feminism is a complex worldview that includes many perspectives, and there are vigorous debates about what defines a "feminist." One school of thought distinguishes feminists who work primarily for civil equality that recognizes the fundamental equality between women and men. Such groups, often called liberal feminists, have been at the forefront of suffrage movements as well as civil rights movements that fight for gains in equality before the law. This view is contrasted with another school of thought that emphasizes the differences that exist between women and men. Commonly known as radical feminists, they argue that liberal feminists fail to recognize the unspoken assumption that women should perform the same as men. In contrast, radical feminists fight for the equal recognition of women's standards as well as men's; they argue that women's ways need to be recognized for their inherent contributions as well. It is a question of standards and assumptions; while radical feminists agree that men and women are equal, they contend that stopping there fails to challenge the continued dominance of a male-centric society.

Feminists have actively challenged notions of "correct" female (and by association, male) behavior that are rooted in custom and tradition. In a related fashion, many women openly confront the notion that politics is the exclusive domain of men. Mexico, for example, has a long feminist history. Some analysts argue that it is Mexico, not the United States, that has been the cradle for feminism in the Western Hemisphere. Sor Juana Inéz de la Cruz, who lived in the 1600s, is said to be the first feminist of the Americas. In large numbers, Mexican women joined the revolutionary armies of Pancho Villa and Emiliano Zapata. Benita Galeana led the first land takeovers by squatters during the Great Depression. She was arrested sixty times and lost her eyesight while on a hunger strike fighting for women's suffrage. Since the 1980s, MAQUILADORA workers have claimed an unusual degree of freedom for themselves, despite the low pay and sexual harassment they continue to face in the factories. Mexican feminists today are fighting for reproductive rights, for better working conditions, and to have violence against women (especially sexual assault and wife battery) taken more seriously. However, in Mexico and in Latin America as a whole, women have not fully harnessed their potential as a political force compared to other interest groups such as labor movements and church groups.

Similar to other sets of activists, groups working to further women's causes disagree about the point of focus for their actions. Some groups accuse others of reinforcing gender distinctions by focusing on issues of family, motherhood, and children, replicating traditional political roles. Engaging in so-called motherist activism (discussed later), groups in Latin America, for example, were challenged by radical feminist leaders because their work focused on practical interests, such as providing meals to deprived children, rather than on more "strategic" issues, including sexual freedom and domestic violence.[34] Yet the mothers' groups, in their emphasis on seemingly practical needs, rallied tens of thousands of activists against military regimes, revealing that the emperor had no clothes. Some argue that women are uniquely placed to fight for the interests of their children, and indeed women have potently harnessed this connection to challenge state norms and policies.

Another debate centers on the relationship between culture and feminism. This has definitely been a theme of contention and division among Latin American, African, and Islamic feminists. Women who work within the system, or within the structure of prevailing religious norms, are accused by others of replicating traditional views that subordinate women, rather than challenging the status quo.

Non-Western variants of feminism have argued that "practical" concerns, including providing meals and healthcare to families, can be just as feminist as the political concerns of other feminists, such as demanding access to political decisionmaking. Adherents to the latter focus, which is considered to be more "strategic" than practical, claim to be working for larger structural changes that would ultimately transform gender relations. But non-Western women do not hold a monopoly on this desire: in Latin America, for example, feminism was central to the effort to delegitimize military rule and re-create CIVIL SOCIETY.[35] Yet other feminist groups, in the face of the same struggles, adopted an explicitly human rights character to their activism. Economic crises and the imposition of austerity programs impelled women to organize and demand relief, filling in the gaps of what government could not (or would not) provide. Maybe some viewed this as practical and too "traditional," but to the women who were organizing, it was feminism at its best.

To be successful, people plan their strategies within existing contexts—sometimes this means radically challenging the system, and other times it means reforming it

Figure 10.5   LGBT Rights in the "Third World"

One of the most personal aspects of identity can also be the most dangerous. Advocates for the rights of lesbian, gay, bisexual, and transgender (LGBT) individuals point out that throughout many countries of the third world, individuals lack the basic freedom to express gender identity or sexual orientation. More than seventy countries around the world consider homosexuality a crime, including five that put people to death for their sexual orientation: Iran, Mauritania, Saudi Arabia, Sudan, and Yemen (as well as some parts of Nigeria and Somalia).[36] In Turkey, a twenty-six-year-old openly gay man was hunted down by his father and killed, in what some sociologists have called Turkey's first public gay honor killing.[37] His death came at the same time that gay clubs and bars were becoming more common and a transsexual pop icon, Bulent Ersoy, was surging in popularity. Uganda's record is particularly severe, where legislation has been passed—with "overwhelming popular support"— to eradicate homosexuality from the country; the sponsor of the bill, who has connections to a largely discredited group of US evangelicals, minced no words as he stated his goal: "to kill every last gay person."[38]

The record on rights is not all negative, however, as Argentina legalized same-sex marriage in mid-2010, becoming the first Latin American state to do so (in a region of the world that analysts have noted is becoming more "gay-friendly").[39] In Mexico the Supreme Court ruled that marriages registered in Mexico City, where same-sex unions are legal, must be recognized throughout the country, providing the potential for nationwide marriage rights.[40] Even though there is no legal protection against discrimination for gay couples in China, more individuals are openly expressing their orientation, even as government censorship and closures of bars and cultural festivals ensue. Researchers have found that the social stigma toward homosexuality in China is grounded less in religious principles than it is in the mandate to marry and continue the family line.[41]

along the edges. Patriarchy and social conservatism are so pervasive, for example, that many women in northern Nigeria believe that reform within Islamic law is the only hope for promoting gender equality. The issue of the Islamic veil captures some of this controversy. Many Westerners associate the traditional headscarf or veil with women's oppression and submission to male authority. Yet for many Islamic women, the decision to wear a headscarf is a conscious choice; the wearing of a veil, or *purdah* (literally, "curtain"), provides them an avenue of expression and even opposition. For some, veiling literally creates a wall that allows women to move through the male world of school and work; it allows a quiet insubordination. In Tunisia, donning a religious veil is forbidden, and many challenge this rule. In Turkey, the Islamic veil is a source of fierce controversy; secular feminists are against it and religious women march for their freedom to wear it. Some women have refashioned traditional styles into a modern fashion of headscarf, granting them expression and individuality. In this sense, women have reappropriated Islamic admonitions for modest dress as a means of heightening their presence and voice.

Clearly, not all women are feminists. In fact, some ardently oppose mobilization and action in the name of equality or women's causes. Some groups, self-proclaimed antifeminists, reject the importance of feminist issues and often agree with gender segregation and clearly defined family roles. They often advocate a culturally conservative position, reaffirming the notion of a predetermined place for women at home, rearing the family, rather than in the marketplace or other public domains of men. Key issues of antifeminists include opposition to abortion and women's employment outside the home.

Each of these approaches, and the actions they inspire, arouse debate about cultural values and standards. Are there universal norms, applicable to all people irrespective of culture, level of development, or social system, or is there merit in an approach referred to as CULTURAL RELATIVISM, in which standards are dependent on relative circumstances?

Elites, Masses, and Legitimacy

It has been implicit in our discussion to this point that power is distributed unequally. Usually in public life, some people hold power and other people are influenced by it. In this chapter, we have emphasized that all people possess ideas about the world around them. It is obvious that in many areas of life, the ideas of some matter more than the ideas of others. In every society around the world, people can be divided into two categories, either the elites (possessing power and influence) or the masses (lacking power and influence relative to the elites). There are always more of the latter. Even though the so-called elites may exercise more influence and authority in economics, politics, culture, or other areas, they are not able to maintain this status indefinitely.

An important term that conveys one of the most fundamental political relationships between elites and masses is LEGITIMACY, sometimes viewed simply as "rightfulness."[42] All leaders, no matter their level, need to be concerned about their legitimacy. It can be viewed as a sense that an individual or group who has power, holds such power properly. Individuals or groups can possess power or influence, but if the people over whom they have influence do not view them as legitimate, their power and influence will likely be short-lived.

Sociologist Max Weber identified three primary sources of legitimacy: tradition, charisma, and legality. Traditional legitimacy is based on cultural precedents established for recognizing authority and power. A tribal chief, for example, bases his legitimacy on this source. Hereditary monarchies, in which some people receive their influence because of membership in particular families, are other sources of traditional legitimacy. The "Mandate of Heaven," possessed by members of the Chinese imperial leadership, is another example of legitimacy that is traditional in nature. Charismatic sources of legitimacy are based on personal attributes that command attention, respect, and often obedience. Charisma is both something that people are said to exhibit, as well as something given to them in the eyes of ordinary people. For example, Ayatollah Ruhollah Khomeini, the former religious leader of the Iranian Revolution, was viewed as a mythical hero to many. Before the 1979 revolution, while he was living in exile (mostly in Turkey, Iraq, and France), people in Iran insisted that they could see his face in the moon.[43] The third source of legitimacy, according to Weber, is legality: establishing seemingly impersonal rules and procedures to determine the recipients of leadership and authority. In this example, elections and laws transfer a sense of legitimacy to individuals and groups.

Legitimacy is what makes political systems last. It transforms raw power into a sense of authority. Without legitimacy, rulers' mandates are enforced out of a sense of fear, rather than a sense of duty or obligation.[44] A lack of legitimacy can cause a government to crumble. In some cultural traditions, there would be signs from the ancestors or the spirits that a leader had lost his or her legitimacy. In imperial China, for example, natural disasters were perceived to be signs that the emperor had lost the legitimacy to rule. In many modern democracies today, legitimacy is based on the popular mandate. Although elections are increasingly being viewed as the legitimizing tool of modern leaders, this has not always been the case, nor do many leaders maintain their legitimacy based on legal means alone.

Do powerful elites really need to be concerned about their legitimacy? Simply put, they do. It is difficult to survive on coercion alone, and leaders need authority in order to accomplish the day-to-day tasks of governing. Coercion and the violence it entails are costly, not only in a crude financial sense, but in terms of morale as well. Certainly, some authoritarian leaders have made extensive use of threats and coercion as a means of maintaining their power. But it is extremely difficult (although not impossible) to maintain power in this manner for long. Leaders in all areas of public life need to develop connections with the masses, and must be able to foster a sense that they are legitimately empowered to make decisions. When citizens no longer feel that the leadership has legitimacy, they are often impelled to act. Ordinary citizens, even in the face of dire constraints on their behavior and threats of coercive responses from leaders, attempt to challenge circumstances that they feel are unjust and illegitimate. While some of these attempts face anguishing defeats, others are successful at challenging the state of affairs and bringing about desired change.

Leaders maintain their legitimacy in a variety of different ways. Ideology plays a key role, as members of the elite attempt to craft views and actions to their liking. The manipulation of ideologies by leaders is particularly acute in TOTALITARIAN systems, in which the government has control over most aspects of people's lives. The use of important symbols, such as buildings, images, linguistic phrases, and historical heroes, is another means by which leaders attempt to promote and increase their legitimacy. In societies that have experienced revolutions, or have had a recent history of revered leaders, paying homage to and noting a lineage from these leaders can be a powerful source of legitimacy, especially in uncertain times. On the fiftieth anniversary of the founding of the People's Republic of China, for example, then-president Jiang Zemin, who was also general secretary of the Chinese Communist Party (CCP), ordered large pictures of himself to be carried on high behind the traditional posters of Mao Zedong and Deng Xiaoping. This rather blatant attempt of demonstrating the source of his authority is not unlike other public relations campaigns in which leaders engage. In examining legitimacy in the non-Western world, one must be careful to avoid connections between legitimacy, stability, and popular content. Just because a pronounced sense of legitimacy may seem to be present in a particular country does not mean that citizens agree with all (or even most) of the actions that their government takes.

Leaders may also promote their legitimacy by providing material gains to the population. Indonesia's former president Suharto based much of his legitimacy, especially in the later years of his rule, on promises to the people that their economic lives would improve. When the futility of this promise was painfully realized in the spring of 1998, however, his legitimacy plummeted, and he was forced from office. This example provides another lesson about the importance of stability. When leaders are successful at maintaining it, for the most part life is stable. When they fail, it can often lead to popular mobilization or other forms of participation, a topic to which we now turn our attention.

Ideas in Action

If they are not acted upon, ideas remain a possibility, rather than an expression of will. In the remainder of this chapter, we examine the next step: when individuals and groups decide to take action based upon their beliefs. We examine forms of political participation, which we define simply as efforts by ordinary people to influence the actions of their leaders.[45] Sometimes activists work within the bounds of legal activity, although oftentimes they attempt to change or break the conventional rules. While in some systems, especially totalitarian regimes, citizens are forced to participate in governmentally sponsored demonstrations, rallies, or protests, for our purposes we only examine participation that is voluntary. Fundamentally, political participation is about communicating preferences to the people who have power and influence (elites).

Certainly, not everybody, even in the most developed democracies, participates. One important characteristic that participants tend to exhibit is a sense of efficacy, which is a sense that one's participation can make a difference. If you believe that by writing a letter to an elected official you are likely to influence her or his point of view, you have a strong sense of efficacy. On the other hand, if you do not vote because you are of the mind that it does not make a difference, you have a low sense of efficacy. Oftentimes, a sense of efficacy also correlates with level of education, as well as socioeconomic security. It takes time to be active and engaged in public life, and few people can afford to take time off from work or be away from family in order to speak at a neighborhood assembly or picket against an unjust action.

How do people participate in their political, social, and economic world? We often think of voting in elections as the primary means of political participation, but in fact this is just one of four primary ways that people can participate in public life: (1) explicit communication, both spoken and written; (2) regime action, including voting and joining political parties or legal organizations; (3) mobilizational action, including demonstrating in social movements or rallies or participating in boycotts or other forms of group resistance; and (4) inaction, by refusing to vote or obey authority, or utilizing the so-called WEAPONS OF THE WEAK. These categories are not necessarily mutually exclusive. In fact, individuals and groups who feel dissatisfied with one type of action, such as normal constituent communication, often decide to pursue another strategy, such as joining a protest.

Spoken and Written Communication

Many citizens decide to communicate with their public leaders, often using simple means such as telephone calls, letters to officials or to the media, speeches, public signs, and increasingly, online petitions, blogs, and social-networking sites. Most officials establish some form of channel to foster communication between themselves and their constituents. In 2010, Nigerian president Goodluck Jonathan announced his plans to run for president on his Facebook page. Even the world's most secretive state, North Korea, is attempting to get in on the game by joining Facebook and Twitter (in

Young and old in Indonesia at a campaign rally for President Susilo
Bambang Yudhoyono (Reuters/Supri)

an attempt to respond to the propaganda war with South Korea).[46] Letters to the media
can be an extremely useful way to communicate dissatisfaction with a leader or policy. Even in the most totalitarian systems, government-controlled newspapers are
designated as receiving points for citizen letters and complaints. Even if the letters
themselves are not published in the "official" media, they are often collected and
distributed for the leadership to read. Petitions—either online or in print—often presented by groups of people, provide another open channel, although not without risk.

Regime Action
The second major category of participation is regime action, or participation that is
overtly designed to support the functioning of the larger political, social, or economic system. This is the type of participation with which most people are likely familiar. In many countries, democratic and nondemocratic alike, citizens are called on

to elect representatives to make decisions in their name. The difference in nondemocratic systems, though, is that there is little if any choice of candidates, or the candidates who are elected fail to exercise power or influence. Citizens are also called on to vote in referendums about issues that affect them, such as the Mexican vote on whether or not the Zapatistas should become a national opposition party.

Political parties stand out as one of the most common vehicles of participation. They develop as groups of similarly minded individuals and organize so that they can influence policy decisions. Parties help individuals identify with issues in public life, and they organize people into action. They also promote a common identity among participants, in some cases helping to bridge ethnic or cultural divides. In democratic and nondemocratic systems alike, political parties form so that the elites can appeal to ordinary citizens. In some countries, until very recently a single party dominated public life, and citizens have had few choices but to belong to the ruling party. In others, a meaningful PARTY SYSTEM has developed in which competing groups of people openly vie for attention and power. Parties often rename themselves (as the Islamic parties in Turkey), craft new coalitions (with other parties as well as constituent groups), and shift power balances, all in the attempt to maintain dynamic links between elites and masses.

Maurice Duverger classified three main types of political parties, based on their style of organization and operation.[47] The first is the CADRE PARTY, in which PERSONALIST REGIMES, often based on friendships and favors, together with factional groupings comprising people with similar approaches who try to stick together, dominate the relatively small group of elites involved in political matters. Often in systems where cadre parties prevail, the right to vote is limited, meaning that political parties do not face the need to justify their ideological positions or policies beyond the groups already possessing power or influence. A second type is the MASS PARTY, which attempts to reach out beyond the walls of power to appeal to less politically engaged individuals and groups. Mass parties have open membership, but their leaders often target specific segments of the population to whom they plan to pitch their ideological appeal: factory workers, intellectuals, peasants, or other groups. In order to maintain their interest and support, mass parties develop local branch offices that provide services and information to their likely constituents. Duverger's third type is the DEVOTEE PARTY, which is dominated by a charismatic leader and a small elite united in forging a revolutionary path. The Chinese Communist Party during Mao's leadership is an exemplar of such an elitist party, even if its rhetoric attempted to cater to a mass audience.

How important are political parties within the non-Western world? In single-party states, such as the PRC, they are the primary venue through which the elites exercise their power. In transforming states, such as Indonesia, the nascent political party system is dominated by personalities and crowded with minute factions. In other countries, including Peru, traditional parties have become virtually extinct. Many leaders sense they are better off without a party than with one. In states where personal relations continue to dominate politics, elections tend to be centered on candidates rather than parties. These systems are marked by extreme electoral volatility, and can easily open the door for populist antisystem candidates who have few qualms about dissolving democratic institutions once they capture the seats of power.

Another type of institution that facilitates the participation of ordinary citizens is the employment organization or union. Independent unions attempt to provide a collective voice to workers. They attempt to promote workers' rights and interests, including sick leave, access to healthcare, and the right to strike, which is restricted in many areas of the world. Unions played an important role in civil rights movements in South Korea and South Africa. In some countries, unions work closely with elites; left-leaning political parties tend to develop strong ties with labor and trade unions. Unions may also serve as the launching pad for oppositional movements and parties. The Movement for Democratic Change (MDC) in Zimbabwe, for example, which has posed the greatest challenge that the ruling Zimbabwe African National Union–Patriotic Front (ZANU-PF) has ever faced, grew out of labor unions. In other countries, governments attempt to co-opt independent expression through the establishment of official, state-sponsored unions. If Chinese workers attempt to organize independently of the CCP-run federation of trade unions, they face almost certain jail time, or are sent to camps for "rehabilitation through labor." The famous big-box stores in China are the only location in the world where Wal-Mart employees may form a union—one that is under the firm supervision of the Communist Party organization (local offices are usually directed by someone from company management).[48] In fact, independent unionization is dangerous business throughout the third world.

Latin America remains an extremely risky place to organize for workers' rights. According to statistics from the International Trade Union Confederation, workers in Latin America face a "climate of extreme violence," with 89 trade union and labor activists' deaths in 2010—making it the most dangerous continent in the world for union activity.[49] In countries reliant on exports, including Nicaragua, El Salvador, Guatemala, Mexico, and Honduras, trade unionists face many restrictions on their ability to strike. Labor repression is also common in many African countries, where 80 percent of worldwide arrests for union activities take place. Finally, in the Middle East, independent trade unions are virtually nonexistent. In this region, the situation is particularly bleak for foreign workers, who make up approximately two-thirds of the labor force in many countries. In most countries in the region, foreign workers are not permitted to join or form any type of workers' union.

Union organizing can also be found among the youth. Children's labor unions, whose origins are found in the New York newsboy strikes against Joseph Pulitzer and William Hearst at the turn of the twentieth century, are vying for a stronger voice in national and international debates about child labor. According to the International Labour Organization (ILO), there are more than 215 million children workers worldwide (and some 100 million adolescents),[50] only a fraction of whom have banded together to form unions in support of their cause. Brazilian street children formed the first modern children's labor union in 1985.[51] Similar groups can be found throughout Africa, Southeast Asia, and India. Children's labor unions are becoming increasingly organized (some now hold international meetings), and they are united in the voice that child labor should not be abolished, but rather reformed.

Mobilizational Action

The third category of participation is mobilizational action, which includes social movements and other forms of collective action by aggrieved groups of people. By definition, this form of participation involves more than one person. People around the world understand the strength that can be found in numbers. When a group of like-minded individuals forms to influence the turn of events around them, they are said to have formed a social movement. We often think of participants in social movements as attempting to change the status quo and bring about a new state of affairs, but in fact many participants in social movements are fighting instead to maintain the current state of life. Social movements form when there are grievances, either because people sense that they are being unfairly singled out or that they are not doing as well as other groups (RELATIVE DEPRIVATION), because they feel that promises, either implicit or explicit, have not been kept (rising expectations), or because they perceive a threat of some sort. There is also a sense that "time is ripe" for change, providing an opportunity structure for action. There are seemingly favorable times for groups of people to engage in collective action, often because of a political or economic transition, unexpected access to power, divisions among leaders, or a decreased likelihood of repression.[52] Changes in the international environment and movements with "spillover effects" also inspire action. Savvy activists develop expectations of the likelihood of repression, and act accordingly.

Social movements can be defined by an issue, such as civil rights or environmental protection, by a core group, such as women's movements or students' movements, or by a common target, such as antiglobalization protests or antimilitary demonstrations. One of the most common characteristics of social movements is that

Figure 10.6 Iran's "Green Movement"

During the summer of 2009, a daring movement played out throughout Iran and the global blogosphere as millions of Iranians took to the streets to demonstrate against the announced results of a presidential election that had been ceded to the incumbent, Mahmoud Ahmadinejad. Protesters from many walks of life challenged the legitimacy of his reelection in a poll that saw 85 percent turnout among eligible voters. In what has been called the "Twitter Revolution," activists engaged in unprecedented use of information communication technologies to gather protesters, adopt last-minute strategies in response to government repression, and spread brutally explicit evidence of the government crackdown—around the world. Webcasts of opposition leaders were broadcast on YouTube, then spread easily through websites, mobile phones, and Bluetooth links. The BBC's Persian-language television service, broadcasting to Iran, received ten thousand e-mail messages daily and six video clips a minute at the height of the anger.[53] The most prevalent image of the movement was that of Neda Agha-Soltan, a young woman who was shot to death during the protests. A witness captured the image on his mobile phone, which was eventually transferred to YouTube (outside of Iran), after which the clip of the dying woman went viral. The day after the election, the state shut down the Internet entirely for half an hour while the authorities struggled to gain control—possibly allowing the Revolutionary Guards to draft Internet-savvy youth to help organize attacks on Twitter and other websites, which led to a "battle for control of the web . . . between governments and individuals."[54]

Green Movement supporters employed humor as a tactic. Responding to the chants of "Death to Israel! Death to America!" at President Ahmadinejad's rallies, supporters of the main opposition candidate, Mir Hussein Mousavi (a former prime minister), shouted "Death to potatoes!" to mock the president's practice of distributing sacks of potatoes to his financially underprivileged supporters.[55] Yet the regime responded with blunt force. One eighty-year-old woman lamented, "They have killed so many of the young and the well intentioned. Even the shah did not kill like this."[56]

they often begin with a narrowly defined issue, and then rather quickly blossom to include other complaints and interests, broadening their appeal to a greater number of groups. Rarely are social movements confined to a single issue, and alliances between sets of activists are common. A group of students begins a protest ostensibly about economic CORRUPTION. Then they are joined by unemployed workers angered by layoffs, and state employees frustrated at the inattention of their government-controlled union. The widespread protests then attract others who are at odds with the regime, including mothers who are confined to the home because of factory cutbacks, migrant peasants who cannot find work for more than a week at a time, and high school dropouts wanting to get in on the action. This situation was part of the story of the widespread demonstrations in China in the spring of 1989.

University students wanting to pay homage to a fallen leader sparked the movement. After other groups joined the students in Beijing and 300 other cities, and after the international media picked up on the unlikely protests, a prodemocracy movement formed. As participants multiplied, the task of the protest organizers increased exponentially. Disagreements about tactics increased, such as whether protesters should stage a hunger strike, whether they should openly confront the regime by blocking Tiananmen Square during an international summit, and whether they should negotiate with other protesting groups. We now know, thanks to extensive documentation and interviews with exiled protest leaders, that a serious factional split developed early on in the movement. Disagreement among movement leaders is common after a protest gets off the ground.

Participants in social movements often disagree about the scope of their protest actions. Do they want to provide a wake-up call to the regime and then return to life as usual, or do they want to bring regime leaders to their knees, attempting to cripple the economic and diplomatic base of the state? Some protesters view dialogue (especially with governments) as "selling out," while others view it as a strategic tactic. Some activists want to forge alliances with other organized social groups, uniting in their common cause of increasing regime TRANSPARENCY and ACCOUNTABILITY. Movements to extend political freedom and promote environmental protection are often linked, either in formal coalitions or because activists cross lines. Concern for the survival of indigenous peoples is often linked to environmental concerns, as in Nigeria with the Movement for the Survival of the Ogoni People (MOSOP), and in Mexico with the Zapatistas. In China, many of the same activists who supported the movements in 1989 have been among the harshest critics of the Three Gorges Dam and other similar megaprojects.

Economic concerns have been a major mobilizing force throughout the non-Western world. For many years, people unable to cope with AUSTERITY PLANS (discussed in Chapter 7) have protested against EXTENDED-CREDIT FACILITIES (ECFs), most visibly in what has come to be known as an "IMF riot." These riots, which often involve looting and burning, are a form of protest that has broken out in India, Jamaica, Egypt, Indonesia, Greece, and Argentina as people find that they can no longer manage with such devastating hardship. Less dramatic but sometimes more deadly versions of IMF riots take the form of mass demonstrations, such as those in Bolivia motivated by fatigue over fifteen years of structural adjustment.

In addition to achieving a desired goal, social movements are important because they provide a sense of identity and belonging to participants. In her studies of

Peruvian women's movements, Maruja Barrig argues that by participating in democratically organized programs such as communal kitchens and milk distribution programs, women develop a sense of solidarity and model behavior that could be extended into other areas of life.[57] To better understand the organization and impact of social movements, we examine two subtypes: women's movements and youth mobilization.

People often think of women's movements being involved in suffrage, or the right to vote, and little more. Women's mobilization, though, has gone well beyond this single cause, and in fact women activists have refused to be held back by the absence of the right to vote. For example, even though Mexico had some of the most vibrant and developed women's networks throughout Latin America as early as the 1930s, it was among the last countries in the Southern Hemisphere to grant women the right to vote.[58] Women's movements, especially in the third world, have been particularly strong at demonstrating that personal issues are indeed political issues. As discussed in Chapter 7, NEOLIBERALISM has contributed to crises and poverty, and women have been channeled disproportionately into low-paid and transitory work. This has led many women to seek participation in community-based and neighborhood organizations to survive as they struggle to fill the gaps created when the state cuts services. Already struggling to support a family, these women face a huge burden without social services to rely on. Yet it sometimes seems that the most burdened and desperate people can mobilize to accomplish huge tasks. For example, women spearheaded the Madres de Plaza de Mayo movement in Argentina, which brought attention to the "disappeared" husbands and sons of the participants, ignited human rights protests, and launched similar movements throughout Latin America. Another example of motherist activism can be found in China following the crackdown on the students in Tiananmen Square. Ding Zilin, whose son was killed on the last evening of the demonstrations as he attempted to vacate the square, and other mothers have staged an international movement to publicize the plight of their children and the brutality of the Chinese government. Although mothers go to the front lines for defense of family and morality, often they are subjected to STATE-SPONSORED TERRORISM, sexual abuse, and humiliation. They face similar discrimination within other participatory channels, including parties and unions that co-opt women into auxiliary chapters. Whether in traditional parties or social movements, women must prove themselves against visible and invisible obstacles. Women in many countries form their own organizations because their demands for equality and justice are viewed as divisive or frivolous.

Women throughout Latin America, especially in Peru and Chile, have established communal dining programs to pool resources and feed the economically poor. During the 1980s, one of the largest social movements in Latin America was the Vaso de Leche, or Municipal Milk, program. Based in Lima, Peru, its participants distributed at least a single serving of milk a day to millions of children. While the military concentrated on progressive and radical rural reform, popular social programs initiated by women attempted to incorporate new groups into public affairs, especially the urban lower class and peasants. Their mobilization was especially critical because of the disastrous economic crises that battered the region throughout the 1980s. In the end, though, they maintained some reliance on government, especially at local levels, for funding. They also received support through international donations, mostly from the United States. These activities are important not only for the services they provided to needy people, but also for the linkages they established between women's groups. They help many women feel a sense of belonging and empowerment, which helps promote active involvement in public affairs that otherwise seem "off limits." The challenge they face for more long-term impact, though, is to be able to organize when not in the face of crisis.

Additionally, college and university students tend to be at the forefront of protests and social movements. Why? Students tend to be skeptical of the norms of government and society, yet optimistic about their ability to make a difference. Many Latin American youth argue that their role is to offer sorely needed answers for the new situations their countries are facing. The traditional model of the party is exhausted; the youth need new organizations capable of responding to demands for a new, more participatory, and flexible political culture. Students tend to be risk-takers, willing to sacrifice time, money, and sometimes their lives in order to make a point. Some have noted a correlation between presence of major universities and presence of social movements, especially in capital cities (Tehran, Mexico City, Beijing). University campuses also can be ideal locales for communication networks. The national university of Peru, San Cristóbal de Huamanga, for example, served as the launching pad for one of the most violent movements in Latin America, Sendero Luminoso. Some student movements to unseat leaders have been successful, such as in Indonesia in 1998 and Iran in 1979, while others have been painfully unsuccessful, notably in Mexico in 1968 and China in 1989.

University students also have a history of political activism in Iran. In November 1979, in the early days of the Islamic Revolution, students were one of the groups leading the seizure of the US embassy in Tehran when fifty-two American hostages were captured. Twenty years later, in July 1999, student-led demonstrations for press reform broke out at Tehran University, spreading to eighteen cities. Sensing an open opportunity caused by widened rifts between Iran's conservative Supreme Leader, Ayatollah Sayyid Ali Khamenei, and the popularly elected but lower-ranking president, Mohammad Khatami, students staged five successive days of protest for democratic reform and press freedom. Students mobilized after the legislature passed a restrictive press law and after conservative leaders ordered the closure of a popular left-leaning Islamic newspaper, *Salam*.

In response, police forces raided the university dorms while students were sleeping, pushing some from multistory windows. In response, even more students joined the protest, using updated twists of slogans from the 1979 revolution. The chant "Independence, Freedom, Islamic Republic," was altered to "Independence, Freedom, Iranian Republic." Most accounts claim that the police killed one student, and approximately twenty more were seriously injured. In addition, nearly a thousand students were arrested for participating in the unrest, and at least four people were sentenced to death, in secret trials, for inciting violence. In July 2000 a military court acquitted the Tehran police chief blamed for leading the charge to violence the year before, inciting a muted but audible outcry from many in Iran and abroad.

Weapons of the Weak

The final type of participation is powerful in its ability to cause disruption through inaction or (on the surface) seemingly inconsequential acts of individual resistance.

If the traditional spaces to which people can turn are denied (unions, political parties, media, protest channels), they learn to turn elsewhere to express their sentiments, especially their grievances. Anthropologist James C. Scott identified weapons of the weak as a way to categorize concealed, disguised, individual resistance. These actions, such as concealing a pig from state officials or falsifying income records, may not garner the same amount of attention as a revolt in the national capital, but they can be extremely effective tools against injustice nonetheless. People pursue less obvious and less explicitly confrontational forms of resistance when open challenge to authority is too risky. In varied contexts, Scott and others draw our attention to "everyday forms of resistance" pursued by dominated groups, such as women, peasants, or other disenfranchised individuals. As discussed in Chapter 4, weapons of the weak were common forms of resistance in struggles for national liberation.

Some analysts have sought to explain why women and other repressed groups in some parts of the world appear to be aloof from politics and less likely to participate in democratic struggles. They argue that in many cases women's political power and participation have declined since the precolonial period. Women's initial response to being politically marginalized during colonialism was resistance. However, this resistance often proved ineffective and was followed by a disengagement from formal politics or withdrawal into a consciously apolitical stance. Instead, women have come to favor private, extralegal channels and institutions including families, secret societies, spirit cults or prayer groups, and traditional women's associations. Additionally, women tend to be more active in regard to socioeconomic issues at the local rather than the national level.

But part of the reason why some groups appear complacent to outsiders is that observers fail to recognize acts of resistance that do not utilize more conventionally recognized channels of protest. Many actors employ weapons of the weak in the face of power, accomplishing in subtle acts what might never be achieved in more traditional routes. Individuals feign support for a cause, while subtly putting a cog in the wheel to block it. Actors can drag their feet, pretend compliance, and organize others to break rules through acts of civil disobedience. As Célestin Monga argues, outsiders often lament the absence of civic participation in African societies because they overlook the long tradition of indigenous activism, what he terms the "anthropology of anger."[59] People get angry when systematically oppressed, and they develop ways of escaping repression. They pretend to accept the rules imposed by authoritarian groups, and are constantly adjusting to escape domination and circumvent coercive strictures. Such participation is GRASSROOTS-BASED and highly creative. Activists subvert the rules by not confronting power directly. These informal methods of participation and protest may be what truly pushes change.

Subversive music is a common form of political expression. For example, one of Africa's most famous Afrobeat musicians, Fela Anikulapo-Kuti, considered music a weapon. While praise-singing is a tradition associated with greats such as King Sunny Adé, Fela invented a new art: abuse-singing. In the late 1970s, Fela took on then-president Olusegun Obasanjo, the military dictator of Nigeria, arguing that Afrobeat was the only music through which people could say what they felt and tell the government what they thought. Fela was beaten and jailed. His seventy-eight-year-old mother was thrown from a second-story window and later died of her injuries. He is followed in these pursuits by his son, Femi Kuti, whose Afrobeat songs attack corrupt politicians and warn about AIDS. One of the most famous heavy metal bands in China, Ordnance, has taken on Beijing authorities for being too soft, and has faced a ban from Chinese airwaves because of lyrics such as "compromising with the United States and Japan is a disgrace."[60]

Another highly influential political forum for dealing with real-life issues such as corruption, drug trafficking, AIDS, and sexism is the *telenovela,* or soap opera, a favorite form of entertainment for millions in Latin America. The *telenovela* is much more influential than the newspaper in Mexico; it is said that writers are using this art form the way Thomas Paine used the pamphlet. As dictatorships have been retired, a flourishing independent medium is taking advantage of the political openness to tackle once-taboo subjects.

Weapons of the weak are seemingly invisible and unthreatening, yet they convey a strong message about the grievances and power of dominated people. Mass abstention can be another discreet weapon of last resort. In expectation of massively fraudulent elections in Peru, the main opposition party encouraged people to stay away from the polls, to spoil the ballots, or to write "no to fraud" on them. Dissidents might slip an encrypted missive into a newspaper article, the true meaning of which becomes clear when the last word of each sentence is read vertically up and down the column. In the middle of a photograph portraying an abundant harvest, "down with dictatorship" is subtly carved in the wheat. By the time these tricks are discovered, it is too late for authorities to pull thousands of magazines or newspapers from the shelves. Another example is found among the women of Iran, who boldly challenge traditional Islamic customs of modesty by requesting cosmetic improvements (including rhinoplasty performed by doctors trained in Cleveland) on the bit of their face that is exposed. Similarly, Iranian women dye their eyebrows and purchase nonprescription contact lenses to challenge societal norms and express their individual identities. Iranian newspapers have carried accounts of teenage girls in Iran who crop their hair short and dress as boys as a way to refuse submission.[61] While these actions may not seem forceful, or overtly political, each is an expression of voice and power in its own right.

Some find their situation so egregious that they perceive their only option to be that of "exit."[62] Increasingly, analysts recognize suicide as an explicit political choice by individuals who feel they have no other option. Women in southeastern Turkey, caught in a rapid and forced migration to the urban areas, attempt suicide at record rates.[63] Women who feel trapped in arranged marriages, or torn between the modern world of the city and their desire to return to more traditional patterns in their rural homes, gain a sense of control over their fate through suicide that they cannot find in life. Unprecedented numbers of Mexicans took their own lives after the devaluation of the peso and the resulting crash of the Mexican economy in 1994. While suicide is usually conducted in private, these cases were unique in their public display; young men, believing they had no chance under the existing economic circumstances to establish a family, threw themselves in front of subway cars. A spate of highly public suicides at factories in China served as a wake-up call to the living and working conditions within some Chinese factories, including at Foxconn, the world's biggest contract electronics supplier, which is a supplier to Apple, Dell, and Hewlett-Packard, among others. Interpretations of these weapons of the weak, which also included employees simply walking off the factory floor, varied, including sociologists' claims that they were signs of a generation rejecting the regimentation of their predecessors who served as the "cheap labor army" responsible for China's economic reemergence.[64] In late 2010, a seemingly quiet act of rebellion caused ripples throughout the Arab world. Mohammad Bouazizi, a vegetable salesman in Tunisia, set himself on fire after a policewoman confiscated his unlicensed cart, slapped him, and spat in his face. His protest and painful death (he lay in the hospital for nearly 10 days before he died), sparked protests that toppled the government of Tunisian president Zine el Abidine Ben Ali, spreading to much of the Arab world.

The management of information is another classic form of everyday resistance. For example, rumor is especially popular and effective in Africa, where oral traditions are highly valued. Rumor has been described as a potent brew of what is not known in the here and now, linked to what may or may not be known by those able to manipulate the supernatural. Rumors are hypotheses; in places where there is no authoritative news or information source, rumors don't just titillate, they are currency.[65] In the last days of Mobutu Sésé Seko's reign in Zaire, rumors about prophecies of his impending doom greatly undermined what was left of the regime's credibility and contributed to its ultimate demise.

Conclusions: Civil or Uncivil Society?

To what can such varied forms of citizen participation and activism lead? Some speak of the potential emergence of a civil society in which citizens are able to enjoy some level of autonomy, or independence, from the government, and a multiplicity of voluntary associations are permitted to form. The belief is that if citizens are able to seek membership in independent associations, absent of government control or influence, this promotes an actively engaged citizenry who adopt a moral sense of obligation to participate in civic causes. With a multiplicity of groups and voluntary associations, people have an increased opportunity to express themselves as well as competing viewpoints and perspectives. This leads many to connect civil society with democracy. This straightforward connection, though, can be misleading.

In many regions of the world, the development of an independent merchant class is viewed as part of a nascent civil society. If people have an area in their life over which the government has no influence or control, this is said to foster an independent, civic identity above political divisions. For example, after the 1985 Mexico City earthquake, the urban poor worked through neighborhood organizations to force the government and World Bank to alter their recovery plans. Similar civic action groups have formed to fight crime and corruption in Mexico and South Africa. The combination of high crime rates and distrust of police competence contributed to the phenomenal growth of one South African vigilante group that has morphed into a private security business, Mapogo a Mathamaga, which is infamous for its use of corporal punishment. This form of mob justice is very popular; Mapogo has branches throughout the country and boasts of thousands of members and that 85 percent of those who display the group's stickers on their premises and property never experience any criminal activity.[66]

High literacy rates and access to independent media promote an independent sense of society, as citizens can educate themselves about alternative ideas and approaches to issues. For example, once the Turkish government's monopoly over radio and television broadcasts was abolished in 1993, citizens suddenly had a huge proliferation of options for information and leisure. The Internet revolution, spawned by changes in communication technology, also has the potential to change people's sense of self, state, and society. These changes are important not only for the options they make available for citizens, but also for the increase in accountability they foster. Some view the development of an increasing space for civil society as a potential birthing ground for democracy, because it promotes the existence of diverse competing groups and encourages citizens to take an interest in and participate in government.

Yet civil society will not automatically be more benign or democratic; given the increased space for organization and mobilization, it is just as likely for antidemocratic groups to form. This is especially, although not exclusively, the case in regimes with a recent history of political and social violence in which individuals were socialized into accepting coercion and repression as a regular mode of behavior. The proliferation of competing groups is not a silver bullet against repression. Observing groups like the Carapintada military leaders in Argentina, and the Inkatha in South Africa, Leigh Payne referred to the proliferation of "uncivil movements" that promote exclusion and violence as a means of competing and gaining power within a democratic system.[67] Such groups are common in a variety of countries, with or without past experiences of AUTHORITARIANISM. They gain influence through the use of threats, legitimating myths, and coalition formation, and no system is immune. Exclusionary movements are capable of securing their demands within the democratic system, so they face no pressing need to overthrow it. But these groups provide an insidious threat to an inclusionary, vibrant democratic society. They use democratic language, institutions, and strategies toward their own uncivil ends. They can transform themselves into political parties with undemocratic goals. The Odua People's Congress in Nigeria, a Yoruba militia that once played a big part in the prodemocracy movement, transformed its message into a hard-line ethnic supremacist agenda. Given the elitist, antipeasant rhetoric common among student demonstration leaders in China, many wonder whether the 1989 movements, had they been successful, would have resulted in a more or a less democratic outcome than exists today.

The presence of these "uncivil" groups and behaviors highlights the value-laden approach to the civil society debate. David Rieff argues that many have used the concept of a civil society, correlated with increased tolerance, expression, and diversity, to welcome groups we approve of.[68] Yet if civil society merely refers to groups who are able to operate independent of the reach of the state, their ideology about mode of action or inclusion of minority groups has nothing to do with it. In this estimation, Serbian war criminal Radovan Karadzic is just as civil as Czech human rights leader Vaçlav Havel. The US National Rifle Association, which the United Nations has refused to admit as a legitimate nongovernmental organization, is as much an agent of civil society as is the International Campaign to Ban Landmines, which has received considerable international financial and emotional support. Rieff, Payne, and others cause us to question the mere proliferation of organizations as a desirable consequence linked to the weakening of political power. As Alison Brysk reminds us, constituents participating in free and competitive elections have returned authoritarian leaders to power in Guatemala, Bolivia, and elsewhere.[69]

11

Linking
Concepts and Cases

Now that you have a sense of the variety of views and actions that are taken in the third world, we present you with evidence from our eight CASE STUDIES so that you can explore these ideas further. As you look at issues of voice and participation in these countries, try to observe patterns of similarity and difference between and among them. What is the impact of history on the development of POLITICAL CULTURE? To what do you attribute differences in the frequency and volatility of expression? In which of these cases can you see generational-based clashes, and what is their source? Which countries have more mobilized civil societies, and which cases appear to be less vibrant? Why do you think this may be so?

Case Study: Mexico

Fifty years ago, poet Octavio Paz described Mexico as trapped in a labyrinth—with a political culture of cynicism and suspicion deeply rooted in the country's history.[1] Part of the explanation for this is that under the Institutional Revolutionary Party (PRI), the Mexican government actively sought to preempt all meaningful citizen participation. Through its use of CORPORATISM, the government attempted to incorporate or co-opt all potentially influential groups in society. Yet today in Mexico, CIVIL SOCIETY is fighting to change that relationship and let Mexico's leaders know that it should be society that dictates and the government that obeys.

   What explains this dramatic shift in political culture, and how far-reaching is this change? As we will see in Chapter 14, Mexico began in earnest in the 1980s a protracted POLITICAL LIBERALIZATION that some say dates back to the late 1960s. A crucial part in the transition to DEMOCRACY was played by civil society. Citizen groups like Alianza Civica fought hard for the DEMOCRATIC TRANSITION. Others, too fearful to speak out, used WEAPONS OF THE WEAK, accepting handouts or attending rallies, but still voting their consciences. Many people mobilized after the 1985 earthquake in Mexico City, after the government's ineffective response left civil society to organize to save their neighborhoods. This disaster was an important watershed event, and since then Mexicans (perhaps simplistically identified as "parochial" in classic civic culture studies) have agitated for change and exercised their democratic rights in a variety of ways.

In 2000, for the first time in over seventy years, Mexican citizens voted in free and fair elections and a party other than the PRI, the National Action Party (PAN), the party of Presidents Vicente Fox (2000–2006) and Felipe Calderón (2006–2012), won the presidency. Founded in 1926, this conservative, probusiness party long opposed the PRI. It has a religious agenda (as opposed to the two other main parties, which tend to be secular) and is socially conservative. It is most popular in Mexico's northern states and very much believes that GLOBALIZATION is the best way to promote economic GROWTH, along with free market, neoliberal reforms. As the incumbent party its popularity has flagged as it has struggled to deal with a range of political and economic challenges. President Calderón will continue to face an uphill battle in the Mexican congress during the remainder of his term in office, since PAN came in second in the 2009 midterm elections (with 28 percent of the vote overall).[2]

The leftist Party of Democratic Revolution (PRD) grew tremendously in influence over the first five years of the democracy, promising to renegotiate the North American Free Trade Agreement (NAFTA), subsidize farmers, and spend more on welfare programs. Most PRD supporters were from the south—the poorest regions of Mexico, those most marginalized by globalization. The PRD was created by Cuauhtémoc Cárdenas (son of former president Lázaro Cárdenas) when he split with the PRI in the late 1980s. Although Cárdenas and some other PRD officials have repudiated defeated 2006 presidential candidate Andrés Manuel López Obrador, it was López Obrador (known as "Amlo") who united the party and who largely personifies it today.[3] However, since 2006 the PRD has lost momentum (it came in a distant third in the midterm elections in 2009) and Amlo's influence has greatly diminished since the heady days immediately following the elections. The PRD's dominant faction sees him as a liability, but for now it appears that no one else in the party can replace him. With or without Amlo, at this point the PRD isn't expected to be a real contender in the 2012 presidential race.[4] Things could change. And at the very least, if it can position itself as a swing vote, the left could play the role of kingmaker in that election.[5]

Certainly one party that will be looking out for such an alliance is the PRI, the party that monopolized political power in Mexico for seven decades and has lost every presidential race since the country made its democratic transition. Currently the PRI is considered center-left, although its IDEOLOGY has fluctuated over time in what is described as the "pendulum effect." Immediately following the 2000 elections, the PRI went into a tailspin and some analysts predicted that the party was dead. Yet since 2000 it has for the most part been the largest party in both houses of congress—and it has continued to win influence because Calderón has had to seek out its cooperation. The PRI's cooperation has often (but not always) been forthcoming, because it doesn't want to be viewed as intransigent; it wants to show that it can make deals and govern.[6] It was rewarded by the voters in the 2009 midterm elections, winning the most votes (37 percent overall). Although this did not give it the majority it would like to have had in the lower house of congress, there is good news for the PRI. Analysts believe that voters turned out to support it because they were nostalgic about the party's ability to get things done. Even though the PRI was corrupt when it ruled the country prior to 2000, it was seen as bending the rules in favor of working people. Since 2000, in PRI-controlled STATES, governors still hand out goods and maintain PATRON-CLIENT RELATIONS. On the other hand, PAN, which is believed to be equally corrupt, is viewed as incapable of leading Mexico out of the economic and security crises it faces. It is often seen as cold and out of touch with the hardships that people are facing.[7]

In its efforts to hold its political representatives accountable, Mexican civil society has remained active. For example, in 2009, citizens frustrated by their lack of choices on the ballot undertook a *voto nulo* ("vote null and void") campaign. This initiative was unique for the speed with which it swept the Internet, urging voters to *voto nulo* instead of voting for any of the candidates for office that year. The activists' argument was that voting for nothing was better than continuing with the politicians who were currently running the country. In the end, it is estimated that 2 million Mexicans canceled their ballots (about 5 percent of all votes on average—and 60 percent in some areas). Because the *nulo* vote crossed party lines, it isn't believed to have affected the outcome of the elections, but it did send an important message. Instead of staying home and not voting, people came out to show their annoyance with the dysfunction of the political system.

Mexican citizens are upset by the recession, the lack of security in the country, and their sense that corruption is as bad as ever.[8] For the most part they turned out to vote for state and local races in 2010, despite the drug cartels' attempts to frighten them away from the polls. Mexicans are demanding that their government continue evolving, moving toward finally realizing the core ideals of the Mexican Revolution. Mexicans have been galvanized to action because, even in this democracy, institutional channels are still not responding to people's needs.[9] As with the *nulo* campaign, some in this movement are practicing civil disobedience precisely because they believe in democracy. And they will use whatever tactics are necessary to demand that the system work for them.

Case Study: Peru

If any generalizations can be made about Peruvian political culture, they are few in number and quickly outdated. However, it has often been said that Peruvians, traditionally identified as having a strong civil society and a weak state, value decisive leadership over institutional checks and balances.[10] Some analysts suggest that this tendency to favor authoritarians goes back to the days of the Inca Empire and centralized rule. Such traditions continued under colonialism—as did militarism, which has been a constant in Peru.

There is a long tradition of military intervention in Peruvian politics; most of the country's nearly 200-year history has been spent under military rule. During much of the 1990s, large numbers of Peruvians supported President Alberto Fujimori's growing AUTHORITARIANISM as a necessity in the country's wars against TERRORISM and inflation. However, by the end of the decade this justification no longer rang true for most people. Peruvians became increasingly divided over what they valued more highly—security or freedom. Although the president still had his supporters, Peruvians were becoming impatient with his excesses. They resisted Fujimori's efforts to overturn the constitution and destroy the integrity of the electoral process. Because of the groundswell of activism that brought Fujimori down, observers argued that the 2001 elections showed that it could no longer be said that civil society in Peru was weak or antidemocratic. It was primarily an urban, middle-class civil society that rallied to prevent *continuismo,* the open-ended continuation in office desired by Fujimori. Prodemocracy gatherings became a tradition each Friday in Lima, where Peruvians expressed their political opinions in a variety of creative ways. For example, groups of women gathered in front of the presidential palace with washtubs, scrub brushes, and aprons to protest how dirty politics had become by symbolically washing the Peruvian flag.[11]

When it comes to civil society coalescing around labor concerns, farmers and miners have been active in Peru. For example, in 2010 farmers fought police and blocked a highway to protest a copper-mine project that they feared would harm the land and water supplies. Elsewhere, coca farmers protesting plans to eradicate their crop seized a power plant and took hostages, affecting power supplies to the regional capital.[12] Miners have also organized against mistreatment by a Chinese mining company, Shougang Corporation. In addition to conflicts with bosses over low wages, workers contend the Chinese treated them like inferiors, refusing to speak directly to Peruvian workers. Employees maintain that the company dumped toxic waste into the sea and never made good on promises to invest in the mine and the town's infrastructure. Strikes and clashes have sometimes turned violent, as private security guards and Peruvian police have opened fire on protesters. In 2009 a construction worker was shot by police. A year later, no one had been held responsible for this death.[13]

It is a similar story for indigenous activism in Peru. Indigenous movements have come and gone for years, often without gaining much traction, but recently they have emerged bigger and more powerful than ever, proving capable of disrupting politics as usual. In Bolivia and Ecuador, using institutionalized as well as noninstitutionalized forms of collective action, Indians have taken down governments. Historically in Peru these groups have been weaker, but over the past few years more than fifty native groups, comprising as many as 300,000 people, have formed networks to join in a movement that has exploded onto the scene as a response to ECONOMIC LIBERALIZATION. Since 2008 they have been facing down a president intent on pushing economic growth by opening up lands (as much as 72 percent) of the Amazon that have traditionally been respected as off-limits.[14] More visible and better organized than they have been in the past, communicating across the jungle to isolated communities via radio, Amazonian indigenous groups successfully called general strikes, closing down roads and rivers to traffic for weeks at a time. They have turned out in the thousands at protests in cities and towns throughout the Amazon. They have even threatened to cut off the supply of oil and natural gas to the capital. These activists insist that the land is theirs and that if the government opens it up to mining, oil, and natural gas companies, a variety of problems will follow, including destruction of the environment and loss of a way of life. From their point of view, this is a life-or-death struggle and they have dug in for a protracted fight—and it is the most serious crisis that neoliberal Alan García Perez's government has had to face.[15]

The García government has responded by claiming that those who seek to keep the Amazon for themselves are selfish and are sitting on resources that the state owns the right to by law—untouched resources that could be used to modernize and develop the entire country. It has sought to win the public's support by using condescending language and conjuring up racist images of indigenous peoples as savages. For example, in 2007 García wrote an opinion piece for the Lima newspaper *El Comercio* titled "The Dog in the Manger Syndrome" (based on Aesop's fable), in which he insinuated that Indians were like dogs preferring to begrudge others what they were not using themselves. The media have continued this tact, calling the Indians *chunchos* (Quechua for "wild ones") and portraying native people as ignorant, uneducated, and incapable of taking part in a national dialogue.[16] On the other hand, trade unions and Peru's Catholic bishops have supported indigenous demands, but tempers have risen and clashes have broken out, such as in 2009, in which dozens of activists (and police) have been killed.[17] The political system has failed to settle the conflict. Worse, some analysts point to the president's suspension of civil liberties and criminalization of peaceful social protest. García has gone so far as to characterize some activists as terrorists. For example, he charged Alberto Pizango, the leader of the Inter-Ethnic Association for the Development of the Peruvian Amazon (AIDESCEP), with sedition and ordered his arrest (Pizango fled the country, taking political asylum in Nicaragua). The president also characterized the indigenous movement as an international conspiracy (backed by Venezuela and Bolivia) to destabilize his government.[18] Such amped-up rhetoric is concerning to some, who fear that this democratic government may be giving security forces carte blanche to resort to extreme measures. There is evidence that they are doing so, as human rights monitors are calling for an investigation of disappearances. The Peruvian congress hoped to reduce tensions by suspending the presidential decrees that set off the protests, but the protesters would not be put off and some of the decrees were eventually repealed.[19] However, the activists held fast, arguing that nothing had really changed because free trade agreements with the United States and China also open the rainforest to exploitation. So far these Amazonian groups have not joined forces with highland Indians (who also know racism, marginalization, and the negative impact of extractive industries). Yet there is plenty of reason for them to do so, and if they do, analysts agree that a united indigenous SOCIAL MOVEMENT in Peru will be a force that can demand territorial and cultural autonomy, if not the suspension of the neoliberal approach to DEVELOPMENT.[20]

Case Study: Nigeria

Often described as a "conglomerate society," Nigeria is composed of more than 250 different ethnic groups whose divisions are complicated by regional, religious, and linguistic identities. For most of the years since independence in 1960, political power, both civilian and military, has been largely under the control of northern Muslims, who resent the southern domination of commerce that dates back to colonialism. On the other hand, until 1999 many southerners felt that they had never had a government that represented their interests.

Since the quick transition to democracy in 1909, several political parties have been hastily formed, but few of them have much of an ideological base. Rather, many Nigerian politicians continue a tradition of manipulating IDENTITY to achieve political power. Fearing loss to a rival, they mobilize populations by asserting their cultural distinctiveness. In this oil-rich country, where political power translates into access to economic resources, politics is viewed as a winner-take-all gamble. Politicians from all regions have propagated myths of irreconcilable differences, while working hard to blur the glaring disparity between rich and poor. This explains why elections in Nigeria, as in many other countries, are fought as mortal combat.[21]

Identity politics were certainly at play in the 1999 and 2003 elections. In 1999 the ideological differences between the candidates were negligible and both candidates were southwestern and Yoruba. In 2003 the southwestern, Yoruba, Christian incumbent ran against a northern Muslim. In each election it was widely suspected that both candidates owed their loyalty to the former military leaders who were providing them with financial support. In the end, in both 1999 and 2003, Olusegun Obasanjo (a retired general) was elected, largely because these backers believed he was someone with whom they could work.

The sense that Obasanjo has been bought and paid for by the northern military ELITE has contributed to a surge in religious and ethnic tensions. Since the return to democracy in 1999 more than 13,000 people have been killed in communal violence, most of it at the local level and over access to land and resources. Much of this killing occurs in an area known as the Middle Belt, which cuts a large swath across the country and reflects the tension between north and south. Conflicts there are often fought between "indigenes" and "nonindigenes" (old-timers versus newcomers) and are based in economic and political rivalries, hardened with a veneer of religious or ethnic hatred.[22] For example, tensions rose when one-third of the country's thirty-six states sought to impose SHARIA (what some consider to be Islamic law) over the objections of the non-Muslim community. In *sharia* courts, several Nigerians received what some considered cruel punishment. For example, after failing to prove that four men had raped and impregnated her, in 2001 a still-breastfeeding teenage mother was flogged 100 times for adultery. Many people, particularly non-Muslims but even some Muslims, consider such actions to be abusive and fear that the northern states are seeking to create an Islamic THEOCRACY in Nigeria.[23]

However, most analysts believe that, for now at least, such fears are overblown. Although Islamic extremism exists in Nigeria, most Nigerian Muslims are moderate and tolerant. They were mortified by the attempt by a young Nigerian, Umar Farouk Abdulmutallab, to bomb a US airliner on Christmas Day in 2009. However, there are others, known as Boko Haram (or dubbed by the press "Nigeria's Taliban"), who believe that Islamic law is not enforced strictly enough in Nigeria. Its members have taken up arms in several northern cities because they are poor, unemployed, and sick of government corruption. Boko Haram, a Hausa expression of disgust with Western education, has grown stronger over the years, testing the capacity of the democratic government. Hundreds of people have been killed in clashes between government forces and these militants, who aim to overthrow the federal government and transform Nigeria into an Islamic state. The government's use of scorched-earth tactics has only emboldened these fighters, who recently blasted their way into a central prison and released all the inmates.[24]

Social conditions in the north are ripe for insurrection, but it is often said that Nigeria's political leaders fear being usurped by each other more than by a popular revolt. Something that may have the potential to touch off instability is actually an arrangement worked out years earlier to promote stability: a "power shift" or "rotation" guaranteeing that presidential candidates from the major regions get a turn (or two) at the presidency.[25] As Obasanjo's retirement neared, Nigeria's power brokers agreed that after two terms of the southwesterner's presidency, it was time for someone different. It looked like the next president would be a Muslim northerner (although those from the south and southeast were pointing out that they had never had a turn). Analysts agreed that because of the advantages of incumbency (money and the backing of political godfathers), whoever won the People's Democratic Party's (PDP) nomination would have a very real edge in the 2007 election. Although there were several contenders (all northern), Obasanjo favored Umaru Yar'Adua, a conservative Muslim governor from the northern state of Katsina.[26]

Yar'Adua became the PDP nominee. When he won the election (under dubious circumstances) in April 2007, Nigeria witnessed the first civilian-to-civilian transfer of power in its history. However, this crowning achievement was followed by crisis. In November 2009, Yar'Adua suddenly left the country for medical treatment without handing over power to his vice president. In February 2010, after seventy-eight days of uncertainty (and infighting between power brokers), the Nigerian senate finally made a bold (and some say unconstitutional) move. It named the vice president, Goodluck Jonathan (a PDP Christian from the southeast), as acting president. When Yar'Adua died two months later, Jonathan was inaugurated as president. However, even before he could take the oath of office, questions swirled regarding Jonathan's right to rule. Many northerners from his own party began agitating for new elections, since according to the practice of rotation, it was still a northern Muslim's turn at the presidency.[27] Jonathan served out Yar'Adua's term, declared broken the arrangement for selection of the PDP nominee, and faced twenty opponents, most notably four northern challengers, for that prized position. Just four months ahead of the April 2011 elections, tensions were running high in the PDP, between those who insisted on continuing the rotation and those who wanted to do away with the system. Some Nigerians worried that reneging on the deal could be destabilizing and dangerous for the democracy. Others welcomed the prospect of a PDP split, arguing that Nigeria had become in effect a one-party state and it was time to reboot. With no other party having a chance of beating the PDP, some argued that the best thing for the democracy would be for the party to divide, allowing for two strong candidates to run in the next elections. That did not happen, but if it had it would have been a first for Nigeria.

Case Study: Zimbabwe

Zimbabwe has a flourishing rural and urban civil society. Its urban civil society had largely come together to support the Movement for Democratic Change (MDC), the greatest threat to the Zimbabwe African National Union–Patriotic Front (ZANU-PF) and its monopoly on power in more than three decades. The grievances that contributed to the MDC's rise had been festering for years. Austerity had turned many people who didn't normally think of themselves as political into activists. At the turn of the twenty-first century, almost all Zimbabweans disapproved of the government's handling of the economy, and three-quarters of those surveyed wanted President Robert Mugabe to resign.[28] The MDC capitalized on this sentiment with its election slogan "Change Everything, Everything Changes." With a focus on political and civil rights, this liberal party called for ending government corruption and increasing TRANSPARENCY, reducing poverty, and strengthening the RULE OF LAW.

The multiracial MDC enjoys a remarkably broad base of support. Although the party grew out of Zimbabwe's trade unions, which are very male-dominant, it included a feminist plank in its campaign.[29] The MDC's core supporters, who compose one-third of Zimbabwe's voters, are the young urban dwellers (the so-called Born Frees) who were either children at independence or born soon after. Mugabe's appeals to black NATIONALISM fall flat with much of this younger generation, who are too young to remember the humiliation and suffering that blacks experienced under white rule. Although members of ZANU-PF have spoken ominously about a "Rwandan solution" for the country's whites, it is undeniable that the membership of the MDC is multiracial. One of its most popular leaders is Roy Bennett, a white farmer who is known to Zimbabweans of all colors as Pachedu, "one of us."[30] Interestingly, voting is based not so much on ethnicity as on an urban-rural split (the MDC is popular in predominantly Ndebele Matabeleland, whereas ZANU-PF has never been well liked there).

Yet there are very real divisions in the country that cut across ethnicity. As opposed to the younger, urban generation of Born Frees, older and rural people have had a hard time ignoring the fact that so many years after liberation, whites continued to hold on to disproportionate amounts of Zimbabwe's most fertile land. Over the years the ZANU-PF government promised that it would address the land question. In the 1980s the government did redistribute some land, but for various reasons the program slowed down, its targets were never met, and farmers who did receive land did not get access to credit and other forms of badly needed support. The same thing happened in the early 2000s and agricultural production dropped even more sharply. Although nearly all the country's 4,500 white farmers were driven off the land, Mugabe's friends were the primary beneficiaries of the latest redistribution. Grossly inequitable landownership patterns (though less based on race) continue to prevail in Zimbabwe—more than a quarter of a century after independence.

What has happened in Zimbabwe is a good example to the world of what happens when crucial questions are left unresolved for decades. For many activists, land has sacred and cultural value as well as productive potential. The effort to reclaim the land is for them not just a development issue but also a restitution and justice issue.[31] While some analysts accuse Mugabe of cynically using the movement to hang on to power, it is important not to forget the very real needs asserted by this social struggle and to recognize that the anger stems from past injustices and deprivation. The reconciliation model promoted by the West has not resulted in justice or reparation. From the point of view of many rural people in Zimbabwe, the neoliberal, laissez-faire approach to land reform must be challenged.[32]

Because the opposition had been supported by the West, the government sought to portray it as the lackey of white farmers and Britain. Although the MDC once threatened to take President Mugabe down in much the same way that Yugoslavian dictator Slobodan Milosevic was finally ousted, until early 2007 Mugabe hadn't had to face the angry crowds. Perhaps this is because Zimbabweans were remembering the lessons of China's Tiananmen Square more than those of Yugoslavia. The MDC's Morgan Tsvangirai once said that he wouldn't call the massive street protests he once threatened, for fear of a bloodbath. It very nearly came to that in 2008, when Mugabe came closer than ever to losing power in a runoff election. To staunch the flow, as hundreds of MDC supporters were beaten, arrested, and murdered, Tsvangirai dropped out of the race. As discussed in Chapter 16, in 2009 the MDC leader decided to try to bring the crisis to a "soft landing" by entering into a coalition government in order to promote power-sharing, stabilize the country, and avoid catastrophe. Tsvangirai has characterized Mugabe as "both part of the problem and part of the solution: we cannot untangle the tentacles of state without him."[33]

For his part, it appears that Mugabe only entered into this unity government to co-opt or demobilize his opposition. He has certainly succeeded in frustrating his opponents and there is some talk about MDC dissidents, trade unionists, and civic activists forming an alliance to press for more substantive change.[34] But it appears that the most notable schism exists in the ruling party itself. For years, analysts have been reading the tea-leaves, attempting to forecast the nearly ninety-year-old president's political successor. In the past few years there has been an unusually public divide within ZANU-PF's politburo, its supreme decisionmaking body. Unable or unwilling to name a successor, in 2009 the politiburo chose Mugabe as party leader for another five-year term.

Some analysts believe that Mugabe may have stayed in power even longer than he prefers, because the president thinks that he's the only person who can win elections and hold the party together. In fact, Mugabe blamed factionalism within the party for the losses in the first round of the 2008 presidential election. Some analysts believe that the top brass would prefer that Mugabe step down, but fear that the party would collapse into warring factions without him.[35] The party divide is based in ego and regional and clan rivalries as well as good old power politics. For example, several years ago the various camps came close to blows over the promotion of Joyce Mujuru as second vice president (a post some see as a steppingstone to the presidency). The veteran liberation fighter Mujuru (also known as "Comrade Spillblood"), backed by her also-powerful husband, retired general Solomon Mujuru, is relatively moderate. But she is no shoo-in for what would be the first transfer of power since independence; there are several other ambitious, hard-line contenders (such as Defense Minister Emmerson Mnangagwa and Justice Minister Patrick Chinamasa) also vying for the job.[36] Still, a transition could happen at any time, and if the party were to turn on itself and split, it could open up a number of new possibilities.

Case Study: Iran

As discussed in Chapter 10, Iranian civil society is vibrant, even in the face of increased repression. The presidency of POPULIST archconservative Mahmoud Ahmadinejad (including his much disputed reelection in 2009) has pitted opposing forces within the country against each other in a visible, documented, and Internet-infused showdown. Ahmadinejad, the first Iranian president since 1981 who is not a cleric, campaigned on a populist platform that spoke to the sense of disenfranchisement and economic woes experienced by many so-called ordinary Iranians, and his rhetoric continues to invite dissension between upper and lower CLASSES in the country, a CLEAVAGE that is increasingly aligning with divisions surrounding the role of Islam in public and private lives.

From their side, religious leaders, sometimes even including Supreme Leader Sayyid Ali Khamenei have tried to limit Ahmadinejad's influence, especially in national security and foreign policy, as they believe the president's policies have been "dragging Iran to the point of quasi-catastrophe," especially in foreign relations.[37] A significant split between many religious teachers and scholars and the Supreme Leader became public during the disputed 2009 election, though, as Khamenei lost the support of many clerics, both for his vocal support of Ahmadinejad, even in the face of substantiated voter fraud behind his reelection, and especially because of the Supreme Leader's support for repression against democracy and human rights activists. Tensions even threatened to bring down the institutional structure of the Supreme Leader, as some religious leaders—including many who had been active at the foundation of the Islamic Republic in 1979—emphasized the human fallibility of any individual who would assume this post.[38] It is striking to note that these challenges to Khamenei came from religious leaders and seminarians.

Although muted somewhat by the conservatives' hold on power, Iranian civil society is fueled by an internal struggle between groups that want to forge a uniquely Islamist path to a modern state and society, and those who envision a modern Iran less hostile to secular demands and more open to Western traditions.[39] One observer even claims that Iranian society is "a culture at war with itself."[40] The integration of religious values and rules with everyday life has long been a struggle among the elite of Iran, especially following the colonial influences of Russia and England. After the Islamic Revolution of 1979 established Iran as a theocracy, this debate was muted. Ayatollah Ruhollah Khomeini often declared that "politics and religion are one" and that Iran's theocracy is "God's government." The implication of this conception puts dissenters in a dangerous space: opposition to the government is de facto opposition to God.

Conservatives today take issue with the accusation that they are trying to go backward. They state that they, too, are interested in reform, just not Western-style reform. In their view, changes in Iran must fit within the context of "Islamic-style" democracy, in which clerics still hold political power befitting an Islamic and not a liberal republic. In the eyes of conservatives, proponents of the "culture of liberalism" are only bankrupting the Islamic Republic[41] and are seen as a genuine threat to the status quo; there are many within Iran—including some religious clerics—who are pushing discussion about the ways in which an active faith life can thrive in a more open society.

Of the many groups pushing for greater change in Iranian politics and society, women and youth stand out. Women were prominent during Iran's constitutional revolution of 1906–1911, and they are once again returning to the public forefront. For example, in 2001 for the first time in the republic's history, a woman ran for president to challenge the orthodox interpretation of Article 115 of the Iranian constitution, which states: "The president should be elected from among spiritual and political men." More than half of university students are women, and curtains no longer divide male and female students within classrooms. Yet this advancement has created both opportunities and dilemmas—it is problematic, for example, for women with degrees to find husbands with the same level of education, and married women still require their husband's permission in order to work outside the home.[42] Until recently, women were barred from men's sporting events (Ahmadinejad made an exception—without consulting the clerics—because of loud demands by female soccer fans).[43]

Some point to a potential "marriage crisis" in the Islamic Republic, as many couples find marriage, with the resulting change in housing status, too expensive or less desirable, and, to the consternation of many religious leaders, are pushing back the average marriage age. (Real estate prices—especially in major cities—have skyrocketed in recent years.) The potential change in sexual mores is viewed as a threat to the spiritual core of the country—the head of Iran's National Youth Organization presaged, "The sexual bomb we face is more dangerous than the bombs and missiles of the enemy."[44] The government's proposal—"semi-independent marriage" in which young couples legally marry but continue living apart in their parents' homes—was rapidly condemned and dropped after especially vocal outcries from women, who saw the scheme as providing the sexual bounty of marriage without social or security status for themselves.[45]

One of the most famous contemporary Iranian women is Shirin Ebadi, a lawyer who champions the cases of women and children and who was jailed for violating Iranian publishing standards by writing about human rights in the Islamic Republic. In 2003 she became the first Iranian and the first Muslim woman to receive the Nobel Peace Prize, much to the consternation of then-president Khatami. Since the disputed 2009 elections (during which time she was an outspoken critic of Ahmadinejad and Khamenei), authorities confiscated her Nobel Prize medal from her safety-deposit box, arrested her sister, and confiscated her husband's passport (only to "return" a forged passport in its place).[46]

Younger citizens, especially university students, have a long history of activism in Iranian politics. Their role is significant, as it is believed that more than 50 percent of the Iranian population is under thirty years of age. College students supported former president Khatami's reform movement, staging boycotts and protests at great risk. Months after the massive crackdown by security forces, students at a respected university boycotted end-of-term exams in solidarity with classmates who remained in prison. This is the segment of the population most adept at using smart phones and the most recent advances in information communication technologies, and they continue to use them to angle their case. Youth were the backbone of the Green Movement in 2009 (discussed in Chapter 10), and they continue to take to the streets to demand change, incurring the wrath of the administration and its security apparatus. They are likely to continue to demand a voice in the increasingly crowded public arena of the Islamic Republic of Iran.

Case Study: Turkey

The expression of opinion in Turkey is a relatively open enterprise, although some significant limits on identity have yet to be dismantled. These restrictions are particularly acute when it comes to the hot topics of modern Turkish life: political Islam and Kurdish activism. Essentially, what does it mean to be "Turkish" in the twenty-first century? Is this an exclusive, secular orientation, molded in the image of the founding father? Or can modern Turks be confident in their public expression of religion and Kurdish heritage? The answer is quite fluid. One poignant citizen stated, "being a Turkish citizen first and foremost means being confused."[47]

Religious SECULARISM was vividly enshrined in the birth of the republic by Mustafa Kemal Atatürk, the self-ordained "Father of the Turks." Since that time, most government leaders and military elites have ardently guarded against the political expression of religion, even though over 95 percent of Turks identify as Muslim. Just in case the government errs in this regard, the military has clearly expressed its willingness to take matters into its own hands. Plotting to replace the country's secular government with an Islamic regime is a crime punishable by expulsion from politics or even, in the most extreme cases, death. In 1997, for example, Premier Necmettin Erbakan was forced to resign after barely a year in office, under heavy pressure from the pro-secular military. Even if some claim that Erbakan has maintained his influence outside his office, despite his banishment from politics for five years, his departure was a strong signal to others who want to mix politics and religion. Yet when the Justice and Development Party (AKP), led by Recep Tayyip Erdogan, won a majority of seats in the legislature in 2002, parliament overturned President Ahmet Necdet Sezer's veto in order to allow Erdogan, who had been banned from office for reading a poem that the courts accused of inciting religious hatred, to serve as prime minister. The influence of his party, which has consistently made campaign promises to dismantle some of the restrictions on religious expression, is at once hailed by some (who believe their rights of religious expression have been unfairly limited by the dominance of secularism) and feared by others (notably the armed forces). There was even an attempt in 2008 to ban the AKP itself from politics—a fate experienced by its predecessors, Welfare and Virtue, among others—over its perceived pro-Islamic pledges.

As discussed in Chapter 10, the headscarf is a visibly divisive symbol in Turkey today, and will likely remain such in the future. In this struggle, several prominent women have exposed the extremes to which some groups are prepared to push the issue. For example, Merve Kavakçi lost her seat in parliament over her donning an Islamic headscarf. Later, her Turkish citizenship was stripped because she had acquired a US passport to travel (Turkish law does not allow dual citizenship). Even young girls who want to publicly express their religious modesty have faced pressure: security forces have been called into Turkish schools to fight against "anti-secular propaganda," refusing to allow students wearing headscarves to enter the school. One observer argued that "headscarves are the emblematic feature" of change in Turkey today, stating that "Islam in Turkey is not so much experiencing an upsurge or revival as it is coming out of the closet," much to the dismay of the largely urban elite who have consistently promoted the clear separation of public and private matters, with religious devotion to remain solidly in the latter. As some women attempt to craft a novel acceptance of their religious identity, a "new consumer culture" has developed around flashy, colorful headscarves and the women who confidently wear them as they go out on the town. While the proportion of women who wear the veil in Turkey declined from 1999 to 2008, more women, including what one observer refers to as "the pious nouveaux riches," do so in public, sometimes prompting heated exchanges.[48]

The ruling Justice and Development Party is pragmatically conservative, although not overtly religious—party leaders liken their movement to the Christian democratic parties of Europe.[49] It has been lobbying on behalf of observant Muslim women who want to be permitted to enter state universities without removing their veil at the gate. Prime Minister Erdogan, whose wife, Emine, wears the headscarf in public, successfully advocated a 2008 constitutional amendment to permit women to cover in universities. One news organization called the loosening of the ban a "quiet revolution."[50] Even though 410 out of 550 members of parliament supported the measure, the Constitutional Court blocked the change, in a decision that cannot be appealed, although some individual universities have quietly loosened restrictions on religious attire in defiance of the court.

As we see with other states in the third world, the youth of Turkey are a sizable and potent group within civil society (approximately half of the population is under the age of thirty). Yet according to a 2008 report from the United Nations Development Programme (UNDP), they are largely "invisible" and unable to develop their full potential.[51] Women have been especially hard-hit—only about 25 percent of women are in the formal labor force, and, with the exception of the field of education, those who are working tend to hold low-level positions. Yet when an issue galvanizes people into the streets, it is often university-aged citizens who are at the forefront, as seen most notably in 1979, 1999, and yet again in 2009.

One element of increasingly uncivil society within Turkey today surrounds the politically sensitive issue of Kurdish nationalism. The Kurds are the only large linguistic minority in Turkey, composing approximately 15 percent of the national population. In 1999, Turkish officials captured Abdullah Öcalan, leader of the Kurdistan Workers Party (PKK), and sentenced him to death for murder, terrorism, and treason. In an attempt to win the support of the European Union, the Turkish parliament banned capital punishment during peacetime, and Öcalan's sentence was commuted to life in prison in 2002; Turkey signed a protocol banning the death penalty in all circumstances in 2004.

Even though there has been much violence surrounding PKK-Ankara relations, the PKK, which is strongest in southeastern Turkey, only speaks for a minority of ethnic Kurds. Most favor peaceful solutions, although, since many Kurdish identity parties (including the People's Democracy Party, the Democratic People's Party, and the Democratic Society Party) are repeatedly banned from political action because of their alleged connections to the PKK, their message tends to be diluted. Regional insecurities fueled by instability in Iraq make progress on the open discussion of Kurdish identity difficult. It was only in 2006 that Turkish state television began broadcasting Kurdish-language programming, for example. The PKK-Ankara conflict is wearing down the patience and sense of security of ordinary citizens, and the Erdogan government has been attempting new initiatives to increase Kurdish language rights and decrease the military presence in Kurdish regions since 2009, with mixed success. One Kurdish intellectual gives quite a bit of credit to the Erdogan government, saying that their "great achievement is that they have left the era of denial in the past. . . . They have declared that there is a Kurdish people and a Kurdish language."[52]

In recent years, authors, journalists, and editors have faced charges under Article 301 of the Turkish penal code, which criminalizes individuals who "insult Turkishness." Authors and journalists (including Turkey's only Nobel Prize recipient, Orhan Pamuk) have been charged with this vague crime for acts such as allegedly insulting Atatürk, having fictional characters discuss Turk/Ottoman complicity in the Armenian genocide of 1915, or even encouraging Armenians to get over their hatred of the Turks. Largely in response to international outcry after Pamuk's fame, the article has been amended, but not abolished, with the target of insult changed from "Turkishness" to "Turkish nation." Large numbers of authors and journalists continue to face trial for their work.

The future of Turkish civil society will remain a balancing act. Major players seeking accommodation include secular-minded Kemalists (backed by the weighty generals), Western-oriented entrepreneurs and business owners, Kurdish nationalists,

Islamists, and publicly observant Muslims and private adherents. Multiple points of view exist, but all too often some voices attempt to ostracize and condemn others. As an urban university student stated, "Turkey is a country which has a big potential to polarize like a streak of lightning."[53] Storms may very well be in the forecast.

Case Study: China

The expression of ideas—especially political—within modern China is limited by the continued dominance of the Chinese Communist Party (CCP). Even though alternative parties exist—they constitute the so-called loyal nonopposition—decisions within China today need the approval of CCP officials. China continues to abide by the Leninist principle of mandating a singular, elitist, unchallenged party. Those attempting to form groups or engage in behavior that can be perceived as formal opposition have been imprisoned for charges including "subverting state power," "divulging state secrets," and "inciting subversion." Perhaps the most well-known Chinese dissident who has been imprisoned for his views is Liu Xiaobo, a former literature professor and activist who has been in and out of detention and labor camps since 1989 and who, despite receiving the 2010 Nobel Peace Prize, is largely unknown within China due to the state-controlled media.

Despite the known risks, there is a strong tradition of dissent and disagreement within China, dating back to the first student demonstrations against the government in the May 4th Movement of 1919. Ironically, some of the same leaders who gathered in Beijing to denounce the Chinese government in 1919 were responsible for violently ending student demonstrations in the nation's capital in 1989. Those demonstrations in Tiananmen Square attracted global attention as university students and citizens from all walks of life protested against inflation, corruption, and the absence of political reform. As the world's television cameras captured the dynamic events taking place in Beijing and other Chinese cities, the government prepared to send tanks to crush the movement, which it ultimately did on the nights of June 3 and 4, 1989.

In addition to explicitly political demonstrations and protests against corruption and the abuse of constitutionally guaranteed rights, increasingly Chinese citizens organize around other collective identities, especially rural farmers and activists of varying religious affiliations. With alarming frequency, Chinese peasants wage protests against illegal levies and fees in the countryside, uneven implementation of the planned-birth policy, and official corruption, among other matters. This is part of a larger pattern of both increased participation from citizens as well as surprising acknowledgment from regime officials. It is believed that there are an estimated 100,000 "mass incidents" (riots and other disturbances) each year.[54] Because of the coverage of crackdowns against major dissidents, many assume that protests in China are risky, rare endeavors. But the risks don't seem to quell the desire to speak out against perceived injustices: witness the protests in Tibet in 2008 and Xinjiang in 2009, among thousands of others taking place every day.[55]

Also, in defiance of state limits on religion, Chinese citizens seek membership in underground Christian churches and other spiritual associations. A recent academic survey conducted by researchers at Shanghai's East China Normal University reported that 31 percent of Chinese self-identify as religious, or approximately 300 million people, challenging the long-stated estimate of 100 million. This figure includes 40 million Christians (although most missionary organizations put the total at nearly 60–80 million), and 200 million believers in traditional Chinese religions.[56] The latitude for religious choice and expression has been front and center in disputes between Beijing and Vatican City (the two states lack formal diplomatic ties), as Beijing asserts its right to appoint and supervise the behavior of Chinese Catholics and the Holy See refuses to acknowledge most CCP-appointed priests and bishops. The tenacity of the dispute points to the broad numbers of Chinese, both in cosmopolitan urban settings as well as in rural communities alike, who seek spiritual communities for expression.

While newspapers and magazines continue to operate under the official sponsorship of the CCP, most observers note a qualitative change in the types of stories covered by the media, as well as the increasing investigatory powers of newspaper and magazine journalists. There are even cases of the central government using state-run media to rein in corrupt local officials, such as after a rash of lead-poisoning broke out in children who lived near a smelting company in the central province of Shaanxi. Reporters from *Xinhua,* the lead news agency in China, covered similar stories in eastern Fujian.[57] Access to the Internet is also creating a wealth of options for Chinese citizens, although the government, with the known complicity of Microsoft, Google, and Yahoo! in some cases, has monitored targeted individuals, even reading their draft e-mails.[58]

As is the case in many other countries of the developing world, the Internet—billed "the great equalizer" by some—is taking China by storm, even as the central government employs legions of censors to attempt to police the discourse. China is now the world's most wired nation, with an estimated 457 million Internet users, and despite the government's "Great Firewall," those Chinese who have the financial means to purchase a virtual private network (VPN) can elude the censors. Even so, Internet service is regularly blocked to regions during and following disturbances—in the western region of Xinjiang, for example, service was not restored until ten months after the ethnic rioting that convulsed the capital, Urumqi. On the day the Internet was restored, many residents took the day off school or work and flocked to Internet cafes to catch up on messages and return to online gaming—imitations of World of Warcraft are by far the most popular.[59] The Internet is becoming the prime source of entertainment for Chinese youth who are bored and frustrated by state-run television and the limits on foreign programs. Facebook, Twitter, and YouTube are blocked, but indigenous social-networking and messaging sites are very successful, especially QQ.[60]

The effects of development on gender in China have been very uneven. Communist leaders inherited a dismal record of attention to women in 1949, and although the situation has improved greatly (baby girls, for example, are no longer forced to have their toes broken to create a small foot through binding), women in China today continue to face many struggles. Traditional attitudes toward girls have been reinforced by the one-child-per-couple policies implemented since the 1980s. Economically, one of the most disturbing trends affecting the mobility of women is the feminization of agriculture, as women are left behind in impoverished rural areas while the men in the family go to the cities in search of more lucrative employment. Women comprise approximately 65 percent of all farmers in China, but earn less than 60 percent of what male farmers earn, a decrease of nearly 20 percentage points compared to just a decade prior.[61] Recognizing this and other seemingly unintended consequences of the population-control policy, the Chinese government has loosened the plan in recent years, permitting two children per couple in major urban areas. Such exceptions had already been permitted in the Chinese countryside, where families with a firstborn girl were permitted to have a second child. Additionally, conspicuous wealth makes some of the penalties irrelevant for families who are unlikely to turn to government-provided social services in the first place, while travel to Hong Kong allows couples to sidestep some of the restrictions.

If we measure civil society in terms of independent organizations, there are challenges: most organizational life is corporatist, and groups need permission from local authorities to form and gather. An area that has been swelling with grassroots participation in recent years has been environmental activism—many estimate that there are more than 3,000 formally registered environmental NONGOVERNMENTAL ORGANIZATIONS (NGOs) in China today. China's first legal nonprofit group was Friends of Nature, an environmental organization founded in 1994. An executive with a group that helps domestic nonprofits in China stated, "Civil society is now a phrase people in China are beginning to understand."[62] Environmental groups have more autonomy than other potential groups, in part because of the severity of environmental problems in China, and in part because Beijing's leaders have recognized the inherent connection between environmental degradation and sustainability of economic growth. Large projects that have received the sanction and funding of Beijing, such as massive dam and water-diversion projects, remain off limits.[63] Despite these limits, though, Chinese citizens continue to find ways to express their opinions and approaches to life in the twenty-first century.

Case Study: Indonesia

Indonesia is a country rich in diversity (which should not be surprising, given its geography of more than 17,000 islands). Rather than viewing linguistic, cultural, and religious diversity as strengths, however, Indonesian leaders and to some extent ordinary citizens view them as threats. Especially during the thirty-two-year reign of General Suharto, any identity that contradicted national unity was squelched. The two biggest offenders were expression of religious division and communism. In fact, until very recently, any printed materials containing Chinese characters could be confiscated, on the suspicion that they might promote communist infiltration. Yet months of protest across Indonesia led to Suharto's dramatic resignation in 1998. The demonstrations, ignited by the enduring economic crisis that had crippled the country, quickly evolved into a referendum on the continued leadership of Indonesia's second president. Throughout the streets of Indonesia's major cities, Suharto was vilified for his corrupt, heavy-handed rule. After they were successful in toppling the president, however, diverse groups of demonstrators faced a dilemma familiar to other activists protesting authoritarian leaders: since organized opposition had been illegal for so long, there were few available networks through which opposition groups could communicate and mobilize.

During Suharto's "New Order" (1966–1998), the only viable electoral force—not technically a political party—was Golkar, a federation of army-sponsored associations and trade unions that served as an umbrella for anticommunist associations and a government-fabricated identity. Opposition parties existed and ran candidates in the People's Consultative Assembly, but their acceptance was always at the discretion of government leaders. Opposition candidates were often refused the right to be seated in parliament, even after their election, and were rarely permitted to staff cabinet positions in Suharto's government. Additionally, government employees were open to charges of disloyalty for joining any party that might challenge Golkar—the source of their bread and butter.[64]

Indonesian civil society includes a variety of semiautonomous groups; truly competitive political parties were first allowed in January 1999, and social movements, which before had been used as tools of the authoritarian state, now mobilize in opposition to the regime or in response to social or political trends that concern them. For example, shortly after Susilo Bambang Yudhoyono (SBY) was reelected in 2009, "Indonesia's Watergate" broke, complete with nationally broadcast tapes of conversations between police and representatives from the attorney general's office purporting to launch a plot to frame the powerful (and popular) national corruption watchdog. Citizens took to the streets, chanting against the police and calling for more meaningful measures against corruption. Groups promoting women's rights (especially condemning domestic violence and lack of economic opportunities) and media literacy (especially concerning the impact of violent programs on youth) have also become more prominent. A more liberal media system is also beginning to develop, even though its freedoms are reined in from time to time. Government repression and increasing veils of secrecy over Jakarta's inner workings have hampered media access. SBY's record is similar to his predecessors'—under his leadership, journalists have been held accountable for new press offenses detailed in the criminal code (rather than the more liberal press law), and new antiterror laws have increased communications surveillance, especially with regard to coverage of the terrorist organization Jemaah Islamiya.

Indonesia is unique in Southeast Asia because of the prominence of Islam as a belief system among its people. In fact, Indonesia is the world's largest Muslim-majority state. Approximately 88 percent of citizens identify themselves as Muslim, and there are almost as many Muslims living in Indonesia as in the entire Arabic-speaking world. Its political institutions are secular, designed to help mediate potential fissures along religious lines. Muslims have long been the standard-bearers of independent organizations in Indonesia; even during the Suharto years, groups of organized Muslims—some with membership rolls in the tens of millions—challenged the regime.[65] Since the landmark 2005 peace agreement that granted Aceh unprecedented autonomy within the republic (the province of Aceh is seen as the birthplace of Islam in Indonesia), formal Islamic courts organized on the principles of Islamic religious law, or *sharia*, have been established throughout the province, which is long known for its orthodox views. Since their implementation in 2006, the *sharia* courts have received mixed reviews—with some women's groups reporting increased harassment of women (including the arrest of three women who gathered in a hotel corridor after a UNITED NATIONS–sponsored seminar on women's rights) as well as detainment of foreign aid workers, both male and female, for meeting with a person of the opposite sex in ways considered inappropriate by the *sharia* police. Others praise the changes, viewing *sharia* courts as proof of the province's autonomy and as demonstrating that it is possible to be both Muslim and modern.[66]

Religious-based cleavages in Indonesia are not new. Formerly, the most serious religious-based conflict had been within Islam, between parties with varying adherence to Islamic law. Violence between Indonesia's Christians, who make up the second-largest group of religious believers, and Muslims, placed the state "on the brink of a religious war,"[67] although activist-representatives of many faiths have been calling on the government to uphold the secular constitution and guarantee the right to freely practice religion.

Indonesian identity is an extremely sensitive topic, and debates over inclusion in this category continue to rage with great ferocity. One region that has faced simmering discontent and discord is West Papua, Indonesia's least-populous province, which prior to 2007 was known as West Irian Jaya. Activists in this heavily militarized region have been subject to much abuse at the hands of the Indonesian military in attempting to respond to separatist demands by some Papuans, whose physical appearance, more Melanesian than Asian, is distinct from that of other Indonesians. A particularly disturbing video surfaced in late 2010 that included one man with a knife up against his throat and another moaning in pain as a burning stick was forced against his genitals.[68] Individuals have been imprisoned for treason after displaying the outlawed Papuan flag, the Morning Star. Similar to many conflicts in Indonesia, the challenges in Papua follow the pattern of coinciding cleavages: in addition to differences in ethnicity and socioeconomic opportunities, a significant religious cleavage exists. Locals are mostly Christian or animist, and clash with the newer, predominantly Muslim residents of the region, whose migration to the island has been encouraged by Jakarta.

Indonesia's population is diverse and dynamic, and in recent years has engaged in the forms of both civil and uncivil activism discussed in Chapter 10. As with our other case studies, Indonesia continues to grapple with contending meanings of citizenship, nationality, and voice.

Now It's Your Turn

Why do you think people turn to political ideologies to achieve their causes? How can ordinary citizens and leaders alike be manipulated by ideologies? Why do you think youth are attracted to particular movements? After reading about some of the forms of activism and expression discussed in this chapter, do you view any actions, such as wearing an Islamic headscarf, differently than you did before? Why or why not? What are some of the seemingly unusual ways in which people are making their concerns known? Why do they choose these methods? How do economic, political, and cultural factors contribute to activism (or lack thereof)?

12

The Call to Arms:
Violent Paths to Change

It's like setting a wolf loose amongst a flock of sheep.
—Former Iranian Basij militia member,
reflecting on the militia's response to internal unrest[1]

Our nation wants unity. It wants no more crying mothers, no more blood and killing.
—Turkish prime minister Recep Tayyip Erdogan, announcing
a plan to end the war between the Republic of Turkey and the
Kurdish Workers Party, 2009 (the plan broke down within the year)[2]

On September 11, 2001, Americans faced violence in a way that most in this country had never experienced. When planes were crashed into the towers of the World Trade Center in New York City, the Pentagon just outside Washington, D.C., and a field in rural Pennsylvania, we witnessed the power of organized violence. As the United States and the world struggled to understand the reasons for these actions, we contemplated a force that has long been used by individuals and groups who feel they have few other ways to express their opinions. In Chapter 10 we discussed people's option of "voice," focusing on ideologies and participation. In this chapter we investigate a particular type of participation that engages the use of violence. We examine a variety of means of violent expression, highlighting the individuals and groups behind the actions and emphasizing the role of governments and militaries, terrorists and revolutionaries. This is an extremely important area of inquiry for the third world, as it is estimated that of the 200 or so wars and other violent conflicts that have taken place since the end of World War II, the vast majority have occurred in the less developed countries.[3]

Some view violence as the breakdown of politics, but we encourage you to view it instead as a tool used by actors to accomplish their goals. Violence is a powerful weapon, used by terrorists, governments, GUERRILLAS, militaries, militias, and activists canvassing the whole gamut of ideological persuasion. While many commonly view the use of violence as a means of gaining territory, such tactics are also often used to exact responses including fear, intimidation, surrender, and subjugation, as we will see in this chapter. The psychological force of violence (or the threat thereof) is perhaps the greatest source of its potency.

Violence can take many forms, and its perpetrators justify it in a variety of ways. Behind violent acts are myriad motivations, aspirations, and justifications—all open to competing interpretations. As students of the third world, we attempt to classify types of actions taken by ordinary people and political ELITES alike, but these labels are often reductionist (overly simplified) and may imply judgment. Take one form of violence with which we have all become more familiar in recent years: TERRORISM. As analysts, we can come up with a clear-cut definition of what we mean by the term—it involves purposeful acts against innocent civilians in order to provoke fear and insecurity. Clearly, some individuals and groups engage in these acts in ways consistent with this view, and they take action without apology—priding themselves as among the world's most renowned terrorists. Yet there are other times when the term is used as a political label to characterize a seemingly unjustifiable action by a group of people. In discussions of this topic, watch carefully the labels that are tossed around; tagging a group as "terrorist" can often fulfill a political agenda to delegitimize a group's perspective. Classifying acts of political deviance is a subjective enterprise.

Terrorist violence is used in many different types of conflict and by many activists of all stripes. Here we will observe terrorism at work, including during warfare, revolutions, and times of peace. The designation of terrorist acts can sometimes be a puzzle; dependent upon one's perspective, the task of defining what exactly "terrorism" is has befuddled many social scientists. As linguist, activist, and political commentator Noam Chomsky once stated, "what is terrorism to some is heroism to others."[4] Sometimes the fiery debate has taken on the language of "freedom fighters" versus "terrorists"—it should not be surprising that groups of people using violence believe that the ends justify the means.

Rather than trying to argue for or against a particular definition, we highlight key components: terrorism is a deliberate organized act, with the goal of inspiring fear. Usually, innocents are victimized, although the definition of who is "innocent" can be manipulated. Terrorists have shown devastating flexibility in both their targets and their tactics, which include bombings, kidnappings, hijackings, and the threats of such actions. They want to gain an audience—attention, even negative attention, is what they seek, in order to publicize their causes. They want to alter opinion and policy. Contrary to popular belief, they're not all after land or material resources. Rather, they sometimes fight bigger, more seemingly abstract issues, such as GLOBALIZATION. The September 11 attack on the United States pointedly targeted two of the greatest symbols of Western wealth and military power: the World Trade Center and the Pentagon. Since attention is what these groups are after, the proliferation of nonstop news reports on television, radio, and the Internet has become an accessible platform. Terror tactics evolve based on the response of societies and governments. In a scenario that seems almost quaint by today's standards, planes used to be commandeered by hijackers to go to Cuba. Nowadays groups are creating weapons of mass destruction out of airplanes. Why? The flexibility of terrorism requires relatively few people to pull it off, and in the twenty-first century it is easier to acquire adequate materials to invoke terror. Maybe the world has become jaded and it takes more to get our attention—which is precisely what advocates of terror and other forms of violence desire.

As we discuss various manifestations of violent expression, watch for the use of threats by perpetrators and for the use of labels by victims, and try to understand the motivations behind competing sides of the issues.

Conflict and War

Why do people, especially in groups, turn to aggressive acts of defiance? There have been many theories to explain when and why people turn to violent means.[5] To some, resorting to violence is a way of dealing with their dissatisfaction over a state of affairs. When facing frustration and unmet expectations, it is argued, people are likely to turn to aggression. Conflict is also likely in societies that experience great change, whether political, economic, or cultural. This can be especially true if that change is uneven, as the fits and starts of life often are. Promises of dramatic improvement are often unfulfilled, leaving some, particularly those who believe they made the most sacrifice in the name of the cause, feeling betrayed. People who believe they have limited options to make their voices heard try to challenge each aspect of security and comfort.

Another explanation, known as the RESOURCE MOBILIZATION approach, emphasizes agents' ability to put together effective leadership and political opportunities for expression. In this view, collective action is taken when the time is right and when the necessary connections between resources and people can be crafted. Because of the power of human agency, though, no single approach can be used to help explain the rise of violent action.

Significant differences, also known as CLEAVAGES, can almost always be found in societies and groups of people. These are based on a variety of factors, including the myriad identities discussed in Chapter 10, as well as perceptions of well-being and fair treatment. Yet these differences are not always viewed as relevant, and they may remain latent for long periods of time. What sparks the change? In other words, what are some of the factors that make cleavages important enough for people to act on, even in violent ways?

One of the issues that alters a situation from low to high priority is the perceived extent of differentiation between and among groups. Many argue that the perception of stark differences between the rich and the poor in a given region or society can often be a source of violence. In the literature on SOCIAL MOVEMENTS and mobilization, this view is referred to as RELATIVE DEPRIVATION. It is one thing if everyone is poor, but if some people are poor and others are very rich by comparison, the likelihood for action is much greater. If there is a strongly held perception that the difference between those who have benefited from a particular policy or program is great, a sense of indignity may impel people to act. As we saw in Chapter 7, the general state of the economy is an important factor that influences individuals' and groups' perception of their well-being and their decisions about action or inaction. In times of economic hardship, especially if policies are perceived as unevenly harming some groups of people, we have observed that some groups will turn to crime, violence, and other disruptive forms of behavior. China, for example, has recently reported a large increase in crime, secret societies, triads, and gangs, accompanied by a rise in unauthorized gun ownership, although official statistics are not collected. Attacks on young schoolchildren are especially shocking. This has especially become a problem in the western reaches of the country, which have benefited less from China's economic boom than southern and coastal regions.

Expectations about changes in lifestyle are also important. If people have little reason to hope for anything from society or government, they often remain passive and largely inactive. But if they are given reason to anticipate more, especially through sacrifice, their hopes increase. Expectations sometimes end up going dangerously unfulfilled. Sometimes there is an ASPIRATION GAP between what one expects and what one can actually achieve or acquire. Exposure to international media that portray a variety of lifestyles and norms, increased interaction with other members of society who live in different circumstances, and especially, elite cues about that way of life can all help create circumstances that widen this chasm. A related idea is the REVOLUTION OF RISING EXPECTATIONS, which people experience as they begin to believe in the possibility and likelihood of positive change, for either themselves or their families. People naturally develop expectations about their future life. For example, many students attend college with the expectation that they will be able to get a good job to support themselves after graduation. Expectations often have a way of increasing in scope, and it is common for people to believe that with hard work and effort, life will get better. If this cycle is broken, and quality of life decreases rather than improves, it can be followed by frustration and disappointment.

Yet the motivation for action is not always as it appears, and people sometimes use unexpected public forums such as sports events and funerals to vent their frustration. Soccer matches have long been fertile ground for the expression of discontent. In what was dubbed the "Soccer War," 6,000 people were killed and 12,000 were injured during the 1969 World Cup qualifying game between El Salvador and Honduras. Frustrated by the perceived lack of fairness of referees during a match in the Democratic Republic of Congo (DRC) after the Congolese lost a World Cup qualifying match to the Italians, fans took to the streets, attacking Chinese businesses because they misperceived that the referee was Chinese (he was from Japan). Chanting "Chinese go home," many used the event to protest Chinese investment in the copper-mining industry throughout the DRC.[6] Funerals have also been known to spark protests and sometimes riots, especially if mourners seek retribution because they perceive that their loved one was targeted.

Others, led by political scientist Arend Lijphart, have assigned importance to the patterns of division existing within society, distinguishing between coinciding and crosscutting cleavages.[7] These expressions are used to characterize whether or not the significant conflicts and areas of difference in society are diffused among varying groups, or are concentrated among particular sectors of society. For example, if the economically poor in a given country also tend to be the religious minority, employees in the service sector of the economy, and predominantly women, this would be an example of coinciding cleavages. In all aspects of differentiation, a particular group of people seem to be getting the short end of the stick. Coinciding cleavages are more volatile, as all of the conflicts are stacked up into tidy groups and it is clear who does not agree with whom. In contrast, crosscutting lines of division help diffuse the conflict: the significant points of difference are spread among multiple groups in society, keeping any one group from perceiving any tremendous amount of injustice. Although real life never conforms to neatly crafted categories, Nigeria is often cited as an example of coinciding cleavages, where differences in religion, ethnicity, and region line up. Yet not all Yoruba are Christian, and of course the regions are not entirely homogeneous. Some Ibo, for example, live in the north. Another example can be found in Mexico, since the south is much poorer, less industrial, and more Amerindian than the rest of Mexico. Again it is an imperfect categorization, since the southern region of Chiapas contains some divisions between Indians who are Protestant and those who are Catholic. The point remains, though: more pronounced divisions can invite greater potential for conflict along these lines. They certainly invite an "us versus them" distinction that can significantly hinder consensus building.

Another factor that influences the potential for violent action relates to the availability of meaningful avenues of expression. Protests and riots are sometimes designed to be turbulent from the outset, but other times they turn violent when participants feel they are being ignored or that it is only through destructive action that their voices will be heard. Yet violence is not always an act of desperation. Ironically, some groups have engaged in violent tactics just as they were about to achieve their goals.[8]

In our discussion of the relevance of differences, we have concentrated mostly on groups smaller than governments and STATES. We now turn to a discussion of types of war, which is usually one of the first categories of violent conflict that comes to mind. Since the eighteenth century, war has been defined as violence between states or between organized groups, with the explicit goals of gaining territory, seeking revenge, or conquering recalcitrant groups of people. The twentieth century has been called the "century of war" because of the dominance of hostile conflict—three times as many people died in war during this century than during all of the prior nineteen centuries combined.[9] Wars produce scarred soldiers, lonely widows, traumatized victims of torture and rape, and political prisoners. Increasingly, the casualties of war are civilians rather than combatants.

There are many different types of wars, and an increasing variety of conflicts are now categorized as such, or as warlike situations, including "nonconventional" wars such as the war on terrorism. Some of the main types of warfare include interstate, civil, guerrilla, and PROXY WARS, as well as wars of liberation waged by ethnonationalists, as also discussed in Chapter 4.

Interstate and Separatist Wars

Interstate wars are the most conventional type of modern warfare, even if today they are no longer in the majority. Wars between states mostly involve traditional militaries, and commonly occur over border disputes, contested landholdings, and perceived threats to security. The legacies of colonialism have often been the source of wars in the third world, with conflicts over borders that fail to recognize significant historical, ethnic, and cultural continuities, and the creation of MULTINATIONAL STATES and stateless peoples. China, for example, has fought border wars with India (1962) and the Soviet Union (1969–1978), and has invaded Vietnam (1979).

One extremely volatile border situation can be found between two South Asian giants, Pakistan and India, in the region called Kashmir. It has been a point of conflict since the departure of the British in 1947; in two full-scale wars and other outbreaks of violence, tens of thousands of people have died on what is viewed as the highest battlefield on earth. A UNITED NATIONS cease-fire in 1949 provided both India and Pakistan a portion of the Kashmir region, which is rich in resources and historical connections, but this compromise barely held—and it is rarely viewed as little more than a temporary solution. The territory controlled by New Delhi, India's only Muslim-majority state, is referred to as Jammu Kashmir, while the Pakistani-controlled territory, also predominantly Muslim, is named Azad (Free) Kashmir. In addition, China, since Pakistan ceded a small tract of land to it in the 1950s, has occupied the northernmost part of the territory (Aksai Chin), even building a road linking Tibet and Xinjiang. Part of the reason for the enduring conflict in the region is that inhabitants themselves are not united in their desire for the future, a common dilemma in border wars. Plans to hold elections in 1995—with the hope of resolving the dispute—were abandoned after an attack on a Muslim mosque. Nuclear tests by both Pakistan and India in 1998 escalated tensions even further, and an attack on the Indian parliament in December 2001 again brought these two Asian states to the brink of war. Multiple peace talks have taken place to attempt to resolve the Kashmir conflict, although there has been dispute about who can legitimately represent the multiple sides involved in the dispute, and violence (both by protesters and by paramilitary forces sent in to quell them) accompanies any effort to resolve the six-decade-long dispute.

One of the most devastating interstate wars in the third world was the eight-year war between two Middle Eastern giants, Iran and Iraq. Claiming over 500,000 lives, it was the longest war in the recent history of the Middle East.[10] Although the conflict began when Saddam Hussein ordered Iraqi forces to invade Iran during a perceived time of weakness for the young Islamic Republic, its origins can be found in historical, territorial, and ideological differences. Even though Iraq initially welcomed the Islamic Revolution of February 1979, it broke relations with the Iranian regime in October of that year, branding it "non-Islamic" for inciting Shiite communities throughout the Gulf to rebel against their regimes.[11] Hussein and many Iraqis feared that the Islamic Revolution would embolden Iran to challenge contested waterway claims and the Gulf region in general. At one point during the war, Iran demanded Hussein's ouster as a precondition for peace talks, flaming internal opposition within Iraq. Iraq's capture of Kharg Island, Iran's principal Gulf oil terminal, in December 1985, quieted anti-Hussein movements within the country.

The war itself was one of the most brutal in the region, as Iran launched so-called human-wave attacks in which hundreds of thousands of civilians, including boys as young as nine years old, were sent to their death in assaults on Iraqi artillery positions. (This has been a strategy used by combatants with large populations, such as China in the Korean War and by both sides of the Ethiopia-Eritrea conflict.) Religiously motivated troops joined the war in their attempt to seek martyrdom; some were even given symbolic keys to a paradise that was promised to martyrs. Iraq responded with mustard and nerve gas agents. Iraq was surprised that Tehran didn't crumble during the initial attacks, and by 1982 began to seek peace. Iran refused these initiatives and attacked across the border, significantly weakening the Iranian military and leading to a long standoff with Iraq. After a prolonged war of attrition, a UN-brokered cease-fire was accepted in 1988. The only border-crossing between Iran and Iraq was reopened in 1999 to allow Iranian pilgrims to visit Shia holy sites in Iraq.

Wars are also fought over contested definitions of states—questioning what amount of territory should be included within internationally recognized borders. In

Figure 12.1 The Kurds

Another important example of separatist conflict can be found in the diverse Kurdish population, who are considered the largest group of stateless people (approximately 30 million) in the Middle East. At least one-fifth of the Kurds live in Turkey, with significant populations also found in Iran, Iraq, Syria, Lebanon, Armenia, and Azerbaijan. Facing widespread persecution since the late 1980s, many Kurds have immigrated to Germany (where they have faced much neo-Nazi violence) and the Netherlands. Contrary to popular perception, the Kurds are not a single, homogeneous group. Kurdish people speak several different, often mutually indecipherable languages and espouse different forms of Islam (although most are Sunni Muslims). Even in a similar fight for autonomy and the creation of an independent Kurdistan (not to be confused with the Iranian province of Kurdistan), rivalries dominate, and thousands of Kurds have died at the hands of other Kurds.

Turkey is the Kurds' main path to the West. Yet depending on the mood in Ankara, one can be sent to jail for broadcasting in Kurdish, running a political campaign on the basis of ethnicity, or too openly advocating a sense of Kurdish pride, which is viewed as a separatist act by some, a terrorist act by others. Since 1984, war between the Turkish government and some Kurds has claimed at least 40,000 lives and driven several million Kurds from their homes. Common interpretations of Turkish law hold the promotion of "hatred between ethnic groups" to include any mention of Kurdish identity. Approximately 1.4 million Kurds live in Iran's remote northwestern province of Kurdistan; about twice that many live elsewhere in Iran. As Sunni Muslims, many Iranian Kurds face oppression from the Shiite regime in Tehran, and Iran's Kurdish Nationalist Movement has been driven into Iraq. Even though Kurds in Iran enjoy relative autonomy, protests since Mahmoud Ahmadinejad's presidency have turned more urgent, especially after five Iranian Kurds were hanged in Tehran, accused of belonging to a political party viewed by the Iranian government as a terrorist organization.[12]

The Kurdish problem has been particularly acute in Iraq. Following the 1991 Gulf War, most Iraqi Kurds (approximately 2.5 million) moved into a semiautonomous northern district, protected by a no-fly zone enforced by the United States and Great Britain. Violence against them, though, began long before the Gulf War. US intelligence estimates that from 1987 to 1988, Saddam Hussein's government used chemical agents to gas to death 50,000–100,000 Kurds.[13] The development of an autonomous Kurdistan in Iraq has helped spur Kurdish pride in other areas of the Middle East. As a community, Kurds have a huge stake to play in the debates over Iraq's future—they are viewed by some as the "kingmakers" of the troubled state.[14]

Chapter 10 we introduced the notion of the NATION-STATE and the existence of areas of tensions in some, although by no means all, multinational states. The preservation of borders and territorial integrity is an ESSENTIAL FUNCTION of states. Yet the modern state has "deterritorialized" many national groups, sometimes because of the artificial demarcation of boundaries, often at the hands of imperial powers. Groups challenge their incorporation into a particular state for a variety of reasons, often relating to issues such as religious expression, ethnic disputes, or pressures relating to natural resources. Of course, few of these issues stand alone. Some indigenous groups, such as the Dayaks and Igorots in Southeast Asia, seek to maintain a traditional, nonindustrial, nonurban life that conflicts with national economic DEVELOPMENT plans of many states. Other groups take issue not with the industrial or economic goals of the government, but rather want to have their own homeland or government. This phenomenon is also known as SECESSION. For most, the goal is either to achieve national liberation from political occupation or to create a new political state. For others, the struggle is for humane treatment, more autonomy, and the right to the

Pro-Kurdish demonstrators join a sit-in in Turkey (Reuters/Murad Sezer)

free expression of their cultural traditions. Sometimes—though not always—this can lead to violent conflict, either in the suppression of the movement (such as China's response to the expression of an independent Tibetan IDENTITY), or in the expression of the need for a new identity. The Sikh community in Punjab, India, seeks a homeland called Khalistan, the "Land of the Pure." To date, India has been hostile to calls for this homeland, which geographically stands at the strategic intersection of India, the People's Republic of China (PRC), and Pakistan.

The results of separatist conflict can be disastrous, including displacement, ethnic cleansing, and genocide. The third world is riddled with the tragedies of such conflict, including the murder of Armenians by Turks (1915), of Kurds by the Iraqis (1984–1991), of Hutu and Tutsi in Burundi (1993–1998), of Tutsi and moderate Hutu in Rwanda (1994), of Hmong by Laotians and the Chinese (1975–1979), and of Africans by Arabs in Darfur (since 2003). Muslim rebel groups have been campaigning for SELF-DETERMINATION in the south of the Philippines, a predominantly Christian state, for more than three decades. One group of Malaysian Muslims, the Moro National Liberation Front (MNLF), fought for the establishment of some degree of self-rule within the autonomous region in Muslim Mindanao, which was established in 1996 (followers of Islam are called Moros or Moors in Spanish). A more famous group of armed Muslims in the Philippines is the Abu Sayyaf Group (ASG), known for kidnapping foreigners and Christian Filipinos, for which it has received large ransom payments. Formed in 1991, it is a splinter group of the MNLF and is rumored to have ties with Al-Qaida. The primary goal of the ASG is to create an "Iranian-style" Islamic state on Mindanao and the Sulu Islands. Yet some caution against viewing these conflicts as rooted in "ancient tribal" or even distinctly religious rivalries.[15] Such conflict, rather, has been stoked by modern power plays or by rivalries that were introduced by external, often colonial powers. It remains true that more groups of people are actively fighting today for new forms of political independence and expression than in decades or centuries past.

Indonesia has also faced much secessionist conflict following independence from the Dutch. The state leadership vigorously pushed nationalist assimilation policies that emboldened resistance. Aceh, a northwestern province on the island of Sumatra with a population of 4 million, has been home to the longest-running and most violent separatist conflict in Indonesia. The Acehnese are considered to be more orthodox Islamic than residents in other regions of Indonesia—after receiving some degree of autonomy, Aceh's leaders opened the first provincial *SHARIA* court in 2003, although there already had been local religious courts to handle family matters.[16] The region is also a major oil and gas producer, and there is a sense of bitterness felt by many Acehnese that Jakarta skims off much of the revenue of the region.[17] The area has been rife with conflict, with murder of innocents by both the Free Aceh (Aceh Merdeka) guerrillas and the Indonesian security forces alike, and the proliferation of gangs operating under the guise of the Free Aceh movement. Following the 2004 tsunami in the Indian Ocean (Aceh was the land closest to the epicenter of the underwater earthquake), new life was breathed into the peace negotiations that had been ongoing since 2000. In late 2006, direct elections for provincial and district leaders were held in Aceh as the Free Aceh movement attempted to morph from an armed insurgency into a political movement.

Civil Wars

Although interstate conflicts are obviously important, an increasing number of battles in the world today are internal. Even some of the major cross-border wars, including those between India and Pakistan, and Eritrea and Ethiopia, trace much of their origins to civil conflict. The third world has been beleaguered by civil wars, including conflicts in Algeria, Angola, Cambodia, Chad, China, Côte d'Ivoire, Laos, Nicaragua, Nigeria, the Philippines, Rwanda, Somalia, Sudan, Uganda, Yemen, and Zimbabwe. Civil wars, which occur within a single country, are known to be among the most brutal and damaging types of conflict, inflicting particularly heavy tolls on civilian populations. Families are often separated in civil wars, either by the outcome of the war or along lines of allegiance. Because of the brutality involved, ill will and the scars of war often continue after the official conflict has ended. Sometimes the estrangement can last for decades or longer.

Civil wars are fought for a variety of reasons. Some researchers are challenging the assumption that the existence of multiple ethnic groups makes a country more prone to civil war. In their study of 127 civil wars from 1945 to 1999, James D. Fearon and David D. Laitin found that irrespective of the ethnic mix, the probability of civil war declines as countries get richer.[18] If these findings hold true, they turn the table on past explanations of conflict and suggest that efforts to promote good government, economic development, and capacity building, including policing, could be successful strategies in war-torn countries. These findings also remove the aura of inevitability that tends to cloud some views of conflict.

Oftentimes, battles rage over which leader or group should rule a country. Such was the nature of the Chinese civil war from 1945 to 1949, which ended with Nationalist Party (Kuomintang, or KMT) forces fleeing to the island of Taiwan and the Chinese Communist Party (CCP) proclaiming the People's Republic of China. Other civil wars are fought between rival leaders or groups. Colombia is a country that was torn apart by civil wars throughout much of the nineteenth century, waged between rival Liberal and Conservative Party leaders, guerrillas, drug traffickers, and other entrenched interests. The ongoing war in Colombia was launched in the mid–twentieth century by a conflict now referred to as La Violencia. This war initially started out as a street riot in Bogotá, following the assassination of a Liberal Party leader and candidate for president. It has worsened as Colombia's problems have mounted: continued elite conflict over the future direction of the country, the deepening and professionalization of the drug trade and the concomitant development of a police force that rivals the military in many ways, and the development of paramilitary groups throughout the country. A war that began between two rival political parties has devolved into an ideological struggle including Marxist-Leninist guerrillas, the military, narcotraffickers, and militias, with significant regional and international involvement. Amnesty International estimates that the conflict has resulted in one of the world's most numerous displaced populations, estimated to comprise as many as 4 million people.[19]

From 1967 to 1970 a civil war was fought in Nigeria in which more than 1 million people died. The declaration of war was the culmination of a series of events, most immediately a pogrom directed against Ibos in the north. Led by Odumwegwu

---

Figure 12.2 Taiwan: Renegade Province or Independent State?

The controversy surrounding the status of Taiwan, just off the southeastern coast of China, demonstrates that in some ways the Chinese civil war of the 1940s still rages. After the Chinese Communists defeated the Chinese Nationalists in the fall of 1949, Chiang Kaishek and his supporters completed their transfer to Taiwan, much to the chagrin of the indigenous population. (An uprising in 1947, prior to the complete arrival by the Nationalists, is believed to have claimed over 20,000 lives.) From their base in Taipei, the Nationalists pledged to "retake" mainland China, up until the death of Generalissimo Chiang in 1975. Major combat was averted largely by the positioning of the US Seventh Fleet in the Taiwan Straits, which separate the two lands. Owing to anticommunist sentiment in the 1950s and 1960s, most of the world, with the exception of France and later Great Britain, refused to recognize the newly minted Communist Party regime as the legitimate government of China—they recognized the Nationalist regime on Taiwan instead. This continued until the early 1970s, when Taiwan exited the United Nations and most countries of the world completed normalization of relations with the People's Republic of China.

Both groups involved in the dispute purported to support "one China," but both the Nationalists and the Chinese Communist Party viewed themselves as the legitimate government of all Chinese people. (Taiwan maintains formal diplomatic ties with just over twenty small states and lacks formal representation within the United Nations.) Former president Lee Teng-hui and his successor, Chen Shui-bian, began to challenge the meaning of Taiwan being part of "one China," much to the consternation of Beijing. Even during the harshest periods, trade links between China and Taiwan flourish: China is Taipei's top export market. Since the election of Ma Ying-jeou in 2008, relations between the two entities have significantly warmed, achieving—even in just the first three months' time—the "most rapid advancement" in a standoff that has existed since the 1940s, including direct charter flights, loosened restrictions on Taiwanese investment on the mainland, and, in general, a lower profile for Taiwan abroad, a challenge that Ma's predecessors routinely pressed.[20]

Ojukwu, the Ibo sought to create "Biafra," an independent and sovereign state carved out of their traditional home in Nigeria's southeast. However, for a variety of reasons, including concern over the loss of the substantial oil revenues coming from the region, the north and west combined forces to resist secession by all conceivable means. Biafra became Africa's most internationalized war in the 1960s as the countries of the world lined up on one side or the other. When the much larger and better-equipped federal army found that it could not prevail against the Ibo forest fighters, it resorted to a policy aimed at starving the Ibo into submission. The blockade had devastating consequences, particularly on women and children. Although they eventually lost the war, the Ibo won international sympathy, as the Biafra conflict was considered by many to be a genocide led by the largely Islamic north against the Christian southeast.[21]

Guerrilla Warfare

The term "guerrilla," deriving from the Spanish word for "little war," refers to troops operating independently of state militaries, and often in opposition to them, following a relatively loose set of methods designed to deceive enemy forces and overcome deficiencies in equipment, force size, and location. In their attempt to damage the LEGITIMACY of a government, guerrilla forces target civilian populations for recruitment. Women soldiers have participated in this form of combat more than other types of warfare.[22] Additionally, there is often an extensive effort, through propaganda, terror, and policies, to win the support and fighting power of peasant populations. Guerrilla groups are known for setting up successful pilot projects, including schools and clinics, to provide services to groups often ignored by the state and to win their support.

In guerrilla warfare, conventional rules of engagement, especially concerning noncombatants, are largely ignored. Policies, both psychological and concrete, are designed to exhaust and demoralize the enemy while recruiting civilians through either fear or persuasion. Battles tend to center around long, protracted campaigns, often from a rural base. Guerrilla tactics are mobile, necessitated by their smaller troop sizes, and often rely on the element of surprise. Revolutionaries who perceive the unorthodox methods of fighting to be their only shot at victory often use guerrilla warfare. Examples include the Chinese civil war and revolution, Fidel Castro's 1959 revolution in Cuba, and Ho Chi Minh's battles against the Japanese, French, and later US troops in Vietnam.

The modern Chinese state was founded largely upon the principles of guerrilla violence. Mao Zedong, the leader of China's 1949 revolution and one of the modern world's leading revolutionaries, was a man of contradictions. He was a poet and librarian, which is how he first encountered Marxist and Leninist theories about revolution. Mao came of age in a China that was on the brink of collapse, worn down by the imperial wars of the late 1800s, the infighting of the warlord period following the collapse of the Qing Dynasty, as well as the economic misery and political uncertainties that follow the end of an EMPIRE. Although Mao was a relatively insignificant participant in the founding of the Chinese Communist Party in Shanghai in 1921, he grew to lead it throughout the revolutionary war with KMT forces, and was the man who proclaimed the beginning of the PRC in Tiananmen Square on October 1, 1949. Throughout the revolutionary war and in wars that followed the establishment of the

Figure 12.3 Something Has Gone Terribly Wrong

Since the ouster of its long-standing dictator, Mobutu Sésé Seko, in 1997, the Democratic Republic of Congo (DRC) has fallen into the abyss.[23] At one time there were at least three rebel movements fighting the government, and six African countries lined up on one of the many sides in this war. Since a 2002 peace agreement, most foreign armies have withdrawn and some rebel groups have transformed into political parties that vie in Kinshasa for seats in parliament. However, the war still rages on in the far east of the country, monitored by the largest UN-peacekeeping force in the world.

The war continues to have a geopolitical element. In many ways it is still a hangover of the 1994 Rwandan genocide. Hutus (many of whom fled to the DRC to escape retribution for their role in the killing) are hunkered down, waiting for the day that they can return to claim power back home. Meanwhile, the now Tutsi-led Rwandan government views these Hutu machinations as threatening and supports armed groups in the Congo out to get them. But at least just as important, the conflict in the DRC has become a battle royal over who will control the region's vast mineral wealth. Many of the riches in question are "conflict minerals," vastly lucrative critical components of computers and iPhones sold worldwide. As a result, most of us are involved in some capacity in this war, whether we know it or not.

As the conflict enters its second decade, no one knows how many people have been killed. Observers estimate that the death toll must be nearing 7 million (which means that the carnage in the DRC ranks with that of the Holocaust). One hallmark of the current war is the massive levels of sexual violence that have accompanied it. Of course, rape as a tool of war is nothing new. But its magnitude in eastern Congo is unimaginable, unprecedented. There the UN estimates that hundreds of thousands of women and girls (as young as eight) have been raped, many of them repeatedly, and often publicly, in front of their families. Sometimes brothers, sons, and fathers are told to rape their own sisters, mothers, and daughters (and the men are murdered when they refuse). It is all too common for victims to be repeatedly raped, taken as sex slaves, or sexually mutilated in ways that can leave them permanently incontinent. The perpetrators of this violence come from all sides in the war; they are believed to be mostly soldiers and militias (some of them foreign-backed). But some civilians have joined in the brutalization as well.

Sometimes when something becomes so widespread, outsiders assume that it must be "cultural" or somehow acceptable. But what is happening in the Congo is by no means cultural or acceptable; after a decade of the unimaginable, the social fabric has broken down. When rapists know that they can operate with impunity and that atrocities will go unchecked, violence comes easily.[24] If the world watches and simply shrugs, perhaps it can be argued that at what point do we count ourselves as complicit?

PRC, Mao advocated a type of warfare known as "people's war," which combined guerrilla tactics with Mao's emphasis on China's "human factors," highlighting the importance of the MASSES and the need to motivate and organize them. Mao often stated that "if our hearts are pure, we will fight with the strength of 10,000 men." The so-called people's war of 1927 to 1949 combined elements of social revolution with a war for national SOVEREIGNTY. From its base in China's northern rural areas, the CCP successfully employed guerrilla tactics to conquer cities, win the support of the population, and reign victorious.

Proxy Wars

Another type of conflict, sometimes referred to as "warfare by substitutes," involves surrogate fighters who are recruited to fight battles that other, often more powerful groups do not want to get involved in directly. Such proxy wars were especially common during the COLD WAR, when the United States and the Soviet Union acted as patrons for wars that were in their interest. The United States propped up anticommunist governments, including Indonesia, South Korea, South Vietnam, and Chile, while the Soviet Union did what it could to support Marxist-Leninist regimes throughout the world, including China (initially), North Korea, and North Vietnam. Recognizing that even the most powerful states or richest groups cannot afford to be in constant war with their enemies, these countries choose instead to support dissenters, separatists, and other potential clients of a rival to avoid mutual assured destruction. During the Cold War, proxy conflicts were used to avoid direct opposition between the superpowers.

The goal of this type of conflict is to wear down the enemy, weakening it by encouraging the waste of resources, without expending a tremendous amount of one's own resources or energy. Surrogate conflict can also include the assassination of political leaders or individuals. It often includes direct sabotage. In the early 1980s, for example, the United States "unofficially" provided support, buttressed by a special operations manual of the Central Intelligence Agency (CIA), to Nicaraguan Contra rebels who were fighting the leftist Sandinista government. Similar efforts were taken by the Soviet Union to encourage North Korea to attack South Korea in 1950.

Some turn to this substitute conflict as a way of improving their own image and to place some distance between themselves and the seemingly unsavory battles at hand. It has been argued that a group known as Islamic Jihad, an offshoot of the military wing of Hamas, was used as a proxy to carry out executions on behalf of the government of Iran, which attempted to improve its international image following its isolation during the 1980s.[25] Similar sentiment was expressed after the thirty-four-day war between Israel and Hezbollah, the Iranian-inspired group within Lebanon, in 2006—just as international pressure was focused on the alleged nuclear weapons program within Tehran.[26] In proxy conflict, nationals are involved usually in training and support, employing private armies in a country to put down revolutionary movements, assassinate critics of the regime, and maintain control. Fidel Castro's Cuba was relatively unusual in sending large numbers of soldiers abroad; since many of the fighters were nonwhite, they were welcomed in many places that the Soviets and the East Europeans were not, including Ethiopia, Mozambique, and Angola.

Proxy wars permit the sponsoring agent to focus on "big picture" events and strategy, while others do the "grunt work" on the ground. For example, the early stages of the US-led war in Afghanistan in 2001 were viewed by many as a form of proxy war, using Northern Alliance and other anti-Taliban forces to do the dirty work while the United States led the air campaign and provided intelligence. The long elusiveness of Osama bin Laden had been attributed to the use of Afghan, Pakistani, and other ground forces who might have succumbed to bribes from bin Laden's associates to permit him to escape the country. As fighting continues, the Taliban is making a resurgence and many old problems remain—*The Economist* even referred to Afghanistan as "a geographical expression in search of a state."[27] In a majority of proxy wars, there are often very real regional conflicts or domestic divisions at the heart, which are greatly amplified by the patronage of outsiders.

Faces Behind the Disruption

So who is responsible for acts of violence? As you might imagine, there is great diversity in the types of individuals and groups who believe their use of destructive means is justified. In this section, we discuss some of the major types of groups involved in belligerent activities. The faces behind the disruption can be as diverse as the forms of violence that are employed. For example, even though men make up the majority of individuals who engage in terrorism, women have frequently joined terrorist groups. Some argue that participation in violent groups provides women a rare outlet for gender equality, an argument that is used to explain women's participation in terrorist organizations and revolutions.[28] In Peru's Shining Path (Sendero Luminoso), large numbers of women participated as equals in the group's apparatus, overcoming the subordinate role and status historically ascribed to them in Peruvian society. And some made it to top positions in the regional command and the National Central Committee, including Abimael Guzmán Reynoso's first wife, Augusta la Torre, who served as the second in command in the organization (Guzmán's second wife, Elena Iparraguirre—also known as Comrade Miriam—also exercised significant influence over the movement, for which she received a life sentence after her third trial in 2006). Women have been active leaders in the Kurdistan Workers Party (PKK) in Turkey, the Palestinian uprising (INTIFADA), the Chechen resistance against Russia, and the Liberation Tigers of Tamil Eelam in challenging the Sri Lankan government, along with an increasing number of other movements. It is believed that as many as one-fourth of Russian revolutionaries in 1917 were women.[29] It was a woman who was sent to assassinate India's prime minister, Rajiv Gandhi, in 1991. In 1970 one female Palestinian refugee, Leila Khaled, almost single-handedly hijacked a commercial plane, evacuating all passengers before she blew it up. Even in the famously patriarchal Al-Qaida, the glass ceiling was shattered when a woman dressed as a man sauntered into a meeting of military recruits and launched an explosion that killed five men and wounded at least thirty—thwarting the profile used by antiterrorist forces around the world to identify perpetrators.[30] The participation and leadership of women cannot be reduced to IDEOLOGY or level of restrictions imposed on them. In Bahrain, where women enjoy some of the most liberated circumstances in the Gulf, young women and girls have joined in arson attacks at local stores, seemingly as a way to belong or to overcome the doldrums of daily life.[31]

Young people have also long been attracted to violence—often drawn to the idea of belonging to a meaningful group that provides direction and identity. We discuss one of the most famous sets of twins—the Htoo brothers from Myanmar—below. But there are others. Shining Path, born in a university setting, appealed especially to students. The most violent stages of China's CULTURAL REVOLUTION employed the use of middle and high school–aged "Red Guards" to terrorize those labeled enemies of the CCP and to foment revolutionary fervor throughout the country. In Zimbabwe, both the Zimbabwe African National Union (ZANU) and the Zimbabwe African People's Union (ZAPU) mobilized entire classrooms of children, who left with their teachers to train as guerrillas. Participants in the Palestinian intifada are believed to be particularly young. Research puts the median age of terrorists in the third world at approximately twenty-two years old. Youth have been active in arson attacks, hand-to-hand combat, sabotage, and suicide missions. Some postulate that their involvement can be explained by the lack of outside commitments that would

Figure 12.4 Legality as a Tool of State Terror

Governments possess many means to craft seemingly "legal" means by which they can impose their will and limit opposition voices. Perceived troublemakers, for example, are often forced into exile: either to remote parts of the country, or outside of the state altogether. In China some dissidents have been released from prison, but they are provided a one-way ticket out of the country and often depart without being able to send notice to their families. Other countries place activists under house arrest in remote areas as a way of keeping them out of trouble. In Myanmar, for example, Aung San Suu Kyi spent nearly twenty years in some form of detention, including prolonged periods of house arrest, before she was released in November 2010. Police brutality is another overt form of state violence; in Turkey, outright abuse at the hands of the police is considered one of the country's worst human rights abuses. Other governments use executions (state-sanctioned murder) as part of routine public policy. Although official statistics are lacking, it is believed that

China annually executes more people than all the rest of the countries of the world combined, though government officials have stated that the numbers of executions have decreased since 2007, when a mandated review by the Chinese Supreme People's Court was initiated.[32] As a supposed deterrent to potential criminals, Chinese officials have executed accused criminals in public arenas, following sentencing rallies that have even been broadcast on television. Iran also has increased its use of capital punishment in recent years, mostly by hanging. Iran executed 146 people in 2010, including Shahla Jahed, the mistress of a prominent soccer player who had been in a so-called temporary marriage (permissible under Shia law) with the man—it was Jahed's own family member who pulled the chair from beneath her during the hanging.[33] Other countries are moving away from capital punishment, including Turkey, which in 2004 signed a protocol banning the death penalty in all circumstances, a move that was part of its accession bid to the European Union.

limit their availability for activities, while others point to youths' propensity for risk-taking, their passion for causes, and their mobility.

Militaries and Militias

In any discussion of the major groups that sponsor violence as a means to achieve goals, we would be remiss if we excluded governments themselves. As sociologist Max Weber highlighted in his classic definition of the "state," one of the greatest powers of governments is their monopoly over the right to use force. This does not mean, of course, that states are the only groups that hold coercive power, nor does it imply that all use of government force is proper or legitimate, but it does accurately imply that governments tend to have the most organized, well-financed, and effective means of making their preferences known. By engaging forces in wartime combat, adopting domestic policies that include executions and punishment, and supporting abductions, assassinations, and forced relocations, it is clear that governments all around the world use violent means to achieve their ends.

As an institution of government, the state military wields tremendous power. Militaries consist of disciplined, organized, and well-funded groups of people with great influence: official armed units are used to implement key directives of governments, often using force. Militaries are found in almost every country of the world. The major exception is Costa Rica, which dissolved its military in the 1950s, even though it still has a small paramilitary force.

Young men under the age of twenty-six nearly exclusively carry out military acts. In World War I, women first donned military uniforms and received military ranking. Yet today in Eritrea and Israel, both sexes are formally required to enroll in military service, and increasingly women participate in noncompulsory military training and combat as well. Just as it is wrong to assume that all women are mothers, it is also a mistake to think that all mothers are peaceniks and opposed to the use of violence to effect change. African women trained with men and fought alongside them in Zimbabwe's war for liberation. In the mid-1970s approximately one-third of the soldiers fighting for ZANU were female, and some of these women held positions of authority over men. In addition, civilian women provided assistance to the guerrillas as their way of fighting. They cooked for the rebels, and because for a while at least women could better avoid the attention of Rhodesian soldiers, they sometimes disguised their bundles as babies and smuggled supplies to guerrilla bases. Just as women participated in the war effort in various ways, so too did they have different expectations about what the coming change should mean for them. ZANU recognized how important women's support was to the struggle and challenged local norms during the war by making an explicit commitment to women's liberation. However, for various reasons since taking power, the liberation government's position has been described as ambivalent at best. ZANU did push through some significant reforms of benefit to women, but there has been no transformation of gender relations.[34]

Increasingly in modern combat, civilians, especially children, are often the group most victimized by warfare. Since 1945, it is estimated that 90 percent of the casualties in war have been civilians.[35] The statistics are even more telling when they are viewed not as raw numbers, but as a trend. Prior to the early 1990s, the ratio of military to civilian casualties was eight to one. In the wars of the 1990s, the trend was reversed: for every military fighter that died in combat, eight civilians perished.[36] Some of this can be attributed to the "civilianization" of war, as noncombatants are increasingly targeted for attack or are innocently caught in the crossfire, or suffer because of the lawlessness and impunity that prevail. In Darfur in western Sudan, for example, Jan Egeland, who served as UN Undersecretary-General for Humanitarian Affairs, argued that it is "more dangerous" to be a woman or child than to be a soldier. Even simply leaving the refugee camp to procure firewood for cooking puts civilians at great risk.[37]

Another development of late-twentieth-century warfare that highlights the changing face of violence has been the inclusion of large numbers of children as active protagonists of warfare. The conscription and detention of children against their will is viewed by some as one of the "least reported" and "least punished" crimes globally.[38] Although difficult to track, it has been estimated tens of thousands of children (under the age of eighteen) fight today as soldiers with government and armed opposition groups in over fifty countries. Most child soldiers are between ages fifteen and eighteen; the youngest age recorded by the Coalition to Stop the Use of Child Soldiers is seven. One expert on the topic claims that child soldiers serve in almost 75 percent of the world's conflicts.[39] The presence of children in combat has become a critical problem in Africa and Asia, although youth are used as soldiers, porters, cooks, messengers, checkpoint guards, sexual slaves, and spies throughout the world. Myanmar has the highest numbers of child soldiers in the world, within both governmental armed forces and nongovernmental groups, and the fighters are often under fifteen years of age. Because of their agility and fearlessness, children have also been employed to do much of the more dangerous work in battle zones, including mine-clearing operations. Not surprisingly, poverty and perpetual cycles of conflict are viewed as some of the main conditions influencing the increase of child soldiers, although the influence of teachers, family, friends, local politics, and culture all play a role as well.[40] The proliferation of "small arms" (discussed in Chapter 18) has also increased the use of child soldiers, as the ease of modern combat has made strength, size, and experience less important. The Russian AK-47, which flooded markets after World War II, only weighs about 3 kilograms in its modern versions; because it is cheap and mobile, it is something an eight-year-old can maneuver with relative confidence, so nearly anybody can become a "soldier."[41]

Even if they are not formal "soldiers" per se, children have been combatants in some of the world's bloodiest conflicts. In the Palestinian uprising, for example, children have been active agitators against Israeli forces, throwing stones and sabotaging units, and they have paid dearly, often with their lives. Some children are forced to take up arms, but others are given little choice in the face of poverty, discrimination, and the pressure to conscript. Human Rights Watch estimates that in some conflicts, namely in El Salvador, Ethiopia, and Uganda, as many as 30 percent of child participants have been female. Pregnancy, often the outcome of gang rape by comrade or enemy soldiers, isn't enough to keep young girls out of combat, either. Young girls have been used as suicide bombers in Sri Lanka and Lebanon, and many girls are allocated to soldiers as rewards, as "wives." In Uganda, children have been forced to brutally beat other children to death, their victims lying face down on the ground, with arms and legs restrained.[42]

Young soldiers receive little or no training. In warfare, children are also subjected to severe punishment, sometimes even harsher than what adults would receive. There have also been reports of widespread juvenile disappearance, extrajudicial execution, and torture. Perhaps because they have a less developed sense of right and wrong, children (in some places known as the "lost generation") are said to commit the worst atrocities. Drugs are also used to make children effective killers. Children want approval, and sometimes they find acceptance in the most violent groups. Often, child soldiers are orphans, who together with street children are particularly vulnerable to recruitment and desperately eager to please adults (even if the adult is responsible for them being orphaned). Most have been traumatized themselves, as witnesses to murder of their families, and are sometimes even forced to participate in ritualized killings. The Revolutionary United Front (RUF) in Sierra Leone, for example, trained its child soldiers by ordering them to kill other children or even their own parents or someone they knew so that they wouldn't fear death or try to escape.

In the Sierra Leone civil war, all sides used children as frontline troops, including Liberia. It is estimated that 30 percent of the soldiers in Charles Taylor's National Patriotic Front, which invaded Sierra Leone on Christmas Eve in 1989, were boys less than seventeen years old. The RUF has forced children into service, kidnapping them and administering drugs to them—including highly addictive cocaine—against their will. Children have also been targeted as willing suicide agents. During the Iran-Iraq War, thousands of patriotic Iranian children were sent to the front lines, holding the symbolic key to a paradise as martyrs. In Sri Lanka, young Tamil girls (often orphans) were recruited by opposition forces and trained as suicide bombers, known as the "Birds of Freedom."[43]

Child soldiers do not always fight for their own country or ethnic group. In the conflict in the Democratic Republic of Congo, for example, children from Namibia and Rwanda were brought into the fray. Children have also been recruited into terrorist and separatist groups. Peru's Shining Path is believed to have forcibly recruited several thousand indigenous children. Child soldiers have also been common in Colombia's nearly fifty-year civil war.

One of the most famous cases of children rebels surrounds the teenage Burmese twins Johnny and Luther Htoo, leaders of the Burmese rebel group "God's Army." Many of the children who fight with this group are orphans of the war in Myanmar. The twins claim mystic powers, including being invulnerable to the personal devastation of landmines and bullets, which are said to "bounce off" the young commanders. They are also said to have invisible soldiers who assist them, and are rumored to have black tongues. Johnny Htoo is said once to have jumped into a stream, after which he was transformed into an old man. He returned to his teenage self after convincing his fellow fighters of his prowess. One of the unique aspects about the group is that these young boys, who became soldiers before they reached the age of ten, have led grown adults into battle. The belief among their followers is that they are not as young as they seem. Rather, in fitting with Karen animist teachings that messiahs will be sent to lead the people through difficult times, they are reincarnations of past revolutionary and legendary heroes. Working in concert with the Vigorous Burmese Student Warriors, God's Army rebels seized hostages throughout Thailand, including once capturing more than 800 patients and staff at a hospital. In the winter of 2001 the twins turned themselves in to police in Thailand, at the age of fourteen.[44]

In Figure 12.5 we present comparative data on militaries in the third world. While we believe this information is a useful starting point, we urge you to consider that countries are notorious for underreporting both the size of their formal military force strength, as well as the amount of budgetary resources committed to the military. One way that governments get around full reporting of their troop strength is by creating paramilitaries and other semimilitary units that are not counted in the official troop total. For example, the PRC, which has undertaken dramatic troop reductions since the mid-1990s, does not include the 1.3 million members of the People's Armed Police (PAP) in its official troop count. After the foundation of the Islamic Republic of Iran in 1979, clerical leaders called for both a standard military to protect the country's borders and maintain internal order, as well as a separate Revolutionary Guard, known as the Pasdaran, to protect the Islamic character of the system. The Revolutionary Guard has fewer troops compared to the regular military, yet is considered the dominant military force and the backbone of major operations. It controls the Basij Resistance force, a volunteer military of approximately 90,000 men and women who, as loyalists to the 1979 revolution, are used to brutally dispel dissent. This ambiguity is one reason why the CIA, in its *World Factbook,* reports the portion of the population available for military service and the portion fit for military service, rather than actual troop numbers. Additionally, globally statistics show that the military averages approximately 0.87 percent of the national labor force. As you can see, despite the fact that China has the world's largest standing army by far, its official military accounts for only 0.37 percent of the labor force, whereas Indonesia and

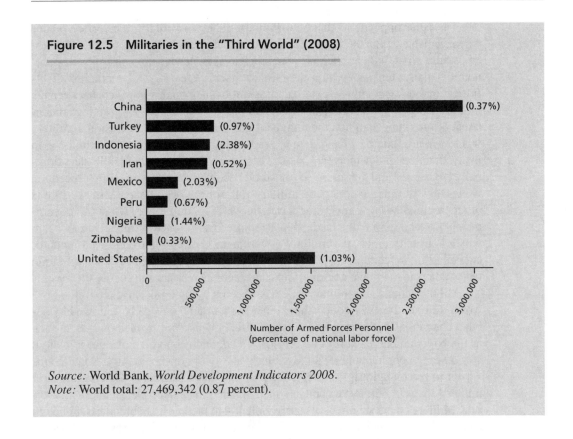

Figure 12.5 Militaries in the "Third World" (2008)

Number of Armed Forces Personnel
(percentage of national labor force)

Source: World Bank, *World Development Indicators 2008.*
Note: World total: 27,469,342 (0.87 percent).

Mexico, both with modest-sized militaries in terms of force strength, show a larger percentage of the overall labor force (both over 2 percent).

Despite relatively generous expenditures for militaries—when compared to spending for healthcare and education, for example—soldiers in the third world tend to be compensated very poorly. As a result, it is common for groups to turn to extortion at roadblocks, kidnapping, bribery, and other malfeasance to supplement their income. Paramilitary police in the restive Indonesian province of Aceh in the early 2000s, for example, received 60 cents a day in compensation from the government, which is less than the cost of a pack of cigarettes.[45] This problem has also been identified with the Chinese police force, which is famous for forcibly collecting bribes in the Chinese countryside, a dilemma that other countries face as well.

The declared goal of the modern military is to provide defense and security for a country. Civilian leadership over the military is recognized as a common value in the world today. In this model, the military is simply one of many interest groups lobbying for its own priorities. This norm is known as civilian rule, which has been violated in many countries, and not only in the third world. So-called professional militaries act on the authority of governments and possess restricted powers to challenge civilian political leadership. They develop particularized areas of expertise, such as challenging external enemies, and keep out of areas beyond their purview, such as political infighting. No military is completely professional in this sense, but we can observe varying degrees of professionalism using this metric.

The polar opposite of this civil-military duality—military rule—often begins when elements within the military sense a crisis. The manifestations of this perceived crisis are varied, but can include societal cleavages, leadership controversies, economic malaise, tensions within the military itself, defeat in war, contagion effects from neighboring countries, external intervention, personality conflicts between the military leadership and political leaders, or simply an easy power grab.[46] In the interest of providing stability, the argument goes, a disciplined, professional military would often be the best candidate to lead an interim transition. Unfortunately, in many situations the perceived "crisis" lasts longer than most civilian leaders originally envisioned and the so-called transition becomes standard operating procedure. Chile, for example, experienced military rule for eighteen years. Military rule is often precipitated by a government overthrow, or a coup d'état, when the governmental leader or part of the leadership is replaced by violence or threat. After a coup, which is usually quick, the military government is often referred to as a junta, or council. Military commanders have then been known to take control of schools, train new soldiers in their own doctrine, and take elaborate measures to silence the masses.

Military coups and military rule have been a common occurrence in the third world. In Iran, the 1921 coup ushered in a "new order," only to be followed by another coup in 1935. Sometimes coups are initially welcomed by the population, such as the Nigerian coup against CORRUPTION, fraud, and economic mismanagement in 1983. Many people applauded the military as saviors of the country. Some coups appear to be contagious, following one after the other. Nigeria experienced several military coups in thirty years and has spent much of its independence under military rule. Military coups are not necessarily violent—in fact most are bloodless, although a particularly brutal coup occurred in Chile in 1973, in which at least 2,000 people died. Turkey is another country with quite a scorecard of coups.

The Ottoman Empire was founded by warriors, and to many this tradition of military dominance rightly continues in the modern Turkish state. Modern Turkey was born of a military coup by the Kemalists in the 1920s, who claimed to be protecting Turkey from Islamic rule (Atatürk himself was a war hero). Turkey has become famous for military interventionism, often ostensibly in the name of DEMOCRACY. Ever since, the military has perceived itself as possessing a special role to defend Atatürk's secular republic. Three more coups followed in 1960, 1971, and 1980. In the 1980 coup, a six-man military junta suspended parliament, arrested leaders, and closed the doors on all parties and independent associations, including unions. The junta also instituted mass arrests and oversaw the drafting of the 1982 constitution, considered to be one of Turkey's most repressive. This power of military regimes to craft democracies that garner favor for themselves, including AMNESTY for their actions after they leave office, is a common occurrence in countries facing activist militaries.[47]

A different type of coup took place in Turkey in February 1997, when the military "encouraged" the resignation of Islamist prime minister Necmettin Erbakan. The prime minister had ruffled many feathers during his tenure, with perceived overtures to Iran, Iraq, and Syria, hosting Islamic shaikhs at his formal residence during the Muslim holy month of Ramadan, and (unsuccessfully) attempting to end the ban on headscarves. After seemingly flagrant Islamic activities in a small town near Ankara marking "Jerusalem night," the military presented Erbakan with a list of measures to limit Islamic expression in Turkey, including the closure of intermediate-level religious schools, which he eventually signed. One military officer even called the prime minister "a pimp" for undertaking the pilgrimage to Mecca as a guest of Saudi Arabia. When Erbakan urged sanctions against the officer, the military refused.[48]

Even in the absence of outright military rule, there are circumstances when militaries wield a tremendous amount of influence, even in the selection of the prime minister or other executives of government. Such persuasion is often made in threats not to support or protect a leader if he violates the wishes of the military. The term PRAETORIANISM is used to characterize states where civilian authorities face such intimidation. Some more simply call it blackmail. The concept derives from the praetorian guards who protected the Roman emperor. Often they would threaten to withdraw their crucial support if they did not get to choose who would be in power. Similarly, through their threats of vetoes and departure, militaries can shape policy.

Unlike most of its neighbors, Mexico has succeeded in establishing an unwritten deal between civilian and military leaders, as long as the military polices itself for human rights abuses and stays out of politics. However, Mexico had a long tradition of military intervention in politics; much of the nineteenth century was known as the age of CAUDILLOS. After the Mexican Revolution, several military figures vied for power. From 1917 through the 1930s, citizen-soldiers ruled, as all of Mexico's presidents during that period had started their careers as officers in the revolutionary army. The military continued to play a very important role in the Institutional Revolutionary Party (PRI) and therefore the government throughout the 1930s. In the early 1940s, President Lázaro Cárdenas began to demilitarize politics by dramatically reducing military expenditures and limiting the military's representation in the party. Since 1943, candidates for president have been automatically disqualified if they have a military background. Over time, the military has largely stayed in the barracks in Mexico, and unlike armed forces elsewhere, the Mexican military has not exploited periods of crisis to expand its influence. Most analysts do not consider the military in Mexico to be an independent political "wild card" in the way that it is in other countries. It is possible that continued instability in Mexico could draw the military into the political arena, but for more than sixty years the state has been largely under the control of civilians.[49]

In many countries of the third world, militaries have a mixed record of achievements and failures. They have been good at providing order and economic GROWTH. Yet they have also racked up a miserable record of human rights protection, especially in circumstances where they rule outright or where they are temporarily installed as an interim government. Some military regimes are characterized as caretaker governments, preoccupied with law and order and less concerned with implementing social changes. Corrective military regimes attempt to create a national identity and promote orderly economic development. Revolutionary military regimes promote the most radical changes of all, highlighting dramatic land reform that is never fully implemented.

Rape has been used as a deliberate military tactic, especially within the strategy of ethnic cleansing, but in other forms of violent warfare as well. It has been common in the wars in Rwanda, Kuwait, Haiti, and Colombia, among other countries. Women and girls are frequently victims of gang rape committed by soldiers and militias. The Khomeini regime in Iran set up so-called residential units to suppress female dissidents. The elite Revolutionary Guard used these outposts to continuously rape women who refused to submit to the regime.[50] In Darfur, females of all ages have been gang raped in front of their families, then butchered and left to die. The United Nations estimates that 15,000 women and girls were raped in the Democratic Republic of Congo in 2009, placing the blame on government troops, militias, and rebels.[51] Rape has also been used as a form of genocide, as male soldiers and paramilitaries have been ordered or allowed to impregnate "enemy" women. Sexual assault has long been part of a purposive strategy to sever women's ties to the community and to strip them of their dignity and pride. It often leads to the complete ostracism of these women. These trends point to the overall sexualization of war in the modern world, and the development of sexual terrorism.

One example of an entrenched, long-running military government is that of Myanmar, also known as Burma. In the late 1950s the Burmese army gained prestige and importance during the country's struggle for independence. In fact, prior to the beginning of its latest crackdown in the late 1980s, it was the police, not the military, who were the most hated institution in the country. But that changed when the military brutally suppressed popular demonstrations against its rule in 1988. Most estimates claim that 3,000–8,000 people were killed in this assault. Popular disgust with the army increased after it was overwhelmingly defeated by the National League for Democracy in the 1990 elections and refused to step aside. The leader of this political party, Aung San Suu Kyi, spent nearly two decades in detention. Universities, closed for nearly twelve years, reopened in 2000 as a small step toward normalcy. The 2008 constitution reserves a quarter of seats in both houses of parliament for the military, which holds a lock on top ministerial positions. As the armed forces seek funding through heroin trafficking, they attempt to maintain at least the appearance of a return to civilian rule, and elections were held in late 2010 (the first since 1990)—even though major opposition parties boycotted the poll to protest military involvement.

In many countries, regular military units are declining in numbers, prestige, and the support they receive. Some cannot escape their tarnished reputation; others appear to be bureaucratic beasts lumbering over sick economies. They are being replaced, especially in areas of conflict, by paramilitary units—relatively autonomous armed groups often in charge of security for an individual person, political party, or institution. To avoid the stigma of the appearance of military rule, some governments are turning to civilian militias to handle their security tasks. These can sometimes be virtual death squads, as we have seen in both Rwanda and East Timor. Their funding comes from the government (although often through covert channels) and they usually report directly to military officials. In some cases, including Colombia, paramilitaries comprise off-duty soldiers and police hoping to pocket some extra cash. Paramilitary units are often launched in an attempt by governments to wash their hands of violent acts. Mexican paramilitary units were used in Chiapas to try to shield the military from criticism for human rights violations. Similarly, in the early 1980s, China created the People's Armed Police, a unit that surged in growth after the crackdown on students in Tiananmen Square in 1989. The PAP, unlike the regular police force in China, is fully armed—it guards government offices, patrols borders, and quells riots and uprisings.

The power of military units can become extremely dangerous in transitional circumstances, such as after the fall of powerful leaders or a change in power, as rogue groups, still possessing weaponry and the desire for influence, attempt to maintain their power and voice. In Indonesia, a paramilitary group formed from former police cadets who failed the four-year officer course. Some believe that this unit—named Gunung Tidur—was responsible for a fatal series of fires during the May 1998 riots that led to Suharto's downfall.[52] Retired generals, upset at their loss of prestige and patronage, were also blamed for bombing a mosque outside of Jakarta in 1999.[53] Similar episodes have been reported in Tajikistan, Nigeria, and elsewhere.

One case in which the power of militias was highlighted was the chaos following the successful referendum on independence in East Timor in 1999. Violence between rival civilian groups, mostly instigated by the government-backed militias, claimed the lives of thousands and destroyed much of the region. The problem continues in West Timor, where tens of thousands of refugees remained for over a year after the referendum. Militias in West Timor continued to intimidate the refugees to keep them from returning to the independent East Timor (now known as Timor-Leste). As one scholar put it, once the refugees depart, the militias no longer have a reason for existence—they provide job security to a group hungry for employment.[54] In the Molucca Islands, the increased numbers of people fleeing sectarian violence there have exacerbated the refugee crisis, where clashes between Christians and Muslims have claimed thousands of lives.

In addition to traditional government militaries and militia groups, privately employed soldiers play an important role in wars in the third world. Mercenaries are as old as war itself, but in today's world their recruitment, deployment, and action is a multimillion-dollar business. Often, these soldiers-for-hire travel from country to country to earn a financial profit. For example, Serb and Ukrainian soldiers trained fighters in the Democratic Republic of Congo. In fact, foreign mercenaries fueled both sides of the conflict in that country. There and in Angola, over eighty companies were used to funnel soldiers into the battlefield. The most famous is the now defunct South African–based company Executive Outcomes, which was hired to provide fighters in both Angola and Sierra Leone to guard mines that are the source of "conflict diamonds," precious jewels that are illegally sold on the regular market and used to finance conflict. In South Africa, after a spike in the number of mercenaries being employed from that country, the government passed legislation making it illegal for citizens to fight elsewhere—without prior approval. In fact, immediately after the fall of Baghdad in 2003, when US commanders couldn't spare any troops to provide security for retired Army lieutenant-general Jay Garner (who had been named director of reconstruction and humanitarian assistance in Iraq), he hired two men from South Africa who were veterans of that country's apartheid-era Special Air Service. The contract that Garner and his successor, Paul Bremer, signed with them was never completed, as it was belatedly discovered that the men were violating South African law. One of Garner's former bodyguards was later arrested in Zimbabwe on suspicion of helping to plot a coup in Equatorial Guinea. The man was released but later convicted in South Africa of violating antimercenary legislation.[55] In Colombia, British Petroleum hired a battalion of soldiers to protect its interests, and mercenaries have been hired to protect Firestone's rubber plants as well. Mercenaries have also been active in a separatist conflict that has been fought in Papua New Guinea since the late 1980s. To put down the insurrection, the Papuan government hired soldiers, euphemistically called "military advisers," from the Bahamas-based corporation Sandline.

Governments may possess a monopoly over the right to use force—which states use both to change circumstances and to promote the status quo—but by no means are they the only promoters of violent change. We now turn our attention to some other groups that advocate or promote aggression to achieve their cause.

Terrorists

Who are terrorists? In the mid-1970s, terrorist expert Frederick Hacker argued that terrorists are usually characterized as criminals, crazies, or crusaders, and that sometimes they are characterized as all three.[56] As discussed at the beginning of this chapter, labeling individuals or groups as "terrorists" can be fraught with difficulty and inaccuracies. Why do people turn to tactics that target civilians? Some trace it to feelings of hopelessness, or the belief that there is no other avenue through which people can express their opinions. Terrorism often involves groups who are struggling for resources. In fact, it has been argued that terrorism takes place because modern war, which requires large militaries, advanced weaponry, and the like, has become a luxury tool of rich countries. All in all, terrorism can be a monetarily cheaper alternative to conventional warfare, and yet, due to its ability to foster fear and insecurity, it can be extremely effective in achieving political objectives. Many different types of terrorist groups can be identified. Terrorists may be associated with political revolutionary movements (including the famed "Carlos the Jackal"), national liberation (or separatist) causes (such as the Philippines' Abu Sayyaf and Sri Lanka's Tamil Tigers), or single-issue campaigns (such as the Animal Liberation Front). Such groups are found along all points of the ideological spectrum, but tend to congregate especially on the extreme left (e.g., Peru's Shining Path) and the extreme right (e.g., Al-Qaida).

Terrorist violence is used in many kinds of political activity. Some distinguish forms of terror by categorizing the targets of such activity. Domestic terrorism involves acts that are based in a single country without significant support from outside sources. Actions by the Free Aceh movement in Indonesia would qualify as ethnonationalist domestic terrorism. The Philippines has several Islamist separatist groups who are especially active in the southern regions of the country, including Abu Sayyaf, famous for kidnappings, bombings, and a plot to assassinate then-president Gloria Arroyo in 2008. The 1996 attack on the Japanese embassy in Lima, staged by the Marxist Túpac Amaru Revolutionary Movement, is another example of domestic-centered terrorism.

In contrast, international terrorism includes terror activity that is not limited to one state. An extremely well-coordinated and sophisticated attack in Mumbai in November 2008 left at least 160 people dead, with more than 300 injured. This attack, a siege throughout India's second largest city that lasted three days, was coordinated by Lashkar-e-Taiba, one of the largest Islamist terrorist organizations in southern Asia, based in Pakistan. The attackers, most of whom were in their early twenties, arrived in Mumbai on inflatable speedboats, armed with Kalashnikovs, hand grenades, and bombs, and proceeded to launch attacks in restaurants, taxis, luxury hotels, a train station, and a Jewish center in Mumbai. The attacks were surprising in both their scope and their preparation: planners used Google Earth to orchestrate their carnage,[57] which was documented in terrifying detail via social-networking sites around the world. One gunman had been instructed by his handler: "Everything is being recorded by the media. Inflict maximum damage. Keep fighting. Don't be taken alive."[58] Only one gunman, Ajmal Kasab, survived, and he was sentenced to death in May 2010.

The deep pockets of international terror networks reach into many different societies as a way of evading detection—transferring funds through the use of promissory notes or other underground methods that require minimal paperwork and are therefore difficult to trace. But it's not all about unmarked Swiss bank accounts. One arrangement is known as *hawala*—which is Hindi for "in trust." This system allows people working in one country to deposit payments (often in currency or gold) at a local office so that a third party can have virtually instantaneous access to the money in another country in a paperless transaction conducted through phone calls and e-mails. Some have described this as the Western Union of the non-Western world.[59] Based in the United Arab Emirates, *hawala* offices are found throughout the Middle East, northern Africa, and Asia. Some banks operating under this system have been accused of funneling profits from customers' fees to terrorist leaders, including Osama bin Laden and other high-ranking members of Al-Qaida, even though the 9/11 Commission confirmed in the latter case that funds were transferred by interbank wire rather than through the *hawala* system.[60] In fact, *hawala* networks have been extremely important in providing financial services and humanitarian aid through NONGOVERNMENTAL ORGANIZATIONS (NGOs) in Afghanistan, with sums reaching as much as $20 million a month.[61]

Another source of creative financing for illicit activities draws on the relationship between drug cartels and terrorist organizations, dating back to the 1970s. Terrorist groups, including the Sunni Taliban regime that formerly ruled Afghanistan, and some extreme Shiite groups in Lebanon, are believed to have financed their operations from the sale of illicit drugs, especially opium.[62] In Peru, Shining Path factions are known to offer protection to local peasants and coca growers. So-called taxes on coca growers and levies on traffickers' flights out of the region have been a primary source of revenue for the Shining Path, whose income is estimated to range between $10 million and $100 million a year.[63]

Prior to September 2001, few Americans had heard of Al-Qaida (meaning "The Base"), even though many were familiar with the name of its leader, Saudi fugitive Osama bin Laden. Al-Qaida, formed in 1988, is a deeply embedded international network of terrorists based in many countries; it supports extremist Sunni Muslim fighters in conflicts around the world, including Chechnya, Tajikistan, Kashmir, and Yemen. But as we have learned since mid-2001, many Al-Qaida operatives live and work in other countries around the world, with significant bases in Germany, the Philippines, Pakistan, and the United States, among others. Some of the stated goals of this network include the overthrow of nearly all conservative Muslim governments, to be replaced by a more virulent form of Islamic governance, and the expulsion of Western influence from the Muslim world, especially the US presence in Saudi Arabia. Even though Al-Qaida members often mention freedom for the Palestinians in their rhetoric, this seems to always take a back seat to their other concerns. In addition to funding its own terrorist activities, Al-Qaida is believed to be the premier funding source for Islamic extremist activities in the world. In 1996, bin Laden publicly issued his "Declaration of War" against the United States, which he and other members of Al-Qaida view as the chief obstacle to change in Muslim societies. It is important to note that while bin Laden and this group claimed to speak on behalf of Muslims around the world, Muslims have nearly universally denounced Al-Qaida's calls for violence and extremism, before and after September 11.

Terrorist groups combine multiple grievances to craft their own unique expression of rage against the status quo. These groups often present a combination of ideologies and demands and then fit their actions to their strengths and circumstances. For example, Uganda's Lord's Resistance Army (LRA), formed in the 1980s, has now become the most deadly militia in Africa. The group was initially led by then–twenty-eight-year-old cult leader Alice Lakwena, and later by her cousin, Joseph Kony, a former Catholic choirboy who is said to be possessed by spirits. First Lakwena (from the mid-1980s) and then Kony (from the late 1980s) promoted the proliferation of gangs, murderers, rapists, and sheer terror, especially in northern Uganda. For nineteen years they fought the Ugandan army, telling young recruits to smear botanical shea butter on their bodies to repel bullets and to sing Christian hymns as they marched straight toward the enemy. They also told recruits that the rocks they threw at soldiers would turn into grenades. After suppression by the Ugandan army, Lakwena fled to Kenya, where she died in 2007. The LRA aimed to recreate the Kingdom of God and establish a state based on the Ten Commandments. In addition to Christian precepts, the group incorporated aspects of both indigenous religions and minor tenets of Islam—Kony announced that Fridays would be a second sabbath, largely as a way to appease his financial sponsors in Khartoum, Sudan. This sponsorship was largely designed to counter Uganda's support of separatists in southern Sudan. Some of the LRA's more unusual tenets, though, including bans on eating the meat of white-feathered chickens and riding bicycles—a primary form of transportation in Uganda—cannot accurately be traced to any of these belief systems. Kony claims that he is instructed by God, and that the LRA is very strict about enforcement: one man was killed for violating the bicycle ban, and LRA soldiers forced the dead man's wife to eat one of his feet or be killed. LRA agents are famous for abducting young teens—as many as 35,000 young girls and boys, according to the United Nations Children's Fund (UNICEF). In 2005 the INTERNATIONAL CRIMINAL COURT (ICC) issued arrest warrants, on charges including twelve counts of crimes against humanity, for Joseph Kony and four LRA associates. These were the first warrants issued by the ICC since its establishment in 2002. In August 2006 the Ugandan government and the LRA signed a truce that many hoped would finally end the nearly two decades of massacres and mutilation in the country. Yet, as of early 2011, Kony remained at large, and the LRA (significantly diminished) now operates from across the border in eastern Congo.

Even though terrorism by independent groups is most common, terrorist methods are also advocated by clandestine agents of governments, through government-sponsored or -supported groups designed to intimidate and repress individuals and groups within society. They often use death squads to threaten and eliminate their enemies. Although states risk being ostracized by the international community by engaging in terrorist acts, this is a gamble that some are willing to take. Increasingly, even if groups are not acting on the orders of a government, they are often acting with its support (ideologically and often financially), giving rise to the term "STATE-SPONSORED TERRORISM." Because of the passion that groups are able to incite for their causes, attempts to isolate state-sponsored terrorists have been incomplete at best.

Figure 12.6 The Israeli-Palestinian Conflict

Perhaps few struggles are more enduring than the ongoing conflict between Arab Palestinians and the Israeli government. This dispute has been the source of five major wars, and has contributed to numerous other regional upheavals, claiming thousands of lives—including children, teenagers, and entire families. The outbreak of conflict, especially following the 1967 Six Day War, has displaced millions of Palestinians, scattering them across multiple states and refugee centers in the region. Terrorist violence has marred all sides in this clash, rife with border disputes, intense religious symbolism, and security concerns. It seems that no one's hands are clean—but each side claims it has been provoked by the other, and both the Israeli government and the Palestinian Authority claim that the injustices of the situation make it difficult for them to control those under their rule. In fact, one of the dangerous turns in the dispute has been the willingness of individuals to take actions into their own hands, sometimes wrapping themselves in nail-studded explosives and taking their own lives—along with the lives of many others—in crowded urban areas. In 2002, Wafa Idris, a volunteer medic with the Palestine Red Crescent Society, was identified as the first female suicide bomber to attack Israel within its borders (she has since been followed by several more). While police attacks and the bulldozing of homes have been commonplace on the Israeli side, suicide bombings have proven to be a weapon of choice for some Palestinians. Shortly after the death of former Palestinian Authority leader Yassir Arafat, in November 2004, Mahmoud Abbas was elected president of the Palestinian Authority. As the Palestinian Authority increased its level of institutionalization, a surprise parliamentary victory was won by Hamas, the Palestinian Sunni Islamist organization famous for both its comprehensive Palestinian welfare programs, as well as its controversial charter that calls for the destruction of the state of Israel. Following its surprise victory, the United States, the European Union, and Israel imposed an economically crippling response that cut all fund transfers and tax receipts. The controversy only emboldened Hamas and its supporters and made many question the West's hypocritical response to a democratically elected government. Following a World Bank report that documented the devastating effects of these measures, monies were again channeled to the Palestinian people through elaborate means that bypassed the Palestinian Authority. Yet a significant schism between President Abbas (whose base is in the West Bank) and Hamas (who remain in control of the Gaza Strip) has presented an impasse for international negotiations, which once again remain in a deadlock over the fundamental issues of borders, security, settlements, and the status of Jerusalem, the city claimed as a holy city to three major world religions: Christianity, Islam, and Judaism.

There is a growing list of known governments that are active in supporting groups beyond their shores: the usual suspects include Iran, Cuba, North Korea, and Syria. Cuba, Yemen, and North Korea have been accused of providing safe haven to hunted terrorists. With the insecurity that follows in the wake of terror attacks, it is tempting to divide the world in two, placing countries that cooperate with the US-led global war on terrorism on one side and those that do not on the other. As we discuss in Chapter 20, the BUSH DOCTRINE implicated any country that supports terrorists, as being terrorists themselves. Such seeming clarity, though, can be misleading. True, there are some countries that invoke sovereignty—the right to control what happens within one's borders—and argue that they will not cooperate in this war on terror, which they claim is just another attempt by the United States to impose its will on others. Yet there are other countries, including the Philippines and Somalia, that are plagued by weak governments that struggle to control their own territory; therefore their assistance would be impotent at best. As much as President

Barack Obama has attempted to craft an effective approach to state-sponsored terrorism, including rejecting the image of the global war against it and reaching out to state leaders across the spectrum and the globe, his approach has been stalled by debate within his own foreign policy team about the best approach, as well as by the political reality of attempting to change policies that had been so central to his predecessor, George W. Bush. Some have wondered aloud whether much has changed, in terms of outcome. One Bush-era lawyer highlighted that "the change in tone has been important and has helped internationally. But the change in law has been largely cosmetic. And of course there has been no change in outcome."[64]

Iran is viewed in the West as a large-scale sponsor of terrorist violence—a charge that leaders in Tehran vehemently deny. The country is suspected of having committed or sponsored assassinations in northern Iraq, attacks against the Kurdish Democratic Party of Iran, and other policies of liquidating the regime's opponents who live outside the country. Iran also stirs the coals with neighboring Iraq by providing safe haven to some of Turkey's PKK operatives. Following the attacks of September 11, the United States argued that it would welcome Iran's support in the war on terror if it withdrew support from perceived terror groups. In fact, the United States needed the support of Iran to help forge ties with the Northern Alliance in Afghanistan. Iran had assisted the Northern Alliance and other anti-Taliban groups through the 1990s, and some viewed their mediation as "essential" to convincing the factions of mujahidin fighters in Afghanistan to work with the United States to topple the Taliban regime.[65] Libya also was long branded an active sponsor of terror. Once behind the wheel of government in 1969, Colonel Muammar Qaddafi sought to launch an Arab-Islamic revolution, for which he trained thousands of foreign terrorists each year in Libyan camps. Among the most famous was Carlos Ramirez Santos, also known as "Carlos the Jackal," who operated on behalf of Libya, Syria, and Iraq until his extradition from Sudan and deportation to France in 1997. By 2003, though, building on the improved relations he experienced after agreeing to turn over the Libyans accused of planting the bomb on Pan Am Flight 103, which killed 207 people, Qaddafi formally declared the existence of his chemical and nuclear weapons programs and invited international inspectors into Libya (although some claim his announcement was in response to the US-led war in Iraq, he had made similar offers, to no avail, beginning in the late 1990s).[66] After the weapons programs were destroyed, the French government followed through on pledges to help Libya build a peaceful nuclear power program, and in 2006 the United States restored diplomatic relations with Libya, removing it from the list of countries believed to be officially sponsoring terrorism.

As mentioned, the view from within each of these countries diverges from the account we are familiar with in the West. Remember that groups engage in violent actions because they believe it is the best way—and sometimes the only way—to be heard. Although Sudan has been accused of assisting or planning much terror activity in the West, Sudanese leaders and citizens alike contend that they have suffered at the hands of Western terrorism as well. Public sentiment in Sudan turned strongly against the West after the 1998 US bombing of the only medicine factory in the country following the Al-Qaida attacks on US embassies in Kenya and Tanzania. Many international organizations (including the United Nations) and leaders in both the Western and the non-Western world have challenged the evidence that was used to justify the attack on this factory, which the Clinton administration argued was being used to produce chemical weapons. UN analyses of the wreckage and the soil around it found no signs of chemical weapons production. Many people, not just in the third world, considered the timing of this attack—the week of the president's appearance before a grand jury—as an attempt to divert attention away from Clinton's own political difficulties. This prompted many to compare the saga with the movie *Wag the Dog,* which had coincidentally been released at almost the same time.

Another way to categorize types of terrorism is by focusing on the tools used to provoke fear or cause damage. While nuclear weapons and their delivery tend to be cost-prohibitive and technologically problematic for many countries of the world, bioterrorism is more within their reach. This leads some to refer to biological and chemical weapons as the "poor man's nuclear bomb" and "great equalizer." Biological weapons, including anthrax, the plague, and smallpox, are viewed as an ideal tool for many terrorists today because their effects take days to appear, making an elusive escape more likely. Yet it can be extremely difficult to contain any outbreak resulting from a biological attack, meaning that the perpetrators may themselves be harmed as well. Such weapons remain dangerous because of their availability and potency: small amounts can wreck havoc on large groups of people. They have already been used as weapons of mass destruction—most effectively by Saddam Hussein's forces against the Kurds in Iraq. Iran, victimized by Iraq's use of chemical weapons during the war between these two countries in the 1980s, is also known to be producing (or preparing to produce) biological and chemical weapons.

Chemical weapons, in the form of mustard gas, tabun, sarin, phosgene, VX, and other agents, are believed to be the easiest-made weapons of mass destruction and are viewed as particularly horrendous because of their invisible and insidious stealth nature.[67] Their ingredients, including pesticides and fertilizers, are readily available. The main obstacle to their effective deployment comes in the difficulty of producing large quantities, as well as a delivery method, because in most cases they must be miniaturized in order to be potently dispensed. As of early 2011, some of the countries included on the US State Department's list of state sponsors of international terrorism (Iran, Syria, and Sudan) are known to possess chemical weapons. Perhaps some of the major countries are not in the best position to condemn such action, though, as the United States and Russia possess the two largest stockpiles of chemical and biological weapons in the world and, despite some progress, have yet to destroy their stockpiles as agreed to in the Chemical Weapons Convention of 1993.[68] In fact, the scourge of these terror agents was introduced by the Western powers, which used them widely in World War I and in the Vietnam War.

Even if conventional nuclear weapons may be out of reach for many states, some believe the world faces an increased threat of nuclear terrorism due to the quantity of materials relatively unaccounted for—including plutonium and highly enriched uranium, as well as the increased number of nuclear-capable states, discussed in Chapter 18. Even if an individual cannot piece together enough material to build a nuclear bomb, it is believed that a group could still build such a device—widely referred to as a "dirty bomb"—to spread radiological contamination. Widespread destruction can be achieved by wrapping radioactive material (including spent fuel rods) around conventional explosives. Once detonated, in the form of a car bomb, suitcase nuke, or other device, the intense radiation will be far more destructive than the blast itself. As of yet, there are unconfirmed suspicions that Iran received or smuggled nuclear materials out of the former Soviet Union. It is extremely difficult to know if Al-Qaida or other known terror groups have access to such materials, although it is highly plausible.

Revolutionaries

One of China's great revolutionaries, Mao Zedong, once emphasized the violence and uprootedness of revolutions in his famous observation that a REVOLUTION "is not a dinner party. . . . A revolution is an insurrection, an act of violence by which one class overthrows another."[69] To elaborate on Mao's prose, a revolution may be defined as a change in regime with the desire to achieve extensive, relatively quick, and often concurrent changes in economic, political, and social structures. Even though many countries claim to hold a revolutionary heritage, if we adopt the conventional definition of revolutions as fundamental transformations in everyday way of life, they are actually fairly rare events. The classic revolutionary states, in which such dramatic changes were implemented, are China, France, and Russia.[70] Revolutions such as these are unlike other changes of power because their goal is to destroy the existing system, often through the use of charisma and violence. In the Chinese and French Revolutions, for example, people even changed their names and ways of referring to others. Following China's 1949 revolution, it was common for people to refer to each other by the egalitarian moniker "comrade" rather than by surname or title.

Yet there have been many attempts to promote revolutions and revolutionary change beyond the three traditional "grand" revolutions. Many countries in the third world claim a revolutionary heritage, including Iran, Mexico, Turkey, Cuba, Peru, and Zimbabwe. Revolutions are often launched from remote regions where governmental groups have less control, and their leaders build their power base through ideological persuasion. Those at the forefront of the revolutionary effort often employ guerrilla tactics, especially the element of surprise, such as when the Zapatistas unexpectedly marched into the city of San Cristobal de las Casas on New Year's Day in 1994. In a nutshell, revolutions are about change.

Revolutions bring new people to power, incorporating groups such as peasants and workers who had otherwise been left out of the process. In this sense, they attempt to "liberate" people—a term that is commonly associated with revolutionary endeavors. Many revolutions are class-based, arising from structural changes that pit one group of people against another. Revolutions can also be born of crises manifested in territorial expansion, economic reorganization, international dislocation, or population expansion. Situations ripe for revolution include those involving widespread misery, oppression, and injustice, combined with either a weak government that is unable to solve the problems facing it or a significant crisis. In these situations, when "push comes to shove," groups who perceive themselves on the losing end of the bargain concentrate their resources and attempt to overthrow the oppressive system. In revolutionary situations, groups demand some role in decisionmaking, whether facing down military rulers, such as in Mexico, Bolivia, or Cuba, colonial regimes, such as in Vietnam and Algeria, or monarchies, such as in imperial China and Russia. In each of these cases, the entrenched elite was unable (or unwilling) to incorporate the new voices without a fight. Revolutions can also follow the collapse of an EMPIRE or regime, as happened with the collapse of the Qing Dynasty in China, the Ottoman Empire in Turkey, and the Qajar Empire in Iran (then known as Persia). A crisis situation unites otherwise disconnected groups to rebel against the status quo and claim power. Successful revolutions often coalesce around a single leader (or small group of leaders) who is able to harness discord into a potent political force.

Sometimes leaders of revolutions are (or become) military leaders as well, including Turkey's Mustafa Kemal Atatürk, Burkina Faso's Thomas Sankara, and Algeria's Houari Boumedienne. Yet not all revolutionary leaders have a military background: Iran's Ayatollah Khomeini was a religious leader, China's Mao Zedong was a librarian, Guinea Bissau's Amilcar Cabral was a census taker, and most people believe that the Zapatistas' Subcomandante Marcos was once a professor. Revolutionary leaders tend to have charisma and come from the relatively privileged classes—many are leaders of the intelligentsia, among the most educated members of society and accustomed to having their say. Yet the harbingers of revolutionary movements often suffer some sort of major setback, experiencing failed expectations or suffering from an aspiration gap, as discussed earlier in the chapter. Many leaders of revolutions face a tumultuous history in their own countries—difficulties they often rectify with a vengeance against their former suppressers.

For example, Khomeini was exiled to Iraq from 1964 to 1968 for criticizing the Shah and allegedly sparking riots. He was later evicted from the Shia holy city of An Najaf by Saddam Hussein. Khomeini viewed himself as uniquely fit to avenge the problems of the West, especially the humiliations wrought on Muslims in the Middle East. Following his victorious return to Iran in 1979—after mass protests against the Shah's regime had long festered—he quickly acted on these ambitions, transforming the Iranian Revolution into an Islamic Revolution.[71] Mustafa Kemal Atatürk, leader of the 1919 Turkish Revolution, also viewed himself as distinctively able to lead his country down a new path. The difference between their approaches was the role of religion in their revolutions: Khomeini believed that an orthodox version of Islam and a rejection of all things Western were the best corrective to Iran's problems, while Atatürk prescribed an unyielding form of SECULARISM to overcome Turkey's challenges. Both rode the rising wave of NATIONALISM in their respective societies.

Another revolutionary who capitalized on nationalist themes was Ho Chi Minh, leader of the modern revolution in Vietnam, whose name means "Bringer of Light." At the end of World War I, when he was a student in France, Ho approached President Woodrow Wilson with the hope that Wilson's doctrine of self-determination would be applied to Vietnam. Wilson turned Ho away. Ho later founded the Viet Minh (whose name is an acronym for the Vietnam Independence League), but died before his dream of a unified North and South Vietnam could be realized, at tremendous cost. Affectionately known by many Vietnamese as "Uncle Ho," he repelled French attempts to regain an Asian empire in the 1950s, and later frustrated US attempts to defeat them in the 1960s and 1970s.

Some revolutionary leaders are already incumbent rulers who overthrow their fellow leaders to establish a new governing system. The Turkish Revolution of 1919 is one such example. Some have called it an ELITE REVOLUTION, or a revolution from above—defined by the swift overthrow of the elite by other members of the elite, limited mass participation, and limited violence.[72] Ellen Trimberger argues that the specific characteristics of elite revolutions, especially their restrictions on the involvement of the masses, can lead to situations in which the military may regularly intervene, which certainly holds true for the coup-riddled experience of Turkey.[73] The Peruvian Revolution (by coup), led by General Juan Velasco Alvarado, may also be described as a revolution from above. Despite these examples of elite revolutions, it is important to note that most are made "from below," incorporating the masses or other disenfranchised groups in an overthrow of the power structure. In fact, the Velasco revolution failed in part because it didn't incorporate the participation of other groups, including the people it meant to serve—the peasants.

Women have been active participants in revolutionary struggles and wars: harboring rebels, moving weapons and intelligence through war zones, staffing health organizations, and carrying rifles. Women served key roles in revolutions in Nicaragua, Palestine, South Africa, Zimbabwe, Mexico, and the Philippines. In the Philippine Revolution of 1896–1902, known as the first anticolonial independence movement in Asia, women gained prominence. As one example, Teresa Magbanua was known as the Filipina "Joan of Arc" for her battles against the Spaniards in the late 1800s. In the Mexican Revolution, both Emiliano Zapata's and Pancho Villa's armies included women revolutionaries, called *soldaderas*. They were originally camp followers who fed soldiers and provided services that the government did not. Gertrudis Bocanegra organized an army of women during the Mexican War of Independence in 1810: she died in 1817 after being arrested and tortured. Women often organized their own units, armed themselves, and fought as soldiers equal to the men. In unprecedented numbers, women participated in every aspect of the anti-Somoza effort in Nicaragua; in fact, they made up 30 percent of the Sandinista army and occupied important leadership positions, commanding full battalions. They were mostly young women, and the men with whom they shared units appeared for the most part to accept them. But after the revolution, women were largely ignored, even betrayed, by the Sandinistas.[74] And although there were female soldiers in Namibia, women never rose to officer status. In Namibia and Zimbabwe, female soldiers were often stigmatized after the war for being "mannish" by carrying guns. When Sam Nujoma thanked the Namibian people for their contribution to the country's liberation, he mentioned women specifically but did not recognize them as fighters.

Despite proclamations of great change, revolutions fade away—they are difficult to sustain. Revolutions require resources (personnel, coercion, money), energy (charismatic leaders and committed followers), and a level of ideological zeal and commitment that few societies can maintain for very long, much to the chagrin of both those who led the revolution and those who suffered losses during it. China's Cultural Revolution is the best example of one leader's attempt to literally "continue the revolution" and maintain its legacy.

Terror often plays a large role in revolutions and revolutionary societies. Because revolutions attempt to achieve dramatic changes, there is little room for dissent or discussion. As with much violent conflict, clear sides are chosen by combatants and bystanders alike. Individuals and groups who are viewed to be against the regime are labeled "counterrevolutionaries," a charge that carries great danger, often tantamount to a death sentence. Especially after it is perceived that there has been some setback to revolutionary progress, terror methods, including torture, isolation, and forced labor, are commonly employed as means of holding on to power and keeping the revolution alive.

One of the most problematic legacies of revolutions is the selection of leadership beyond the revolutionary generation. Succession is an issue in many countries of the non-Western world, but especially in those with a revolutionary heritage. Leadership transition in nondemocratic states is rarely orderly. Leaders tend to seek to rule for life, and few mechanisms are put in place to choose their replacements until a crisis precipitates change—which means that leadership turnover happens during times of instability. Plato hypothesized that such circumstances, often deriving from chaotic mass rule, produce authoritarian despots. Deng Xiaoping's death in 1997 passed with barely a hiccup, because Jiang Zemin had been given almost eight years at the helm under Deng's steady hand and continued hold on (informal) power. The formal transfer of power from Jiang Zemin to Hu Jintao in 2002–2003 was similar in some ways, masking the fact that Jiang still controlled the reins, albeit from behind the scenes. Even after the titles of power were conferred to Hu Jintao, the leader of China's so-called fourth generation, Jiang and his protégés continued to exercise power for at least a year afterward. The groundwork for the next transition within the PRC, set for 2012–2013, has already been prepared: by mid-2010, Xi Jinping and Li Keqiang had each received promotions to key military and party posts. In Cuba, many express uncertainty about life after Fidel Castro, an uncertainty that was already apparent even when Castro's uncharismatic brother Raul assumed control during an ongoing "temporary" transfer of power after one of Fidel's health crises in July 2006. In South Africa, even though there was plenty of worry as Nelson Mandela neared retirement, his protégé, Thabo Mbeki, was able to provide a sense of continuity. However, since then tensions have grown, as Mbeki's second term was cut short due to party infighting. And in North Korea, in the months surrounding the elevation of one of reclusive leader Kim Jong Il's sons, Kim Jong-Un, tensions in the region were significantly heightened, especially after North Korea launched artillery attacks against a South Korean island along the disputed maritime border. Some observers believe the actions, part of a larger pattern of North Korean aggression, demonstrated a less than enthusiastic embrace by the Korean military of Kim's designated successor.[75]

Do revolutions often accomplish what their leaders set out to achieve? Since revolutions claim to promote fundamental transformations in power relations, it is important to assess their gains. Few revolutions are total failures, but few accomplish most of their explicit goals, either. In the early years of a revolution, it is common to observe significant attempts at land distribution and social change, employing at least the rhetoric, if not the reality, of equality. Castro, for example, appeared to be confronting machismo with laws requiring men to help with domestic responsibilities, but the laws were rarely enforced. Most revolutions also produce at least some form of leadership change, although one tyrant may simply be replaced by another, or by someone even more despotic.[76] The ruling groups in power after the revolution rarely deliver on the grand pledges they used to mobilize people to join in the first place.

Social stratification is rarely decreased in postrevolutionary societies—rather, the bureaucratic malaise and the expansion of state power that tend to follow revolutionary conflict often increase the gap between rich and poor.[77] Revolutions in the third world have an especially poor record of promoting equality and increased freedom, even if some redistribution of wealth or land reform actually takes place, such as in China and Cuba. In China, Cuba, and Nicaragua, one form of inequality was simply replaced by another, as the former landlords became poor and party leaders became more comfortable. Pledges to promote sexual equality, as well, are often relegated to lower status after the revolution is won, leading many to argue that promises of gender equality are formulated only to secure support of women during the revolutionary fight. In Namibia and Zimbabwe, promises of gender equality were "postponed" in order to appease still-powerful traditional (patriarchal) interests that the vulnerable revolutionary governments needed as allies. In the dangerous attempt to create "new" societies and new cultural foundations, and to do this quickly, huge groups of people often get caught in the crossfire. Although the statistics remain hotly debated, it is estimated that 2–3 million people died during Pol Pot's disastrous communist revolution in Cambodia, and at least 1 million died during the revolutionary fervor in Vietnam. Mao Zedong went to the grave with many deaths on his shoulders: some estimate that as many as 60 million people died in China as a result of his rule.[78]

Due to these broken promises, postrevolutionary societies often face great difficulty dealing with the revolutionary heritage they inherit, and governing groups in these societies tend to be defensive and reactionary. For example, in Iran in 1981, two years after the Islamic Revolution, the government crushed the so-called Marxist mujahidin after they purportedly bombed the Islamic Republic's office in Tehran. The mujahidin had been part of the coalition that overthrew the Shah in the first place, but they quickly fell out of favor with Khomeini and his supporters. The new government executed 6,000 of its members and supporters, and thousands of ordinary people answered the virulent call to attack the "enemies" of Islam. Training camps were established, including one camp in Tehran that was reserved for women trainees only.[79] In Mexico, Cuba, and China, the complex legacy of revolutionary leaders has proved a formidable challenge to the ruling regime that follows it, especially when groups ruling in the name of a revolutionary heritage seem to abandon prior goals and pledges.

To conclude our discussion of revolutions and revolutionary heritage, we compare two revolutions that continue to shape life in the third world. Both the 1979 Iranian Revolution and the 1949 Chinese Revolution were extremely popular with the population. In China, this support was sustained, for the most part, until the crackdown on the students in 1989. In Iran, the "grand coalition" quickly collapsed. Even though it was estimated that approximately one-fifth of the Iranian population demonstrated against the regime of Mohammad Reza Shah Pahlavi in December 1979, the euphoria ended shortly after it toppled the Shah's regime.[80]

The execution of the 1979 Iranian Revolution was rapid, while the Chinese Revolution was drawn out over twenty-two years of warfare before the PRC was established in 1949. Both revolutions took time to consolidate. In fact, most issues in both societies today emanate from the struggle of trying to be "modern" and relatively integrated without losing the hard-fought gains of the past. Both revolutions replaced imperial eras, even if there was a thirty-eight-year interim period in the case of China. The Iranian Revolution rid society of an unpopular monarch who had already once been deposed, ending 2,500 years of dynastic rule. In China, the Qing Dynasty had collapsed in 1911, but rival groups and factions, including political parties, warlords, and millennial cults, sparred over the country's future throughout most of the transition.

In their attempt to shoot for the moon, revolutionaries sometimes create new problems for themselves and those who follow them. Leaders in both Iran and China, for example, realized that their calls for "revolutionary" families to have many children as a way of prolonging the revolutionary spoils soon created a painful drain on public resources. Mao encouraged population growth throughout the 1960s and early 1970s, yet mandated limits on family size in the late 1970s. In the 1980s, Iran's population jumped from 34 million to more than 50 million. As a result, Iran has introduced one of the world's most comprehensive family-planning programs, making every form of birth control available free of charge and requiring couples to pass a family-planning course before they can legally marry. This initiative prompted the health ministry to send officials door-to-door, with clerics issuing FATWAS to approve intrauterine devices and vasectomies.[81]

Both postrevolutionary societies are now evaluating the modernization of their regimes and the ways that they can continue revolutionary rhetoric while reaching out to other countries. The Iranian Revolution is undergoing an "Islamic Reformation"—defining the proper relationship between Islam and the modern world.[82] Iran leads the Islamic world in this debate, publicly challenging precepts everywhere from the courtroom and editorial pages to the cinemas and blogs. And clerics convicted of taking the debate too far have become celebrities among the ordinary population, especially since the Green Movement of 2009 (discussed in Chapter 10). Ever since the death of Mao Zedong in 1976, Chinese leaders have rethought their revolutionary saga, once even stating that Mao was 80 percent correct and 20 percent wrong in his handling of Chinese affairs. After Deng Xiaoping pushed China to open its doors to the outside world, Chinese began to question their revolutionary rhetoric more than ever. Few communist cadres had considered rehearsing their memorization of Mao's quotations while sitting at a Starbucks or Kentucky Fried Chicken.

What was accomplished by these two revolutions, grand in scale if not in achievement? In both China and Iran, literacy rates increased dramatically, especially among the youth. Between 1970 and 1990, literacy in Iran topped 90 percent, even as the population itself had doubled.[83] China also achieved dramatic improvements in literacy and healthcare between the 1940s and the 1970s, especially in the countryside. Revolutions in both countries provoked fearful responses from nearby states. Turkey blames the rise of PKK terrorism and separatist claims on the Iranian Revolution, and many of China's Southeast Asian neighbors, led by Indonesia, formed the Association of Southeast Asian Nations (ASEAN) as a way of combating a possible domino effect of communism throughout the region. Obviously, new cadres of leadership entered the ranks in both countries as a result of their revolutions. As the postrevolutionary generation gives way to the post-postrevolutionary leadership, the combination of pragmatism and revolutionary legacy that is used to justify their rule may become increasingly difficult.

Conclusions: Whither Violence?

Is the world more violent today than in the past? Those who argue that it is point to the end of the largest military buildup the world has ever seen, the Cold War, and the resulting widespread availability of weapons—to governments, individuals, and organized groups alike. They also find evidence in the renewal of latent issues, such as separatist movements and ethnic violence that were earlier suppressed by authoritarian regimes—as we have witnessed in Yugoslavia, Rwanda, Nigeria, and Indonesia. There are also those who maintain that the world today is no more violent than in the past. They point to current moves toward strengthening regional and international norms against violence, despite the violent nature of governments throughout time and the ongoing determination of violent revolutionaries and terrorists. However the question is answered, it is up to you to weigh the evidence and decide.

As we have shown in this chapter, the use of violence as a means of implementing change is not always ideologically, religiously, or culturally based. Nor is it always the usual suspects (the "criminals, crazies, or crusaders") who are the perpetrators of violence. State-sponsored violence, domestically and internationally, makes up a large proportion of violence in the world today, Western and non-Western alike. Our discussion has also highlighted that it is not only so-called extremists who engage in violent acts. Some groups and individuals feel that it is only through hostility and aggression that they can get the respect, attention, and credence they deserve.

It is tempting when looking at these issues and actors to be reductionist: to claim that the tactics of revolutionaries, terrorists, and government fighters are evil, that actions are always based in fanaticism, or that violence is always irrational. One does not have to condone the use of violence to evaluate such actors on their own terms and attempt to understand why they take the actions they do.

While many see violence as the only way to resolve a situation, it is difficult to make the transition beyond violence. The use of violence is often, although by no means always, self-perpetuating. People are forced to take sides, defining "enemy" groups and dehumanizing neighbors, colleagues, and fellow citizens. Following times of discord and disruption and attempts to move beyond them, there is a great sense that past "scores" need to be settled.

13

Linking
Concepts and Cases

As we have discussed, violent expression can take many forms and derives from many different motivations. In what ways is conflict expressed differently in the countries that we are studying? What are the main sources of discord and how are they expressed? Do you observe any significant differences between the STATES that were established via revolutionary or liberation wars and those that were not? How do the power and role of the military in each of these states impact the operation of government or the expression of dissenting opinion? What legacies of past conflict can you observe in these states at the beginning of the twenty-first century? Based on what you already know about our cases, what type of situation do you expect to find in each of these countries? For example, given what you learned about CIVIL SOCIETY in Chapter 10, what expectations do you hold for the expression of violence in each of these states?

Case Study: Mexico

It is undeniable that in some parts of Mexico, violent crime is a serious problem and that levels of insecurity have grown over the past few years. It is not unusual today to hear that Mexico is facing its greatest crisis since its revolution due to the violence unleashed by organized crime. The drug trade in Mexico has flourished for some time. Fifty percent of the cocaine entering the United States came through Mexico in 1990—today 90 percent of it does, as the power center has shifted from Colombia to Mexico. Over the years the trade has become more lucrative (the trade in Mexico is estimated to be worth $25 billion a year), more competitive, and bloodier. In response, in 2006 President Felipe Calderón declared a war on drugs.[1] He has called in 40,000 army troops and succeeded in some high-profile drug seizures, arrests, and extraditions. However, as one kingpin is removed, intergroup competition soars as his lieutenants fight to succeed him. Today it is estimated that there are at least seven different drug-trafficking organizations (plus splinter groups) vying for supremacy and control of territory. The stakes are high because (as Calderón put it) Mexico is next door to the biggest drug addict in the world.[2] As the cartels continue their infighting, they have become increasingly brazen and gruesome in their attacks, assassinating each other and terrorizing ordinary people (including uploading videos of mutilations, beheadings, and the like, to YouTube). As of March 2011, the Mexican government confirmed that nearly 35,000 people (many of them ordinary folks caught in the crossfire) have been killed in drug-related violence—in just over four years.[3] More than thirty reporters have been killed or disappeared in that time period, and more of those who continue to work admit to practicing self-censorship (in an effort at self-preservation). Because the government is unable to protect journalists, the Juarez newspaper *El Diario* printed an extraordinary front-page open letter to the mafias in 2010, asking them to explain what it is that they want (since the mafias are the de facto authorities in Juarez).[4]

In 2008 a US Joint Forces Command report suggested that Mexico was on the cusp of becoming a failed state, at risk of rapid and sudden collapse. This brought a storm of controversy (as did Secretary of State Hillary Clinton's comparison of Mexico's conditions today to Colombia's narcostate insurgency two decades ago). President Barack Obama joined the Mexican government in immediately denying the comparison, arguing that Mexico is not a failing state; it is a DEMOCRACY that is taking action "just in time."[5] Not all Mexicans agree; as rates of violence escalate and levels of security plummet, more people are feeling that the government can't protect them and that the war is too costly. According to one poll, three out of four Mexicans feel less secure than they did a year ago and fewer than 20 percent believe that President Calderón's war on drugs is succeeding.[6] Partly this is because the violence often seems so random.

Fewer Mexicans buy Calderón's reassurances that the rising violence is a sign that progress is being made. Although some in the Mexican and US governments insist that what Mexico is facing is not a political insurgency, these mafias do mean to influence politics. According to Shannon O'Neil, Mexico's transition to democracy disrupted the long-established understanding between the traffickers and the government that defined the rules of the game in a way that allowed business as usual to go on with limited government interference. The compact was broken; because the government (now democratic) is taking on the cartels, the drug lords have decided to undermine the democracy.[7] They seek to hijack the democratic process, bombing campaign offices, assassinating candidates and government officials, and scaring voters away from the polls. Despite this, Mexicans have bravely continued to turn out in relatively large numbers to vote against candidates believed to have ties to organized crime.[8]

Mexican citizens are doing their part, and as hard as he is fighting the cartels, Calderón must do more to fight CORRUPTION in his own government. On Transparency International's Corruption Perceptions Index, Mexico's ranking dropped from 89 to 98 from 2009 to 2010—indicating that it is perceived as more corrupt.[9] Although some doubt his ability to make significant changes in the time he has left in office, President Calderón has attempted to rectify the problem in a variety of ways. He has sought to create a unified command, revamping the municipal and state police forces (since it is at these levels that police are the most vulnerable to mafia influence) to work more closely with federal police and troops. His reforms include improved pay and training and weeding out bad cops.[10]

In terms of RULE OF LAW, there is also room for improvement. The judicial process is slow and ineffectual, criminal defendants are generally not presumed innocent, and tortures, rapes, disappearances, and murders continue in Mexico as they have for years. Although there are some who are honest and humane, for years police and soldiers have operated with impunity because the military polices itself. Even before the current war on drugs began, in 2006 the United Nations Committee Against Torture raised concerns about military and police abuse, particularly the rape and arbitrary detention of protesters in Mexico.[11] As of early 2011, Mexico's human rights commission had identified more than 4,800 complaints against the military since 2006. Such complaints are rarely investigated, let alone prosecuted; when they are it is done in secret military tribunals and the outcomes are hardly ever publicized. But the United States has pressed President Calderón to hold the military accountable and Calderón has responded. In 2010, Calderón proposed that civilian trials be held for soldiers accused of some serious crimes such as rape, but that military authorities would continue to have jurisdiction over arbitrary killings and beatings. Under this plan the military would remain the initial investigator of all accusations and would determine which cases are handed over to prosecutors. Not surprisingly, human rights activists are disappointed by the limited nature of the reforms. Tellingly, the military fully supports them.[12]

Perhaps it is understandable that so many people believe that the Mexican government should take a more comprehensive approach to the problem of violent crime (committed by state and nonstate actors). Some Mexicans contend that programs aimed at repairing Mexico's social fabric, which has been torn apart, would be more effective than a military approach in reducing violence. Others have demanded more internal audits of the security forces and increased civilian oversight, improved collection of data on these forces, and other steps to hold the police and armed forces accountable.[13] However, years ago, in a quid pro quo deal struck in 1946, Mexican officers agreed to stay out of politics as long as the security forces were placed beyond scrutiny. As a result, the Mexican military has been unique in its willingness to let civilians rule. Admittedly, this is a less than perfect arrangement, but Mexico is one of the few countries in Latin America that hasn't had a coup in nearly a century. And this is one record that few Mexicans want broken.[14]

Case Study: Peru

In the 1980s a horrendous civil war was heating up just as Peru was making an attempt at democratization. Just as civilians were resuming power, a leftist insurgency movement, Sendero Luminoso (Shining Path), began its attacks.[15] Some time earlier, in the impoverished region of Ayacucho, an obscure philosophy professor, Abimael Guzmán Reynoso, had begun to command a following. A personality cult developed around Guzmán; "President Gonzalo," as he was called, considered himself to be the "Fourth Sword of Marxism" (after Marx, Lenin, and Mao). To his followers, this philosopher king was incredibly charismatic. His first supporters were university students and recent graduates—young people from the middle and upper-middle classes seeking social mobility and frustrated by the country's prolonged economic crisis. What became a fanatical GUERRILLA movement was in many ways more a religion than a political entity; Guzmán's followers were true believers, remarkably devoted to the cause.[16]

Although the Shining Path's IDEOLOGY drew from Marxist philosophy, this was unlike other Latin American revolutions in that Guzmán disdained the Cuban model and rejected Soviet assistance. Rather, Guzmán studied in China and claimed his movement to be orthodox Maoist.[17] Like Mao, Guzmán sought to mobilize the peasantry for a rural revolution. However, the comparison pretty much ends there.[18] According to Guzmán, Peru's social order had to be destroyed to make way for a new one, and this required killing 10 percent of the civilian population. The guerrillas fought a vicious war in the countryside and the cities, killing not only soldiers and government officials, but also DEVELOPMENT workers and popular community leaders whom the Shining Path considered sellouts. The more violence the better, argued the rebels; it was only after purification through bloodshed that Peru would become a Maoist utopia. In this effort, these true believers did their best; it is estimated that in twenty years of terror the government forces (including militias) and the guerrillas killed almost 70,000 Peruvians and that the Shining Path was responsible for about 54 percent of the fatalities.[19]

But the military did its part to add to the death toll as well. The governments of Fernando Belaúnde (1980–1985) and Alan García (1985–1990) adopted similar responses to the insurgency. They declared states of emergency, suspended constitutional guarantees, and to varying degrees turned the war over to the military. Thousands more civilians were killed in the crossfire between Shining Path and the security forces. In its zeal, the military committed gross human rights violations against anyone suspected of being a member of the Shining Path. President García made a few feeble attempts at controlling the military, but without much success. In part this was because both Belaúnde and García alternated between two approaches to the insurgency. They never could decide whether to fight an Argentine-style dirty war, or to pursue a developmentalist solution, offering massive social assistance and promoting economic development to root out the fundamental causes of the insurgency and win over the population.[20]

On the other hand, President Alberto Fujimori (1990–2000) was very clear on this point. This president favored a no-holds-barred, draconian approach. After his self-coup of 1992, Fujimori effectively became a dictator in a civil-military regime. One of the first things he did was to expand the military's legal prerogatives to match its actual prerogatives. In return for its loyalty, Fujimori gave the military absolute control over the counterinsurgency program. As a result, in 1992 Peru was identified as having the highest rate of disappearances of any country in the world.[21]

It was this free rein that Fujimori credited with his victory over TERRORISM. In September 1992 not only was Guzmán captured in a hideout above a Lima dance studio, but so were the master computer files for the entire organization. This amounted to a bonanza; police rounded up more than a thousand suspects within a few weeks. Yet even more crucial, the government succeeded in totally destroying Guzmán's mystique. Placed in a cage and dressed in a striped prison uniform, "President Gonzalo" was revealed on television as a meek, paunchy, middle-aged man with thick glasses.[22] Because so much of the Shining Path's power was based in the personality cult centered on Guzmán, this dramatic change in persona proved devastating to the movement—at least for a while.

A 2003 Peruvian TRUTH COMMISSION report found that there were more than 70,000 victims of the war between 1980 and 2000. According to the report, the Shining Path was responsible for the majority of deaths and disappearances, but 37 percent of these crimes were perpetrated by state security forces and paramilitaries.[23] Although the commission called for trials of the members of the armed forces accused of atrocities, as of 2010 only a few officers have been held accountable for their actions during the war (although former president Fujimori was found guilty in 2009 and sentenced to twenty-five years in prison for ordering death squad killings and kidnappings).[24] Beyond also having blood on their hands, another reason Fujimori deferred to the armed forces was because even mild criticism of the military was taboo—out of fear that it might provoke a coup. Since the return to democracy, Peru's presidents have been careful not to be perceived as encroaching on military autonomy. Although civilian authorities have made some progress in managing the size of military budgets and played a greater role in directing security policy, it would be difficult to argue that they have strongly asserted civilian control over the military. For example, a 2005 law disallowed civilian courts from holding hearings on military matters, thus making it harder to prosecute the military for human rights violations.[25] In violation of its obligations under international law, the García government issued more decrees in 2010 that in effect provided blanket amnesties for most abuses in recent history—conveniently including those committed during his first presidency (since, according to declassified US government documents, during his first term [1985–1990] García ordered the assassinations of suspected leftists).[26]

Meanwhile, the Shining Path is back. It has reorganized and split into two factions operating in different parts of Peru. Both groups are believed to have departed from the Maoist ideology of the original Shining Path. They reportedly have less revolutionary zeal than their forebearers and appear to have reinvented themselves as part insurgents and part illicit drug entrepreneurs. The original group was also involved with coca back in the day, but today it is a major focus. Otherwise, relatively little is known about members of the new Shining Path.[27] This new group is well disciplined and well armed, and it knows the terrain of the rural highlands. The insurgency has gradually become more aggressive in recent years; it is estimated that it carried out more than a hundred attacks in 2009 (the most in a decade), killing at least three police officers and twenty-six civilians.[28] Continuing the tradition of granting the military the autonomy to fight insurgents as it sees fit, the García government has intensified counterinsurgency efforts, authorizing emergency powers, suspending civil liberties, and granting the armed forces additional authority in the parts of the country where the guerrillas operate. Perhaps the estimated 350 guerrillas who compose this force are more of a threat to the war on drugs than a terrorist threat. However, Peruvians must experience a collective shudder whenever they hear talk of a return to war.[29]

Case Study: Nigeria

For almost five decades Nigeria has suffered under several cycles of civilian and military rule. Since the country's independence in 1960, two government leaders have been assassinated and there have been six successful coups, with many more failed ones. The military has spent more time in power than have civilians, and when civilians have ruled, it has mostly been at the discretion of the armed forces.[30] The 2007 presidential election was crucial, because if the incumbent were barred from running again, there would have to be a transfer of power. In Nigeria no civilian leader had ever left office voluntarily. Both previous experiments with civilian government were overthrown by the military before it ever came to that.

Without a doubt, the armed forces have been the dominant political actor in Nigeria since they first took power in 1966. Lacking any sense of professionalism, the military does not serve civilian authority; rather it considers itself to be above all other institutions. Instead of being apolitical, the Nigerian military has morphed into an armed political party.[31] Even if it is "above" all other institutions, it is hardly isolated from the country's myriad social and economic divisions. Rather, the military itself has a long history of internal disputes and is factionalized, with cliques taking power to promote the interests of one particular ethnic or regional group against another.

For years the military has been divided into a series of personal loyalty pyramids led by corrupt senior "military godfathers." These "militicians" have found that the surest route to controlling the country's vast oil wealth is through control of political office.[32] Much of this fortune is concentrated in Nigeria's southeast. When the Ibo, the largest ethnic group indigenous to the region, declared their intent to secede and create their own independent country—Biafra—Nigeria descended into a civil war that raged from 1967 to 1970. Despite the overwhelming force of the Nigerian military, it was frustrated in its efforts to put down the insurrection. It reacted with stunning brutality, quarantining the southeast to starve out the rebels. More than 1 million Ibo died before it was all over—most of them civilians, many of them women and children. Although in the end the military government prevailed, Nigeria had come perilously close to breaking up. The Biafran War was used to rationalize giving the military even more power, and it grew dramatically in size and strength starting in the 1970s.

Other than a short, highly dysfunctional experiment with civilian rule from 1979 to 1983, military dictators continued to rule the country in a game of musical chairs. The middle to late 1990s were marked by the most predatory rule the country had ever seen, under General Sani Abacha. Yet even by 1999, when the military appeared finally ready to allow civilians another try, it was not entirely ready to return to the barracks. It began looking for ways to impose control without resorting to a coup. During the entirety of Nigeria's latest DEMOCRATIC TRANSITION, retired generals have played a strong hand in deciding who would take the reins of power. Some analysts contend that these political godfathers were determined that Nigeria's next president be a former military officer and that they handpicked Olusegun Obasanjo for the job.[33] During his two terms Obasanjo worked hard to emphasize his role as a civilian president. However, since he was part of the military, no one knew better than Obasanjo how entrenched it was; the military had helped him return to power for his second term, and he knew he couldn't push too hard. Obasanjo made it through his two terms unscathed, but many feared that the vacuum created by the sudden departure of his successor, Umaru Yar'Adua, for medical attention in 2009–2010, might trigger a coup. Goodluck Jonathan managed eventually to be installed as (and elected) president, but he cannot be sure that the military is united behind him; there is concern that a crisis could be sparked by the tensions surrounding the April 2011 elections.[34]

A long-standing crisis for which all three presidents have needed the military's backing is the conflict in the Niger Delta. Located in southeastern Nigeria, the Delta region comprises 70,000 square kilometers of mostly marsh and creeks. Its inhabitants contend that this environment has been ruined by the oil industry and that this has cost them their health and their livelihoods; they have for too long been mistreated as their oil wealth is taken from their states to bankroll the rest of the country. Nigerian writer Ken Saro-Wiwa was martyred in the late 1990s for making peaceful demands on behalf of one group indigenous to the Delta, the Ogoni. This multidimensional war that has run intermittently since has cost an estimated $1 billion a month in lost revenues and slowed Nigeria's oil production by as much as 30 percent.[35] As a result, Angola has surpassed Nigeria as Africa's number one oil exporter.

Given the country's dependence on oil exports, this conflict poses a mortal threat to Nigeria's economy. President Obasanjo sought a military solution against the various guerrilla armies, militias, and gangsters that were carrying out kidnappings, pipeline bombings, and piracy. However, the military found itself bogged down in the Delta; as it resorted to scorched-earth tactics, residents were caught in the crossfire, with thousands killed and injured. One group of insurgents, the Movement for the Emancipation of the Niger Delta (MEND), has served as an umbrella, uniting various groups against the government (some of which were originally created by local politicians to serve as private armies and to rig elections). MEND is not the first armed insurgency to challenge the government in this part of the country. Yet it has proven itself more sophisticated, better armed, and more capable of better-coordinated attacks than previous groups. The number of raids on the oil industry spiked in 2007 and 2008 as MEND claimed that it was fighting for "total control" of the region's oil.[36]

After the failure of a major military offensive in May 2009, President Yar'Adua broke with his mentor, Obasanjo, and pursued a radically different approach in this war. Yar'Adua conceded that many of the militants' demands were justified and offered them a cease-fire and AMNESTY. He promised to pay fighters who were willing to lay down their weapons ($13 a day) and rehabilitate them. He also pledged to spend $1.3 billion to promote economic development by building roads, schools, and hospitals. It is estimated that approximately 10,000 fighters (including many senior commanders) took Yar'Adua up on the deal, and oil production began to rise again as infrastructure was repaired.[37] However, the president's sudden death meant months of government paralysis. The amnesty deal was left incomplete, and many of those who accepted it are losing patience as they wait for the government to make good on its part of the deal. At least one faction of MEND has broken the cease-fire and resumed its war on the oil industry. Analysts believe that this group was behind an unprecedented attack directed at President Jonathan in the capital, Abuja, in October 2010—far from the usual battlefield. Jonathan responded by pledging to ramp up the amnesty program and promised to make peace in the Delta his top priority. Because he is from the Niger Delta, some analysts believe that he could be more successful in brokering an end to the conflict than his predecessors. Jonathan may have the knowledge of the area and the political will to build on the truce, but the question is, will he have the time?

Case Study: Zimbabwe

Chimurenga is a Shona word that has great salience for all Zimbabweans. It has a number of meanings, but it generally refers to revolution, war, struggle, and resistance. In the First Chimurenga War, in the 1890s, the Shona and Ndebele fought against the loss of their land to white settlers. The result was the Second Chimurenga War and its focal point for Africans also was land—in this case reclamation of what was theirs. This second war is what most people consider to be Zimbabwe's war for liberation, and it was revolutionary in its aims, although not necessarily in its outcome.

Two nationalist movements led the liberation war, the Zimbabwe African People's Union (ZAPU) and the Zimbabwe African National Union (ZANU), an off-shoot of ZAPU formed in opposition to it. In 1963 the armed wing of ZANU, the Zimbabwe African National Liberation Army (ZANLA), sent its first group of soldiers to China for guerrilla training. China continued to support ZANU throughout the liberation war, and the Soviet Union provided assistance to ZAPU's armed forces, the Zimbabwe People's Revolutionary Army (ZIPRA). Meanwhile, the West for years largely stood behind the white governments—in effect leaving the Africans little choice but to turn to the communists. This was perfect for white Rhodesians, who joined white South Africans in portraying themselves as the last bulwarks against black communism. Consequently, with the involvement of external actors, Zimbabwe's struggle became for many outsiders a COLD-WAR PROXY WAR.

Justified as a necessary response to the "communist threat," the white government put the country under a state of emergency that would last fifteen years. ZAPU and ZANU were banned and their leaders, including Joshua Nkomo of ZAPU, as well as ZANU's Robert Mugabe and others, were held in detention for nearly a decade. Realizing that the conflict would be protracted, black nationalists knew that they would need a strong base of support and set about mobilizing the MASSES for it. It was not difficult to raise peasant consciousness—the loss of their land was an issue of great importance for most people. However, as the years dragged on, civilians became increasingly caught in the crossfire. As communities began to tire of the drain of war, conflicts between the guerrillas and their hosts became more common.

All of this was a problem for both ZIPRA and ZANLA, which most analysts today consider more alike than different. While the two groups had their disagreements, both armies were led by nationalists who appealed to Africans as Zimbabweans rather than as Shona- or Ndebele-speakers. Neither liberation army was ethnically homogeneous, but because they tended to recruit from their different areas of operation, they became identified in that way—ZANU as primarily Shona, ZAPU as Ndebele.[38] Despite the rivalry between them, in 1976 the two parties joined forces in an uneasy alliance known as the Patriotic Front (ZANU-PF).[39] With this and other factors working in their favor, the guerrillas escalated their assault. By 1979 the white government was so weakened that it was forced to negotiate a peace. The Patriotic Front was ready for an end to the carnage as well; although approximately 1,000 whites died defending Rhodesia, it is estimated that some 30,000–80,000 people—mostly black civilians—died in the war for liberation.[40]

However, not long after independence Zimbabwe was back at war; this time the struggle was between the victors. For years there had been tensions between ZANU-PF and ZAPU, but relations became hostile after the 1980 elections, in which ZANU-PF won control of the government. Although each blamed the other for provoking the violence, the four-year civil war that followed clearly had an ethnic dimension. The Fifth Brigade, an entirely ZANU and Shona-speaking elite military unit, was set loose to find dissidents in Matabeleland, a heavily pro-ZAPU region. The countryside was ravaged as the military used scorched-earth tactics. By the time a unity accord was brokered in 1987, between 8,000 and 30,000 more people had been killed, most of them Ndebele civilians.[41] In 1980, Robert Mugabe, a guerrilla fighter and ZANU leader, was elected president in Zimbabwe's first democratic elections.

Since the late 1990s, Zimbabweans have again been braced for conflict. Faced with the strong democratic challenge posed by the Movement for Democratic Change (MDC), the government has resorted to a variety of tactics. The government's Operation Murambatsvina (Operation "Drive Out Filth") bulldozed the homes and businesses of more than 700,000 people in Harare and other cities. Although the government says it was cracking down on illegal activities and promoting public order, others contend that this mass eviction was ZANU-PF's effort to stave off a possible uprising by dispersing the political opposition, mostly the urban poor.[42] Activists have been attacked, kidnapped, tortured, and murdered. The government's supporters have roamed the countryside intimidating anyone even thinking of supporting the MDC.[43]

What has the military had to say about all of this? The Zimbabwe National Army was formed in 1980 by integrating the three rival armies (ZANLA, ZIPRA, and the Rhodesian security forces). Although in many ways it remains a revolutionary army, Zimbabwe's military has until recently been considered relatively professional. However, in the past few years as the government has become increasingly desperate to hold on to power, it has become militarized. Members of the military hold powerful positions not only in ZANU-PF, but also in the cabinet, parliament, and state agencies. After soldiers rioted in late 2008 over low pay and high inflation, the Mugabe government decided to secure the army's loyalty by giving it the right to plunder. The cash cow in question now is the Marange diamond fields in eastern Zimbabwe, discovered in 2006. Containing the most extensive deposits in Africa, characterized by one expert as a freak of nature, the Marange fields contain one of the highest concentrations of diamonds in the world. With the blessing of the ruling party, the military has moved in, clearing the area by attacking illegal miners, and killing hundreds of them.[44] Despite attempts through the Kimberley Process and other mechanisms to characterize this loot as "blood diamonds" (and prohibit its sale), the Zimbabwean government fought hard and won the right to export millions of carats of these gems on the world market—at an estimated value of $1 billion to $1.7 billion a year.[45]

Though the military seems sated for now, no one is entirely sure what it will do in the future. Since rumors of a coup plot in 2001, Mugabe has consistently favored officers with the highest-ranking posts within the party. The military is now better placed to play the role of kingmaker, and it appears that Mugabe has maintained the loyalty of its commanders. However, there must be growing concern among these commanders about the post-Mugabe future. Not only are a number of these soldiers vying to lead ZANU-PF after Mugabe is gone, but they are also seeking an amnesty deal from the (understandably reluctant) MDC, to protect them from prosecution for political crimes. These are times of great uncertainty, and it appears that the troops are drawing up a contingency plan—should the party fall out of power.

Case Study: Iran

Iran's history of coups, revolution, and violence runs deep. The country's periods of major strife and unrest were each propelled by similar issues: opposition to a corrupt, unjust king, and resentment against the intrusion of foreign powers. Legacies of these struggles linger today. The debate over Iran's revolutionary legacy and the meaning of its status as a THEOCRACY in the modern world, however, is far from an elite-dominated CLEAVAGE. It is a debate central to most public disputes in Iranian society today.

The Iranian military has always been a patron to the powerful. In 1925, after the fall of the Qajar Dynasty, Reza Khan took the historical title for Iranian kings—"Shah"—adopting the name Reza Shah Pahlavi. With Turkey's Mustafa Kemal Atatürk as his model, the new monarch promoted secularization and limited clerical powers. Pahlavi alienated several groups—especially the religious clergy—in stripping the clerics of land and control of schools, ending polygamy for women, and giving women the right to vote, work, and have abortions. He led from 1925 to 1941, ignoring constitutional limits and using the military to suppress any unrest that threatened to challenge his rule. His son, Mohammad Reza Pahlavi (Shah from 1941 to 1979), continued the reign of absolute power. In the early 1950s there were attempts to challenge the Shah, but with assistance from the United States and Britain he regained full power in a coup d'état against the extremely popular prime minister, Mohammad Mossadeq.

During his tyrannical rule, Mohammad Reza Pahlavi led Iran into an era of GROWTH, with Iran's economy becoming one of the largest in the Middle East by the mid-1970s. But policies that benefited the rich while failing to incorporate unions, intellectuals, and religious leaders led to dashed expectations and increasing perceptions of RELATIVE DEPRIVATION. In particular, there was a REVOLUTION OF RISING EXPECTATIONS with the higher prices for oil in the 1970s, and then an ASPIRATION GAP—as only the Shah and his cronies saw the proceeds. Frustration and aggression simmered and began to hit a breaking point with widespread inflation. Facing increasing calls for reform that would incorporate larger segments of the Iranian population, the Shah buckled down: in 1975 he formed the Resurgence Party (Hizb-i Rastakhiz) from his military connections. Citizens were given the choice to join the party or depart the country. In an attempt to rein in the clerics, the Shah then declared that he was both political leader of the state and spiritual guide of the community, complete with an announcement of the coming of a new civilization that would surpass Sweden in terms of overall human development by the year 2000.[46] The Shah replaced the Muslim calendar with a new royalist calendar, disregarded SHARIA law by raising the minimum age for marriage, and ordered universities not to register women who insisted on wearing the Islamic chador. Each of these moves enraged religious leaders and increased their cries against the moral laxity of the country.

Further, the Shah provoked Sayyed Ruhollah Musavi Khomeini—a cleric whose given name means "Inspired of God"—and his followers when the government published an article ridiculing the cleric in January 1978. Religious demonstrations in the holy city of Qum followed, and the government's violent response left many demonstrators dead, launching a cycle of demonstrations every forty days, concurrent with the ritual in Shia Islam for a religious ceremony to take place for forty days after a death.[47] The continuation of demonstrations, a major movie-theater fire exacerbated by a slow state response, and Khomeini's inflammatory speech commemorating the end of the holy month of Ramadan coincided to lead the country toward revolution. In November 1978 the Shah—who at this time was very ill—placed Iran under military rule. His demise was hastened by his appeal for assistance from the West, and the quick collapse of his own military. Because the system was corrupt to the core, it fell apart easily. What followed was nearly a spontaneous revolution that included many diverse groups from Iranian society. Women wore the veil (declared illegal in 1936) to protest against the Shah and the debauchery of the

West. It was an unusual revolution in several ways, being urban in origin, involving relatively little bloodshed, and resulting in the creation of a rightist theocracy that was retrogressive in nature.

One of the biggest surprises of 1979 was the departure of the Pahlavi military after the Shah left for the United States in January. Islamic revolutionaries provided security when airports reopened to allow the exiled Khomeini to return from Paris. Khomeini capitalized on popular discontent—especially among the youth—and successfully urged the military to wholly desert the monarch. The Ayatollah purged the military of monarchists loyal to the Shah by dismissing 12,000 personnel, most of whom were officers, in an attempt to "Islamicize" the military.[48] He then created the Pasdaran, or Revolutionary Guard, and later the Basij, a paramilitary resistance force that provided volunteers for the "human wave" attacks during the war with Iraq. Members of the Basij (also known as the "Mobilization of the Oppressed") remain the regime's chief enforcers, and are known for their brutality. The Pasdaran was created in 1979 to protect the Islamic character of the system. As a capstone to the revolution, Khomeini activated traditional claims, inspired by seventh-century political philosophy, that gave religious leaders divine right of protection, and established their supremacy over both political and spiritual matters. It was the Shah's SECULARISM that had most aggravated Khomeini and his followers, and their revolution called for a new role for Islam in the political state—the establishment of a theocracy. The LEGITIMACY of clerical leaders, while increasingly questioned by some segments of Iranian society today, has been a bedrock of the Islamic Revolution.

Iran's sponsorship of international terrorism is a major source of strained relations with many powers. Iranian support for Hezbollah (Party of God), a radical Shiite Muslim group based in Lebanon and known to be responsible for attacks against the United States (notably the attack on the Marine barracks in Beirut in 1983), is a point of great contention. Hezbollah is known to aspire for a theocratic state along the lines of the Shiite theocracy in Iran, and leaders in the organization maintain close contact with the Iranian Supreme Leader, who serves as a spiritual and political mentor of sorts. President Mahmoud Ahmadinejad received a hero's welcome during his first state visit to Lebanon in November 2010, during which he praised Hezbollah as a "model for Lebanon and the rest of the world."[49] Iran also has significant financial and military ties with Hamas (Islamic Resistance Movement). This Sunni Islamist group receives its major funding from Iran, especially since the United States and the European Union cut off funding after Hamas's victory in Palestinian parliamentary elections in 2006.

As president, Ahmadinejad has capitalized on divisive issues, both to craft a new Iranian image abroad and, perhaps more important, to rally a sense of conviction within his own population. A former officer in the Revolutionary Guard and member of the Basij, Ahmadinejad has consistently denied the historical existence of the Jewish Holocaust, and has insisted on his country's right to develop a nuclear program (ostensibly for the provision of energy rather than weapons). Because of the sanctions imposed on Iran for the development of its nuclear program, in addition to the decades of US-led arms embargoes against the country, Iran's military (one of the largest in the Middle East) is relatively low-tech, and it has been forced to rely on smuggling efforts to find spare parts for much of its major equipment.[50] Despite being somewhat out-of-date, the Iranian forces still have a menacing presence in the region.

Because of Iran's theocratic rule, enemies of the regime are defined to be enemies of God. One of the Iranian regime's most famous pronouncements of decided enemies was Khomeini's 1989 FATWA (religious injunction) against Salman Rushdie, author of the seemingly sacrilegious *Satanic Verses*. This decree provided a sum of over $2 million (plus expenses) for efforts to kill Rushdie. Even though Iranian leaders distanced themselves from the decree in 1998, and attempts on Rushdie's life have failed, attacks on his collaborators have had mixed success; a suicide bomber sent to London accidentally blew himself up in a hotel room, the book's Japanese translator was stabbed to death, and attempts on the lives of the publishers were made as well. Other enemies include political dissidents, such as Shapour Bakhtiar, the last prime minister under the Shah, who was murdered in Paris in August 1991. As many as 200 émigrés are believed to have been abducted, from many countries of the world.[51] Violence played an integral role both in the collapse of the Pahlavi Dynasty and in the continuation of the Islamic Republic. As cleavages continue to deepen, and Iran searches for a more active stage in regional and world affairs, the possibilities for political disruption remain.

Case Study: Turkey

The fundamental role of the military and its attempt to maintain a central role in modern Turkish politics may be one of the biggest areas of change in Turkey in recent years. The Republic of Turkey has long been a state sustained by an activist military: since 1960, there have been four significant military interventions in national politics. As discussed in Chapter 11, the primary sources of discord in Turkey, and the main motivation for military intervention in the past, are the public expression of religion and perceived challenges to the official version of Turkish NATION-ALISM, especially those posed by the separatist Kurdistan Workers Party (PKK).

Mustafa Kemal Atatürk, founder of the Turkish Republic and its first president, is viewed as a military hero who put the final nail in the coffin of the theocratic Ottoman Dynasty, which had lasted six centuries. Mustafa Kemal, as he was known before 1923, was a decorated military commander in the Ottoman army, enraged, like most Turks, by the Greek (and other foreign) occupation of Anatolia, or Asia Minor. After winning the Turkish War of Independence against the Greeks in 1922, the secular republic was established. Atatürk, or "Father of the Turks," as he was later known, left a legacy of national pride, republican government, and secularism—a heritage that the Turkish military has adopted as its organizational duty to maintain.

The military has a deep history in Turkish politics, and its influence, autonomy, and power are unique among the world's democracies. The interventionist role of the military is also one of the main stumbling blocks in Turkey's application to join the European Union (EU). It is a sizable force—Turkey possesses the second largest army in the North Atlantic Treaty Organization (NATO). Since 1923, military leaders have wielded significant influence in the political arena. There are, however, some signs that the relatively unchecked influence of the military in Turkish affairs may be waning, both in practice and in popularity. As guardians of the secularist legacy of the state, the armed forces have consistently received the most favorable rankings among public institutions within the Republic of Turkey, though this support has shifted recently, with the percentage of the population who believe the military is having a "very good" impact declining from 57 percent in 2007 to 30 percent in 2010.[52]

Despite recent claims that past coups and military interventions are historical remnants, recent events have again shone light on the penchant of the armed forces to seize political power. When Abdullah Gül, the republic's first president with an Islamist-leaning background, took office in 2007, the army posed a "thinly veiled coup threat" to step in if necessary.[53] Evidence has also recently surfaced that in 2003, shortly after the election of Prime Minister Necmettin Erbakan, a pro-Islamist politician who has riled secular leaders for decades, senior military officers (both serving and former) prepared to launch a so-called Sledgehammer to destabilize the country and justify a military coup in the face of a perceived growing Islamist threat. This elaborate scheme, which army leaders said was only a training exercise, included attacking mosques in Istanbul and provoking Greece to down a Turkish plane over the Aegean Sea. More than forty officers—including seven admirals and four generals—were arrested in February 2010; thirty-one were eventually charged with conspiring to overthrow the government. These moves were significant because they marked the first time that an elected government and system of civilian courts possessed the upper hand vis-à-vis the military.[54] Arrests in 2008, related to the state's so-called Ergenekon undercover case against counterguerrilla organizations with suspected links to the security forces, heightened citizens' sense of illegal activities, including assassination plots against the prime minister, in the name of protecting the secular state.[55]

In addition to responding to internal threats from the perceived rise of radical Islam or Kurdish separatism, the military, not surprisingly, mobilizes for perceived external challenges as well. The greatest of these, as viewed from Ankara, is the threat from Greece. Turkey boasts a 100,000-man Aegean army, first deployed in 1975 to face down offshore Greek units only miles away. Disputes over sea-lanes, air rights, and mostly barren islands have brought the two countries to the brink of war, most recently in 1996. Following improved relations between Greece and Turkey in 1999, a retired admiral recommended disbanding the Aegean force, attracting overwhelmingly negative attention in the domestic media and in Turkish security circles.[56]

Turkey's most dominant instance of state-sponsored violence has been its response to the volatile issue of the Kurdish Workers Party, founded in 1974 as a Marxist-Leninist insurgent group. While some, including Iran, view the PKK as the legitimate representative of an ethnic group, the Turkish government argues that the PKK is a terrorist organization that threatens the existence of modern Turkey (both the EU and the United States have also formally designated the PKK as a terrorist organization). In its struggle with the PKK, Ankara has forcibly moved noncombatants, turned a blind eye to extrajudicial killings and torture, and limited freedom of expression, including cultural and linguistic expression.

The PKK, whose goal is to establish an independent Kurdish state, has stood accused of murdering innocent civilians, terrorizing Turkish cities and tourist sites, and attacking Turkish targets abroad, especially in Western Europe. In execution style, the PKK has murdered entire families (including infant children) and attacked schools in Kurdish regions, burning buildings and executing teachers. Its activists are diverse: armed with Kalashnikov rifles, approximately one-third of PKK fighters observed in a recent camp were women.[57] Its targets have also included more moderate Islamists and other Turks—especially Kurds who do not agree with PKK aims—who refuse to give money to their cause. It may seem ironic that most of the civilians murdered by the PKK were themselves Kurds, whom the PKK accuses of acting in complicity with the Turkish state. This points to a central conundrum faced by Kurds throughout the Middle East: intense rivalries between competing groups have prevented any unity of action.

Similar to the fate of Peru's Shining Path after Abimael Guzmán's capture, the dramatic arrest of Abdullah Öcalan in February 1999 limited—but did not curtail—the activities of the PKK. Öcalan went on the run after the PKK was expelled from Syria in October 1998. He was captured in February 1999 in Nairobi, Kenya, and renounced the armed fight for Kurdish independence six months later. Öcalan remains a formidable force, even from jail. For example, he called off the 2009 cease-fire from his prison cell.[58] Cease-fires between the PKK and Ankara have in fact been on and off since Öcalan's capture in 1999, and violence, which has claimed more than 40,000 lives on both sides, has come in fits and spurts. Most agree that any lasting solution is dependent upon the status of other Kurds in the region, notably Iraqi Kurds.

Historically, violence fared prominently in Turkish life, and more recently, as new interpretations of Turkish IDENTITY contend for inclusion, the use of nonpeaceful means to settle disputes has been common. Debates on both public and private expression in the republic are likely to continue in Turkey, even if the formal institutions of violence seem more tempered today than in years past.

Case Study: China

Similar to many of the countries we have studied, China has had multiple revolutions rather than a single revolutionary moment. Yet strangely enough, especially for their fervently anti-imperial character, both of China's major revolutions incorporated Western ideas, only later adapting "Chinese characteristics." The first revolution took place in 1912, after the last dynasty of China, the Qing, collapsed. Sun Yat-sen, a Christian medical doctor known as the father of modern China, planned the revolution from Tokyo, Honolulu, Vancouver, and London. Yet the revolution, led by the Nationalist Party (KMT), failed to consolidate, due partly to the focus on establishing a limited republic, and partly to Sun's illness and premature death in 1925, after which China descended into regional chaos. Warlords, individuals who had accrued military and political power over small regions of the country during the unrest that accompanied the collapse of the dynastic period, engaged in violent attempts to regain control over their fiefdoms. Out of this, another Nationalist leader, Chiang Kaishek, rose to the fore. Twice the KMT worked together with the younger, inexperienced, and ill-equipped Chinese Communist Party (CCP), and twice the Nationalists betrayed them, to dire consequences. In the second United Front, as their alliances were called, the KMT and the CCP worked together, some would say in a halfhearted manner, to expel the Japanese, who had invaded the north of China. It was during this conflict—in which the Nationalists gained the reputation as a corrupt band of soldiers who would quickly flee from the advancing Japanese—that the CCP gained the support of many of China's ordinary people. This was especially true in the countryside, which was the main recruiting ground for the fledgling CCP. Even though Mao Zedong was hardly a key member at the first party meetings in Shanghai in 1921, by the late 1920s he had begun to emerge as a revolutionary hero and cultural icon who would impact China, and all of Asia, like no other man. Yet victory over the Nationalists in China's civil war (1945–1949) was not enough. In Mao's attempt to "continue the revolution," he launched the country into a state of virtual civil war during his so-called CULTURAL REVOLUTION. Even though the main campaigns of the ten-year movement, designed to promote absolute equality and cleanse China of foreign and Confucian influence, were primarily confined to China's major cities, the period is referred to as "the ten dark years," which no Chinese living on the mainland escaped. This decade of unrest—a "planned revolution" of sorts—was rife with purges, public denunciations, propaganda, and ideological fervor.

In the relative calm of the post-Mao period, with economic reform taking precedence over ideological expediency, societal conflict, suppressed by earlier campaigns and a near-complete lack of choice, has begun to resurface. Societal violence has also resurfaced, in ways and numbers not seen since the last years of the imperial periods. Abduction, robbery, drug smuggling, and sex industries—often involving young girls kidnapped from the countryside—are all on the rise. In a dramatic return to the way social matters were handled during the Cultural Revolution, recent attempts at public shaming of prostitutes in Shenzhen—in which women and their alleged clients are paraded in the street, with loudspeakers bellowing their names and misdeeds—have been criticized for violating the privacy of those accused.[59]

In contemporary politics, the role of China's People's Liberation Army (PLA) in governing is difficult to discern, because the institution is so closely intertwined with the CCP. In fact, the PLA, founded in 1927, follows in a long line of military involvement in politics: military commanders established many Chinese dynasties. It is common to hear that the CCP commands the gun, meaning that the PLA is subordinated to the party. Mao himself argued in 1927 that "all political power grows out of the barrel of a gun," and later that "the party commands the gun, while the gun shall never be or must never be allowed to command the party." Leaders since Mao, though, have attempted to limit party influence over the military, even though Deng Xiaoping, as chair of the Central Military Commission, effectively utilized PLA units to clear Tiananmen Square in 1989. Both Jiang Zemin and Hu Jintao rose to national prominence with weaker ties to the PLA. Yet they successfully courted military clients and were careful to avoid alienating PLA commanders in policy decisions. It is a matter complicated even further by the phenomenon known as "wearing multiple hats"—important political figures holding several posts at the same time. As an example, President Hu Jintao concurrently holds the posts of general secretary, chairman of the Central Military Commission, and president. Yet not every soldier or even military officer is a member of the Chinese Communist Party.

The PLA, in true guerrilla fashion, had won over the "hearts and minds" of the Chinese people during the postimperial struggle, especially in response to the Japanese invasion in the 1930s. As its name suggests, it was the PLA, whose lifeline was the CCP, that broke China's painful cycle of international humiliation at the hands of the imperial powers. Yet to many today, the Chinese military is synonymous with the crackdown on the students in Tiananmen Square, discussed in Chapter 11. For outside observers, it is difficult to understand the profound sense of shock that most Chinese citizens experienced when the army, "their" army, turned so violently against unarmed students in the square in June 1989. Leaders in Beijing had to activate PLA units from north-central China to clear the square, since the original troops, who had trained near Beijing University in the summers, were persuaded by the protesters to avoid firing their weapons.

Espionage is part of the daily business of militaries and governments, but recent Internet hacking has raised the prospects of China becoming a leader in cyberwarfare—part theft of intellectual property and part sophisticated military tactic. Perhaps even more concerning, though, is the role of hundreds of thousands of civilian hackers engaged in the so-called China syndrome[60]—breaking into foreign websites, including those of the White House and the US Department of Labor—especially after major incidents (such as the collision between the US and Chinese jets in 2001). The US Pentagon acknowledges the "steady progress" of the Chinese military in developing online-warfare techniques, in part, perhaps, to make up for an underdeveloped military, relative to US capabilities.[61]

Another type of violence has demanded attention in recent years: attacks against individuals and groups, especially the rash of school attacks spanning three months in 2010 (five attacks in all, killing seventeen people and wounding nearly a hundred). In one of the school attacks, a villager gruesomely hacked to death seven kindergartners, a teacher, and the teacher's elderly mother. In each of the attacks the assailant was a middle-aged man wielding knives, hammers, or other tools and acting alone.[62] One of China's most well-known bloggers, Han Han, has written that some of these attackers may view their assaults as an effective way to take revenge on a society "that has no way out."[63]

Owing to China's vast size and regional distinctions, the PLA at the beginning of the twenty-first century remains both factionalized (along ideological lines) and regionalized. Targeting both outer space and the deep waters, it is attempting to branch out beyond its long-held strength in numbers to become a diversified fighting force. China continues to modernize its revolution in all major areas of life—social, economic, military, and political alike.

Case Study: Indonesia

Since the late 1990s, Indonesia has faced considerable turmoil, from a major financial crisis to the loss of territory, bloody ethnic and religious conflict, as well as devastating natural disasters. Violence, in its many forms, has seeped into many of these challenges. Indonesia has long struggled with a military that takes matters into its own hands, especially during perceived times of crisis. Prior to the 2000s, military involvement was formally included in the bureaucracy at every level of civil government. Indonesian armed forces have traditionally filled in when there was a vacuum of civilian leadership (including building roads and linking regions to electrical grids), only withdrawing formally from politics in 2004, when their reserved seats in parliament were rescinded. The special forces, known as Kopassus, exert a special influence over the civilian government, and have been accused of gross human rights violations, especially in response to activists in East Timor, Aceh, and Papua, where separatist tendencies have ignited. The fragile religious balance in many regions, held together before by the regime's *pancasila* (literally, "five principles") doctrine, began to unravel—to disastrous outcomes. Riots, led by discontented students and angry middle-class Indonesians, broke out as Suharto clamped down on political expression in the mid-1990s, closing media outlets and political party offices, and later called in the military to quell economic riots in 1998. Suharto's first three successors failed to learn many valuable lessons about the instability caused by relying on the military to put down civic unrest; B. J. Habibie, Abdurrahman Wahid, and Megawati Sukarnoputri each made clear, in statements and actions alike, that they put much trust in the military apparatus as a means of preserving the stability of the Indonesian state. President Susilo Bambang Yudhoyono (SBY), a retired general and former security minister who received years of training at US army bases, has the reputation of a man careful to call on the gun. With many crises across the archipelago, he has had many opportunities to restrain the use of force.

Although Muslims in Indonesia are overwhelmingly moderate, Muslim extremism in Indonesia has been on the rise since the late 1990s. Democratic openings and international events have combined to encourage such groups, which were repressed during the Suharto years, to speak out. One extremist Islamist group, Jemaah Islamiah (Islamic Organization), was implicated in the October 2002 attack on a nightclub in a resort area of Bali, which left nearly 200 people dead. This group, known for its desire to establish an Islamic state combining Malaysia, Indonesia, Singapore, and parts of the Philippines, is purported to have links to Al-Qaida, a charge its leaders deny. The Bali attacks killed many foreign tourists and severely curtailed the dominant tourist industry in the area. Jakarta was rocked by twin suicide bombings against luxury hotels frequented by foreigners in July 2009 (only ten days after SBY's reelection), and again an association with Jemaah Islamiah was alleged. The target of the 2009 attacks may have been a weekly gathering of Western businesspeople convened by "Mr. Indonesia," James Castle, who has long promoted Indonesia as a wise investment destination. Even if the attacks, which included the Jakarta Marriott (also the site of a car-bomb attack in 2003), weren't against Mr. Castle's group, the Marriott is "an iconic landmark that represents American ownership," in the words of one terrorism expert.[64] President Yudhoyono has made the fight against terrorism a priority of his administration, though many fear that splinter terrorist groups, in Aceh and other remote regions, are mobilizing for action. One major Jemaah Islamiah figure, logistics chief Riduan Isamuddin (also known as "Hambali") remains in US custody in Guantánamo, Cuba. Events of late, including the discovery of a significant terrorist training camp in Aceh and headline-grabbing bank robberies that are believed to be sources of financing for extremist training, suggest to some that there is a shift in targets of religious extremism in Indonesia. While foreign tourists were once the primary target, the Indonesian state itself, including police and even the president, is increasingly viewed as the enemy.[65]

Separatist violence has also challenged Indonesia in recent years, most visibly surrounding the East Timorese vote for independence. Turnout during the August 1999 poll was outstanding—98.6 percent of those eligible, of whom 78.5 percent rejected INTEGRATION with Indonesia. Prior to the referendum, violence was a tool used by both sides; pro-integrationists were murdered, as were pro-separatists—often with machetes. The Indonesian military had encouraged nationalist organizations and anti-independence sentiment since the 1970s.[66] Pent-up anger burst onto the scene when the vote actually took place. After the referendum, violence became rampant, with government-sponsored militias engaged in "political cleansing."[67] The UNITED NATIONS estimates a total death toll as high as 7,000, with up to 300,000 people displaced during the postelection violence (all of this in a population of 850,000).

Aceh province, on the western tip of Indonesia's largest island, Sumatra, has also faced separatist violence—in which nearly 15,000 people are believed to have died. After the devastating tsunami in 2004, peace talks resumed and an autonomy agreement was crafted. Developments reached a milestone when the first direct elections for provincial leaders in Aceh were held in December 2006, in which a former rebel leader walked away victorious.

Another area ripe with insurgent strife is Western Papua (known until 2007 as West Irian Jaya), on the Indonesian half of the island of Papua New Guinea (this western portion of New Guinea is home to two Indonesian provinces: Papua and Western Papua). This province provides a classic example of the forced incorporation of a culture that has been sustained because of economic interests (the region has the world's largest copper and gold mines). Although the region was incorporated, as was the rest of Indonesia, by the Dutch, many of the indigenous Papuan people, who are distinct from the dominant Javanese throughout Indonesia, believed they would achieve their independence after the Dutch left, especially after the Dutch agreed to grant them self-rule. The Dutch formally transferred control of Papua to the United Nations, and then to Indonesia, with an agreement that indigenous Papuans would be able to decide, within six years, whether or not to remain part of Indonesia.[68] Indonesian military forces occupied the land in 1963, and the referendum on independence has never been permitted to take place. Papuan separatists have maintained their own flag, the Morning Star, as a unifying symbol. Violent disputes surround this symbol, and prominent activists have been imprisoned and beaten for displaying it: Indonesian law states that only the Indonesian flag (known as the Red and White) is permitted to fly over its territory. An autonomy law was promulgated in 2001 that earmarked some relevant government posts for native Papuans and guaranteed that up to 80 percent of the mineral wealth from the region would be returned to it. The murder of a prominent Papuan leader later that year placed the long-term viability of the accord in doubt, and Megawati effectively killed the deal when she issued a unilateral decree dividing Papua into three regions in early 2003.[69] Many years later, the legality of this partition remains disputed, both in Indonesia and beyond. This and other flashpoints across Indonesia are likely to continue to challenge political, military, and civil society leaders for years to come.

Now It's Your Turn

What has been the effect of catastrophic violence in the countries that have experienced it? What do you think it takes to become a revolutionary leader? Why are some leaders more successful than others at rallying people to implement change? Do any of our country case studies seem ripe for revolution? How would you compare the various responses of these governments to revolutionaries or perceived insurgents? Why do you think some people believe that violence is the only solution to their dilemmas? What would it take for you to adopt violent means of expression?

14

Ballots, Not Bullets:
Seeking Democratic Change

Nigerians treat power as a mistress, and something we would not want to share with anybody, not even a friend. —*Kayode Eso, retired Supreme Court justice*[1]

A country without free elections is a country without a voice, without eyes, without arms. —*Octavio Paz, writer*[2]

As you read in Chapter 12, violent conflicts and the military's tendency to assume political power pose a variety of problems for many countries. This certainly has an effect on political performance and the prospects for DEMOCRACY in all of the regions we discuss. Ethnic and religious strife, as well as other divisions, create very real problems for governments—both democratic and nondemocratic. In the most difficult cases, even SOVEREIGNTY, the STATE'S right to exist, is contested. As in the cases of Israel and Somalia, there are often profound differences over who should be part of a political community or what should be its territorial boundaries. In a democracy, citizens agree that the government can make legitimate claims to their obedience. However, if the military or another powerful group of people does not accept these demands as legitimate, this poses serious problems for the viability of the government. Until such claims are resolved, democracy is imperiled, if not impossible.

What Is Democracy?

But before we can talk about how difficult it is to sustain, we should first ask ourselves, what is democracy? What makes a country democratic? Let us first say that there is wide disagreement over what should be emphasized when defining democracy. There is no single archetype for democracy, no single, unique set of institutions that are characteristic of democracy. In this chapter we will limit ourselves to a discussion of political democracy, as opposed to social or economic conceptions of democracy. As you will soon see, within political democracy there are different kinds of constitutional systems, and democracies vary widely in levels of citizen participation, access to power, checks and balances, governmental responsiveness to popular demands, party strength, and political pluralism. Therefore, in defining democracy we need to be as general as possible to allow for the many systems that are differently democratic.[3]

However, for all its variations, certain minimal criteria must be met for a political system to be considered democratic. Although governments satisfy these criteria to different degrees (and none of them perfectly), three conditions are commonly named as essential to any democracy: the existence of competition, participation, and respect for civil liberties. With the identification of these common denominators we can begin to define democracy. Democracy is one type of political system. As opposed to systems of AUTHORITARIANISM, in which decisionmaking power is concentrated in the hands of a few and authority is unchallengeable, democracies are based in the decentralization of authority. In democracies citizens take part in making the decisions of government. Put more simply, democracy is a system of governance in which citizens hold their leaders accountable for their public actions. ACCOUNTABILITY is ensured through open competition for office. Democracy institutionalizes competition for power through elections that are free, fair, and held on a regular basis.[4]

But another important part of competition is inclusiveness, which demands a high level of political participation in the selection of leaders and policies. Where government makes room for people to add their voices, the political process has been

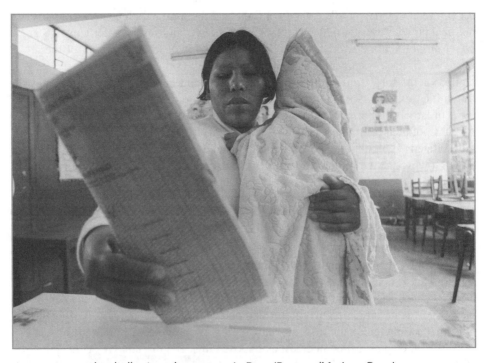

A woman casts her ballot in a shantytown in Peru (Reuters/Mariana Bazo)

opened up to promote effective political participation.[5] In a democracy, citizens should be able to influence public policy. At its core, democratization entails the accommodation of a wide range of opinions. For a country to be considered a democracy, there must be room for a lively and vibrant CIVIL SOCIETY, with active parties, trade unions, and religious and cultural groups that operate independently of the regime. Of course, it is also expected that people will be free to organize and express themselves without worry of harassment or imprisonment. This is necessary to satisfy the democratic requirements of both participation and competition.

Therefore, participation is expressed as the right of all citizens to take part in the democratic process. "Taking part" can mean any number of things, but it must at the very least include the right to political equality. In democracies there should be very few restrictions on the citizen's right to vote or run for office. No one should be excluded because of gender, ethnicity, religion, CLASS, or sexual orientation. Neither should there be a property or literacy requirement for citizens to participate in the process. The greater the number of people who are denied citizenship and whose opportunities are hurt by such denial, the more unlikely states will be able to achieve a CONSOLIDATION of democracy, or make it durable. Democratic governments will take pains to be inclusive, to ensure collective as well as individual rights, to ensure that minority and traditionally oppressed groups have equal representation, and to ensure that the votes of all citizens are weighted equally (one person, one vote).[6]

The term "free" is often used synonymously with the term "democratic." According to the human rights organization Freedom House, the number of countries defined as "free" nearly doubled from 69 in 1989 to 120 in 2000, but fell significantly, to 87, by 2010. This was the fifth consecutive year that the organization reported a decline in this category (the longest downhill run since Freedom House began the report four decades ago). Less than half the world's population lives in countries ranked as free; in terms of regions, the Middle East is the least free, but Latin America and Africa have witnessed declines as well. The only region that has reported some (modest) progress is Asia, particularly due to improvements in the Philippines.[7]

What kinds of improvements? Countries, or to be more precise, political systems, that are termed "free" generally allow for a high degree of political and civil freedoms, but they do so to varying degrees. Some people offer up the sheer number of elections held in the late twentieth century as evidence that a democratic revolution has taken place. They identify elections as the watershed event marking the DEMOCRATIC TRANSITION and treat democracy as an event rather than a process. This is problematic for a variety of reasons. Elections can sometimes result in a setback for democracy, especially if antidemocratic candidates are elected or if divides are deep and elections are perceived as win-or-lose events. This is why democracy must be rooted in a POLITICAL CULTURE that promotes popular participation, one that tolerates differences and accepts the consensus.[8]

Although there have been significant setbacks over the past few years, it is remarkable that between 1990 and 2005, forty-four of forty-eight countries in sub-Saharan Africa held multiparty elections, compared to only four African countries in 1990.[9] In East Asia in the 1980s, only Japan was considered democratic. As of 2009, there were five more states in that region holding multiparty elections: South Korea,

Mongolia, Indonesia, Taiwan, and Timor-Leste.[10] However, elections alone do not make a democracy. Rather, democracies have electoral and nonelectoral dimensions. Be careful not to fall for the FALLACY OF ELECTORALISM, or the tendency to focus on elections while ignoring other political realities. Many countries have gone through the motions of elections, yet power remains in the hands of an oligarchy or the military. Or there are civilian leaders but without broad, unconditional, mass support for democracy or a clear disavowal of authoritarianism.[11] As we will see, Peru, Mexico, Turkey, and Indonesia have made significant progress in some areas of political and civil rights, but there are still other crucial reforms that these countries need to address. How rulers come to power is important, but just as important is the strength of democratic institutions and whether they can hold elected leaders accountable for their actions. In determining the success of a democratic transition, it is more important to ask whether the RULE OF LAW prevails and whether an independent, impartial judiciary guarantees the protection of political and civil rights, rather than simply relying on the "litmus test" of elections. As of 2010, there were 115 ELECTORAL DEMOCRACIES around the world.[12]

Democracies that pass a more comprehensive test are commonly known as LIBERAL DEMOCRACIES. As opposed to the minimal framework of electoral democracies, liberal democracies are based on a deeper institutional structure that offers extensive protections for civil and political rights—individual and group liberties such as freedom of thought and expression, freedom of the press, and the right to form and join assemblies or organizations, including political parties and interest groups. Where civil rights are protected, people feel that they have the freedom to participate in the political process. Democratizing societies will encourage civil society to flourish, and encourage political parties and interest groups to organize without constraint. Again, there are no perfect democracies. No country completely lives up to all the standards listed here. And what can start as a major political transformation can turn out in a variety of ways.

For example, transitions frequently become sidelined by disputes between democrats over the meaning of freedom, the best constitutional and electoral system, or whether to organize as a unitary or federal state. All democracies, even the most established ones, must continuously work to improve their democratic practices. For example, the economic inequality that exists in the United States (and in every democracy to some degree) has the effect of skewing political power. Despite claims of political equality, the affluent are "more equal than others," because they can use their resources to exert disproportionate influence over policy.[13]

Because of problems with democratic practice, often the line between democratic and nondemocratic regimes is unclear. Several countries are hard to place because they may satisfy some requirements of democracy but not others. For example, Turkey has made some major reforms. Its formal structures may be democratic, but in practice its constraints on free political activity complicate the issue. Governments that are characterized as "free" or "democratic" commonly experience isolated violations of civil liberties or occasional electoral malpractice. However, they are considered democratic because they meet certain minimal standards (e.g., it must be possible for the ruling party to be voted out of power through a fair electoral process, with basic freedoms continuing into the future). New democracies differ markedly from one another, with varying strengths and weaknesses. Since a "third wave" of

Figure 14.1 Respect for Political and Civil Rights: How Our Cases Rate

Freedom House is a highly respected non-governmental organization that monitors democratization and human rights worldwide. As part of its work the organization rates every country based on its respect for political rights and civil liberties. Here is how our case countries ranked in 2009:

Mexico: Free
Peru: Free
Nigeria: Partly free
Zimbabwe: Not free
Iran: Not free
Turkey: Partly free
China: Not free
Indonesia: Free

Source: Freedom House, *Freedom in the World 2010.*

democratization began in 1974, more than eighty countries have made significant progress toward democracy. However, contrary to popular belief, there is no end point at which a country can be said to have "attained" democracy. It should be expected that it will take some time for appropriate political systems to be created, and that they will evolve at least partly in response to political failures. For example, Mexico had been ranked as "free" for several years, but in 2010 Freedom House dropped its rating to "partly free," largely because of problems associated with its ongoing drug wars.[14]

Therefore, democratization is something that should be understood as an ongoing, dynamic process instead of a singular achievement. Just as we recognize that some countries may come closer to fitting the democratic ideal than others, we must recognize that a similar continuum exists for their less-than-democratic counterparts. In the end, most governments fall somewhere in between the two poles of democracy and TOTALITARIANISM, an extreme form of authoritarianism. Many governments allow for more freedoms than do rigidly totalitarian regimes, but these freedoms are so few that such governments cannot adequately qualify as democracies. As you will see in the next chapter, there is an unusually large array of names for those systems that fall somewhere in between. For example, many third world governments, including those of Nigeria and Iran, are termed DELEGATIVE DEMOCRACIES: they are neither liberal democracies nor full-blown dictatorships. Delegative democracies are sometimes called democratic because they have an outward appearance similar to that of their more democratic counterparts. However, delegative democracies are led by ELITES whose commitment to democracy is contingent and instrumental, not routinized, internalized, and principled.[15] Delegative democracies are a peculiar form of democracy; through fair elections a majority empowers someone to become the embodiment and interpreter of the nation's interests. No, this doesn't sound very democratic, but as Guillermo O'Donnell contends, delegative democracies are more democratic than they are authoritarian. What is important to remember is that even though some governments are doing a better job of promoting certain aspects of democracy than are others, the success is relative and the work is ongoing.[16]

Background to the Transition

As mentioned earlier, starting in the 1970s and accelerating through the 1990s, a number of what were sometimes characterized as stunning political changes occurred throughout the world, including the third world. The winding down of the COLD WAR coincided with a period of what some called a global democratic revolution, as a "third wave" of prodemocracy movements rose up not only in Europe, but also in sub-Saharan Africa, Asia, Latin America, and to a lesser extent the Middle East (the Middle East and North Africa's third wave mostly came later, with the "Arab Spring" of 2011). Some analysts have characterized the past two and a half decades as a critical historical moment, "the greatest period of democratic ferment in the history of modern civilization."[17] Much of this commotion grew out of an *ABERTURA,* or a political opening, associated with a mix of reforms. Countries undertaking such reforms are often described as experiencing a POLITICAL LIBERALIZATION. Periods of political liberalization are generally associated with a variety of changes such as greater press freedoms, greater freedom of assembly, and the introduction of legal safeguards for individuals. People living in countries experiencing a political liberalization witness the release of most political prisoners, the return of exiles, and perhaps most important, a growing tolerance of dissent.

At the end of 2010, nearly 43 percent of the world's population was living in countries that could claim to be broadly democratic, with 35 percent living in countries characterized as "not free" (more than half of them living in China alone). With a few staggering exceptions, the full-fledged dictatorships so common during the Cold War have virtually disappeared.[18] However, not all governments that can be described as "broadly democratic" are necessarily headed toward democracy. As O'Donnell has noted, not all processes culminate in the same result. For example, at times over the past decade, China and Iran have been said to have liberalized politically, but this does not mean that they are democratizing or are in the process of a democratic transition. China and Iran do not appear to be on their way toward adopting the kind of political system that the West usually considers democratic. And in both countries, even as gains are made, they can be quickly retracted (as happened with Iran's Green Movement in 2009). On the other hand, what was remarkable about the last quarter of the twentieth century was not only the sheer number of countries that made political reforms, but also the number that began a democratic transition of one kind or another. In understanding how so many countries arrived at this point, it is important to recognize that each country's situation is unique; its citizens are responding to a particular set of historical challenges and socioeconomic problems. Consequently, no single set of determinants can satisfactorily explain the origins and evolution of democratic transitions throughout the third world.[19]

As you will recall from Chapter 10, some analysts emphasize the significance of internal factors in understanding change. Their interest is the roles played by domestic actors, whether elites or masses, in the dramatic political events we've been describing. The preceding chapters have demonstrated how people around the world are being mobilized by a variety of pressures. Citizens have demanded the opening of political space in which a variety of new relationships can be crafted. Not all of these groups are mobilized by democratic interests, yet whatever their goals, new forms of social mobilization and patterns of state-society relations are emerging in which relationships of power and accountability are redefined. Yet often it has been

Figure 14.2   Is Democracy Universally Desirable?

Operating under the assumption that "all good things go together," starting in the late 1980s donor countries began pressuring aid recipients to show that they were making political as well as economic reforms. The targets of these reforms frequently criticized such interference with domestic politics, for a variety of reasons. One problem was that developed countries, with their emphasis on political and civil rights over economic and social rights, were arbitrarily assigning certain values as democratic. Advocates of what is called the "Asian values" argument contend that democracy is a Western concept not traditional to most of the world's cultures. Just as cultures that contain a democratic tradition have a better chance of making democracy work, those having little or no experience with democracy face significant disadvantages. These analysts argue that democracy has failed to take root in much of the world because it is not generally accepted there. They contend that it is ethnocentric to assume that democracy is a universal value, because under this definition, democratic values (such as individualism) are unique to the West.[20] Moreover, the West's insistence on respect for democracy, political and civil human rights, and environmental concerns is hypocritical, since its own progress in these areas leaves much to be desired. Such an argument is difficult to dispute. Yet democratic principles are hardly unique to the West, just as the authoritarian impulse is scarcely restricted to the non-Western world.[21]

political elites who have played crucial roles in the political transition. Frustrated over their inability to govern effectively or faced with a crisis of LEGITIMACY, civilian and military leaders have on occasion stood aside to allow for democratic change. Once the transition is under way, elite commitment to democracy (or the lack of such commitment) has often played a large role in its success or failure.

Other analysts emphasize the role played by economic forces in promoting political change. They contend, for example, that the industrialization and economic success of South Korea and Taiwan created in these countries an environment conducive to democratization. There and elsewhere, as the middle class has grown, these citizens have become more politically conscious and vocal in demanding political and civil rights. However, around the world it is more common to find that political change has occurred as people have struggled to cope with devastating economic crises. There are cases from all four regions we study in which the hardship associated with austerity incited popular protests that nearly brought down governments, democratic and nondemocratic. In the immediate post–Cold War period (and since), such demonstrations often persuaded authoritarians to initiate political reform—or at least to affect the appearance of reform.

Although the political liberalization of some countries predated the end of the Cold War, external pressures associated with its demise (such as the withdrawal of superpower support for authoritarians) are recognized as another factor driving reform. Yet even now the governments of many third world countries continue to be highly extroverted; their survival depends on foreign patronage. As discussed in Chapter 7, since the 1970s, in return for aid, international organizations such as the INTERNATIONAL MONETARY FUND (IMF) have directed developing countries to impose economic reforms on their increasingly disgruntled populations. However, after the Cold War ended, donor countries began to insist that third world governments initiate political reforms aimed at promoting "good governance"—increasing the accountability and TRANSPARENCY of government.[22] This is the "all good things go together" argument: proponents of NEOLIBERALISM tend to assume that economic GROWTH and democratization complement each other and are mutually reinforcing (although there is still disagreement about which comes first).[23] However, the developed countries have never been consistent in their demands for political liberalization; the vigor with which such calls were made varied depending on the target of reform (e.g., for strategic and economic reasons, most Middle Eastern countries were largely exempt from donor attention).

A variety of other external factors have also been used to explain the recent political changes experienced in so much of the world. Some analysts credit the dramatic events of the late twentieth century to a zeitgeist (or "spirit of the times"), unique to the immediate post–Cold War era, because at that moment in history democracy appeared to be breaking out all over the world and democratic IDEOLOGY had no serious contenders. This zeitgeist is believed by some to have contributed to a snowballing or demonstration effect as authoritarian governments toppled like dominos.[25] Analysts interested in this facet of change argue that among states closely linked by culture, geography, or some other shared experience, the more successful a transition in any one country in the group, the more likely we are to see similar political change among the other members of that group. This effect has been magnified by the revolution in communications, in particular satellite television, which

Figure 14.3   When Islamists Win Elections

Algeria's experience (and, more recently, that of the Palestinians) has been a lesson for many people seeking change in predominantly Muslim North Africa and the Middle East. Under a variety of pressures for political liberalization, Algeria's authoritarian government allowed democratic elections in 1991. A number of parties organized to participate in these elections, among them the Islamic Salvation Front (FIS), an umbrella party representing many smaller Islamist groups. When the FIS was poised to win a strong majority of seats in a second round of parliamentary elections in early 1992, the Algerian government (with the tacit backing of France and the United States) voided the elections, declared the FIS illegal, and set out on a campaign to portray all Islamist contenders for power as a threat to democracy in Algeria and to the West. Supporters of this policy argued that Islamists were totalitarians in disguise, adopting the rhetoric of democracy only to gain power. What happened in Algeria confirmed views of the West as hypocritically supporting democracy only when in its own interests.

In 2006, after the Palestinian movement Hamas won a surprise landslide victory in parliamentary elections, the United States led a group of Western states that immediately set out to isolate and undermine the new democratically elected government (designated by the United States as a terrorist organization because of its attacks on Israel). Similarly, the West was criticized as slow to support the 2011 Lotus Revolution in Egypt, as it feared the Islamist Muslim Brotherhood would move into the vacuum created by President Mubarak's departure. While such a response may seem reasonable to some, this perceived ambivalence about democracy is problematic—particularly in the Middle East. Whether the United States likes it or not, the Islamist appeal has grown and exists in all Arab countries, and this may be as much due to sympathy for the Islamist program as it is based in resentment of corrupt government and Western hypocrisy.[24]

allows outsiders to watch events literally as they unfold. The intriguing role that this technology plays in political change is only one part of an "international diffusion effect" (what some call the "Twitter effect"), which can change leaders' expectations, affect crowd behavior, and even alter the balance of power almost overnight. Although such effects have mostly been associated with the military coups and the collapse of civilian rule, during the past three decades the information revolution has also worked to support a resurgence of democracy.[26]

After the Transition:
Consolidating and Deepening Democracy

One way to understand the resurgence of democracy is to think of it as occurring in phases. Of the political systems that are democratizing, some are just making the transition from authoritarian rule and beginning to establish democratic regimes, such as Mexico and Nigeria. On the other hand, while they vary in terms of the quality of democracy, South Africa and Ghana, South Korea and Taiwan, and most of Latin America are well into a second phase of democratization, known as CONSOLI-DATION. When is a democratic transition complete? According to analysts Juan Linz and Alfred Stepan, it is complete when there is sufficient agreement about the political procedures to produce an elected government. It is complete when a government comes to power as the direct result of a free and popular vote, and when this government has the authority to generate new policies. Finally, a democratic transition is complete when we can be sure that the executive, legislative, and judicial power generated by the new democracy is not subservient to other bodies such as the military. Most important perhaps, all politically significant groups agree to abide by the procedural rules of the game. In effect, a democracy has progressed from transition to consolidation when no significant political groups are seriously trying to overthrow the democratic regime or secede from the state.[27] These are the democratic rules and procedures that must be established before one can begin to speak of consolidation.

Even when a transition can be described as complete, there are still many tasks that must be accomplished, conditions that must be established, and culture (attitudes and habits) that must be developed before democracy can be considered durable, or consolidated. How do we know when a democracy has been consolidated? Analysts admit that it is easier to recognize consolidation by its absence. Unconsolidated regimes are fragile, unstable, and plagued by signs of disloyalty. Beyond this it is hard to define consolidation, because no single indicator other than general stability serves as its marker. We know that the road to consolidation is a long and complicated one. Perhaps the simplest way of telling if consolidation exists is if democracy has become "the only game in town." The majority of people believe that the system is a good one, and that it is the most appropriate way of governing collective life.[28] When this is the case, the regime enjoys broad and deep levels of popular legitimacy.

When a democracy is consolidated, the issue for government is no longer how to avoid democratic breakdown. You know you have a consolidated democracy when, even in the face of extreme economic or political hardship, the overwhelming majority of people believe that any political change must occur through the democratic system.

All political actors have become accustomed to the idea that political conflict will be resolved according to the established rules, and convinced that violations of these rules will be ineffective and costly. In other words, when it is consolidated, democracy becomes a habit; it is routinized and widely accepted. This takes years of practice—some political scientists argue that two generations of uninterrupted democratic rule must pass, allowing the rules of the game to be refined, tested, and strengthened. In Latin America, for example, although several others are consolidating, only Uruguay and Costa Rica are widely considered to be consolidated democracies.[29]

How do we ensure that democracy lasts that long? Democratic stability is promoted when the rights of the political opposition and minorities are safeguarded. That may sound counterproductive, especially where divisions are deep, but analysts tell us that conflict becomes less intense as it is contained within institutional channels. Most important, over time there is a change in the political culture of elites and masses, as commitment to the democratic framework is no longer simply instrumental but rather a commitment based in principle. As democracies consolidate, we gradually see within them the development of what some analysts call a "civic culture." Although mutual trust between potential opponents, willingness to compromise, and cooperation between political competitors are all identified as key components of civic culture, the particulars of any democratic political culture will vary by country.[30] In general, though, as consolidation proceeds, political elites and the masses gradually internalize democratic values and develop habits of tolerance and moderation. Rights become realities and there is an agreed standard of fairness. Of course, this balanced political culture is only likely to occur where inequalities are relatively low and people can afford not to care too much about politics—and such circumstances do not yet exist in most new democracies. As one analyst put it, "The trick, then, is for democracies to survive long enough—and function well enough—for this process to occur."[31]

In other words, consolidation is another breakthrough of sorts. It is fostered through a combination of institutional, policy, and behavioral changes and is an important achievement for any budding democracy. Yet just because a regime is consolidated does not mean that it is immune to future breakdown. Any number of crises could occur to make a nondemocratic alternative attractive and undo even a consolidated regime. One way of avoiding such breakdown is by recognizing the intimate connection between consolidation and the deepening of democracy. This qualitative shift is sometimes described as a third phase of democratization. Democracies are deepened as they improve, by promoting equality and extending to more citizens the opportunity for participation in political life. By this definition, even older, more established democracies may still become more democratic. All democracies can be improved—that is, made more responsive and representative.[32]

At this stage countries often find themselves in a Catch-22 situation. In what is sometimes called "the democratic dilemma," democracies need to be deepened in order to fully consolidate. However, the deepening of democracy can undermine the prospects of consolidation. Deepening democracy means addressing social and economic inequalities, and this is likely to threaten elite interests and provoke an authoritarian reaction. Consequently, in the short term at least, the most stable democracies are also often the most superficial ones—the ones that forestall necessary changes to minimize the risk of coup. Ironically, because they are defective, "shells of what they could be," these democracies ultimately fail.[33] Incapable or unwilling to deal with the problems of massive inequality, they are vulnerable to "reverse waves" or democratic breakdowns. Such democratic breakdowns should be expected, just as they followed the first and second waves of democratization earlier in the twentieth century. These reverse waves have been traumatic times for human rights and international peace; they gave rise to fascist and communist regimes in the period between World Wars I and II, as well as military dictatorships in the 1960s and 1970s.[34]

Is there any indication that the world is headed in this direction again? By the start of the twenty-first century there were troubling signs that support for democracy in some developing countries was eroding. The expected reverse wave appeared to be hitting Latin America, the region furthest along in its transition. For example, a 2001 survey of eighteen countries conducted by the highly respected polling organization Latinobarómetro found an unprecedented and sharp decline in popular support for democracy throughout much of the region. However, by 2005, satisfaction with democracy was growing generally in the region and by 2010 it was highest in Uruguay, Costa Rica, and Chile. The 2010 poll found Latin Americans to be very optimistic about democracy; 61 percent of those polled agreed that they preferred it to any other form of government. One major finding of the 2010 survey was that the numbers of optimists had grown from three years earlier, and pollsters attributed at least some of this to the relatively good economic performance of the region. In relation to our case studies, 40 percent of Peruvians agreed that their country was making progress, compared to only 25 percent of Mexicans.[35]

Interestingly, according to the latest Latinobarómetro poll, South Americans tended to be more satisfied with the way democracy was working in their countries than were Central Americans, whose economies weren't doing quite as well and who expressed a great deal of anxiety about the rising crime rates in their countries (however, this was a concern of many people; nine out of ten Latin Americans surveyed stated that they feared being the victim of a violent crime). However, popular support for democracy continued to be lowest in Paraguay, where a strong authoritarian streak remains: 33 percent of Paraguayans polled stated that in certain circumstances an authoritarian government might be preferable to a democratic one. Paraguay's numbers on this question were significantly higher than those found anywhere else. Still, as positive as they were about democracy generally, 47 percent of Latin Americans stated a willingness to consider a return to authoritarianism if it would be able to deal with the problems of public insecurity.[36]

While such findings are striking, analysts of the 2010 report insist that the lesson to take away from all of this is that democracy is slowing but steadily consolidating. And Latin America's experience is hardly unique. The same questions posed in Asia and Africa elicited similar responses. In its survey of thirteen East Asian countries, Asian Barometer found that the majority polled (outside of China) supported democracy, but that because so many people had little experience with democratic politics and because neither authoritarianism nor democracy were credited with being particularly effective at improving their lives, to some degree many people embraced both authoritarianism and democracy concurrently. This is likely the case elsewhere as well. While seven out of ten of those surveyed in nineteen African countries in 2009 said that democracy was always preferable to other forms of government, 60 percent agreed that they saw government more as a parent than as an employee, and their own role in relation to government as children rather than bosses.[37]

Such a relationship hardly provides the best foundation for a successful democracy, but leaders, given the pressures weighing on them, might find it useful. Since the end of the Cold War, third world leaders have been faced with donor pressure to democratize (in addition to juggling myriad preexisting and new social, economic, and political crises). These pressures and crises have been managed in a variety of ways. The result, however loosely defined, is a fascinating array of variations on democracy. Catherine Boone identifies the most common manifestations of this crisis management as REFORM, RECONFIGURATION, and DISINTEGRATION. In the next section and continuing into the next chapter we will describe these forms of crisis management as practiced in the third world. However, the particulars vary by country, and whether a political system has reformed, reconfigured, or disintegrated can at least in part be explained by the structural differences among states. Individual decisions must also be factored in, as people worldwide make choices and take actions in response to the unique predicaments they face. In other words, just as the extent of the crisis each country faces is a function of the relative weakness of the regime and the strength of the pressures bearing on it, so too is the outcome.[38]

Reform

To review the fundamentals, for a political system to be considered a democracy it must be based in certain principles such as participation, representation, accountability, and respect for human rights. No government has a perfect record in this regard; however, some countries have made more progress in certain areas than in others. Long-standing, well-established democracies exist in India, Costa Rica, Botswana, Mauritius, and a handful of other non-Western countries. Given the diversity of these countries, it should come as no surprise that no single set of institutions, practices, and values embodies democracy. Similarly, various mixes of these components produce different types of constitutional systems. However, most democracies operate under some variant of the PARLIAMENTARY SYSTEM or the PRESIDENTIAL SYSTEM. Although US citizens are most familiar with the presidential system, which is also found in much of Latin America and scattered throughout Africa and Asia, the largest democracy in the world, India, has a parliamentary system, and parliamentary systems are the norm in Europe.

This is significant, since some analysts argue that the choice of constitutional design and electoral system may impact the quality and stability of democracy. There are pros and cons to each constitutional system, and each system involves some trade-offs. Analysts disagree about which is best for developing countries. One group, led by Juan Linz, argues that although the presidential system has worked well for the United States, its record in low-income countries is more problematic. The presidential system tends to concentrate power in the executive branch, perhaps making the president too strong and (where there is little commitment to democratic values or practices) facilitating the abuse of power. In Peru, Zimbabwe, South Korea, and elsewhere, presidential systems have been associated with executive coups (self-coups) and executive strikes against democracy.

This is one of "the perils of presidentialism," based in the tendency for executives in presidential systems to view themselves as having authority independent of the other branches of government. Even when they have won by the slimmest of margins, presidents are more likely than prime ministers to find opposition in the legislative branch irritating and to consider it an interference with their mission. Not all presidential systems suffer from this problem, but where presidentialism exists, whoever is elected president believes he or she has a mandate, or the right to govern as he or she sees fit. Under such circumstances, the executive is constrained only by the "hard facts of existing power relations" and the constitutionally limited term of office.[39]

It might appear that such an approach does not build a strong basis for the development of democratic institutions. Not only does presidentialism adversely affect the quality of democracy, but it is also commonly viewed as a major factor contributing to democratic breakdowns. Part of the reason for this is lack of capacity: while a strong executive is capable of making rapid decisions, it is often less proficient at coping with crises. For example, Nigerian president Umaru Yar'Adua was so unimpressive and invisible in his first year in office that he was nicknamed "Baba Go-Slow."[40] Still, some presidential regimes (including Nigeria's) have survived extremely difficult challenges. But where there is presidentialism, gridlock (resulting from the mix of a domineering president and a newly assertive legislature) is more likely. And some analysts contend that presidencies tend to be more rigid and are less likely to avail themselves of the creative approaches demanded by most crises.[41]

Fearful that mounting problems will overwhelm a weak or inexperienced government, voters tend to create presidentialist regimes, as they frequently flock to candidates who promise to save the country. Such leaders appear to be strong, courageous, and above partisan interests. This image is very seductive, especially for people who have lived through difficult or uncertain times. Consequently, we should not be shocked by the frequency of presidentialism. It is important to remember that democratic elections are not an end unto themselves. Newly democratizing countries can be expected to continue on in a transition that is not necessarily linear in its progression. There is rarely a simple trajectory from authoritarian to democratic rule; transitions are often longer and more complex. This is in part because the values and beliefs of officials are embedded in a network of inherited power relations and do not change overnight. This helps to explain why elections in newly democratizing countries can be such emotional and high-stakes events. Often the candidates compete for a chance to rule virtually free of all constraints. After the elections, voters are expected to become passive cheerleaders for all of the president's policies.[42]

For these reasons, parliamentary systems are described by Linz as better suited for most countries. According to Linz, parliamentary systems are more stable and more representative than presidential systems. In parliamentary regimes the only democratically legitimate institution is parliament. The executive's authority is completely dependent upon parliamentary confidence. As opposed to presidential systems (in which the executive is usually selected through direct popular elections), in parliamentary systems there is no worry about executives reaching out to appeal to people over the heads of their representatives.[43]

However, Donald Horowitz argues that parliamentary systems can actually end up more polarized and coalitions can end up more unstable than they are in presidential systems, and that this can impede the business of governance. Unlike presidential systems, parliamentary governments risk periodic crises (known as votes of "no confidence") that can result in the ousting of executives and the disruption caused by new elections. On the other hand, Linz argues that what appears to be instability in parliamentary governments can actually be a benefit: since parliamentary systems are more flexible, they are self-correcting. Moreover, Linz contends that fragmentation is not a problem unique to parliamentary systems. Because there are fewer incentives to make coalitions in a presidential system, gridlock is a persistent problem and the legislative and executive branches end up competing against each other rather than working together. Although coalitions and power-sharing are possible under such systems, more often the institutional rivalry associated with the separation of powers in a presidential system can be extremely destabilizing, especially for unconsolidated democracies.[44]

The tendency of presidential systems toward majoritarianism (in which majorities govern and minorities oppose) makes politics a winner-take-all ZERO-SUM GAME. Because it creates a sharp divide between the government and the opposition, majoritarianism aggravates divisiveness in countries where it is already a problem. What one wins, the other loses. However, the zero-sum nature of majoritarian politics is also associated with parliamentary systems such as those of Britain, India, Jamaica, and Sri Lanka. In parliaments dominated by a single majority party, this party controls both the executive and legislative branches. Consequently, the prime minister may end up having more effective power than that of the typical president.

Still, not all parliamentary systems are majoritarian. Some forms of parliamentary government tend to be multiparty and to create governments built on what is called a consensus model. As opposed to the sharp divides of majoritarianism, the consensus model found in Turkey and most of continental Europe attempts to share, disperse, and restrain power in a variety of ways. For example, under the consensus model a parliamentary government can promote the creation of broad coalition cabinets and an executive-legislative balance of power. According to Linz, in such parliamentary systems the executive is more accountable before the legislature. This is important, since in deeply divided societies it is crucial that particular groups not be excluded. Government must work to build consensus and give everyone a stake in the system by encouraging coalitions. Yet in presidential systems gridlock is not always the rule and conciliatory practices are not unknown. Actually, some analysts argue that the mode of election (such as single member versus proportional representation) is more important in fostering conciliation and consensus building than whether the constitutional system is parliamentary or presidential.[45]

An additional factor considered in these debates concerns another aspect of rigidity versus flexibility. The proponents of presidential systems argue that the rigidity of fixed presidential terms is an advantage as opposed to the uncertainty and instability that are characteristic of parliamentary politics. However, there are also disadvantages to the inflexibility of presidential systems. Not only is reelection possible only on a fixed term, but it is also very difficult to impeach or remove a president from power before his or her term is over. As a result, the country may be stuck with a "lame duck" government that has lost public confidence and support. Or, because of fixed terms and limits on reelection, experienced and capable leaders must step down at the end of their terms.

Conversely, advocates of parliamentary systems say that such systems are advantaged by their greater flexibility and adaptability. With a vote of "no confidence," in which the majority of members of parliament vote to "censure" the prime minister, the legislative branch can force new elections to be called at any time to turn out an executive who has lost popular support—without regime crisis. And popular, effective executives can be retained indefinitely, whereas a president may be required to retire just as he or she is becoming an adept leader. Moreover, because in presidential systems the executive is both head of government and head of state, there is no constitutional monarch or ceremonial president who serves as a moderating influence on the executive (as there is in parliamentary systems). Although it is increasingly the case in parliamentary systems as well, presidential systems tend to place a heavy reliance on the personal qualities of a single political leader. Again, Linz argues that this is risky, especially in countries where there is an authoritarian tradition.[46]

In the end, consideration of a country's history and culture is crucial in the selection of a constitutional system, since the issue of "fit" is so important. Lack of synergy between a country and its constitutional system can greatly undermine popular support for democracy. Some countries have switched from one type of constitutional system to another in an effort to get it right: Zimbabwe and Nigeria have replaced parliamentary with presidential systems (Zimbabwe has returned to a parliamentary system, but with the president as head of state and head of government and a prime minister as co–head of government), while many Latin American countries suffering from presidentialist politics have considered adoption of parliamentary forms of government. Still, some analysts argue that the constitutional system matters little, since the differences between the two types of systems are exaggerated—both systems have succumbed to military coup and single-party rule. They add that perhaps other factors, such as political culture or the economy, are more important than institutional choice in promoting durable democracies. The one thing these political scientists seem to agree on is that any system involves some trade-offs.[47]

As you will see in the sections that follow, no matter if it is presidential or parliamentary, democratization must be based on certain bedrock principles: DEMOCRATIC INSTITUTIONALIZATION, political competition, and various forms of horizontal and vertical accountability. Beyond this, there is room for an enormous variety of formal and informal rules and institutions within what we broadly recognize as democracy.[48]

Democratic Institutionalization

Political systems are classified as democratic as long as they have made or are making observable progress toward what is often referred to as democratic institutionalization. In order for democratic systems to be long-lasting and meaningful, democratic institutions must be crafted, nurtured, and developed.[49] When democratic institutions are strong, the processes of government are established and less vulnerable to nondemocratic intrusions (for example, military takeovers). Under such circumstances, citizens and leaders alike can develop reasonable expectations about the rules and procedures of government, which are "above" the whims of individuals or groups. In other words, the rules should be stable and formalized—they should not vary dramatically based on which particular leader is in office. This development of regularized processes is often referred to as institutionalization. Through their various functions, institutions ensure participation, representation, accountability, and respect for human rights.

Democratic institutions are often thought of as the formal, concrete organizations (such as the executive, legislative, and judicial branches of government, as well as political parties and civil society) that are the principal means through which citizens select and monitor democratic government. Yet other democratic institutions are more procedural, such as regularized patterns of interaction that are widely accepted and practiced, like electoral rules, the checks and balances of presidential systems, or the rules governing the transfer of power. Whatever their form, democratic institutions promote (in one way or another) the individual's right to participate in the political life of the community. In their particular capacities, each institution in a democracy serves a critical function.[50]

Political Competition

Political competition is a procedural part of democratic institutionalization. It involves much more than the right to form parties or to take part in elections. For example, in order for parties and candidates to freely compete for political office, they need access to the media, just as citizens need independent sources of information. Individuals and parties seeking power know that positive press and advertising are crucial to any campaign. For example, most analysts of Mexican politics agree that television coverage of the 2006 presidential campaign in Mexico was a deciding element in the vote. Media-savvy parties enlist public relations firms to create commercials full of slick images. They hire US spin-doctors to manipulate sound-bites so as to put their candidate in the best light. However, they also run extremely negative campaigns, including Internet smear campaigns. Mexico's 2006 presidential race was one of the most acrimonious in Mexican history. More than one analyst has suggested that leftist contender Andrés Manuel López Obrador lost his early lead (and ultimately lost the election) because he was effectively defamed as a danger to the middle class.

Beyond access to the media, political competition is based in the principle that political parties must be free to organize, present candidates for office, express ideas, and compete in fair elections. Even in democracies, political parties vary enormously in the way in which they select the candidates they put forward; some (such as Nigeria's ruling People's Democratic Party) are the product of insider wheeling and dealing. To help safeguard the process from undue influence of elites, more democracies are developing rules concerning campaign finance, including ceilings on how much money private individuals and groups can contribute to political parties and candidates. Strict enforcement of limits on donations and other aspects of party financing is a necessity. In Mexico, prior to recent reforms, one candidate reportedly spent twenty times the legal campaign limit. This problem has continued, as parties went beyond the limits in the 2006 election.[51]

Campaign finance reform is just one aspect of a number of procedural elements meant to safeguard democracy. Although governments vary widely in terms of these procedural elements (such as when elections are to be held), in democracies the procedures for holding governments accountable are well established and respected. Regular, free, and fair elections are taken for granted in democracies. While elections are often upheld as an indicator of freedom, and they can be an important part of a democracy, in and of themselves they hardly guarantee that a country is democratic. Remember the electoral fallacy: even nondemocratic states may hold elections.

Whether it is the first election or the fiftieth, the orchestration of free and fair elections is a complicated undertaking. This can be quite difficult in a country without reliable transportation and communication facilities, or with an enormous population

Figure 14.4   Elections in China

While it should be clear that elections are an extremely important component of democracy, the existence of competitive elections alone is not sufficient evidence of the stirrings of a democratic transition. In the People's Republic of China, for example, truly competitive elections at the local level have taken place since the mid-1980s, although these have been confined to villages and to county-level people's congresses. (Three townships have also experimented with elections, although these moves have been "discouraged" by Beijing.) At the village level, citizens now elect members of "villagers committees" every three years. These committees are officially nongovernmental organizations, since villages are not a formal level of government. They manage public affairs and social welfare, help maintain public order, and promote economic development, primarily through job creation. By 2010, elections had taken place in more than 600,000 villages, reaching 75 percent of the Chinese population.[52] International observers, many under the auspices of the Carter Center, have followed the election campaigns and have consistently noted a level of competition and campaigning previously unknown in China. Political parties other than the Chinese Communist Party (CCP) are not allowed, but candidates are able to run as independents, though the nomination of candidates is tightly controlled. Approximately 40 percent of elected candidates do not in fact run under the CCP banner.

Observers have noted concerns about voter privacy: people routinely mark their ballots from their seats, rather than using private booths. As this is common practice, people who would attempt to use the more private polling booths might raise suspicion among their fellow villagers. Most analysts believe that these elections have been implemented less to promote democratic sentiment and more to facilitate control over unruly agents in the countryside. Talk about expanding the polls to higher levels of governance (e.g., townships) have stalled. Giving peasants the opportunity to vote out corrupt Communist Party officials is believed by the government to be enough, for now—particularly if it helps citizens to view the government as more legitimate.

(India has over 714 million voters). The investment of a great deal of time, money, and effort is necessary long before election day to lay the basis for a legitimate result. Free and fair elections require the creation of an independent electoral commission as well as neutral poll workers and multiple international and domestic observers. Too often electoral commissions (even in transitioning democracies) are nominated and funded by the executive branch. Yet the reputation of such a commission must be beyond reproach as it undertakes the tedious and painstaking work that is critical to the honesty of any vote. In Mexico, a disputed election in 1910 led to the first major social revolution of the twentieth century. Some feared that it might come to this again as citizens poured into Mexico City in 2006 to protest the decision of the country's federal electoral commission in the closest election in Mexican history.

Where no good census exists, just the registration of voters is an enormous task. Sometimes, as in Nigeria, taking a census can be a massive logistical undertaking and a political landmine. Fears that a census will lead to the redrawing of the political map (and redistribution of wealth and power) have resulted in mass rioting in more than one country. Consequently, Nigeria went fifteen years without a headcount, from 1991 to 2006.[53]

Throughout the third world, political parties are using social networks to publicize electoral malfeasance, and electoral commissions are developing computer programs to organize electoral rolls and prevent fraud. But even these computer programs must be strictly monitored. To protect against fraud and to demonstrate his dedication to democratizing the process, former Mexican president Ernesto Zedillo adopted reforms to ensure that his country's electoral institute was truly nonpartisan. Billions of dollars were spent to compile a reliable list of eligible voters in Mexico. The adoption of national identity cards for the first time afforded millions of women (and others who were less likely to have a driver's license or other form of official identification) the opportunity to vote.

In preparation for the April 2011 elections, Nigeria's voter lists had to be replaced because they included many fictitious names as well as names of deceased individuals. In an effort to help produce a more valid list, the Nigerian government plans to display voters' names on the Internet and is encouraging citizens to text-message the commission with complaints about irregularities.[54]

Where citizens have had little or no experience participating in free and fair elections, voter education is a necessity. Beyond ensuring that they have access to the information required to make an informed decision, voters must understand the ballot and be able to indicate their choices. Where a large proportion of the population is illiterate, this requires designing a ballot using symbols or photographs of the candidates as well as the written word. Furthermore, there are a number of practices that democracies use to help ensure that there are no irregularities at the polls or with the count. Voting in most of the world is low-tech; ballots are marked by hand or with fingerprints. Voting using fingerprints helps to cut down on fraud, since the ink stains the skin for a few days and helps deter anyone who might wish to vote twice. Steel ballot boxes with padlocks were used to suggest that the elections could not be stolen and were the fashion in the 1980s in most Latin American countries. For symbolic and practical reasons, transparent ballot boxes are favored in countries as different as Iraq, Zimbabwe, Egypt, and Mexico. As Mexico democratized, it invested in new voting booths. Outfitted with curtains, these booths were a break with the past in that they were designed to accommodate only one person at a time and ensure the privacy of the voter. The impact was enormous: for the first time in their lives, Mexicans could be sure they were voting without someone looking over their shoulders. Similarly, Haiti boasted of its first free and fair election in 1990 with the Creole slogan, "As clean as a knife through a potato."[55]

Beyond efforts to guarantee privacy, local and international election observers must be trained and posted in sufficient numbers to help ensure the fairness of the process. A large part of this involves things like making sure that the process is orderly, that there is no intimidation at the polls, and that no one who is registered to vote is turned away. People often wait for hours to vote in mile-long lines, as turnout for elections is much higher in many third world countries than it is in the United States, where it is not unusual for fewer than 50 percent of registered voters to cast their ballots—even in presidential elections. In addition, the electoral commission must ensure that there are enough ballots at the polls, collect and tabulate the vote accurately (done by hand in most countries), and report the results in a timely manner (as delays tend to draw suspicion and raise tensions).

Taken together, these procedures help to ensure that an authentic democratic transition is under way. For countries experiencing their first democratic elections, or FOUNDING ELECTIONS, these are historic events. They often symbolize a departure from authoritarianism and dramatically demonstrate the power of a mobilized citizenry. In many ways the 2000 presidential vote in Mexico, although the conduct of elections had improved greatly since 1997, symbolized such an event. Virtually everyone agrees that this was the freest and fairest vote ever. The result served as an indicator of the authenticity of Mexico's democratic transition: the governing party allowed itself to lose the elections. It was a surprise for many; the victory by challenger Vicente Fox put an end to over seventy years of uninterrupted one-party rule. There was similar jubilation when democratic elections were held in Nigeria in 1999, after fifteen years of military dictatorship. Likewise, the parliamentary elections in Indonesia in 1999 were celebrated as the freest since 1955.

While founding elections mark an important watershed event, most analysts agree that it is the second round of elections that is a more vital step toward consolidation, especially if they result in an orderly transfer of power. Many Nigerians were concerned that their second experience with elections, in 2003, would pose the greatest challenge for their new democracy. To their relief, it went relatively smoothly, compared to their experience a decade earlier, when the presiding dictator, who was unhappy with the result, quickly ended a democratic experiment.

Although there are "dominant-party democracies," such as in Botswana, in which there has never been a transfer of power because one party has always won elections, these countries are also widely regarded as democracies. For as long as the possibility of change through election exists, the system is democratic. Still, for most countries the transfer of power from one party to another is a crucial part of the transition to democracy.

Beyond these procedural elements and general principles, there are a number of other qualities we expect to see in countries making a democratic reform. Some analysts focus on the recruitment of candidates and argue that a democratizing country must allow for the people's representatives to be drawn from an "open" political elite. Candidates for office in democracies are often sensitive to accusations of being part of an "old boys' club" and portray themselves as part of a new "breed" of leaders, capable of making real change. For example, Ahmet Necdet Sezer was the first president in modern Turkish history who was neither an active politician nor a military commander (he was chief justice of the Constitutional Court). Furthest removed from the old boys' club is probably Michelle Bachelet, who in 2006 became the first woman elected president of relatively conservative Chile. Bachelet—a pediatrician, an agnostic single mother with three children by two men (one whom she never married), and the daughter of a general who died in prison under the dictatorship—had never before held elective office.[56] "Outsider" candidates such as Bachelet appeal to voters because they offer the prospect of change; they draw people looking to break the hold of traditional political elites.

Whereas the idea of any elite dominating politics is perhaps antithetical to the democratic ideal, the fact remains that the economically rich have a disproportionate hold on power in both democratic and nondemocratic governments. Yet by "open," it is hoped at least that democratic systems will be more accessible to newcomers, more concerned with the interests of the general public, and more likely to work for the interests of the majority. At the very least, because in democratic systems the political elite can be held accountable to the voters, we can assume that those who are elected will try harder to make good on their promises.

Horizontal Accountability

Horizontal accountability refers to the imperative for various political actors from the different branches of government to work together. The idea is that no branch should overstep its boundaries and seek to dominate the others. In reality, maintaining (or establishing) horizontal accountability is usually about the legislative and judicial branches seeking to limit executive power. This is not quite as true for parliamentary systems, which have a fusion of powers: voters select the legislators (the members of parliament), who then select (or create) the executive (the prime minister). On the other hand, presidential systems are distinguished by a separation of powers in which each branch of government is independent of the others. Voters in presidential systems directly select the executive as well as the legislators, which can result in divided government (voters have a proclivity to split the ballot) and potential gridlock from power-sharing between the executive and legislative branches.

From the executive point of view, any number of obstacles can interfere with a leader's ability to make good on his or her promises. Ironically, the democratic process itself is likely to be identified as one of those obstacles. For example, President Fox, although he appeared to have won a clear mandate in 2000, in reality had extremely limited powers; his policy initiatives became mired in gridlock because his party did not have a majority in the Mexican congress. President Calderón (with much less of a clear victory in 2006) was able to make an unlikely alliance with the Party of Democratic Revolution (PRD) to win governorships away from the Institutional Revolutionary Party (PRI). But almost all of his proposals were diluted or defeated in the legislature, since he was hard-pressed to generate the two-thirds majority necessary for the major political reforms he had in mind (e.g., establishing a system of runoff voting for the presidency, which would have averted the 2006 crisis and given the winner a stronger mandate).[57]

This may all sound very frustrating, but in presidential systems, decentralization produces a separation of powers, allowing for checks and balances on the executive. In Nigeria, Olusegun Obasanjo was constantly at odds with a fractious national assembly. Although his party controlled both houses, the president was known to refer derisively to the young, ambitious lawmakers dominating that body as "children" who were causing him no end of trouble. Deadlock over the budget resulted in policy paralysis; disbursements were put on hold and salaries went unpaid. For their part, the "children," who had campaigned for Obasanjo, soon felt excluded by him. They accused the president of being more authoritarian than democrat, a "my way or the highway" general.

Of course the social and economic crises that the Nigerian and other governments have inherited from their authoritarian predecessors reinforce certain practices and ideas about the proper exercise of political authority. Moreover, dominant political cultures may value decisive leadership over institutional checks and balances. As mentioned earlier, presidentialism is likely to develop where a state of constant crisis has generated a strong sense of urgency. As a parentlike figure, the president (and sometimes the prime minister) tends to become the embodiment of the nation—benevolent guardian and defender of its interests. Because of their stature, presidents may come to see other institutions such as the legislature and courts as nuisances that interfere with the full authority delegated to them.[58]

What we're describing as presidentialism can occur in parliamentary systems as well. For example, Turks voted in a referendum in 2010 for a number of constitutional amendments, including one to allow the parliament more power to appoint judges. Prime Minister Recep Tayyip Erdogan supported the plan as a way to rein in what is seen as a highly politicized judiciary that has consistently overstepped its boundaries, a move that would be helpful for Turkey's accession to the European Union. Critics charge that the changes amount to an effort by the ruling Justice and Development Party (AKP, which controls the legislative and executive branches) to seize control of the judiciary, remove this essential check on government, and secure all power (in effect creating a "civilian dictatorship" with explicit religious undertones).[59] While executives in delegative democracies can often move faster because of the relative lack of horizontal accountability, it is up to the leader to shoulder the burden of a country's tremendous problems—and should the leader fail, it is perceived as entirely his or her fault.

Vertical Accountability

One of the cardinal rules of democracy is "you can't stay in power by doing nothing." No democracy is likely to be consolidated without high levels of support offered by legitimacy, and no democracy will garner high legitimacy rates without some degree of effective governance. As mentioned earlier, one of the two most commonly understood components of good governance is accountability. But there are two kinds of accountability: horizontal and vertical accountability. By vertical accountability, we refer to a government's relationship with its citizens. The more responsive a government is to popular demands, the more satisfied people will be with the way government works and the more they will support it through hard times. The better the government is at promoting the general welfare, the more that people will trust it, believe the system to be a good one, and remain committed to it.[60] Initiatives associated with vertical accountability include capacity building, establishing the rule of law, reconciling group conflict, and maintaining civilian control over the military.

Capacity building. The ability to strategize, prioritize, and carry out state functions to improve people's lives, or capacity building, is a crucial test for most new democracies. One measure of a government's capacity is its ability to deliver public services. Yet although people commonly cite effectiveness as a highly valued attribute of governments, democracies don't necessarily make for the most efficient of administrations. And decisive action is even more difficult for democracies under economic strain. As discussed in Chapters 6 and 7, undemocratic governments have sometimes proven to be quite capable of delivering not only services, but also economic growth. It could be argued that when it comes to capacity building, democracies are disadvantaged in that, by definition in this type of political system, a variety of actors must be consulted in decisionmaking. Consequently, democracy tends to be a messy and slow business. New democracies certainly face many challenges, and one of the first things their leaders must learn is to restrain expectations. New democracies are often expected not only to stabilize economies and promote economic DEVELOPMENT, but also to make good on promises of political freedoms and representativeness. They are to be accountable to their citizens, establish order, and promote the rule of law.[61] Beyond that, there are more mundane expectations of new democracies as well. The problem is that often these governments do not inherit usable bureaucracies and therefore lack the administrative capacity to make progress in providing services, implementing policy, and so on. Elected government should at the very least be capable of performing what are commonly regarded as ESSENTIAL FUNCTIONS: collecting taxes, providing a sense of security throughout the country, and enforcing the law, as well as designing and implementing policies responsive to the majority. Some analysts expand the definition of essential functions to include concern with the population's economic and social well-being. This typically includes demands for the supply of public goods (such as the rehabilitation of communications and transportation systems, or the provision of sanitation and electrification). Unless democracy can provide these things, it is unlikely to be viewed favorably for long. But for economic reasons if nothing else, this is out of reach for many governments.

Newly elected governments not only face economic shortfalls, but also often find it extremely difficult to pick up the pieces after years of mismanagement and abuse. It is extremely difficult to increase governmental capacity when the infrastructure has decayed beyond the point of viability. People become bitter where there are long lines for gasoline (especially in countries that are major exporters of oil), or where the electricity and telephone systems are unreliable. Newly elected democratic governments know that they don't have much time to prove themselves. Where citizens have spent years under wasteful authoritarian rule, many expect to see a DEMOCRACY DIVIDEND, a general improvement in quality of life and standard of living in just a few years' time. Yet turning around an economy often takes longer, and although some populations have demonstrated impressive patience, sooner or later they are likely to become frustrated if the benefits of change don't materialize. Under such pressures to perform, communication with the masses is of the utmost importance, and leaders who lose touch with their constituencies soon find themselves out of work. In much of the world, the appeal of POPULIST authoritarians may grow as more people sense that democracy isn't meeting their expectations.

Analysts suggest that democratic transitions are greatly affected by economic factors in a variety of ways. Certainly other factors come into play, but several consecutive years of negative economic growth lessen the chance of survival for a democratic regime (or a nondemocratic regime, for that matter). Poverty and economic inequality are key obstacles to democratization, and many countries that have experienced economic misery have fallen to what is called "the totalitarian temptation" in the search for alternatives. However, poverty does not guarantee failure. Some low-income countries such as Uruguay have completed their transitions and consolidated their democracies despite hardship. The oldest third world democracy, India, is often characterized as a puzzle in that it retains democratic governance against all odds—poverty, entrenched caste and religious divisions, and other problems. Certainly such hardship makes these democracies more prone to risk, but a few cases show that it is possible for democracies to survive. To a great extent the ability to survive depends on whom the population blames for the economic problems, and the perceived desirability of political alternatives. Even where democratic government appears to be getting off to a slow start, as long as most people believe that democracy is the best political system for them, it can survive even under difficult economic conditions. If, however, people and their leaders believe democracy itself is compounding the problem, or that it is incapable of remedying the situation, democratic breakdown is likely.[62]

One of the first initiatives of any new leader (democratic or not) is to attempt to bond with the masses by blaming the country's problems on the previous administration. It is common for candidates to be elected based on their promises to fight CORRUPTION—the abuse of power for private gain. Corruption is a problem shared by all forms of government in virtually every country in the world, including the oldest democracies. Indonesian president Susilo Bambang Yudhoyono's government tried to demonstrate this commitment by arresting more than eighty former government officials and ministers. Some of these arrests ended in convictions, including for a member of the president's family. However, since the start of his second term, Yudhoyono's credentials as "Mr. Clean" have been questioned. His popularity has plummeted (from a 90 percent approval rating in 2009 to 48 percent in 2010), as he has been accused of stacking the country's anticorruption commission with yes-men and protecting members of his own entourage.[63]

Such accusations are not uncommon. Nigeria's former president Obasanjo was accused of using his anticorruption zeal in a witch hunt to target his political opponents. When Nuhu Ribadu, his respected anticorruption czar, appeared to be on the verge of accusing powerful state governors of unheard-of levels of grand corruption, Ribadu was demoted, received death threats, and fled into exile. This is a shame, since in 2003 Nigeria was identified by Transparency International, an international watchdog group, as the most corrupt country in the world (Somalia took the title in 2010. Nigeria ranked 134th out of 178 countries; the higher the number, the worse the corruption).[64] It is said that Nigeria's national treasury was empty when Obasanjo took office. Switzerland has cooperated in freezing more than $600 million in funds stolen from Nigeria. Yet this is only the tip of the iceberg; it is estimated that the last dictator alone, Sani Abacha, looted the treasury of up to $8 billion.[65]

Yet fighting corruption by promoting accountability and transparency is crucial if democracies are to progress. In old and new democracies alike, pervasive official misconduct can contribute to democratic breakdown. Bribery, extortion, influence peddling, and other scandals can greatly damage political legitimacy and disillusion people, alienating them from the political process. Clearly, the most stable countries of the world are the least corrupt (and vice versa).[66]

How can corruption be reduced? Most experts recommend a broad strategy based around the idea of increasing TRANSPARENCY, which can be understood in a number of interrelated ways. In one crucial sense, it means openness, particularly in terms of spending and budgetary matters. During Mexico's liberalization, the government began declassifying information and publishing the federal budget in full (something that had traditionally been cloaked in secrecy). In Nigeria, the Obasanjo government came to power promising to make the process of awarding government contracts transparent. His successor, Umaru Yar'Adua, promised personal transparency, offering to reveal his personal assets at the beginning and end of his term.[67] Likewise, in countries improving their transparency, it is common for presidential discretionary or "secret" funds to become not so secret, and to be cut or abolished altogether.

Accountability is not only about punishing wrongdoers but also about reducing the incentive to steal. Compared to other Asian countries, Indonesia ranks somewhere in the middle (more corrupt than Singapore, Thailand, and the Philippines but less corrupt than Japan and South Korea). In an effort to confront the problem, President Yudhoyono raised the wages of civil servants, since low pay is believed to encourage graft.[68] Another approach is raising the risks and costs associated with corruption. It means that from top to bottom, from high-ranking officials who treat the state treasury as a private source of wealth, down to police and petty officials who supplement their meager incomes with *una mordida* (a bite) or *bakshish* (a gift), government actors must no longer be allowed to violate the law with impunity, and will be prosecuted if they do. Governments must improve the ability to detect extortion and other abuses so as to better expose, punish, and disgrace those guilty of misconduct. However, the problem in many countries is all-pervasive; too often, graft is understood as the only platform for attaining dreams of wealth and success. Those who are making their way up the ladder find that "fear of the unknown" fuels corruption; they are determined to take their cut before they lose their footing on that ladder.[69] The police are the government actors most likely to demand bribes; daily petty extortions from them and other civil servants hit the poorest the hardest. According to a 2009 Transparency International report, in Cameroon, Liberia, Sierra Leone, and Uganda, more than 50 percent of respondents admitted to paying a bribe in the preceding year. According to Transparency International, corruption exists everywhere, but is most rampant in Africa and the Middle East. This is a real threat to democracy, since corruption is said to impact the psyche of a nation, breaking trust and creating cynicism. If people don't expect much from government, this limits democracy's life expectancy.[70]

Establishing the rule of law. There are important distinctions between rule *of* law and rule *by* law. Rule by law is commonly employed by authoritarian regimes to repress populations—to crack down on "enemies of the state." On the other hand, rule of law is one of the core functions of a high-quality democracy. Though not easy to define, because it comprises several elements (and there is disagreement over what these elements are and how they should be prioritized), at its most basic the rule of law provides the foundation for the enjoyment of political rights and civil liberties. It means that no one is above the law. The government is ruled by law and subject to it. Certainly rule of law can be compromised and there can be gaps or flaws in its operation (in the laws themselves, in the application of the law, in access to the judiciary and a fair process). It is probably best to conceptualize rule of law as existing on a continuum, in that some democracies have made more progress than others in establishing it.[71]

Therefore, there are several different elements that work together in the rule of law. Whether that means making it safe for people to walk around their neighborhoods at night or a policy of zero tolerance for official corruption, strengthening the rule of law is a tremendous challenge for many democratizing regimes. A decade into Mexico's democracy, three in ten citizens say that they've been victims of crime (but only one in ten reports it). Perhaps this is because an estimated 90 percent of crimes in Mexico go unpunished.[72] Although analysts disagree about whether crime rates have actually risen since the transition to democracy in several Latin American countries, they confirm that the fear of crime has definitely increased. In Argentina and Mexico, fear of crime has become a major election issue and thousands have protested the lack of public security.[73] Around the world, public frustration with democratic governments' inability to impose the rule of law has also led to vigilantism. In some places this amounts to community-based policing, necessary where the government has in effect ceded significant powers to local communities. For example, in 2006 Liberia was so terrorized by armed gangs (overwhelming the capacity of the police) that the justice ministry called on the population to form vigilante groups to protect themselves.[74]

Liberia is hardly the only country whose government is unable to guarantee public security. However, the rule of law also means that legal systems in democracies should be able to guarantee predictable and impartial treatment from governmental agents, including the police, the military, and judges. This poses a major challenge for many governments, especially where these public servants have long traditions of acting with impunity. Within Mexico, the culture of corruption within the police force (and the military, which serves as a national police force) is so institutionalized, so ingrained, that many people consider the police to be the worst criminals. In 1997 the army general appointed to head Mexico's war on drugs turned out to be on a drug cartel's payroll. Ten years later it was no different; in 2008, the country's highest-ranking official ever arrested—Mexico's antidrug czar—was found to have been collecting $450,000 a month for providing the cartels with information on the government's war on drugs. In Egypt, under the Mubarak regime, the security forces were given broad powers to arrest people without charge and detain them indefinitely. There and elsewhere, officers see themselves as enforcers for the government, not public servants. They are above the law, rarely punished for abuses.[75] Human rights groups in Nigeria and other transitioning democracies report similar problems, with security forces involved in sexual brutality, disappearances, and extrajudicial killings. One way of promoting public security is for democracies to curb the power of ministries of the interior, the agencies whose role it is to police the police, which have often earned the nickname "Ministry of Fear." People need to be able to trust the police as public servants and they need to have confidence in the administration of justice.

A strong, efficient, and independent judiciary is another decentralizing institution crucial to the success of both parliamentary and presidential systems. Transitioning democracies must improve performance when it comes to ensuring not only personal security, but also that disputes are settled quickly and fairly. Citizens should not have to fear arbitrary arrest or being left to rot in overcrowded prisons while awaiting charge. A powerful judiciary—professional, depoliticized, and largely free from executive or other partisan interference—can be the greatest protector of a democratic constitution and source of democratic legitimacy. It is the ultimate guarantor of the rule of law.[76] Yet analysts recognize the judicial branch to be one of the democratic institutions that take the longest to create, and progress is probably most accurately measured by degree. In China, for example, although there have been some reforms, it is still not uncommon for judges to lack even the cursory legal training that lawyers receive; in 2008 a party veteran with no formal legal training was appointed chief justice of the Supreme Court, and a former Court vice president was sentenced to life imprisonment for taking nearly $575,000 in bribes.[77] The Chinese Communist Party still controls the judiciary, directing verdicts and sentences. Torture is widespread and coerced confessions are routine; trials are frequently closed to the public (particularly in politically sensitive cases).[78] These are just a few of the challenges for democracies seeking to impress citizens with a sense of vertical accountability. According to Freedom House, the most significant declines in freedom between 2005 and 2009 were related to rule of law. Too many judicial systems remain weak, unable to act independently and rule impartially. These glaring failures greatly limit the potential for the institutionalization of democratic gains in many countries worldwide.[79]

Reconciling group conflict. As Robert Dahl notes, at its base the exercise of democracy is the institutionalization of conflict.[80] Unlike autocrats, democratic leaders, because they are accountable to the people, must spend a great deal of their time at least appearing to be responsive to the interests of groups with conflicting interests. States are not independent of ethnicity, class, gender, and other interests, but the legitimacy of democratic governments is partly derived from their ability to appear to be independent of these interests, to modify conflict, and to build consensus. Yet democracy has an inherent paradox: it requires both representativeness and conflict, but not too much of either. Democracy must allow for competition, but only within carefully defined and accepted boundaries. Reconciling group conflict is at the heart of democratic politics, but the ability to do this doesn't happen overnight. New democracies must work to promote understanding and contain conflicts so that CLEAVAGES don't tear their countries apart. As mentioned earlier, democracy is institutionalized competition for power. However, if that competition is too intense, the system can break down entirely. It is therefore crucial that new democracies find mechanisms to mitigate conflict and promote consensus. They must do this in a way that works successfully to pull together all the core principles of democracy: participation, representation, accountability, and respect for human rights.[81]

Cleavages are found in every country in the world. They tend to run along lines of class, ethnicity, religion, region, and party. Ethnicity, because it is wrapped up in issues of IDENTITY, is often seen as the most difficult type of cleavage for a democracy to manage. In MULTINATIONAL STATES, compromise is difficult, and in deeply divided plural societies, ethnicity is often thought to predetermine access to power and resources. What one group wins, another group fears it will lose—and fear of exclusion is not an unreasonable concern, given the experience of many countries. Elections become a desperate struggle between parties, as well as ethnic groups, regions, even religions. The rules matter little, since to lose political power is to lose access to virtually everything that is important. Under these circumstances the potential for polarization is such a real threat that some analysts hold out little hope for democracy where divisions are deep and identity has been politicized.[82]

Democratic governments must therefore attempt to manage or soften this conflict in a variety of ways. As described in more detail in Chapter 12, they can attempt to generate crosscutting cleavages—to find common ground between groups—as well as work to moderate political views and promote tolerance and cooperation. Another way of mediating these pressures is through institutional designs that encourage the decentralization of power. Federal systems of government may be crucial to the survival of democracy where cleavages are deep, since they allow for more autonomy and responsiveness at the local level. They also diminish the winner-take-all character of politics by facilitating greater representation of minorities and other marginalized groups. Conflict may be reduced and interethnic accommodation promoted through other efforts to reconcile historical differences. The protection of minority rights may go a long way toward managing deep divides—for instance, through the recognition of more than one official language, respect for a variety of legal codes, and toleration of parties representing different communities. A number of countries, such as South Africa, have been relatively successful in managing tensions by skillfully crafting democracies that take into account the particular mix of cultures and identities contained within their territory. Some analysts suggest designing coalitions, like Bosnia-Herzegovina's, that allow for a sharing or rotating of power. More commonly such efforts have the goal of ensuring that all people have equal rights to citizenship, and protecting the rights of minorities to retain their own culture, religion, and language. But coalitions are hard to build; South Africans and Bosnians will attest that the divisions in their countries are still very real. Yet ethnic groups that are allowed to share power are much more likely to view a democracy as legitimate.

Unfortunately (and often tragically), in a ploy to win election, some politicians actually encourage "tribalism" and manipulate issues of ethnicity to their own political advantage. It may not be possible to dissipate tribalism by generating crosscutting cleavages (so that the identity and interests of one ethnic or religious group are spread among different classes or regions). In Nigeria, cleavages often coincide, and people are divided by region, ethnicity, and religion.[83] As a result, reconciling group conflict often poses a nearly impossible task for many newly elected governments.

In addition to political cleavages concerning ethnicity and religion, there are also often deep divides over matters concerning women's equality. Although for various reasons some women have also been known to support authoritarians, others have been at the forefront of prodemocracy movements, in part because they expect that democracy's emphasis on human rights will include them and their children. In some cases they have been correct in this belief. As the *abertura* has unfolded, political space has gradually opened to women in several countries. For the first time ever, women were allowed to vote and stand as candidates in Kuwait's 2006 parliamentary elections (although it was not until 2009 that four women won seats).[84]

The lesson here is that simply allowing previously disenfranchised groups the right to participate in elections as candidates and voters is not enough to result in a true *abertura*. Affirmative action to guarantee women's representation in political bodies may be one way of prodding such an opening. Taiwan has an electoral system that reserves 10–25 percent of the seats in legislative bodies for women. India, Peru, and several other countries have adopted quotas as well. Some might argue that quotas are the only way to press toward gender parity in political representation: of the twenty-three countries in which women have attained the critical mass of at least 30 percent of legislative seats, eighteen of them have had quotas. But even when such rules exist (as they do in some form or another in ninety-five countries), they often go unenforced. The proportion of parliamentary seats occupied by women increased on average by 8 percent between 1998 and 2008. The average proportion of women in parliament worldwide is 17 percent. All regions have to varying degrees moved toward equal representation since 1995, but men still outnumber women by more than five to one in legislatures around the world. The United Nations Development Fund for Women (UNIFEM) estimates that at the current rate, it will take two generations before the number of women in parliaments worldwide approaches parity.[85]

Rwanda, Sweden, and South Africa are the countries with the largest proportions of women serving in parliament; in terms of regions, Latin America takes the lead. In 2009, women held 40 percent of the seats in the Argentine legislature, making it (along with Cuba) a world leader. Reforms in the United Arab Emirates (UAE) and Tunisia have added some women to the political ranks, but in much of the Middle East and Oceania, women's representation remains very low (in Saudi Arabia there are no women in parliament). In general, countries without quota laws are electing women, but more slowly and less steadily.[86]

Yet increasing the formal representation of women doesn't guarantee that the distribution of political resources will change. Moreover, although women are often thought to be less corrupt and more connected to the people, this is not necessarily so. It is clear that women politicians (who often see themselves as needing to conform to succeed) are not usually in a good position to challenge the existing system, which is resistant to change.[87] Even in what appear to be bold political reforms, such "progressive" legislation is mostly a formality that has meant very little change in the lives of women. Liberalizing governments have also been known to extend women's economic rights, such as the right to own property, or the right to equal pay for equal work. But these reforms as well have often disappointed because of a government's failure to implement the new laws or to put resources into programs promoting equality. Democratic and nondemocratic governments commonly include a ministry or department specifically established to deal with "women's issues." However, it is rare for such offices to hold much power; in most cases they are marginalized and the women heading them are mere tokens in otherwise overwhelmingly male cabinets. Although it could be argued that women's status has generally improved in most regions, progress has come very slowly. Moreover, there continues to be great unevenness in women's experience of gender equality, both between and within countries, based on regional, class, ethnic, and other divides.

As you can see in Figure 14.6, the United Nations Development Programme (UNDP) has developed a composite measure to examine the opportunities that are made available to women in countries around the world. This index, called the Gender Empowerment Measure (GEM), provides a detailed look at the prospects women face in terms of health and educational well-being, as well as economic and political participation and decisionmaking. An examination of the GEM rankings for more than a hundred countries shows that overall, the world is doing a better job at narrowing inequalities in healthcare and education than it is regarding economic and political participation. Interestingly, not all first world countries are more equal than those in the third world: higher levels of income are not necessarily correlated with expanded opportunities for women. As a 2010 study for the World Economic Forum asserts, no country has eliminated the gender gap. The Nordic countries have had the most success. For the first time in five years the United States broke into the top 20 (ranked 19th out of 134, up from 31st in 2009), largely because of the number of women in leading roles in the Obama administration and improvements in closing the wage gap. The United States is now in league with Canada, Latvia, and Trinidad and Tobago, whereas France (46th), Greece (58th), and Italy (74th) are rated relatively poorly on gender empowerment, behind countries such as Lesotho (8th), the Philippines (9th), and South Africa (12th). Yemen comes in last, with supposedly the largest gender gap in the world.[88]

A look at our CASE STUDIES in Figure 14.6 shows that even China, which has the most favorable GEM ranking, at 38, still has far to go in promoting gender equity. Although the economic participation gap is on its way to closing (74 percent of Chinese

Figure 14.5 Shattering Stereotypes

As difficult as it is to achieve gender parity in the legislative branch, progress in electing female executives is even slower. In 2000 there were a total of nine female heads of state or government worldwide. A decade later there were fourteen. Although the West assumes that it is more advanced in this regard, some of the first female heads of government and heads of state in the modern era have actually come from the "third world":

- Sirimavo Bandaranaike of Sri Lanka is considered to be the "dean" of women's leaders. She was the world's first elected female prime minister, serving in that post from 1960 to 1965, 1970 to 1977, and 1994 to 2000.
- Indira Gandhi was prime minister of India from 1966 to 1977 and 1980 to 1984, when she was assassinated. Pratibha Devisingh Patil is the current president of India, the first woman elected to the office, in 2007.
- Benazir Bhutto became Pakistan's elected prime minister in 1988 at the age of thirty-five. The first woman elected to head a modern Islamic state, Bhutto served as prime minister twice and was removed from power twice on corruption charges. In 2007, two weeks before the elections that were likely to return her to power, she was assassinated while leaving a campaign rally. Her widower, Asif Ali Zardari, was elected president in 2008.
- Megawati Sukarnoputri of Indonesia (2001–2004) and Corazon Aquino (1986–1992) and Gloria Macapagal Arroyo (2001–2010) of the Philippines became the presidents of their countries, replacing men ousted for incompetence and corruption. Megawati lost her bid for reelection. There were several coup attempts against Aquino and attempts to impeach Arroyo, but both Filipina presidents served out their terms.
- Ellen Johnson-Sirleaf, Africa's first directly elected female leader, took office in 2006. Known as the "Iron Lady" for her resilience in the face of political persecution, this former

World Bank economist is leading the reconstruction of Liberia after a debilitating fourteen-year war.
- Cristina Fernández de Kirchner is Argentina's first elected female president (the second female president to serve). Isabel Perón, who was elected vice president, assumed the presidency (1974–1976) upon her husband's (Juan Perón's) death. Fernández is the first democratically elected head of state who replaced a spouse (without his death). She succeeded her husband, Nestor Kirchner, in 2007, and theirs was often characterized as a presidential marriage, as the former president openly served as his wife's closest adviser.
- Dilma Roussef, once a young radical who had been imprisoned (and reportedly tortured) by Brazil's military dictatorship, was elected Brazil's first female president in 2010. A protégé of former president Luiz Inácio Lula da Silva (she served as his minister of energy and chief of staff), Roussef is expected to continue and expand upon her predecessor's social welfare policies, adding her own pledge to universalize access to electricity for all of Brazil's citizens by 2015.
- Bangladesh, Chile, Costa Rica, Nicaragua, Belize, Jamaica, Bahamas, Dominica, Saint Lucia, Trinidad and Tobago, Guyana, Haiti, Rwanda, Turkey, and Kyrgyzstan are some of the other countries that have elected female presidents or prime ministers.

Certainly some of these women have come to office by making a name for themselves. But in high- as well as low-income countries, the family name sometimes opens doors for women (and men too) and serves as an important entrée into politics (Hillary Clinton was hardly the first). Many female presidents and prime ministers have risen to prominence at least partly because they were the widows or daughters of male political leaders (Corazon Aquino, Indira Gandhi, Violeta Chamorro, and Benazir Bhutto are just a few examples).

women work outside the home), the wage gap is glaring: in China women earn the equivalent of 68 cents to every dollar a man earns. In terms of the political representation gap, China has slipped to 53rd place in the world (from 16th in 1997). Women now hold less than a quarter of all seats in China's parliament. Although

Figure 14.6 Measuring Gender Empowerment (2008)

	GEM Rank	Seats in Parliament Held by Women (percentage of all seats)	Female Labor Force Participation	Ratio of Estimated Female-to-Male Earned Income
China	38	21	74	.68
Mexico	68	22	46	.42
Peru	74	29	61	.59
Nigeria	—	7	39	.42
Turkey	77	9	26	.26
Iran	98	3	32	.32
Indonesia	100	12	53	.44
Zimbabwe	105	18	61	—

Sources: UNDP, *Human Development Report 2010.* Data on ratio of estimated female-to-male earned income from UNDP, *Human Development Report 2009.*

some are making more progress than others, in developed and less developed countries (including democratic ones), men continue to dominate government. Despite claims to the contrary, most governments are not representative of all "the people." Even relatively progressive governments have broken their promises to women (not to mention other historically marginalized groups) for a variety of reasons, most notably to avoid challenging traditional patriarchal interests.[89]

Sonia Alvarez points out that states are slowest to work on particular types of issues defined as private, outside the "proper" realm of politics. According to UNIFEM, only a fraction of countries (fewer than 5 percent) specifically criminalize rape in marriage—and even then, the perpetrator is charged in fewer than one in ten cases.[90] It is only in the past three decades that well-established liberal democracies have begun to deal with sensitive issues of social relations, including spousal rape, sexual harassment, and other forms of violence against women. For example, Turkey did not criminalize marital rape and sexual harassment in the workplace or introduce more punitive sentences for sexual crimes until 2004.[91] Turkey is by no means unusual; most newly established democracies would rather delay dealing with such issues because of the controversy surrounding them. In Mexico, for example, violence against women is pervasive and its perpetrators operate with impunity. Since 2007 the federal government of Mexico has established a special federal prosecutor's office for crimes against women, and twenty-eight states have enacted legislation aimed at improving the legal system's response to sexual assault and domestic violence. But this is a huge undertaking that most Mexican states have indicated little interest in implementing.[92] Therefore, while the *abertura* offers a range of possibilities perhaps once unheard of, the window of opportunity has only partially opened. Interestingly, sometimes it is the less-than-democratic regimes that can push through policies promoting gender equality. Ironically, in democracies, through a process that is supposed to foster inclusion and consensus building, the promotion of human rights, especially women's rights, may be set aside in the interests of "unity."

Civil control over the military. As discussed in Chapter 12, in the face of growing instability, civilian leaders have often sent in the police and even the military to restore order among unruly crowds. Unless they find some other way of building legitimacy, these leaders become heavily dependent on the support of the security forces. However, the military often views itself as the supreme arbiter of the national interest. Its concern over civilian inability to impose calm in the midst of a political or economic crisis has on occasion prompted the military to take matters into its own hands.

A government that must continually look over its shoulder out of fear of an army takeover is in an extremely precarious situation. Many new democracies find themselves coexisting with powerful militaries and must take care not to challenge their prerogatives. Ideally, freely elected democracies would not be constrained or compelled to share power with other actors, including the military. Democratically elected governments should have unquestioned and full authority to generate new policies or carry out their core functions. Therefore, it is crucial that militaries be removed from politics and firmly subordinated to civilian control. MILITARY PROFESSIONALISM, or the military's depoliticization and recognition of civilian supremacy, is absolutely critical to the survival of democracy. The military must view itself as serving the civilian government, not as the definer and guardian of the national interest. This can be achieved: Mexico's military is not considered a threat to civilian control, and it looks like the Turkish and Indonesian militaries are declining in influence as well (although they have by no means been neutralized as political actors).

Unfortunately, few countries experiencing a democratic transition can rest fully assured that the military accepts this subordinate role. Where the transition was preceded by a military regime (or a military-dominated regime), unless it is eliminated by foreign intervention or by revolution, the security forces will still hold a powerful place in government during and after the transition. The military is a crucial part of the government that the new democracy must attempt to manage. Many new regimes have made efforts to establish civilian supremacy, with varying degrees of success. Although ultimately the goal is for military decisionmaking to be subject to civilian control, leaders must consider the military's power in determining when and how far to push reform. As Nigeria began its democratic transition in 1999, analysts agreed on the need to reduce military prerogatives, although they disagreed about whether Obasanjo was the man to do it. Wary of other former military leaders who might stage a comeback, Obasanjo purged some army officers associated with the Abacha regime. However, many Nigerians suspect that Obasanjo owed his presidential win to military financiers and doubted he had the will to make significant reforms in civil-military relations. During Obasanjo's time in office, soldiers committed massacres without worry of prosecution, in part because the president didn't want to provoke a coup. A power vacuum was created when Obasanjo's successor, President Yar'Adua, left the country for medical treatment without transferring authority to his vice president. Nigerians held their breath, wondering if the military would stay out of the matter (it did). Perhaps this is a sign that Nigeria's democracy is consolidating, since experts warn that if this scenario had played out ten years earlier, it would have almost certainly led to a coup. Although Jonathan was favored to win, two of the top contenders for the presidency in April 2011 were men who ruled not that long ago as military dictators (Ibrahim Babangida and Muhammadu Buhari)—and remember, former president Obasanjo was a member of that club as well. In Nigeria as in many other democracies, getting (and keeping) the military out of power is a formidable task.[93] In the end, persuading the military to stay out of politics may sometimes necessitate AMNESTY deals that excuse its members from ever facing punishment for their abuses of human rights. This can truly amount to a deal with the devil, as it so often leads to a culture of impunity (among other problems) later on.

Presidents Abdurrahman Wahid and Megawati Sukarnoputri of Indonesia also struggled to gain control over the military, not just the official forces but also the (often more reckless) militia units throughout the country. They are both now gone, but the influence of the military remains. Indonesia's current president, Susilo Bambang Yudhoyono, a former army general, has ostensibly limited the political role of the armed forces, but they remain responsible for widespread abuse (notably in Papua and Aceh) and have yet to be held accountable for past crimes. Some members of the Indonesian special forces division, known as Kopassus, have been convicted of gross human rights abuses, but continue, according to critics, to commit crimes with impunity.[94] This is not uncommon; during political transitions the military is often in a position to negotiate the terms of its withdrawal so that it retains nondemocratic prerogatives. Ironically, such deals may be a political necessity—to get the military out of the presidential palace—but in the long run they greatly limit the possibilities for consolidation.[95] Consequently, until the possibility of a coup d'état becomes remote, no system can be considered durably democratized.

Conclusions: When the Transition Turns Out to Be the Easy Part

Where democratic experiments have been attempted and failed, it is impossible to identify a singular cause for their failure. The lesson is that we cannot assume there will be a simple, unilinear advance to democracy in the third world, given the heterogeneities and inequalities that exist there. As we've seen in Nigeria, democracy can suffer serious setbacks. As we celebrate the countries embarking on their democratic transition, perhaps our interest should be the substance of their institutions, at least as much as their sustainability. It is crucial that we find ways to support the deepening of democracy, and avoid undermining it, if we are to improve the chances of its consolidation.

15

Political Transitions: Real or Virtual?

Zimbabwe is mine. —*Robert Mugabe, president of Zimbabwe*[1]

Elections in Peru have never been a ballroom dance.
—*Rafael Roneagliolo, election monitor*[2]

Given the difficulties associated with the DEMOCRATIC TRANSITIONS described in the preceding chapter, it is important to recognize that transitions can be tough, protracted, and inconclusive. Many countries that began a POLITICAL LIBERALIZATION have already returned to AUTHORITARIANISM, while others hang on precariously, under serious threat. The so-called transitions we see in many countries may be more virtual than real. Transitions can be co-opted, controlled, or aborted.[3] As we will see in this chapter, it is not unusual for authoritarian governments to seek to legitimize their rule through elections. They are not above affecting the appearance of reform and will go to any lengths to hold on to power. However, with some important exceptions, authoritarians have tended to perform poorly. In Somalia and a handful of other cases, years of authoritarian rule have aggravated various divides to such an extent that the STATE itself has disintegrated or collapsed. As we will see, more than a few states today are at risk of imploding or failing.

What Is "Virtual Democracy"?

One could say that there are as many different types of authoritarian systems as there are democracies. They can be right-wing and conservative, seeking to maintain the status quo or even turn back the clock to an idealized time, or they can be left-wing and radical, promoting transformative change. What we see among communal dictatorships, THEOCRACIES, and POPULIST dictatorships (to name only a few forms) is that even governments that reject the democratic transition are scrambling to preserve their positions. They are under varying degrees of pressure from donors to at least affect the appearance of reform. Although these nondemocratic regimes share some important qualities with DELEGATIVE DEMOCRACIES, their leaders are solidly authoritarian.

335

Whereas executives in delegative democracies dominate the other branches of government, the authoritarians described here subvert the entire democratic process. They may not appear quite as repressive as old-style authoritarians. The levels of repression today may not rank equally in terms of severity and magnitude with what occurred during the height of the COLD WAR. Still, in reconfiguring systems, there are significant restrictions on participation, competition, and civil liberties. They may have elections, but they are patently unfair. In Algeria, for example, when it appeared that the "wrong party" was about to win in 1992, the government canceled the elections. In Côte d'Ivoire, one of the incumbent's campaign slogans in 2010 was actually "We win or we win," and this was one promise he made good on, refusing to give up power after more Ivoirians voted for his opponent than for him.[4] Reconfiguring regimes ban parties at will, and restrict most political organization and competition. Although Egyptian president Hosni Mubarak (in power since 1981 and known as "the last pharaoh") was elected for a fifth time by a landslide, it helped that the main opposition party had been banned and that his challenger had been just recently released from prison after spending three years there. Reconfiguring regimes are repressive of civil and political freedoms. Like the Mubarak government, they may go to great lengths to appear democratic (Egypt's president hailed the 2010 parliamentary elections as a milestone for DEMOCRACY), but they strenuously avoid any real political reforms, sometimes until it is too late, as Mubarak and many of his neighbors are learning.[5] Often, governments don't even bother to make it look like an election; they openly interfere with the campaign process and seek to further their political goals by establishing control over television, radio, and newspapers. Authoritarian governments have routinely imprisoned and tortured journalists who are critical of their policies. According to Reporters Without Borders, Iran is the Middle East's biggest prison for journalists and Netizens. In Iran it is said that there is "freedom of speech, but not freedom after speech."[6] In much of the world it is not uncommon for journalists and bloggers to be arrested, imprisoned, and tortured. "Preventive measures" including torture and assassination have been used in Egypt and Algeria against all those opposed to the government. Those targeted include large numbers of Islamists—both those directly implicated in violent action as well as moderates committed to nonviolent means for change.[7]

And the leaders of these countries are frequently quite unabashed about their behavior. They often make EXCEPTIONALIST claims that the rules don't apply to them. President Robert Mugabe has declared that he will rule Zimbabwe until he is 100 and signed into law a constitutional amendment that allows him to choose a successor should he ever decide to retire midterm.[8] Conservatives in Iran say that they want reform, but that it must be in the context of an "Islamic-style" democracy in which conservative clerics still hold political power, befitting of an Islamic, not a liberal, republic. Although these leaders deny the impact international pressure has on them, many are sensitive to their image overseas and few can face down the threat of sanctions. In effect, what many leaders have created is what has come to be known as "donor democracy." In order to keep the flow of aid open, these "democratic authoritarians" must look like they're making respectable progress at "getting politics right." From their point of view, getting politics right may actually mean putting stability first, especially where experiments in democracy have been associated with CORRUPTION, inefficiency, instability, and economic chaos. This is the government's point of view in China, which along with Iran is one of a handful of countries that need not much concern themselves with appearances.

Both Iran and China claim to be pursuing their own versions of democracy. In China's case, it is a socialist democracy, "with Chinese characteristics." In Iran's case, at least until its handling of the Green Movement in 2009, Iran's THEOCRACY could arguably be more democratic than the governments of its neighbors (and Western allies) in the Middle East. Leaders of Iran and China insist that their countries are exceptional and will not follow the path of other countries. They continue to buck trends toward democratization, writing off Western democracy as "a great lie" or "bourgeois liberalization" that they hope to keep far from their borders.

Yet only a handful of countries have been able to ignore or contain Western pressures for reform. Because of its size and perceived power, China can scorn Western advice on good governance and still rest assured of the continuation of benefits such as most-favored-nation status and membership in the WORLD TRADE ORGANIZATION (WTO). Because there is always someone eager to buy its oil, Iran has so far been similarly well placed to evade Western pressures for democratization (and it has apparently handled pressures for change from within, at least for now). Until recently, most Middle Eastern governments have not had to bother reconfiguring, because of their oil and because they are relatively pro-Western. Out of fear that democracy might produce governments that are not so compliant, the West has done little to pressure Saudi Arabia and the other Gulf states to democratize. However complacent the West may have been about its Arab allies, to varying degrees they are corrupt and unpopular—and they are having an increasingly difficult time holding off internal pressures for change.[9] Fewer and fewer dictators can ignore these pressures. Instead, through the use of manipulation and deception, some have become impostors, making what can only be called a pseudotransition. The result is the creation of a virtual democracy or semidemocracy in which formal democratic political institutions exist to mask the reality of authoritarianism. Again, what they are doing is in effect crisis management. Authoritarians must come up with new survival strategies as the old ones become less viable. Although some, such as Bahrain, Yemen, and Syria seem to have no problem with it, others find it harder to portray themselves as new democrats and meanwhile fall back on the old strategy of mass repression. Except for a few oil-rich regimes, they can no longer afford to co-opt the opposition with pork barrel items because of an INTERNATIONAL MONETARY FUND (IMF) requirement for economic reform. Instead, they try to create new friends, mobilize old ones, and find new ways to channel and control participation. Often this results in only the most superficial of changes. Of course, each government varies in the degree to which it uses these strategies, reflecting a unique historical context as well as donor response, and this combination of factors explains the variation in results.[10]

Reconfiguration

Perhaps more remarkable than the reforms described in the preceding section is the story of how less-than-democratic leaders have scrambled to hold off pressures for real change by simply appearing to be more democratic. According to Catherine Boone, this scramble can be described as a RECONFIGURATION, which can play out in any number of ways.[11] Reconfigurations are not in themselves necessarily bad things or nonevents. Even the most incremental steps or alterations can accumulate into substantial reform, if not transformative change. Simply the fact that regimes are squirming to renovate or reconfigure is evidence that the pressures upon them offer the potential for more substantive change. Reconfiguring systems may become more democratic or authoritarian. The outcomes will vary because they will be shaped by the choices made by individuals and groups operating under the constraints unique to each country.[12]

Despite the fact that they can come in many different shapes and sizes, there are certain qualities associated with reconfiguring regimes. As we will see, reconfiguring regimes centralize power in the hands of one or a few. They are personally appropriated states, in which the leader becomes interchangeable with the government. With little or no ACCOUNTABILITY, such governments easily fall prey to the temptations of corruption. To ensure that they retain their position and affect the appearance of LEGITIMACY, they practice what we characterize as "low-intensity democracy." When they can't win elections fairly, they are not above drawing from a bag of tricks—even resorting to various means of repression. Because of their overreliance on the military, reconfiguring regimes often end up as "hard states," which may work to keep them in power in the short term, but ultimately leaves them vulnerable to collapse.

Women voting in the 2009 elections in Iran (Reuters/Caren Firouz)

Centralization of Power

Ironically, authoritarians justify their centralization of power as a way to secure their countries from collapse. The leader argues that the country is in crisis, and therefore every institution that might interfere with the effective exercise of power must be controlled. For example, during the Cold War, dictatorships kept judiciaries weak and submissive—so as not to be distracted with questions of constitutionality. However, some courts appear to be taking all this talk about democracy seriously, rendering decisions that proclaim that they cannot be bought or repressed into submission. Yet in virtual democracies, this is often a thankless task. Although Zimbabwean courts have continually attempted to demonstrate their independence, the president's policy has been to disregard court orders. Judges have been physically harassed and the government has refused to guarantee their security. Vacancies are left unfilled as many independent judges in Zimbabwe have (in one way or another) been forced to resign, but the courts still occasionally act independently; they have dismissed TERRORISM charges against human rights activists and members of the opposition party because state security forces had abducted and tortured them. However, the security forces retaliated by arresting the magistrate who ordered the release of Roy Bennett (a popular white opposition leader facing terrorism charges).[13] In Iran, the Supreme Leader appoints the head of the judiciary, who appoints senior judges. Frequently trials are closed, confessions are coerced, and the accused are denied access to legal counsel. In the aftermath of the Green Movement in 2009, hundreds were convicted in a televised series of mass show trials, none of which met international standards for justice.[14]

Authoritarians typically demonstrate a similar predilection toward forcing the legislative branch of government into line. For years the parliaments and congresses serving such regimes have in one manner or another become rubber stamps for executive initiatives. There is a dual track of power in Iran and China. In both countries there is a government hierarchy of executive power. But running parallel to most institutions and often trumping the government is the true locus of power in each country. In Iran, the clergy and its institutions are supreme. In China, it is the branches (and "small groups") of the Chinese Communist Party.

Occasionally, however, governments playing at democracy have made the mistake of allowing their hold over the legislature to get away from them. In the 2008 elections in Zimbabwe, Mugabe's party for the first time lost its majority in the parliament. Under increasing pressure after he very nearly lost the presidential elections that year (winning only because the opposition candidate pulled out of the election to boycott in protest of election violence), Mugabe entered into what many see as a faux power-sharing agreement, creating the post of prime minister for Morgan Tsvangirai. The resulting unity government established in 2009 has largely been run by Mugabe, a wily strategist who has worked the deal to his benefit at every turn. What happens in such cases in reconfiguring regimes is that either the executive has deluded himself into vainly believing that popular support would continue his party's domination at the polls, or he has simply proven unable to control the outcome in the way he could in the past. In Mugabe's case, it appears that, at least for now, he's played the opposition, forcing it into a loveless marriage.

Personally Appropriated States

As you will recall from the first chapters of this book, most (but not all) third world countries have long histories of authoritarian government that go at least as far back as the colonial period. The result is now a tradition of arbitrary and unchecked power operating in both civilian single-party states and military dictatorships. Whether headed by a civilian or military leader, such governments can best be described as PERSONALIST REGIMES or "personally appropriated states." By this we mean that there is such a consolidation of power in the hands of one individual that this leader comes to personify the nation. Personality is a big part of being able to pull this off. Personalist leaders tend to be exceptionally charismatic, or at least have a talent for making people believe that they have a near-mystical ability to know what is good for the country. To prove it, such a leader will try to portray himself as a populist, "a man of the people." An example is Mahmoud Ahmadinejad, the fiery nationalist president of Iran, who won a surprise landslide victory in the 2005 elections. But when he was handed a second term in 2009 (despite allegations of widespread fraud), it led to widespread demonstrations, which were met with a vicious crackdown by security forces.[15]

At least in his first run for the presidency, Ahmadinejad's style worked: a mix of Robin Hood economic populism (promises to fight for the poor and strip power from the rich and privileged) and Islamist hero (accusations that the United States is practicing nuclear apartheid). China's prime minister Wen Jiaobao, also known as "Grandpa Wen" or "the crying prime minister," has become a familiar face alongside rescuers at the site of natural disasters, hugging kids and offering sympathy to survivors. He even has a popular Facebook page, with smiley-face emoticons left by admiring supporters, many of whom are Chinese living overseas. Attempts by political ELITES to appear to be "regular guys" may be all about winning trust in government (which isn't as crucial for authoritarians as it is in democracies, but it doesn't hurt).[16] It is certainly easier to do when one can manipulate the media with censorship.

During the Cold War, many of these leaders literally appointed themselves "president for life." Or, as in the case of the previous rulers of Iraq and Syria, they groomed their sons to succeed them in "hereditary republics." For years President Mubarak was believed to be preparing his son, Gamal, to eventually inherit the presidency. Because the military (which we all know now has a preeminent place in decisionmaking) expressed reservations about this, however, one of the first things that the elder Mubarak did to buy more time was announce that Gamal would not seek the presidency.[17] Others have so far more successfully constructed a system that guarantees their personal control into perpetuity. In 2005 President Mugabe's party "won" the two-thirds majority needed for him to change the Zimbabwean constitution, so that when this octogenarian is ready, he can personally install his successor without even calling for elections.[18] Since the end of the Cold War, with some notable exceptions, the West has for the most part become less patient with this kind of behavior from its erstwhile allies.

Corruption

During the Cold War, what sustained such long-standing regimes, besides superpower support, was often a combination of co-optation and repression. Now as then in these PATRIMONIAL regimes, the leader plays the role of the benevolent but stern father. Under the continuation of a very old tradition in much of the world, PATRON-CLIENT RELATIONSHIPS are based on reciprocity. The patron allocates resources and in return the client owes the patron his or her political loyalty. Consequently, in China some local governments have been described as mafia states allied with gangs. Chinese president Hu Jintao spoke of the need to tackle corruption in the Communist Party, which he characterized as "rampant." In many ways the Sichuan earthquake in 2008 revealed the extent of this problem, as widespread corruption is believed to have fatally compromised construction of schools and other buildings (nicknamed "tofu buildings"), some of which crumbled, killing 70,000, many of them schoolchildren.[19] In Zimbabwe, where the majority of citizens live on less than one dollar a day, the bash for President Robert Mugabe's eighty-sixth birthday is estimated to have cost half a million dollars.[20]

Another example of how this patron-client system works is illustrated by the relationship between potentially politically relevant interest groups (such as trade unions or peasant organizations) and the government. CORPORATISM is most associated with fascism in Nazi Germany, but it has several different meanings. Usually associated with some form of authoritarianism, its conservative advocates claim that it offers an alternative path to LIBERAL DEMOCRACY and socialist TOTALITARIANISM. In many of the highly personalist regimes in Latin America in the 1960s and 1970s, corporatism took the form of "bureaucratic authoritarianism," in which the military joined with technocrats to promote order and GROWTH. Whatever its variant, corporatism is unique to no single part of the world; it tends to grow wherever there are long traditions of powerful state rule. Corporatism describes the behind-the-scenes relationship between a governing party (or state) and various organized interests or sectors. It is built around a relationship of reciprocity in which the party seeks to control interest groups by recruiting, partially including, or co-opting them. The interest group affiliated with the state gets recognition as an "official" organization, the only one with the right to speak on behalf of a specific group. Although the state defines the powers of these organizations, the organizations do attain some of their objectives, and the state gains a new base of support. While part of the deal is that the interest group must drop at least some of its demands, some groups argue that they are being pragmatic in embracing such relationships, since the only alternative may expose them to massive government repression. Those who place a premium on stability and maintenance of order view corporatism as a benefit; however, under corporatism the MASSES are left out, and change, if it comes at all, is likely to be slow.[21]

Not only does this kind of co-optation swing elections, but patronage networks also often result in gross governmental excess and a distortion of priorities. In the worst cases, they amount to kleptocracies, in which leaders and their cronies help themselves to the nation's treasury and resources. During Indonesian president Suharto's thirty-two-year reign his family accrued a personal fortune estimated at $15–35 billion. The former president, with great fanfare, was placed under house arrest, but the charges against him were later dropped, ostensibly for health reasons (and reopened briefly in June 2006). His youngest son, Hutomo (Tommy), who held a monopoly on clove processing and controlled many key national industries, was sentenced to eighteen months in prison for a corrupt land deal. He was later sentenced to fifteen years for ordering the murder of a judge who had convicted him on corruption charges. Tommy was freed on "conditional release" after only four years.[22] This was the first time a member of that family had ever been convicted of a crime. Suharto died in 2008, having never fully faced corruption charges due to poor health, and he was buried with full military honors. Few Indonesians were satisfied with the light-handed treatment of the Suharto clan.

Elites also benefit materially when sweetheart deals with MULTINATIONAL COR-PORATIONS create a windfall—and a CLASS of multimillionaires. This appears to already be happening in Afghanistan, where more than $1 trillion in untapped minerals such as gold, copper, iron, and lithium promise to make it one of the most important mining centers in the world. Evidently, the gold rush has already started; in 2009 Afghanistan's minister of mines was convicted of accepting a $30 million bribe in return for awarding China the rights to a copper mine. Also in 2009, Afghan citizens paid $2.5 billion in bribes, equaling 23 percent of the country's gross domestic product, and a UNITED NATIONS survey found that a majority of Afghans consider public dishonesty to be more of a problem than the war. Meanwhile, President Hamid Karzai's government has blocked investigations of his supporters, who have been implicated in a range of scandals, from real estate to drug deals. In fact, graft is so systemic that it is said to provide the Taliban with their primary recruiting tool.[23] Such nepotism and cronyism is hardly a post–Cold War phenomenon. But it has proliferated since the 1990s as political leaders distribute valuable assets and lucrative state contracts to key allies and clients through the privatizations called for by neoliberal reforms. Of course, the extent of corruption varies widely by country. It is important to remember that no government in the world is completely honest. In some countries the corruption can be characterized as the "politics of the belly," in reference to grossly underpaid civil servants who moonlight or take bribes in order to make ends meet. Elsewhere, there may be a long tradition of gift-giving or nepotism, but the government still manages to function. However, in the most predatory states, corruption is so pervasive that the system is rotten. Ultracorrupt states (some of the worst today are said to be Somalia, Myanmar, Afghanistan, and Iraq) are often notorious not only for their private use of public resources, but also for their lack of capacity and incompetence.[24]

Low-Intensity Democracy

Yet despite these failures, reconfiguring regimes are hard to overthrow. Their leaders operate under what Phillip Huxtable calls "the universal law of politics": those in power strive to stay in power.[25] Few authoritarians willingly relinquish the reins of government to anyone but a handpicked successor. Instead of caving in to Western pressures, the "reform" they seek to initiate is entirely on their own terms, with their own timetables, and within the constraints they impose.[26] One common sleight of hand is to rush elections through before the opposition can organize or unify quickly enough to compete against the incumbent. The result is what we call "low-intensity democracy," in which there may be great fanfare about the coming democratic reforms. A new constitution may be created, opposition parties may be legalized, and elections may be held—but the reform process itself is hijacked. Elections are carefully calculated to produce the victory of the incumbent, who can then resist further change by claiming the popular mandate.[27]

There are a variety of ways of accomplishing this besides garden-variety practices such as stolen or stuffed ballot boxes, or turning away registered voters while allowing unregistered voters to cast their ballots (often more than once). Although many US voters were alarmed to learn in 2000 that many of these irregularities have occurred in their own elections, the United States isn't the only place where entire graveyards of the deceased have "voted." Many people around the world vote under the watchful eye of a party functionary. In Indonesia under President Suharto, people were required to vote at work. Their ballots were opened on the spot and tallied on a large board visible to all.[28]

Moreover, the national electoral organizations established by governments are often funded by (and working for) incumbents. International and domestic election observers watch elections to report rule violations and interference with the democratic process, including intimidation and violence at the polls, irregularities in vote counting and tallying, and lack of objectivity at polling stations (i.e., who gets to vote without proper documentation). In one of the worst cases in recent history, in Peru, observers sent by the Organization of American States (OAS) left in protest over the Fujimori government's handling of the 2000 elections. In the first round of voting, for example, the number of ballots cast reportedly exceeded the number of registered voters by 1.4 million. In Peru it is said that the Fujimori government administered the results in a "step-by-step" coup. There and in other countries that are more or less democratic, the collection of ballots can only be described as chaotic, as computer systems have been said to break down for hours or even days, resulting in highly suspicious delays in the count.

Mobilization Through Repression

Not only do reconfiguring regimes interfere with their opponents' ability to campaign for office, but they also themselves run campaigns that are divisive and polarized. In a climate of economic hardship, incumbents can successfully portray democratic politics as a ZERO-SUM GAME and play up fears, accentuating divisions along ethnic, religious, and other lines to mobilize the public. For years President Mugabe and the Zimbabwe African National Union–Patriotic Front (ZANU-PF) aggravated divisions between urban and rural dwellers to mobilize support. With their hold on power threatened by liberal, prodemocracy movements often centered in the cities, reconfiguring regimes like Mugabe's strike out at their enemies to disperse the opposition (for example, "Operation Drive Out Trash" razed the homes and businesses of 700,000 city dwellers in 2005).[29] Reconfiguring regimes also fall back on their long-established networks of rural support. Despite the fact that they too have been affected by budget cuts, systems of patronage (alliances with local and regional power brokers in the countryside) are often more institutionalized and therefore slower to break apart. Because poverty is often most pronounced in rural areas, the people living there fear losing what little state support they receive. As a result, rural areas are often major bastions of support for governments attempting to reconfigure.

Besides manipulating rural-urban divides, reconfiguring governments may encourage a resurgence of ethnoregional or religious ideologies in order to mobilize populations and divert attention from the government's failures. As a result, ethnic conflict often worsens under authoritarian rule. Over the years, Mugabe has been accused of cynically manipulating ethnic and racial divides to maintain his power base. NATIONALISM may also be used to divert attention from the government's failings by identifying scapegoats as the source of the country's problems. For example, leaders may exaggerate the threat by certain out-groups, either foreign or domestic, or hold them responsible for the country's problems. President Mahmoud Ahmadinejad blamed Iran's massive unrest in 2009 on Western provocateurs, attributing the protests to an international conspiracy seeking to promote a soft revolution.[30]

In the Peruvian elections of 2006, Alan García was able to squeak past his closest challenger by suggesting that his opponent was a puppet of Venezuelan president Hugo Chávez. García successfully portrayed himself as the only candidate willing to stand up to Chávez and appealed to Peruvians' nationalism, warning them not to let a foreigner dominate the country. For his part, Chávez has mobilized his base by appealing to many Venezuelans' anti-Americanism and demonstrating his willingness to confront the United States.[31] In Zimbabwe, Mugabe originally blamed white farmers for the country's problems. Britain and the opposition Movement for Democratic Change (MDC) were also scapegoated. In speeches, Mugabe corrupted his main challenger's name to "Tsvangison," making it English-sounding to Zimbabweans, and called him a "tea boy," insinuating that Morgan Tsvangirai was a British stooge.[32] In fact, Mugabe blames the British government and Western sanctions for most of Zimbabwe's current political and economic problems.

In terms of enemies at home, it is not uncommon for women, homosexuals, immigrants, or minorities to be blamed for economic hardship, political instability, or a "decline in values." To legitimate their rule, reconfiguring regimes lash out at all kinds of enemies—real or invented. In an effort to appeal to conservative traditional and religious elements, authoritarian leaders commonly call for a reassertion of IDENTITY. For example, authoritarians are notorious for manipulating "family values" and reinforcing traditional conceptions of women's proper role. Whereas some women are mobilized by conservative appeals to their "innate" commitment to the family and morality and have even supported military coups against democratic governments, those women who do not or cannot conform to "traditional" roles are designated as traitors. In countries around the world women are stigmatized and even attacked for their inability or unwillingness to stay within the boundaries set for them by the patriarchal order.

Dictatorships worldwide have issued crackdowns for many of the same reasons. Whether it is the imposition of "protective legislation" that denies women access to employment, or reproductive controls that refuse them access to contraception or abortion, what reconfiguring leaders are doing is building political alliances, more specifically partnerships with traditional and conservative elements. For example, in Iran, the Basij, a voluntary militia created after the Islamic Revolution, is known for targeting homosexuals, women, and ethnic and religious minorities. The Basij was responsible for the 2009 shooting death of Neda Agha-Soltan, the young Iranian woman whose murder on a Tehran street was broadcast all over the world, and who has become a martyr of the Green Movement.[33] Although there is no agreement on whether Agha-Soltan was simply in the wrong place at the wrong time or whether it was no coincidence that she was female, we do know that around the world the politics of exclusion only work to heighten social tensions and violence. As we can see in the worst cases of this, such as Rwanda, scapegoating deepens already-existing divides and renders the prospects for a more authentic democratization at some point in the future all the more difficult.

Hard States

As states weaken and CLEAVAGES resurface, the possibility of state collapse grows. Where leaders stubbornly refuse to stand down, the ensuing instability is used as a justification for a more repressive authoritarianism. Kim Jong-Il, who has literally starved North Koreans into submission, is a classic example (his government arguably stands alone as the most repressive in the world today). It could be argued that Robert Mugabe has just been using a lighter touch in Zimbabwe for the past decade. When President Mugabe lost the first electoral round in a head-to-head race against his opponent in 2009, he unleashed such an onslaught of violence on opposition supporters (more than 200 were killed and thousands tortured) that their candidate, Morgan Tsvangirai, decided to withdraw before the runoff.[34] Although Tsvangirai would likely have won the elections if they had continued (and been the least bit free and fair), he withdrew to save his supporters, fearing that Mugabe might order another massacre like the one that killed tens of thousands of people in Matabeleland in the 1980s. Governments that commit such atrocities are described as "hard states." In such cases, authoritarianism itself risks becoming the cause of state collapse. Not to be confused with strong states, hard states such as North Korea, Yemen, and Myanmar become totally dependent on the military for their survival. In many of these countries the government may have a civilian façade, but the military has an overwhelming influence—it is the only thing propping the government up.

As we have seen in the preceding two chapters, the civil and military spheres in much of the world are not as distinct as they are in consolidated democracies. Howard Wiarda and Harvey Kline argue that such a separation is not traditional in much of Latin America, where an alternation in power between military and civilian rule was for many years the norm. Even today, it is not uncommon for constitutions in Latin America to assign militaries the right, even the obligation, to intervene in the political process under certain circumstances. Similarly, executives are often constitutionally afforded extensive powers to bypass the legislature, and until relatively recently judicial review was not part of the Latin American legal tradition.[35] Consequently, it should be of little surprise that given the upheaval of the 1960s and 1970s, most Latin American countries (including El Salvador, Chile, Brazil, and Argentina) were rapidly becoming hard states. And Latin America was hardly unique.

In China this tendency is called "resilient authoritarianism." While some point to the recent significant growth in the number of antigovernment demonstrations in China as a sign that the government will soon collapse or democratize, it is just as likely that these demonstrations will prod the government to make just the reforms necessary to survive. Instead of being a sign of a state's declining power, such modification may actually work to enhance administrative efficiency, further entrenching the government's rule—as we have seen with villagers' committees' elections. Even in the face of mass discontent, such regimes can continue to consolidate power as long as the core leadership can avoid factional struggles and keep the support of the military and police.[36] However, under these and similar circumstances it is not unheard of for authoritarians to lose this crucial source of support. The security forces step in to fill the political vacuum and to establish order—if nothing else.

While it is common for military leaders to promise a transition to democracy, most coups should be viewed as nothing more than yet another reconfiguration. There are some cases, such as Nigeria, where (at least for a while) it appeared that the promised transition did finally take place. As mentioned in Chapter 14, some people are skeptical about Nigeria, and doubt the military will ever truly turn over power to civilians, because (as in too many cases) such transitions are delayed, incomplete, or temporary. Sometimes military leaders simply reconfigure themselves as civilian candidates for president, hold staged elections, limit the ability of the opposition to compete, and (if all else fails) rig the results. More often, as is feared in Nigeria, the military just continues to govern from the wings. When this is the case, it should fool no one. It amounts to merely another manifestation of virtual democracy.

Disintegration

When the reconfiguration gets out of control, when the government will not budge in the face of overwhelming opposition and divisions within the military render it unable or unwilling to prevent a breakup, the result is a crisis of governance, or at worst a DISINTEGRATION. So far, outright disintegration has been the least-frequent outcome associated with this period of crisis management. It is much more common to find countries on the cusp of failure, characterized as "weak" or "failing" states. Yet even those categorized as failed states may not collapse. Most states that fall into these categories are in sub-Saharan Africa, but they can be found in a few other places as well (besides Nigeria, the states characterized in 2010 as most at risk for failing were Iran, Guatemala, and Honduras; none of these countries actually took the plunge—that year, anyway). All told, there were an estimated seventy-seven countries identified as at "high" or "very high" risk of social unrest in 2010. The countries making this list were vulnerable because of a mix of factors: a high degree of income inequality, rising ethnic tensions, and low levels of public trust in institutions (to name just a few). Interestingly it is the "intermediate" regimes—neither consolidated democracies nor hardcore authoritarian regimes—that are believed to be the most susceptible to turmoil. Adding to the odds, many of the countries already at high risk have also been hit hard by the Great Recession. Forecasters expected troubles to come to a head in 2010 or 2011, because political reactions to economic distress historically have been delayed.[37]

What differentiates a weak state from a failed state? According to Stuart E. Eizenstat, John Edward Porter, and Jeremy M. Weinstein, the difference isn't so much about poverty per se as it is about lapses in three critical functions of government: the provision of security (and preserving SOVEREIGNTY over the territory), the provision of basic services, and the protection of civil freedoms. Weak states are deficient in one of these areas, while failed states are not capable of fulfilling any of the three.[38] However, facing internal and external demands for substantive change, weak states (such as Somalia prior to 1991) can quickly erode and collapse, becoming failed states (such as Somalia since 1991). In 2010, analysts listed Sudan, the Democratic Republic of Congo, Afghanistan, Iraq, and Zimbabwe as weak—in the process of decay and on a long slide toward disintegration.

According to I. William Zartman, disintegration is best conceptualized as a long-term degenerative disease. Countries in decay are in varying stages of decline, but what they have in common is state paralysis: they can no longer perform the functions that make them states. Under such circumstances government retracts and the countryside is left on its own. The state becomes a shell; there is no sovereign authority. Power is up for grabs and warlord politics, or rival power centers, play increasingly larger roles in people's lives. There is a breakdown of law and order and organized violence becomes generalized. The effect is societal collapse. People retreat into ethnic nationalisms or religious affiliations as a residual source of identity and organization, and no single institution can claim to receive the support of or exercise control over the people living there.[39] Under such circumstances, even the firmness of national borders becomes vulnerable, and the fracturing or breakup of states becomes even more likely. Analysts tell us not to be surprised if such a pattern emerges over the next few years, as previous waves of democratization have been followed by reverse waves of democratic breakdown.[40]

But the degenerative disease that so many states are experiencing does not always prove fatal. A cure or more likely a remission is possible. Some states may survive political turbulence of the kind described, exist on the brink of collapse, and still emerge with new vigor. More analysts are arguing that given the arbitrary boundaries demarcating states, perhaps in some instances fragmentation is not a bad thing. Juan Linz and Alfred Stepan make the interesting point that in order to have a democratic regime, there must first be a viable state.[41] While we must never forget the human tragedy so often associated with disintegration, for some countries disintegration is increasingly being thought of as a necessary first step—before democratization can even be considered. Given the foundation of a more viable state, democratic forces may then regroup and substantive reforms can begin. Although external actors need to be kept in mind for the considerable role they play in shaping outcomes in weak states, what may prove to be more crucial to their recovery is the ability of CIVIL SO-CIETY to rebound. Even a collapsed state can come back from the dead. To some degree, Rwanda is an example of this. The inhabitants of a territory must come together to restore faith in government and to support the successor government. If they can do this, what is left of the state may recover its balance and return to more or less normal functioning. However, if the pieces do not come back together, warlord politics is a likely fate of many weak states. Still, nothing is preordained. Even weak states evolve differently and no outcome is inevitable.[42]

Conclusions: Is a Reverse Wave Ahead?

Most leaders have acceded to internal and external demands for political liberalization not only in a variety of ways, but also to varying degrees, depending on the intensity of the pressures they face. Some leaders have been willing to make the reforms necessary to build the base for a still-fragile democratic system. And while a strong economy is an asset, even democracies in some of the poorest countries, against all odds, have proven to be impressively resilient. Elsewhere leaders have made partial changes, or reconfigured the political system in such a way as to maintain their own power bases. To varying degrees, authoritarians of diverse stripes have affected the appearance of change. During this period of intense reconfiguration and reform that the world is experiencing today, there are some states that appear to be explicitly bucking the liberal democratic trend. In the case of China, for example, one specialist characterizes efforts by prodemocracy activists as the "lessons of failure."[43] Certainly China is not alone in this category, in its ability to hold off change, even if we are living in a "democratic age."

Still other political systems have disintegrated (or may yet disintegrate) under the cumulative effect of the pressures already described. Because they are so fragile, some democracies will struggle and eventually fail. Does this sound like the situation in any of our country case studies? A firestorm was created in 2009 when a

US Joint Forces Command report listed Mexico along with Pakistan as at risk of rapid and sudden collapse.[44] Nigeria also remains at risk; not even a decade into its democratization, its ranking on the Failed State Index has worsened since 2008. If this already challenged and rapidly delegitimized democracy continues to find itself unable to deal with factionalized elites and address group grievances and uneven DEVELOPMENT, it could mean the end of civilian rule—whether through military coup or civil war.[45]

Ironically, given the current climate, it is the reconfiguring regimes (like Zimbabwe, perhaps) that are more likely to survive, at least in the short term. Despite donor talk about the importance of good governance, it is the virtual democracies that are best placed to enforce the economic reforms the donor countries so desire. Perhaps the worst thing for democracy is for developed countries to accept an incumbent's portrayal of political reform as destabilizing and dangerous. Unwilling to budge on neoliberal economic reforms or fearful of political vacuums, too often donors lower the threshold for their political expectations. They back off from demands for reforms such as respect for civil rights, agreeing with authoritarians that perhaps the people "aren't ready yet."

In this time of overstretched budgets and fear of Islamism, it is more likely that donors will choose to sit back and accept such rationales. Yet in the case of authoritarians, we know from history that the more repressive a government is, the more likely it will threaten its neighbors, as well as its own people. It is also important not to forget the lesson of Somalia—states left to fail can pose a world of problems for all of us. Therefore, as Larry Diamond and Marc Plattner observe, it is in our interests to do everything we can to nurture and support fragile democracies.[46] There is nothing inevitable about the triumph or persistence of democracy. Even consolidated democracies can decay if there is a long period of incompetent leadership. In the end, it is important to remember that there are a wide variety of possible outcomes to the transformations under way.

International pressure alone did not create this third wave of democratization, but if international support for it should wane, the viability of already frail democracies will be further diminished. It is therefore crucial that the international community provide the support necessary to preempt a third reverse wave, by assisting these democracies in their deepening and CONSOLIDATION.[47]

16

Linking
Concepts and Cases

Great variation exists among our eight CASE STUDIES in terms of history, economy, and society. In the following pages we will briefly review each country's recent political history, using examples to illustrate some of the concepts discussed in the preceding two chapters. As you read these case studies, look for the major similarities and differences of experience—especially in regard to their REFORM, RECONFIGURATION, or DISINTEGRATION. Keep in mind that because of the dynamic nature of politics, it is likely that some things have changed since this book was published, so further research may be needed to answer some of the questions posed here.

Where, and why, would you locate each case on the continuum from consolidated LIBERAL DEMOCRACY to authoritarian regime? Why do you think some countries are taking the reformist route while others reconfigure? What are some of the ways in which government leaders attempt to hold on to power? To what extent have the military, the economy, and the existence of pluralism complicated transitions, or CONSOLIDATION?

In which cases has the population appeared to choose the order provided by AUTHORITARIANISM over the instability associated with DEMOCRACY? What are the major supports and constraints for democracy in each country? Where have the constraints become crises, and which are the most prone to disintegration? Which governments are suffering from the worst crises of EFFICACY? Have they been able to overcome these problems? What are some of the ways countries have attempted to undo decades of CORRUPTION? Of those that have made the most progress toward democracy, how have they achieved their success? Conversely, how are the reconfiguring regimes faring now? Which of these countries have made progress toward deepening democracy? In what ways are they accomplishing this?

Case Study: Mexico

Over the past few decades, Mexico has been engaged in one of the world's longest and most dramatic DEMOCRATIC TRANSITIONS. Until 2000, Mexicans had lived for seventy-one years under a government controlled by the Institutional Revolutionary Party (PRI). Politics in Mexico was for generations a ZERO-SUM GAME in which all formal power was centralized under the control of one party. Although this was no democracy, many Mexicans appreciated the relative stability their country enjoyed under the PRI.

Still, since the 1970s, certain factions in the PRI recognized the need for political reform, which occurred in fits and starts. By the mid-1990s it had become clear to many Mexicans that the relative stability provided by one-party rule could not make up for the excesses that came with it. Mexico was experiencing a series of LEGITIMACY crises, most notably associated with an economic collapse in 1994 and a civil war in the south. In addition, Mexicans were rocked by a number of major scandals and were no longer able to overlook the pervasive corruption within the government. Many Mexicans felt threatened by a growing lawlessness in the country, much of it linked to Mexico's newly prominent position in the international drug trade. Moreover, Mexico's economic difficulties and growing inequalities were contributing to a situation in which stability could no longer be ensured.

At about the same time that all this was happening, the United States, Mexico, and Canada were moving toward the creation of the North American Free Trade Agreement (NAFTA). Yet its passage was delayed in the US Congress because of a number of concerns, including questions regarding the antidemocratic character of the PRI government. In the end, a combination of internal and external pressures convinced PRI technocrats (so named because of their foreign-trained expertise in economics and careers built in the bureaucracy rather than the party or politics), including President Ernesto Zedillo, to move forward with a "silent revolution," or gradual democratization of Mexico. The biggest fight Zedillo had on his hands was with entrenched elements within his own party, known as the "dinosaurs," an old guard who wanted to maintain the PRI's absolute control of power.

Despite the internal struggles, political and economic reform proceeded. The legislative elections of 1997 marked a watershed event, in that for the first time the PRI lost its majority in the Mexican congress. Yet it was President Zedillo's dramatic break with the tradition of the *dedazo* (or "the tap of the finger," in which the outgoing president handpicked his successor) that opened up the political space for Mexicans to take part in truly democratic elections.[1] There were some irregularities, but in many ways this election amounted to Mexico's second revolution—after seven decades of uninterrupted rule, the PRI lost and actually allowed itself to be removed from power.

The personality dominating this "electoral revolution" was Vicente Fox of the conservative National Action Party (PAN). Fox campaigned hard in appealing to the average Mexican's dissatisfaction with politics as usual, and he won by a clear margin. Just as surprising as the result of the vote was that the transfer of power was remarkably smooth. However, with a term limit of six years, Fox had precious little time to demonstrate to Mexicans that he could make good on his grand promises. Although the economy did remain relatively stable and the government made some inroads against corruption, Fox's record is widely considered disappointing.

Ironically, part of the reason that President Fox failed to meet the people's high expectations was *because* Mexico's democracy was working—since 2000 it has become stronger, more accountable, and more transparent. Still, the presidential election of 2006 was extremely divisive, characterized by an unusual amount of US-style mudslinging. For months up until the election it looked as if Mexicans would choose by a landslide their first leftist president, Andrés Manuel López Obrador, a POPULIST former mayor of Mexico City who had been highly critical of the failures of both Fox and the PRI. However, in the last weeks of the campaign, another career politician, the conservative, Harvard-educated Felipe Calderón, came from behind to win. López Obrador called foul and demanded a recount, claiming that the election had been stolen from him by a conspiracy of government and business ELITES backing Calderón. It took two months before Mexico's federal electoral tribunal came to the unanimous decision that Calderón was the rightful winner. In this country with a long history of fraudulent elections, López Obrador suspected a continuation of the tradition and refused to accept defeat. Worse, in the months after the painful and protracted election was decided, it appeared that nearly one-third of Mexicans were disillusioned with democracy—and it was not uncommon to hear Mexicans question whether they had a democracy at all.[2]

This lack of legitimacy is very dangerous for any new democracy, and Calderón hardly had a mandate: he won by less than 1 percentage point. Whether the country would remain governable is still a good question. Mexico's only other experience with genuine democracy was very brief (it lasted from just 1911 to 1913 before collapsing into the Mexican Revolution).[3] Moreover, the imperial presidency that was once the norm is over; Mexican presidents now have less power than any of their predecessors. As discussed in Chapter 13, public support is declining for the issue that Calderón has pursued most vigorously, the war on drug traffickers. Calderón attempted to push through a variety of reforms (in the state energy monopoly, in taxes, and in education), but he hasn't been very successful at breaking the gridlock and making the deals necessary to get them approved in the Mexican congress.[4] His party lost badly to PRI in the 2009 midterm elections; the PRI is now the largest party in the legislature and it isn't predisposed to helping Calderón.[5] The PRI won nine of the twelve governorships but lost in some states that had been thought reliably pro-PRI. As a result, some analysts call the 2010 elections a draw—and the best indicator of what's to come. The good news is that voters are holding their representatives accountable—and sending the message that no party has a lock on their votes.

Given the state of the economy and plummeting approval rates for Calderón's war on drugs, many analysts believe that PAN will lose the presidency in the next vote. The PRI believes that it has the momentum; as of late 2010, Enrique Peña Nieto, a telegenic young PRI governor of the state of Mexico, was considered the frontrunner. But the PRI's showing at the polls for the legislature won't necessarily translate into a presidential victory (the PRI did well in the 2003 midterm elections but then came in a distant third in the 2006 race).[6] Thus, the most that can be said for now is that there's a good possibility of a PRI presidency in the near future—and if the next president is PRI, he (or she) will have to deal with a legislature and judiciary that may have something new—a mind of their own.[7]

Case Study: Peru

Whereas most of the rest of Latin America has continued on with a POLITICAL LIBER-ALIZATION dating back to the early 1980s, Peru reversed course—and has since reversed itself again. Although it wasn't a smooth ride, until 1992 Peru was undergoing a democratic transition and was on the same path as many of its neighbors. Not exactly a liberal democracy, most analysts agreed that it had made some progress toward

DEMOCRATIC INSTITUTIONALIZATION. But because it has so consistently swung back and forth between authoritarian and democratic rule, Peru came to be known as an "intermittent democracy."[8]

Based on his experience in a war on drugs, two GUERRILLA insurrections, and hyperinflation, Alberto Fujimori, the democratically elected president of Peru, determined that democratic dialogue was inefficient. Extraordinary circumstances called for extraordinary actions. Frustrated with the limitations placed on him by the checks and balances of Peru's democratic institutions, in 1992 Fujimori assumed for himself the powers of a military dictator. With the assistance of Peru's National Intelligence Service and the military elite, Fujimori concentrated power in his own hands, declared a state of emergency, and dismantled democratic institutions by closing the congress and purging the judiciary. By 1995 he had vanquished his enemies, turned the economy around—and been reelected by a landslide. Although there is room for disagreement as to why Peruvians were willing to surrender their hard-earned but still somewhat restricted democratic liberties to Fujimori, even his enemies admit that the president was able to provide Peruvians with a sense of stability relatively unknown in the Andean region.

While appreciative of the order he provided, by the late 1990s Fujimori was second only to Fidel Castro as the longest-sitting head of state in Latin America. The government had crossed the line from DELEGATIVE DEMOCRACY into authoritarianism and Peru could no longer meet even the minimum qualifications of democracy once Fujimori determined that there was no one else capable of running the country.[9] The president pulled out all the stops and ran what is widely agreed to be the dirtiest campaign and election in the country's history. In the end, large numbers of Peruvians, and most of the world, refused to recognize the result of the 2000 election, in which Fujimori declared himself the winner in his race against CIVIL SOCIETY leader Alejandro Toledo.[10]

Ultimately it was a corruption scandal that brought Fujimori down. Although mysteries still abound concerning who actually held power in Peru and the military's role in what some call a "clandestine coup," crowds celebrated the president's faxed resignation from Japan in November 2000. (Fujimori later became the first Latin American president found guilty of human rights abuses in a court in his own country. He was sentenced to twenty-five years in prison in 2009 for authorizing kidnappings and massacres.) After a short transitional phase, in 2001 the new presidential election came down to a race between two candidates. Traditional political parties are virtually extinct in Peru. Instead, it is more common to find candidate-centered movements closely identified with a single personality or "flash parties," because they are disposable and vanish almost as quickly as they appear.[11] The contest was between prodemocracy activist Alejandro Toledo and former president Alan García. Toledo (from whom Fujimori had stolen the elections just months before) came out the victor, narrowly winning a five-year term as president.

As the leader of this new democracy, it was crucial that Toledo do everything he could to avoid the pitfalls of the past and work to rebuild democratic institutions, restore the credibility of the judicial system, and establish the RULE OF LAW. However, Toledo was confronted with several problems at once, and the broadly based unity that had once bound those opposed to Fujimori rapidly evaporated.[12] Although Toledo will probably not be remembered as a great president, there were some improvements during his tenure: Peruvians enjoyed more political and civil liberties, the rule of law was strengthened, Peru's institutions were showing signs of more independence and more ACCOUNTABILITY, and the country was in better shape economically than when Toledo took office in 2001 (although the majority of Peruvians had not seen much benefit).[13] Although his government wasn't a disaster, it did not make much progress in fighting corruption, controlling the military, or restoring Peruvians' faith in politics. According to one analyst, Peru was like a spouse who had been cheated on: there was a lot of hurt and mistrust.[14]

It is probably just as well then that Peruvian presidents are prohibited from seeking two consecutive terms, since by the time of the 2006 election, Peruvians looked set to elect Ollanta Humala, a former army officer and populist nationalist political outsider promising an abrupt about-face. However, Peruvians are known for waiting until the last minute to make their decisions regarding their vote, and consequently it is almost impossible to predict election outcomes. In the end, Humala lost to disgraced former president Alan García because he was the least-worst choice (a popular saying at the time compared the two candidates as a choice of "cancer or AIDS").[15]

Having made his political comeback, President García was a changed man (at least ideologically speaking) the second time around. Having moved to the center-right of the POLITICAL SPECTRUM, he pursued a pro-market, pro-US policy that aggressively sought foreign investment and economic growth. Bolstered by world demand and higher prices for its commodities, few other countries in Latin America experienced as tremendous an economic boom as did Peru. Although poverty rates dropped by 15 percent, not everyone shared in the good times (or agreed with the president's methods). Despite the fact that his popularity ratings were some of the lowest of any president in the region (at 35 percent) toward the end of his term, García was actually talking about a third comeback, in 2016. In the meantime, the race for the April 2011 election was shaping up to be tightly contested, with a crowded field that included a number of figures from the past: Ollanta Humala (on the left), former president Alejandro Toledo (a centrist), and (on the center-right) Keiko Fujimori, the deposed dictator's thirty-five-year-old daughter, who vowed to pardon her father if she is elected president. Two other contenders were Luis Castañeda (a centrist former mayor of Lima) and pro-business former finance minister Pedro Pablo Kuczynski.[16] Just a month ahead of the elections, Toledo was the frontrunner, but he, Fujimori, and Castañeda had lost some ground while Humala (appearing more centrist) and Kuczynski were gaining on them. However, hardly anyone who knows Peruvian politics was willing to predict the election's outcome, except to guess that there would be a runoff in June (because no one looked strong enough to win in the first round), that the transfer of power would be smooth, and that (as much as Peruvians say that they're sick of him) whoever is elected will likely continue García's market-friendly policies.[17]

Case Study: Nigeria

As discussed in Chapter 5, Nigeria has come through a nightmare to begin its democratic transition. And in what is surely a case of truth being stranger than fiction, a born-again former military dictator led the way. Until this latest experiment with democracy, in 1999 Nigeria had spent only ten of its nearly forty years of independence under civilian rule. Earlier experiments with democracy failed in the midst of intense political crises, polarization, incompetence, and a lack of economic DEVELOPMENT. Nigerians have endured incompetent and corrupt civilian governments; they suffered worse through a civil war and through coup after coup, but the country hit bottom during the five years it spent under the dictatorship of Sani Abacha (1993–1998).

It is difficult to briefly relate just how venal this government was. Those with political power amassed enormous fortunes from the country's oil wealth, to such a degree that Nigerian POLITICAL CULTURE has been described as "prebendal," or based on the systematic abuse of state office and resources for individual and group gain. This is hardly a fair characterization of the Nigerian people, since most of them received nothing from these transactions. Under both civilian and military rule, the vast majority of Nigerians have been permanent outsiders.[18] For years, those who dared speak out against the government and its abuses were harshly repressed.

Yet in what has been described by many Nigerians as divine intervention, in June 1998 Sani Abacha suddenly dropped dead (reportedly of a massive heart attack). By that time the military had tired of the exercise of government and was willing to give civilians another shot. To create what would become known as the Fourth Republic, Nigerians poured into the voting booths in February 1999. They elected representatives at all levels of government, including the presidency. And although observers cited many electoral abuses, they accepted the results because the irregularities did not appear to be systematic. Olusegun Obasanjo won, the military remained in the wings, and Nigeria began its fourth experiment with democracy.

Most observers agree that Obasanjo and his People's Democratic Party (PDP) won by a landslide in imperfect though basically free and fair elections. Yet from the outset there were serious challenges to Obasanjo's ability to govern. The country itself appeared to be fragmenting, and the population was becoming increasingly frustrated with the government's lack of capacity. However, 2003 was hailed as a "judgment year," an important test for democracy in Nigeria in its first civilian-run elections in twenty years. Obasanjo was reelected with 62 percent of the vote and Obasanjo's PDP continued to hold most seats in the House of Representatives and senate. However, the process was marked by political violence and widely regarded as at least partially rigged.[19] A long tradition of discord, suspicion, and cynicism continued in the Fourth Republic.

Much of the public dissatisfaction with the government stemmed from the sense that the leaders of this democracy cared more about themselves than about the people. Toward the end of Obasanjo's second term, Freedom House ranked Nigeria as "partly free," citing a decline in civil and political rights and a variety of problems including threats against the media and unions.[20] There was not much evidence that democratic consolidation had begun, as there appeared to be little agreement on the rules of the game. Between 2000 and 2005, Nigerians' trust in their president fell from 77 to 26 percent, and their satisfaction with democracy fell from 84 to 26 percent.[21] By the end of 2006, Nigeria had managed to survive without a coup and without breaking apart, but the country's democracy, for a variety of reasons, was not consolidating.

Several attempts at what some would call manipulating the democratic process followed. Obasanjo proposed amending the constitution so that he could have a third term, but legislators shot this idea down.[22] Political insiders did make progress in institutionalizing a deal for a rotating presidency to be shared between regions—

and successfully installed retired generals among the top candidates for the April 2007 presidential race. If pulled off smoothly, this contest would mark another milestone in Nigeria's history. No democratically elected Nigerian president had ever before handed power over to another democratically elected leader. The elections were chaotic but held on schedule—and they were widely described by international observers as the most fraudulent since the return to civilian rule. Among other things, until days before the elections it was unclear who the candidates would be, and on election day some of the candidates' names were left off the ballot. Ultimately, Obasanjo's pick, Umaru Yar'Adua, was declared the winner, with over 70 percent of the vote. Although the alternation in power marked a turning point in Nigerian history, the country is a dominant-party democracy (both houses of parliament and three-quarters of the governorships are all predominately PDP, which has won every presidential election since 1999). So given the circumstances, the outcome was hardly surprising but not quite the triumph for democracy that many hoped for: it amounted to one member of the governing party merely handing power over to another.[23] A more significant achievement for Nigeria's democracy will be when one party steps aside for another to take power.

Yet that seems many years away. Because Yar'Adua was elected under a cloud of suspicion, questions of legitimacy dogged him. During his roughly two and a half years of rule, Yar'Adua became known for his commitment to the rule of law and TRANSPARENCY but made little progress toward promoting these ideals. Admitting that there were problems with the elections that brought him to power, Yar'Adua did initiate a reform of the electoral process to ensure more credible results in the future. He chose a different course from that of his mentor, Obasanjo, in resolving the Niger Delta conflict, as described in Chapter 13. Yar'Adua's successor, Goodluck Jonathan (whose father says that he chose this name because he had a feeling that his son would be lucky), only had about a year left in his term to make good on his pledge to continue his deceased predecessor's policies.[24] As this book went to press, Jonathan was running as the PDP candidate in the April 2011 election—and was almost certain to be the next president. It took more than luck for this Pentecostal Ijaw from the southeast to take the nomination, since as far as many people are concerned, Yar'Adua's death meant that northern Muslims hadn't finished their turn at the presidency. More concerning, a win for Jonathan in 2011 would violate the unwritten deal regarding a two-term presidential rotation between regions—a deal that is (arguably) responsible for sustaining the longest period of civilian rule since independence.

Case Study: Zimbabwe

Since the overthrow of white minority rule in 1979, Robert Mugabe and his party, the Zimbabwe African National Union–Patriotic Front (ZANU-PF), have effectively dominated the country's politics. To be fair, it should be pointed out that when he was first elected, this hero of the war for liberation inherited from colonial Rhodesia a highly centralized state and powerful security force. Over time, the president has reconfigured in a variety of different directions. For years now he has claimed that the country is democratic, yet he has made a determined effort to undermine Zimbabwe's democratic institutions since the mid-1980s. Through alternating policies of co-optation and repression, Mugabe has so far been largely successful at controlling his opponents.

Until about a decade ago, Mugabe could count on the full cooperation of the legislature in this effort, since party loyalists held virtually all the seats in the House of Assembly. However, by the late 1990s, internal and external pressures forced the president to undertake a reconfiguration. Not wanting to be seen by the world as a dictator, Mugabe very much needed the prestige of legitimacy, and believed he could obtain this with the pretense of democracy. However, at about this time a new opposition group, the Movement for Democratic Change (MDC), was rapidly gaining popularity in the cities. Meanwhile, the economy was in shambles and Mugabe, desperate for foreign aid, knew that the parliamentary elections due to be held in 2000 had to at least appear to be democratic.

Recognizing these realities, Mugabe met these expectations partway. He did not outlaw opposition parties, but did not intervene in preelection violence aimed against them. In the elections that followed, irregularities were attributed to all sides, but human rights organizations report that ZANU-PF supporters were particularly violent—beating, gang-raping, and killing opposition candidates and their supporters. If the right to campaign is as important as the right to vote, then clearly these elections were marred from the start. Yet here again is evidence of a reconfiguration: Mugabe permitted the opposition a partial success. Perhaps it was just part of the democratic façade erected to assuage donors, but for the first time in two decades, ZANU-PF actually lost its two-thirds majority.

Since then, the Mugabe government has become more adept at crushing any checks on its authority. The government threatened to ban the MDC (the only opposition party of any significance), and party leader Morgan Tsvangirai was tried for treason, a crime punishable by death (he was acquitted). In 2005 the eighty-one-year-old Mugabe crowed that he would remain in power as president until the age of 100, and events since then suggest that he is intent on keeping his word. For the 2008 presidential elections, whether due to mounting internal and external pressures or to Mugabe deluding himself that he could actually win, the government continued to reconfigure. However, when it appeared that for the first time in three decades Mugabe would actually lose power—he came in second place to Tsvangirai in the first round of the vote—the president and his party reverted to old tactics. The lead-up to the runoff elections in June was so bloody that Tsvangirai pulled out to save his supporters, and Mugabe, in a one-man race, celebrated victory with 85 percent of the vote.[25]

After months of pressure from Zimbabwe's neighbors, the country's three main parties: ZANU-PF, the MDC-T (the main branch of the MDC, led by Tsvangirai), and the MDC-M (a smaller faction of the MDC, led by Arthur Mutambara) agreed in February 2009 to form a unity government. Power was supposed to be shared between Mugabe (in his sixth term as president and head of state), Tsvangirai (the prime minister and head of government), and Mutambara (the deputy prime minister). Despite grave reservations, Tsvangirai entered into the pact, as he put it, "to change the fronts on which we wage the struggle."[26] He did so to stabilize the country and get a new constitution approved that would make way for elections supervised by an independent electoral commission. However, despite the terms of the deal, Mugabe holds the reins of power (leaving Tsvangirai with responsibility but no power). Although they were supposed to divide up the posts, Mugabe controls all the key ministries, the security forces (including the police), and state media. He has even appointed party loyalists as governors in every province.[27] "Power-sharing" has been a rocky road, as it has become increasingly clear to everyone (particularly Tsvangirai) that the MDC is being played. There has been some progress, as the unity government is given credit for improving the economy. However, this government was recognized by all parties all along as a marriage of convenience, designed to last only for eighteen to twenty-four months, until a new constitution can be written and elections held. As this book went to press, no date for elections had been set, but with the clock on this arrangement winding down, Mugabe was reportedly champing at the bit to complete the constitution, call quick elections, and end the power-sharing charade.[28]

In imagining Zimbabwe's future, several scenarios come to mind—all of them hinging on the next elections, which Mugabe has threatened to call in 2011, but the MDC, African Union, and others say must wait until a new constitution and electoral reforms are adopted (not likely until 2012 or 2013). As hard as it may seem to fathom, a continuation of some form of the status quo (with Mugabe as the candidate in the next less-than-democratic elections) is a good possibility. Some analysts expect that ZANU-PF's plan is for Mugabe to win (using whatever means necessary) and then pass the torch to a successor who will look out for party interests.[29] Another scenario is that the elections are actually free and fair. If Mugabe is the candidate (and he says that this is his intention), it is unlikely that he could actually win a fair race (a survey in late 2010 found that of those who were not too fearful to reveal whom they supported, 32 percent would vote for Tsvangirai and 18 percent for Mugabe).[30] But as hard as it is to imagine a clean election, it is almost as hard to visualize Mugabe losing the presidency and stepping aside graciously for anyone else to take the oath of office. It's a possibility, but it's not the end of the story that most would expect. A third scenario centers on Mugabe's sudden departure from power. In an interview in September 2010 the president reportedly sat slumped in his chair and appeared distracted.[31] According to the current constitution, if the president fails to complete his term, the legislative branch will act as an electoral college, choosing someone from parliament to complete his term (and remember, the 2008 parliamentary elections gave the MDC a slim majority). Sooner or later, Mugabe will be out of the picture, and ZANU-PF will either retrench into a hard-line dictatorship or be faced with the necessity of putting up a candidate who can win votes.

Case Study: Iran

Iran is a country gripped by contradicting visions of its transitional goals. As a society built on revolution, it has undergone cyclical changes, especially in its relationship with the Western world. The 1979 revolution, which overthrew Shah Mohammad Reza Pahlavi, sought to overturn the attempts at "Westernization" and establish an indigenous Islamic Republic under the leadership of Ayatollah Ruhollah Khomeini. Former president Ali Akbar Hashemi Rafsanjani is often credited with maneuvering Iran through a murky decade of economic struggles and international isolation, and concurrently launching the country in an *ABERTURA*-type direction. This helped promote a reform movement embodying limited pluralism that gained prominence during Mohammad Khatami's presidency from 1997 to 2005. Khatami campaigned on a reformist platform calling for relaxed social and cultural norms, mild openness to

Western culture, and the inclusion of women in governance. Yet this movement activated a powerful conservative reaction, from both leaders and citizens. This prepared the foundation for Mahmoud Ahmadinejad's surprise election in 2005, after securing 62 percent of the vote in a runoff with former two-term president Rafsanjani in what analysts have labeled one of the most dynamic contests in Iran's history.[32] Ahmadinejad, a former governor of a remote province who had been Tehran's mayor for less than two years before he rose to the presidency, is most definitely a populist more than a pluralist.

Power in the Islamic Republic has long been concentrated in a single leader or small group of leaders who are not accountable to democratic procedures (the elected president, for example, is "head of government," but the more powerful position is "chief of state," held by the Supreme Leader). Elections in Iran are competitive, participatory, and raucous. Candidates for parliament have to cross a minimum 25 percent threshold of the vote, so it is not unusual to have runoffs. Political parties cannot participate in elections, although some "political groups" have won legal recognition since 1997. Candidates must first muster the support of the Council of Guardians, set up in 1979 to interpret legislation and ensure its conformity with the sacred law of Islam. This twelve-person group, whose members are all appointed to power (six by the Supreme Leader), approves all legislation before it becomes law. Additionally, the council determines whether or not candidates are eligible to serve in public office, before they withstand the public votes—the council disqualified all but 4 of the more than 475 candidates running for the presidency in 2009.

A key issue in Iran's political development is the lack of separation of powers—Iran has virtually no horizontal accountability between institutions. The Supreme Leader, for example, is answerable to the religious jurisprudence of the Assembly of Experts, which is designed to limit threats to the Supreme Leader's supremacy. Both the president and elected members of parliament are subordinate to the Supreme Leader, currently Sayyid Ali Khamenei. The major organizations, including public security, military, and broadcasting units, are not accountable to the executive or legislature. Within the judicial system, there is not even an attempt to feign autonomy. Judges are held to both political and religious qualifications. Religious judgments *(FATWAS)* cannot be repealed by civil courts. The Supreme Leader has veto over everything. For example, Iran's Supreme National Security Council voted in favor of improved relations with the United States in 2000, but Ali Khamenei vetoed the motion.[33]

The disputed 2009 elections (Iran's tenth presidential ballot) signaled a defining blow to the already weak façade of any meaningful form of democracy in Iran, illustrating yet again that elections (alone) do not constitute a democracy. In the eyes of most, the widespread electoral fraud revealed the hollow nature of reform at the top in Iran. Voter turnout was heavy, estimated at 85 percent, and opinion polls released just prior to the final count showed a neck-in-neck race between Ahmadinejad and Mir Hussein Mousavi, the former prime minister (before the post was abolished in 1989), who is also a painter and an architect. Few could believe the official announcement, shortly after polls closed, that Ahmadinejad had won by a 28-point margin. The concerns around the election demonstrated that Iran is certainly experiencing a virtual democracy, as discussed in Chapter 15. Members of the clergy, some supporting Ahmadinejad, others in Mousavi's camp, issued *fatwas* and opinions on the disputed results. Yet the problems go beyond a flawed presidential election. Many began to openly question the utility of having a Supreme Leader, especially when Ayatollah Khamenei appeared impotent in the face of a genuine political crisis. Dissension and a feeling of malaise spilled over into the ever-important discussion of the decline of the national soccer team when a radio call-in show encouraged listeners to provide an explanation for the decline in soccer—supporters of the Green Movement who had rallied behind Mousavi mobilized yet again.[34] As one analyst put it, this moment in Iran "was not a 'Third World' version of Bush v. Gore in 2000."[35]

Reformists have been, and will likely continue to be, frustrated by the clerical leadership that blocks many of the changes they desire. We must be careful, though, not to assume that all clerical and other "religious" leaders and activists hold the same view. Many so-called deeply religious individuals within the Islamic Republic are fundamentally opposed to the actions of the Council of Guardians or the Supreme Leader. Iranian clergy have, at various times, served as both supporters and opponents of social and political movements in Iran, with a long tradition of clerical involvement in popular freedom movements.[36] It seems increasingly obvious that the voices who consider such core questions as the importance of NATIONALISM, the scope of individual and social freedoms, and the role of religion and politics are not going to disappear. Indeed, it is accurate to claim that they have been on the Iranian political agenda for over a century.[37] These competing forces are likely to continue to battle it out as Iran forges its way through the twenty-first century.

Case Study: Turkey

The Turkish Republic has undergone multiple phases of political development since its establishment under Mustafa Kemal Atatürk in 1923. Under his leadership, the country experienced dramatic change, especially in social life. Atatürk took pains to foster a modern, secular state united under the singular leadership of the Republican People's Party (RPP). His successor, Ismet İnönü, permitted party contestation, largely in response to UN concerns, but the PARTY SYSTEM struggled for decades in order to become fully embedded within Turkish politics. Struggles remain. It seems that Turkey has embraced democracy, but not necessarily pluralism.[38]

Until quite recently, Turkey was cited as an example of a delegative democracy: a system dominated by personalism in national politics and plagued by weak institutional relationships, especially a lack of meaningful horizontal accountability, and weak political parties. Changes that have been motivated in large part by European Union (EU) demands for accession have strengthened the democratic character of the Republic of Turkey, including recent changes to the Constitutional Court (which has had a history of banning political parties for a perceived Islamic character) as well as the curtailing of the military's penchant for stepping into politics, as discussed in Chapter 13. The institution of the Turkish presidency, traditionally a secular figurehead for the republic, is changing: constitutional changes adopted in 2007 and 2010 now call for direct election of the president (rather than parliamentary appointment), the establishment of a five-year, once-renewable term for the chief executive (replacing the single seven-year term), and removal of some of the privileges the military enshrined in the constitution, promulgated after the 1980 coup. It was not that long ago (2007) when the military annulled the first round of a presidential election, framed as a "bullet aimed at democracy" by many.[39] Even beyond this most recent series of constitutional amendments, the division and balance of powers in the republic are less than clear. The Constitutional Court, for example, has a long history of banning political parties, including the Welfare and Virtue parties, and almost banned the current ruling party, Justice and Development (AKP), in 2008.

Turkish leaders face two dominant struggles that challenge the regime's ability to handle opposition groups in a democratic framework. First is the lively debate between those who want to preserve Turkish SECULARISM, enshrined in the Kemalist doctrine, and those who seek a greater role for Islam in national life. Even nationally elected leaders can be forced off the scene for the appearance of publicly promoting religious values. The government's handling of Kurdish nationalism has been the other lightning rod of criticism and potential risk of democratic losses.

Similar to many of the countries we are studying, leaders in Turkey are attempting to battle corrupt political actions that challenge regime legitimacy. The initials of the current ruling party, the AKP, mean "pure," and the party has vocally campaigned, with quite a bit of success, on promises to root out corrupt elements within the government. The judicial system, despite recent reforms, remains influenced by governmental appointments and promotions, and rigid executive control over financing, even though amendments adopted in 2010 pledge to curtail their role.

The Turkish constitution has been subject to great scrutiny and amending, most recently in mid-2010. This set of twenty-six amendments, backed by the ruling AKP, were designed in part to increase parliamentary control over the army and the judiciary. They also ended the practice of expelling members of parliament if their actions could be included in grounds to ban a political party. The amendments, which were approved by a margin of 58 percent in favor to 42 percent against, also repealed the article barring prosecution of people in power after the 1980 military coup, and make the military more accountable to civilian courts (the ratification vote took place on September 12, 2010, the thirtieth anniversary of the coup). Yet depending on whom you ask, the amendments have either strengthened civil society, bringing Turkey closer to EU norms, or placed the judiciary closer to the AKP and, by association, religious control, ending the secularist emphasis of the regime. Of particular concern to opposition parties, for example, is the amendment that calls for parliamentary appointment of Supreme Court judges. The final outcome may actually make the political landscape more treacherous, as a former Turkish ambassador to the United States stated: "politics will polarize and harden further . . . the ruling party will become even less receptive to the opposition, and the opposition will use tougher words and approaches to undermine the government."[40]

While Turkey has clearly moved out of the zone of authoritarianism that marks many countries in the region, it remains a country short of consolidated democracy. As we have observed with the military and some aspects of the educational system, in Turkey the "seeds of authoritarianism [are] embedded in many institutions and rules."[41] Religion will continue to be a divisive issue within the republic, as well as the greatest challenge to pluralism and democracy in the state. As this book went to press, both political leaders of the Republic of Turkey are privately Muslim yet unapologetic supporters of Turkish citizens who are more religiously minded and who desire more public expression of their views. Can Prime Minister Recep Tayyip Erdogan and President Abdullah Gül work to incorporate newly confident citizens, many with roots outside of urban Istanbul, who desire public expression of their spirituality, without provoking the sensitivities of the traditionally influential secularists? As these leaders and their controversial AKP stand for parliamentary elections (due to take place no later than July 2011), they face an increasingly polarized and emboldened body politic on many fronts.

Case Study: China

Life for ordinary citizens in China is freer than it has ever been since the commencement of the People's Republic. Yet the most accurate way to characterize the changes that are happening in this country would be to emphasize the leadership's reconfiguration of political and social life—changes mostly introduced by Deng Xiaoping in the 1980s. As a victim of Mao Zedong's ideological and personal purges himself, Deng set out to depersonalize Chinese politics and place the country again onto the path of "normalcy." There is certainly a great deal of change taking place, and in many senses political relations in China are increasingly institutionalized. Some of the biggest developments are happening at the local levels, including elections for local committees and congresses. Yet the biggest hindrance to true political liberalization (on a national scale) is the dominance of the Chinese Communist Party (CCP), and especially the lack of separation between party and government in almost all public affairs. Political stagnation stands in stark contrast to the dynamism of the Chinese economy, which has captured the attention of many since the 2000s began. As a PBS documentary recently asked, "China's economy has evolved, but has its government"?[42] The answers are complex.

Chinese elite politics has been dominated by strong personalities. People commonly refer to generations of leaders: Mao Zedong led the first generation, Deng Xiaoping the second, and Jiang Zemin the third, with Hu Jintao now leading the fourth. Hu's consolidation of power stretched from 2002, when he was named general secretary of the CCP, to 2004, when he replaced Jiang Zemin as chairperson of the Central Military Commission, gaining effective control of the party, the state, and the military. Because it proceeded along predictable lines, it was a momentous transition that points to the increased institutionalization of Chinese succession politics, albeit in a decidedly nondemocratic fashion. The wheels are already turning for the next major transition of elite leaders, with the fifth generation set to take the stage in 2012, when it is widely expected that the current vice president, Xi Jinping, will be named CCP secretary, and 2013, when Xi will most likely be named president. Leaders are handpicked years in advance to help avoid ugly power struggles that could endanger the party's sense of legitimacy among the population.

Government and party leaders vigorously emphasize the "unity of the Chinese nation" and the dangers of instability and chaos if this unity is challenged. Yet this harmony is not as prevalent as leaders would like their people to believe: China is an extremely decentralized country with a surprisingly weak central government that has a difficult time enforcing its mandate at the local levels. Until recently, the central government had difficulty even collecting tax monies from its provinces. Central leaders today battle the seemingly rampant corruption that challenges not only the façade of harmony but the precarious legitimacy of the regime as well. Hu has used the corruption campaign to sack the former party secretary of Shanghai, to wild applause from many citizens. But other, lower-level corruption indictments have exhibited political undertones—one central minister was removed, implicated ostensibly for graft, but also coincidentally after he questioned Prime Minister Wen Jiabao's plan to rein in China's overheated economy.[43]

A natural disaster in the spring of 2008 revealed to many outside of China both the deep roots of corruption throughout the country as well as the devastating human toll from it. This earthquake, which occurred months before Beijing hosted the 2008 Summer Olympic Games, killed at least 68,000 people (rendering nearly 5 million additional people homeless), including many children who were attending school in shoddily constructed buildings at the time of the tremor. Immediately after the earthquake, allegations of corruption began, made clearer by the fact that school buildings, even many that had been recently constructed, had collapsed in a heap of dust while nearby buildings were left standing, unscathed. Many of these buildings consisted of what locals called "tofu buildings," which resemble jiggling blocks of the soft bean curd that serves as a staple in many East and Southeast Asian diets. The Chinese construction sector, in general, operates under a cloud of deep suspicion. The Supreme People's Procuratorate, the major prosecuting agency of the central government, announced in 2009 that bribery in urban construction cases accounted for nearly 40 percent of all the business bribery it dealt with during the first six months of 2009, with three-fourths of the bribes being marked "major or serious" cases involving more than $7,000.[44] The Chinese construction boom of the late 1990s and early 2000s was ripe for hasty deals that went unregulated and largely, in the absence of a calamity, unnoticed.

Many challenge any sense of meaningful participation in China because of what is lacking: elections at the provincial and national levels, competitive political parties that promote the articulation of varied interests, and a separation of powers between governmental and party institutions. Yet others argue that, underneath the surface, Chinese citizens are developing ways of influencing decisionmaking, building what Kevin O'Brien and Lianjiang Li have termed "rights consciousness"—the promotion of a sense of efficacy and involvement in local and even national affairs.[45] Importantly, this behavior is most prominent in the Chinese countryside, where the bulk of the population remains today. The type of protest culture that O'Brien and Li document may not change national policy priorities, but it has potential to grow into an ingrained sense of power among the population in the face of unjust leaders.

Change is clearly the name of the China game—one recent book even referred to the state's current iteration as "China 2.0" to distinguish it from earlier monolithic versions of the People's Republic.[46] Calls for reform emanate from leaders and citizens alike, although the meaning of "reform" is certainly in the eye of the beholder. Even party elders have called for restrictions on the freedom of speech, and Prime Minister Wen Jiabao, the popular leader who, as Zhao Ziyang's assistant in 1989, approached students in Tiananmen Square to urge them to back down, told CNN that calls for "the people's wishes for and needs for democracy and freedom are irresistible."[47] The type of regime this is likely to produce will depend upon the complex narratives yet to be written in the world's most populous state.

Case Study: Indonesia

The politics of transition in Indonesia began with a bang: following the resignation of President Suharto in May 1998, the country embarked on an uncertain path of reform. The post-Suharto leadership inherited a series of grave problems, headlined by a great sense of betrayal, corruption, and hopelessness that followed the economic collapse of 1997. The degree of challenge was so high that *The Economist* has since stated that, following Suharto's fall, "the very integrity of the country seemed in doubt."[48] A key turning point in this effort to jump-start political progress was the 1999 parliamentary election, characterized by Freedom House as "reasonably free although not entirely fair." The rainbow of parties able to compete during this election was a vivid departure from the past, when Suharto's political machine, Golkar, dominated. Out of this election, a ruling coalition formed, led by a presidential team made up of leaders from two competing parties. Yet the least of the problems Abdurrahman Wahid and Megawati Sukarnoputri faced was their differing party loyalties, even though eventually it was Megawati's Indonesian Democratic Party that pressed for Wahid's resignation. They needed to clean out a political system infested with corruption, tame a military accustomed to wielding considerable influence, and manage an economic recovery often made worse by international demands. In 2004, after three disappointing years of slow and erratic reforms during Megawati's presidency, Susilo Bambang Yudhoyono (SBY), a former army general who had served as Megawati's minister of security, was elected in Indonesia's first direct election for president (prior executives were elected by the legislature, which was composed of a combination of elected and appointed officials). This election, along with the 2005 peace deal between Jakarta and rebels in Aceh province, caused Freedom House to upgrade Indonesia's 2006 rating to "free" (a rating it has held since) and highlight the country's progress toward democratic consolidation. In fact, some have said that Indonesia "is arguably the most open, democratic and pluralistic society in the region."[49]

It seems difficult to overstate the importance of the 2004 presidential elections in Indonesia. Turnout (almost 80 percent) was impressive, and they were executed without violence.[50] Five candidates ran in the initial election, with former president Megawati facing SBY in a runoff. SBY won comfortably with 60 percent of the vote. SBY, who in addition to his former military service is also a lifelong music enthusiast with three romantic pop albums to his credit, won reelection to a second five-year term in 2009. Tallying the vote is a hugely complex operation in Indonesia, as the state has more than 175 million registered voters spread across 17,000 islands. As these representative institutions continue to become stronger, it will remain increasingly difficult for analysts to question the compatibility of Islam and democracy. As *Time* magazine put it, the elections in 2009 "silenced skeptics who doubted whether Indonesia—with its diversity of islands, religions and ethnicities" was fit for democracy.[51]

Despite these achievements, Indonesia consistently ranks as one of the most corrupt countries in the world (in 2009, Transparency International ranked Indonesia 111th out of 180 countries surveyed for its Corruption Perceptions Index). This ranking, continuing under the administration of "Mr. Clean," as SBY is known, demonstrates the endemic nature of such behavior (Transparency International once called former president Suharto the "greatest kleptocrat of all time").[52] Corruption colors many aspects of daily life in Indonesia, from renewing a driver's license to banking. Today, citizens especially distrust the police and the judiciary—dubbed the "court mafia" by many citizens.[53] The military is still viewed with disdain, and former abuses have yet to be rectified. To date, no senior military leaders have ever been convicted for their abuses of power during the Suharto era or since.[54]

If democracy is the acceptance of conflicting points of view, then events throughout the restive western province of Aceh since 2006 point toward significant gains throughout the country. Devastated by the tsunami that struck just off the coast of Aceh in 2004, Acehnese activists again went to the table with the Jakarta leadership (with the help of the government of Finland) to cement a peace deal that culminated in regional elections for governor. Irwandi Yusuf, a former rebel leader who had been jailed for treason (he escaped when the prison was destroyed by the monster wave in 2004), campaigned against former enemies, including military personnel and representatives from the Jakarta establishment, pulling ahead in large part because of his unique ability to work with both sides of the bitter conflict.[55] Yusuf played a fundamental role in the peace talks, just as he had in fomenting the thirty-year insurgency that claimed an estimated 15,000 lives. The 2009 parliamentary elections included local Acehnese parties, counting among the candidates former anti-Indonesian rebels. The Aceh Party (the leading local party, which consists of many former insurgents) staunchly refused to discuss independence from Indonesia along the campaign trail, a path feared by many Indonesians outside of Aceh. The successful elections increased the sense of legitimacy, both for the peace process in Aceh, and for Jakarta's tolerance of the peace process as well, even though tensions persist and mistrust lingers.

Despite these impressive gains (as well as the belated acceptance of Timor-Leste as an independent state), analysts still raise the specter of potential state disintegration. National IDENTITY as an "Indonesian" remains a relatively new concept for most people, who are distinct from other Indonesians in terms of language, culture, history, and religion. The cautious words of a government spokeswoman during the debate over East Timor in 1999 remain in the hearts of many across the archipelago: "Indonesia is an abstract concept, based on the former Netherlands East Indies. If we start allowing different parts to break away, it will be dismembered before we know where we are."[56] As discussed in Chapters 14 and 15, the consolidation of democracy can be more difficult and complex than the genesis of democratic change, and struggles surrounding identity and inclusion mar this lengthy process. Due to the arbitrary enforcement of defamation laws, widespread self-censorship in the media, and an overall "climate of fear" surrounding the discussion of powerful forces within the country, Human Rights Watch argues that Indonesian democracy remains on "shaky ground."[57]

The citizens of Indonesia have struggled through a tremendously difficult path following the downfall of their strong-willed authoritarian leader. Changes in political structures and attitudes give rise to cautious optimism for the future of the world's fourth most populous state. As SBY continues in his second term as president, we shall see if he exceeds the assessment of the *Jakarta Post:* "The president who didn't mess it up."[58]

Now It's Your Turn

After considering the problems of democratization described in this chapter, how do you think democracy can be made more sustainable? In your view, what are the most important factors in determining the overall success or failure of a democracy? Given what you know of these cases, do you find the Western model of democracy's divisiveness appropriate here? Could this model be applicable for much of the third world? What would you think are the challenges of having a democratic system during a crisis situation? What would be its benefits? Do you think it likely that political liberalization alone can address the needs of countries experiencing great economic and political instability? Are there any circumstances in which you believe disintegration might be a better outcome? Why?

PART FOUR

Beyond the Nation-State

Today more than ever, we live in a global economic, political, and cultural world, in which no country is an island completely isolated from the influence of other regions. The geographical lines that divide governments are in many ways less important today than they were at the beginning of the twentieth century. This development has profound effects on the issues that face us all, as well as on the institutions through which we handle these issues. In the chapters that follow, we examine some of the issues that are decidedly multinational if not global in scope, and discuss some of the institutions, both regional and global, that have developed in response.

17

Sovereignty and the Role of International Organizations

We the peoples of the United Nations, determined to save succeeding generations from the scourge of war . . . and to reaffirm faith in fundamental human rights, in the dignity and worth of the human person, in the equal rights of men and women and of nations large and small, and to establish conditions under which justice and respect for the obligations arising from treaties and other sources of international law can be maintained, and to promote social progress and better standards of life in larger freedom . . . have resolved to combine our efforts to accomplish these aims. —*Charter of the United Nations*

Among many developments in the past five decades, few parallel that of the increased interconnectedness of the world's STATES and of issues that affect citizens of the globe. We begin this chapter with a discussion of the role of states, acting not alone but rather in regional and global organizations, with special attention to the UNITED NATIONS. What are some of the issues that these organizations have tackled? Have they achieved much success? Next we discuss groups that have organized independently of governments, by highlighting the development of NONGOVERNMENTAL ORGANIZATIONS (NGOs) in the world today. We conclude with discussion of some of the major global challenges facing our world, and discuss the capacity of NGOs at the regional and international level to resolve these issues.

The rise of groups outside of the traditional NATION-STATE in part has led to a rethinking of the idea of national SOVEREIGNTY, commonly understood as government's autonomy or independence to act, especially within its own borders. The legitimate authority over any given territory, usually viewed as the entitlement of the state, includes the right to self-defense and the determination of its own destiny. The principle of sovereignty implies a degree of NONINTERVENTION in one's affairs. Yet recent leaders have argued that state sovereignty may be limited when countries are unable (or unwilling) to protect their citizens from crimes against humanity, which include ethnic cleansing, mass rape, and genocide (or the systematic decimation of people). This approach, known as the RESPONSIBILITY TO PROTECT, promotes awareness of the state's need to shield its citizens from harm. It also calls on the international community to support the UN and other organizations in establishing an early warning capacity to help prevent such atrocities in the first place. How can the international community respond to mass executions within other countries, or the systematic rape and torture of vulnerable groups? How should other countries respond? These are not new questions in international relations. Rather, they are reminders that the questions surrounding our past inaction in the face of mass violence, especially the Holocaust, have not all been answered, and that the controversy over how and when to intervene in others' affairs still haunts our world.

Despite the euphoric claims of globalism and our interconnected twenty-first-century world, systematic torture and the murder of specifically targeted groups of people continue to take place today, and we continue to struggle with how to respond. Does sovereignty mean that government leaders can violate the human rights of individuals and groups within their borders? As we discuss below, some now argue that humanitarian needs in countries or regions permit (or even require) the response of other countries, including a military response. Yet a central tension remains: Do problems that cross national borders demand an international response? What if the problem is confined within a single state? Are other countries justified to take action, in the name of promoting human rights? How should this response be coordinated, implemented, and monitored? This approach poses many other questions: What degree of suffering warrants a response from others? Under what conditions is international action justified? Who has the LEGITIMACY to carry out such actions? How are the objectives of intervention determined? Is unilateral action, undertaken by a single state or group, justified as long as it is in the name of humanitarian needs? Does a multilateral approach, involving the coordinated effort of multiple governments, necessarily make an action more legitimate? The answers to these questions have the capacity to dramatically change the way in which nation-states and the governments that lead them view themselves and their roles.

To this point in the book, much of our discussion has centered on the role of state actors. Yet recognizing the principle of INTERDEPENDENCE, supranational organizations that go beyond single nation-states have taken a more active role in international affairs. Some of this action is taken by groups of governments who willingly forgo some degree of their independent sovereignty in order to accomplish particular goals. Other action is taken by nongovernmental actors who organize not around their governmental IDENTITY, but rather around a particular cause or interest. Both types of organizations are increasingly prominent on the world stage.

International Governmental Organizations

INTERNATIONAL GOVERNMENTAL ORGANIZATIONS (IGOs) comprise official representatives of states who gather to discuss responses to issues and conflicts that affect the world community. We have already discussed two prominent IGOs, the INTERNATIONAL MONETARY FUND (IMF) and the WORLD BANK, which were both established at the 1944 Bretton Woods conference. In this section we discuss the role of IGOs and other multilateral institutions in resolving global issues. We focus on both regional and global IGOs as a tool of fostering cooperation among governments. One important feature of IGOs is that their memberships comprise official governmental representatives, and their goals are to calibrate the policies of like-minded states as well as to solve contentious issues that arise between conflicting state policies and goals. These goals are different from those of the other major type of organizations discussed in this chapter, the nongovernmental organizations.

Each of these organization types poses different challenges for the third world. Often, less powerful countries are excluded from decisionmaking structures within these organizations, either explicitly or implicitly. This contradiction of universal membership is most stark with respect to the United Nations, in which each state is guaranteed a relatively equal voice in some chambers, most notably the GENERAL ASSEMBLY, but not others, including the much more powerful SECURITY COUNCIL. The lack of TRANSPARENCY—clear, publicly available decisionmaking processes—challenges both the participation of many states and groups as well as the perception that actions taken by these organizations are positive. Many of these organizations are undergoing reform to fix these drawbacks, but formidable obstacles remain.

Regional Organizations

Over the past several decades there has been a proliferation of regional economic blocs, free trade areas, CUSTOMS UNIONS, and COMMON MARKETS. Since the late 1970s the impetus for this GROWTH has come from both the desire to form regional trade organizations as well as a defensive response to GLOBALIZATION. Regionalism is a framework of cooperation, with an indefinite duration, intended to include multiple issues, most often economic or security-related in nature.[1] The latter part of this explanation captures the transition that has touched many organizations in the third world; quite a few began with an initial focus on economics and trade within a defined (although not absolute) geographical space, and are now adopting other complementary agendas as well.[2]

A few observations on regional alliances focus our attention on some of the unexpected aspects of these organizations. Sometimes, former enemies (or countries with continuing hostilities) seek alliances as a way to formally move beyond their conflict. In Latin America, for example, Peru is a member of many regional organizations to which countries it has had past disputes with also belong, including Ecuador and Bolivia. The Association of Southeast Asian Nations (ASEAN) began largely in response to the regional perception of the growing communist threat in Southeast Asia. ASEAN's predecessor, the Southeast Asia Treaty Organization (SEATO), was distinctly strategic in focus. Member states within this organization continue to hold competing views on a variety of issues, including economic growth, the environment, and threats to security.

Another regional organization that originally brought together states in the larger interest of promoting stability and a common defense is the Southern African Development Community (SADC). The SADC was established in 1980 to provide political and economic protection against the apartheid regime in South Africa (which itself joined the SADC after its independence in 1994).[3] From the start, members recognized the gains to be had through consultation and cooperation. The SADC has been praised for its realistic priorities for regional planning.[4] Leaders have promoted small-scale irrigation over grandiose dams, as well as the use of appropriate technology, including attempts to combat widespread deforestation by developing more fuel-efficient stoves and alternative energy sources for cooking pots. As we find in other regional organizations, members have benefited from functionalist arrangements on technical matters, including efforts to sustain tropical forests, curtail the illegal trade in ivory and diamonds, promote the repatriation of refugees, and manage the distribution of limited natural resources, including through oil and natural gas pipelines. The fifteen SADC member states have expressed an interest in closer economic INTEGRATION, including the promotion of a free trade area, a customs union, and a common market—work that has been plagued by nontariff barriers, poor transportation infrastructure, and inadequate energy supplies.[5]

Increased interaction and contact can have many unintended consequences. Just as regional organizations developed to promote greater economic integration or cooperation in security matters, less formalized interaction has helped to promote regional solidarity through personal and cultural exchanges. For example, South American member states of Mercosur, also known as the Common Market of the South, have begun exchanges of mayors, provincial governors, and students, and Spanish is now obligatory in Brazilian schools as a way to promote regional cohesion.[6] An agreement signed with the Andean Community of Nations in December 2004 furthered such integration. This regional organization (now representing more than 270 million inhabitants) formed in the absence of developed linkages among states, and is now considered one of the main economic blocs of the world.

Two other prominent regional actors, ASEAN and the Organization of American States (OAS), had their genesis during the COLD WAR, forming as alliances to combat the rise of communist governments. Both organizations have moved beyond this ideological focus in the post–Cold War era, with ASEAN welcoming its former nemesis, China, on a consultative basis. Current member states of ASEAN, formed in 1967, are Brunei, Cambodia, Indonesia, Laos, Malaysia, Myanmar, the Philippines, Singapore, Thailand, and Vietnam, with consultative status held by the "dialogue partners": Australia, Canada, China, the European Union (EU), India, Japan, New Zealand, the Republic of Korea, Russia, and the United States. The China-ASEAN Free Trade Area was established in January 2010 to further increase regional integration, prompting some fears about international competition among Indonesian farmers.

With the commencement of the ASEAN Regional Forum (ARF) in 1994, the noneconomic aspect of the organization has again been highlighted. This component of ASEAN was developed in order to promote peace and security in the Asia-Pacific region. Greater participation by China will be needed in order to bring more power to the association. Now with twenty-six members, the ARF has become a high-profile forum for discussing security issues across the region.

The OAS, the preeminent organization for the Western Hemisphere, began with an agreement among member states in 1948, and the organization was launched three years later. All thirty-five countries in the region are official members, although the current government of Cuba has been denied its attendance rights since 1962, largely at the demand of the United States. US dominance of the OAS during the Cold War meant that the organization focused on isolating Marxist governments and fighting against leftist rebels. Since the end of the Cold War, the emphasis has shifted greatly. The priorities of the OAS today are to preserve and strengthen DEMOCRACY through the promotion of social justice, human rights, and good governance, and to provide solutions to the debt crises many member states face. Despite the presence of many regional economic organizations in Latin America, the OAS has also helped promote microenterprise and telecommunications trade, while shining attention on abuses of labor rights and the need to promote SUSTAINABLE DEVELOPMENT throughout the region. The OAS has been a major diplomatic player and peacemaker in the region as well, most notably helping to cool tensions between Ecuador and Peru in the mid-1990s. It also was a leading regional voice in challenging Alberto Fujimori's hijacking of Peru's presidential elections in 2000, and suspended Honduras from the organization after a constitutional crisis in 2009. Honduras was expelled from the OAS after a military coup ousted President Manuel Zelaya. Against the wishes of the Honduran Supreme Court, President Zelaya proceeded with a nonbinding poll on drafting a new constitution, which many believed would have ended the term limits that would have forced him from power. The pajama-wearing president was whisked away on an airplane and promptly replaced by a new civilian president. For the first time in the organization's history, the OAS invoked the part of its charter that calls for the suspension of a member for an "interruption of democratic order."[7] This focus on democracy was not as prominent, though, as OAS states lifted the ban (in place since 1962) on Cuba's membership in June 2009 (an invitation that Havana promptly rejected).

In Africa, the premier regional organization is the African Union (AU), which succeeded the Organization of African Unity (OAU) in 2002. Few mourned the loss of OAU, scorned by many as the "dictators' club" for its failures to protect citizens against tyrannical leaders.[8] AU architects hope that it will one day operate along the lines of the European Union, with a pan-African parliament (launched in 2004), a central bank (with plans for a common currency by 2023), and an AU-wide court of justice. With the same members and many of the same problems as its precursor organization, the African Union has a stronger charter (but not yet larger funds) to promote integration between the fifty-three African member states (covering the whole continent and several island states, with the exception of Morocco). Reflecting its commitment to democracy, member states of the AU must promise to hold free elections. Reflecting on past weaknesses of the AU and similar multilateral institutions, by design the African Union is attempting to limit the gross abuse of power in the name of state sovereignty. The AU is extremely unusual in that it has explicitly established its right to intervene against genocide or gross human rights abuses in any member states. Peacekeeping forces under AU command were mobilized in Burundi and Darfur in 2003, and the African Union/UN Hybrid Operation in Darfur (UNAMID), an unprecedented mission, was deployed in 2008. Like its predecessor, UNAMID has sorely lacked troops and equipment, and faces much resentment and mistrust, as many civilians are frustrated by its lack of effectiveness.

Besides traditional security issues, the other major focus of the AU is the improvement of living standards for citizens across the continent. In this light, the New Partnership for African Development (NEPAD) was proposed by former presidents Thabo Mbeki (South Africa) and Olusegun Obasanjo (Nigeria) and other government leaders in 2001. The idea behind this ambitious recovery and antipoverty plan, now under the auspices of the AU, is for developed countries to reward African states that practice good governance (which involves transparency, ACCOUNTABILITY, and similar reforms) with not only debt relief, but also increased aid and investment as well as freer trade. Through independent "peer reviews" of performance, African governments will encourage each other to follow a program of agreed standards aimed at remedying institutional deficiencies and promoting sustainable development. It's a work in progress, and one that will take time, resources, and determination to implement.

Other IGOs bring together states across multiple geographic regions in order to highlight a common identity or cause. One of the largest IGOs in the world today is the Organization of the Islamic Conference (OIC), which encompasses fifty-seven states across four continents and includes nearly one-third of the members of the United Nations—from Albania and Nigeria to Guyana and Indonesia. (Despite the presence of approximately 175 million Muslims in India, its membership has been blocked by Pakistan.) The goals of the OIC, founded in 1969 after an arson attack against Al-Aqsa Mosque in Jerusalem, are to promote cooperation among members, safeguard Islamic holy sites, and eliminate racial discrimination and colonialism. Trying to coordinate such a diverse group of states, even though unified by religious identity, has proven quite difficult, and while the OIC has carved out an important role as a facilitator of discussion among states, it has also lacked the teeth to implement decisions made within its chambers. In part because of its broad reach, the organization has suffered some famous disputes among members, and has been unable to unite even on some key proposals, including following up on promises for aid in the aftermath of natural disasters and implementing a coordinated economic policy toward the state of Israel.

How can membership in a multilateral organization, with either a regional or a global scope, change conduct within a country? Turkey's decades-long attempt to join the European Union provides a possible test case. Turkish leaders submitted their formal application for full membership in 1987, but the EU did not accept Turkey as a candidate until December 1999. Formal accession negotiations did not begin until 2005, and it is unlikely that Turkey will be able to complete the full accession process before 2020.

What is holding up Turkey's coveted EU membership? Its continued sparring over the divided status of Cyprus (an EU member since 2004) exacerbates the tension. (The European Union requires Turkey to fully open its ports to Cypriot shipping, a demand that Ankara has said it will meet only after the European Union starts direct trade with the Turkish Cypriot community that resides in the northern region of Cyprus under Turkish control.) Additionally, member states have expressed concerns about human rights in Turkey, especially its troubled record on freedoms of speech. Sections of the Turkish penal code, which place significant limits on citizens' right to speak openly about ethnicity and nationality, have been particularly concerning, as authors have been charged for violating this law in both fiction and nonfiction alike. The role of the military in Turkey's constitution and civil administration also opens Ankara to criticism. In an effort to acquire EU membership, Turkey's parliament has enacted some reforms that could have favorable outcomes for the respect of human rights: military judges have been removed from civilian courts, longer prison terms have been established for those guilty of torture, and barriers preventing prosecutors from easily muting unpopular voices within government have been removed. Most significant, the parliament has also banned the use of capital punishment during peacetime. Many within Turkey are growing weary of the demands for change coming from the European Union, and believe that the republic will likely be permanently excluded from EU membership because of the Union's status as a "Christian Club," as elaborated by former EU Commission president Jacques Delors. Opinion polls within Turkey show that support for EU membership is waning. Turkey may provide a good study of both how some domestic decisions are influenced by the desire to acquire membership in broader associations, as well as the difficulties in expansion and absorption of new members from the perspective of multilateral organizations.

The United Nations

Among the myriad international organizations that exist in the twenty-first century, the United Nations, founded in the immediate aftermath of World War II, stands alone as the most universally recognized. Its goal, as stated in the UN Charter, is intricately tied to the period from which it grew: to "save succeeding generations from the scourge of war." Its predecessor, the League of Nations, a product of World War I, was largely unsuccessful in reaching this goal, as World War II broke out within two decades of its establishment. While the causes of the League's failures are still hotly debated, many have identified one of its key weaknesses as the granting of equal voice to every member state. This, some argue, failed to accurately reflect differences in power and influence. Today's United Nations comprises 192 member states, following the admission of Montenegro in 2006, and its organizational structure gives greater influence to some countries than others—an issue we will return to later. The main headquarters of the UN are in New York City, with principal offices in Geneva (headquarters of offices for human rights and disarmament), Vienna (headquarters of offices for drug-abuse monitoring, criminal justice, peaceful uses of outer space, and trade law), and Nairobi (headquarters of offices on human settlements and environmental programs). Through its committees, agencies, assemblies, and related organizations, the United Nations gathers leaders to debate and define policy goals, set standards, and monitor compliance with internationally agreed programs in pursuit of its overarching goal—to promote the peaceful resolution of conflict throughout the world.

The UN Charter, signed in 1945, outlines the principles of COLLECTIVE SECURITY, state sovereignty, and the equal rights of SELF-DETERMINATION of all peoples. Collective security embodies the concept that states can impede an aggressor state by binding together in a cooperative framework. The goal of such action is to prevent conflict, but if conflict does occur, aggression is met with a united force of collaborators. It is a tactic that combines the pooled resources and power of united countries, seemingly indicative of "world opinion," with the threat to use force if security and peace are threatened. During the Cold War, collective security took a back seat to the old power politics the UN was designed to replace; the one collective security action was that taken in Korea from 1950 to 1953, made possible only because the Soviet Union boycotted the Security Council to protest the exclusion of the People's Republic of China from the United Nations. The force was commanded by a US general whose orders came from Washington rather than the United Nations per se. The operation of collective security was more evident in action taken following Iraq's invasion of Kuwait in 1990, when the powerful, veto-wielding, permanent members of the Council all acquiesced in agreement to combat the invasion. Again, though, this action must be viewed only as a limited example of collective security, especially given the commanding role of the United States during the war. The doctrine of self-determination, although incompletely applied, has been an important force for non-Western peoples within the United Nations. In a nutshell, the concept embodies the belief that all peoples of the world have the right to rule themselves, rather than being ruled by external, colonial powers. The processes of decolonization, spearheaded by African and Asian representatives to the UN, led to the peaceful independence of many states, especially in the 1950s and 1960s. However, as discussed in Chapter 4, the remnants of colonialism, including the vestiges of imperial governments, continued well into the twentieth century. Chapter XI of the UN Charter establishes a pivotal role for member states regarding "non-self-governing territories." Members of the United Nations have a responsibility to assist in the establishment of self-government where it does not yet exist. The independence of Namibia in 1990 is one of the most unusual cases of UN-supervised decolonization. Formerly known as South West Africa, the territory was placed under the responsibility of the United Nations, rather than being given status as a member state, in 1950, after South Africa refused to administer the territory as it previously had under the League of Nations system. More recently, this aspect of the Charter has enabled the United Nations to assist in the development of newly self-governing states, such as East Timor (now known as Timor-Leste), which achieved its independence from Indonesia in 2002. Currently, less than twenty non-self-governing territories remain under the tutelage of a United Nations member state, with the United Kingdom and the United States as the dominant administering authorities.

One of the most important General Assembly resolutions passed in the United Nations is the 1948 UNIVERSAL DECLARATION OF HUMAN RIGHTS (UDHR). The development and acceptance of this document have helped to promote a wide-ranging body of human rights law, including treaties that recognize economic, social, cultural, political, and civil rights. Articles 1 and 2 of the Universal Declaration state that "all human beings are born equal in dignity and rights" and are entitled to rights "without distinction of any kind such as race, color, sex, language, religion, political or other opinion, national or social origin, property, birth or other status." Through its committee structure, fact-finding missions, international conferences, and advocacy, the UN attempts to promote these ideals in all of its work.

Organization of the United Nations. The main structures within the United Nations include the General Assembly, the Security Council, the Economic and Social Council (ECOSOC), and the International Court of Justice (ICJ), the principal judicial organ. The General Assembly, in which each member state is represented, makes recommendations in the form of nonbinding resolutions. Some committees of the UN write reports analyzing the implementation of standards and solutions, or propose new organizations to monitor situations. The main aim of the UN is to promote consensus, and this work is achieved through the laborious and detailed processes of drafting resolutions that have the support of a plurality of state representatives. Although all nonbudgetary resolutions in the General Assembly are nonbinding, they highlight steps that governments should take to resolve conflict and promote peace and prosperity, and elements of resolutions are often incorporated into the national laws of the supporting countries. The General Assembly is the most procedurally democratic arm of the United Nations, since each state gets one vote, irrespective of size, power, or prestige. From the speeches and debates within the General Assembly, we can ascertain a great deal about the voice of world opinion.

One of the most visible agencies of the UN is the Security Council, which can initiate binding action, including final approval of the General Assembly's choice of SECRETARY-GENERAL, the chief administrative officer of the United Nations. Additionally, the Security Council recommends states for membership to the General Assembly. The Secretary-General, referred to by some as the "punchbag in chief,"[9] is appointed by the General Assembly on the recommendation of the Security Council for a five-year, renewable term. Since 1946, half of the Secretaries-General have come from countries in the third world: U Thant, of Burma, who served from 1961 to 1971; Javier Pérez de Cuéllar, of Peru, from 1982 to 1991; Boutros Boutros-Ghali, of Egypt, from 1992 to 1996; and Kofi Annan, of Ghana, who led the organization from 1997 to 2006. Ban Ki-moon, a former South Korean minister of foreign affairs and trade, became the eighth Secretary-General of the United Nations in January 2007, and the second man from Asia to hold this post.

As the name implies, the Security Council is designed to deal with threats to peace and security. It convenes a meeting at the call of any member state that feels threatened or violated, and it often summons representatives of conflicting sides to present their case to the chamber. Representatives on the Security Council are often required to make very rapid decisions that carry great weight. In circumstances determined to constitute "threats to the peace, breaches of the peace, or acts of aggression," as defined by CHAPTER VII of the UN Charter, the Security Council can order binding action, including economic sanctions or the use of armed force. In the post–Cold War era, the Security Council has been more activist, especially in terms of peacekeeping and humanitarian issues.

There are two sets of countries that sit in the Security Council. Reflective of their strength, the five post–World War II powers—the United States, the Soviet Union, the United Kingdom, France, and China—were given permanent, veto-power seats in the Security Council.[10] These countries are known as the permanent five members (P-5). This privileged position was given to the powerful countries of the mid-1940s to recognize their importance at the time of the UN's birth, a lesson taken from the experiment with the League of Nations. Granting these countries a veto over substantive (not procedural) matters bestows on them a tremendous amount of power; a single no-vote by any of these five countries will halt any action taken by the Security Council. Members' use of their veto power has fluctuated across time, with vetoes being used much more frequently to block action during the Cold War than since the 1990s. The most frequent invoker of the veto has been Russia (formerly the Soviet Union), with 124 vetoes from 1946 to 2008. The United States ranks second in its use of vetoes, registering 82 since 1946. China has used vetoes the least, tallying only 6 since 1946.[11] Yet even if the veto is rarely used today, the threat of its action can certainly change policy proposals and influence the topics that are brought to the Security Council for discussion. It is a powerful tool that the vast majority of member states do not have, nor are they likely to have in the future.

The second group within the Security Council consists of ten other states, elected by the General Assembly on a temporary, two-year rotating basis, without veto power. Some voices, within both the Western and the non-Western world, argue that this structure is outdated and needs to be modified, both to more accurately reflect the balance of power in today's world, and to be more representative of non-Western countries. As *The Economist* put it, "An increasingly unrepresentative, anachronistic Security Council speaks with diminishing authority."[12] Western countries dominate its membership. Most glaringly, no Muslim-majority country has a lasting seat within this powerful chamber—Turkey and Indonesia are consistently raised as the most likely claimant of the so-called Muslim seat on the Security Council. Former Secretary-General Kofi Annan, among others, frequently called for increasing the size of the Security Council to give it more diversity and a stronger voice for developing nations. According to the proposals, an enlarged Security Council could include a permanent seat from each region of the developing world, including, for example, permanent (nonveto) positions for Africa, Asia, and Latin America to be rotated among states in these regions. Currently, there is a regional focus to the election of nonpermanent members; five are elected from Africa and Asia combined, one from Eastern Europe, two from Latin America, and two from Western Europe and other areas. Another proposal for a larger Security Council could include permanent states irrespective of regions. Brazil, Germany, and Japan are the states most often cited, because of their realized or potential economic strength, although US president Barack Obama expressed his support for India's permanent representation on the Security Council during his visit to India in November 2010 (much to the surprise of many). Germany and Japan also argue that they contribute more financially to the UN than Russia, China, Great Britain, and France, making them deserving of a more permanent voice in the UN's chamber of power. The challenge is crafting a Council that is "large enough to be representative, but small enough to do business."[13]

Any change in the makeup of the Security Council will require an amendment to the UN Charter (which has happened only twice since 1945), and is likely to take a long time. Gaining the approval of the current P-5 is only the first step, to be followed by approval and ratification by two-thirds of all UN member states. In addition to P-5 concerns, opposition to Security Council enlargement also comes from less powerful states that are not currently represented in the Security Council, but that fear the power such a change could give to their adversaries. Pakistan, for example, opposes any proposal that might give India a role. Iran favors an increase in geographic representation, but wants to limit the exercise of veto power. Argentina, Bangladesh, Malaysia, and Egypt oppose any new members to the Security Council—often because they do not favor particular candidates for this new membership. The number of competing reform proposals, and the fierceness of both support and opposition for these plans, demonstrate the power of the Security Council as well as widespread distrust of a group that increasingly operates behind closed doors. At best, today's Security Council represents the world power structure as it was in 1945, heavily favoring the victors of World War II in an institution designed to give equal voice to all states. At worst, it is an enduring legacy of big-power politics that operates without systematic input from the majority of people whom it is designed to serve.

Both supporters and critics commonly discuss the need for UN reform. Within the UN system, advocates point to the need to modify structures and operating procedures to accommodate the increased membership, mandate, and visibility of the services the organization provides. In just over sixty years, membership mushroomed from 50 original member states to 192, with very few fundamental changes in between. Trying to create a unified, efficient, and streamlined approach to the wide variety of crises (political, humanitarian, environmental, and others) to which the United Nations responds, proves difficult, as each situation has unique needs and vulnerabilities. The committee charged with reviewing UN operations—convened by the Secretary-General himself—has concluded that UN programs and responses are often "fragmented and weak," lacking the capacity to enforce plans and proposed solutions.[14] After a series of high-profile blunders, including an "oil for food" scandal that reached all the way to former Secretary-General Kofi Annan, all agree that stricter financial management within the organization is necessary. The problems associated with being a consensus-driven body can also impede the work of the organization, as was seen in the Geneva-based Human Rights Commission, which was replaced by a smaller Human Rights Council in 2006. The new council includes a process for reviewing the human rights situation in all countries that are members of the General Assembly, and selects its members through a simple-majority vote of all Assembly members rather than by approving regional slates as in the past. These changes were designed to help minimize the presence of human rights violators on the council, and counter their ability to avoid criticism by gaining a seat. The new council also meets throughout the year—rather than the six-week session of the old Human Rights Commission—as a way to respond to crises and highlight the continuous importance of human rights protection.

Another area of controversy within the United Nations surrounds its expanding mandate to take action in countries in the name of humanitarian relief or responsibility to protect. One of the fundamental questions plaguing UN strategies is the hot topic of intervention: When and how should a global body respond to crises in another state's affairs? Since the end of the Cold War, the United Nations has increased its activism, first in military opposition to the Iraqi invasion of Kuwait, and later with involvement in internal conflicts in the former Yugoslavia, Somalia, Cambodia, El Salvador, the Democratic Republic of Congo, and East Timor, among others. The fundamental right to sovereignty of all states—the almost sacred principle upon which the United Nations is based—is enshrined in the UN Charter. State leaders who resist UN action in their countries predictably invoke this principle, which helps explain why there has been no UN response to humanitarian crises in Tibet (due to China's objection) or Chechnya (over Russia's opposition). It has also plagued the crafting of an effective response to the ongoing crisis in Darfur, which we discuss later.

As a large, global body consisting of representatives from almost every country of the world, what can the United Nations realistically accomplish, in addition to providing a forum for discussion and diplomatic solutions to problems? The primary modes of influence available to UN actors include censure, economic sanctions, and intervention, either with or without military backing. These actions are permissible under Chapter VII of the UN Charter, which authorizes the Security Council to take enforcement measures to either maintain or restore international peace and security. During the Cold War, Chapter VII provisions were invoked twice: to impose economic sanctions on the white minority regime in southern Rhodesia in 1965, and to impose an arms embargo against the South African apartheid regime in 1977. The latter set of sanctions is now viewed as the most comprehensive package implemented under Chapter VII provisions. They were lifted with the end of apartheid in 1994.

Sanctions imposed under Chapter VII authority have been a more common tool in the post–Cold War era. They have been invoked against Iran, Iraq, the former Yugoslavia, Libya, Haiti, Côte d'Ivoire, Liberia, Rwanda, Somalia, Angola, Sudan, and Sierra Leone, with consideration of sanctions in many other cases. Sanctions can be either mandatory (all member states face risk of punishment if they do not comply) or voluntary. Their imposition is nearly always controversial, because they risk harming ordinary citizens more than powerful leaders. In their favoritism of one group over another, they can prolong and deepen existing conflict. In Bosnia, for example, economic sanctions tied the hands of the Bosnian Muslims while the Bosnian Serbs were being rearmed by Serbia. Sanctions can also worsen already difficult situations faced by civilian populations. In part due to the widespread recognition of the human toll of sanctions against Iraq from August 1990 to March 2003, the Council approaches sanctions and their utility with great caution. Since the mid-1990s the United Nations has applied more selective or targeted sanctions, banning financial transactions, travel, or arms trade in an attempt to bring countries in line with the desires of the international community.

Peacekeeping operations. The term "United Nations" often conjures an image of the so-called peacekeepers—the people who wear the famous "blue hats." Yet the processes of "keeping the peace" in areas marred by conflict have fundamentally changed. As the plan was originally designed in the late 1940s, soldiers participating in PEACEKEEPING OPERATIONS (PKOs) were supposed to keep warring parties separated, provide monitors between former combatants, or guarantee a cease-fire, as they did in the first UN peacekeeping mission, designed to observe the Arab-Israeli truce in 1948. (Peacekeeping is a much more elaborate process than peacemaking, which is viewed as bringing the warring parties to agreement. Ideally, but not always, peacekeeping forces pick up where the peacemakers leave off.) Peacekeeping troops can fight only if attacked, and they can remain only as long as all warring parties agree to their presence.

Before we discuss their tasks, let's clarify who the peacekeepers are. The UN Department of Peacekeeping Operations coordinates the work of approximately 124,000 uniformed personnel globally, serving in fifteen operations on four continents as of early 2011 (this represents a ninefold increase in PKO troops since 1999, and more responses are always on the horizon).[15] Since 2006, the United States has been the largest deployer of UN-mandated forces, a trend that is likely to continue past 2011, as President Obama pledged an additional 30,000 troops in late 2009.[16] The United States is followed by Pakistan and Bangladesh as the next largest troop contributors. PKO forces are also often drawn from regional groups, in the attempt to avoid aggravating conflict by inviting "outsiders" into local conflicts. Some have proposed increasing the contingency of so-called regional cops, which are funded internationally but sanctioned by the United Nations to enforce Security Council mandates. They could provide the legitimacy of the international community but place the onus on self-interested, local agents.

The United Nations has supported sixty-three peacekeeping operations since 1948, with prominent PKO missions responding in Haiti, Sudan, the Democratic Republic of Congo, East Timor, and Cyprus. Peacekeepers have also been involved in the coordination of administrations in Kosovo (where they operate parallel to the North Atlantic Treaty Organization [NATO], which handles military matters). Responsibilities placed on the individuals who don the blue helmets of the United Nations, a color explicitly chosen because it is not worn in combat, are likely to increase in the future.

Yet peacekeeping has become a dangerous business, especially in immediate postconflict situations, when the presence of peacekeepers is largely unwelcome. For example, following the 1999 election in East Timor, a UN-sponsored relief office in West Timor was stormed by angry crowds, and the bodies of three UN workers (from the United States, Croatia, and Ethiopia) were burned in the streets. The United Nations and international diplomats expressed disappointment in the outcome of the trials for these deaths, as the accused were tried for "mob violence resulting in death" rather than manslaughter. This was particularly disturbing after the defendants openly admitted complicity in the aid workers' deaths, expressing national pride rather than remorse.[17]

In addition to the danger, peacekeepers often have a limited mandate. In 1995, Dutch peacekeepers stood helplessly by in Srebrenica, Bosnia, as Serbs murdered thousands of Muslim men and boys. And the mostly Belgian UN force pulled out of Rwanda at the start of the genocide in 1994, after a number of their own were killed. PKO missions are limited by financial constraints as well. Many states demonstrate a tremendous lack of commitment, especially financial, refusing to pay even when they vote to authorize a mission. The United States shoulders much of the blame in this regard: even though it has long been the single largest financial contributor to the UN, it has also, since the 1990s, refused to pay a significant portion of its PKO dues, pressing for reforms instead.[18] The trend is just beginning to reverse: timely payment of dues to international organizations was one of Obama's campaign promises, although he faces resistance in the US Senate. While some see bureaucratic waste, others see efficient investment. As Ambassador Susan Rice, the US permanent representative to the United Nations, claims: "If the US was to act on its own—unilaterally—and deploy its own forces in many of these countries, for every dollar that the United States would spend, the UN can accomplish the mission for twelve cents."[19]

Another common problem is that the presence of peacekeepers can give citizens a false sense of security, while the forces themselves lack the real power to intervene (or bring new problems with them). As a devastating outbreak of cholera ravaged crisis-weary Haiti in mid-2010, serious allegations—initially rebuffed by the UN—charged PKO forces as responsible for the disease. As this book went to press, Secretary-General Ban Ki-moon had ordered an investigation after it was revealed that participating soldiers (from Nepal) had not been tested for cholera prior to their deployment.[20] An even darker side of PKOs is emerging, as troops have been implicated in charges of sexual exploitation, human trafficking, and abuse. UN officials call the sexual violence in Congo the worst in the world.[21] PKOs are impotent at best, complicit at worst: "Despite more than 10 years of experience (in Congo) and billions of dollars, the peacekeeping force still seems to be failing at its most elemental task: protecting civilians."[22] Unfortunately, the debacle involving the impotence of UN forces in Congo (during which women in their eighties were repeatedly gang-raped while peacekeepers were deployed nearby) seems to reflect a pattern of neglect throughout Africa as well. One observer has called Congo "the U.N.'s crowning failure" and "the African equivalent of Afghanistan" because of the conflict's violence and complexity.[23]

These challenges within peacekeeping operations are related to UN interventions more generally. The UN and related agencies need better staffing and processes in order to collect information and respond to, even potentially prevent, outbursts of violence that require international action. Following the crisis in Rwanda in 1994, former Secretary-General Annan (who was at the time of the genocide the head of the UN's peacekeeping office), repeatedly argued for the need for better intelligence-gathering. While increased intelligence capacity might be necessary, many view this assertion by Annan (which Bill Clinton supported) to be a halfhearted attempt to excuse the explicit decision not to take action in Rwanda even after evidence of the coming genocide was made available to the Secretary-General. If peacekeeping missions need anything, critics argue, it is better equipment, common training for interoperability, and updated maps: UN troops got into trouble when they became lost in Sierra Leone's countryside and their radios did not work.

One comprehensive strategy, suggested by Francis Deng, the Secretary-General's Special Adviser for the Prevention of Genocide, comprises three phases: monitoring developments to draw early attention to an impending crisis; interceding in time to avert the crisis through diplomatic initiatives; and mobilizing international action when necessary. Ideally, problems should be addressed and solved within domestic frameworks, with international involvement only after the failure of internal efforts. In some cases, where the consequences of delay are grave, the international community may need to act earlier. But crisis-induced reactions are often more symbolic than effective in addressing the causes of conflict, as we've learned from Somalia and elsewhere. External intervention is a major intrusion. Though some will welcome it because of the promise of tangible benefits, we should expect peacekeepers to encounter resistance on grounds of national sovereignty or pride, so the justification for intervention must be reliably persuasive, if not beyond reproach. Deng says that the difference between success and failure is the degree of spontaneous acceptance or rejection by the local population.[24]

Another struggle in responding to crises is the lack of a streamlined process that allows for quick and efficient action. Currently, only after the Security Council has authorized an intervention, and only after the host country has agreed to that intervention, can the Secretary-General and General Assembly then begin assembling a collection of troops from countries that volunteer them. The requirement for host-country authorization is at least partly to blame for Sudan's long refusal to allow African Union troops to be replaced by UN peacekeeping forces, even though hybrid forces were also proposed for consideration. Many have highlighted the need for a trained army ready for emergency intervention. One proposal calls for a rapid reaction force that would be composed of up to 15,000 personnel, including military, police, medics, and conflict transformation specialists, and could be ready to deploy within forty-eight hours of Security Council authorization. Standby units have long been discussed within the United Nations, but their actualization has taken on greater urgency following the Rwandan genocide and the continuing crisis in Darfur.[25] While concerns surround the creation, maintenance, and potential misuse of such a force, recent intervention failures may be enough to overcome past objections.

Additionally, as mentioned, there is a growing sense among many that some issues, particularly the most egregious violations of human rights, require humanitarian intervention by the world community. The United Nations has been one of the most active organizations in coordinating the implementation of, and transition

Figure 17.1   Genocide in Rwanda . . . and Darfur?

A clear-cut case of genocide took place in Rwanda in the 1990s, during which the international community made a deliberate decision not to intervene to halt the conflict. The UN pulled its limited troops out of the region in April 1994 after Belgian peacekeepers were killed—and just as the genocide was beginning. By the time it was over, more than 800,000 people were dead. Within the United Nations, the United States blocked a proposal for further UN intervention, even though Nigeria, Tanzania, and Ghana each offered to send peacekeepers to the region. Bill Clinton's response was that the United States would send troops to peacekeeping missions only if they were limited in scope: the UN could not get involved in every dispute.[26]

This case is appalling not only in its numbers, but also in the speed with which the mass murders were conducted; perhaps 250,000 of Rwanda's Tutsi were murdered in just over two weeks, in what may accurately be termed the "fastest genocide rate in recorded history."[27] One scholar estimates that the daily killing rate during the Rwandan genocide was five times that of the Nazi death camps.[28] The UN's commanding general in Rwanda claimed that the presence of 5,000 well-armed troops could have saved many of these lives. Or, had the United Nations Assistance Mission for Rwanda (UNAMIR), which was confined to the capital city Kigali, been reinforced and expanded, as the government of Belgium initially requested (and the United States and Britain blocked), many believe the genocide could have been averted.

Apparently, willingness to act is exactly what's missing yet again when it comes to Africa. This time the killing is in Darfur, in the dry reaches of western Sudan. Again, the casualties are mostly "African" civilians, and the killings are committed mostly by the "Arab" Janjaweed militia (the term *janjaweed* translates roughly as "devils on horseback"), which is supported by the Sudanese government. A rebel group launched an attack on a government installation in early 2003, claiming to represent the interests of the marginalized African farmers of the mostly Fur and Zaghawa ethnic groups. The government's response, which included turning the Janjaweed loose to terrorize African populations, has been draconian. The rapes and murders of Africans of all ages by their Arab assailants are often reportedly accompanied by racist slurs and even branding. Interestingly, as in Rwanda, it matters little to the killers that they and their victims share the same religion (in Darfur, the overwhelming majority of the population is Muslim).

While most reports on the conflict would have us believe that it is an ethnic or racial divide that fuels the violence, the roots of the conflict are complex, involving disputes over resources and power-sharing as much as anything else. Not all the Arabs Darfuris are bad and not all the African Darfuris are good: some Arabs have refused to take part in the carnage and have themselves been victimized. The African rebel groups have turned on each other, with many innocents caught in between. No one really knows how many people have been killed, although a common estimate runs to approximately 300,000 (with 2.7 million more displaced throughout the country or taking refuge in neighboring Chad and the Central African Republic).

Three hundred thousand dead does not quite add up to genocide, according to a United Nations report. While the investigators allowed that "genocidal acts" may have been committed in Darfur, and some atrocities may be based "in genocidal intent," in this crucial report the UN basically gave itself a pass (in terms of responsibility for action). "African solutions for African problems" became a convenient mantra, as the entire matter was turned over to the newly formed (and inadequately funded) African Union. A total of 7,000 African Union peacekeepers were sent to monitor the situation—in a territory the size of France. Meanwhile, an interesting mix of private actors (including conservative Christians, MTV, and an array of Hollywood activists) were finally able to rally enough world opinion to persuade the leaders of the UN Security Council that there could be political consequences if they continued to ignore what so many had come to see as the first genocide of the twenty-first century.

It is due to the pressure of world opinion that a hybrid UN-AU operation of 22,000 has

Figure 17.1 continues

Figure 17.1 continued

finally hunkered down in Darfur, attempting to do what earlier peacekeeping operations could not. Since 2007, the International Criminal Court has issued arrest warrants (including one for genocide) for President Omar al-Bashir and several others on both sides of the conflict. For years now, various peace deals seeking to end the conflict in Darfur have been struck and then set aside. Meanwhile, the rebel armies have splintered, making it all the more difficult to corral the interested parties into a comprehensive peace that adequately deals with conflicting demands regarding power-sharing, compensation for injuries, and security guarantees. Although the fighting in Darfur has continued (and escalated in 2010), the world's attention has turned largely elsewhere in Sudan, from the west to the south. There, everyone is waiting to see if a 2005 peace deal that ended another, much longer war (one in which 2 million, mostly civilians, died) will hold long enough to result in the July 2011 independence of Africa's newest state, the Republic of South Sudan. While our focus shifts to the south, Darfur becomes "the forgotten war"—but remains chaotic, dangerous, and unresolved.[29]

beyond, humanitarian response teams. No longer is the United Nations a neutral arbiter along buffer zones. The defining point it faces now is a clearer, more universal acceptance of its new role, particularly in response to emerging needs. Two of the most prominent examples of humanitarian intervention by UN peacekeeping forces came in response to Saddam Hussein's attacks against ethnic Kurds in Iraq, and Slobodan Milosevic's attacks against ethnic Albanians in Kosovo (the latter mission was later abandoned after NATO launched a war campaign). Yet there is a disturbing pattern of neglect and inaction in other cases. In Sierra Leone, for example, the UN ignored the conflict for far too long, and then tried to broker a peace deal on the cheap by forcing what has come to be called the "see no evil" treaty down the government's throat. This plan, condemned by Mary Robinson and the UN Human Rights Commission, gave high-ranking cabinet positions control of the diamond fields and AMNESTY to the Revolutionary United Front (RUF), known for its "Operation Leave No Living Thing" and trademark mass amputations. To add injury to insult, the UN then sent in a handful of temporary cops, who managed to get themselves captured and held hostage by one of the parties to the peace treaty. The painfully slow response by the United Nations to what some consider genocide in Darfur most pointedly calls into question the international community's sincerity when it said "never again."

The need for a coordinated international intervention arises, according to one point of view, because powerful nations do not have direct interests at stake, and are therefore unwilling to get involved. There is often a delay, during which time rebel forces may try to "finish the job" before "outsiders" arrive. Humanitarian intervention, especially, requires distinguishing between the "good guys" and the "bad guys," and it is not always clear which side is the most deserving of support. Sometimes intervention can strengthen the weaker side, giving it little incentive to compromise and prolonging the conflict that troops were sent to end. As we have seen in many cases, noble intentions can lead to disastrous consequences, especially if they are not backed up with sufficient international determination, including military force, finances, and the willingness to stay until the problem, sometimes intractable, is solved. To underscore the complexities surrounding these issues, in Figures 17.1 and 17.2

Figure 17.2   The Timorese Referendum for Independence

Indonesia occupied East Timor for almost twenty-five years following its military invasion of the former Portuguese colony in 1975. In 1998 the newly appointed interim leader of Indonesia, President B. J. Habibie, indicated he might grant some flexibility in the consideration of a referendum on East Timor's status. Facing minimal pressure from Australian prime minister John Howard, Habibie announced in January 1999, much to the disdain of his military commanders, that the vote would take place sooner rather than later. His announcement was met with immediate opposition in his own country, on the part of military leaders and ordinary citizens alike. The UN supported the election, with a great deal of assistance from Portugal as well, during which the East Timorese voted overwhelmingly in favor of independence. The response by Indonesian militia was brutal. Almost half (some say three-fourths) of the population was displaced, as many people were rounded up and sent to refugee camps in West Timor (400,000 of 825,000 residents). There were accounts of widespread rape and torture. Facing threats from the United States and the United Kingdom that they would halt future arms sales indefinitely,

and block millions of dollars of support from the International Monetary Fund, Indonesia submitted to the presence of a UN peacekeeping operation, under Australian command. The peacekeeping portion of the operation, which attempted to create and sustain an entire civilian administration in a region that has long been unstable, was rife with problems from the beginning. In September 2000 three UN refugee workers were killed in West Timor, where over 100,000 refugees remained more than a year after the referendum. This violence forced the evacuation of hundreds of other workers because of security concerns. After East Timor, which later changed its name to Timor-Leste, achieved its formal independence in May 2002, the final UN support mission in East Timor withdrew in May 2005, replaced by an integrated peacekeeping operation to support the government. Its mandate has been extended annually since 2008 to assist in the capacity building of this young, fast-growing state, and UN peacekeepers are scheduled to depart in 2011. Although Timor-Leste made *Foreign Policy*'s list of "most failed states" in 2010, it was referenced as "the most uplifting story on this dismal list," with declining violence and hope on the horizon.[30]

we briefly discuss two cases of UN intervention: one mission in which the PKO was shut down precisely at the dawn of tragedy, and another mission that was sent in following a UN-sponsored referendum for independence.

Most of the problems with PKOs are exacerbated by the fact that we ask peacekeepers today to do much more than their original mandate—they are called on to clear landmines, monitor elections, seize weapons, enforce international law, contain violence, protect civilians, supervise postwar reconstruction, and arrest war criminals.[31] Peacekeepers have been placed in charge of disarmament operations as well, a mix of policing and military operations that is untenable at best. Where is the line between keeping the peace and quelling unrest? Increasingly, peacekeepers are forced to walk this dangerous line. The accumulation of tasks by PKO forces has been challenged by both the financiers of the missions, but more importantly by the recipients of the action, who often have little if any say in operations in their own country. The other view is that humanitarian interventions smack of imperial control because of the particularistic politics that are involved in each case. "Humanitarian" may sound well and good, but these interventions are also designed to achieve political objectives.[32] Such actions for the international community are taken in uncharted territory, and often have unintended effects. As we have seen, peacekeeping and humanitarian intervention can clearly make a bad situation worse.

Some interventions have exacerbated or prolonged crises, since they diffuse the specific interests that foreign powers, such as France or the United States, seek to project or protect. While participants ostensibly need to be impartial, the longer multinational forces stay, the greater the danger of loss of impartiality and therefore effectiveness in carrying out their mandate. Mission mandates need to be clear and achievable: an imprecise mandate is a recipe for confusion and a worsening of the crisis. Often the immediate purpose of humanitarian interventions is to deliver relief. But to have a lasting impact, such missions must move beyond Band-Aids to promote more substantive change, which can be a massive undertaking.

Lasting peacekeeping also includes state reconstruction, a focus that was ignored in Rwanda after efforts failed so miserably in Somalia. In a sense, peacekeepers are asked to engage in a complex process of engineering, including the preventive work that could be done by other agencies within the UN. Societies torn apart by strife need a comprehensive approach that pays more attention to the conditions that led to the crisis in the first place. Also, peacekeeping efforts especially need to encourage the rebuilding of CIVIL SOCIETY, which, as discussed in Chapter 10, emerges rather than being created. The processes of peacekeeping need to provide protections for minority groups and individuals, as well as reassure people that it is acceptable to express opinions without fear of reprisal. The RULE OF LAW, or the impartial and universal application of legal norms, must gradually prevail. A lesson we have learned from mistakes in past operations is that we cannot rush to elections: nascent parties need time to consolidate, form platforms, and present them to voters. In addition there is a huge need to defuse armed movements, which is a controversial undertaking and difficult to implement. When major portions of the society feel unsafe, they are unlikely to surrender their sometimes only means of defense to outside intruders in the name of "making the peace." Otherwise it will be easy for disenchanted groups to reject election results, with or without violent means, and voters will have little choice but to vote on the basis of ethnic or religious identity. Elections held under the wrong conditions can be a real setback for democratization.[33]

The United Nations and social development. In recent years the crisis-response aspect of the United Nations has received much of the limelight. The world community, however conflicted, has strongly voiced its conviction that governments (and agents acting in the name of governments) may be held accountable for actions within their own borders. The UN and its agencies have also been at the forefront of attempts to promote international law and universal principles. Since its inception in 1945, a key aspect of the United Nations has been its promotion of peace through programs designed to enhance the well-being and development of the world's population. One aspect of social development it has attempted to tackle is child neglect and abuse. Many children are forced to forgo daytime educational opportunities to make money on city streets, shining shoes, washing cars, or collecting recyclables. Educational programs under the auspices of the United Nations Children's Fund (UNICEF) allow these street children to receive an education in the evenings. As discussed in Chapters 6 and 10, child labor is a huge (and complex) problem in the third world.

The Convention on the Rights of the Child (CRC), adopted in 1989, is perhaps the most broadly signed convention in the world (the only two UN member states that haven't ratified it are Somalia and the United States). Establishing the standards that all civilized countries should attempt to meet in caring for their children, the CRC is comprehensive in scope, promoting four core principles: nondiscrimination; devotion to the best interests of the child; the right to life, survival, and development; and respect for the views of the child.

Among other things it calls for the protection of children from abuse and abandonment, as well as the provision of basic needs, including prenatal healthcare. The CRC urges governments to abolish prejudicial treatment of children, including treatment before they are born. Although the convention does not directly address the issue of abortion, it can be read to challenge the use of prenatal sex selection, a practice in which parents choose to abort female fetuses and carry male fetuses to full term, which is especially evident in China and India. In China, where traditional preferences and low-tech means have been accelerated by its "one child" population policy and cheap, accessible ultrasounds, preferential sex selection (before and after pregnancy) has distorted the gender ratio in the country.

The United Nations has also been a pivotal IGO in promoting the rights of women. As one example, in the 1940s, women's rights were viewed as something separate from the universal human rights of all people. Largely due to efforts of the UN and related agencies, this status changed by the 1990s to completely incorporate, in theory at least, women's rights within the notion of universally applicable human rights.[34] One of the most important documents attempting to institutionalize these ideas is the 1979 Convention on the Elimination of All Forms of Discrimination Against Women (CEDAW).

The convention, which has the force of international law, has been ratified by 186 of the member states of the United Nations and is considered to be the most wide-ranging attempt to eliminate discriminatory acts against women. Many refer to it as the "International Bill of Rights of Women," in that it establishes minimum standards for combating prejudice based on gender. It is also the only human rights treaty that affirms the reproductive rights of women. The convention recognizes that socially defined gender roles require provisions against discrimination and abuse that go beyond equal treatment of men and women. CEDAW asserts the inhumanity of torture and cruel and degrading treatment, and stresses that intimate violence is no less severe than violence committed by the state. It also focuses on the need to combat military sexual slavery, workplace abuse, and violence in the family. CEDAW condemns the use of rape as a tool to humiliate women and their communities. Of the countries on which we focus, seven have ratified the document: China (1980), Mexico (1981), Peru (1982), Indonesia (1984), Nigeria (1985), Turkey (1985), and Zimbabwe (1991). The United States joins Iran, Sudan, Somalia, Nauru, Palau, and Tonga in not yet having ratified the treaty, and is the only industrialized country in the world to hold this dubious honor. This document served as the springboard for the commencement of global conferences on women, held in Mexico City (1975), Copenhagen (1980), Nairobi (1985), and Beijing (1995). Each of these events, and meetings held to monitor the implementation of proposals from each conference, sparked a related increase in the number of women-related NGOs and networks of organizations designed to investigate and resolve issues, including marriage and reproductive rights, healthcare and educational inequities, and physical, sexual, and psychological abuse, in times of both peace and conflict, faced by women.[35] In fact, at each UN-sponsored world conference on women, a meeting in conjunction with NGO representatives was held as a way to complement the work of the conference and increase networking opportunities made available to all participants.

Activists in each country have used the force of CEDAW to accomplish varying aims. Many signatory states have altered their constitutions and national laws in order to enter into compliance with the treaty. In Nepal, CEDAW has empowered women to push for stiffer penalties for rape, as well as legislation that, for the first time, codifies women's right to inherit property. In Botswana, CEDAW was used to challenge citizenship laws under which children of a woman married to a foreigner were not considered citizens of the state (even though children of a man married to a foreigner were granted all the rights of citizenship). In Afghanistan, legislation to eliminate violence against women was based on CEDAW components, notably making rape a crime for the first time in the country's history as well as nullifying forced marriages and early marriages without consent of the female partner.[36]

In 1994 a special rapporteur on violence against women was appointed. This has enabled more direct investigation and advocacy on behalf of the rights enshrined in CEDAW. For example, the rapporteur conducts field visits to countries that have ratified CEDAW to investigate claims of breaches of the human rights of women and girls, acting as an advocate and working to ensure proper punishment. Additionally, since an optional protocol took effect in December 2000, women may bypass their national governments and complain directly to the United Nations. The most prominent case to use this optional protocol, which has been ratified by seventy-eight countries, is the inquiry into the murders of nearly 300 women in Ciudad Juárez, Mexico (whose deaths still remain a mystery).

The United Nations and justice: tribunals, truth commissions, and courts. The United Nations and other IGOs have been integral in dealing with violent legacies of states in transition and international crimes against humanity. This work demonstrates the enabling role that international organizations can play in assisting countries during transitional periods. There are two primary types of institutions designed with this type of mandate: war crimes tribunals and TRUTH COMMISSIONS.

Criminal tribunals are established nationally (and sometimes internationally), often following the breakup of a regime or the end of a war or other act of aggression. Two of the most famous such tribunals were the Nuremberg and Tokyo trials following World War II. Yet these initial tribunals, though international in name, were largely controlled by the victorious Allied powers to prosecute aggressors from the defeated Axis states.[37] War tribunals are based on the Geneva Conventions, and attempt to locate and prosecute "persons responsible for serious violations of international humanitarian law." Ad hoc international criminal tribunals have been established to investigate the war in the former Yugoslavia (operating since 1991) and the genocide in Rwanda (operating since 1997).

In March 2003 the United Nations established an international criminal tribunal to prosecute former Khmer Rouge leaders in Cambodia. Justice has been particularly slow-going in the investigations of the more than 1.7 million deaths during the 1975–1979 Khmer Rouge period. In fact, it wasn't until mid-2010 that the first senior member of the Khmer Rouge regime was sentenced (Kang Guek Eav, also known as "Duch"). He was the only one of five defendants to acknowledge guilt, admitting to overseeing the torture and killing of more than 14,000 people. Duch, who was sixty-seven years old at the time of his sentencing, will likely serve only nineteen years of his thirty-five-year sentence, even though he was convicted of both war crimes and crimes against humanity, because the tribunal took into account time already served (and he may be eligible for parole in twelve years). As many of the likely defendants enter their twilight years (and some of the most brutal Khmer Rouge leaders have already died), many fear the time for achieving any sort of justice is running out.

Tribunals are quite concrete—their goal is to investigate claims of human rights violations and atrocities, to hold trials, and to punish responsible individuals. A major part of the investigation of such tribunals includes the perusal of murder sites and purported mass graves in which aggressors attempted to conceal the evidence of their crimes. One of the difficulties faced by the Rwandan tribunal, based in Arusha, Tanzania, is the sheer number of accomplices and perpetrators of the crimes—tens and possibly hundreds of thousands—which is "beyond the capacity of any justice system to arraign and judge," in the view of one analyst.[38] Additionally, some of the accused have launched websites, inciting fear that pictures taken illegally in the courtrooms, or even the names of witnesses, could dangerously become public knowledge.[39] Because the operation of tribunals is often a very slow process, some of the accused have been released because of time limits. By 2010 the Rwandan tribunal had completed fifty trials and convicted twenty-nine persons, including the first genocide convictions under international law, such as against Jean Kambanda, the prime minister at the time of the carnage. Journalists and media employees accused of inciting hatred before and during the genocide also stand accused. But the Rwandan tribunal is not the only institution working for justice in this carnage. In April 2001, in a Belgian court, four Rwandans (a university professor, a businessman, and two nuns) were indicted for murders committed during the 1994 genocide.[40] All countries that have signed the Geneva Conventions are obligated to empower their courts with the jurisdiction to try individuals accused of torture, war crimes, and crimes against humanity. Even so, few of these countries have enacted the necessary domestic legislation.

In the Yugoslavian tribunal, rape and sexual enslavement were prosecuted as formal crimes for the first time, although Yugoslavia was hardly the first place where rape had been used as a weapon of war. At the Nuremberg trials these crimes were not included, because the organizers didn't want to hold the defendants accountable for something that they themselves could be accused of. The Yugoslavian tribunal recognized, after hearing testimony from girls as young as twelve, that rape constitutes a form of torture and should legitimately be considered a war crime and a crime against humanity. Three soldiers received sentences ranging from twelve to twenty-eight years for their crimes in the eastern Bosnian town of Foca.[41] This has been an important precedent for other tribunals, with the Rwandan tribunal being the first to convict for rape as a war crime.

For these tribunals to be established, governments must grant their approval, and oftentimes the logistics of a tribunal need to be approved by the affected national legislatures. While this can provide a lengthy hindrance to the commencement of tribunals, an opening is usually found after a change of regime or the death of an authoritarian leader. For example, a breakthrough was made in 2000 when US senator John Kerry successfully brokered an agreement between the Cambodian government and the United Nations to begin investigating the Khmer Rouge massacre. This agreement became possible only after Khmer Rouge leaders voluntarily surrendered to Cambodian authorities in 1998 and 1999. Indonesia repeatedly rejected calls to establish a tribunal for East Timor that would investigate the human rights abuses that occurred in the territory during the 1975–1999 Indonesian occupation. Former president Abdurrahman Wahid once stated that even if former general Wiranto, who is widely blamed for either ordering or failing to stop the militia violence, were convicted, he would be pardoned in the interest of maintaining national harmony. In response to widespread pressure to bring the responsible parties to justice, Indonesia established an ad hoc human rights tribunal, which has been largely dismissed as a meaningless façade. The United Nations established a Serious Crimes Investigation Unit to hear trials concerning alleged crimes against humanity in Dili, the capital of Timor-Leste, but Jakarta has virtually blocked action in this regard by refusing to extradite the accused. Although the investigatory unit has already processed more than eighty cases, it is unable to prosecute Indonesian military figures. Finally, in 2002, the Commission for Reception, Truth, and Reconciliation in East Timor was founded, and within three years it had produced a lengthy report detailing abuses, but it too has been under pressure to promote reconciliation rather than justice.

To prosecute war crimes committed in Sierra Leone's civil war since 1996, the United Nations has supported the creation of the Special Court for Sierra Leone. This court is a hybrid national and international tribunal that was established jointly by the government of Sierra Leone and the United Nations. Eleven persons associated with the three major warring factions have been indicted. They include Charles Taylor, who was arrested in 2006 after years of evading capture—living a life of luxury most of that time in Nigeria under an amnesty that ended the war. Taylor is most renowned for supporting a rebel group that drew heavily on child soldiers and regularly employed mass rapes and severing the limbs of civilians among its tactics. He and the others who have been indicted face charges of war crimes, crimes against humanity, and violations of international humanitarian law. Taylor becomes only the second former head of state ever to be charged with war crimes—second to Slobodan Milosevic, the former Serbian president who died while in custody in The Hague after five years in prison. (Sudanese president Omar Hassan al-Bashir became the first sitting head of state to receive an arrest warrant, in 2009.) A key controversy concerning this court was determining the youngest age at which a war crimes suspect could be tried. After heated debates between the government, which wanted all persons no matter their age to be tried, and UNICEF, which argued that no one under eighteen should be tried, especially because the youngest of the perpetrators were often drugged and coerced into fighting, a compromise was reached allowing the court to try persons older than fifteen. However, anyone under eighteen will be tried in a separate juvenile chamber and those found guilty will be sentenced to community service, foster care, or other forms of rehabilitation.

The initiative to establish the INTERNATIONAL CRIMINAL COURT (ICC) began in 1948 to address a need to replace ad hoc, conflict-specific tribunals with a permanent war crimes tribunal. The ICC, which entered into force July 1, 2002, does not replace national courts, but rather serves as a court of last resort when they are unwilling or unable to handle cases. The idea of such a court was tabled by superpower politics during the Cold War, but was resurrected in the early 1990s. In 1998, 160 states signed an agreement to create this permanent court (with the conspicuous exception of the United States, which has expressed concern that politically motivated cases will be brought against it). The ICC, which deals only with crimes committed after its establishment, is located in The Hague, with the International Court of Justice. (The ICJ is empowered to hear cases waged between governments, while the ICC allows individuals and groups to prosecute individuals for genocide, war crimes, and crimes against humanity. Additionally, the ICJ is a civil court, while the ICC prosecutes criminal cases.) At the ICC, established under the Rome Statute, a panel of eighteen judges hears cases—with the maximum allowable penalty of life imprisonment. The ICC is designed to put on trial not only the most notorious abusers of human rights, but their assistants and orderlies as well. In its first years, a handful of prominent indictments were handed down, the suspects all from African states: Joseph Kony, leader of the Lord's Resistance Army (LRA) in Uganda; Thomas Lubanga, former leader of the Union of Congolese Patriots militia in Ituri, Democratic Republic of Congo; and President Bashir, minister of humanitarian affairs and alleged leader of the Janjaweed militia during the atrocities committed in Darfur, Sudan. Three rebel leaders have also been summoned to appear before the court. Additionally, former Liberian president Charles Taylor was transferred to custody in the ICC in 2006 even though the trial is being held under the mandate of the Special Court for Sierra Leone. Political and security concerns about holding the trial in Freetown, Sierra Leone, prompted this move to The Hague. Now that the ICC is a permanent fixture in international law, it is hoped that Security Council politicking over the establishment of ad hoc tribunals will be averted. Already, many have noted a positive trickle-down effect from the establishment of the ICC, as national and international courts gain prominence and the immunity of corrupt leaders no longer seems absolute.[42]

Somewhat similar to international tribunals, truth commissions are designed to air grievances about past wrongs committed by individuals or groups as a way to prevent future crimes against humanity, to restore a semblance of "normalcy" after periods of unrest, and to promote a human rights culture. Yet truth commissions are different from war crimes tribunals in a few very important ways. Trials are designed to punish, and may deprive individuals of life, liberty, or property. Truth commissions vary in their aims; they often seek to promote individual and structural healing, piece together past reality, and establish a historical memory so that it can never be denied. Because they are separate from courts of law, truth commissions do not usually have the right of subpoena; they are less bound by concerns of DUE PROCESS and may admit hearsay and other forms of evidence that would be unacceptable in a war crimes tribunal.[43]

The most widely known truth commission is the Truth and Reconciliation Commission of South Africa. However, other truth commissions (some dating back to the 1970s) have been established in Haiti, Guatemala, Uganda, Bolivia, Argentina, Zimbabwe, Uruguay, Chile, Nigeria, and the Philippines. Not all truth commissions are the same, and few follow the model established in South Africa, which granted widespread amnesty to participants in exchange for their role in the investigation. Some of these commissions, such as the ones in Guatemala and El Salvador, are established under UN auspices, while others are domestic initiatives alone. Some, but not most, allow amnesties. A few truth commissions are established for the primary purpose of honoring those hurt by abuse and promoting closure, while others gather information and pass it on to courts for prosecution. Truth commissions are generally established after a civil war, or after an authoritarian government steps aside, as part of a DEMOCRATIC TRANSITION. Timor-Leste fits this description. Its truth commission, known as the Commission for Truth and Friendship, makes creative use of local customs. Those who are accused of the most serious crimes will be brought before courts, but because there are too many people to handle, the approximately 10,000 East Timorese who participated in lesser crimes with Indonesian-backed militias will come before the truth commission. Many of these people are hiding out in West Timor, afraid they might be lynched if they return home. For those who want to come home, the truth commission will bring them before local village councils. If they admit their crimes and apologize, they will be sentenced to community service. According to local custom, they will then be safe from acts of revenge.

Some critics of truth commissions characterize them as "some-of-the-truth commissions" or "Kleenex commissions" that do more harm than good. Many people resist the idea of granting amnesties to individuals who admit to committing atrocities, in return for their cooperation with the commission. The trade-off is viewed as necessary in order to allow a more complete airing of misdeeds, including public testimony that often allows victims (or their families) to confront the perpetrators of the crime. Several truth commissions have televised their proceedings. They vary over whether they provide the names of those who come forward. Despite their differences, the goal of truth commissions is to make sure that the acts of injustice cannot be ignored, even if, in the end, the commissions breach justice by "letting some people off the hook."[44] For a variety of reasons, truth commissions often face powerful resistance and need money, a broad mandate, and high-level backing if they are to succeed. South Africa's Archbishop Desmond Tutu, in his justification for amnesties in the South African trials of apartheid leaders, argued that criminal justice can be sacrificed if it leads to a greater sense of social justice.

* * *

As you can see, the tasks before the United Nations are enormous, and some may say nearly impossible to achieve. Many around the world, including leaders within the organization itself, are increasingly questioning the relevance of the United Nations, especially as powers beyond the formerly dominant United States and European states assert their role, making compromise more difficult. Secretary-General Ban Ki-moon, who is eligible to renew for one more term after December 31, 2011, has faced much criticism for leading the United Nations into an "era of decline."[45] Many question whether the most well-known IGO is "at the center of global responses" to the big problems facing the world as it moves toward "mini-lateral cooperation" of smaller coalitions of big countries instead; as one analyst put it, the UN is no longer "the only game in town."[46] Organizations such as the GROUP OF 20 (G-20), with more manageable memberships and less pomp, may actually provide more latitude for discussion and negotiation among world leaders.

As one historian (who also serves as an informal adviser for Secretary-General Ban) stated: "The U.N. is not the sun of the international solar system; everything doesn't revolve around it. But it is the final reference point on most issues, which have to come to the U.N. for legitimacy."[47]

It should be clear that international governmental organizations have played a pivotal role in the world community, sometimes fostering cooperation among governments, and other times taking action against governments that are perceived to be violating universal norms of conduct. All organizations have their limitations, and generally IGOs are constrained by the fact that they are established by governments to act in the interest of governments. This means that they are beholden to the interests and concerns of powerful elite groups, and that political agendas, as we have seen, tend to predominate over the humanitarian interests that they profess to promote. And despite the talk of inclusion and equal voting privileges for small states as well as big states, weaker governments of the third world can get caught in big-power agendas that limit their voice and ability to take action. In the end, while states participating in IGOs give up some degree of sovereignty in order to work in concert with others, that power can be snatched back when considered necessary. We now turn to another type of collaborative organization—groups of people who organize outside state authority to promote particular agendas in the global community.

International Nongovernmental Organizations

In Chapter 6 we discussed the influence of some NGOs, namely MULTINATIONAL CORPORATIONS. International NGOs are private, transnational associations of individuals or groups that organize around a shared interest or understanding, and have strong ties to civil society, which we introduced in Chapter 10. NGOs are extremely diverse, in their size, organizational structure, and range of interests. Their numbers exploded in the 1980s, to the point that many countries have thousands, if not tens of thousands, of NGOs or affiliates. Even though scarce resources for programming and advocacy present formidable obstacles to groups in the third world, NGOs have a strong presence. They include universities, civic organizations, churches, and other religious institutions. You are probably aware of many such organizations, even if you do not identify them as NGOs per se: Habitat for Humanity, the International Federation of Red Cross and Red Crescent Societies, the International Planned Parenthood Federation, Greenpeace, Oxfam, WarChild, Amnesty International, Catholic Relief Services, Lutheran World Relief, Bread for the World, Save the Children, and Goodwill Industries International are just some of the most widely recognized. These organizations are powerful in that they help countries incorporate ideas into national (and international) policies and programs. They are also vital in shaping and conveying public opinion to large gatherings of policymakers. They may be national or international in scope. NGOs are often able to open previously closed discussions or bring attention to taboo topics, including violence against women, the environmental toll of free trade, and child labor. NGOs rarely work alone. Rather, they work together with other organizations and with governments in order to promote their causes, often by hosting international meetings in conjunction with other associational conferences, such as those of the United Nations, a presence that has increased dramatically since the early 1970s.

What can NGOs accomplish that national governments cannot? NGOs such as Amnesty International have been especially critical in exposing human rights abuses and educating citizens about their rights, with less of the government interference that mars the work of peacekeeping missions. NGOs work in dangerous circumstances and under many rules, and they are often subject to retaliation. Often, these organizations voice impatience with the slow action of government-based organizations. Non-governmental organizations are less beholden to bureaucratic and electoral interests, and they have power that IGOs such as the UN, which is bound to act only on the expressed interests of its members through the Security Council, do not. Even though they are made up of individuals and interest groups, their target audience is most often the governments of countries or world opinion. Many of the issues that we have discussed throughout this book have NGOs associated with them. For example, the Global Alliance Against Traffic in Women is a wide-reaching NGO with a presence in each major region of the world. Some of the programs it has sponsored include the networking of Burmese women's groups along the tense Thai-Myanmar border, as well as the coordination of training workshops and the publication of handbooks on human rights in multiple languages. Sometimes it takes a committed group of people organized in an association independent of the government to be able to distribute such materials to groups who need them most. Human Rights First is another widely recognized NGO that works at both the grassroots and global levels to connect skilled professionals with the people who could most benefit from their expertise and resources.

One of the best-known associations of NGOs dedicated to the promotion of human rights is Amnesty International. Its success, in part, is due to a wide-reaching network of local (often university-based), national, and international offices. One of the key areas that Amnesty International focuses on is advocacy for individual political prisoners and prisoners of conscience—people who suffer persecution for their beliefs. Amnesty International has been particularly effective in targeting governments, through annual reports and policy papers that reveal violations of universal standards of human rights. Additionally, its members coordinate campaigns for the release of political prisoners throughout the world, and spearhead an international campaign against the use of capital punishment. One of this organization's greatest strengths is its work in raising the awareness of particular issues by publicly turning the spotlight on countries that abuse human rights.

Another NGO that campaigns for humanitarian issues and also works "on the ground" is the International Federation of Red Cross and Red Crescent Societies (IFRC), part of the larger International Red Cross and Red Crescent Movement, which also includes the International Committee of the Red Cross (ICRC) and the more than 180 national Red Cross and Red Crescent Societies around the world. This is a highly acclaimed and almost universally accepted set of organizations that works largely independently of governments so that it can remain impartial in handling humanitarian crises during times of both peace and war. Because the IFRC is not tied to any official government, or even to the United Nations, it can accomplish tasks or change its mandate without needing to muster the will of the international community or the consensus of multiple nation-states. Unlike the campaigning organizations discussed above, the IFRC attempts not to change opinion, but rather to take action, promoting the most universal perspective of humanity—protection and humane treatment of all individuals, even combatants wearing enemy uniforms.

The International Red Cross and Red Crescent Movement's record of humanitarian interventions is quite impressive. The complexities facing refugees, particularly related to legally defined "genuine refugees" versus "DISPLACED PERSONS," serve as a case in point. The ICRC has successfully procured legal exemptions to allow its

A woman carries her sick child to a clinic for internally displaced people in Darfur, Sudan (Reuters/Mohamed Nureldin Abdallah)

representatives to come to the aid of displaced persons in conflict-ridden areas, where other international organizations, notably those affiliated with the UN, lack jurisdiction to respond.[48] It has also been quite active in repatriating prisoners of war, including 10,000 Iraqi prisoners held in Iran.

The ICRC, based in Geneva, Switzerland, has been absolutely pivotal in promoting global cultural values, especially related to times of war. In fact, as an NGO it was a key player in the drafting and signing of the first Geneva Convention in 1864, also known as the "Red Cross Convention," which when combined with follow-up conventions provides the universally acknowledged rules of warfare. The ICRC stressed that states need to protect the worth and dignity of individuals "even when this is most difficult and costly for states."[49] It has also been instrumental in advocating the need for quality medical care, even during times of strife, and especially for the protection of medical-care providers who identify themselves in war-torn areas with the recognizable symbol of either the red cross or the red crescent.

Yet not all NGOs attempt to maintain the neutrality of the International Red Cross and Red Crescent Movement. Two NGOs that attempt to promote advocacy within particular substantive topics—medicine and journalism—irrespective of geopolitical borders, are the Paris-based associations Doctors Without Borders (Médecins sans Frontières [MSF]) and Reporters Without Borders (Reporteurs sans

Frontières [RSF]). MSF was founded in 1971—in the aftermath of the Biafran war in Nigeria—to publicly challenge the neutrality of the IFRC. The organization unites medical professionals around the world in order to provide medical training and emergency assistance, especially in areas of conflict. In 1999, MSF won the Nobel Peace Prize for its humanitarian work with victims of wars, famine, and other disasters. MSF has also been very active in refugee issues, particularly in camps and temporary settlements. MSF doctors have served in Vietnam, Lebanon, Afghanistan, Kosovo, East Timor, and elsewhere. Their work includes both prevention and treatment. For example, MSF doctors have been working with local community leaders in Nigeria in an attempt to fight malaria in the Niger Delta, where the disease is endemic. Prior to the genocide in Rwanda in 1994, individuals associated with MSF tried to make the signals of the coming onslaught known. In fact, the MSF called for a military intervention in this conflict, the first time in its history that it took this step. MSF is famous for its fierce independence, but it does not attempt to appear neutral in the face of conflict. One struggle mission participants underscore is that their provision of assistance often supports, if not outright strengthens, the cause of the crisis in the first place. Yet bound by the Hippocratic Oath of medicine, MSF doctors feel obliged to treat all human beings, irrespective of their crime or intentions.

The goal of RSF, founded in 1985, is to publicize threats to the free flow of information in an increasing number of forums, especially by highlighting the arrest and torture of journalists who suffer because of their profession. The organization uses Article 19 of the UDHR as its basis and, like many other NGOs, consults regularly with the United Nations. It publishes an annual report of press freedoms in countries around the world, highlighting the arrests, kidnappings, imprisonment, torture, and murder of journalists. Not surprisingly, many reporters suffer these fates when they investigate and attempt to report on CORRUPTION, abuse of power, or drug trafficking, especially if they highlight the complicity of politicians. More than half the member states of the United Nations impose limits on freedom of the press. Turkey is notorious for attacks on journalists, and there are many reports of media employees being tortured while in Turkish custody. In Nigeria, especially under previous regimes, journalists have been harassed, kidnapped, and subjected to other forms of pressure and obstruction for trying to cover contentious issues. According to the RSF, Iran and China are considered the biggest prisons for journalists in the world, with China holding the dubious distinction of arresting the most "Netizens" (seventy-two) in 2009, outranking Vietnam and Iran, which have each cracked down on Internet dissidents recently as well.[50]

A new direction in press freedom that RSF and other NGOs are pressing is the free flow of information on the Internet. Increasingly, many non-Western countries are imposing restrictions on communication via this channel, by installing filters that block access to websites, forcing computer users to register, or sharply limiting access for all citizens, as discussed in Chapter 10. RSF publishes annual lists of "Enemies of the Internet," which detail access restrictions as well as punitive efforts taken against individuals who use this medium to express their views.

Other NGOs promote environmental causes. The better-known environmental NGOs include the Nature Conservancy, Greenpeace, and the World Wildlife Fund. These are huge, multinational organizations with very large budgets to accomplish advocacy, education, and mobilization around environmental issues. These NGOs, even more than others, have linked arms with similar-minded organizations in networks to accomplish great feats. Greenpeace, for example, states that one of its primary goals is to stop the "chemicalization" of the planet, especially by ending the threat of nuclear weapons and nuclear power as well as other forms of "dirty" technology, and to limit ozone depletion caused by the production and use of greenhouse gases. In 2004 it launched a campaign against the Kimberly-Clark Corporation, producer of the popular Kleenex brand, for the destruction of ancient boreal forests in order to make their famously soft product. It has also been highly critical of genetically modified organisms and crops. Yet Greenpeace is also linked with other human rights and environmental organizations that promote responsive government and biodiversity. Greenpeace has offices in forty-one countries, with an especially strong presence in East Asia, Western Europe, and North America, and some presence in South America.

Churches and religious institutions are other examples of NGOs that have crossed over into multiple issue areas in order to promote human welfare. The Catholic Church, for example, is a widely recognized NGO with a high degree of activism in the third world, directly and through its many institutions. One of these is Caritas, which attempts to promote Christian ideals of social justice and charity by working with and for impoverished peoples. Like many NGOs, Caritas is part of an international-level umbrella organization, but most of its work is increasingly being conducted at the regional, even the state, level. Another religiously affiliated NGO is the International Association for Religious Freedom (IARF), which, having been established in 1900, predates many other NGOs. The goal of the IARF, which is one of many NGOs affiliated with the United Nations, is to promote the universal right of freedom of religion. The IARF includes peoples of many faiths, including Buddhists, Hindus, Humanists, Sikhs, Universalists, Christians, and indigenous peoples, in its advocacy and operation. The IARF has linked arms with many other initiatives and NGO networks, participating, for example, in the Jubilee 2000 effort to increase third world debt relief for the most impoverished nations.

NGOs have become increasingly prominent within state networks of global power and influence in recent decades. They serve a particularly prominent role within the United Nations, where they increasingly work in a consultative capacity.[51] Although NGOs are currently confined to ECOSOC committees, without any formal access to the General Assembly and its committees, there is much pressure to change this. In fact, the IFRC, the ICRC, the Inter-Parliamentary Union, and the Sovereign Military Order of Malta each have special observer rights in General Assembly sessions, and NGOs are finding ways to influence each chamber of the United Nations. Within the United Nations, NGOs cannot vote, because they do not represent a state, but they are welcomed as participants in most UN debates because of their grassroots experience and data, which states may not be able or may not have the desire to gather. As interest groups, they actively lobby delegates when the General Assembly is in session, and organize parallel meetings when the UN sponsors global conferences on special topics. They also provide connections between grassroots citizenry and international diplomatic channels that otherwise do not exist. Additionally, NGOs work with UN agencies in the field, taking on massive grassroots tasks that the overburdened and overly bureaucratized UN agencies would be less able to accomplish. For example, over 500 NGOs work with the United Nations High Commissioner for Refugees to intervene in crisis situations where refugees are involved.[52] An NGO's inclusion under consultative status, however, can be blocked by UN member states.

While we have emphasized the role of nongovernmental organizations at the international level, it should be noted that much of their work is implemented by regional and national NGOs working in concert. One of the main strengths of NGOs is their ability to foster partnerships and alliances with groups of similar interest, some civic, others government-based, in order to accomplish their goals. For example, the Inter-African Committee on Traditional Practices Affecting the Health of Women and Children, which is a network of affiliates in twenty-six African and three European countries, has worked to raise awareness of female genital cutting by concentrating on public awareness campaigns and educational opportunities in communities.

We have discussed a wide array of organizations, both national and international in scope, with differing levels of expertise and involvement. Increasingly, many question whether these organizations are necessary, or even relevant. To be sure,

---

Figure 17.3 NGOs: When Politics and Sports Mix

Another nongovernmental organization that exerts much influence on countries' behaviors is the International Olympic Committee, which decides the host country for this premier international event. Landing a spot as the host of the Olympic Games is the envy of many third world countries. Athletic events and their related organizations can also serve as a tool for multilateral international influence. As the film *Forrest Gump* humorously memorialized, it was an amateur ping-pong tournament between China and the United States that led to the commencement of formalized relations between these two countries in the early 1970s. China, for example, recently hosted the 2008 Summer Olympic Games, with much fanfare and controversy. Many openly questioned whether it was appropriate that China, a country notorious for its human rights abuses, should have the honor of hosting one of the world's major sporting events. These cries grew louder after Beijing cracked down on Tibetan rights protesters, who mobilized on the forty-ninth anniversary of the uprising against Chinese rule. The Olympic torch relay—across six continents—became a cat-and-mouse game between authorities and protesters attempting to douse the flame. There were widespread calls for a boycott against the Beijing games, which did not materialize (although film director and producer Steven Spielberg very publicly withdrew—prior to the unrest in Tibet—from his role as official artistic adviser to the Games, after being unable to persuade Chinese leaders to pressure the Sudanese government to end the violence in Darfur).[53]

Yet the sporadic inclusion of non-Western states as hosts of global sporting events reveals again how marginalized the third world can be, even in organizations that are ostensibly designed to include all of the world's citizens in nonpolitical affairs. For many non-Western states, the idea of recruiting, training, and completely sponsoring an internationally competitive sports team is an absurdity, given the financial struggles that many of these states face. Nor have such seemingly apolitical venues been immune to political struggles: South Africa was banned from the Games from 1960 until 1992 because of international response to the apartheid regime. Cold War politics also reared its ugly face at the Olympic Games. In 1980, President Jimmy Carter ordered the US Olympic team to boycott the Summer Games in Moscow to retaliate against the Soviets for their invasion of Afghanistan (in return, the Soviets boycotted the 1984 Games in Los Angeles). North Korea and Cuba both skipped the 1984 and 1988 Games as a political statement. China threatened to boycott the 1996 Games in Atlanta if it was not selected as host for the 2000 Games, and over allegations of drug use among Chinese athletes. Sometimes politics and athletics do go hand in hand.

they have both strengths and weaknesses. Perhaps, though, the increasing push from many countries, especially those within the third world, to join and become active members in these organizations, is a sign of some level of vitality. Taking the United Nations, for example, nearly every state that is eligible for membership has sought a seat in this world body—the only states that lack membership are the Vatican (which holds observer status) and several "microstates" with extremely small populations.[54] Including more voices makes things messier, but perhaps more inclusive as well. The struggle to balance representation, efficiency, and productivity takes on more urgency as the global community faces ever more complex challenges to life in the twenty-first century. It is to those issues that we now turn.

18

Global Challenges— and Responses

You cannot cut a deal with Mother Nature.
—President Mohamed Nasheed of the Maldives,
whose Indian Ocean state could be submerged by
rising waters by the end of the twenty-first century[1]

As we have discussed throughout this book, STATE borders have less salience, or meaning, than ever. Either because boundaries are more permeable, or because problems cross borders so readily, many issues take on a cross-national, even global, dimension. The question becomes, then, what are the best methods to approach these far-reaching issues? First, we take a brief look at some of the key global issues of our world today. Because of the scope and breadth of these issues, many believe that real solutions to these problems can be found only in a multilateral response, meaning the conduct of activities by three or more states. Since the 1970s, many global approaches have been designed, built on the recognition that the solutions of global problems would need the cooperation and input of the international community.

Environment

If there is a single issue that most clearly demonstrates the interconnectivity of this planet's residents, it is the issue of our global environment. Pollution, whether in the form of air, water, land, or otherwise, is not confined to artificially designed political borders. Fish swim in shared waters, moving between the sovereign areas of particular states and the universal seas. Air damaged in one region often worsens as it travels to another, irrespective of human-drawn borders. Often the impact of environmental degradation does not affect the individual or group that engages in it, but rather neighbors near and far. Even though there has been improvement in recent years, smog from illegal slash-and-burn farming on the Indonesian islands of Sumatra and Borneo routinely blankets Thailand, Malaysia, and Singapore—forcing schools to shut down and residents to curtail basic activities—as farmers blatantly ignore government prohibitions.[2] Most scientists agree that modern environmental problems are initiated and worsened by human activity.

Yet the problem of transborder pollution is only one piece of the environmental issue. Population centers in the third world, already strained by limited resources and increasing urbanization, will face greater pressures in the coming decades as today's world population of nearly 7 billion people swells to more than 9 billion by 2050, with nearly all of that increase projected to be in developing countries.[3] Additionally, the world is host to weather-related natural disasters that tend to defy efforts of prevention, including extreme bouts of heat or cold, as well as severe events such as hurricanes and tsunamis. The disastrous tsunami that was triggered by an earthquake off the west coast of Indonesia on December 26, 2004, claimed the lives of nearly 280,000 people and destroyed the livelihoods of 3 million. In the summer of 2010, Pakistan faced its worst flooding in eighty years, with most estimates reporting 20 million people affected (and a death toll ranging from 1,300 to 1,600). Recovery from the 2010 earthquake in Haiti, which claimed nearly 230,000 lives, was made more difficult by flooding and landslides that many attribute to population concentration, deforestation, and climate change.

Other environmental issues place clearer culpability on human behavior, with clearly uneven impacts being felt in developing versus developed countries. The divide between cause and impact—the "people most at risk from climate change live in countries that have contributed the least to the atmospheric buildup"—runs counter to the notion that "we're all in this together" and points to another way of viewing an extremely unequal world.[4] Deforestation, caused in part by increased agriculture and changing food patterns among humans, is believed to account for up to 20 percent of all greenhouse gas emissions. Stepping up after facing years of criticism, Indonesia is leading the way in this area, having pledged a two-year moratorium on deforestation in 2010.[5] The availability of safe drinking water dominates environmental agendas in many regions of the developing world. Access to safe, clean water is a political issue in many regions of the world, even though most estimate that it only costs about $25 to provide an individual in the developing world with safe, clean water for the rest of his or her life.[6] With over 260 rivers either crossing or marking international political boundaries, the potential for conflict over this necessary natural resource is ripe—in fact, nearly 80 percent of all violent disputes over water resources around the world have occurred in the Middle East.[7]

The Food and Agricultural Organization (FAO) of the United Nations estimates that only about 20 percent of agricultural land in developing countries is irrigated; more land will be needed to sustain an increase in food production. Additionally, water control could be used as a form of ecoterrorism if, for example, one government attempts to block the water supply from a river or other source from traveling to another region. Turkey, for example, controls the waters of the Tigris and Euphrates, on which both Syria and Iraq are dependent. Dams being built in southwestern China are draining water tables and worsening droughts not only in China but also in Thailand and Myanmar, leading to calls for water reform.

Environmental issues provide a good example of the theoretical construct known as the "free-rider" problem, which shows that individuals (or groups) can benefit from attempts to solve a problem without contributing to its cause. Similarly, people can attempt to skirt limits or constraints designed to decrease the depletion of a particular resource without being caught. This provides individuals and groups little incentive to put forth the effort or the resources to solve problems, which is the main reason why issues such as environmental degradation need larger, global responses in order to successfully combat further decay. Exacerbating this free-rider problem is the long-term view on change: we may not see the lasting effects of changes made today for many years to come. This delay in results often limits people's sense of urgency for taking action now, and underscores the need for global organizations and specialized institutions that can reach large audiences to take leadership. While there are many internationally organized and supported environmental programs, many of them coordinated through the United Nations Environment Programme (UNEP), the UN's support for grassroots activism is more empowering and often more successful than larger-scale events. The Greenbelt Program in Kenya, now an international movement, provides one vivid example. Led by Wangari Maathai, activists organized women to replant 30 million trees while providing much needed education on indigenous and women's rights, as well as on the importance of sustainable agriculture. Maathai and other activists were imprisoned for their work—including when they protested the construction of a sixty-story office tower in the middle of a Nairobi park. For her leadership in environmental and other issues, Maathai was awarded the 2004 Nobel Peace Prize. In a similar example of grassroots activism, the Chipko movement in India mobilized thousands of women to embrace trees and advocate conservation as a way to prevent erosion, flooding, and famine resulting from widespread logging.

Many are familiar with the problem of global warming, also known as the GREENHOUSE EFFECT, brought on by industrial emissions that trap heat close to Earth's atmosphere and contribute to higher average temperatures across the planet. These phenomena are not natural—they are consequences of human consumption patterns. Although the actual degree increase is debated (and based on future models), there is agreement that the average global temperature is increasing. The greatest greenhouse gas–emitting nations include China, the United States, India, and Brazil. As industrialization and urbanization continue, emissions will also continue to rise. China's demand for energy is producing a surge in emissions, as the International Energy Agency now "projects that China's emissions of energy-related greenhouse gases will grow more than the rest of the world's combined increase by 2020."[8]

International conferences to discuss sources of the problems and potential solutions have been held since the mid-1980s. After meetings in Montreal (Canada) in 1987, governments committed to reducing all substances, but especially human-made materials, that deplete the world's ozone layer. At the Rio de Janeiro (Brazil) meetings in 1992, greater cooperation was forged between developed and less developed states, promoting "common but differentiated" responsibilities for the environment. The expressed goal is to foster all countries' right to DEVELOPMENT while chipping away at a growing problem at the same time. The spirit of Rio was widely adopted as a workable solution to environmental issues, and further negotiations led to a comprehensive first set of actions that were approved at the Kyoto (Japan) conference in 1997. Signatories agreed to reductions in greenhouse gas emissions, differentiated by their economic status: the lion's share of the responsibility is placed on developed countries, from which the largest portion of harmful emissions originates. The Kyoto Protocol to the United Nations Framework Convention on Climate Change requires thirty of the most developed countries to cut combined emissions of greenhouse gases by an average of 5 percent below their 1990 levels by 2012 (less developed countries will be required to reduce emissions during the second "commitment period," at a later date). The allowance of different emission rates, based on level of development, has led to some bizarre bargaining proposals from developed countries, which seek poorer, low-emissions states to participate in a "trade" of emissions rights for a price. Despite oft-voiced concerns about the inequities posed by this solution—which activists claim is merely skimming the surface of what truly needs to done to accomplish genuine change—the Kyoto Protocol entered into force in February 2005, seven years after it was first signed. Even though 161 states have signed and ratified the agreement, major gaps in enforcement remain, with China, India, and Brazil exempt from targets temporarily, and the United States operating completely outside of the Kyoto decisions. Some have argued that the emphasis of Kyoto, on defensive reductions rather than proactive developments of alternatives, was the crux of the challenge, although finding a workable replacement to the protocol has proven extremely difficult.[9]

In 2007 in Bali, a two-year process to prepare for major meetings in Copenhagen in 2009 was begun, in the hope of crafting a binding agreement to follow the Kyoto Protocol. Frustration reigned at the gathering of 45,000 politicians and policymakers, who failed to produce a replacement treaty when the negotiations deteriorated into discussion of matters of intent rather than legally binding obligations. States promised financial commitments to tackle climate change and most of its effects by 2020, although the bulk of the money would come from the private sector, whose investment declined quite rapidly. Leaders of some developing countries believed they were being bullied into an agreement for the sake of reaching a conclusion, and that their concerns and limitations were not being heard. Tension between the United States and China (which had recently traded hats as China surpassed the United States as the world's leading emitter of greenhouse gas emissions) were palpable. Diplomatic slurs revealed the dissension in the room: Chinese prime minister Wen Jiabao left the Copenhagen conference center, sent underlings to meet with President Barack Obama in his stead, and launched a meeting with Brazilian and Indian leaders without Obama being present.[10] The sentiment of one observer seemed to capture the evaluation by many: "Copenhagen was a disaster. That much is agreed."[11]

The Cancún, Mexico, meetings in 2010 were less tense, yet on a smaller scale than many had hoped for. Leaders agreed to the creation of a "green fund" to help developing states make changes in energy consumption and production to cope with climate change, although there remains a "significant gap" between countries' promised reductions in emissions and the targets that most scientists believe need to be met to tame the global temperature rise.[12] Annual meetings are on the books as a way to continue both discussion and the creation of binding targets. Many are keenly aware that the tasks before them are enormous, yet they are attempting to temper expectations. As the editorial board of *The Economist* noted, "It would be wonderful to solve climate change with a global deal. But no such thing looks remotely achievable."[13] It seems that many of the unilateral and regional attempts to mitigate climate change, as we see in the cases of Indonesia and Brazil, may outpace the multilateral approach, especially as big-power politics continue to get in the way.

There are also many large-scale efforts to protect biodiversity in the rainforests, rural areas, and beyond. Tigers, for example, have become extinct in the wild in Cambodia, China, North Korea, and Vietnam, with the majority of the only 1,000 breeding female tigers in the wild now found in India, Russia, and Indonesia. Scientists warn that without radical action, tigers could join other animals on the extinction list.[14] A key document framing these efforts is the Convention on International Trade in Endangered Species of Wild Fauna and Flora (CITES). In force since 1975, CITES is viewed as one of the largest and most effective conservation agreements ever promulgated, with 175 states as official parties to the convention. Its goal is to prevent the adverse impact of trade on vulnerable species of animals and plants, ranging from elephants, rhinos, and chimpanzees to orchids, cacti, and caviar. Yet this effort is controversial. In an attempt to limit the poaching of elephants for their ivory tusks, CITES banned all forms of ivory trading in 1989. However, since 1997 Zimbabwe and a number of other southern African countries have fought and won the right to sell off their legal stockpiles of ivory, known as "white gold," and use the money to pay for their elephant conservation programs. This limited legal trade has opened up a loophole that dealers can easily exploit. Poaching operations have again become rampant, especially in Nigeria, the Democratic Republic of Congo, and Chad. Efforts to regulate the international trafficking of endangered wildlife sometimes pit environmentalists against those dependent on the income created by such trade, who call for an end to Western colonial environmentalism. To many, the question is about priorities: Which is more important—combating rural poverty or conserving cacti?

The Human Rights of Refugees and Global Migrants

The people of the world are on the move, especially in the third world. Some estimates claim that recently as many as 15 million people have fled their countries in an attempt to escape violence, persecution, or warfare. An additional 25 million more may be considered DISPLACED PERSONS—people who have left their homes but remain in their countries, often in makeshift camps that lack even the basic necessities to live. They are overwhelmingly women and children (over 80 percent), with unique vulnerabilities. Refugees and displaced persons are common targets for exploitation and harassment by soldiers, militia members, and even refugee camp officials. Not only do these uprooted people need assistance in the short term, including food, shelter, clothing, and protection, but they face daunting long-term needs as well. Refugees cannot remain as such forever; the vast majority desire repatriation in their home country, or asylum in a country of choice that would allow them to start their lives relatively anew.

Some of the key source countries of human displacement include Afghanistan, the Philippines, Sudan, Burundi, the Democratic Republic of Congo, Somalia, Vietnam, and Colombia. As Mexico is for the United States, Turkey has become a gatekeeper of sorts in recent years for illegal immigrants traveling from the third world to Europe. Because of tighter restrictions on immigration within the European Union, Turkey has become a transit route of choice for immigrants from India, Afghanistan, Pakistan, and many African states. Human traffickers, known in China as *shé tóu* (snakeheads) or *polleros* (chicken herders) in Mexico, rake in huge quantities of cash: while the average price a Mexican pays to cross into the United States is $1,500, and Central Americans pay $6,000, the starting price for Chinese is $30,000 (many pay double this price).[15] It is a lucrative, sometimes comprehensive business that thrives on the risks some people will take in the hope of a better life. Snakeheads working to move people out of China offer services that take care of everything from purchasing a passport, to escorting their client through transit points, to setting up fraudulent marriages—profiting as much as $40,000 on a single client.[16]

Since its establishment in 1951, the United Nations High Commission for Refugees (UNHCR), which twice received the Nobel Peace Prize (1954 and 1981), has been the main international agency to assist people in these processes. One of the major responsibilities of the UNHCR is to find "durable solutions" for the world's refugees. This includes searching out possibilities for repatriation, through voluntary return to their homeland, integration into another country via the granting of asylum, or resettlement in a third country. Unfortunately, the tasks facing this agency, and others related to the handling of refugees, are increasing.

As discussed in Chapter 12, much conflict in today's world is different; it is often, although not exclusively, targeted at civilians, using displacement and systematic violence, hatred, fear, and other psychological weapons. The Democratic Republic of Congo, Sudan, Angola, Indonesia, Sri Lanka, Iraq, and Afghanistan are just a few areas in our world today where concentrated pockets of people are not safe in their own home communities, and where there have been large-scale movements of people within or outside their countries. For the most part, conflict within each one of these regions is confined to single countries; they are wars within, rather than between, NATION-STATES. The internal nature of these conflicts, over which states can claim SOVEREIGNTY, makes a response by the outside community more difficult, because aggressors (and their supporters) may frame it as an unwelcome invasion into internal matters. World leaders struggle to cope with these changes and with these forms of violence. In the case of international refugees, it is illegal under international law to force "genuine" refugees to return to the country from which they fled, even though the United States and other countries have done so. But how should international organizations respond?

Much attention within the United States has been focused on migration from Latin America, especially Mexico. Until the mid-1980s most Mexican migrants made their way to Mexico City in search of opportunities. However, a disastrous earthquake and a long economic crisis pushed migrants to go farther in search of work. While many are concerned about the costs to the communities left behind—such as the prolonged separation from family—this out-migration serves as an important source of income for these countries, as wages are sent home in the form of remittances. In addition, where there is high unemployment with few prospects, out-migration functions as a safety valve, releasing pressure on already overburdened governments. Even where unemployment is relatively low (until the Great Recession, Mexico had a relatively low unemployment rate), as long as the wage differentials are as high as ten to one (as they are on average between the United States and Mexico), people will continue to leave their countries. The United States and other developed countries have attempted to build the walls higher and to militarize the borders to cut down on illegal migration—the "Great Wall of Mexico," part of a series of several barriers strategically placed along the southwest border of the United States, seems to be doing little to curb illegal immigration. The Spanish government erected a ten-foot-high fence around Melilla, a contested territory off the coast of northern Africa that has become a major crossing point for migrants, in order to keep out people attempting transit from Morocco or sub-Saharan African countries. How-ever, these actions have only forced people to find ever more difficult and danger-ous routes.

Terminological debates about "types" of refugees capture the emerging prob-lem: while a technical definition exists, based in the 1951 UN Convention Relating to the Status of Refugees, many feel it is far too narrow and that it fails to provide an accurate picture of modern migration. This difficulty is only compounded by the complex reasons that people flee: some, although they are believed to be a minority, seek better economic opportunities. Of course, it is often difficult to untangle indi-viduals' motivations, and economic rationales can be as much about "pure survival" as they are political. Others fear political persecution and violence. In fact, many flee violence for a safe but poverty-filled future. The reasons people pack up may be diverse, but their situation as displaced people tends to be uniformly dangerous. Many trade one set of insecurities for another when they seek asylum in countries experiencing conflict. The Convention Relating to the Status of Refugees confines the status of "refugee" to "a person who, owing to a well-founded fear of being per-secuted for reasons of race, religion, nationality, or membership of a particular so-cial group or political opinion is outside the country of his nationality and unable, or, owing to such fear, is unwilling to avail himself of the protection of that country."

Yet the numbers of displaced persons, trapped in their own countries, fleeing from persecution, and often forcibly relocated, may outnumber the official count of refugees. Most estimates of internally displaced persons place the global total at around 25 million—and this does not include another 25 million who are victims of natural disasters—although there are formidable difficulties in quantifying such peo-ples. This has been the case because people (and governments) have used an overly restrictive definition of who is a refugee. Today, individuals are forced to seek safety because of their gender, their sexual orientation, their beliefs, or their region of ori-gin. Others are economic, political, or wartime refugees. The simmering situation in the war-torn Darfur region of Sudan, discussed in Chapter 17, has produced nearly 3 million displaced persons, some of them internally displaced within Sudan and others who have crossed the border into neighboring countries, where they often face continued persecution.

Population density and government programs to relocate people can cause sim-mering tensions to explode. In Central Kalimantan, the Indonesian part of the island of Borneo, tensions flared between the Dayaks, native to the region, and the Madurese, who had been resettled from the crowded southeastern coast of Java. Eco-nomic tensions increased the perception by many Dayaks that the government was offering favors to the Madurese. In an often-bloody conflict that included decapita-tions of many who were slain, government troops fled as they got caught in the cross-fire.[17] Once again, the survivors of this attack will flee, leaving what some had adopted as their second or even third home: many have spent more time "on the run," looking for a place to settle, than they have ever spent living in a single place.

Refugee camps are not the "safe havens" that many might expect. Officially, displaced people are the responsibility of their home governments, which in many cases are the source of their persecution in the first place. Examples of violence are widespread, including assault, gang rape, sexual mutilation, and torture, perpetuated by organized crime, military police forces, antigovernment activists, local residents, humanitarian workers, peacekeepers, and even the refugee community itself.[18] This violence is a frightening expression of part of the underbelly of GLOBALIZATION. Afghan refugees in Iran have been attacked and killed by mobs. Indonesian militias routinely raided refugee camps in West Timor, stoning, beating, and sometimes killing displaced citizens from the east. Burmese refugees in Thailand were attacked when Burmese military representatives crossed the border and destroyed their camp, killing some, injuring scores, and leaving many without any shelter in an already perilous situation. Children, who make up large numbers of the refugee populations around the world, are forced to educate themselves, or put up with woefully inadequate makeshift schools. They end up finding other ways to spend their time, including adopting various survival tactics such as the illicit distribution of drugs, weapons, and sexual favors.

In other areas, internal refugees are holed up in internment camps, ostensibly for their own safety, but in reality to prevent them from aiding the opposition groups that purportedly threaten government or other powerful forces. Whole families have been murdered while they slept in such camps. Refugees are being "warehoused," or confined to camps or segregated settlements for five years or more, oftentimes while being denied basic rights enshrined in the Convention Relating to the Status of Refugees. Refugees in a protracted situation without any lasting end in sight have the right to employment, freedom of movement, and education, although these privileges, including basic noninterference in personal affairs, are rarely afforded them.[19] Entire generations have grown up as refugees—the NONGOVERNMENTAL ORGANIZATION (NGO) Doctors Without Borders reports that more than 400,000 Sudanese and 2 million Afghans have stayed in camps and other so-called temporary shelters for more than twenty years.[20] People already facing tremendous dislocation and vulnerabilities get lost in the shuffle as attention moves beyond their prolonged plight.

Contrary to popular belief, it is other third world states that serve as the host countries for refugees. The ratio of refugee population to total population in less developed states, especially Iran, Pakistan, Kenya, and Guinea, is much higher than the ratio in the developed countries, including Germany, the United States, and Canada. Combined, countries with annual incomes (per person) of less than $2,000 host more than two-thirds of all refugees, while states with per capita incomes over $10,000 host only 4 percent of the world's refugees.[21] Economic struggles and high unemployment rates have motivated Western and non-Western governments to reject new arrivals, confine refugees to camps and prisons, and even deport them.

Another dark side of migration can be found in human trafficking. One of the fastest-growing criminal enterprises and a multibillion-dollar industry, trafficking in humans is second only to the illicit smuggling of drugs. While the forms of exploited labor in which these individuals engage are varied—including domestic work, mail-order brides, illicit adoptions in the first world, and street-begging to finance third parties—the majority of trafficked peoples are forced into commercial sex enterprises. Although both males and females are subject to this form of forced labor, it is estimated that the vast majority (80 percent) are female, and up to 50 percent are minors—with an estimated 1.2 million children trafficked each year, mostly into prostitution.[22] These data do not include those who are forced into forms of labor within their own countries, or internal slaves. Individuals are literally traded between and within developing countries, and also to economically developed countries, where they are often lured by hopes of finding work as waitresses, models, or entertainers. However, once under the control of the sometimes vast criminal enterprises that run these rackets, they work in bondage as SWEATSHOP laborers, prostitutes, or domestic servants.

Children are viewed as a desirable commodity in this abhorrent industry fueled by misconceptions. Popular myths that children are free of AIDS and that sex with a virgin can cure disease have greatly contributed to the growth of this form of child labor in nearly every corner of the world. The chaos that follows large-scale disasters provides opportunities for this illicit trade to flourish; after Haiti's January 2010 earthquake (the worst in the region in 200 years), it is believed that over 1.2 million children were directly affected. It is estimated that prior to the disaster, 2,500 children were trafficked each year from Haiti across the border into the Dominican Republic to work as domestic labor, in begging cartels, and in the pornography and sex industry. With children lost or separated from their families (or families so desperate that they abandon their children), many are rightly concerned about an escalation in child trafficking following the earthquake.[23]

Healthcare and Disease

In Chapter 7 we discussed the connection between health and poverty. The deprivation of citizens in the third world, sometimes due to economic malaise, violence, and war, has in many cases led to the complete failure of public health systems. The UN has drawn an explicit link between financial well-being and health, stating that "poverty is an important reason that babies are not vaccinated, clean water and sanitation are not provided, drugs and other treatments are unavailable, and mothers die in childbirth."[24] Consistently, the leading causes of death around the world include heart disease, respiratory infections, AIDS, diarrhea, tuberculosis, and malaria.

Health crises demonstrate the world's deepening INTERDEPENDENCE in at least two very stark ways: first, diseases cross increasingly porous borders without consideration of economic, political, or other status; and second, they require the coordinated response of multiple actors, including state and nonstate alike. One vivid example of the health vulnerabilities that have been deepened by globalization is the potential for another flu pandemic that, even if it does not reach the mortality levels of the 1918 "Spanish influenza" outbreak (which claimed 40–50 million lives worldwide), could still lead to an estimated 2–7 million deaths and significantly disrupt life in every country of the world.

One of the first tests of recently developed global plans to respond to a disease pandemic was the outbreak of what later became known as severe acute respiratory syndrome (SARS), in 2003. This mystery illness, which presented as a flulike condition, was first discovered in Vietnam, and within two weeks of the initial diagnosis following the death of a Toronto man, the World Health Organization (WHO) issued a global alert. It was later discovered that the outbreak had begun two months earlier in one of China's southern provinces, and that the epicenter of the disease was one of Hong Kong's major hotels where a Chinese doctor who had treated some of the earlier cases fell ill. Because of the port city's status as a major transit point in Asia, and the rapidity with which cases spread from Asia to North America, the response by the WHO and governments was swift—regulating air travel, monitoring healthcare workers, and quarantining anyone believed to be a carrier of the virus.

Despite frightening pictures of people with ventilated masks covering their mouths in major cities across multiple continents, efforts to control transmission of the syndrome were successful. DNA analysis quickly uncovered the genetic code of the disease, its spread was halted, and, even though it claimed approximately 750 lives globally, there were no confirmed cases of the disease by late 2004.

Similar to other deadly strains of viruses, the latest feared viral culprit, known alternatively as "avian influenza" or more simply "bird flu," began in China. Bird flu is one of sixteen known subtypes of the influenza virus. This particular strain was directly transmitted from birds to humans in Hong Kong in 1997, and the disease spread throughout Asia in 2004. In just two years, human infections multiplied, hitting Vietnam, Cambodia, Thailand, Indonesia, Turkey, Azerbaijan, Egypt, and Djibouti, with outbreaks among poultry populations in many other states. Concerns about this particular virus, scientifically known as H5N1 for the combination of two specific proteins appearing on its surface, surround its reach within the poultry population (it has already caused the largest poultry outbreak on record, devastating many local economies) and its ability to mutate and become more virulent. Indeed, H5N1 is feared as a strain with pandemic potential because of its possible mutations and adaptation into a virus that is contagious among humans and for which humans would lack natural immunity. Even if this variant of the flu does not mutate to become easily transmissible between humans, the WHO and other health agencies view an impending flu pandemic of some type as very likely, and "once a fully contagious virus emerges, its global spread is considered inevitable."[25] The H1N1 (also known as "swine flu") pandemic in 2009 reignited this debate, even if, in the end, that particular strain did not become the crisis many feared. This outbreak started in Mexico and the United States, and quickly spread worldwide.

Many people view the struggle over medicines and vaccines to be part of the classic struggle between haves and have-nots. Similar to many of the issues that we have examined in this book, there are few simple solutions. Although many efforts have been undertaken at the global level, most have not yet been effectively implemented on the ground. For example, a global program launched in 1988 to completely eradicate polio through a wide-reaching vaccination plan cosponsored by the WHO has been stalled by lack of medical professionals in needed areas, lack of political will to implement national programs, and even rumors. Although in 1998 only approximately 6,000 active cases of polio remained, in recent years there have been serious setbacks. Nigeria is now home to half of the world's known cases of polio (1,600 in 2010), and other countries are reporting their first active cases in years, sometimes decades, such as Tajikistan, Uganda, Mali, Togo, Ghana, Kenya, and Côte d'Ivoire.[26] National governments have signed documents and proclaimed their commitment to eradicating the disease, but their pronouncements go unheeded or are sorely underfunded. As with so many challenges, polio knows no human-made borders, and because infection does not always lead to paralysis, there may be many more cases lying dormant than policymakers and activists realize.

Attempts to contain the spread of tuberculosis by 2015—highlighted as one of the UN's MILLENNIUM DEVELOPMENT GOALS—have also encountered difficulties, with the National Institute of Allergy and Infectious Diseases estimating that one-third of the world's population is infected with the tuberculosis bacterium and at higher risk for developing the active disease.[27] Because of the difficulties in achieving perfectly consistent treatment (some regimens call for eleven different pills every day for two months), cases of "untreatable" drug-resistant tuberculosis have been registered around the world, including in eastern Europe, the United States, and southern Africa.[28] The tuberculosis vulnerability of HIV-positive individuals makes this development particularly worrisome. Despite this, Jeffrey Sachs, who directs the Earth Institute at Columbia University and serves as special adviser to the United Nations on the implementation of the Millennium Development Goals, contends that it would only require residents of the richer regions of the world to donate the cost of one cup of Starbucks coffee per year to eradicate this gigantic killer.[29]

One of the most prescient examples of how the global healthcare crisis is disproportionately affecting the third world is the HIV/AIDS pandemic. In 2006 the world acknowledged a quarter century of living with AIDS—highlighting the sobering reality that its spread, especially in the third world, continues. The United Nations has created an agency devoted entirely to the problem, and even the SECURITY COUNCIL has labeled HIV/AIDS a threat to international peace and security. Progress has been made, though, as the numbers of new HIV infections and deaths from AIDS are falling globally, down nearly 20 percent since the peak of the epidemic in 1999.[30]

Much controversy has surrounded AIDS medications regarding their availability and cost and the development of generic alternatives. Yet some doctors suggest that we need to worry less about the cost of the drugs and more about the shortage of condoms (for males and females alike). Even this most basic means of prevention is out of reach of the poorest who need it, despite the large sums of money that governments, international agencies, and nongovernmental organizations are spending.[31]

Perhaps more governments need to follow the examples of Uganda and Thailand, and break taboos by instituting aggressive public education campaigns. Uganda was one of the most open countries in terms of HIV acknowledgment in the 1980s, when even in the United States and many European countries, leaders were slow to discuss the epidemic, or falsely believed it was a disease that affected only homosexual communities. In South Africa, which continues to experience one of the most severe epidemics of AIDS, although new infections there are starting to slow, former president Nelson Mandela surprised many with his candor when, in an attempt to help stimulate more accurate public discussion about the disease, he announced that his son had died of AIDS. Others, such as Botswana, which has consistently ranked as among the countries with the highest rates of HIV infection, test all patients entering clinics or hospitals. However, we should not underestimate how difficult this can be, since many political and religious leaders often object to the explicit language that is necessary to inform people about how the disease is transmitted, or how widespread it has become. In many countries, conservatives block the distribution of female condoms or vaginal microbicides (which a woman can use with or without her partner's cooperation or knowledge), which they believe contribute to promiscuous behavior. Adding to the tragedy is the fact that very often women are already infected before they become aware of their HIV status. AIDS has now become the leading cause of death and disease among reproductive-age women worldwide, and in sub-Saharan Africa, more than half of those living with HIV/AIDS are women.[32]

Screening for HIV infection is physically and financially inaccessible for many people worldwide. Yet testing is crucial. There are programs that provide pregnant women with a short course of anti-AIDS medicines, such as AZT, a failed cancer drug that can delay the onset of AIDS. With testing and counseling, because mother-to-child transmission of HIV can be virtually eliminated through the use of such drugs, safe delivery practices, and the safe use of breast milk substitutes, pregnant women can play a huge role in containing the spread of HIV.[33] However, as important as such programs are, they are limited in their effectiveness. If state leaders and NGOs are indeed committed to providing treatment to all who need it, a commitment that is questionable at best, another pitfall emerges: How will governments of the developing world provide for those so-called medical pensioners whose life is prolonged, albeit by the regular delivery of drugs and support facilities? In most cases, a basic health infrastructure must be built where none exists. Expensive laboratory work must be done on a continual basis to monitor this complicated regimen of drugs. Otherwise, it is feared that drug-resistant strains will develop, as they have for malaria and tuberculosis.

Still, we need to remember that the anti-AIDS drugs now available offer treatment, not a cure. And they do nothing to prevent transmission of the disease. Prevention and education remain critical in this process, despite their expense. But the failure to treat the disease will lead to even higher costs that we cannot even begin to tabulate. The first step to treatment and prevention is awareness of one's HIV status, which is why some of the most successful programs have promoted simple, confidential testing—both to encourage quick treatment and also to decrease the likelihood of infecting others. Prevention efforts are targeting some surprising enablers of the disease. The United Nations has identified soldiers as major carriers of HIV and, alarmingly, discussed the role of international peacekeepers in continuing the spread of this deadly virus.[34] Since 1981, when the disease was first recognized within the medical community, more UN peacekeeping troops have died of AIDS (or will soon die) than have been killed in combat.

Clearly, none of these issues can be understood in isolation. Health is a multi-faceted aspect of daily living, directly impacted by socioeconomic status, opportunities for education and employment, and interconnected social and political realities, among other factors. And it's not just the headline-grabbing ailments that cause suffering and premature death around the world—tens of thousands of people in the third world die each day of complications from childbirth, diarrhea, asthma, and other conditions that are closely connected to the lack of basic healthcare resources. Yet there can be apathy among citizens of the developed world about third world health problems such as diarrhea, even though more than 1.5 million children die of the dehydration caused by this ailment every year.[35] This is entirely preventable, and does not require complex deals between global drug companies or fistfuls of pills, just oral rehydration therapy and basic sanitation. Even though high-profile rock stars aren't likely to devote a world tour to building more toilets around the world, the construction of basic latrine systems could go a long way toward curbing unnecessary deaths. One study found that more than a third of the world's population lack such basic latrine systems, and that more than a billion of the world's people scoop their water for drinking, washing, and cooking from sources polluted by human and animal excrement.[36]

One other example of the differences in healthcare between the developing world and the developed world can be found in cigarette smoking and both the availability of education related to the known ill effects of smoking on health and the types of marketing campaigns used. As a global antismoking treaty (the Framework Convention on Tobacco Control—ratified by 171 states) is debated by public health leaders around the world, the well-funded tobacco industry is facing off with health officials in developing countries who are attempting to limit the marketing of tobacco products, including placement of noticeable warnings about the known ill effects of smoking. As customers in the United States and Europe are consuming fewer cigarettes, the tobacco companies are working to pick up sales in the developing world—and are still maintaining a 2 percent increase in sales each year worldwide.[37] With support from the WHO, individuals and governments have been encouraged to take legal action against cigarette companies, and lawsuits have been started in Brazil, Nigeria, and Turkey, among other countries. Indonesia, the world's fifth largest cigarette market, faces less regulation on advertising and marketing, a fact that was shockingly evidenced when a video of a chain-smoking two-year-old-boy in Sumatra went viral on the Internet.[38] Smoking rates in Indonesia increased by nearly 50 percent in the 1990s, and it is now estimated that 60 percent of adult men smoke (rates for women, which have historically been as low as 5 percent, are steadily increasing). Indonesia receives $2.5 billion from Philip Morris International in excise taxes on cigarettes, and tobacco jobs remain a vital part of the state's economy.[39]

How important is the lack of basic healthcare around the world? Some have argued, at least in the case of the HIV pandemic, that it was only after scientists emphasized the security and political implications of the continued spread of the disease—rather than "simply" a humanitarian catastrophe—that many political leaders took notice.[40] Jeffrey Sachs has argued that AIDS and malaria in Africa may be larger obstacles to economic GROWTH than debt, which is already crippling.[41]

Weapons Proliferation

The proliferation of weapons is an issue of increasing concern in the post–COLD WAR era, in which larger numbers of states are deciding to invest resources to acquire conventional weapons as well as nuclear and other weapons of mass destruction (WMDs). Without doubt, conventional weapons—weapons that lack chemical, biological, or nuclear components—are dangerous, but their impact is limited. The advent of the nuclear age in the 1940s changed all this, as the destruction of the entire planet became a possibility. While from the 1950s to the 1980s a limited number of large and powerful states pursued nuclear weapons, the tide seems to be changing, and some have claimed we are currently living in a "second nuclear age."[42] While Western militaries dominated the world for the past 200 years, we now face a distinct shift in the balance of power as non-Western states, particularly throughout Asia, acquire weapons to challenge Western dominance. Especially concerning are the WMDs, an umbrella category describing weapons that incorporate nuclear, biological, chemical, and radiological agents that can, as their label suggests, bring harm to large groups of people in one blow. One of the gravest dangers of WMDs is the difficulty of their detection; a sufficiently lethal dose of agents could be loaded into a container and shipped, largely undetectable, anywhere around the world. Unfortunately, multibillion-dollar efforts by the United States to provide antimissile defensive systems only exacerbate the desire and urgency to build weapons that can evade such error-prone mechanisms. There is much uncertainty about WMDs. Yet what is certain is that the atmosphere is a much different one than of DETERRENCE based on "mutual assured destruction" that marked the nuclear race during the Cold War. Now, individuals and groups can wreak havoc on a population without endangering themselves and with a much broader blanket of anonymity.

Many believed that the end of the Cold War in the late 1980s would lead to a safer, less militarized world. This has not been the case. Especially within the richer countries of the third world, the acquisition of advanced weaponry, with which comes attention and inclusion in the world's "elite nuclear club," has significantly increased since the mid-1990s. In 1998 alone, India detonated five atomic bombs, followed by Pakistan's own tests; North Korea fired a multistage rocket over Japan; and Iran, India, and Pakistan each tested intermediate-range ballistic missiles. China has deployed short-range missiles aimed at Taiwan and fortified its longer-range missile system. Throughout Asia and the Middle East—Israel, Syria, Iraq, Iran, Pakistan, India, China, and North Korea—the military focus is shifting "from infantry to disruptive technologies" based on chemical, biological, and nuclear weapons capable of delivery by ballistic missiles.[43] Since 2006, two states in particular—North Korea and Iran—have tested the limits of the Nuclear Non-Proliferation Treaty (NPT), which has been in force since 1970.

The NPT has been formally supported by 189 member states of the United Nations. Its weaknesses and contradictions, though, were highlighted by the tit-for-tat nuclear tests by India and Pakistan in 1998, two of the states that have neither signed nor ratified the NPT, and by the openly secret "basement bomb" arsenal possessed by Israel, which remains an unofficial nuclear weapons state. Even before North Korea became the first country to withdraw from the NPT in 2003 (it is notable that South Africa is the only NPT signatory to formally dismantle its nuclear weapons program, which it completed in 1994), many countries have challenged the relevance of the NPT, which restricts the legal possession of nuclear weapons to states that tested nuclear weapons prior to 1967, when discussions that led to the NPT began. Increasingly, it appears that "nonproliferation" is becoming a quaint term with little punch behind it. Mohammad El Baradei, former director-general of the International Atomic Energy Agency (IAEA) and 2005 recipient of the Nobel Peace Prize, captured the hypocrisy poignantly, characterizing the original nuclear weapons states (United States, Great Britain, France, Russia, and China), in their failure to comply with their own promises to ultimately eliminate their own stockpiles, as an offensive group who continue "to dangle a cigarette from their mouth and tell everyone else not to smoke."[44]

The need for energy is at least the official justification for the recently overt uranium enrichment within Iran, a nuclear program that has its roots in US assistance to the administration of Reza Shah Pahlavi in the 1950s. Although President Mahmoud Ahmadinejad continuously asserts Iran's right as a signatory of the NPT to enrich uranium for domestic energy consumption, many within Iran and beyond have raised eyebrows at these intentions, especially given the president's fiery language toward Israel, stating on multiple occasions that is should be "wiped off the map." Iran became a "nuclear capable" state in the spring of 2006, when Ahmadinejad personally announced that Iranian scientists had enriched small quantities of uranium. Although the POPULIST president has rallied much domestic support around this enrichment program, fueled by strong denouncements in the West, it is not yet clear whether he has the support of the true wielders of power within his country, the clergy and the Council of Guardians. Supposedly, Supreme Leader Ayatollah Ali Khamenei signed a *FATWA* forbidding the production, stockpiling, and use of nuclear weapons, stating that "we fundamentally reject nuclear weapons."[45] Nevertheless, Iran is again under the sanction of Security Council resolutions designed to limit the state's ability to obtain the equipment, technology, and finance to support a nuclear program. Beyond the Security Council resolutions, in 2010 the United States passed even more targeted restrictions against Iran, including legislation that is aimed to block companies that do business in Iran's energy sector from trading in the United States.

Iran's interactions with China have raised particular concern. China is believed to be a major supplier of component parts necessary for the development of Iran's nuclear program, including the pressure gauges that are critical to the operation of a centrifuge.[46] (China was accused of playing a fundamental role in assisting Pakistan with the latter's development of a nuclear weapon in the 1970s, although many argue that Beijing is now working to take a more responsible approach to the export of sensitive technologies, even if enforcement is lacking.)[47]

Other moves have been made by North Korea, under the leadership of the reclusive, bouffant-sporting Kim Jong-Il. A landmark attempt to end the active nuclear weapons program in North Korea was signed with the United States in 1994 (known as the "Agreed Framework"), with the United States providing power reactors and oil in exchange for the supervised conclusion of this weapons program. In 2002, Kim confirmed the suspicions of many by restarting the country's main nuclear reactor at Yongbyon and forcing two UN inspectors to leave the country. Since 2002, tensions have continued to rise as North Korean leaders assert their "right" to nuclear development and warn in their weighty "doomsday" talk of impending nuclear war brought on by the enemies of the North Korean regime. Six-party talks hosted by China (also including representatives from South Korea, Japan, Russia, and the United States) since 2003 have, at times, decreased immediate tensions in the region, although they have produced little of substance to date. These talks were expanded to include Germany in autumn of 2009. More than once, a potential trade of nonaggression promises from the United States for an end to North Korea's pursuit of nuclear weapons technology has been floated, to no avail. Others, including Japan and South Korea, have provided energy supplies—including electricity and technology for various reactors—in the hope of stalling the regime's march toward nuclear weapons. Despite these efforts, the noose around the North Korean economy and society tightened following two sets of UN sanctions imposed after missile tests in July 2006 and an underground nuclear test in October that same year, both of which were backed by the North's lone ally, China. Allegations of illicit deals, including the sale of SCUD missiles to Yemen and heroin to Australia, have helped marginalize Kim and his regime even further, which many believe explains some of the motivation for his continued agitation.

Tensions were heightened once again throughout 2010: the North sank a South Korean warship (killing forty-six soldiers), and then unveiled a previously unknown uranium enrichment facility—with 2,000 centrifuges—to a visiting Stanford scientist. North Korea then attacked a South Korean island just 13 kilometers from the

North Korean coast, which killed two South Korean soldiers and two South Korean civilians. It is always difficult to discern the motivation behind such acts, but most analysts believe the moves were connected to the unveiling of Kim's heir-apparent, his youngest son, Kim Jong-Un. As with all of the other issues covered in this chapter, actions in one state have domino effects in others—the immediate fallout from North Korea's provocative nuclear tests included loud calls within Japan and South Korea to seek greater deterrence themselves, which could potentially lead to a renewed arms race in northern Asia.

Although almost all the governments of Latin America are democracies and there are no major conflicts between them, some (such as Costa Rican president and Nobel Peace Prize winner Óscar Arias) fear that this region may be headed for an arms race as well. Two decades ago the United States prohibited arms sales to the region, which was dominated by military dictatorships notorious for their abuse of human rights. However, recognizing the political and economic progress the region has made since then, President Bill Clinton ended the ban in 1997. Since 1997 the United States has made available large packages of sophisticated weaponry for use in Colombia. In addition, Venezuela, Chile, Peru, Brazil, and other countries in the region have made multibillion-dollar arms purchases from Russian, Spanish, US, and other manufacturers. Although the George W. Bush administration warned that Venezuela's spending spree was a threat to others in the region, few analysts characterize the region as caught up in an arms race, as its military spending has been among the lowest in the world (1.3 percent of gross domestic product in 2004, regionally). Still, President Arias points out that since 2004 there has been a real shift in spending, as Latin American countries spent $24 billion on weapons and troops that year (up 8 percent from a decade earlier). If this trend continues, Arias cautions, Latin Americans may end up getting their priorities wrong.[48] National pride may propel these countries to militarize and to shift more of their budgets away from education and other needs, to the detriment of their overall human development goals.

Such escalations are hardly novel, yet a new development related to an aspect of arms proliferation is their location. Increasingly, the world has the capability to wage an arms race unlimited by the globe; it is taking place in space, through the placement of satellites, radar systems, and arms above Earth's atmosphere. The United States was the only delegation within the Conference on Disarmament to oppose the establishment of a committee on the prevention of an arms race in space. Currently, most weapons systems employed in outer space are for defensive purposes. The increasing presence of these weapons, though, threatens to challenge the integrity of past arms control agreements. As the United States and Russia are joined by China in the race to explore outer space, these challenges are likely to increase. China is the third country to have placed one of its citizens in space, and the country is working to build a space station, conduct a lunar landing by 2025, and send probes to Mars and Venus.

Another type of weapon that greatly impacts ordinary people, especially the rural poor of the third world, is landmines. They have been used on a large scale since World War I, and the problems surrounding them are many, including their long life-span after war or conflict ceases. Masterfully hidden during conflict, they remain concealed today by overgrown foliage, tending to victimize innocent civilians who are unsuspecting of their presence (most researchers estimate that 80 percent of landmine casualties are civilians). The people most likely to encounter mines are the economically poor, especially peasant farmers and their children. Complicating matters even more, many of the mines are washed out of the ground and deposited elsewhere, often on previously cleared land. Additionally, a mine can cost as little as $3 to make, and over $1,000 to clear. There are millions of active mines scattered in over seventy countries on every continent, although Africa is the most heavily mined continent on Earth. People have been killed or injured by landmines in every country in southern Africa, with the exception of Lesotho and Mauritius. It is believed that Somalia, Ethiopia, Eritrea, and Sudan each have 500,000 landmines, with 250,000 in Rwanda. It is currently estimated that there is one mine for every fifty-two people in the world.[49] Landmines have exacted a huge human toll in many war-scarred countries, especially Angola, Afghanistan, Cambodia, Mozambique, and Vietnam. In addition to the physical toll they take when they explode, their presence also denies people the use of land that could be vital to their subsistence.

If there is one topic that demonstrates the interconnectedness between NGOs, IN-TERNATIONAL GOVERNMENTAL ORGANIZATIONS (IGOs), and national governments in recent years, it is the International Campaign to Ban Landmines (ICBL), an international effort including over a thousand organizations based in sixty countries. The coalition was awarded the 1997 Nobel Peace Prize for its efforts. In March 1999 the most quickly promulgated arms treaty in history, known as the Ottawa Treaty, entered into force, banning antipersonnel landmines. This treaty, in the works since 1971, was finally adopted in 1997 in a novel process: it abandoned formal UN channels and explicitly incorporated voices from NGOs. As a result of the "back doors" that were used to move the process along, many refer to the Ottawa Treaty as a "breakaway treaty." The final process took only a little over a year to conclude.[50] Even though a larger area was cleared of landmines in 2005 than ever before, casualties from mines (mostly civilian children) rose to more than 7,000, an 11 percent increase over previous years.[51] Even with 151 countries committed to the treaty, at least three governments still actively employ landmines in their battles—Burma, Nepal, and Russia—and important players such as China, Russia, Israel, and the United States remain outside of its requirements.

The International Committee of the Red Cross (ICRC), in cooperation with countries such as Canada (which spearheaded the effort), South Africa, Belgium, and Norway, as well as multiple IGOs and NGOs, worked on this treaty, which has been ratified by 112 governments around the world. Former mine producers that have signed the Ottawa Treaty include Brazil, Canada, Chile, Nicaragua, Peru, South Africa, Thailand, Uganda, and the United Kingdom. The remaining mine producers that oppose the treaty include China, Cuba, Iran, Iraq, Russia, Serbia, Singapore, the United States, and Vietnam. The treaty prohibits the use, stockpiling, production, and transfer of antipersonnel landmines. In addition, the campaign has established an international fund, administered by the United Nations, to promote and finance victim assistance programs, and promotes awareness programs, all in the effort to eradicate the mines worldwide.

As if the problem with major weapons systems weren't enough, the presence of small, portable weapons—such as machine guns, assault rifles, and hand grenades—is on the rise. Indeed, these are the weapons—rather than nuclear bombs—that are responsible for most of the injuries and deaths in today's world. Small-arms proliferation seems to be out of control and free trade and open borders have only expanded it. It is estimated that over $10 billion worth of automatic rifles, machine guns, mortars, and other light arms are sold each year. It may not sound like a lot in terms of money, but this trade is extremely deadly. Some analysts estimate that the Rwandan genocide was carried out with less than $25 million in imported arms,[52] with much of the killing done with a huge cache of machetes imported from China, whose military is known for exporting small weapons throughout Africa. Technical improvements in the manufacturing of weapons, which make them lighter and easier to conceal, exacerbate the problem. This trade in small arms is illegal, and difficult to track or control. No one, not individual countries, not the UN, keeps good records on the small-arms trade. And there's no international movement for this issue like there is for landmines. However, recognizing that the black market in these weapons assists drug cartels, urban gangs, and GUERRILLAS, the Organization of American States (OAS) has attempted to curb the trade. The OAS began a program of registering guns to help track where they ended up, establishing uniform procedures among its members.[53] At the global level, the United Nations hosted a conference on the illicit trade in small arms in July 2001. It was a controversial meeting, as the agenda only included the illegal trade of arms, so that the big dealers, including the United States, Russia, and China, wouldn't lose a huge export industry.

Some regional attempts to contain the arms trade have been promoted by the OAS, the African Union, and the European Union. A major global initiative targeted to change the behavior of arms-providing states is Costa Rican president Óscar Arias's International Code of Conduct on Arms Transfers. Arias, who crafted a Central American peace plan barring outside aid to guerrillas in El Salvador and Nicaragua in the 1980s, brought together sixteen other Nobel laureates with international nongovernmental organizations to present this initiative to the United Nations. The plan calls for developed countries to refuse to sell arms to countries that violate basic human rights or are involved in armed aggression or TERRORISM. If such a plan were to be implemented, it could dramatically change the global weapons landscape. For example, the United States routinely ships weapons to countries whose militaries are known to be abusive, including Colombia, Turkey, Indonesia, Saudi Arabia, and Egypt. Such trade would be barred under the proposed code. It also calls for all countries to report their weapons sales and purchases to the United Nations, under the current system of voluntary compliance. Arias points out that if 10 percent of the world's military spending, approximately $1 trillion annually, were spent on human development, preventable disease and hunger could be ended, and education and sanitation could be made universal. In 2008, 147 member states of the United Nations voted to move forward with work on the treaty, with only the United States and Zimbabwe voting against it.

Conclusions: The Future of Global Capacity for Response

What are the advantages of responses by global or regional actors? Multilateral responses can give less powerful countries a stronger voice because they can find strength in numbers. In the United Nations, for example, two-thirds of all member states are developing countries. Although there are limits to what individual countries can achieve, as we have seen, the sheer number of third world countries represented in the UN provides a channel for diplomatic influence that they cannot find elsewhere. Multilateral efforts can also compel action when individual states either will not or cannot comply, due largely to financial constraints. Multilateralism can also promote an internationally acceptable setting in which nations can more freely negotiate in an atmosphere of compromise and diplomacy, which would be more difficult to achieve with individual states.

Yet an "international community" seems to exist more in symbol more than reality. Contrary to the exasperated claims of some, we do not have a world government, nor are we close to achieving one. The coordinated response of major powers is about as close as we have come to a singular community in action, and this response has been limited. Much of the world, especially the powerful countries, continues to frame matters in terms of major powers and large countries, as has been evidenced in more than one of the issues discussed in this chapter.

What differences exist between regional and global responses? Because of the limited scope and number of actors, it may be easier to build consensus for action within a regional context, although this is not always the case. For global responses, consensus (or at least verification of the absence of opposition) takes more time to craft. For some regions, assembling an intervening force would be difficult, because of historical or contemporary problems that make no one trustworthy. The larger organizations bring more economies of scale and more people to the table, but they are also more bureaucratically cumbersome—a common criticism of the United Nations—and it is easier in the larger global organizations to leave out voices of the disenfranchised and less powerful. Or, even if the opportunity to speak and participate is present, many of the non-Western countries feel they still have no teeth in these institutions. Regional organizations and specialized NGOs overcome some of these problems of size, but they can also lack influence and might. Yet even international organizations such as the United Nations do not have compelling force; more powerful countries can bypass the UN if they feel their sovereignty would be impeded. The clearest recent example of such diversion was the action of the North Atlantic Treaty Organization (NATO) in Kosovo taken on behalf of the Albanian Serbs: the US-led coalition bypassed the Security Council because China and Russia would have vetoed the measure as an unwanted and unwarranted intrusion of state sovereignty, though the UN did later take on a role, providing a Security Council resolution and sanctioning a peacekeeping force.

Yet an overarching concern for the non-Western world, in the face of much multilateral activity, is the responsiveness of such forces to the needs and concerns of the less powerful. Organizations, large and small, make decisions affecting individuals, who have little or no impact on the process. The need to include disparate, less powerful voices is especially magnified at higher levels. While the problems inherent in this enterprise have been brought to our attention through street demonstrations against the WORLD BANK and the INTERNATIONAL MONETARY FUND, the same is true with the United Nations and nongovernmental organizations that take action in the name of the people. How to make such organizations more representative and more accountable will remain a huge task for the future. If these institutions are perceived to be overtly partisan, they will lose their LEGITIMACY and ability to act. Multilateral institutions are favored because they seemingly prevent (or at least limit) the impulse for self-interest or self-delusion. But they are problematic because, in the search for consensus, they can sit idly by while massacres, such as those in Darfur, take place. Faced with changing conceptions of sovereignty and global action, many speak of a forthcoming "borderless world." Yet perceptions from the third world contend that some borders, especially economic, social, and power distinctions, remain as sturdy as ever, if not stronger.

19

Linking
Concepts and Cases

We have discussed a wide range of issues and concerns in the preceding few chapters. To illustrate these ideas further, it may be useful to consider the following questions as you study the cases. What different postures toward the international community do you observe the leaders of these countries taking? What are the perceived trade-offs between isolation and INTEGRATION? Do you observe any differences between how leaders may want to be seen and how they are actually perceived? What do countries seek from international or regional cooperation? What regional or global issue stands as a priority for each of these countries? In which countries has the international community tried to alter behavior through the threat of punitive action? Why have some attempts been more successful than others?

Case Study: Mexico

When he was elected in 2000, President Vicente Fox hoped that part of the "democracy premium" gained from the political transition would allow for significant changes in Mexico's relations with the rest of the world. In some ways the newly democratic government was more innovative and successful in its foreign policy than in any other area. Energized by his surprise win, Fox adopted an unusually ambitious and activist foreign policy agenda. This marked a break with the past. With a few notable exceptions, for decades the Institutional Revolutionary Party (PRI) took an isolationist approach to the world. Under the Estrada Doctrine (named after a foreign minister), the PRI chose a policy of NONINTERVENTION in the affairs of other countries. It rarely condemned other governments or spoke up against human rights abuses. PRI governments were careful to uphold the principle of SOVEREIGNTY so as to keep others from discussing Mexico's own record.

Mexicans had hoped that their celebrated democratization would be treated as an asset and give the country the credibility it needed to play a larger role on the world stage. President Fox promised a more mature foreign policy, which he defined as a more engaged approach. He believed that Mexico was ready to take a much more active role in world affairs, especially through activities within the UNITED NATIONS. Mexico was a founding member of the UN, but over the years Mexican governments have considered the UN to be dominated by developed countries and

421

been distrustful of it. For more than twenty years, they chose not to compete in SE-CURITY COUNCIL elections for rotating membership. Upon coming into power, however, Fox campaigned for Mexico to take over for Jamaica in a nonpermanent seat within the Security Council and won it in 2001. Moreover, under Fox and Felipe Calderón, Mexico became a supporter of UN reform, urging that a permanent seat in the Security Council be created for Latin America. In another break with past policy, these democratic Mexican governments expressed their willingness to consider sending noncombat personnel to provide support services as part of international PEACEKEEPING OPERATIONS (PKOs). Prior to this time, because of concerns that a more active role would violate the country's tradition of noninterference in the affairs of others, Mexicans had participated in peacekeeping operations only in El Salvador after the war there, as highway patrol officers.

As mentioned, part of Mexico's reluctance to take a more active role in the world was motivated by a desire to deflect outside criticism of its own undemocratic record. Now this was no longer a concern. Based on the progress his country had made, Fox argued that Mexico was ready to become a "proactive defender of human rights" abroad.[1] Fox moved Mexico toward this goal when, in 2005, it became the 100th country to ratify the convention creating the INTERNATIONAL CRIMINAL COURT.

Perhaps an even bigger test of the president's determination to depart from the principle of nonintervention was Mexico's willingness to criticize others for their human rights abuses. Such a proactive stance would amount to one of the biggest foreign policy changes undertaken by the new government. It would not be easy (nonintervention is named as a central principle in the Mexican constitution), but it appears that the shift has occurred. For example, under the PRI, Mexico was one of the few Latin American countries that consistently refused to join the United States in denouncing Cuba. However, during the Fox administration, Mexico voted at the UN to criticize Cuba's human rights record. As a result, Mexico's relationship with Cuba sank to its lowest point in many years. After a series of incidents and accusations, both countries withdrew their ambassadors.[2]

Given their ideological differences, it should not be surprising that President Fox also had difficult relations with Venezuela's Hugo Chávez. Diplomatic relations were broken after Chávez accused Fox of being submissive to the United States, and Calderón won votes in the tight presidential race by demonizing his rival, López Obrador, as an acolyte of the Venezuelan president. Relations between the two governments continued to sour as, during the Mexican elections crisis of 2006, Chávez refused to recognize Calderón as the rightful winner.

As President Fox sought to assume center stage in more arenas and took a more active role for Mexico as a spokesman for Latin America, tensions with other countries in the region (including the United States) sometimes grew. President Calderón has spoken of his desire to repair these relations. Since Calderón became president, Mexico and Cuba's relations have been repaired and are now described as cordial. Under Calderón, Mexico and Venezuela have resumed diplomatic relations and exchanged ambassadors. Calderón has also indicated that he would like to see Mexico serving as a bridge between the United States and left-leaning governments in the region, such as Nicaragua, Ecuador, and Bolivia.

In addition to improving relations with its Latin neighbors, in recent years Mexico has worked hard to reduce its dependence on the United States by diversifying its economic ties. Besides entering into trade partnerships with more than fifty countries, Mexico is increasingly visible at forums such as the GROUP OF 20 (G-20), arguing against protectionism and for increased funding for the INTERNATIONAL MONETARY FUND (IMF). In 2009 Mexico was again elected into a nonpermanent seat on the UN Security Council, raising its international stature. Although Mexico has been outspoken on Gaza, the Honduran coup, and other matters, one global issue on which Mexico has become a leader is climate change. In part this is because Calderón (who is a former energy secretary) has taken a personal interest in the matter. Hosting an environmental conference in Cancún in 2010, he called on high- and low-income countries (particularly the United States and China) to stop blaming each other for the problem of global warming and to accept shared responsibility for it. Mexico is seeking to serve as a bridge between developed and developing countries on the issue. The Mexican president has proposed a "third way" for countries like Mexico: commit to reductions in greenhouse gases in return for technology transfers and aid from the big polluters. Calderón has also called for the creation of a "green fund" to aid poorer countries in reducing their emissions and adapting to climate change, and has set an ambitious goal to halve its emissions by 2050 (compared to 2002 levels), a pledge that Calderón intends to keep (with foreign assistance). Mexico is the only low-income country to publish a full inventory of its greenhouse gas emissions (the world's fourteenth largest economy, it produces 1.5–3.0 percent of global emissions). Its comprehensive strategy to reduce emissions, which includes ambitious tree-planting efforts, has contributed to its "very good" score on the Climate Change Performance Index, which rates countries on their greenhouse emissions and policy. In 2010 Mexico was ranked 11th out of 60 countries (behind Brazil, Sweden, and Germany but far ahead of the United States, which was ranked 53rd).[3] In sum, since Calderón has become president, Mexico has been out in front, taking leadership and serving as a role model on the issue of climate change. Although he doesn't attract nearly as much attention as Brazil's Luiz Inácio Lula da Silva or Venezuela's Chávez, Calderón has significantly shifted his country's role on the international stage and Mexico has stepped up to shape the world's agenda.

Case Study: Peru

Peru has long had ties with the United States and other countries, but the Andean STATE's primary international interest has been its relationship with its neighbors. In that relationship, Peru has wavered and often appeared irresolute. On the one hand, it has asserted its desire for regional cooperation. The country took an early interest in promoting inter-American solidarity at the 1826 Panama Conference. At the Lima Conference of 1847–1848, Peru joined Bolivia, Chile, Colombia, and Ecuador in calling for a defensive alliance and eventual confederation. On the other hand, despite being a longtime member of the Organization of American States (OAS) and the Andean Community of Nations (CAN), Peru has had an on-and-off relationship with its neighbors. It has welcomed the economic cooperation that comes with integration, but has never pursued it fully. It is only an associated member of Mercosur; as such it receives some preferential treatment but does not have full voting rights or complete access to the markets of full members. Peruvian governments have sometimes expressed their interest in joining Mercosur as a full member and establishing a common foreign policy among CAN members. At other times, however, Peru has threatened to quit such integration efforts altogether.

Such capriciousness toward its neighbors may be explained by a history of difficult relations in the region. As much as it recognizes the need for cooperation, Peru has just as consistently asserted its desire for independence and determination to pursue what it views as its national interest. As a result, Peru has often found itself in competition with its neighbors—all of which are seeking commercial advantage. The IRREDENTIST conflicts that have divided the region are based in Spain's failure to mark clear boundaries between its administrative units during colonialism. Consequently, Peru has had long-standing border disputes with Chile and Ecuador. Relations with Chile have been tense since the 1879 War of the Pacific, in which Peru lost large tracts of land to Chile. Peru and Ecuador have fought a series of brief wars for the past six decades over a sixty-mile stretch of Amazonian territory that was never well demarcated. In addition, Peru is challenging Chile's control over a maritime boundary that gives it rights over a rich fishing area. Peru has taken its case to the International Court of Justice, which is expected to hand down a ruling in 2012.[4]

Peru's dispute with Ecuador over the Cenepa River Basin (known as the "Alsace-Lorraine of the Andes") dates back to the early nineteenth century and is centered on questions of territory, water, and mineral rights. For Ecuador, the Cenepa provided the country with badly needed access through the Amazon to distant markets and the Atlantic. But Peruvian presidents treated control of the Cenepa as a matter of national pride. Following a brief conflict in 1995 that resulted in an indecisive outcome, mediators from Brazil, Argentina, the United States, and Chile were able to set the matter to rest in 1998, ending one of the longest disputes in the region.

Although relations have improved in recent years, Peru's conflicts with Chile and Ecuador have proven to be highly politicized, emotionally charged issues that have periodically disrupted inter-American relations. For example, the Peruvian government and press often accuse Chile of being imperialist, acting arrogantly toward Peru, viewing itself as "successful" and "modern," and putting down Peru as "backwards," "uncivilized," and "poor."[5] Peru's relations with Venezuela and Bolivia (in particular, the personal animosity between Presidents Alan García, Hugo Chávez, and Evo Morales, respectively) can best be described as a cold war. On more than one occasion, García has accused Chávez of interference in Peruvian domestic politics and even of fomenting unrest by supporting violent protests by various antigovernment groups.[6] Although it is unlikely that Peru would come to blows with these two countries, the name-calling has at times been fierce—in part because their ideological differences are stark (Chávez and Morales are leftists and highly critical of the United States whereas García embraces the United States and NEOLIBERALISM). In Peru's conflicts with Chile and Ecuador (as well as with Venezuela and Bolivia), each side blames the other for behaving aggressively. Meanwhile, analysts have accused all the governments involved of making their border disputes into nationalist issues to divert public attention away from domestic problems. Some say that a recent spy scandal, in which a Peruvian intelligence official was charged with selling military secrets to Chile, is an example of this.[7]

Although the war of words is not over, a least for now it appears that most of Peru's border disputes with its neighbors have been put to rest. However, regional rivalries were not helped by the Fujimori government's huge military budgets, or its purchase of fighter jets. Some analysts believe that such actions pushed the region perilously close to an arms race—and a dangerous and unnecessary waste of precious funds, given the fact that the parties involved are democracies that pose no serious security threat to each other. For the past several years, though, flush with cash from the higher prices they've received for their exports, several countries in the region have spent billions on weapons purchases. Venezuela and Brazil are two that Peru has called out for this, but in particular it has been Chile's arms acquisitions that are causing Peru some concern. As a result, García has called for a military nonaggression pact in South America that would cut arms purchases and promote more TRANSPARENCY and confidence-building measures.[8]

For all its thorniness with its neighbors, such statesmanship can be characteristic of Peru. As a small to medium-sized power, Peru has been impressively active in a variety of capacities. It sent approximately 200 peacekeepers to Haiti as part of an international effort aimed at establishing stability in the region's poorest country. Its diplomatic corps has long enjoyed a reputation of being first-rate. Peruvian career diplomat Javier Pérez de Cuéllar served two terms as UN Secretary-General, from 1982 to 1992. Peru was also instrumental in the crafting of peace accords that ended long-standing wars in more than one Central American state. It played a leadership role in the negotiation of several multilateral conventions, including the Law of the Sea conferences. Backed by several NONGOVERNMENTAL ORGANIZATIONS (NGOs), Peru has successfully negotiated two debt-for-nature swaps with the United States to fund conservation work in its western Amazonian rainforests. As Peru moves toward consolidating its DEMOCRACY, look for similar accomplishments, and for Peru to return as a voice for the non-Western world at the UN, in the NON-ALIGNED MOVEMENT (NAM), and in other international arenas.

Case Study: Nigeria

Nigeria is known as the giant of Africa. It is Africa's largest democracy and the continent's second largest economy. Nigeria is also a regional power—and some believe it to have the potential to be a superpower. However, during the last years of the Abacha government, Nigeria had become an international pariah of sorts, isolated for its role as a hub in the transshipment of illegal narcotics and slapped with a variety of minor sanctions for its human rights abuses. That status has changed dramatically since Nigeria's latest attempt at democracy in 1999, as the country has resumed its traditional place in international politics. A founding member of the Organization of African Unity (OAU) and one of the first countries to hold the chairmanship of the OAU's successor, the African Union (AU), Nigeria has taken an interest in a variety of issues that do not directly affect the country, such as Western Sahara and Darfur. These efforts have won it the title "Africa's leader" and for many years Nigeria was viewed as the voice for the region at international forums. Nigeria has assumed leadership roles in a number of INTERNATIONAL GOVERNMENTAL ORGANIZATIONS (IGOs), including the Organization of Petroleum Exporting Countries (OPEC) and the Commonwealth. Since independence the country has been a major contributor of troops to more than twenty-five UN peacekeeping missions—in the

Democratic Republic of Congo, Lebanon, Iran, and Iraq, among other countries. If Africa ever attains a permanent seat on the Security Council, there is a good chance that two old rivals, South Africa and Nigeria, would campaign hard for it.

Because it is such a giant, what happens in Nigeria affects much of the rest of the continent. Democratic CONSOLIDATION in Nigeria would contribute positively to the POLITICAL LIBERALIZATION throughout the region. On the other hand, a return to AUTHORITARIANISM and continued fragmentation in Nigeria would undoubtedly contribute to state decay and DISINTEGRATION in neighboring countries. Thus the relationship goes both ways. Nigerian leaders have taken the position that their country cannot achieve its economic goals if West Africa is unstable. Consequently, Nigeria has imposed what some call a "Pax Nigeriana." It has played the role of regional power broker in the Economic Community of West African States (ECOWAS), and has claimed West Africa, where Nigeria has its greatest security concerns, as its sphere of influence. Willing to violate the OAU's principle of noninterference in the internal affairs of others, Nigeria has viewed itself as an arbiter of both civil and interstate disputes—to the point that some characterize it as being HEGEMONIC.[9] When it went into Liberia it was the first African country ever to intervene in the affairs of a neighbor not threatening war. After years of sending troops to intervene in the civil war in Liberia, it went on to Sierra Leone, where Nigeria led the 1998 intervention by the ECOWAS Monitoring Group (ECOMOG), a multilateral armed force. Ironically, Nigerian dictator Sani Abacha sent 15,000 soldiers to reinstall a democratically elected government in Sierra Leone. Although some questioned Nigeria's motives, it should be noted that in the late 1990s Nigeria spent more on international peacekeeping operations in Africa than did the United States, Britain, or France. It is said to have participated in every single UN peacekeeping mission. Nigeria has been willing to do what the "world's leaders" have shied away from.[10]

Darfur is the perfect example of this. For years a skeletal crew of 7,000 ill-equipped (and often unpaid) African Union peacekeepers (mostly Nigerian and Rwandan) served mostly as a token international presence, often unable to do much more than bear witness to the atrocities committed against civilians. Nigeria intervened in Guinea-Bissau and elsewhere to quash military takeovers. And the country has played a leading diplomatic role in Africa, attempting to broker peace talks in Côte d'Ivoire, Sudan, and Zimbabwe. In 2006, it was Nigeria that helped to convince Liberian warlord Charles Taylor to step down from power by offering him refuge. It was also Nigeria that turned Taylor over to an international tribunal, to be tried for crimes against humanity. Under Olusegun Obasanjo, Nigeria gave South Africa some stiff competition for the title of Africa's ambassador to the world.[11]

Obasanjo clearly enjoyed basking in his glory as Africa's chief diplomat, and Nigerians are sometimes said to have an exaggerated view of the importance of their country on the world stage. That role has diminished significantly since Obasanjo's retirement, given Umaru Yar'Adua's long illness and the distractions regarding Goodluck Jonathan's right to replace him as president. For example, although Nigeria was elected to serve as a nonpermanent member on the UN Security Council in 2009, the Yar'Adua and Jonathan governments were not able to make much of the opportunities to lead. Many of its West African neighbors are experiencing political crises, but, in a departure from past practice, Nigeria has held back from its traditional inclinations. It did not overturn the 2009 coup in Niger or intervene to stabilize

Guinea or Guinea-Bissau (and this has greatly diminished the ability of ECOWAS to respond to events). As of early 2011, it could be a similar story in Côte d'Ivoire; without Nigeria's participation, ECOWAS would have a hard time making good on its threat to intervene against an intransigent incumbent who refuses to step down after losing elections.

It was a hard pill to swallow when Nigerians, having become accustomed to the limelight as leaders of Africa, learned that one of their countrymen had attempted to take down a US airliner in 2009 on Christmas Day (the so-called underwear bomber). Nigerians were stung by their country's inclusion on terrorist watch lists and many felt that their country had no place on a roll-call that included Yemen and Iran.[12] Perhaps the most significant indicator of changing fortunes for Nigeria, though, is that instead of heading up interventions around the world, President Jonathan is reportedly considering asking for international assistance in quelling the so far intractable conflict in the Niger Delta. If the United States or another power were to actively intervene in this war (even at the government's request), it would mark a huge shift in Nigeria's view of itself—and its role on the world stage.

Case Study: Zimbabwe

Because it is a relatively small, landlocked country, most people might expect Zimbabwe to be relatively uninvolved in foreign affairs and very inward-looking. However, Zimbabwe has long had a special place on the international stage. The fate of Rhodesia was a recurrent topic at UN meetings for years. Since the country's independence, the Zimbabwean government has been unusually vocal at international forums. A leader of the frontline states bordering South Africa, Zimbabwe was key in the anti-apartheid movement (and suffered for it). Similarly, Zimbabwe was punished by the United States when it refused to vote alongside the superpower at the UN. On the other hand, for being willing to stand up to the leader of the Western world, Zimbabwe's President Robert Mugabe won the admiration of many non-Western people.

However, toward the end of its first quarter century in power, the Mugabe government's relationship with the rest of the world was deteriorating very rapidly. For years now, many analysts have been concerned that Mugabe is taking the country down with him—just when it appears that Zimbabwe may need the world most. No doubt, Mugabe is looking for a new circle of friends. The most important of these is China. Through its "Look East" policy, Zimbabwe has found a new sponsor (one that is far less likely to lecture on human rights or democracy). It is a mutually beneficial relationship. Zimbabwe needs an alternative source of aid, credit, and foreign investment; China is seeking to expand its political influence and its markets. In addition, its industries are hungry for Zimbabwe's mineral products.[13]

Meanwhile, for most of the past decade the Zimbabwean economy has continued to spiral downward, and Mugabe has lashed out at all who are critical of him. Much of this criticism from the West has come since 2000, when Zimbabwe began a controversial land reform. Led by Britain, the United States and other Western countries criticized the government's handling of land reform and the growing deterioration in human rights.

Yet Mugabe's response to such concerns has been to strike out in defiance. He has especially singled out Zimbabwe's former colonizer, Britain, for his anger. Mugabe has argued that because it was the British whose policy created the problem, Britain has an obligation to pay for the land redistribution and reform. Britain points out that over the past two and a half decades, it and the United States have paid millions of dollars for land reform (the Zimbabwean government says it needs billions). The donors argue that they finally suspended the aid because the land being transferred wasn't going to the poor, but to Mugabe's cronies.

As a result, for the past decade, relations between Zimbabwe and Britain have been at their lowest point since independence. Mugabe has accused Britain of sponsoring the Movement for Democratic Change (MDC), seeking to govern the country "by remote control."[14] After Zimbabwe expelled a group of election observers sent by the European Union (EU) in 2002, the West agreed on a range of punitive measures against the Mugabe government. These measures include a ban on arms sales, but most are targeted sanctions, such as a travel ban and a freeze on the foreign bank accounts of Mugabe and the political ELITE. Although a bit more has begun to trickle in since Mugabe formed a unity government with the opposition in 2009, most Western DEVELOPMENT aid and loans to Zimbabwe have not resumed. Donors are providing some humanitarian assistance, but they have been hesitant to resume large-scale aid until they see more economic and political reforms—even though it is estimated that Zimbabwe will need tens of billions of dollars to rebuild and stabilize the country. Prime Minister Morgan Tsvangirai's pleas for the West to restore normal relations and for the help to come now have fallen on deaf ears. Meanwhile, Mugabe is crowing about how ineffectual his rival has turned out to be. Sanctions haven't been lifted, and the president offers this as proof that rich countries don't want Zimbabwe to develop.[15]

Zimbabwe has taken less heat from other corners. Although it was one of the first countries ever to be suspended from the Commonwealth, a club that included Britain and its former colonies, some members, especially African governments, feel that Britain and the United States have gone too far in vilifying and isolating Zimbabwe. The leaders of the region's two most powerful democracies, Nigeria and South Africa, have long feared that such a public trouncing is actually only worsening the situation. It is the view of many Africans that years of international sanctions and isolation have failed to prod the Mugabe government into compliance; many analysts call instead for "constructive engagement" or a less heavy-handed approach from the international community.

This is a position long espoused by most (not all) of the members of the Southern African Development Community (SADC), which played a crucial role in persuading Tsvangirai to join the unity government in 2009. Although Zimbabwe's neighbors have been criticized for being "soft" on Mugabe, there are a number of reasons to explain why they prefer quiet diplomacy. First, it is important to understand that throughout southern Africa, Mugabe will always be lionized as a liberation hero.[16] However, reportedly the SADC is losing patience with the stalemate in Zimbabwe and wants a roadmap for free and fair elections. Some African leaders (such as Botswana's Seretse Khama Ian Khama) have criticized Mugabe, saying that it sets a terrible precedent to allow incumbents who have stolen elections to remain in power.[17]

None of Zimbabwe's neighbors are happy about the situation next door. South Africa in particular is worried that Mugabe's actions will scare foreign investors away from the region. Mbeki's successor, Jacob Zuma, appears to be somewhat less protective of Mugabe; he has publicly called on the president to respect democracy and human rights. But Zuma has also asked for the West to repeal the sanctions on Zimbabwe, arguing that they threaten the unity government's viability.[18] It can't be surprising that Mbeki (and now Zuma) have chosen to proceed carefully. Given Zimbabwe's still-fragile economic recovery, a reverse could contribute to the country's collapse and more misery for a people already beset with problems. It certainly is not in South Africa's interests for things to go this far, given the hundreds who were flooding into the country daily until recently and the hundreds of thousands (if not millions) of Zimbabwean refugees who would almost certainly pour across its borders if conditions worsen. For these reasons Zimbabwe has become a crucial test for South Africa and the world. The question for those fed up with the status quo is this: How to help Tsvangirai help Zimbabwe—without helping Mugabe?

Case Study: Iran

Iran, similar to many countries of the third world, is struggling to find its way in the international community. Since the mid–twentieth century it has vacillated between the US-led, post–World War II alliance system, to isolation after the 1979 revolution, to a gradual and conflicted opening of arms to the international community. Former president Mohammad Khatami softened Iran's image abroad, including in the West, even making overtures to the United States. His successor, Mahmoud Ahmadinejad, has charted a stronger role that doesn't shy away from confrontation.

Iran has long contended as a regional leader in the Middle East, angling by the mid-2000s to be a "regional superpower."[19] This rise predates Ahmadinejad's ascendancy. The collapse of the Soviet Union increased the regional importance of Iran by allowing the restoration of ties between the Caucasus and Central Asia. These newly independent states, concerned about their survival, found an economic and security patron in Tehran. Hezbollah—armed and trained by Iran—waged a short yet successful war against Israel in 2006, in a conflict viewed by many as a proxy showing of Tehran's growing assertiveness. Finally, the post–Saddam Hussein reorganization of Iraq, in which the formerly suppressed Shiite majority has gained prominence, provides perhaps the largest boost to Iran's clout within the region. One analyst argues that the Shia revival in post-Hussein Iraq has achieved "what Iran's revolution had failed to do"—namely pose a serious challenge to Sunni Arab domination in the Middle East.[20] Because of its conflict with Iraq, the other regional fixture, Tehran is now poised to assume the leadership it never achieved in its early years.

Since the birth of the Islamic Republic in 1979, one of the most important issues facing Iran was its animosity toward Iraq, a tension that erupted in a devastating war from 1980 to 1988. This conflict ended more out of exhaustion than anything—Iran grudgingly accepted UN Security Council Resolution 598, which called for the cessation of hostilities and the exchange of prisoners of war—and Ayatollah Ruhollah Khomeini compared signing the resolution to "drinking poison."[21] Many believed that once the secular Sunni leader Saddam Hussein was out of the picture, closer ties between Iran and Iraq (dominated by religious Shiite Muslims) could form.[22] From Ahmadinejad's seat, he hopes to unite Shiites and Sunnis in a grand anti-US alliance, promoting a brand of POPULISM that Prince Hassan of Jordan has labeled "an alternative to CIVIL SOCIETY in the Middle East."[23] Attempts by many in the Western world to isolate the Islamic Republic may marginalize Iranian leaders even more, perhaps feeding into this phenomenon.

The biggest issue that has raised Iran's profile in the international community (remember that some say bad publicity is better than nothing) is its controversial uranium enrichment program. This development, pursued in secret for eighteen years before being disclosed by a dissident group in 2002, has been the source of defiance from Tehran and furious resistance from nearly everyone else, including Egypt and Saudi Arabia, which publicly called on Iran to cease its dangerous cat-and-mouse game with the international community.[24] Russia had provided assistance for a new nuclear complex and, even prior to the 2002 revelation by insiders, many believed that Iran had an active nuclear weapons program. Iranian leaders maintain the assertion that the program is for domestic energy needs alone—although many within the international community doubt this. The international response has been loud but slow to exercise much force, as many countries, including UN permanent-member states Russia and China, maintain that economic sanctions against the regime would cause too much pain for the civilian population (and harm their own business deals with the regime as well). Security Council sanctions, which necessitate the lack of disapproval from all UN permanent members, have been watered down in order to avoid a veto, and other multilateral sanctions (implemented by the United States, the EU, South Korea, and Japan) remain limited. Iranian leaders continue to insist they will never give up their right, as signatories to the Nuclear Non-Proliferation Treaty, to enrich uranium and produce nuclear fuel, with one key member of Tehran's foreign policy team forcefully stating, "We are the only country in the Middle East . . . that has the capability to produce the fuel. Nobody should ask us to dump this capability."[25] In reality, each round of UN Security Council sanctions related to its nuclear program, which since 2006 have targeted uranium processing, related research and development, the import and export of nuclear material and equipment, and in 2007 a ban on all arms exports, though perhaps slowing the country's nuclear and ballistic missile work, are not serving as an absolute deterrent.

Iran was a charter member of the United Nations, and it has a rocky history of ties with the organization. Its leaders strongly condemned UN failings during and after the war with Iraq in the 1980s. In 1987 moderate president Ali Khamenei portrayed the UN as "a paper factory for issuing worthless, ineffective orders."[26] More recently, the populist Ahmadinejad has used his face time at the UN to sharpen his country's anti-US credentials and its leadership of the Muslim world—he has much to gain in the eyes of many by clearly painting himself as everything that the US leaders are not. In claiming to speak for the Muslim world, Tehran has long supported the proposal that an Islamic country be made a permanent member of the Security Council during future reforms. Iranian leaders continue to raise their profile with the United Nations, including being elected to the UN Commission on the Status of Women in mid-2010, even as Iran faces nearly annual censures within the GENERAL ASSEMBLY on its human rights record, including "pervasive gender inequality and violence against women."[27]

The Islamic Republic of Iran has the potential to exert great influence—regionally and internationally. It is increasing its connections with Russia and Turkey, and extending more connections to Brazil, Gambia, Uganda, and China. Domestic debates on the pros and cons of greater incorporation into the world community, regional RECONFIGURATION and insecurities, and continued international tensions surrounding Tehran's policies will frame what direction this influence will take.

Case Study: Turkey

Turkey's status as both a metaphorical and a physical "bridge" between Europe, the Middle East, and Central Asia is clearly reflected in the country's regional and international memberships and activities. As a border state to continents (Europe and Asia) and civilizations (Islamic, secular, Western, and non-Western), Turkey is greatly impacted by affairs that surround it. Turbulent regional issues have dominated much of Turkey's multilateral ties. Mustafa Kemal Atatürk's statement "peace at home, peace in the world" continues to evoke a modern sense of priority that captures much of Turkey's views on regional and global issues.

Turkey's human rights challenges certainly have the potential to stain its international (and regional) reputation. Turkey has long sought membership in the European Union, and its applications were consistently rejected from 1987 to 1999. The biggest area of concern from the EU is Turkey's human rights record—the situation seems only to have worsened as talks, which began in 2005, continue. Even though the more recent stumbling block in accession talks seems to be Turkey's relations with Cyprus, concerns over its human rights record, especially in the areas of freedom of expression and women's rights, remain.

Additionally, Turkey still refuses to officially recognize its genocide of over 1 million minority Christian Armenians between 1915 and 1923. Large numbers of Armenians were either methodically massacred or forcibly sent to Syria, where many died of hunger in the desert. Foreign legislatures, including the French National Assembly, the European Parliament, the Belgian Senate, and the Russian Duma, have each called on Turkey to recognize the Armenian massacre as genocide, and similar resolutions in the US Congress have been debated for years. Talk of this period, even in fictionalized accounts, puts the speaker at risk for being prosecuted under Article 301 of the Turkish penal code for "insulting Turkishness." Journalists, authors, and others have faced charges under this article, including Orhan Pamuk, the 2006 recipient of the Nobel Prize for literature—even though, largely because of the prominence afforded him with the Nobel, the charges against him were dropped.

Many of Turkey's leaders, especially within the current administration, have made progress toward EU membership a central goal. Yet Turkey's contentious drive for EU membership is currently losing favor among ordinary Turkish citizens. As an environmental director (in an organization backed by the EU) lamented, "Businesses and local governments ask us 'Why are we negotiating if we don't know whether we will ever be accepted?'"[28] While most candidate countries leave the tough environmental requirements for the end of their accession work, Turkey has tackled them early, in part because so many other areas of negotiation have been closed. Yet even with their fits and starts, aspirations for EU membership have had a significant impact on policy changes within the republic, including abolition of the death penalty and adoption of constitutional reforms that removed some of the perceived infallibility of the military.

Turkey's relations within the United Nations continue to be challenged by multiple issues, including the Kurdish question, the status of Cyprus, and its own shifting alliances. As discussed in Chapter 10, one of the Turkish leaders' most pressing domestic concerns is the Kurdistan Workers Party (PKK). Other countries and multilateral institutions have taken on this issue as well, in part because of concerns of overzealous persecution by Turkish authorities of ethnic Kurds, and in part because of the international borders that are affected by this ethnic group. Iraq, Iran, and Syria also have significant Kurdish populations, many of whom lead rival groups to the PKK. For this reason, it was in Turkey's interest to gain favor with the world community by assisting in their protection, at the same time that they were limiting the punch of one of their own "problem groups." As long as competing Kurdish forces were active around Turkey's borders, the PKK's power would be in check. Turkey's ability to maintain such a balance, though, often complicates its own tensions. The dilemma faced by Turkey is huge: an independent Kurdish state would only aggravate its own problems, but instability faced by Kurds in Iraq would send hordes of refugees across the Turkish border, which doesn't bode well for Ankara either. Any operation to protect Iraqi Kurds required the use of Turkish air bases, and struck a sensitive chord among some Turkish military leaders, who feared that this international protection of Kurdish nationals, with the complicity of the Turkish government, could eventually be replicated in Turkey as well. Many fear that the eventual creation of an autonomous Kurdish state could create an even greater security problem for Ankara.[29] When sweetheart deals with rival Kurdish groups across Turkish borders collapsed, the military crossed over into Iraqi territory to destroy PKK bases, prompting outcries from every direction: the Iraqi Kurds, who were caught off-guard, the Iraqi government, whose territory was violated, as well as Turkey's global allies.

Cyprus, an island in the eastern Mediterranean Sea that has been divided into a Turkish-influenced north and Greek-influenced south since 1974, is another irritant in Turkey's global reputation. In 1974, following an attempted military coup on the island by a group favoring union with Greece, Turkish forces landed on Cyprus under the guise of restoring calm to protect the minority Turkish population on the island. The Turkish incursion was met with immediate UN condemnation from the Security Council, which criticized Turkey's intrusion into the sovereign Republic of Cyprus. A peacekeeping operation has been supervising the cease-fire and maintaining a buffer zone between ethnic Turkish residents in the north and ethnic Greeks in the south. The goal of the dialogue, which was reinitiated in 1997, is to foster a resolution in this standoff between the Greek Cypriot National Guard and Turkish forces, which number over 20,000. Turkey continues to express extreme dissatisfaction at the continuation of this peacekeeping operation, which, in lieu of a political settlement, remains in place.

Within this environment, leaders of the Justice and Development Party (AKP) are working to promote a "zero problems" foreign policy of trying to cultivate as many global friendships as possible. This has included outreach to Armenia, including the normalization of relations, despite the fact that this remains the "most problematic relationship in Turkey's neighborhood policy."[30] Revising its COLD WAR direction, Ankara's relations with Russia have substantially improved since Recep Tayyip Erdogan came to power in 2002. Turkish leaders are also charting a more visible role for the state in the North Atlantic Treaty Organization (NATO), evolving from a "wing country" on the geographic perimeter of the Western alliance to, especially since the war in Afghanistan, a more central player.[31] Turkey's role in NATO is pivotal for its Western shift, even as it remains one of only two members of NATO that is not also part of the EU (Norway is the other). Another element of this zero-problems approach has included the forging of a fuel-swap deal, alongside Brazil, with Iranian leaders over its enriched uranium. As we discuss in Chapter 21, this approach has raised eyebrows around the world, especially in Washington.

Each of these dilemmas demonstrates the bind facing Turkish decisionmakers. As they attempt to integrate more with global institutions and with their neighbors to the west, they face increased pressure in their domestic dealings, as well as possible misperceptions abroad. Turkish leaders are clearly charting a larger, more engaged role for the country. As Foreign Minister Ahmet Davutoglu stated in a recent interview, pursuing the zero-problems approach "doesn't mean that we will be silent in order to have good relations with all parties."[32] Few expect much silence from Ankara in the coming years.

Case Study: China

China views itself as a global player, especially since its economic transformation of the mid-1980s. Indeed, many analysts, Chinese and non-Chinese alike, predict that China is the most likely country to become a superpower in the twenty-first century.

Regionally, Chinese leaders continue to play an important role in bringing reclusive North Korea into greater participation in the world community, especially by hosting the six-party talks (which include China, the United States, North Korea, South Korea, Russia, and Japan) designed to manage Pyongyang's nuclear weapons program. China's attempts to stabilize the North Korean situation are largely out of self-interest—estimates vary, but it is believed that during particularly difficult times, such as the winter months, as many as 500 North Korean refugees cross the border into northeastern China each week. Beijing has also been a leading advocate of closer ties between North and South Korea, widely referred to as the "Sunshine" policy. Ironically, China has much security to lose if North and South Korea reunify—a united Korean peninsula could reopen major power surges for influence, and could invite a strong US presence on China's northeastern border. Even though China officially laments the presence of more than 28,000 US troops in Korea, their withdrawal could have a potentially destabilizing effect. The People's Republic of China (PRC) has also attempted to play the mediator role in the ongoing dispute (the fires of which it helps fan) between India and Pakistan, especially following their nuclear tests in the spring of 1998. China (allied with Pakistan) views itself as an important balancing force to India, which is allied with the United States. Beijing perceives India to be its greatest threat, which helps explain the assistance the country has provided to Pakistani leaders in the development of long-range missiles that could carry nuclear weapons.

China's military might catches the world's attention and its recent achievements in outer space continue that pattern. Beijing forces used a medium-range ballistic missile to shoot down an aging weather satellite in 2007, and China launched a robotic lunar orbiter in 2007 and again in 2010. The Japanese government recently issued an explicit warning about China's military growth, adjusting Tokyo's long-term regional defense policy in response to Beijing's increasing military spending, military modernization campaigns, and increased naval assertiveness in the East China and South China Seas, in which are located many hotly contested islands believed to be rich in natural resources.[33]

Beijing is also becoming an increasingly important player in the Middle East. Part of this is driven by trade and energy—Chinese trade with the Middle East nearly doubled between 2005 and 2010 (China is now Iran's largest trading partner), and Beijing is actually the largest importer of Middle Eastern oil, importing 23 percent of all of Iran's oil.[34] (Domestic demand for energy rises approximately 15 percent each year.) Chinese banks and construction companies are also closely involved in major projects throughout the region. Some were surprised when Beijing supported UN sanctions against Iran: it is likely that Beijing voted for UN sanctions out of fear of the impact of an arms race in the Middle East, which would endanger the flow of oil from Saudi Arabia and Iran.

With its increasing economic might, China has become the arms supplier of choice to many non-Western countries, especially those that are otherwise barred from being able to purchase these items. Among its most exported items are guns (especially AK-47s), leg-irons, anti-riot equipment, and armored vehicles.[35] These items, which the most economically developed states stopped producing years ago so they could focus on more sophisticated weapons systems, have found their way onto some of the world's bloodiest battlegrounds, including Sudan and Myanmar. In a move that was once an integral part of the pre-1978 playbook of the People's Republic, when China donated free weapons to countries supporting its revolutionary cause, Beijing uses these sales to deepen its credentials in the developing world and promote itself as a counterbalance to US hegemony.[36]

In the United Nations, Chinese delegates tend to view themselves as the self-proclaimed leaders of the developing countries, in large part because of the power they hold with their veto option in the Security Council. PRC diplomats use this veto infrequently, but strategically, often to lash out at Taiwan's supporters. For example, in February 2000, China vetoed a resolution to extend the peacekeeping operation in Macedonia, because Macedonia had recently recognized Taiwan as an independent country. It has taken similar action against Guatemala, often voting against any measure the state sponsors, because Guatemala has lobbied other UN members for the admission of Taiwan to the UN. While from its soapbox China often preaches the importance of sovereignty, this claim is never meant to include the territory of Taiwan, for which the principle of Chinese territorial integrity is deemed much more important. China is not likely to budge on the contested issue of Taiwan's relationship with the United Nations anytime soon. These acts have impelled others to bend to China's will—South Africa, for example, switched its diplomatic recognition from Taiwan to China in 1997, in part because it hoped the move would garner China's support for a new permanent seat on the Security Council. Some have accused China of using its UN permanent-member power irresponsibly, especially as Beijing helped stall UN action in Sudan's troubled Darfur region.[37] From Beijing's point of view, China was speaking up for Sudan's sovereign right to control what happens within its borders.

China has had a very vocal role in the ongoing debate over UN reform in general, but especially in debates over possible reform of the Security Council. Beijing supports enlargement of the Security Council (and surprisingly endorsed Germany and Brazil as two potential newcomers), while closely guarding its own spot as the lone "Asian seat" within the chamber (not wanting to see either Japan or India emerge as regional rivals).[38] In debates over the future of the United Nations, Beijing's voice is well placed to carry much weight.

As China continues to promote its political, economic, cultural, and military ties with other developing countries, including the use of its so-called soft power to market its own "brand" of affairs, its reach and influence are likely to increase.

Case Study: Indonesia

In the past, Indonesia was a pivotal regional actor, with aspirations toward becoming the leader of countries that refused to line up with either the United States or the Soviet Union. In this latter goal it was a catalyst in efforts to organize non-Western countries during the Cold War. Throughout the 1990s and early 2000s the instability of the Indonesian state, rocked by economic, political, ethnic, and natural crises, aroused concern among its neighbors in the region and within the global community alike. Under the leadership of Susilo Bambang Yudhoyono (SBY), and in the face of more stability, Indonesian leaders have been charting a more engaged path, regionally and globally, promoting the image that, in the words of their president, the country has "1000 friends and zero enemies."[39]

Throughout the Cold War, Indonesia was a proud "holdout" during the superpower-dominated contest, occupying a position that became known as "rowing between two reefs." Indicative of this approach, which is different from neutrality, Indonesia was a founding member of the Non-Aligned Movement, an organization of developing countries that formed in 1961 in opposition to the bipolarity of the Cold War. The NAM grew out of a joint conference of African and Asian leaders in 1955, known as the Bandung Conference, named for the Indonesian city in which it was held. In the face of rising superpower tensions, and the division of many countries into blocs that supported either one side or the other, leaders of many former colonial countries gathered to convey their assessment of world affairs. Since the 1960s the NAM has provided a forum to discuss decolonization, debt relief, total nuclear disarmament, and UN Security Council reform. The organization has also sent fact-finding and relief missions to conflict zones, including Somalia and Bosnia-Herzegovina. All the while, members of the organization claimed independence from the "East-West ideological conflict," concentrating instead on North-South economic CLEAVAGES. Yet even though Indonesian leaders publicly proclaimed "an active and independent foreign policy," the 1965 anticommunist coup won it the favor and support of many of the Western powers—especially the United States. Although the NAM is less independent than it claims to be, it remains a valuable forum for many non-Western countries. In the 2009 summit, for example, which was held in Egypt, members again called on the United Nations to be more truly representative of the smaller countries of the world community.

Ideological and ethnic tensions exist between Indonesia and its giant neighbor to the northwest, China. For almost four decades, this animosity was dominantly ideological in nature, as Indonesia was the focal point of anticommunist struggle in the region. As discussed in Chapter 17, much of the impetus for forming the Association of Southeast Asian Nations (ASEAN) in the late 1960s was to fortify an anticommunist alliance among states in the region. This focus gradually subsided, though, and China now holds "dialogue status" within the organization. Indonesia views its neighbor's increasingly active role in ASEAN in ZERO-SUM terms: as Beijing becomes more influential, Jakarta's level of influence is likely to wane. Indonesia's treatment of its sizable ethnic Chinese population has long been a focal point of tensions between the two countries. In the riots of 1998 and thereafter, ethnic Chinese communities throughout Indonesia—especially Chinese women—have been targeted in mob attacks, mass rape, and discrimination. Ethnic Chinese business communities in Indonesia have been scapegoated as well, especially as Indonesian families watch their disposable income plummet.

Multilateral institutions, especially the United Nations and the International Monetary Fund, have played a key although not always positive role in Indonesia since 1997. As discussed in Chapter 7, IMF demands for the financial bailout package in 1998, after the collapse of the Indonesian currency, led to wide-scale looting and riots across the country. As the Great Recession unfolded in 2008, SBY stated bluntly that his country "will not follow the IMF's formula in coping with the global financial crisis. . . . We still need to learn from that experience (of a decade ago)."[40]

Indonesia's relations with the UN in recent years have mostly surrounded the independence of East Timor in 1999 and the violence that ensued. Regionally, Australia was a main player in urging Indonesian president B. J. Habibie to call for the East Timor referendum, and the Commonwealth also provided a large number of peace-keeping troops in the aftermath of the vote. Despite the passage of time and the achievement of sovereignty within the country now known as Timor-Leste, the dust has yet to settle. Members of the international community demanded that Indonesia establish a war crimes tribunal for the East Timor violence, but then-president Abdurrahman Wahid feared a surge of NATIONALISM, which he argued could completely unravel the state. Perhaps he was in touch with common sentiment across the country, as many Indonesians viewed those accused of atrocities as "patriots" rather than criminals.[41] Calls for the tribunal lessened after Wahid's argument received the endorsement of UN Secretary-General Kofi Annan. As a result, Indonesia organized a reception, truth, and reconciliation commission in East Timor that was designed to be weak—its final report, released in January 2005, chalked up the atrocities within East Timor to the behavior of "rogue elements" within the military. For its part, the United Nations did establish a Serious Crimes Investigation Unit, but it too has been largely impotent. Many shake their head at the realization that Suharto, widely believed to be responsible for two times as many deaths as Saddam Hussein and Slobodan Milosevic combined, has been able to escape any and all wheels of justice.[42]

Indonesia has started to become a major player in Southeast Asian affairs, and its recent outreach to Australia and China seems calculated to ensure Indonesia's presence throughout Asia for decades to come. As the world's fourth most populous state, ringed by some of the globe's busiest fishing lanes, Indonesia possesses global influence. A major arms deal with Russia, penned in 2007, seemed to verify Indonesia's aspirations to ensure important ties for years to come. Yet as *The Economist* pointed out, domestic challenges could derail its future ambitions: "a failure to prosper at home would turn the spotlight away from Indonesia's desire to solve global problems, and towards its capacity to generate them."[43] The islands of Indonesia may stand at a crossroads.

Now It's Your Turn

What significant events or issues would you add to this discussion that have become prominent since this book was published? Have any of the concerns covered in this chapter been significantly resolved—or have any situations dramatically worsened? What role do you believe truth commissions serve in promoting peace and justice? If you were the leader of a country torn apart by conflict, how would you best prescribe picking up the pieces and moving on? In your mind, have any recent events warranted an international tribunal or the commissioning of a peacekeeping operation? Are there any countries that seem to be impacted by regional or global matters more than they are able to influence affairs themselves? How differently would you look at some of the IGOs and NGOs studied in this chapter if you were a resident or a leader in one of these third world countries? Some people argue that, in general, the richer the country and the more its economy is geared toward trade, the more active and complex its foreign policy. The corollary would then be that the poorer the country, the more focused its leaders tend to be on domestic issues. Do you find this to be the case with the countries studied here? Why or why not?

20

Dealing with a Superpower: "Third World" Views of the United States

America's unipolar moment has passed.
—The Economist *on United Nations reform*[1]

The United States has been the "global rule-maker . . . that doesn't always play by the rules." —*Fareed Zakaria, journalist*[2]

Living As the Lone Superpower

Leaders are noticed. As the leading military and political power in the world, the United States possesses both great influence and great responsibility. In responding to and solving global problems, the role of the United States is critical, but certainly not always benign. Many American students are surprised to hear that the United States is viewed with both respect and contempt beyond its borders. Some have a difficult time seeing that actions of the United States are viewed as threatening to many, because Americans tend to believe that their actions are taken in the name of some larger, more noble cause. Yet it is important to remember that others take actions, some of which we deem irresponsible or even reprehensible, with seemingly good motivations as well.

In the early decades of the twenty-first century, it seems that the United States stands as the world's strongest country, the world's lone superpower. Yet many are openly questioning the durability of this status, especially given the reemergence of China. Whether or not it is technically accurate by definition, many view the United States as an EMPIRE—willing and able to exert influence beyond its borders. Sometimes this happens in the pursuit of a worthy goal. Other times, US actions have been less noble. One particularly controversial example may help illustrate this dilemma. Since the early 1950s, US presidents have intermittently considered some form of missile defense as a way to protect the United States and some of its allies from attack, including, by the 1980s, investigation of the feasibility of a space-based system of DETERRENCE. Yet this pursuit, which requires the United States to break hard-won arms accords, is viewed by other STATES as a unilateral expansion of already dominant US capability, since it would neutralize others' ability to respond defensively to a US attack. Initiatives to extend the military arms race into outer space, including space-based lasers and interceptors, add to this perception.

Another example can be found in US trade laws. With domestic legislation sanctioning Cuba and Iran, the US government attempts to economically punish not only these states, but also countries (and private corporations) that do business with them. The US embargo against Cuba, in place since 1962, is the most enduring trade limitation in modern history, despite the fact that it has very little support beyond Washington. Every year since 1991, the GENERAL ASSEMBLY of the UNITED NATIONS has overwhelmingly passed a nonbinding resolution condemning the embargo, with two and sometimes three countries siding with the United States on the issue. The US perspective, reiterated early in President Barack Obama's term, is that the United States will trade with Cuba after it shows signs of political reform. As an editorial in *Newsweek* argued, "The embargo is the perfect example used by anti-Americans everywhere to expose the hypocrisy of a superpower that punishes a small island while cozying to dictators elsewhere."[3]

The United States has also staked out the position that countries should not do business with known terrorists, a contention voiced more strongly after the events of September 11, 2001. The perspective beyond US borders, though, is that the United States does not have the authority to tell other countries with whom they should be conducting business. US sanctions against Iran, meant to strengthen SECURITY COUNCIL sanctions in 2010, have received mixed responses around the world. India's secretary of foreign affairs stated that "unilateral sanctions recently imposed by individual countries [could] have a direct and adverse impact on Indian companies, and, more importantly, on our energy security."[4] China and Russia have expressed similar concerns, primarily in response to business interests. These actions increasingly are causing countries to claim that the United States is invoking EXTRATERRITORIALITY, or the attempt to impose one's rules and laws outside of one's own sovereign territory.

The criticism expands well beyond US trade interests. The US treatment of detainees at the Guantánamo Bay naval base has evoked similar calls. This prison camp, built on contested US territory in Cuba, began detaining alleged terrorists in 2002, riling human rights activists around the world and propelling many of those held into legal limbo—the names and nationalities of the detainees were not released until 2006, after a Freedom of Information Act request was filed by media outlets. Nearly five years after the camp opened, after the US Supreme Court branded the detention unconstitutional, the Bush administration reversed its previous decision that, because of the unique characteristics of the US war on TERRORISM, these individuals were ineligible for protection under the Geneva Conventions. When pictures surfaced documenting overt abuse of prisoners at the hands of US soldiers at Abu Ghraib prison in Baghdad, and gruesome accounts of the killing of twenty-four Iraqi civilians in Haditha in retaliation for a roadside bomb that killed one Marine, many wondered aloud whether these scandals were representative of a larger US approach, rather than isolated incidents.

Some perceive the United States as a government that abides by laws only when it is useful, while attempting to force others to follow US laws and policies, even in foreign countries. In this sense, many countries of the world believe that the United States holds an EXCEPTIONALIST view of its place in the world. The examples are plentiful. The United States condemned the Iraqi invasion of Kuwait in 1990, yet the same US leaders had ordered the invasion of Panama in 1989 in order to capture President Manuel Noriega and try him for criminal drug operations in the United States. The United States produces the most greenhouse emissions of any other country in the world, yet US presidents have sought exceptions from international environmental treaties designed to combat these ills. The lack of US support for the INTERNATIONAL CRIMINAL COURT (ICC), discussed in Chapter 17, including the demand that US military personnel be exempt from its jurisdiction, is yet another case in point. Even though the United States had won an agreement on amendments to protect Americans from frivolous suits, Washington suspended military assistance to thirty-five countries for failing to immunize Americans from prosecution by the ICC.[5] US leaders rejected international protocols on germ warfare and demanded amendments to an accord on the illegal sale of small arms. Even if these policies do not convey a growing sense of isolationism, as some claim, there has been a clear increase in US unilateralism—even prior to the globally unpopular Iraq War.

There are still other examples. In 1997, President Bill Clinton, facing pressure from the Pentagon, refused to sign the Ottawa Treaty, which outlaws landmines, because an exception for the Korean peninsula was not granted. In 1999 the US Senate rejected the Nuclear Test Ban Treaty because—even though US leaders have made clear that they would like the rest of the world to halt weapons development—they don't want to have their own hands tied. On the grounds that outsiders would be able to call for inspections in an imperfect system, President George W. Bush also discarded the biological weapons draft protocol from 1972 (which 143 countries, including the United States, had ratified), and opposed international efforts to limit the trade in small arms. At the same time that pressure was building on Iran, which as a signatory to the Nuclear Non-Proliferation Treaty (NPT), was not permitted to develop nuclear energy programs, the United States crafted a sweetheart deal to provide nuclear technology to India, which is not party to NPT, and therefore, per international agreements, cannot legitimately receive this technology. It is more difficult to lead by example if one keeps breaking the rules, and others are bound to challenge this power: "If America wants to bind China into the rule-based liberal order it promotes, it needs to stick to the rules itself. Every time America breaks them—by, for instance, protectionism—it feeds China's suspicions and undermines the very order it seeks."[6] The hypocrisy of US actions becomes glaring in the eyes of some, as a Chinese diplomat shared: "When you tell us that we support a dictatorship in Sudan to have access to its oil, what I want to say is, 'And how is that different from your support of a medieval monarchy in Saudi Arabia?'"[7]

The United States also faces criticism for failing to provide support to international movements promoting the same rights and privileges that Americans espouse the world over, including women's rights. As discussed in Chapter 17, the United States is the only industrialized country not to have ratified the Convention on the Elimination of All Forms of Discrimination Against Women (CEDAW). Ratification of the convention, which the US delegation helped draft in 1979, has been caught up in domestic politics and concern by some critics that UN committee members would have authority over private decisions and US laws (which they would not, due to the principle of SOVEREIGNTY). The US Senate Foreign Relations Committee even supported ratification of the convention in 2002, but the full measure, which is vehemently opposed by the pro-life lobby, was never introduced to the full Senate for a vote. This has not only harmed the credibility of the United States in some circles, but it has been used by others to deny women's rights in other countries as well. As one Afghani activist testified before the US Senate Judiciary Committee in 2010: "Even in Afghanistan . . . conservative elements use this [US failure to ratify] to attack women's rights defenders. They say that if the United States believes in women's rights as a universal right, why haven't they signed on to CEDAW?"[8]

Additionally, the United States often withholds support for international organizations that conduct work seen as being in opposition to the policy goals of some interest groups in the country—even if the action is perfectly legal in other societies of the world. One clear example of this is the US condemnation of organizations that provide family-planning or abortion services. US presidents Ronald Reagan, George H. W. Bush, and George W. Bush each denied funding to any agency that views abortion as a policy option, describing themselves as taking a moral stance on such "right to life" issues. Meanwhile, the same leaders sided with businesses to oppose international efforts to eliminate child labor. The United States refuses to sign treaties prohibiting the use of child soldiers, and, until the US Supreme Court ruled the practice unconstitutional in 2005, remained one of the few countries in the world that executed juveniles. To many, the contradiction is glaring.

Such actions have contributed to much of the animosity, mistrust, and ill will the United States encounters worldwide. Sometimes this hostility is manifested in condemnations of US actions, or the exclusion of the United States from international bodies. In the spring of 2001, for example, the United States for the first time failed to be reelected to a seat on the UN Human Rights Commission (which former first lady Eleanor Roosevelt helped create in the late 1940s). Shortly thereafter, the United States lost its seat on the UN's International Narcotics Control Board—the primary drug enforcement commission in the United Nations system. Some interpreted the Narcotics Board vote to be an expression of dissension against US drug control policies. After these actions, both of which resulted from secret ballots, some countries' leaders expressed a sense of justice. It is important to emphasize that it was not only countries from the third world that voted the United States out of these seats: negative votes included US allies in the Western, developed world. On the Human Rights Commission, country representatives expressed dissension related to US votes on issues we have discussed throughout this book.

The vocal criticisms of the United States became deafening after the US-led invasion of Iraq in 2003. The war had been justified in large part by US vice president Dick Cheney's so-called 1 percent doctrine—if there were even a 1 percent chance of terrorists acquiring weapons of mass destruction, the United States would be justified to act preemptively. This didn't sit well with the world, even with many US allies. Assisted by the so-called coalition of the willing, which included only a fraction of the world's states that had supported the 1990 invasion, this action was explicitly taken without UN approval because of the lack of support from even US allies within the Security Council's veto-wielding countries (notably France). Bush and the leading voices within his administration became wildly unpopular around the world, and the former president has been accused of doing more harm to America's image and its global relations than any other US president in recent history.[9]

Under President Obama, has America's image been restored? Pollsters have spoken of a perceived "Obama effect," or a boost in pro-American sentiment, since his election in 2008. There have been noticeable gains in positive public opinion toward the United States, as measured by the annual polling by the Pew Global Attitudes Project. President Obama receives more popular ratings in countries around the world than he does in the United States, and "opinions of the US, which improved markedly in 2009 in response to Obama's new presidency, have also remained far more positive than they were for much of George W. Bush's tenure."[10] Yet President Obama still finds himself needing to make the case that the United States is not at war with Islam, a sign that the ghosts of the Iraq War will linger long after the final US forces pull out. US leaders, as they did during the Bush administration, continue to go to great efforts to make sure that the war on terrorism is perceived as a war against religious extremism rather than a war against Islam, as some have attempted to frame it. In his speeches throughout the Middle East, President Obama has stated multiple times: "The United States is not and never will be at war with Islam. In fact, our partnership with the Muslim world is critical in rolling back a fringe IDE-OLOGY that people of all faiths reject . . . America's relationship with the Muslim world cannot and will not be based on opposition to al-Qaeda."[11] However, just as we sometimes conflate individual actions as representative of a culture or government more largely, efforts by a fringe group led by Florida pastor Terry Jones to burn a Quran on the anniversary of the September 11 terrorist attacks received a fierce response, from governments and civilians, around the world.

Shifting from Anti-Americanism to "Post-Americanism"?
Following the events of September 11, 2001, it became common to discuss the ways the world had permanently changed. While it certainly is true that few Americans will view themselves or their personal safety in the same way for a very long time, many

A banner protesting Obama's visit reads, "Beware the evil agenda of the United States in Indonesia" (Reuters/Beawiharta)

voices in the third world argued that it wasn't the world, but rather the United States and its self-image that have been changed by those tragic events. Although both the method and the magnitude of the actions on that day shocked many, much of the world has lived for a long time in fear of violence and terrorism.

The drop in sentiment toward the US government came hard and fast. In the weeks following September 11, the Bush administration crafted a wide-reaching coalition of support, uniting many countries of the world, Western and non-Western alike, against terrorism. Indeed, few countries explicitly condemned the US- and British-led strikes on Afghanistan, which began approximately one month after the attacks on the United States. Yet after the war was launched, some expressed apprehension over the emergence of the BUSH DOCTRINE, which divided the world neatly in two: linking any country that "supports" terrorists to be on the same playing field as terrorists themselves.[12] While it may be temptingly simple to view the world in such stark terms, reality is rarely that clean-cut, as is evident in the CASE STUDIES presented in this volume. In their efforts to support the US coalition in the war in Afghanistan, many countries, especially Pakistan, Turkey, and Indonesia, invited intense opposition among their own populations.

The tone was ratcheted up another notch when preemptive action—acting on the threat of an attack—became a principal component of Bush's foreign policy. President Bush then labeled Iran, Iraq, and North Korea as part of an "AXIS OF EVIL" in his 2002 State of the Union address. This call provoked angry responses not only from these countries, but from others as well, including US allies in Europe and countries that supported the US war on terrorism.[13] It was perceived particularly offensively within Iran, the country that had, just weeks before Bush's speech before both houses of the US Congress, been so integral in helping the United States topple the Taliban in Afghanistan (by mediating between the United States and the Northern Alliance).[14]

If US credibility around the world was significantly drained throughout the 2000s, is anything starting to change? Facing intense criticism about a lackluster foreign policy approach that seemed to be accomplishing little, Secretary of State Hillary Clinton proposed that we are now entering a "new moment" in US foreign policy, highlighting the essential nature of US leadership at the same time that she envisioned new and different ways of leadership.[15] President Obama has sketched out a very ambitious foreign policy agenda, including eliminating nuclear weapons and elevating the concern about climate change to a top priority linked to global security. The conclusion to the war in Afghanistan will be critical—for perceptions of the United States, for stability in the region, and for its impact on terrorism regionally and globally.

The United States has long been a vocal voice for the promotion of liberty and human rights around the world. Is this changing? The Turkish minister of foreign affairs, Ahmet Davutoglu, presented one interpretation of changes since 2001: after September 11, the United States worked to "establish an international order based on a security discourse, thus replacing the liberty discourse that emerged after the collapse of the Berlin Wall" in 1989.[16] Pundits commenting on the strengths of the United States point to its status as a flexible society, open to competing views and welcoming of other peoples and cultures.[17]

Journalist Fareed Zakaria has claimed that we are moving into a "post-American world." He contends that for the first time many can remember, the charge is not

An Afghan girl watches a US soldier on patrol in Kandahar (Reuters/Erik de Castro)

being led by the United States, and that the world is experiencing "tectonic power shifts" as new powers rise.[18] While the United States maintains its dominance in the areas of military and politics, power is shifting in other dimensions, including industrial, financial, social, and cultural power.

As sentiment toward the United States continues to rise and fall, as it likely will, we encourage you to approach these perspectives critically—to try to understand the sources of some of the views expressed. One does not need to agree with a view in order to try to understand it, and most perceptions are based on a combination of facts and fears. It is not un-American to attempt to see the world through others' eyes; in fact, such an exercise is likely to increase commitment to the ideals on which the United States was founded and that it continues to foster. We must be cautious, though, with broad generalizations that, for example, attribute the anger against the West to some vague notion of "Islamic civilization." Most countries in the world show only pockets of anti-American fury, and the rage found in much of the Arab and Islamic world is a relatively recent development since the 1970s.[19] While the roots of these feelings of discord are indeed complex, they stem in large part from the fact that almost every Arab country today is less democratic than it was four decades ago—and that the United States is seen as one of the main forces continuing to prop up corrupt, elitist governments. US policies toward Afghanistan, Iraq, and the Israeli-Palestinian conflict remain very unpopular around the world, with more countries with majorities of citizens disapproving of US policies than approving of them, significantly so in regard to US approaches toward Lebanon, Egypt, and Jordan.[20]

Figure 20.1 Could the Next Superpower Come from the "Third World"?

As history has shown us, a single country cannot remain the preeminent power forever. Empires based in Greece, Rome, Turkey, and China once ruled large regions of the world, seemingly unchallenged. Increasingly it looks as though the next major power could come from the third world. Many point to the People's Republic of China as the rising superpower for the twenty-first century.

To many, China's outsized role in world affairs is not surprising. Yet it is important to remember that, as Ken Lieberthal put it, "until very, very recently China was fundamentally a regional player and marginally a global player," with the change taking place around 2008.[21] If China is successful in its reemergence as a global superpower, it would be the first nation in history to have gone into decline after a period of greatness, only to recover its former glory.[22] Power and influence are often in the eye of the beholder, and many may assume that China is more powerful than it actually is. For example, a *Wall Street Journal*/NBC poll found that "more Americans expect China to be the world's leading nation 20 years from now than expect the United States to be."[23] There are misperceptions at play here as well—surveys in late 2010 revealed that many Americans wrongly believed that the Chinese economy was larger than the US economy.[24] As is true with any matters of human agency, though, be careful with assumptions: few things are inevitable in the world of politics. The jury is still out on whether China's reemergence can be sustained and what external role the country may assume.[25]

India, with its impressive economic growth, diplomatic influence, and dominant regional presence, is also making a play. It appears to be emerging from its nonalignment to become a "swing state" in the global balance of power—developing strong partnerships throughout Asia and the Middle East, and with Western powers as well. Brazil is also viewed as a rising power, alongside Russia. Even Jacques Martin, who has strongly argued that China will dominate the next century, makes room for other players, stating: "If the twentieth-century world was shaped by the developed countries, then that of the twenty-first century is likely to be molded by the developing countries, especially the largest ones."[26] "Superpower" or not, it seems clear that power in the twenty-first-century world is becoming dispersed, rather than concentrated in one country, region, or worldview.

21

Linking
Concepts and Cases

In the preceding chapter we discussed how variously situated third world countries have attempted to deal with the United States as a superpower. We focused on how the Obama administration had the potential to change non-Western views of the United States. Has Obama been able to significantly alter US relations with the non-Western world generally, but in particular with our cases? What is the likely future trajectory for bilateral ties with these countries? Which issues are more or less likely to be important in the next five to ten years? Would you characterize the foreign policy of the Obama administration (compared to that of his predecessors) as one of "change"—or continuity?

Case Study: Mexico

"Poor Mexico. Poor United States. So far from God. So near to each other." This is novelist Carlos Fuentes's spin on a saying attributed to a Mexican dictator notorious for opening the country to foreign domination.[1] Yet it expresses the ambivalence many Mexicans have about living next door to the United States, which is known throughout Latin America as "the colossus of the north." Mexico's foreign policy is dominated by its relationship with the United States, and Mexico is so often described as having a love-hate relationship with its neighbor that the saying has become trite. Although Mexico is increasingly recognized as influencing US styles and tastes, the influence of US culture in Mexico is almost unavoidable. Many Mexicans fear losing their IDENTITY in the shadow of the enormous power of the United States. As one analyst put it, this proximity means that Mexico and the United States are prisoners of each other's problems.[2]

The Mexican-US relationship is one of INTERDEPENDENCE, yet it is not and has never been one of equal dependence. Since the North American Free Trade Agreement (NAFTA) was instituted in 1994, cross-border trade between Mexico and the world's largest economy has boomed. Mexican exports to the United States were worth $292 billion in 2008. Mexico depends on its neighbor to buy 80–85 percent of its exports, and it invests more there than in any other country. Mexico's tourism industry depends on the 15 million Americans who visit every year. Mexicans and Mexican Americans transfer approximately $25 billion each year to family in Mexico (these remittances are Mexico's second largest source of foreign exchange). On the other hand, Mexico is the second biggest consumer of US exports and hundreds of thousands (if not millions) of US jobs depend on Mexican consumers.[3]

With their two economies so closely linked, there is no doubt that what happens in one country affects the other. However, for years Mexico has been treated by the United States as a junior partner.[4] President Felipe Calderón has carried on his predecessor's desire to craft a new partnership with the United States that reflects the profound political and economic changes in his country since the mid-1990s. President Vicente Fox set the stage for this new relationship by clearly letting the United States know that the annual ritual of US certification of Mexico's cooperation with drug control efforts was offensive and humiliating. Such assertiveness reflected a new self-confidence evident since the democratic elections in 2000. As former foreign minister Jorge G. Castañeda put it, "We are not scared of engaging the US anymore."[5]

For Mexico, engaging the United States means discussing problems that have been festering for years. Too often the United States has treated Mexico as a source of its problems and never considered how it might be contributing to troubles in Mexico. As mentioned in Chapter 13, Mexico has the misfortune of living next door to the world's biggest drug addict. The United States constitutes 5 percent of the world's population but uses two-thirds of its drugs.[6] From Mexico's perspective, it helps that President Barack Obama has admitted that the United States shares in the responsibility for the drug violence in Mexico. In addition to continuing with the Bush-era military assistance provided through the 2008 Merida Initiative (the largest aid package in the hemisphere since Plan Colombia, allocating $1.4 billion over three years to help in Mexico's drug war), Obama is expanding it, shifting some funds to promote police training and judicial and other reforms aimed at addressing socioeconomic problems that recruit for the traffickers. The Obama administration is also strengthening efforts at demand reduction (i.e., drug education and treatment programs in the United States).[7] However, from Mexico's standpoint, the disbursement of these funds has come too slowly and the United States has not made enough progress on curtailing the shipment of weapons (particularly the semiautomatic assault rifles used in drug violence) from the United States to Mexico. Ninety percent of the guns used by Mexican traffickers originate in the United States.[8]

From Mexico's point of view, at least as important as the drug war is the issue of migration. Concerned about the increasing dangers faced by Mexicans seeking work in the United States, Fox had hoped to deepen NAFTA by negotiating open borders between member countries, much as is the case in the European Union (EU). The Mexican president tried but was unable to make it easier for the estimated 6.6 million Mexicans (62 percent of all unauthorized immigrants) living illegally in the United States to obtain temporary legal work and to extend to them protections that they do not currently enjoy.[9]

Prior to the September 11, 2001, terrorist attacks on the United States, President George W. Bush appeared receptive to the idea of a limited reform that would reduce illegal immigration without threatening the welfare of US citizens. However, in the months following September 11 it became clear that migration issues had been moved to the back burner. At first, Fox declared that he was prepared to be patient, but nearly a decade later Mexico was feeling abandoned and relations with the

United States were strained, although still good. Mexicans were united in their indignation when, in 2006, to curtail illegal immigration, President Bush signed a bill to erect a 700-mile fence along their common border.[10]

Meanwhile, despite Obama's campaign promises of comprehensive immigration reform, there was no progress on the issue in the first two years of his presidency. Republicans who had sponsored such bills in the past were no longer willing to touch the immigration issue, particularly given the American mood associated with the recession. Unemployment rates in the United States have remained near 10 percent nationwide for the second year of the Obama administration, and many Americans blame undocumented workers for taking precious jobs. Many Mexicans consider such views to be sheer hypocrisy—US citizens often won't accept the kind of work that many undocumented workers perform. Americans want the benefits of cheap Mexican labor, but they don't want to let Mexicans enter the country legally. In effect, for citizens of Mexico and the United States, the immigration problem remains divisive and unresolved. Many Mexicans expected that Obama's presidency would usher in a new era in Mexican-US relations. So far this hasn't happened, leaving them feeling cynical and disappointed.

Is there a way to get around these hard feelings? According to Jorge Castañeda, it is only when democracies work together that a more equitable relationship is possible.[11] First of all, it is important for Americans to understand that it is very much in the interests of the United States for DEMOCRACY to work in Mexico. However, improving the security situation of its neighbor will mean dealing with a number of facets of their relationship simultaneously; these problems cannot be resolved piecemeal. It will be impossible to make progress in curtailing drug violence without also dealing with trade and immigration.[12] This complicates the task, and agreement between these two democratic states is likely to become more difficult than it has been in the past because a democratic Mexico means that the Mexican president is also constrained by his own constituency.[13] It is important to remember that now more than ever, Mexico's president cannot appear to be a "yes man" to the United States. From Mexico's perspective, it is crucial that the United States accept and understand this.

Case Study: Peru

In many ways Peru is a pivotal country for the United States. Today it is recognized as one of the strongest allies of the United States in South America. However, the Peruvian-US relationship has had its ups and downs, and at times that relationship has been strained. Since the mid-nineteenth-century guano boom, the United States has had significant economic interests in Peru. Over the years these interests have expanded into political and strategic areas. Peru has accommodated US interests and supported the United States on a host of regional and international issues. But Peru has been disappointed in its expectations of receiving reciprocal treatment. As a result, some Peruvians have become distrusting and resentful of the extensive US presence and interference in their country's internal and external affairs.

During the COLD WAR, Peru was viewed by the United States as a highly sensitive security zone. Since then, the country has been of particular importance to the United States as the Andes have become a major battlefield in the US war on drugs. In the 1980s, US forces worked closely with local police in crop eradication and drug interdiction in Peru, Bolivia, and Ecuador. By the early 1990s, the war on drugs was the centerpiece of US policy in the region and Peru became a major recipient of US military assistance. Some economic aid was set aside for crop substitution and "alternative development," with the view that drug eradication was a DEVELOPMENT issue. However, the brunt of economic assistance was conditioned on the Peruvian government's cooperation in the use of a military approach to fighting the drug war. US "Andean strategy" aimed to cut off the cocaine trade at its source of supply. For several years, it appeared that this strategy was working, as coca cultivation in Peru plummeted in the late 1990s. The Clinton administration celebrated the end of Peru's status as the world's biggest producer of coca leaf—well aware of the trade-offs involved.

Given the stated support of the United States for democracy worldwide, this relationship was problematic. While US administrations have insisted that there is no trade-off between fair elections and the war on drugs, many Peruvians have doubted the sincerity of such claims.[14] For many, US policy toward Peru during the 1990s was best described as ambivalent. Convinced that counternarcotics operations in the region could not continue without Alberto Fujimori's support, the United States overlooked the growing AUTHORITARIANISM of his government. Humanitarian and drug-fighting assistance continued as the democracy eroded because the United States feared that the instability associated with the drug war in Colombia could spread to Peru. Although US military assistance was appropriated only to fight the drug war, some of this money was diverted by Peru for use in its war against the Shining Path (Sendero Luminoso) GUERRILLAS, under the argument that the terrorists were playing a central part in the drug trade. Consequently, the United States became an important ally for the Peruvian government in its civil war.

By the time Peruvians put a stop to Fujimori's "re-reelection" in 2000, President Bill Clinton was relieved at his old ally's resignation. Putting its previous reticence behind it, the United States then called for a rapid restoration of democracy. To some degree this inconsistent approach favored by the United States can be explained by the fact that it has had competing priorities in the Andes.

This amounted to a mixed blessing for the democratic governments of Peru. Democratization has been relatively successful in most Latin American countries, but it is arguably tenuous in Peru and in the entire Andean region, where the US war on drugs is concentrated. While Plan Colombia's supporters argue that the drug trade is responsible for the weakness of democracy in the region, others are concerned that US policy has resulted in a further militarization of these countries, along with concerning violations of human rights. Since 1999 the United States has spent more than $7 billion on this program. Plan Colombia is institutionalized; this is a security relationship that is not expected to end anytime soon. However, President Obama has indicated an interest in spending less on a military solution and placing more emphasis on providing socioeconomic assistance to get at the roots of the problem. However, given budgetary pressures it is possible that funding for such programs will be cut in coming years.[15]

Certainly since before Obama's time, US priorities have been shifting—everywhere else, the war on terror has taken precedence over other concerns. Would the war on TERRORISM displace the war on drugs in Peru? According to a former US ambassador to Peru, the war on terrorism and the war on drugs are a lot alike. In neither case is the United States likely ever to win a final victory, but the consequences of not dealing with these problems could be even worse than waging a war without end.[16] And in the Andes, there have long been connections between narcotrafficking and terrorism. At this point no one is saying that there is much of a chance of an attack on the United States from the region, but the combination of guerrillas and drug lords makes for plenty of instability. Although most analysts discount the threat a newly reconstituted Shining Path poses for Peru, recent attacks suggest that the Shining Path is regrouping (mostly with money from drug trafficking) and acting more like a cartel than a guerrilla movement. Moreover, indications are that Peru is no longer winning its war on drugs. In what some have described as the "balloon effect," as one drug producer gets squeezed, production shifts to another part of the region. For example, although there was a significant dip in coca production in the late 1990s in Peru, in that same period there was a proportional increase in production in Colombia. Since then, eradication efforts have been more successful in Colombia, while coca production in Peru recovered and continued to rise. In 2010 Peru unseated Colombia as the number one producer of coca in the world (recapturing the title it held in the mid-1990s),[17] in effect setting back the drug eradication effort by fifteen years. But instead of arguing the futility of this approach, President Alan García has complained that Peru doesn't get enough assistance compared to Colombia and has stated that he would welcome more US military aid (including US military trainers) to combat drug trafficking. US counternarcotics aid to Peru amounted to $71 million in 2010. By arguing that we can't separate the war on drugs from the war on terror, Peru's president hopes to catch our attention.[18]

Are there any lessons Peru can teach the United States on how to fight a war on terrorism? Until recently it was thought that with its draconian military solution, the Fujimori government had won its fifteen-year war on terror. Yet it is increasingly recognized today in Peru that the trampling of civil rights in the name of security led to the imprisonment of hundreds of innocents. The no-holds-barred war on terror may have only created martyrs and contributed to long-term problems, as these groups were never destroyed, just forced into dormancy. And now they're back. This is bad news for everyone, particularly those Peruvians caught in between.[19]

Case Study: Nigeria

Frankly, despite its enormous significance, US presidents have generally shown little interest in Nigeria, or in Africa for that matter. Bill Clinton was the first US president to visit Nigeria since Jimmy Carter's trip in 1977. Yet Nigeria is too big to ignore. Only South Africa rivals it as a regional superpower. Described as Africa's equivalent to Brazil, India, or Indonesia, Nigeria is vital to US interests for several reasons. It was until recently the largest oil exporter in Africa (as of early 2011 it was second only to Angola), and the fifth largest supplier of oil to the United States, exporting approximately 2 million barrels a day.[20] In addition, with a population of approximately 150 million, it is not only the region's most populous country, but also the largest market in sub-Saharan Africa, full of tremendous trade opportunities. One in six Africans is Nigerian. And present-day Nigeria is part of the region that was home to the ancestors of most African Americans. Still, the United States generally defers to Europe when it comes to African affairs. Although Nigeria has historically been more closely tied to Britain, that may change as the United States seeks a strategic partner and an alternative to Middle Eastern oil in Africa.

Until recently the US approach to Nigeria was described as paradoxical, alternating between close diplomacy and benign neglect.[21] The Nigeria-US relationship hit its lowest point after it became clear that the results of the presidential elections of 1993 would never be respected. However, despite claims by the United States about its concern for the democratic process, in the mid-1990s it was Nigeria's role in the international drug trade that provoked the most serious US response. Not a major producer of narcotics, Nigeria has become a leading hub in the transshipment of drugs from Latin America and Asia to the United States and Europe. In the 1990s, Nigerian "swallowers," or human couriers, were believed to be responsible for nearly 40 percent of the heroin entering the United States. In response, the United States placed sanctions on Sani Abacha's government—which in turn basically thumbed its nose at the world. Since 1999, however, Nigerian governments have cooperated with international efforts to curb the flow of drugs, and although the country is still a hub for their transit, it has been removed from the US government's list of major drug producers.

But as bad as things got, neither side was willing to use oil as a weapon. The United States wanted to buy it from Nigeria, and Nigeria wanted to sell it to the United States. To protest Nigeria's massive human rights abuses during this dictatorship, Randall Robinson, head of the African American lobby TransAfrica, together with others, called for a boycott of Nigerian oil. However, despite these efforts, the United States and Western allies never seriously considered an oil boycott, arguing that sanctions on oil from Iran, Libya, and Iraq were already driving up prices. Meanwhile, US oil companies joined others in dramatically increasing their investments in Nigeria. That hypocrisy, coming from the world's so-called democratic leader, disappointed and angered many Nigerians who had hoped for more.

Although the United States did not press as hard as some would have liked, US relations with Nigeria during the Abacha years were probably worse than with any other regional power, except for Iran. However, all that changed with the DEMO-CRATIC TRANSITION in Nigeria in 1999. Nigeria has been brought back into the fold. Since its return to democracy, US-Nigerian economic ties have grown. Not only did the United States support the debt relief described in Chapter 9, but US companies such as Chevron and Exxon-Mobil are two of Nigeria's largest investors. US-Nigerian trade has grown steadily over the past decade, and was valued at $42 billion in 2008. Nigerian goods such as cocoa and cotton have duty-free access to US markets until 2015 under the African Growth and Opportunity Act (AGOA)—although the vast majority of what Nigeria sells in the United States under AGOA is oil and natural gas.[22] As the United States also needs to diversify its oil dependence away from the Middle East, its relationship with Nigeria and other African oil and gas producers is likely only to grow. Currently, Nigeria supplies 8 percent of US oil imports (half of the oil Nigeria currently produces). Oil analysts predict that 25 percent of US oil imports will come from Africa by 2015.[23]

Another factor that makes the US-Nigerian relationship more important than ever is security cooperation. Nigeria is West Africa's unrivaled military power. The United States wants a moderate ally in the region and recognizes that Nigeria is a regional powerhouse essential to any international effort to stabilize not only West

Africa, but the continent. Since the debacle in Somalia in 1993, the slogan "African solutions for African problems" has become popular in the West. There are certain problems in Africa that the United States cannot ignore, and one convenient compromise is to promote Nigeria's role as a regional peacekeeper, since it is cheaper to train and equip Nigerian troops than it is to send US forces.

The United States is not only increasing its arms sales and military training in Nigeria, but also is seeking to establish informal bases through which it could quickly deploy US troops and equipment to Africa. Nigeria is a member of the US-sponsored Trans-Sahara Counterterrorism Partnership, through which the United States provides assistance to African governments and in return seeks cooperation in the global war on terror. This program has been criticized by some who predict that it will be used by unpopular regimes against political opponents they choose to characterize as terrorists. It does not take a great deal of imagination to see how this could play out against the Movement for the Emancipation of the Niger Delta (MEND), whose efforts have led to production declines of over 20 percent.[24] Energy security is clearly a critical US interest; US military planners have already mentioned the scenario of intervening in Nigeria to ensure the security of that country's oil fields.[25] On the other hand, that may not be the approach favored by the Obama administration, since during his candidacy Senator Obama was a supporter of the AMNESTY deal described in Chapter 13.[26]

Just as Obama's campaign emphasized change, change can be used to describe US-Nigerian relations since 1999. As mentioned earlier, that relationship changed dramatically with the transition from military to civilian rule, and it has generally been close ever since. For the first several years of Nigeria's latest experiment with democracy, the United States was often willing to look the other way when the government faltered, because of the sense that the country was headed in the right direction. Because of the combination of US security and economic interests in Nigeria, the Bush administration was even willing to accept the outcome of the less-than-democratic 2007 elections. However, those elections appear to have marked a milestone of sorts, as US-Nigerian relations have perceptibly cooled since then.[27] Although the Obama administration has maintained all the same economic, diplomatic, and military ties, many observers interpreted his decision to visit Ghana on his first trip to Africa as head of state, as a message for Nigeria. On this trip, President Obama emphasized Ghana's record on good governance and how it should serve as a model to others. This caused some Nigerians to wince, yet others applauded the US president's unstated message: Nigeria needs to do better. For better or worse, though, what happens in Nigeria does affect US interests—and it is one country that Americans are likely to hear much more of in future years.

Case Study: Zimbabwe

It could be argued that the United States has been on the wrong side of history in much of southern Africa. During the Cold War the United States at various times directly and indirectly supported white governments in the region, for economic as well as strategic reasons. US paranoia that Africans were procommunist became a self-fulfilling prophecy, as black nationalists had nowhere but the Soviet Union and China to turn. This did not make for an auspicious start to relations between the

United States and the new government of Zimbabwe. Although the United States welcomed Zimbabwe's independence in 1980 with a significant aid package, relations between the two countries cooled quickly. This difficult relationship fell to its lowest point in the mid-1980s and again at the turn of the twenty-first century. At times the Zimbabwe-US relationship has been marked by outright hostility.

Yet it must be recognized that in the early years of his rule, Robert Mugabe defied skeptics and managed to create in Zimbabwe something of a success story. Mugabe was willing to compromise his socialist principles and followed a pragmatic course, resisting militant demands. Agricultural production was impressive, and the government promoted a policy of racial reconciliation. To the shock and dismay of whites who had predicted that the country would collapse without their leadership, Zimbabwe continued to be a strategic asset in southern Africa, an anchor of stability in the region.

However, Zimbabwe-US relations could be described as a train wreck waiting to happen. At independence, Zimbabwe was eager to assert itself in international forums. As an aspiring leader of the third world in the Non-Aligned Movement (NAM) and as one of the "frontline states" opposed to the racist government in South Africa, Zimbabwe was determined to shape its own policy. The government had taken an outspoken stance in criticizing US policy, especially US policy toward apartheid South Africa. From Mugabe's point of view, not only was the United States failing to assist the black majority in its efforts to oust the racist government, but it was also collaborating with the racists. In a variety of well-publicized speeches, Mugabe denounced US policy as hypocritical, asking why the United States wasn't sanctioning the apartheid regime when it was willing to use sanctions to promote change in Nicaragua, Poland, and Libya. Over time, the rhetoric became more hostile, as the Mugabe government accused the United States of sponsoring terrorism, and of "international bullyism," for supporting apartheid-backed rebels in Angola, Mozambique, and elsewhere.

The last straw, though, came when Zimbabwe indicated that it would vote its own conscience at the United Nations on issues important to the United States. In an attempt to force Zimbabwe back into line, in 1983 the United States slashed foreign aid to the country from $75 million a year to $45 million. After a Zimbabwean diplomat vented his anger on former president Jimmy Carter, aid to Zimbabwe was frozen in 1986. In both these cases, Mugabe demonstrated a character trait that defines him even today. Ever defiant, he is notoriously resistant to Western pressure. In the 1980s Mugabe described the US policy as tantamount to blackmail. Swearing that Zimbabwe would be no one's puppet, Mugabe famously proclaimed that Zimbabwe "would rather be poor, eat grass, and be sovereign."[28]

Although relations gradually improved and aid resumed in the years that followed, by 2001 the relationship was again at a low point. In response to then–US secretary of state Colin Powell's condemnation of Mugabe's "totalitarian methods," Mugabe told the United States to leave Zimbabwe alone and mind its own business. In response, the US Senate passed the Zimbabwe Democracy and Economic Recovery Act of 2001. Instead of general trade sanctions, which have been criticized as hurting the poor, these are targeted, personal sanctions. Much like the European Union, the United States imposed an arms embargo, as well as travel and economic sanctions against Mugabe, his family, his associates, and other senior government officials.

As political conditions worsened in 2002, the United States cut aid flows and bilateral trade worth millions. President Mugabe responded that such policies were racist, coming from a racist government that knew nothing of democracy. In 2005 US secretary of state Condoleezza Rice blasted Zimbabwe, calling it one of six outposts of tyranny. As Zimbabwe became more isolated from the West, it joined countries such as Iran in asking "who is the West to judge us?"[29]

Over the years the Mugabe government has described its efforts as a continuation of the liberation struggle and reminded the world that Zimbabwe is nobody's colony. On this point the president has received the sympathy of other countries, many of which also worry that the United States has gone too far in interfering in the internal affairs of sovereign states.[30] According to Mugabe, not only has the United States been promoting a regime change in his country, but it is also to blame for the suffering of millions of Zimbabweans. He has accused the United States (as well as Britain and the United Nations) of withholding aid—most notably much-needed medicines to fight HIV/AIDS—until Zimbabwe bends to US HEGEMONY (the Bush administration, for its part, stated that it excluded Zimbabwe from such programs because it didn't trust the Mugabe government with the money).

President Obama's approach to Zimbabwe has been a continuation of the Bush policy of isolation. Within days of Obama's inauguration, there was talk of the United States leading a diplomatic initiative in the UN SECURITY COUNCIL to persuade Russia and China to join in pressuring Mugabe with more extensive sanctions. The Obama administration was reportedly unenthusiastic about the idea of a unity government, but the Security Council plans were dropped after the deal for a coalition government was announced in February 2009. A few months later, Prime Minister Morgan Tsvangirai was greeted warmly at the White House with a pledge of $73 million in aid for the country. Obama listened to Tsvangirai's plea to normalize relations, but his position is that as long as Mugabe holds the reins of power, the United States will not change its policy. As of early 2011, the targeted sanctions remain intact. And although many of Mugabe's strongest critics now believe that a policy of engagement would help move the country toward the goal of truly free and fair elections, Obama remains skeptical, concerned that Mugabe is just trying to use Tsvangirai to fund Zimbabwe's recovery—and that he'll simply dispose of the prime minister when he's through with him.[31]

Case Study: Iran

With the more recent history of strained ties between Iranian leaders and the United States (the BBC calls the relationship "one of the most antagonistic in the world"),[32] it may be tempting to discount their significant relations prior to the Islamic Revolution. Such an omission would be a mistake, though. In fact, the coziness of the Shah with Western leaders after World War II is indeed the source of much of the mistrust that has permeated the relationship since. The Iranians viewed the West, especially the United States, as double-talking supporters of a corrupt and antidemocratic regime. Iran long considered the United States its archenemy, and the animosity on both sides, especially after 1979, when hostages were taken at the US embassy in Tehran after President Jimmy Carter permitted the Shah to seek refuge in the United States, was fierce. Yet increasingly, neither side can ignore the other. Iran's access to oil in the Persian Gulf solidifies its status as a central player in Middle Eastern affairs. Even though US influence in the region may wane in the future, US support of Israel, which Iran and some other Muslim states find very troubling, will continue to color whatever type of relationship unfolds between Tehran and Washington.

Since 1980 the United States has lacked diplomatic ties with Iran; Pakistan represents Iranian interests in Washington, and Switzerland represents US interests in Tehran. Other Western powers, however, have normalized their political relations with Tehran. In 1999 the United Kingdom (the last EU country without a diplomatic emissary to Iran) exchanged ambassadors with Iran. Within the Islamic Republic, however, the weekly jeers of "death to America" continue. Anti-Americanism remains a central part of the Iranian leadership, especially in the eyes of both President Mahmoud Ahmadinejad and Supreme Leader Sayyid Ali Khamenei, who often references the "global arrogance" of the United States.[33]

Under the fiery POPULISM of President Ahmadinejad, Iran's desire to challenge US hegemony is stronger than at any time since the revolution. In fact, as one analyst reminds us, the other major part of Ayatollah Ruhollah Khomeini's 1979 revolution, in addition to the establishment of a THEOCRACY, was a "declaration of independence" from US and British control.[34] Ahmadinejad views himself in precisely this frame. It appears that there was at least a slight chance for things to have been otherwise, as during the short period between the invasion of Afghanistan in October 2001 and the US State of the Union address in January 2002, when there was a consensus within Tehran that the Islamic Republic should normalize ties with the United States.[35] Now, even though the bipartisan (US) Iraq Study Group has explicitly recommended working with Iran to stabilize the situation in Iraq,[36] it appears that the two sides will continue to hurl tense rhetoric and insults at each other.

Almost all commercial transactions between the United States and Iran are banned, under a 1995 executive order that was reinforced with the 1996 Iran-Libya Sanctions Act. This US law imposes penalties on foreign firms that invest in either Iran or Libya, which both stand accused by the US government of supporting terrorism. As tensions over Iran's uranium enrichment programs increased, these limitations became even more wide-ranging. It is not only the clerics in Tehran who are bothered by these actions: India, Russia, and European governments including Germany and France have expressed their displeasure at this perceived US meddling in their financial affairs.

The major concern from the US perspective is Iran's connection to terrorist groups and its weapons proliferation, including the uranium enrichment program—the ostensible reason why Iran was included in George W. Bush's "AXIS OF EVIL" in 2002. Iran had been officially placed on the US State Department's list of state supporters of terrorism in 1984. And because of US antiterrorism laws, US representatives to INTERNATIONAL FINANCIAL INSTITUTIONS oppose Iranian applications for loans to assist in the country's debt relief.[37]

The United States alleges Iranian complicity in the bombing of US Marine headquarters in Beirut (1983), and in the 1996 Khobar (Saudi Arabia) bombing of US military barracks, which killed nineteen members of the US Air Force. Iran has also been implicated through its ties to the Shiite group Hezbollah, even though Tehran insists they are not substantial.

Iran's concerns with the United States are as deep-rooted as the counterperspective. Iran views the United States as the source of most of its problems—there is much remaining anti-American sentiment tied to the Central Intelligence Agency–engineered coup that toppled the popular government of Prime Minister Mohammad Mossadeq in 1953, as well as to US support for the unpopular regime of Shah Mohammad Reza Pahlavi. After the Islamic Revolution of 1979, hundreds of millions of dollars' worth of military equipment, which the former Shah had ordered and paid for, was embargoed, and the financing was impounded. The decision to permit the ailing Shah to enter the United States was viewed by many ordinary Iranians as part of a larger, Western, anti-Iranian conspiracy to again restore a dynasty. Iranian animosity only increased after President Ronald Reagan's decision to support Saddam Hussein during the 1980–1988 Iran-Iraq War, and continued while the United States attempted to maintain its influence in the region, which often necessitated hostile acts toward Iran. For example, in July 1988 a missile fired from a US vessel shot down an Iranian plane flying to Dubai, and 250 Iranians were killed. Iranian leaders were also upset that the international community seemed to take little action against its neighbor, Iraq, which had killed tens of thousands of Iranians with chemical weapons. Iran alleged that German chemical firms were assisting Iraq with its production of weapons of mass destruction.[38] Iranian leaders believed they were snubbed at the conclusion of the Gulf War, as they were excluded from postwar discussions, even though they tacitly assisted the effort to oust Saddam Hussein from Kuwait. Iranians also believe that the United States is unduly and unfairly hindering the development of the Iranian economy, which had already been battered during the eight-year Iran-Iraq War. Even though Iran is the second largest oil producer in the Gulf today, US containment efforts have hurt its energy sector. Iranian leaders feel that they are adrift in a hostile international environment that has been made so largely by efforts of the United States.

What is the outlook for the future? Iranian leaders will continue to be divided over how to accommodate Western power without losing their Islamic identity. Potential rapprochement with the United States will not be entered into lightly—and its likelihood was significantly hampered after Bush's inclusion of Iran in the "Axis of Evil." To some, the inclusion of Iran was ironic, not only because of Iranian mediation between Washington and the Northern Alliance shortly after September 11, but also because of the Islamic Republic's key role in the 2001 Bonn negotiations that established the Afghani interim government, when the United States and Iranian delegations "were practically hugging and kissing each other," according to one observer.[39] Since Ahmadinejad's election in 2005, the situation has substantially cooled. The United States has led the effort within the UN to sanction Tehran for its uranium enrichment program, and it has consistently stated that Washington, indeed the world, cannot tolerate a nuclear Iran. Since 2006, representatives of the permanent five members of the UN Security Council, together with Germany, have been meeting with Iranian representatives to attempt to find a compromise over Iran's uranium enrichment program. (Iran has spoken about formally including Brazil and Turkey in future discussions as well, especially after it negotiated a nuclear fuel-swap deal in May 2010.) Discussions within the US foreign policy establishment about possible normalization of relations were met with solid resistance within the Bush administration. Even as the showdown over uranium enrichment deepened, the Obama administration extended an olive branch to Iran, and critics say that Iran has yet to offer anything in return. Normalization now seems but a distant possibility, at the same time that the search for a workable relationship between Tehran and Washington seems ever more important.

Case Study: Turkey

Ties between Turkey and the United States have long been dominated by a mutually beneficial strategic partnership. The relationship seems to be encountering some growing pains. In recent years the two countries have been characterized as "pliable allies" (as Turkey reliably followed the US lead during the Cold War),[40] as "awkward partners"[41] (shortly after the Iraq War began in 2003), and more recently as "Frenemies" (as Ankara strengthens its role in the Middle East, challenging some US positions within the region).[42]

The United States and Turkey have long had linkages, and their formal relationship was established in 1930. Under the spirit of the Truman Doctrine, since 1947 the United States has provided more than $20 billion in economic and military assistance to Turkey. For over fifty years, the US-Turkish relationship has been based on Turkey's desire to foster good relations with the United States in return for Turkey's provision of military bases within reach of the tense regions of the Middle East. (Yet oddly, only five presidents—Dwight Eisenhower, George H. W. Bush, Bill Clinton, George W. Bush, and Barack Obama—have visited the country.) Turkey was a "frontline state" against the Soviet Union in the Cold War, and against Iraq in the Gulf War of 1991. It has been a member of the North Atlantic Treaty Organization (NATO) since 1952, in which Turkey serves as the "east anchor"—two NATO headquarters are in Izmir.[43] Ankara is working within NATO to land a significant missile-defense command center in Izmir, rather than at Ramstein base in Germany, as a way to cement its pivotal role within the alliance.

From Turkish ground, the United States has been able to exert pressure throughout the region. For years, the United States used Incirlik air base in southern Turkey to patrol the no-fly zone in northern Iraq. The relationship faced its greatest strain in 2003, as the Turkish parliament, concerned about Washington's commitment to a unified Iraq—especially with regard to the Kurds—refused US access to its bases for the Iraq War in 2003.

Much strain has been introduced to Turkish-US ties because of Ankara's changing roles within the Middle East, especially including Turkey's increasingly combative approach to Israel and the warming of ties between Ankara and Tehran. As one analyst put it, Turkey is no longer the compliant partner it was in the Cold War.[44] Turkey is a pivotal state in the region—in terms of geography, population, and economic power. In part, it is exerting this influence through its "zero problems" foreign policy, discussed in Chapter 19. Yet these policies also challenge US interests. Turkey's condemnation of the Israeli blockade of Gaza has long strained ties between the two states, even before nine Turkish citizens were killed on an Istanbul-organized flotilla that attempted to break the blockade in May 2010. Turkey's increased ties with Iran have also raised eyebrows in Washington, especially after Recep Tayyip Erdogan referenced his "good friend" Mahmoud Ahmadinejad[45] and Turkey voted against the UN sanctions resolution aimed at Iran's nuclear program. Yet while the United States sees the Turks operating against US interests in the region, Ankara views its regional diplomacy a bit differently: "The Americans create havoc, and we are left holding the bag."[46]

Sources of domestic friction between the United States and Turkey include human rights, especially the treatment of the Kurdistan Workers Party (PKK) and the assessment of the Armenian genocide. Additionally, Turkey's attempts to normalize relations with two of its border states, Iraq and Iran, have raised US ire, especially Turkey's support for a pipeline carrying Iranian gas to Turkey. The United States has also expressed concerns over Turkey's role in drug trade and trafficking, especially in the eastern and southeastern sections of the country, through which drugs from Iran pass en route to Europe. The United States offered aid (approximately $500 million) for Turkey's anti-narcotrafficking efforts, but it was rejected by Ankara because it was conditioned on human rights improvement. Ankara was put in a particularly untenable position during the US-led war in Afghanistan, and remains on shaky ground in supporting the ongoing war against terrorism. As a secular state with an Islamic majority, Turkey is particularly prone to criticism for supporting the United States in its "war against Islam," as some have perceived the war against terrorism. Nonetheless, the Turkish government remains guardedly allied with the United States in these efforts. It will not be an easy balancing act to maintain for long, though, and it is important to recognize Turkey's own fragile domestic situation. Two-thirds of Turks opposed the US-led war in Afghanistan and Ankara's support of it. Many were concerned that the actions had the real potential of triggering war between Christians and Muslims.[47] Turkey's complexities were in the spotlight in the lead-up to the war in Iraq, as the Turkish parliament rebuffed the US offer of billions of aid dollars in return for allowing US troops to be stationed in the country. The situation's complexity is best understood by returning to the Kurdish question. The most fervent supporters of the United States in Iraq are the Kurds, putting the country at odds with Ankara in its battle against a domestic Kurdish insurgency largely fueled by the Iraqi Kurds along Turkey's southeast border. Turkey views the increasing autonomy of Iraqi Kurdistan as a direct threat to its own border security and state unity. The United States needs both sides—it cannot afford any more enmity within Iraq, while at the same time it looks to its longtime strategic partner in Turkey, which increasingly feels isolated from the West. The importance is heightened as Washington considers the future of the Middle East in the post–Iraq War period, turning to Turkey to forge a workable Middle East diplomacy, especially with Iran and Syria—relationships that Turkey is fostering in large part because of their shared struggle with the Kurdish question.[48]

As with many of the Turkish issues discussed throughout this book, Turkish-US relations are embedded in the country's ongoing efforts to define itself between the European and Islamic worlds. Turkey's international response—and regional activism—are predicated on competing domestic concerns to promote secularization, guard against Islamic extremism, and develop a larger role for the Turkish Republic in regional and international matters. Whether or not the ties will become the "model partnership" hoped for by President Obama remains to be seen.[49]

Case Study: China

The United States opened a formal diplomatic relationship with the People's Republic of China during the 1970s, under the leadership of staunchly anticommunist president Richard M. Nixon. Previously the United States had supported the rival of the Chinese Communist Party, the Nationalist Party, which had been exiled to Taiwan after its defeat in 1949. Nixon's rationale for rapprochement with China, for which he faced much criticism, was that one could view the world in terms of a "strategic triangle" encompassing the United States, China, and the Soviet Union. Opening formal ties with China would exploit hostilities between the two communist giants and ultimately, it was hoped, limit the influence of communism throughout the world. After the 1970s the US relationship with China, like the relationship between most Western powers and China, became centered on its commercial strengths, especially the vast market that it provided for Western goods and services. This financial focus continues, although its importance may wane as China exerts its growing strength in other arenas.

For the past two decades, China-US relations have had cycles of highs and lows, from Tiananmen Square (1989), to Bill Clinton's successful China tour (1998), to the bombing of the Chinese embassy in Belgrade (1999), to the collision of a Chinese jet with a US Navy surveillance plane (2001), which killed the Chinese pilot and resulted in China detaining the US crew for nineteen days. In the wake of the Great Recession, as China finds new, more confident footing as a country rich with financing for countries in need, it is clear that Sino-US relations are entering a new era. The relationship that began in the 1970s as a Cold War compromise is clearly now facing tensions as China's power and influence rise.

As the Hu Jintao administration pursues a path it identifies as "peaceful rising," the United States has expressed concern over deepening Chinese relations in Latin and South America (especially Venezuela and Brazil), the Middle East (Iran and Saudi Arabia), and Africa (Sudan and Zimbabwe).[50] These ties are in addition to China's increased visibility in Asia, in what one former US official responsible for Asian policy termed "filling in" as US attention moved elsewhere.[51] Beijing's plan to craft a "peaceful rise" on the world stage, it was argued, would refute the model employed by other former great powers, which based their gains on the exploitation of others.[52] This explicit challenge to the "strings attached" approach of the United States is still being played out today as China exerts its so-called soft power throughout the third world.

Many within the Chinese foreign policy establishment have framed US behavior as arrogant, self-interested, and imposing—the behavior of a hegemon. Beijing continues to find fault with US policy toward North Korea, even as North Korea continues to escalate tensions in China's own backyard (and beyond). Beijing has faced heightened expectations, as the closest thing to an ally that Pyongyang has, to pressure the "Hermit Kingdom" for a solution. As host of the six-party talks, Beijing's ability to get North Korea to return to the table in sporadic intervals shows some level of influence—although a sustained and verifiable solution to North Korea's determination to go nuclear may be more than Beijing can muster.

In the future, it is likely that Sino-US tensions will continue, as the world's strongest power and the most likely country to rival that unchallenged power continue to bump elbows (and spy planes). The Chinese suspect that the United States is determined to limit the development of their country and influence; this belief is based on US efforts to arm Taiwan, and other perceived challenges to Chinese SOVEREIGNTY, including meeting with Tibetan leaders in the halls of the White House.

A "deep freeze" seemed to set in during 2010 as China protested US arms sales to Taiwan (a staple since the 1980s) more forcefully than usual, and as US defense secretary Robert Gates was refused his request to stop in Beijing during his travels in Asia.[53] On key foreign policy issues, especially North Korea and Iran, Beijing and Washington appear to be advocating for different values, and China's assertiveness regarding disputed territory in the South China Sea is alarming others in the region.

Yet China's status as a tremendous trading partner is the focal point of most of its bilateral ties, and its relations with the United States are not much different. But how long trade can continue to gloss over important differences between the two, and perhaps more important, how a financial showdown may repair itself, remain to be seen. China is the largest creditor of the United States, holding the largest supply of US Treasury securities. As the US trade deficit with China ballooned to over $225 billion by mid-2010, cries for currency revaluation and more open access for US goods on the mainland were heard. China's leaders (and society) are increasingly assertive on the global front, and how the dominant world power accommodates these changes will have much impact on China's future actions.

Longtime China-watcher Kenneth Lieberthal, of the Brookings Institution, recently stated, "Clearly, the narrative in US-China relations has turned distinctly negative."[54] The list of major global issues that cause strife among leaders in both countries includes trade, currency reform, North Korea, Iran, and the environment—hefty issues to be sure. Yet despite all of the friction, there is no doubt that Beijing's ties with the United States are the most important piece of its foreign policy.

Some claim that a "G-2" assemblage of Washington and Beijing is forming as the two great powers of the early twenty-first century seek common strategic interests, perhaps at the expense of their own allies. Others suggest that it is time for the United States to "de-friend" China, or at the very least recognize that the US relationship with the world's emerging superpower is not all that unique compared to China's relationship with key allies of the United States, including the European Union and Japan.[55] Somewhere between these two extremes, Washington and Beijing will craft a working relationship that is likely to shape the outcome of many pressing global issues over the next decades.

Case Study: Indonesia

Indonesia's ties with the Western world have long been strained. Some of this derives from Indonesia's experience with the Dutch and its prolonged fight for acceptance as an independent state. As a founder of the Non-Aligned Movement in the 1960s, Indonesia positioned itself to be largely independent of the West, and indeed sometimes in opposition to it. The latter part of the Sukarno era was very anti-Western and specifically anti-American. After the 1965 anticommunist coup, in a period of US history that remains under scrutiny, the United States cultivated a close relationship with Suharto's Indonesia, viewing it as a regional stronghold against communism. Yet Western powers maintained a cozy relationship with Suharto at great cost, ignoring human rights atrocities and propping up a military regime, all in the name of regional stability. Since Suharto, the inconsistencies of the Indonesia-US relationship have become more visible and have been exacerbated by instability throughout the archipelago. In its war on terrorism, the United States views Indonesia as a critical strategic ally, the "voice of moderation in the Muslim world," as one US State Department official put it.[56] This badge, though, is uncomfortable for many ordinary Indonesians.

The unfolding of events after September 11, 2001, put Indonesian leaders in a very tight spot, especially with US leaders. Political newcomer Megawati Sukarno-putri stepped into office in the summer of 2001 with more than a handful of domestic challenges, and her job became even more difficult after the commencement of the US-led wars in Afghanistan and Iraq. As the leader of the state with the world's largest Islamic population, her support of Washington rankled some Indonesian citizens. Many viewed her initially unqualified support of US efforts to be blasphemous against the Islamic people. As the war on terrorism waged further, this perception grew stronger. In 2004 a respected Indonesian survey institute found that 55 percent of Indonesian citizens believed that the United States was at war with Muslim countries, rather than with terrorists who happen to be Muslim.[57] When George W. Bush made a six-hour stop in Indonesia in 2006, for example, some demonstrators chanted, "We hope Bush dies."[58]

In part because of his childhood connections to Indonesia, many expected President Barack Obama to extend a closer US relationship to this major Southeast Asian state. (Obama lived outside of Jakarta for four years as a young boy, attending both Catholic and public schools; one of the elementary schools he attended erected a statue of him on its grounds.) After having twice postponed his first official state visit, he returned to Jakarta in November 2010 to both cheering and jeering crowds, praising Indonesia as a model of pluralism and democracy. In a deeply personal speech in Jakarta, Obama stated (in both English and Indonesian), "Indonesia is part of me."[59] Yet he faced skepticism from many. As Pew Research Center studies report, since 2000, Indonesians' views of the United States have fluctuated quite a bit, with favorable views of the United States bouncing from 61 percent in 2002 to 15 percent in 2003 (shortly after the US-led invasion of Iraq), 37 percent in 2008, and 63 percent in 2009.[60]

China fares prominently in the strategic calculations of leaders in both Washington and Jakarta. The United States served as a buffer for Indonesia during the early decades of the Chinese communist revolution. Increasingly the United States is turning to its alliance with Jakarta in part to help counterbalance the influence of Beijing. This multipronged approach, and the power it gives to Jakarta, are not lost on Indonesia's (or China's) leaders. While President Susilo Bambang Yudhoyono (SBY) has promoted an amicable relationship with the United States (he participated in military training in the United States in the 1970s and 1980s), his administration has also sought favorable relations with China and Russia, in part to avoid US supervision and influence. Memories of US embargoes on weapons and military training, in place from 1991 until 2005, remain vivid. Senior military leaders, including former defense minister Juwono Sudarsono, have made no secret of the fact that Jakarta will happily turn to Russia and other suppliers to avoid scrutiny. The United States lifted the embargo and prior restrictions on military training to demonstrate an open hand to Indonesian citizens, especially as Washington watched its perception in the Muslim world plummet.

Yet many Indonesians resent their country being characterized solely as the "moderate Muslim state." Despite an uptick in Islamic observance and piety in

Indonesia since the late 1990s, many Indonesians remind outsiders that there are six official religions in the diverse country, its politics are secular, and Indonesia is not all that connected, either diplomatically or culturally, to the Middle East. Foreign Minister Marty Natalegawa bristled at US stereotypes, stating, "We are not an Islamic country"[61]—many patriotic Indonesians do not view Islam to be a fundamental characteristic of their core identity. Diplomatically, efforts to frame Indonesia as the model for others could be quite counterproductive. As the editorial board of the *Christian Science Monitor* put it, Indonesia's "natural tendency toward moderating other Muslim lands could be jeopardized every time an American president exploits that role."[62]

Indonesia's relations with the Western world, dominated by its ties with the United States, are most definitely changing from the days when Jakarta orchestrated the global movement to chart an independent path. Because of the US president's connections to the country, many believed Washington and Jakarta would develop a special alliance under Obama's watch. The path that these changes portend, however, remains to be seen. As it is increasingly seen to be a country caught between the United States (which emphasizes Jakarta's credentials as the world's third largest democracy and as a model of democracy in an Islamic country) and China (which emphasizes its economic ties with the world's fourth most populous state), it seems Indonesia has come full circle. In the 1950s it was caught between the superpowers of the United States and the Soviet Union. Today it again finds itself straddling two large powers with somewhat conflicting worldviews.

Now It's Your Turn

How do recent events complement or challenge the material presented in the case studies? If you had to brief a US government delegation on the perceptions of a particular bilateral relationship between the United States and the third world, what issues and perspectives would you highlight? Do you believe that many Americans understand or can agree with some of the concerns expressed by peoples in the third world? Why or why not? How would you explain the animosity expressed in some corners of the world toward the United States? What do you think are the sources of the love-hate relationship between the Western and non-Western worlds? If you had to outline a policy plan for future US relations with one of the countries studied here, what would it entail? How would this proposal be different if you were to chart it from the perspective of the third world country?

PART FIVE

Conclusion

22

Are We Living in a New Era?

You must be the change you want to see in the world.
—*Mahatma Gandhi, Indian political and spiritual leader (1869–1948)*

Our world in the early twenty-first century is rife with potential conflicts as well as potential new alignments. Interactions between the governments, societies, cultures, and economies of the Western and non-Western worlds may very well chart whether this future follows a path of peace and prosperity or stagnation and decline. If there is one lesson that we have highlighted throughout this book, though, it is that it will take an increased recognition of all of the world's peoples in order to craft any meaningful, lasting solutions to the current challenges we face, and to those that we do not yet envision.

In recent years, there has been a good deal of conversation about the ways in which the world has changed since the end of the superpower COLD WAR conflict, the onset of the third wave of DEMOCRACY, and the events of September 11, 2001. With some distance now from each of these periods, we have the chance to discern lessons learned and opportunities missed. In the wake of the September 11 attacks, for example, then–UN Secretary-General Kofi Annan said that one of the lessons of that day that had not received much attention was that we can't ignore inhumane conditions in the rest of the world. The economic and social problems of others have a direct impact on US national security (and world security). Annan is joined by many others who argue that TERRORISM isn't the only scourge threatening world security. According to former Costa Rican president and Nobel laureate Óscar Arias, "terrorism is one of many challenges to humanity, but the basic threats to world peace are poverty, inequality, illiteracy, disease, and environmental degradation."[1]

As the global economic slowdown continues to unfold, each of these threats seems to take on an even more urgent tone. Now more than ever it seems we need a truly multipronged strategy for curbing the appeal of violence and extremism. Sickness, for example, is closely related to political instability; countries with high infant mortality rates are more likely to fall into civil wars. The absence of political voice or economic opportunity serves as an "incubator" for terrorists. The lack of access to safe drinking water leads militaries to battle. Poverty worsens as economic stagnation deepens and assistance falters. As we contemplate policy responses to the threats we face, it seems that we need to move beyond the spread of nuclear weapons and the threat of terrorism, to the root causes of conflict. Many argue that we need to do whatever we can to reduce the number of "failed states" (e.g., Somalia, Pakistan and Afghanistan), since the combination of long-term grievances, masses of refugees, horribly uneven DEVELOPMENT, lack of human rights, and security challenges is known to produce human misery and political conflict. US defense secretary Robert Gates has argued that "dealing with such fractured or failing states is, in many ways, the main security challenge of our time."[2] Yet a coherent strategy is lacking.

What is to be done? The question can be raised in terms of foreign aid, which could be a much more effective instrument for change than it has been. Used in the proper way, foreign aid can be one of the best weapons against violence. For example, George W. Bush supported debt relief and provided aid through programs such as the President's Emergency Plan for AIDS Relief (PEPFAR), viewed by some to be one of the major foreign policy achievements of his administration, which has continued under Barack Obama.[3] But this assistance, which makes antiretroviral therapy accessible to more than 2 million Africans, has been extremely limited, and continued funding will likely be flat at best, despite President Obama's stated support as well as widespread recognition of the program's success. A *Wall Street Journal* op-ed jointly penned by Madeleine Albright and Colin Powell, two former US secretaries of state, highlights the fundamental connection between richer and poorer countries and the imperative to maintain our awareness of INTERDEPENDENCE: "Our country's economic health and security are inextricably linked to the prosperity and security of the rest of the world . . . (even in the midst of an economic crisis) pulling back from global engagement is not an option."[4]

The other major tool for influence is the military. With the Marshall Plan, the United States once recognized how poverty bred instability and that promoting the development of other countries was a national security issue for the United States. However, during the Cold War, US foreign aid was used to promote stability by propping up dictators—Washington's assistance to Indonesia's Suharto fits this mold precisely. The United States needs to remember the important role that aid can play in promoting stability, but this time it must not use it just to bribe authoritarians into helping in the war on terror. There is a high price for such a policy: the United States it is still paying for cozying up to the Shah for all those years. US policies in Pakistan and Afghanistan—if seen to be promoting security over human rights—risk similar blowback.

Joseph Nye's concept of "soft power," or the ability to influence others by attracting them to one's values, ideals, and norms, is increasingly tendered as a way to understand a country's (or organization's) appeal and leverage. Nye has argued, "When Washington discounts the importance of its attractiveness abroad, it pays a steep price."[5] In a sense, soft power is about public diplomacy. It is something that, as of late, the Chinese have been more aggressively promoting than the Americans, especially throughout the developing world, with investment and engagement across Africa, the Middle East, and increasingly in South America.[6] Few have claimed that soft power is a ZERO-SUM GAME, but China's offering up of an alternative to US policies is quite attractive to some countries that are frustrated with perceived US meddling and infringement. And a recent report contended that "the US has reserves of soft power that it has underused in recent years."[7]

For many people around the world, including some of its closest allies in the West, the United States lost the moral high ground with its unilateral actions during the 2000s. This was most clear when the United States and Great Britain, with clear disapproval from a majority of their colleagues—friend and foe alike—within the UNITED NATIONS, waged war against Saddam Hussein and his purported weapons of mass destruction—which have never been found. As Richard Haass, president of the Council on Foreign Relations, said about this decision, "the full consequences . . . cannot yet be measured."[8] As much as many believed President Obama would bring a completely new approach and, by connection, new perceptions of the United States, significant changes have yet to be realized. As the United States works its way out of the global recession, it again faces accusations of EXCEPTIONALIST behavior in the ways it is approaching financial issues. This was most evident at the GROUP OF 20 (G-20) summit in South Korea in 2010 when China, South Korea, and Germany each presented steadfast challenges to US economic policies (especially the Federal Reserve's infusion of further stimulus funds into the economy), producing a "smack down" in the words of the *Christian Science Monitor.*[9]

As this book goes to press, a new military campaign in Libya has begun. The United States is withdrawing its final (noncombat) forces from Iraq, yet the war in Afghanistan rages on (the US troop presence will likely continue until at least 2014). Even as timetables for an ultimate withdrawal from Afghanistan are debated, many are openly questioning, even after the death of Osama bin Laden, what objectives have been achieved in a conflict that has surpassed the Vietnam War as the longest war in US history. Long after the last foreign troops leave Afghanistan, their imprint will be felt throughout the region and around the world. What balance of values and policies will follow? From where will the next major challenges to peace, security, and freedom emerge? As you likely realized long before reading this book, we live in a world that is always changing. What kind of change will you be?

Acronyms

ACFTA	ASEAN-China Free Trade Area
AGOA	African Growth and Opportunity Act
AIDESCEP	Inter-Ethnic Association for the Development of the Peruvian Amazon
AKP	Justice and Development Party (Turkey)
APRA	American Popular Revolutionary Alliance (Peru)
ARF	ASEAN Regional Forum
ASEAN	Association of Southeast Asian Nations
ASG	Abu Sayyaf Group (Philippines)
AU	African Union
BRICs	Brazil, Russia, India, China
CAN	Andean Community of Nations
CCP	Chinese Communist Party
CCT	conditional cash transfer
CEDAW	Convention on the Elimination of All Forms of Discrimination Against Women
CIA	Central Intelligence Agency (United States)
CITES	Convention on International Trade in Endangered Species of Wild Fauna and Flora
CIVETS	Colombia, Indonesia, Vietnam, Egypt, Turkey, South Africa
CRC	Convention on the Rights of the Child
DC	developed country
DRC	Democratic Republic of Congo
ECF	extended-credit facility
ECOMOG	ECOWAS Monitoring Group
ECOSOC	Economic and Social Council (UN)
ECOWAS	Economic Community of West African States
EPZ	export processing zone
EU	European Union
FAO	Food and Agricultural Organization (UN)
FDI	foreign direct investment
FIS	Islamic Salvation Front (Algeria)

G-20	Group of 20
GATT	General Agreement on Tariffs and Trade
GDI	Gender-Related Development Index
GDP	gross domestic product
GEM	Gender Empowerment Measure
GNI	gross national income
GNP	gross national product
HDI	Human Development Index
HIC	high-income country
HIPC	highly indebted poor country
IAEA	International Atomic Energy Agency
IARF	International Association for Religious Freedom
IBRD	International Bank for Reconstruction and Development (World Bank)
ICBL	International Campaign to Ban Landmines
ICC	International Criminal Court
ICJ	International Court of Justice
ICRC	International Committee of the Red Cross
IFI	international financial institution
IFRC	International Federation of Red Cross and Red Crescent Societies
IGO	international governmental organization
ILO	International Labour Organization
IMF	International Monetary Fund
IPCC	Intergovernmental Panel on Climate Change
JEI	Jamaat-e-Islami (Pakistan)
KMT	Nationalist Party (China)
LDC	less developed country
LGBT	lesbian, gay, bisexual, transgender
LIC	low-income country
LLDC	least–less developed country
LRA	Lord's Resistance Army (Uganda)
MDC	Movement for Democratic Change (Zimbabwe)
MDGs	Millennium Development Goals
MDRI	Multilateral Debt Relief Initiative
MEND	Movement for the Emancipation of the Niger Delta (Nigeria)
Mercosur	Common Market of the South (also known as Mercosul)
MNC	multinational corporation
MNLF	Moro National Liberation Front (Malaysia)
MOSOP	Movement for the Survival of the Ogoni People (Nigeria)
MSF	Médecins sans Frontières (Doctors Without Borders)
NAFTA	North American Free Trade Agreement
NAM	Non-Aligned Movement
NATO	North Atlantic Treaty Organization
NEPAD	New Partnership for African Development
NGO	nongovernmental organization

NIC	newly industrializing country
NIDL	new international division of labor
NIEO	new international economic order
NIMBY	"not in my backyard"
NPT	Nuclear Non-Proliferation Treaty
OAS	Organization of American States
OAU	Organization of African Unity
OECD	Organization for Economic Cooperation and Development
OIC	Organization of the Islamic Conference
OPEC	Organization of Petroleum Exporting Countries
P-5	permanent five members of the UN Security Council
PAN	National Action Party (Mexico)
PAP	People's Armed Police (China)
PDI-P	Indonesian Democratic Party–Struggle
PDP	People's Democratic Party (Nigeria)
PEPFAR	President's Emergency Plan for AIDS Relief
PKI	Communist Party of Indonesia
PKK	Kurdistan Workers Party (Turkey)
PKO	peacekeeping operation
PLA	People's Liberation Army (China)
PPP	purchasing power parity
PQLI	Physical Quality of Life Index
PRC	People's Republic of China
PRD	Party of Democratic Revolution (Mexico)
PRI	Institutional Revolutionary Party (Mexico)
RPF	Rwandan Patriotic Front
RPP	Republican People's Party (Turkey)
RSF	Reporteurs sans Frontières (Reporters Without Borders)
RUF	Revolutionary United Front (Sierra Leone)
SADC	Southern African Development Community
SAP	structural adjustment program
SARS	severe acute respiratory syndrome
SBY	Susilo Bambang Yudhoyono (Indonesia)
SEATO	Southeast Asia Treaty Organization
SOE	state-owned enterprise
UAE	United Arab Emirates
UDHR	Universal Declaration of Human Rights
UDI	Unilateral Declaration of Independence (Rhodesia)
UNAIDS	Joint United Nations Programme on HIV/AIDS
UNAMID	African Union/United Nations Hybrid Operation in Darfur
UNAMIR	United Nations Assistance Mission for Rwanda
UNCTAD	United Nations Conference on Trade and Development
UNDP	United Nations Development Programme
UNEP	United Nations Environment Programme
UNHCR	United Nations High Commission(er) for Refugees
UNICEF	United Nations Children's Fund
UNIFEM	United Nations Development Fund for Women

VPN	virtual private network
WHO	World Health Organization
WID	women in development
WMD	weapon of mass destruction
WTO	World Trade Organization
ZANLA	Zimbabwe African National Liberation Army
ZANU-PF	Zimbabwe African National Union–Patriotic Front
ZAPU	Zimbabwe African People's Union
ZIPRA	Zimbabwe People's Revolutionary Army

Glossary

abertura A Portuguese term borrowed from the Brazilian experience, describing a political opening that may or may not lead to democratization. *See* **political liberalization**.

absolute poverty The term used by the United Nations to describe dire material hardship, a standard of living beneath human dignity. It is a crushing poverty in which people lack access to the basic necessities of life such as food, clean water, shelter, and healthcare.

accountability A characteristic of democracy existing when government is held responsible for its actions. Governments that are promoting accountability seek to control corruption not only by reducing the incentive to steal, but also by raising the costs and risks of official misconduct and demonstrating to the population that no one can violate the law with impunity.

acephalous society A "headless society" or "stateless society" in which there is no full-time executive; rather, groups of people are governed by committee or consensus.

amnesty A pardon granted by governments to individual and often groups of offenders as a gesture of reconciliation, often during a transition or change of regime.

aspiration gap Disparity between what is desired or hoped for and what can be attained. This concept helps us understand the consequences of unmet expectations.

austerity plan Another name for structural adjustment, denoting the hardship associated with implementing such measures. *See* **structural adjustment program**.

authoritarianism A nondemocratic political system in which the ruler depends on coercion rather than popular legitimacy to remain in power. Such systems are characterized by their abuse of human rights. Power is concentrated in the executive branch of government, and executives act with little if any interference from legislatures or judiciaries.

"Axis of Evil" The phrase included in President George W. Bush's 2002 State of the Union address to label Iran, Iraq, and North Korea as threats to world peace due to their attempts to obtain nuclear, chemical, or biological weapons and their alleged support of terrorism.

bottom-up approach An approach to change or development in which policies or projects are initiated and directed from the grassroots or masses.

bourgeoisie Originally from the French word *bourg* for "market town," this became a prominent term of analysis in Marxist socialism, separating the working class (known as the proletariat) from the landowning merchant classes and capitalist entrepreneurs (known as the bourgeoisie). In the Marxist framework, it is the bourgeoisie who will be eliminated by class struggle to produce a classless, communist society. *See also* **proletariat.**

BRICs Brazil, Russia, India, and China; a grouping used to refer to the world's fast-growing emerging economies that are also taking a greater role in political forums. Other countries are sometimes added to the grouping (such as South Africa, South Korea, and Mexico), contributing to an alphabet soup of acronyms.

Bush Doctrine President George W. Bush's foreign policy approach following the terrorist attacks of September 11, 2001. He conceptually divided the world community into two categories—those who support terrorists versus those who fight terrorists. The doctrine may be summed up in his statement that "either you are with us, or you are with the terrorists." In many parts of the world, this simplification was rejected as self-serving and unreflective of the complexities of the twenty-first century.

cadre party A type of political party dominated by personality-driven cliques and factional groupings that depends on local notables to choose and groom candidates. Cadre parties are recognized for their limited recruitment and are often found in states with limited voting rights. The term "cadre" has also been used to refer to the most dedicated members of a political party.

case study A detailed examination of a particular phenomenon or institution (in this context, a state). A method that seeks to find and demonstrate causal connections by tracing them through a series of cases, which are then compared.

caudillo A political strongman, often a member of the military.

Chapter VII The section of the UN Charter that permits the Security Council to "order binding action, including economic sanctions and the use of armed force." It sets enforcement mechanisms to prevent or deter threats to international peace. So-called Chapter VII authority has been used often since the end of the Cold War to justify intervention in conflict or unstable circumstances.

civil society Generally refers to voluntary social interactions between individuals that are independent of the government. Civil society organizations are commonly recognized as intermediaries between the government and the family. As a concept, civil society (also known as public space) includes nongovernmental organizations, social movements, and professional associations.

class (social) A number of people or things grouped together. A group of people who are linked together because of certain things held in common, such as occupation, social status, or economic background.

cleavage A socially supported division between groups in society who are significant enough to have forms of expression. Cleavages are often based on ethnicity, socioeconomic factors, or gender. Scholars have highlighted two dominant patterns of such divisions. Coinciding cleavages are clear and distinct, in which multiple competing viewpoints or points of division line up in clearly divided categories, presenting a situation that is more ripe for conflict. Crosscutting cleavages are mixed between and among various groups, producing an outcome in which cleavages are dispersed throughout society; therefore, those seeking support from the population must appeal to a wider variety of groups.

Cold War The period of intense US-Soviet rivalry that ran from World War II until the dissolution of the Soviet Union in 1991. Although this antagonism was played out in many different ways across every part of the world, it is known as being "cold" because, fearing nuclear catastrophe, the two parties never engaged in direct military confrontations.

collective security The principle that aggression against one state is taken as an aggression against all. Agreement to collectively resist aggression against another is a founding idea of the United Nations. Collective security arrangements are pursued by states in the hope of deterring threatening action.

common market Allows for the free circulation of goods, services, and capital between member states.

comparative advantage Liberal principle that holds that efficiency is maximized through specialization in production.

comparative studies This approach seeks to comprehend the complexity of human experience by adopting an eclectic, multidisciplinary approach. It utilizes the comparative method to produce generalizations that describe, identify, and explain trends—and even predict human behavior. This approach identifies relationships and interactions between actors, as well as patterns of behavior, by making comparisons (of two or more countries or of one country over time) to find similarities and differences in experience.

comprador The indigenous elite who dominate the economies and politics of many non-Western countries. They often enter into sweetheart deals with foreign interests—at great cost to the local majority.

conditional cash transfer (CCT) Government programs that make cash assistance to poor families conditional on a receiver's actions and are often related to child welfare (e.g., assistance of $35 a month to parents who take their children to a doctor for medical checkups or who enroll them in school). Such programs, if well designed and implemented, serve as a long-term investment in human capital and development. CCTs exist in a variety of forms in more than thirty countries.

consolidation Said to exist when democracy has put down deep roots and is durable—when democracy "is the only game in town." Democracies become consolidated by becoming more inclusive, by respecting human rights, and by guaranteeing equal representation to minorities and other marginalized groups. Stability, citizen loyalty, and a widespread belief that the system is good are all signs of consolidation.

convergence Said to be attained when less developed countries "catch up" with developed countries.

corporatism Terminology describing relations between groups and political authority; government restricts the development and operation of independent organizations. In corporatist systems, society is divided by functions (such as unions, professional associations, etc.), and government attempts to coordinate society by balancing groups that must negotiate with government for legal or economic benefits.

corruption Official misconduct or the abuse of power for private gain. A problem in both developed and less developed countries that has contributed to the breakdown of both military and civilian governments as populations call for accountability and transparency.

cross-national analysis A study comparing two or more countries in order to make larger generalizations.

cultural relativism The view that worldwide there is no commonly held morality. Rather, human rights and other ethical issues vary depending on the group, and consequently the promotion of any set of moral codes as somehow universal is misplaced and imperialistic.

Cultural Revolution Formally called the Great Proletarian Cultural Revolution, a chaotic period in modern Chinese history, officially from 1966 to 1969, when Chairman Mao Zedong directed the Red Guards to attack officials to prevent the spread of capitalism and materialism. Many individuals (especially businesspeople and intellectuals) were sent to the Chinese countryside to "learn from the peasants," while others were sent to "reeducation" camps to have their problems rectified. Most analysts today argue that the chaos of the Cultural Revolution did not truly end until Mao's death in 1976.

customs union A form of economic integration in which states agree to promote trade among members by eliminating tariffs and nontariff barriers, and to cooperate to protect their producers by setting a common tariff against nonmember states.

delegative democracy A political system that has an outward appearance of being democratic, and is more democratic than authoritarian. However, such systems are led by elites whose commitment to democracy is said to have limits. In delegative democracies, the executive claims to personify the nation's interests and therefore has the exclusive right to interpret them.

democracy (political) "Government by the people," existing in several variations and operating through different kinds of constitutional systems. A type of government or political system that is based on a decentralization of power and built on the principle of popular sovereignty: in democracies people choose their representatives, who compete for political office through free and fair elections held on a regular basis. Consequently, citizen participation and respect for civil liberties are integral to democracy, as citizens must have the freedom to hold political leaders accountable for their actions.

democracy dividend Popular expectation that after years of abuse, the transition to democracy will bring an economic expansion, an end to corruption, and an improved quality of life. There is usually much goodwill created by a democratic transition; however, this honeymoon is often short-lived and the resulting disillusionment is dangerous for fragile new democracies.

democratic institutionalization The process of crafting, nurturing, and developing democratic institutions to ensure participation, representation, accountability, respect for human rights, and so on. Institutionalization refers to the development of regularized processes; as democratic institutionalization occurs, "the rules of the game" become stabilized and formalized.

democratic transition A phase of political liberalization in which a political system is democratizing (opportunities for political participation and competition are expanded, free and fair elections are scheduled, and so on). Not every political liberalization results in a democratic transition, and not all democratic transitions result in democracy—they can turn out many different ways.

deterrence Defense policy in which a country attempts to prevent attack by threatening credible retaliation. The logic of deterrence is that an initiating action will cause mutual suicide. The greatest deterrents are considered to be nuclear weapons—the mere possession of nuclear weapons is believed sufficient to deter an enemy, because unless a country's entire nuclear arsenal could be wiped out by a first strike, the destruction caused by the inevitable retaliation would be too great a price to pay.

development There is little agreement on how best to describe development. The UN defines political development as "the achievement of a stable democracy that promotes the economic well-being of its citizens in an equitable, humane, and environmentally concerned manner." Some identify it as a process associated with increasing humans' choices and opportunities. Development is now widely recognized as promoting material and nonmaterial forms of well-being; it is associated with improved living standards, although it rests on political participation and human security and is concerned with the distribution of and access to resources. Often confused with "growth," development should be understood as both a process and an end.

devotee party Type of political party that is dominated by a charismatic leader.

disintegration When political reconfiguration spirals out of control. Divides are aggravated by internal and external demands for change, the military's unwillingness or inability to prevent a breakup, and the state's inability to meet demands for change. Weak states are said to "implode"—to decay and collapse from within.

displaced persons People who are forced to flee their homes but who have not crossed internationally recognized borders. The numbers of internally displaced people are often higher than official counts of refugees, and are considered to be more reflective of the magnitude of human suffering.

divide and conquer A common means of colonial conquest in which a usurping power sets two parties against each other, aggravates tensions to the point that the parties bleed each other dry, and then moves into the vacuum. Also known as divide and rule.

due process The expectation that certain procedures must always be followed in making policy; guarantees of fair legal procedures designed to protect the rights and liberties of individuals.

economic liberalization Neoliberal economic reforms that dismantle government controls and promote opening up economies to foreign trade and investment. Also known as market reforms.

efficacy An attitude about one's competence to effect change; a perception of ability or the sense that one's participation can make a difference. A sense of efficacy is an important factor in the decision to be engaged in public affairs—people with a strong sense of efficacy are more likely to be active in civic life than those who believe their actions would be worthless. The antonym of efficacy in this sense would be "alienation."

elite revolution Special type of revolution that is rapid and swift, with minimal participation by those outside of the initiating core and with limited violence. Also known as revolution from above.

elites Those who hold more power than others, whether cultural, political, economic, social, or otherwise. According to elite theory, elites are always outnumbered by those ostensibly holding less power, oftentimes referred to as the masses. Elites possess certain advantages, of wealth, privilege, education, training, status, political power, and the like.

empire The largest, most complex form of state organization, distinguished from a chiefdom by the size of the territories and the populations it controls. Empires are usually vast and impose a centralized government or single sovereign over a collection of different communities or nations. Empires often dominate regional and international trade; known for their large militaries, they frequently amass great riches through conquest and demands for tribute.

essential functions The most basic duties expected of elected governments, such as collecting taxes, enforcing laws, designing policies, and being responsive to the majority.

exceptionalist A belief or behavior that demonstrates the view that one's group is different from the norm, and therefore above the rules by which others are supposed to abide. An exceptionalist view of a group or event emphasizes the singular, unique qualities of whatever is being examined—making it seem that any particular circumstance is difficult to compare to another.

export processing zone (EPZ) A special trade area established by less developed countries to attract foreign investment. In the hope of creating jobs, obtaining technology transfers, and other benefits, EPZs offer low or no taxes and guarantee cheap, docile labor and minimal government regulation or interference with regard to health or environmental codes or the repatriation of profits.

extended-credit facility (ECF) Initiated in 2010, an International Monetary Fund (IMF) program that provides financial assistance to countries experiencing serious balance of payments problems. In consultation with the IMF, countries agree to implement a set of reforms aimed at reducing poverty and promoting economic growth in order to qualify for loans and other assistance. The successor to the poverty reduction and growth facilities and structural adjustment programs (SAPs), ECFs are said to be more flexible, with more streamlined conditions, and designed in consideration of each country's own development strategies and social objectives.

extraterritoriality Imposing one's rules and laws outside of one's own sovereign territory. Extraterritoriality was invoked during the colonial period; now, many developing countries view the United States as attempting to return to this state of affairs by insisting that foreign countries abide by US laws or policies.

fallacy of electoralism The mistake of focusing on elections as "proof" of democracy and ignoring other political realities.

fatwa A religious judgment issued by Muslim clerics.

formal sector The "above-ground" part of the economy (as opposed to the informal sector), calculated into gross domestic product.

founding elections The first elections marking a democratic transition, symbolizing a departure from authoritarianism.

Four Tigers Hong Kong, Singapore, South Korea, and Taiwan—distinguished by their record of strong growth rates and their shared reliance on state capitalism.

General Agreement on Tariffs and Trade (GATT) International economic organization formed to help liberalize and manage global trade after World War II. Established to promote the rules of conduct for free trade (such as lowering tariff rates and discouraging protectionist policies) and to provide a forum for the resolution of trade disputes. GATT was eventually overwhelmed by the growth in the volume of world trade and was replaced with the World Trade Organization (WTO) in 1995.

General Assembly An organ of the United Nations in which each member state is represented; it is primarily a deliberative organization centered around debate and discussion. Some matters, including those on peace and security and the admission of new members, require a two-thirds majority; others are adopted by a simple majority. Decisions of the General Assembly have no legally binding force on governments, but they represent the weight of world opinion.

globalization Describes the world's increasing interconnectedness, particularly in regard to communications, economies, and cultures, and associated with faster and greater international flows of trade, investment, and finance as well as migration, cultural diffusion, and communication—more specifically, a process describing the spread of capitalism and "modernization" worldwide. Alternatively viewed as a positive force that promotes development and brings the world closer together, or as a negative phenomenon contributing to worsening underdevelopment and the homogenization of the world's cultures.

grassroots-based approach An approach that is designed, implemented, and controlled by local communities. Often lauded for being not only more democratic in principle but also more effective in operation. *See* **bottom-up approach**.

greenhouse effect An increasingly substantiated theory that Earth is experiencing a gradual rise in temperatures and that this is due to human activity. This global warming is associated with buildup of greenhouse gases (most notably carbon dioxide), which are released by the burning of fossil fuels. As these waste gases collect in the upper atmosphere, the sun's heat becomes trapped, warming the planet (much like glass traps heat in a greenhouse). Although scientists continue to disagree about the rate of warming, most highly respected climatologists expect that if trends continue, the greenhouse effect will contribute to massive alterations in climate, which will contribute to a variety of consequences, some of them near cataclysmic.

Group of 20 (G-20) Founded in 1999, the G-20 is a forum that brings together finance ministers and central bank governors from the leading industrialized and emerging market economies in a regular dialogue to discuss a range of key issues in regard to the global economy. Together the partners constitute 90 percent of the world's gross national product, 80 percent of world trade, and two-thirds of the world's population.

growth A summation of economic performance referring to an increase in the volume of trade or economic output of a country, measured by gross domestic product (GDP), gross national income (GNI), or gross national product (GNP). Growth is usually a key indicator of a healthy economy, measured against the previous performance of each national economy, not a single worldwide standard (e.g., a 10 percent growth rate in a small economy, albeit impressive, actually indicates a smaller amount of absolute economic activity than a single-digit growth rate in a larger economy).

guerrilla From the Spanish, literally "little war." Guerrillas are loosely organized, nonuniformed combatants, often small in number. Guerrilla tactics are mobile and swift, incorporating the element of surprise with sabotage, hit and run, and ambush, all in violation of conventional laws of warfare.

hegemon A strong, controlling force that attempts to impose its preferences on others. Used in discussions of international affairs to describe the dominance of a specific country. If the nineteenth century was the period of British hegemony, the post–Cold War era is one of US hegemony, with the United States being the sole remaining superpower.

highly indebted poor country (HIPC) A country falling into this category is eligible for a program of debt relief if it makes the required neoliberal economic reforms.

human security Defined as the absence of structural violence, which is understood as widespread poverty and other forms of economic, social, and environmental degradation. Human security is a new but increasingly recognized understanding of security that goes far beyond issues of armaments and territorial security. It addresses individual and collective perceptions of present and potential threats to physical and psychological well-being.

identity The collective aspect or characteristics by which a person or group is known. Humans have multiple identities that they choose to emphasize, depending on context. Common identities uniting people in action include race, class, gender, and region.

ideology The belief systems of individuals and groups; a linked set of ideas that describe the world, help people understand their role within society, and arouse them to take action, whether to change or preserve the existing situation.

import substitution industrialization (ISI) A development strategy especially popular in the mid–twentieth century that seeks to diversify economies and lessen the dependence of less developed countries (LDCs) on foreign imports of manufactured goods. It encourages industrialization headquartered within LDCs by subsidizing and protecting local producers from foreign competition.

informal sector Also known as the informal economy, the informal sector is a shadow economy comprising semilegal or illegal activities that are unreported, unregulated, and untaxed—and therefore not included in the calculation of a country's gross domestic product. Because it is so often the case that their opportunities in the formal economy are limited, women compose a large number of informal-sector workers.

integration A process that increases the quantity and quality of interconnectedness between countries through small or large steps; promotes cooperation between countries based on common security or economic concerns. For example, the European Union began in the 1950s (as the European Economic Community) as an agreement on coal and steel and over the years has moved increasingly toward the creation of a single market—the world's largest.

interdependence A political and economic relationship based on mutual vulnerability between two countries, each of which is sensitive to what happens in the other. The term implies that even developed countries are bound to less developed countries by interdependence, as opposed to those who characterize the relationship as one of dependence—largely the dependence of less developed countries on developed countries.

International Criminal Court (ICC) The world's first permanent international criminal court, the ICC was established by the Rome Statute in 1998 and entered into force in 2002. More than a hundred states have ratified the Rome Statute in recognition of the Court's authority. The Court resides in The Hague, where this independent entity serves as a mechanism for trying individuals accused of committing the world's most serious crimes: war crimes, crimes against humanity, and genocide.

international economic system The network of world trade, which is based on the remains of what was known as the Bretton Woods system. Formed in the post–World War II period, this international economic system has been dominated by developed countries under US leadership. Bretton Woods gave lip service to liberal economic policies such as open economies and free trade. However, even its most ardent advocates routinely practiced protectionist policies that have hamstrung the development of less developed countries. Consequently, critics of this system argue that it is structured to benefit the already rich, to the detriment of the poor.

international financial institution (IFI) An organization that governs fiscal matters within and between states. Most IFIs (such as the International Monetary Fund and the World Bank) promote the neoliberal agenda and are run by developed countries—with very little input from the less developed countries over which they have tremendous influence.

international governmental organization (IGO) An organization with two or more member states that may serve as a forum for discussion to promote cooperation on either regional or functional (issue-oriented) matters. The largest IGO is the United Nations; however, IGOs can be very limited in scope and membership as well.

International Monetary Fund (IMF) Central to the world financial system, this international organization is dedicated to promoting market economics. Established soon after the 1944 Bretton Woods conference, the IMF is a global lending agency originally created to aid in the postwar recovery of Europe and Japan. Rich countries continue to dominate the IMF, which operates under a weighted voting system based on the amount of money members donate to the organization. The IMF is charged with several responsibilities, including stabilization of exchange rates and promotion of fiscal conservatism. One of its most important roles is to assist with balance of payments problems, and in this capacity it serves as an international credit bureau—for countries. Just as is the case with individuals, countries are assigned credit ratings. If the IMF blackballs a country, it will have a very difficult time obtaining credit—from the IMF or from any IFI, for that matter. On the other hand, in order to remain in good stead with the IMF, countries must accept conditionality, or demonstrate their willingness to submit to neoliberal economic reforms such as those promoted through extended-credit facilities.

international political economy The study of the interrelationship between politics and economics at the international and transnational levels; examines how international politics affects the world's economies and how economics affects international political relationships. Advocates of this approach contend that an understanding of international political economy is necessary since economic factors shape most areas of political life. International political economy focuses on issues such as world markets, global financial institutions, and multinational corporations.

intifada From the Arabic, meaning "shivering" or "shaking off." The term was first applied to the Palestinian uprising against Israeli occupation from 1987 to 1993, in protest of killings near a Palestinian settlement. Another intifada began in the fall of 2000.

irredentist war A form of violent interstate conflict stemming from a nation's efforts to redraw political boundaries to include territory considered its homeland or to unite with its people living on the other side of a border.

jihad From the Arabic, signifying "struggle." Although it has recently been taken to narrowly mean a "holy war," its more accurate meaning encompasses the internal struggle that faithful Muslims undergo in their attempts to contend with the challenges facing them. Jihad also encompasses the requirements for a permissible and legitimate war, similar to other faith traditions' teachings on justifiable combat.

legitimacy The popular perception on the part of large numbers of people that the government, its leaders, and its policies are valid, right, just, and worthy of support. A legitimate regime is not necessarily the same as a legal regime, nor does it mean that a regime is democratic. A political regime is legitimate when it is accepted by the majority of its citizens as right and proper enough to be obeyed in most instances. Legitimacy can be achieved through all sorts of means, including propaganda, clientelism, and coercion.

legitimate trade The trade of raw materials in Africa, which Europeans began to pursue more ardently to serve the needs of industry. For a variety of reasons, by the early nineteenth century the "legitimate trade" had displaced the "illegitimate trade" (the term abolitionists had used for the slave trade) along the African coast.

liberal democracy A political system that has undertaken (and continues to undertake) comprehensive political reform in which democratic institutions are routinized and internalized and civil and political rights are protected—so much so that democracy is said to be "consolidated."

liberation theology A movement that started within the Catholic Church in Latin America and has spread to other Christian churches and regions of the world; an action-oriented ideology that promotes social justice through local activism. Liberation theology teaches that the cause of poverty is capitalism, and that the Church should lead a revolution to establish governing systems that will redistribute wealth, end all forms of imperialism, and promote democracy. It was especially popular throughout the 1980s, but has faced opposition because of its use of Marxist revolutionary ideals.

mandatory system The system for administering the territories taken from Germany and its allies after World War I, under Article 22 of the Charter of the League of Nations. The League appointed states such as Britain, France, and South Africa to help prepare the mandates for their eventual independence, yet in many cases the mandatory system was considered no more than "a fig leaf for colonialism." Later, when the mandates became trust territories administered by the United Nations, the mandatory powers were held somewhat more accountable for their actions.

maquiladora A subsidiary of a multinational corporation that assembles imported parts and exports manufactured goods; originally the assembly plants that have proliferated along the US-Mexican border since the implementation of the North American Free Trade Agreement (NAFTA). However, the term is now sometimes used to describe such enterprises wherever they exist in the non-Western world.

mass party A type of political party that attempts to be as inclusionary as possible, oftentimes attempting to incorporate less politically engaged individuals and groups into the political process. Mass parties are marked by a formal nationwide structure, and are used to mobilize large groups of voters.

masses Relative to the elites, the masses are those who lack power and influence and who always outnumber the elites; the vast majority of the population in a country tend to be lumped into the category of the "masses" or the "common people."

mercantilism A precapitalist stage of development marked by accumulation of capital and accomplished through trade and plunder on a worldwide scale. This aggressive economic policy was the guiding force behind the conquest of many areas; it provided the capital base for Europe's industrialization. In its more contemporary form, mercantilism describes the situation when a power seeks commercial expansion to achieve a surplus in its balance of trade.

military professionalism Critical to the survival of democracies, this term refers to the military's depoliticization. Where it exists, coups d'état are unthinkable, as the military recognizes the supremacy of civilian rule and views itself as serving civilian government.

Millennium Development Goals (MDGs) A global action plan to end poverty by 2015. The plan comprises eight goals such as halving the percentage of people who go hungry, promoting universal primary education, and reducing the loss of biodiversity. Agreed upon in 2000 by 189 countries at the United Nations Millennium Summit, the plan provides a blueprint for ending poverty and a pledge to galvanize the world into achieving it.

mother country Another name for a colonizing country; its use denotes the exclusive ties that bound the colonies to the mother country much like an umbilical cord. Also refers to the parental role the colonizers portrayed themselves as playing in the non-Western world.

Multilateral Debt Relief Initiative (MDRI) An enhancement of the highly indebted poor countries (HIPC) initiative, the MDRI cancels the eligible debt of the poorest countries that have "graduated" or completed their HIPC requirements. Under this program, monies saved from the cancellation of this debt are to be used to meet the Millennium Development Goals.

multinational corporation (MNC) A business enterprise headquartered in one country (usually a developed country) with activities abroad stemming from direct foreign investment located in several countries. As MNCs conglomerate and form near-monopolies, international trade is increasingly dominated by a handful of corporations. Enormously powerful because they are so flexible, they can readily move capital, goods, and technology to fit market conditions.

multinational state A political unit of organization that includes two or more ethnic or national groups. Largely due to colonialism's arbitrary boundaries, a nation may or may not reside within the political boundary of a state, thereby producing a multinational state.

nation-state A term that combines the ideals of two concepts. A nation is considered to be a group of people who recognize a similarity among themselves because of common culture, language, or history. Nations often but do not always coincide with political boundaries of states, thereby producing multinational states. A state is considered to be a political entity with legal jurisdiction and physical control—an internationally recognized government.

nationalism A set of political beliefs that center around the shared sense of characteristics attributable to a group of people known to each other as a nation. Nationalism has been used to promote the interests and needs of a particular group of people, and has been a particularly strong rallying force, both uniting and dividing groups.

neocolonialism A term used to describe the condition from which many non-Western states today suffer, as they continue to be indirectly controlled by their former colonizers or other developed countries; said to exist because less developed countries operate under so many of the constraints of colonialism that they are considered independent only in name.

neoliberalism The contemporary version of procapitalist liberal economic strategy, which holds that all benefit from an open economy and free trade, or the unencumbered movement of goods and services between states. It is the dominant view held by the governments of developed countries and most international financial institutions, such as the World Bank and the International Monetary Fund. Neoliberals fervently believe that globalization is a positive force and that the current international economic system based on free competition can work for all if countries will just embrace it. Most third world countries then must adopt the proper reforms, promote openness, and prepare for a period of austerity to get their economic houses in order.

new international division of labor (NIDL) Whereas the "old" international division of labor described the relationship between developed and less developed countries, with the former as producers of manufactured goods and the latter as producers of raw materials, the "new" division points to a shift in the product cycle, with an increasing number of less developed countries moving into manufacturing while developed countries become dominated by the service sector.

new international economic order (NIEO) A comprehensive attempt by less developed countries to reform the international economic system. Debated in the 1960s and 1970s at the United Nations Conference on Trade and Development (UNCTAD) and other forums, the Group of 77 called for a series of changes (from increased foreign aid, to a code of conduct for multinational corporations, to elaborate efforts to stabilize the price of exports from less developed countries) aimed at "leveling the playing field" of opportunities for development. Although some of the proposals continue to be discussed today, only marginal changes have come of the NIEO so far.

newly industrializing country (NIC) Also known as a new industrial economy or an emergent economy. NICs are countries such as China, Mexico, South Korea, and Taiwan that in the past few decades have shifted from agrarian to increasingly industrial economies, due largely to strong state intervention and investment by multinational corporations. The high productivity of the cheap labor force in these countries has enabled the NICs to compete aggressively in the international market with developed countries, effectively driving their textile and other sectors out of business. *See* **Four Tigers**.

Non-Aligned Movement (NAM) Formed in 1961 in opposition to the polarizing tendencies of the Cold War, the NAM is an alliance of over a hundred countries that shunned military alliances and coalitions with other states—especially the dominant powers during the Cold War, during which time the NAM advocated the neutrality of its members. Prime Minister Jawaharlal Nehru of India, President Josip Broz Tito of Yugoslavia, and President Gamal Abdul Nasser of Egypt founded the movement as a vehicle for non-aligned countries to come together to solve mutual problems without benefit of military alliance. A summit is held every three years.

nongovernmental organization (NGO) A private association of voluntary membership that works together to accomplish set goals. The numbers of NGOs in the world exploded throughout the 1980s, and continue to swell. General examples of NGOs include universities, churches, and civic and professional associations. Increasingly at the global level, the "on the ground" competency of NGOs is being recognized in policy- and decisionmaking. One of the foremost examples of the partnership between NGOs and international organizations was the Ottawa Treaty process, which was born of the efforts of the International Campaign to Ban Landmines.

nonintervention Not interfering in the internal affairs of other countries; associated with sovereignty, nonintervention is an international principle traditionally thought to promote international stability.

parliamentary system A democratic constitutional system in which citizens select members of parliament, and executive authority is dependent on parliamentary confidence. Variously characterized as flexible and unstable, gridlock is much less likely in a parliamentary than in a presidential system. Since the majority party in parliament selects the executive, the prime minister can usually be confident that his or her initiatives will be warmly received by the legislature. In a parliamentary system, new elections are called by the prime minister, and can be called at any time (within a certain time frame). As opposed to presidential systems, effective executives can be kept in power indefinitely. However, the system is self-correcting for executive abuse, since the legislative branch can censure and rid itself of an errant executive with much more ease than the painstaking process of impeachment necessary in a presidential system.

party system Referencing the collection of political parties in a given state or region—analysts often distinguish between single-party systems and multiparty systems, based on the number of active and viable parties in the regime. For example, a one-party-dominant system is one in which there are political alternatives but in which a single party exercises a near-monopoly on power, either due to the lack of alternatives or because of the overwhelming support of citizens. A multiparty system is one in which there are two or more major contenders for power.

patrimonialism A form of governance that exists when the ruler treats the state as his or her own personal property. Appointments to government office are assigned on the basis of loyalty to the ruler, who plays the role of a benevolent but stern parent, often through a mixture of co-optation and repression.

patron-client relationship A method of co-optation based on a relationship of reciprocity in which the powerful patron (a leader, party, agency, or government) allocates resources to his or her clients (the people) with the expectation that the clients will pledge to the patron their political loyalty.

peacekeeping operation (PKO) A noncombat military operation mandated by the UN Security Council and sent into conflict areas in an attempt to promote a peaceful transition. PKOs consist of outside forces acting on the consent of all major belligerent parties. Their tasks range from keeping apart hostile parties to helping them work together peacefully. PKOs have monitored cease-fires, created buffer zones, and helped to create and sustain nascent political institutions. PKO forces are often distinguished by their famous "blue helmets."

personalist regime Also known as a personally appropriated state—an authoritarian style of government. This regime exists when a single, highly charismatic individual, who represents him- or herself as the personification of the nation, holds unchecked power. It may exist under civilian or military rule, when the leader seeks to guarantee his or her personal control in perpetuity, as "president for life" or through a hereditary republic.

political culture The context out of which political action is taken, recognizing the importance of systems of values and beliefs. While few people would deny that culture impacts people's views on politics and government, it has been difficult to articulate the precise connections between these variables and political outcomes. In 1959, Gabriel Almond and Sidney Verba identified three root (or "civic") cultures in the countries they studied: participant, subject, and parochial.

political liberalization A process of political reform based on the extension of civil and political rights, and the promotion of a more open political system. Signs that a system is liberalizing politically include a variety of changes, such as an increasing tolerance of dissent and the release of political prisoners. Although they are often associated with democratization, not all political liberalizations will result in democracy. Also known as an *abertura*.

political spectrum Conceptual map used to compare and contrast political ideologies. Along a horizontal line, ideologies are listed according to their views on change, the role of government in economic matters, and the relationship between religious institutions and their place in politics. The modern convention of the "left-right" political spectrum derives from legislative arrangements in the National Assembly of France, when those who supported the monarch and the Catholic Church sat on the right of the monarch, and those who favored democracy and revolution sat on the left.

populist An agenda, political party, campaign, or image designed to appeal to the "common people" rather than to the minority elite, rallying them around a shared sense of belonging and promising many things. The term was originally used to describe political movements in Europe at the end of the nineteenth century that appealed to the rural poor. The term is now used to describe mass political movements, or party platforms that purport to represent sentiment akin to the collective voice of ordinary people on social and economic issues.

praetorianism Military supremacy in politics; a type of increased involvement by soldiers in politics when military officers threaten or use force to influence political decisions and outcomes. The term derives from the praetorian guards of the Roman Empire, who were established as a unit to protect the emperor but who abused their power to overthrow and select the emperor themselves.

presidential system A type of democratic constitutional system in which citizens directly select both their legislators and their executive. Because the executive and legislative branches are elected separately, it is not uncommon for one party to hold the presidency and another to dominate the legislature. As a result, gridlock is much more likely in a presidential than in a parliamentary system. Although there are checks and balances between the various branches of government, the executive is relatively independent of the legislature, and power tends to concentrate in the executive. The rigidity of a fixed presidential term means that it is harder to remove an errant executive from power, and effective executives are constitutionally prohibited from serving beyond the prescribed term.

proletariat The socioeconomic group (or class) identified in Marxist socialism, defined by their relationship to the means of production. The proletarians are the workers who will unite together in revolutionary zeal to overcome the more powerful and entrenched bourgeoisie. Karl Marx argued that most workers own nothing but their labor (unlike artisans, who may own their machinery or tools). The proletariat is commonly called the working class.

proxy war A type of warfare undertaken by the superpowers during the Cold War. In an attempt to avoid the massive casualties associated with mutual assured destruction, the superpowers took sides in conflicts around the world, choosing intermediaries and supplying and arming them to play out the East-West rivalry with less risk of escalation to nuclear war.

reconfiguration A form of crisis management in which governments take very small steps or affect the appearance of reform while maintaining significant restrictions on civil liberties, political participation, and competition. Analysts maintain that reconfiguration is not necessarily antidemocratic in nature—even incremental steps may add up to more substantive reforms, which may in turn contribute to democratization.

reform (political) *See* **political liberalization**.

relative deprivation A comparative statement that reveals the sense that individuals or groups are not doing as well as other groups.

relative poverty Denotes a trend in terms of the gap between rich and poor countries. While some countries have made progress in eliminating absolute poverty, rising incomes during the economic boom of the 1990s have actually contributed to widening inequality overall. Consequently, while absolute poverty is said to have declined, for many less developed countries relative poverty has increased.

rescue package An assortment of loans, credits, and other forms of aid offered by the International Monetary Fund and other international financial institutions to countries suffering from massive economic dislocation (such as much of Asia during the "Asian flu" of the late 1990s). Aimed at stabilizing these economies, such packages are offered, however, only to countries willing to accept certain conditions, such as a neoliberal series of economic reforms.

resource mobilization A conceptual approach to collective behavior and social movements that emphasizes the resources necessary for success, taking into account both the material and the nonmaterial needs of participants in collective action.

responsibility to protect (R2P) An evolving international norm establishing the right of humanitarian intervention. In response to then–UN Secretary-General Kofi Annan's 2000 call to establish a global consensus on when such interventions should occur, UN member states adopted R2P as a key principle of international affairs at the 2005 World Summit. The principle emphasizes the responsibilities of sovereignty, which include protecting their populations from coordinated acts of violence, especially war crimes, crimes against humanity, and genocide. Under R2P, if a government is unable or unwilling to guard the safety of its citizens, the international community has a responsibility to help or intervene, using diplomatic channels and even military force as a last resort.

revolution Meaning "to turn around," a revolution is the attempt (often sudden) to promote fundamental change in political and social institutions of society, often accompanied by violence and economic and cultural upheaval.

revolution of rising expectations The recognition that improvement (often in the economy, but also in life choices and options) is often not as great as predicted or promised. Leaders often deliver inflated promises to their people, and rapid change can often increase hopes and desires for the future. The concept of "rising expectations" is used to distinguish from the "revolution of falling expectations," in which people anticipate a bad future and the future turns out to be even worse than expected.

rule of law A situation in which the power of individuals is limited by a supreme set of rules that prevent arbitrary and unfair actions by governmental officials. A reliance on written rules to govern and operate, rather than on the vice and virtue of rulers.

secession The act of withdrawing or breaking away from some organized entity such as a nation, as when Bangladesh seceded from Pakistan in 1971.

Secretary-General The chief administrative officer of the United Nations. The Secretary-General is nominated by the Security Council and elected by a two-thirds majority in the General Assembly for a five-year renewable term. In addition to presiding over the United Nations, the Secretary-General has become increasingly more visible in mediating and responding to global issues outside UN organizations. Kofi Annan, of Ghana, served from 1997 to 2006. His successor is Ban Ki-moon of the Republic of Korea.

secularism The separation of civil or educational institutions from ecclesiastical control; the act of de-emphasizing spiritual or religious perspectives in political, cultural, or social life.

Security Council The most powerful organ within the UN system. Its representatives include five permanent members (the P-5), which have veto power, and rotating members that do not have veto power. The ten nonpermanent members are elected to two-year terms by the General Assembly. Under the UN Charter, the Security Council possesses as its primary responsibility the maintenance of international peace and security. The Council works to achieve this through many means: mediation, cease-fire directives, and the use of peacekeeping forces, to name a few.

self-determination The right of a people who share cultural ties and live in a given territory to choose their own political institutions and government. A central international political concept of the twentieth century associated with nationalism and anticolonial movements.

sharia Sometimes known as *shariat,* from the Arabic, meaning "way" or "road." *Sharia* is Muslim religious (or canonical) law based on rules for moral conduct developed over the first few centuries after the death of the prophet Mohammed. *Sharia* governs both the individual and social lives of believers, and provides followers with a basis for judging actions as good or evil. Despite debates over the degree of observance and the role of authorities for enforcement, most agree that a common understanding of *sharia* unites most Muslims around the world.

social movement Human beings with a common purpose engaged in discussion and action designed to bring about change. Social movements are responses to a perceived state of affairs and often identify specific groups in society as the source of the problem to be rectified. Oftentimes, collective actions stimulate a countermovement in response.

sovereignty Freedom from foreign control; a principle widely accepted in international law that speaks to a state's right to do as it wishes in its own territory; a doctrine that holds that states are the principal actors in international relations and the state is subject to no higher political authority. Also refers to widespread international acceptance of a particular country's control of territory.

state An organized political entity that occupies a specific territory, has a permanent population, is controlled by a government, and is regarded as sovereign. Currently there are approximately 190 recognized states worldwide. *See* **nation-state**.

state capitalism An economic system that mixes capitalism with government planning; private enterprise accounts for most of the country's economic activity, but the government intervenes on the side of business with subsidies and other supports aimed at promoting domestic producers' competitiveness on the world market.

state society A centralized form of political organization; an outgrowth of the sedentarization of human populations, the intensification of agricultural production, and population booms. State societies are distinguished by increasing social stratification as classes emerge and power is centralized in the hands of full-time political leaders.

This broad category includes many different forms of political organization, from simple, small states to immense empires.

stateless nation A group of people (with a shared identity based on language, ethnicity, religion, or common heritage) who consider themselves to have no country to call their own; people without citizenship in any state.

stateless society A smaller, decentralized grouping of the type in which the earliest humans lived. It is relatively democratic in that power is shared and there are no full-time political leaders. Also known as acephalous society.

state-owned enterprise (SOE) A business that is owned and operated wholly or partially by the government. In many countries, SOEs have been concentrated in sectors thought vital to the national economy. They were built from nationalized properties, as an attempt to reclaim a country's resources from foreign domination or to promote import substitution industrialization. Throughout much of the world, SOEs have been large employers. However, they have been criticized as notoriously inefficient drains on state budgets. Also known as state-owned industry.

state-sponsored terrorism (or state terror) Violent methods used by government forces or vigilante groups acting with at least the tacit approval of state officials to intimidate and coerce people, often the state's own citizens.

structural adjustment program (SAP) The neoliberal prescription offered by international financial institutions to indebted countries. As a condition for international assistance (*see* **rescue package**), countries must commit to an SAP, usually a three- to five-year program that includes a variety of reforms associated with economic liberalization (e.g., privatization, devaluation of currency, cutting social spending, raising taxes, welcoming foreign investment, etc.).

structuralism A school of thought that includes a range of opinion from radical to reformist. Structuralists share the view that the current international economic system works to the benefit of the already rich and that globalization is inherently disadvantageous to poor countries. Structuralists are highly critical of neoliberal programs, which they see as dooming much of the world to underdevelopment.

sustainable development An approach that considers the long-term impact on the environment and resources of current development strategies.

sweatshop A place of labor, usually a factory. The term is used derisively to describe a business establishment profiting from inhumane working conditions.

terrorism The use of violence or the threat of violence and intimidation to achieve aims and spread a message. Terrorists aim for symbolic targets to manipulate adversaries and to achieve political, religious, or ideological objectives.

theocracy From the Greek, meaning "government of God"—a system of rule based on religion and dominated by clergy. Rules are often inspired by some form of holy book.

top-down approach As opposed to a bottom-up approach, top-down policies are ostensibly aimed at benefiting the majority and are initiated by elites.

totalitarianism A full-blown dictatorship, marked by the severity and magnitude of the state's interference in the lives of its citizens. In totalitarian systems the state, guided by an overarching ideology, attempts to exercise absolute control over virtually every aspect of citizens' lives. Power is concentrated in the hands of the leader or party and dissent is not tolerated. There is no right of political competition or participation, leaders are not accountable for their actions, and the state violates civil and human rights with impunity. Classic examples of totalitarian states include fascist regimes such as Nazi Germany, as well as Communist Party–dominated states such as Joseph Stalin's Russia and Mao Zedong's China.

transparency A policy promoted to reduce corruption; exists when the government is open about its spending and budgetary matters, and people are encouraged to report misconduct.

truth commission An official mechanism launched usually during periods of political transition to investigate wrongs of the recent past, especially human rights abuses. Truth commissions represent attempts to deal with the past by promoting the public acknowledgment of wrongdoing, sometimes as an alternative to criminal prosecution. There are multiple models of truth commissions, which vary in the scope of crimes examined, mandate and investigation, and the types of justice employed. Most truth commissions are established to achieve an accurate historical description of what took place, to promote reconciliation, and to help promote more durable democracies by creating a culture of human rights. Truth commissions are viewed by many as but one part of the complex healing process after periods of trauma, but much disagreement about their long-term impact remains.

United Nations Preceded by the League of Nations, the UN was founded in 1945 as an international governmental organization that now includes almost all of the world's states. It provides a forum at which complaints are heard and conflicts are discussed and sometimes resolved. The UN is also involved in promoting human development through the work of its specialized agencies, which promote standards for world heath, education, and the environment in addition to commonly accepted terms for trade and commerce.

Universal Declaration of Human Rights (UDHR) The most comprehensive international statement on human rights. With over thirty articles pertaining to a wide array of political, civil, economic, social, and cultural rights, the UDHR was put forward in 1948 as a general resolution of the United Nations.

universalism The view that conceptions of human rights and morality do not depend on whether a group or culture recognize them as such; rather, these principles are universal. Universalists argue that human rights are timeless, global in relevance and scope; there is a common morality that applies across cultures, and human rights are an entitlement all people share—no matter who they are or where they live.

vanguard party Literally the "leading" party—Vladimir Lenin's term for the Communist Party, supposed to take a front role in the overthrow of capitalism and transition to communism. Lenin prescribed that a single, elite, highly disciplined party would be necessary to lead the revolution of the proletarians, or the workers. Lenin's idea of a vanguard party has been used by Marxist socialist states such as China and North Korea to argue against the creation of competing political parties, producing a monopoly of control with which other socialists disagree.

weapons of the weak Forms of confrontation that often go unnoticed because they tend to be concealed, disguised, or subtle—employed by the ostensibly powerless, including women, minorities, and peasants. Commonly used tactics include rumor, deception, hoarding, and suicide.

World Bank Also known as the International Bank for Reconstruction and Development (IBRD), the World Bank was formed as part of the Bretton Woods system in 1944, along with its counterpart organization the International Monetary Fund (IMF). Like the IMF, the World Bank is controlled by developed countries, as voting power is based on a country's financial contribution to the Bank. Its responsibilities are wide-ranging; although it was originally created to fund the reconstruction of postwar Europe and to promote a stable international economic system, it now focuses its efforts on long-term loans and projects in the non-Western world and more recently in Eastern Europe and the former Soviet republics.

World Trade Organization (WTO) Founded in 1995, the WTO is an institution designed to promote free trade and mediate trade disputes; an updated and expanded product of the General Agreement on Tariffs and Trade (GATT), which focused on manufactured goods. Compared to GATT, the WTO has much more extensive monitoring and enforcement powers, although some less developed countries fear that this international governmental organization is working primarily for the benefit of developed countries.

zero-sum game A situation in which there can be only one winner and one loser. One actor's gain is another's loss (as opposed to non-zero-sum game, in which all can be winners or all can be losers).

Notes

Preface
1. Jim Lobe, "Zoellick Sees End of 'Third World,'" *Inter-Press Service,* April 14, 2010; Ian Morris, "Here Comes the East," *International Herald Tribune,* December 21, 2010; Roger Cohen, "The Age of Possibility," *International Herald Tribune,* November 29, 2010.
2. Ibid.; Clay Risen, "The 2000s Were a Great Decade," *New York Times,* December 19, 2010.

Chapter 1
Comparing and Defining Worlds
1. Henry Louis Gates, "'Authenticity' or the Lesson of Little Tree," *New York Times Review of Books,* November 24, 1991, p. 30.
2. Alfred Sauvy, "Three Worlds, One Planet," *L'Observateur,* August 14, 1952.
3. Cited in Lesley Wroughton, "'Third World' Concepts No Longer Relevant," *Reuters,* April 14, 2010.
4. Andre Gunder Frank, *Capitalism and Underdevelopment in Latin America* (New York: Monthly Review Press, 1967).
5. Samuel P. Huntington, *The Clash of Civilizations and the Remaking of World Order* (New York: Simon and Schuster, 1996).
6. Naomi Chazan, Peter Lewis, and Robert Mortimer, *Politics and Society in Contemporary Africa* (Boulder: Lynne Rienner, 1999).
7. Frank L. Wilson, *Concepts and Issues in Comparative Politics: An Introduction to Comparative Analysis* (Upper Saddle River, NJ: Prentice Hall, 1996).
8. David J. Elkins and Richard E. B. Simeon, "A Cause in Search of Its Effect, or What Does Political Culture Explain?" *Comparative Politics* 11, no. 2 (January 1979).
9. Monte Palmer, *Comparative Politics: Political Economy, Political Culture, and Political Interdependence* (Itasca, IL: F. E. Peacock, 1997).
10. Colin Leys, *Underdevelopment in Kenya: The Political Economy of Neo-Colonialism, 1964–1971* (London: Heinemann, 1975).
11. Thomas Friedman, *The Lexus and the Olive Tree* (New York: Farrar, Straus, and Giroux, 1999).
12. Howard J. Wiarda and Harvey F. Kline, *An Introduction to Latin American Politics and Development* (Boulder: Westview, 2001); Austin Sarat and Thomas R. Kearns, "The Unsettled Status of Human Rights: An Introduction," in *Human Rights: Concepts, Contests, Contingencies,* eds. Austin Sarat and Thomas R. Kearns (Ann Arbor: University of Michigan Press, 2001); Edward W. Said, *Reflections on Exile* (Cambridge: Harvard University Press, 2001).

13. Thomas L. Friedman, "Global Village Idiocy," *New York Times,* May 12, 2002.

14. Joshua S. Goldstein, *International Relations,* 4th ed. (New York: Longman, 2001).

15. Michael E. Porter, "Attitudes, Values, Beliefs, and the Microeconomics of Prosperity," in *Culture Matters: How Values Shape Human Progress,* eds. Lawrence E. Harrison and Samuel P. Huntington (New York: Basic, 2000).

16. Friedman, *The Lexus and the Olive Tree.*

17. Ibid.

18. Jack Donnelly, *International Human Rights* (Boulder: Westview, 1998).

19. Richard H. Ullman, "Human Rights: Toward International Action," in *Enhancing Global Human Rights,* eds. Jorge I. Domínguez et al. (New York: McGraw Hill, 1979).

20. Michael Ignatieff, *Human Rights as Politics and Idolatry* (Princeton: Princeton University Press, 2001).

21. The UDHR gives equal time to both individual and group rights; it recognizes that protections, privileges, and opportunities not only are for individuals, but also should extend to the family, community, nation, and other groups.

22. Amartya Sen, "Democracy as a Universal Value," *Journal of Democracy* 10, no. 3 (July 1999); Ignatieff, *Human Rights as Politics and Idolatry.*

23. Vojin Dimitrijevic, "Human Rights and Peace," in *Human Rights: New Dimensions and Challenges,* ed. Janusz Symonides (Brookfield, VT: Ashgate, 1998); Ullman, "Human Rights."

24. Hilary French, "Coping with Ecological Globalization," in *State of the World 2000,* ed. Lester R. Brown (New York: Norton, 2000).

25. UN News Centre, "Deforestation in Decline but Rate Remains Alarming, UN Agency Says," March 25, 2010, www.un.org; Elizabeth Mygatt, "World's Forests Continue to Shrink," Earth Policy Institute, April 4, 2006, www.earth-policy.org; United Nations Environment Programme (UNEP), "About International Year of Biodiversity," 2010, www.unep.org.

26. UNEP, "Climate Change: Introduction," n.d., www.unep.org (accessed March 23, 2011).

27. Steve Connor, "Global Warming Fastest for 20,000 Years—and It Is Mankind's Fault," *The Independent* (London), May 4, 2006; "Intergovernmental Panel on Climate Change," *New York Times,* February 9, 2010; Al Gore, "We Can't Wish Away Climate Change," *New York Times,* February 27, 2010.

28. Lester R. Brown, foreword to *State of the World 2001,* eds. Lester R. Brown and Linda Starke (New York: Norton, 2001); Christopher Flavin, "Rich Planet, Poor Planet," in *State of the World 2001;* UNEP, "Climate Change."

29. Darren Samuelson, "China: We're No. 1 in Greenhouse Gas Emissions," *Politico,* November 24, 2010, www.politico.com.

30. Joint United Nations Programme on HIV/AIDS (UNAIDS), *UNAIDS Report on the Global AIDS Epidemic 2010,* www.unaids.org.

31. Ibid.

32. Elizabeth Reid, "A Future, If One Is Still Alive: The Challenge of the HIV Epidemic," in *Hard Choices: Moral Dilemmas in Humanitarian Intervention,* ed. Jonathan Moore (Lanham: Rowman and Littlefield, 1998).

33. UNAIDS, *UNAIDS Report on the Global AIDS Epidemic 2010.*

34. United Nations Population Fund (UNFPA), "Preventing HIV/AIDS," www.unfpa.org; UNFPA, "Fact Sheet: Young People and Times of Change," August 2009, www.unfpa.org.

Chapter 2
Precolonial History

1. Octavio Paz, "Critique of the Pyramid," cited in Ana Carrigan, "Chiapas: The First Postmodern Revolution," in *Our Word Is Our Weapon: Selected Writings of Subcomandante Marcos,* ed. Juana Ponce de Leon (New York: Seven Stories, 2001), p. 428.

2. Roland Oliver, *The African Experience* (Boulder: Westview, 1999); Robert W. July, *A History of the African People* (Prospect Heights, IL: Waveland, 1992).

3. Oliver, *The African Experience*.

4. Milton W. Meyer, *Asia: A Concise History* (Lanham: Rowman and Littlefield, 1997).

5. Benjamin Keen and Keith Haynes, *A History of Latin America* (Boston: Houghton Mifflin, 2000).

6. Ibid.; Peter Bakewell, *A History of Latin America* (Malden, MA: Blackwell, 1997).

7. Meyer, *Asia*.

8. Ibid.; Rhoads Murphey, "The Historical Context," in *Understanding Contemporary China,* ed. Robert E. Gamer (Boulder: Lynne Rienner, 1999).

9. Keen and Haynes, *A History of Latin America*.

10. Ibid.; Irene Silverblatt, *Moon, Sun, and Witches* (Princeton: Princeton University Press, 1987); Susan Migden Socolow, *The Women of Colonial Latin America* (Cambridge: Cambridge University Press, 2000).

11. Keen and Haynes, *A History of Latin America*.

12. Inga Clendinnen, *Aztecs: An Interpretation* (Cambridge: Cambridge University Press, 1995); E. G. Parrinder, "Divine Kingship in West Africa," *Numen* 3 (April 1956): 111–121.

13. Michael E. Smith, "Life in the Provinces of the Aztec Empire," *Scientific American Special Edition* 15, no. 1 (February 2005); Huo Jianying, "A Recollection of the Splendor of the Tang Dynasty," *China Today* 50, no. 11 (November 2001); Basil Davidson, *Africa in History* (New York: Simon and Schuster, 1995); David Morgan, *The Mongols* (Oxford: Wiley-Blackwell, 1990).

14. John Man, *The Great Wall* (Cambridge, MA: DaCapo Press, 2008); Laura Laurencich Minelli, *The Inca World: The Development of Pre-Columbian Peru, A.D. 1000–1534* (Norman: University of Oklahoma Press, 2000).

15. Meyer, *Asia*.

16. Murphey, "The Historical Context."

17. Ibid.

18. Simon Martin and Nikolai Grube, *Chronicle of the Maya Kings and Queens: Deciphering the Dynasties of the Ancient Maya* (London: Thames and Hudson, 2000).

19. Minelli, *The Inca World;* David N. Keightley, *The Origins of Chinese Civilization* (Berkeley: University of California Press, 1983); Paul Johnson, *The Civilization of Ancient Egypt* (New York: Harper Collins, 1999).

20. G. Mokhtar, conclusion to *UNESCO General History of Africa: Ancient Civilizations of Africa,* ed. G. Mokhtar (London: Heinemann, 1981).

21. Ironically, the largest states were often the most fragile, disintegrating much more easily than smaller states (and even stateless nations), which proved to be more cohesive and durable. Stateless societies on the frontier, such as the Chichemecas in northern Mexico and the Araucanians in southern Chile, took the longest to conquer. Small, mobile groups able to live off the land were hard to suppress—until in some cases the Europeans decided that it just wasn't worth it.

22. July, *A History of the African People.*

23. Maurice Collis, *Cortés and Montezuma* (New York: New Directions, 1999).

24. Magbaily Fyle, *Introduction to the History of African Civilization* (Lanham, MD: University Press of America, 1999); John Hemming, *The Conquest of the Incas* (Boston: Houghton Mifflin Harcourt, 2003).

25. J. E. Inikori and Stanley L. Engerman, *The Atlantic Slave Trade* (Durham, NC: Duke University Press, 1992).

26. Meyer, *Asia;* David Landes, *The Wealth and Poverty of Nations: Why Some Are So Rich and Some Are So Poor* (New York: Norton, 1998); Murphey, "The Historical Context"; Edward L. Farmer et al., *Comparative History of Civilizations in Asia* (Reading, MA: Addison-Wesley, 1977).

Chapter 3
Colonialism: Gold, God, Glory

1. Hilaire Belloc, "The Modern Traveller," cited in Margery Perham II, *Lugard: The Years of Authority, 1899–1945* (London: Collins, 1960), p. 45.

2. David Landes, *The Wealth and Poverty of Nations: Why Some Are So Rich and Some Are So Poor* (New York: Norton, 1998); Jared Diamond, *Guns, Germs, and Steel: The Fate of Human Societies* (New York: Norton, 1997).

3. A. Adu Boahen, "Africa and the Colonial Challenge," in *UNESCO General History of Africa: Africa Under Colonial Domination, 1880–1935,* ed. A. Adu Boahen (London: Heinemann, 1985).

4. Peter Bakewell, *A History of Latin America* (Malden, MA: Blackwell, 1997); Diamond, *Guns, Germs, and Steel;* Landes, *The Wealth and Poverty of Nations.*

5. This terminology was used by Ali Mazrui in his video series *The Africans,* no. 4, 1986.

6. Milton W. Meyer, *Asia: A Concise History* (Lanham: Rowman and Littlefield, 1997).

7. Mark A. Burkholder and Lyman L. Johnson, *Colonial Latin America* (New York: Oxford University Press, 1998).

8. Walter Rodney, "The Colonial Economy," in *UNESCO General History of Africa;* Emory C. Bogle, *The Modern Middle East: From Imperialism to Freedom, 1800–1958* (Upper Saddle River, NJ: Prentice Hall, 1996).

9. Bogle, *The Modern Middle East.*

10. Benjamin Keen and Keith Haynes, *A History of Latin America* (Boston: Houghton Mifflin, 2000).

11. Meyer, *Asia.*

12. Edward L. Farmer et al., *Comparative History of Civilizations in Asia* (Reading, MA: Addison-Wesley, 1977).

13. Susan Migden Socolow, *The Women of Colonial Latin America* (Cambridge: Cambridge University Press, 2000).

14. Keen and Haynes, *A History of Latin America.*

15. Boahen, "Africa and the Colonial Challenge"; Farmer et al., *Comparative History of Civilizations in Asia.*

16. Farmer et al., *Comparative History of Civilizations in Asia.*

17. Whereas the colonizers often argued that they had intervened to end anarchy and bring peace to the inhabitants of the territory, in fact the colonizers encouraged fissures and played different groups off each other, to prevent unity and ensure their continued dominance.

18. Not yet democracies themselves until well into the twentieth century, the Spanish and Portuguese certainly never claimed to be promoting self-rule for their colonies in Latin America.

19. Peter Mansfield, *A History of the Middle East* (New York: Penguin, 1991).

20. Keen and Haynes, *A History of Latin America.*

21. Some traditional authorities refused to cooperate with the Europeans. A Peruvian curaca, Jose Gabriel Condorcanqui, opposed Spanish abuses of the Indians and led the largest colonial rebellion in all of Spanish America.

22. Bakewell, *A History of Latin America;* Boahen, "Africa and the Colonial Challenge"; Keen and Haynes, *A History of Latin America.*

Chapter 4
Independence or In Dependence?

1. Julie Frederikse, *South Africa: A Different Kind of War* (Johannesburg: Ravan, 1987), p. 30.

2. Mahmood Mamdani, *Citizen and Subject: Contemporary Africa and the Legacy of Late Colonialism* (Princeton: Princeton University Press, 1996).

3. Jay Kinsbruner, *Independence in Spanish America: Civil Wars, Revolutions, and Underdevelopment* (Albuquerque: University of New Mexico Press, 2000).

4. Benjamin Keen and Keith Haynes, *A History of Latin America* (Boston: Houghton Mifflin, 2000).

5. David Landes, *The Wealth and Poverty of Nations: Why Some Are So Rich and Some Are So Poor* (New York: Norton, 1998); Adam Hochschild, *King Leopold's Ghost* (Boston: Houghton Mifflin, 1998); David M. Davidson, "Negro Slave Control and Resistance in Colonial

Mexico," in *People and Issues in Latin American History,* eds. Lewis Hanke and Jane M. Rausch (New York: Markus Wiener, 1993).

6. Edward L. Farmer et al., *Comparative History of Civilizations in Asia* (Reading, MA: Addison-Wesley, 1977).

7. Susan Migden Socolow, *The Women of Colonial Latin America* (Cambridge: Cambridge University Press, 2000).

8. Ali A. Mazrui, "Seek Ye First the Political Kingdom," in *UNESCO General History of Africa: Africa Since 1935,* ed. Ali A. Mazrui (London: Heinemann, 1993); Farmer et al., *Comparative History of Civilizations in Asia.*

9. Mazrui, "Seek Ye First the Political Kingdom."

10. Peter Bakewell, *A History of Latin America* (Malden, MA: Blackwell, 1997).

11. Mark A. Burkholder and Lyman L. Johnson, *Colonial Latin America* (New York: Oxford University Press, 1998); Emory C. Bogle, *The Modern Middle East: From Imperialism to Freedom, 1800–1958* (Upper Saddle River, NJ: Prentice Hall, 1996).

12. Laith Kubba, "The Awakening of Civil Society," *Journal of Democracy* 11, no. 3 (July 2000).

13. Bakewell, *A History of Latin America.*

14. Burkholder and Johnson, *Colonial Latin America;* Keen and Haynes, *A History of Latin America.*

15. Bogle, *The Modern Middle East;* J. Isawa Elaigwu, "Nation-Building and Changing Political Structures," in *UNESCO General History of Africa.*

16. Burkholder and Johnson, *Colonial Latin America.*

17. Landes, *The Wealth and Poverty of Nations.*

18. Ibid.

19. Farmer et al., *Comparative History of Civilizations in Asia.*

20. A. Adu Boahen, "Colonialism in Africa: Its Impact and Significance," in *UNESCO General History of Africa.*

21. Keen and Haynes, *A History of Latin America.*

22. Ibid.; Boahen, "Colonialism in Africa."

Chapter 5
Linking Concepts and Cases

1. Lynn V. Foster, *A Brief History of Mexico* (New York: Facts on File, 1997).

2. Peter Bakewell, *A History of Latin America* (Malden, MA: Blackwell, 1997); Benjamin Keen and Keith Haynes, *A History of Latin America* (Boston: Houghton Mifflin, 2000).

3. Richard Graham, *Independence in Latin America* (New York: McGraw Hill, 1994).

4. Bakewell, *A History of Latin America;* Keen and Haynes, *A History of Latin America.*

5. Ibid.

6. Mark A. Burkholder and Lyman L. Johnson, *Colonial Latin America* (New York: Oxford University Press, 1998).

7. Bakewell, *A History of Latin America;* Keen and Haynes, *A History of Latin America.*

8. Peter Flindell Klaren, *Peru: Society and Nationhood in the Andes* (New York: Oxford University Press, 2000).

9. Quoted in ibid., p. 43.

10. The Spanish *mita* built on Inca practice, but there were crucial differences. For the Inca, *mita* was part of a larger social contract in which reciprocal benefits linked the community and state. For the Spanish, however, *mita* was purely exploitative, as the state provided no return to the community.

11. According to Peter Klaren, however, the state did offer some limits on colonial expropriation. For example, indigenous people could appeal to colonial courts for relief, and some became adept at resorting to Spanish legal institutions to defend their interests. But such policies served as safety valves, effectively strengthening the system against radical or revolutionary challenges. Klaren emphasizes that because the system did sometimes rule on

behalf of oppressed groups, this in no way vindicates or balances the colonial legacy, which is overwhelmingly negative. Klaren, *Peru.*

12. Klaren, *Peru.*

13. Ibid.; Burkholder and Johnson, *Colonial Latin America;* Graham, *Independence in Latin America.*

14. Cynthia McClintock, *Revolutionary Movements in Latin America* (Washington, DC: US Institute of Peace, 1998).

15. Keen and Haynes, *A History of Latin America.*

16. Quoted in ibid., p. 43.

17. Klaren, *Peru.*

18. Ibid.; Washington Office on Latin America, "Deconstructing Democracy: Peru Under Alberto Fujimori," February 2000, www.wola.org.

19. Keen and Haynes, *A History of Latin America;* Klaren, *Peru;* Thomas E. Skidmore and Peter H. Smith, *Modern Latin America* (New York: Oxford University Press, 1992).

20. Michael Crowder, *The Story of Nigeria* (London: Faber and Faber, 1978).

21. Robin Law, "The Oyo-Dahomey Wars, 1726–1823: A Military Analysis," in *Warfare and Diplomacy in Precolonial Nigeria,* eds. Toyin Falola and Robin Law (Madison: University of Wisconsin–Madison Press, 1992).

22. Peter M. Lewis, Pearl T. Robinson, and Barnett R. Rubin, *Stabilizing Nigeria* (New York: Century Foundation, 1998).

23. Karl Maier, *This House Has Fallen: Midnight in Nigeria* (New York: PublicAffairs, 2000).

24. Ian Phimister, *An Economic and Social History of Zimbabwe, 1890–1948* (London: Longman, 1988).

25. Ibid.

26. Other groups, such as Asians and Coloureds (biracial people today known as "brown Zimbabweans"), were also subjected to the color bar, although they generally had more advantages than blacks. Although the black-white struggle dominates most analyses of Zimbabwe, these groups also played a significant though often covert role in the liberation struggle.

27. Phimister, *An Economic and Social History of Zimbabwe.*

28. Ibid.

29. In the 1920s, *The Watchtower* prophesized the Second Coming and claimed that a whirlwind would blow whites and nonbelievers away.

30. Phimister, *An Economic and Social History of Zimbabwe.*

31. Ibid.

32. Ibid.

33. Ibid.

34. Masipula Sithole, "Zimbabwe: In Search of Stable Democracy," in *Democracy in Developing Countries: Africa,* eds. Larry Diamond, Juan Linz, and Seymour Martin Lipset (Boulder: Lynne Rienner, 1988); D. E. Needham, E. K. Mashingaidze, and Ngwabi Bhebe, *From Iron Age to Independence: A History of Central Africa* (London: Longman, 1985); Victor de Waal, *The Politics of Reconciliation: Zimbabwe's First Decade* (Trenton, NJ: Africa World Press, 1990); A. J. Wills, *An Introduction to the History of Central Africa: Zambia, Malawi, and Zimbabwe* (New York: Oxford University Press, 1985).

35. Elton L. Daniel, *The History of Iran* (Westport: Greenwood, 2001).

36. Mike Edwards, "The Adventures of Marco Polo, Part I," *National Geographic,* May 2001; Daniel, *The History of Iran.*

37. Daniel, *The History of Iran.*

38. The title "Shah" reappropriates a pre-Islamic Iranian title for "king."

39. Daniel, *The History of Iran.*

40. Ibid.

41. Stephen Kinzer, *Crescent and the Star: Turkey Between Two Worlds* (New York: Farrar, Straus, and Giroux, 2001).

42. Douglas A. Howard, *The History of Turkey* (Westport: Greenwood, 2001).

43. Quoted in Kinzer, *Crescent and the Star,* p. 4.

44. Ibid.

45. Ibid.

46. As one person put it, "In this country it is allowed to say bad things about God, but not about Atatürk." Kinzer, *Crescent and the Star,* p. 36. Similar sentiment was also expressed in a recent modern history of Turkey: "If indeed a country can be said to be the creation of a single individual, then Turkey is a new country, the creation of Mustafa Kemal Atatürk." Howard, *The History of Turkey,* p. 1.

47. Lucian W. Pye, *China: An Introduction,* 3rd ed. (Boston: Little, Brown, 1984).

48. Much of the story surrounding the Great Wall is based in legend. While some smaller walls were built prior to the Qin Dynasty, and joined together during the Qin emperor's reign, the bulk of the wall was completed during China's Ming Dynasty (1366–1644), and significantly renovated thereafter. There is evidence to challenge its status as part of China's ancient past. Historian Arthur Waldron has produced extensive research challenging the myth behind the wall, citing, among other points, that even though Marco Polo traveled extensively throughout the region in the thirteenth century, he made no mention of the structure. Similarly, contrary to popular beliefs, the Great Wall cannot be viewed from space, at least not without significant satellite magnification. Yet perceptions of the wall's visibility from space predate space travel by humans—*Ripley's Believe It or Not* made the claim as early as 1930. See David C. Wright, *The History of China* (Westport: Greenwood, 2001).

49. Pye, *China.*

50. Barney War, "Teaching Indonesia: A World-Systems Perspective," *Education About Asia* 3, no. 3 (Winter 1998).

51. Milton W. Meyer, *Asia: A Concise History* (Lanham: Rowman and Littlefield, 1997); Björn Schelander and Kirsten Brown, *Exploring Indonesia: Past and Present* (Honolulu: Center for Southeast Asian Studies, 2000).

52. Schelander and Brown, *Exploring Indonesia.*

53. Meyer, *Asia.*

54. Robert Cribb and Colin Brown, *Modern Indonesia: A History Since 1945* (New York: Longman, 1995).

55. Chris Manning and Peter van Diermen, "Recent Developments and Social Aspects of *Reformasi* and Crisis: An Overview," in *Indonesia in Transition: Social Aspects of Reformasi and Crisis,* eds. Chris Manning and Peter van Diermen (Singapore: Institute of Southeast Asian Studies, 2000).

Chapter 6
Growth and Development: A Progress Report

1. United Nations, *2000 Millennium Report* (New York, 2000).

2. World Bank, *World Development Indicators 2010,* www.worldbank.org; "Opportunities for Convergence and Regional Cooperation," United Nations Economic Commission for Latin America and the Caribbean, February 2010, www.eclac.org; UN Food and Agricultural Organization, "The State of Food and Agriculture, 2009," www.fao.org; World Bank, "Economic Crises Taking a Toll on Children," April 7, 2010, www.worldbank.org.

3. World Bank, *World Development Indicators 2010;* "Counting Their Blessings," *The Economist,* January 2, 2010; World Bank, "The Global Outlook in Summary, 2008–2012," Summer 2010, www.worldbank.org.

4. World Bank, "The Global Outlook in Summary."

5. Jose Antonio Ocampo, "The Global Challenge of Inequality," *IDS Bulletin* 38, no. 2 (March 2007); "The Elusive Fruits of Inclusive Growth," *The Economist,* May 15, 2010.

6. World Bank, *World Development Indicators 2010;* Central Intelligence Agency (CIA), *World Factbook 2010,* www.cia.gov; Andrew Jacobs, "China's Army of Graduates Faces Grim Prospects, with Few Jobs in Cities," *New York Times,* December 12, 2010; James M. Cypher and James L. Dietz, *The Process of Economic Development* (New York: Routledge, 2009).

7. United Nations Development Programme (UNDP), *Human Development Report 2000* (New York, 2000).

8. World Health Organization (WHO), "Countdown to 2015," www.who.org.

9. WHO, "Countdown to 2015, Decade Report," 2010, www.whoqlibdoc.who.int; UNDP, *Human Development Report 2010,* www.hdr.undp.org.

10. "High-Speed Internet Gap Between Rich and Poor Widening, UN Office Warns," *UN News Centre,* November 12, 2009; Nicholas D. Kristof, "I've Seen the Future (in Haiti)," *New York Times,* December 5, 2010.

11. UNDP, *Human Development Report 2000.*

12. WHO, "Countdown to 2015, Decade Report"; World Bank, "Development in a Changing Climate," *World Development Report 2010,* worldbank.org.

13. Antoine Van Agtmael, "Industrial Revolution 2.0," in *Annual Editions: Developing World 10–11,* ed. Robert J. Griffiths (New York: McGraw Hill, 2010).

14. Fareed Zakaria, "The Rise of the Rest," *Newsweek,* May 3, 2008.

15. United Nations, *Millennium Development Goals Report 2010,* June 15, 2010, www.un.org.

16. Ugo Panizza, Federico Sturzenegger, and Jermin ZeHelmeyer, "International Government Debt," Discussion Paper no. 199 (Geneva: United Nations Conference on Trade and Development [UNCTAD], June 2010); Cynthia Roberts, "Polity Forum: Challenges or Stakeholders? BRICs and the Liberal World Order," *Polity* no. 42 (December 7, 2009).

17. Anup Shah, "Poverty Around the World," *Global Issues,* March 1, 2010, www.globalissues.org.

18. World Bank, "Development in a Changing Climate"; Merrell Tuck, "New Data Show 1.4 Billion Live on Less than US $1.25 a Day, but Progress Against Poverty Remains Strong," August 26, 2008, www.web.worldbank.org.

19. CIA, *World Factbook 2010,* www.cia.gov.

20. Keith Bradsher, "China's Trade Surplus Climbs to $28.7 Billion," *New York Times,* August 9, 2010.

21. David Barboza, "China Passes Japan as Second-Largest Economy," *New York Times,* August 15, 2010.

22. Amartya Sen, cited in Nicholas D. Kristof, "Stark Data on Women," *New York Times,* November 5, 1991.

23. United Nations Population Fund (UNFPA), "New Report Analyzes Skewed Birth Ratios in Vietnam," September 9, 2009, www.unfpa.org; UNFPA, "Asian Son Preference Will Have Severe Social Consequences, New Studies Warn," October 29, 2007, www.unfpa.org.

24. Rana Foroohar and Susan H. Greenberg, "The Real Emerging Market," *Newsweek,* September 21, 2009.

25. United Nations Educational, Scientific, and Cultural Organization (UNESCO), "Education for All," *Global Monitoring Report 2010,* www.unesdoc.unesco.org.

26. United Nations Development Fund for Women (UNIFEM), "Making the Millennium Development Goals Work for All," www.unifem.org; UNESCO, "Education for All."

27. International Labour Organization (ILO), "Global Employment Trends for Women," 2008, www.ilo.org; United Nations Children's Fund (UNICEF), "Gender Equality: The Big Picture, 2007," www.unicef.org.

28. Sylvia Chant, "Poverty Begins at Home? The State of the World's Children, 2007," UNICEF, December 2006, www.unicef.org.

29. Moises Naim, "Globalization," *Foreign Policy* 171 (March–April 2009).

30. World Trade Organization (WTO), "What Is the World Trade Organization?" www.wto.org.

31. World Bank, *World Development Indicators 2010.*

32. Thomas L. Friedman, *The Lexus and the Olive Tree* (New York: Farrar, Straus, and Giroux, 1999).

33. United Nations, *Millennium Development Goals Report 2010.*

34. UNDP, *Human Development Report 2005.*

35. World Bank, *World Development Indicators 2010;* "Waiting for a Trade Policy," *New York Times,* July 5, 2010.

36. Samuel T. Ledermann and William G. Moseley, "The WTO's Doha Round and Cotton," *African Geographic Review* no. 126 (December 1, 2007); Oxfam, "Burkina Faso: Cotton

Story," n.d., www.oxfam.org (accessed March 23, 2011); Sallie James, "The US Generalized System of Preferences," Cato Institute, Center for Trade Policy Studies, November 16, 2010, www.scribd.com.

37. Ledermann and Moseley, "The WTO's Doha Round and Cotton"; Sewell Chan, "US and Brazil Reach Agreement on Cotton Dispute," *New York Times,* April 6, 2010.

38. Thomas L. Friedman, "Protesting for Whom?" *New York Times,* April 24, 2001.

39. Daniel Griswold, "The Blessings and Challenges of Globalization," Cato Institute, September 1, 2000, www.cato.org.

40. Jackie Smith and Timothy Patrick Moran, "WTO 101: Myths About the World Trade Organization," in *Annual Editions: Developing World 01–02,* ed. Robert J. Griffiths (Guilford, CT: McGraw Hill and Dushkin, 2001).

41. Neil MacFarquhar, "African Farmers Displaced As Investors Move In," *New York Times,* December 21, 2010.

42. Larry Elliott, "Economics: Poor Nations Ride High on Commodity Boom," *The Guardian* (London), May 10, 2006.

43. World Bank, *World Development Indicators 2010.*

44. Alexei Barrionuevo, "A Mine of Riches and an Economic Sinkhole," *New York Times,* September 11, 2010.

45. Naomi Mapstone and Javier Blas, "Fishmeal Prices Soar to All-Time High," *Financial Times,* April 26, 2010.

46. World Bank, *World Development Indicators 2010.*

47. Joshua S. Goldstein, *International Relations,* 4th ed. (New York: Longman, 2001).

48. Lydia Polgreen and Marlise Simon, "Rejected by Europe, Global Sludge Ends in Tragedy for Ivory Coast," *New York Times,* October 2, 2006; "Help Urged for Ivory Coast Waste," *BBC News,* November 24, 2006.

49. US Bureau of Labor Statistics, "International Comparisons of GDP per Capita and per Employed Person," Division of International Labor Comparisons, July 28, 2009, www.bls .gov; CIA, *World Factbook 2010.*

50. World Bank, *World Development Indicators 2010.*

51. Tracey Keys and Thomas Malnight, "Corporate Clout: The Influence of the World's Largest 100 Economic Entities," *Global Trends,* 2010, www.globaltrends.com.

52. Marc Gunther, "Fortune: Global 500," July 8, 2010, www.cnnmoney.com; World Bank, "2009 GDP," *World Development Indicators Database,* September 27, 2010, www .data.worldbank.org.

53. World Bank, *World Development Indicators 2010;* UNCTAD, "Global FDI Inflows Continue to Slide in 2009," September 17, 2009, www.unctad.org.

54. Kathleen Schalch, "Study Finds American Firms Doing Business in China Are Not Improving Conditions for Chinese Workers," National Public Radio, *All Things Considered,* May 5, 2000.

55. "China Labor Tests Its Muscle," *New York Times,* July 13, 2010; "The End of Cheap Chinese Labor?" *The Economist,* July 18, 2010.

56. Vikas Bajaj, "Bangladesh, with Low Pay, Moves in on China," *New York Times,* July 16, 2010; Julfikar Ali Manik and Vikas Bajaj, "Dozens Killed in Bangladesh Fire," *New York Times,* December 14, 2010.

57. "Secrets, Lies, and Sweatshops," *Bloomberg Businessweek,* November 27, 2006.

58. Schalch, "Study Finds American Firms Doing Business in China Are Not Improving Conditions for Chinese Workers."

59. Friedman, "Protesting for Whom?"

60. Goldstein, *International Relations.*

61. ILO, "World Day Against Child Labor," International Programme on the Elimination of Child Labor, June 12, 2010, www.ilo.org; "No Minor Issue," *National Geographic,* November 2010.

62. Manik and Bajaj, "Dozens Killed in Bangladesh Fire"; Frank Jack Daniel, "Mexico: Mexican Strikes Cripple Mines, Mills, and Refineries," *Reuters,* March 2, 2006.

63. International Labor Rights Forum, "Sweatshop Hall of Shame 2010," www.labor rights.org; Global Investment Watch, "Ikea, Wal-Mart, Target, and Kohl's Sleeping Easy While Turkish Workers Suffer," May 18, 2009, www.globalinvestmentwatch.com.

64. David Barboza, "In Chinese Factories, Lost Fingers and Low Pay," *New York Times,* January 15, 2008.

65. International Labor Rights Forum, "Labor Rights Abuses Continue on Firestone Liberia Rubber Plantation," July 28, 2009, www.laborrights.org; Ruthie Ackerman, "Firestone's Superbowl Fumble," *The Nation,* February 18, 2008, www.thenation.com.

66. Goldstein, *International Relations.*

67. Help Stop Child Slavery, "Overview: Child Slavery Today," n.d., www.helpstopchild slavery.org (accessed March 23, 2011).

68. Beatrice Newbery, "Labouring Under Illusions," in *Annual Editions: Developing World 01–02.*

69. Ibid.

70. Aislinn Simpson, "Baby Formula Recall in China After Infant Death," *The Telegraph* (London), September 13, 2008, www.telegraph.co.uk.

71. Marc Gunter, "Wal-Mart Sees Green," *Fortune,* July 26, 2006, www.cnnmoney.com.

72. Donald G. McNeil, "At Front Lines, AIDS War Is Falling Apart," *New York Times,* May 9, 2010.

73. World Bank, *World Development Indicators 2010;* World Bank, "Global Monitoring Report: Trade, Aid, and the IFIs," 2010, www.worldbank.org.

74. Joseph Kahn, "Losing Faith: Globalization Proves Disappointing," *New York Times,* March 21, 2002.

75. Kofi A. Annan, "Trade and Aid in a Changed World," *New York Times,* March 19, 2002.

76. World Bank, *World Development Indicators 2010;* "Why Should They Believe Us?" *New York Times,* April 24, 2010; United Nations, *Millennium Development Goals Report 2010.*

77. World Bank, *World Development Indicators 2010.*

78. "Rich Must Not Cut Aid to Poor to Balance Budget—UN," *Reuters,* September 20, 2010; United Nations, *Millennium Development Goals Report 2010.*

79. "Why Should They Believe Us?" *New York Times.*

80. Eckhard Deutscher and Sara Fyson, "Committing to Effective Aid: Why Can't Donors Walk Their Talk?" Development Outreach, World Bank Institute, February 2007, www.worldbank.org.

81. Sarah C. Sullivan, "Poll: Americans Have Inflated View of Foreign Aid," *PBS Newshour,* December 6, 2010, www.pbs.org.

82. World Bank, *World Development Indicators 2010;* CIA, *World Factbook 2010.*

83. World Bank, *World Development Indicators 2010.*

84. Jubilee USA Network, "Why Drop the Debt?," 2007, www.jubileeusa.org.

85. Jubilee Debt Campaign, "The Debt Crisis," n.d., www.jubileedebtcampaign.org (accessed March 23, 2011).

86. Jubilee USA Network, "Why Drop the Debt?"

87. World Bank, *World Development Indicators 2010.*

88. "Increase Production, Exports to Generate Foreign Currency," *The Herald,* September 15, 2005; "IMF Gives Zimbabwe Back Its Voting Rights," *Radio France Internationale,* February 22, 2010.

89. Jubilee USA Network, "Why Drop the Debt?"; "Ending the Cycle of Debt," *New York Times,* October 1, 2004.

90. Susan George, *The Debt Boomerang: How Third World Debt Harms Us All* (Boulder: Westview, 1992); "Development Funds Moving from Poor Countries to Rich Ones, Annan Says," *UN News Centre,* October 30, 2003; Jubilee Debt Campaign, "The Debt Crisis."

91. Eduardo Galeano, *Open Veins of Latin America* (New York: Monthly Review Press, 1973).

92. Jubilee USA Network, "Debt Slavery Is Foreign Aid in Reverse."

93. "Debt Relief Lifts Aid to Record Highs in 2005—OECD," *New York Times,* April 4, 2006; World Bank, *World Development Indicators 2006.*

94. Emilio Sacerdoti and Philippe Callier, "Debt Relief Yields Results in Niger," *IMF Survey Magazine,* January 25, 2008.

95. "Oxfam Applauds Zambia's Free Health Care," *Ottawa Citizen,* April 1, 2006; Jubilee USA Network, "Debt, Poverty, and the MDGs," 2007, www.jubileeusa.org.

96. World Bank, *World Development Indicators 2010;* United Nations, *Millennium Development Goals Report 2010.*

97. "Prudence Can Win," *The Economist,* May 30, 2009.

98. Panizza, Sturzenegger, and ZeHelmeyer, "International Government Debt"; "Seeing the World Differently," *The Economist,* June 12, 2010; United Nations, *Millennium Development Goals Report 2010.*

99. World Bank, *World Development Indicators 2010;* Panizza, Sturzenegger, and ZeHelmeyer, "International Government Debt."

100. "Why Should They Believe Us?" *New York Times;* United Nations, *Millennium Development Goals Report 2010.*

Chapter 7
A New and Improved Structural Adjustment?

1. Quoted in "States of Unrest," *New Internationalist* no. 365 (March 2004), www.newint.org.

2. Thomas L. Friedman, *The Lexus and the Olive Tree* (New York: Farrar, Straus, and Giroux, 1999), p. 294.

3. Ross P. Buckley, "Improve the Living Standards in Poor Countries: Reform the IMF," *Emory Law Review* 24, no. 1 (April 1, 2010).

4. Sam Perlo-Freeman, Olawale Ismail, and Carina Solmirano, "Military Expenditure," *SIPRI Yearbook 2010,* Stockholm International Peace Research Institute, November 23, 2010, www.sipri.org.

5. Ibid.; "Mission: Possible," *The Economist,* April 11, 2009.

6. "Austerity Alarm," *The Economist,* July 3, 2010; "Counting Their Blessings," *The Economist,* January 2, 2010.

7. Steven Mufson, "In China, Too, a Health Care System in Disarray," *Washington Post,* October 29, 2009.

8. Organization for Economic Cooperation and Development (OECD), "Economic Survey of China, 2010: Improving the Health Care System," February 2, 2010, www.oecd.org; Elisabeth Rosenthal, "Without 'Barefoot Doctors' China's Rural Families Suffer," *New York Times,* March 14, 2001.

9. Tan Eelyn, "China Fights Growing Problem of Tuberculosis," *Reuters,* January 5, 2010.

10. Michelle Chen, "China Sees 2010 Trade Surplus Less Than $190 Billion," *Reuters,* November 13, 2010.

11. Nancy Birdsall, "Managing Inequality in the Developing World," in *Annual Editions: Developing World 01–02,* ed. Robert J. Griffiths (Guilford, CT: McGraw Hill and Dushkin, 2001).

12. Tom Evans, "'Water Justice' Advocate: Don't Privatize," January 8, 2010, www.cnn.com; Juan Forero, "Who Will Bring Water to the Bolivian Poor?" *New York Times,* December 15, 2005.

13. Jason Beaubien, "Change Proposed for Mexican Oil Monopoly in Crisis," National Public Radio, *All Things Considered,* May 21, 2008; Michael Slackman, "Egypt Concedes to Resistance on Privatization Push," *New York Times,* June 27, 2010; Vikas Bajaj, "As India Sells Assets, Political Tensions Rise," *New York Times,* February 24, 2010.

14. US Department of State, "Background Note: China," August 5, 2010, www.state.gov; "Re-Enter the Dragon," *The Economist,* June 5, 2010.

15. "Non-SOEs Employ 80% of Industrial Workforce," *Xinhua News Agency,* November 23, 2009.

16. "Whatever Happened to the Food Crisis?" *The Economist,* July 4, 2009; Heather Timmons and Hari Kumar, "Protests over Fuel Costs Idle Much of India," *New York Times,* July 5, 2010.

17. Steve H. Hanke, "Regime Change?" *Forbes,* June 5, 2006, www.forbes.com.

18. "Zambia: The Hard Road to HIPC Completion," *Africa News,* January 6, 2005; Jubilee USA Network, "A Silent War," 2007, www.jubileeusa.org.

19. This is ironic, since of the least-liberalized countries in the region, the People's Republic of China was also the emerging economy least affected by the Asian crisis. In a remarkable exception to neoliberal rules, China has not been subjected to an austerity plan, and in the meantime it soaks up the largest amount of the world's foreign investment.

20. Sewell Chan, "Perils Remain Despite Recovery's Pace, IMF Head Says," *New York Times,* April 25, 2010; "Mission: Possible," *The Economist;* Center for Global Development, "London Summit Q&A with Nancy Birdsall," March 30, 2009, www.cgdev.org.

21. World Bank, *World Development Indicators 2010,* www.worldbank.org; US Department of State, "Background Note: Ghana," September 17, 2010, www.state.gov; David White, "Stuck in Poverty After 40 Years of Aid," *Financial Times,* November 25, 2004.

22. United Nations Development Programme (UNDP), *Human Development Report 1999,* www.undp.org.

23. "Zambia: The Hard Road to HIPC Completion," *Africa News,* January 6, 2005.

24. Andrew Jacobs, "China's Army of Graduates Faces Grim Prospects, with Few Jobs in Cities," *New York Times,* December 12, 2010.

25. "Africa's Cities to Triple in Size," *BBC News,* November 24, 2010; United Nations Population Fund (UNFPA), "Urbanization: A Majority in Cities," May 2007, www.unfpa.org.

26. Anna Tibaijuka, "Message from the Executive Director," *Urban World* 2, no. 3 (June 2010), www.unhabitat.org.

27. Don Butler, "Tipping the Balance," *Ottawa Citizen,* June 17, 2006; Jonathan Hari, "Lives of Grime," *The Independent* (London), July 14, 2006.

28. "Happy Planet Index Ranks Country As One of Unhappiest," *Africa News,* July 16, 2006.

29. Barnaby Phillips, "Nigerian Police Having Problems Keeping Oil from Being Stolen," National Public Radio, *Morning Edition,* July 19, 2000.

30. Yao Lu, "China's Floating Population," Institute for Social and Economic Research and Policy (ISERP), 2010, www.iserp.columbia.edu; "350 Million Migrant Workers by 2050, Report Says," June 27, 2010, www.china.org.cn.

31. Miriam Mannak, "Informal Sector Also Needs Skills Training," *Inter-Press Service,* June 11, 2008.

32. UNDP, "Living Up to Commitments," *UNDP Annual Report 2009,* www.undp.com.

33. Valentine Moghadam, *Gender and National Identity: Women and Politics in Muslim Societies* (London: Zed, 1994).

34. Virginia M. Moncrieff, "Afghanistan Election: Woman Candidate Braves Retaliation with Presidential Run," *Huffington Post,* June 23, 2009.

35. Moghadam, *Gender and National Identity.*

36. Human Rights Watch, "The Damaging Debate on Rapes of Ethnic Chinese Women," September 8, 1998, www.hrw.org.

37. Mica Rosenberg, "Mexico City Smog Hurting People's Sense of Smell," *Reuters,* June 4, 2008.

38. Gordon C. Chang, "The Best and Worst of Times for China's Environment," *Forbes,* June 9, 2010, www.forbes.com.

39. "Official: Flooding in China Kills 79 with 347 Missing This Year in Worst Toll in Decade," *Associated Press,* July 10, 2010; US Energy Information Administration, "China: Background," Country Analysis Briefs, July 2009, www.eia.doe.gov.

40. Susan George, *The Debt Boomerang: How Third World Debt Hurts Us All* (Boulder: Westview, 1992).

41. "The Other Oil Spill," *The Economist,* June 26, 2010.

42. "Nigeria," *Monga Bay,* February 4, 2006, www.mongabay.com; John Vidal, "Nigeria's Agony Dwarfs the Gulf Oil Spill. The US and Europe Ignore It," *The Guardian* (London), May 30, 2010.

43. Joshua E. Keating, "The World's Ongoing Ecological Disasters," *Foreign Policy* (July 16, 2010).

44. "The Price of Cleanliness," *The Economist,* October 24, 2009; Bill McKibben, "Climate Change," *Foreign Policy* 170 (January–February 2009).

45. Graciela Chichilinisky, "Financial Innovations and Carbon Markets," *UN Chronicle* 66, no. 3 (January 8, 2009); Bradley C. Parks and J. Timmons Roberts, "Inequality and the

Global Climate Regime: Breaking the North-South Impasse," *Cambridge Review of International Affairs* 21, no. 4 (December 2008).

46. Bank Information Center, "World Bank Loans Exacerbate Climate Change," February 10, 2009, www.bicusa.org.

47. Peter Bossard, "The Forgotten Downstream Victims of Large Dams," *Huffington Post,* June 18, 2010; David Stoez, Charles Guzzetta, and Mark Lusk, *International Development* (Boston: Allyn and Bacon, 1999).

48. Korinna Horta, "The World Bank Group and the Chad-Cameroon Oil and Pipeline Project," Bank Information Center, June 2010, www.bicusa.org.

49. Maria Cheng and Christina Okello, "Tons of Bushmeat Smuggled into Paris, Study Finds," *Huffington Post,* June 17, 2010; Biosynergy Institute, "The Bushmeat Project," 2004, www.bushmeat.net; Sharon Begley, "Is That an Alligator in Your Suitcase?" *Newsweek,* June 18, 2010.

50. World Health Organization (WHO), "Malaria," Fact Sheet no. 94, April 2010, www.who.int.

51. United Nations, *Progress Towards the Millennium Development Goals, 1990–2005,* www.unstats.un.org.

52. World Bank, *World Development Indicators 2010;* Megan Rowling, "HIV Patients, Health Workers in Poor Nations Fear Treatment Cuts," *Reuters,* July 16, 2010.

53. WHO, "MDG 4: Reduce Child Mortality," *WHO Health Topics,* 2010, www.who.int.

54. United Nations, *Progress Towards the Millennium Development Goals.*

55. Steven F. Hayward, "The China Syndrome and the Environmental Kuznets Curve," *Environmental Policy Outlook,* December 21, 2005, www.aei.org.

56. WHO, "MDG 5: Improve Maternal Health," *WHO Health Topics,* 2010, www.who.int; WHO, "Maternal Deaths Worldwide Drop by Third," *WHO Media Centre,* September 15, 2010; UNFPA, "Advocacy and Fundraising Documents: What Does a Dollar Buy?" *UNFPA Global Population Policy Update,* August 27, 2004; Denise Grady, "Maternal Deaths Decline Sharply Across Globe," *New York Times,* April 13, 2010.

57. WHO, "Measles," Fact Sheet no. 286, December 2009, www.who.int.

58. "HIV Epidemic 'Halted,' Says UN," *BBC News,* November 23, 2010.

59. Ibid.; Joint United Nations Programme on HIV/AIDS (UNAIDS), *UNAIDS 2010 Global Report,* www.unaids.org; Sheryl Gay Stolberg, "College Campuses Produce New Style of AIDS Activist," *New York Times,* November 30, 2010.

60. World Bank, *World Development Indicators 2010.*

61. US Department of Labor, "Forced and Bonded Child Labor," July 26, 2006, www.dol.gov; Anti-Slavery International, "Child Labor," May 5, 2006, www.antislavery.org.

62. George, *The Debt Boomerang.*

63. Roberto Fendt, "The Brasilia Consensus: A New Model for Development?" Center for International Private Enterprise, September 27, 2004, www.cipe.org.

64. "The Gloves Go On," *The Economist,* November 28, 2009.

65. "Interview with IMF Managing Director Rodrigo de Rato," *People's Daily Online,* July 9, 2004, www.english.peopledaily.com.cn.

66. Steven R. Weisman, "IMF Votes to Enhance Power of China and Others," *New York Times,* September 19, 2009; International Monetary Fund, "Factsheet: IMF Quotas," March 11, 2010, www.imf.org; "IMF Board Approves Far Reaching Governance Reform," *IMF Survey Magazine,* November 5, 2010.

67. "A Slow Maturing of Democracy," *The Economist,* December 12, 2009.

68. Joseph Kahn, "International Lenders' New Image: A Human Face," *New York Times,* September 26, 2000.

Chapter 8
Alternative Approaches to Development

1. Quoted in Elisabeth Malkin, "Economic Decline Lifts the Prospects of a Vocal Populist," *New York Times,* February 4, 2009.

2. Quoted in "Breaking the Poverty Cycle," *Asiaweek,* October 13, 2000.

3. Jorge Nef, *Human Security and Mutual Vulnerability* (Ottawa: International Development and Research Centre, 1999).

4. United Nations Development Programme (UNDP), "A Decade to Eradicate Poverty," in *Annual Editions: Developing World 01–02,* ed. Robert J. Griffiths (Guilford, CT: McGraw Hill and Dushkin, 2001); John Tessitore and Susan Woolfson, eds., *A Global Agenda: Issues Before the Fifty-fourth General Assembly of the United Nations* (Lanham: Rowman and Littlefield, 1999).

5. Dot Keet, "Alternatives to Neoliberal Globalization," Transnational Institute, October 2010, www.tni.org.

6. Joseph Stiglitz, *Making Globalization Work* (London: Penguin, 2006).

7. World Bank, "Social Safety Nets: Lessons from Rich and Poor Countries," April 24, 2009, www.worldbank.org.

8. Stiglitz, *Making Globalization Work.*

9. Julius E. Nyang'oro and Timothy M. Shaw, "The African State in the Global Economic Context," in *The African State at a Critical Juncture: Between Disintegration and Reconfiguration,* eds. Julius E. Nyang'oro and Timothy M. Shaw (Boulder: Lynne Rienner, 1998); Theodore H. Cohn, *Global Political Economy: Theory and Practice* (New York: Longman, 2000).

10. Michael Hardt and Antonio Negri, "What the Protesters in Genoa Want," *New York Times,* July 20, 2001; Thomas L. Friedman, "Evolutionaries," *New York Times,* July 20, 2001.

11. Nyang'oro and Shaw, "The African State in the Global Economic Context"; Daniel Kauffmann, "Aid Effectiveness and Governance: The Good, the Bad, and the Ugly," Development Outreach, World Bank Institute, February 2009, www.worldbank.org; "Meanwhile, in Another World," *The Economist,* February 9, 2002.

12. Meredith Woo-Cumings, "Introduction: Chalmers Johnson and the Politics of Nationalism and Development," in *The Developmental State,* ed. Meredith Woo-Cumings (Ithaca: Cornell University Press, 1999); Jorge G. Castañeda, *Utopia Unarmed: The Latin American Left After the Cold War* (New York: Knopf, 1993).

13. Elisabeth Malkin, "At World Forum, Support Erodes for Private Management of Water," *New York Times,* March 20, 2005.

14. Adebayo Adedeji, "Popular Participation, Democracy, and Development: Is There a Dialectical Linkage?" in *Nigeria: Renewal from the Roots? The Struggle for Democratic Development,* eds. Adebayo Adedji et al. (London: Zed, 1997).

15. "More Is More?" *The Economist,* June 12, 2010; Nancy Birdsall, *Cash on Delivery: A New Approach to Foreign Aid with an Application to Primary Schooling* (Washington, DC: Center for Global Development, 2009).

16. United Nations Development Fund for Women (UNIFEM), "Making the MDGs Work for All: Gender-Responsive Rights-Based Approaches to the MDGs," November 2008, www.unifem-eseasia.org.

17. Adedeji, "Popular Participation, Democracy, and Development."

18. Celia W. Dugger, "Peace Prize to Pioneer of Loans to Poor No Bank Would Touch," *New York Times,* October 14, 2006; Grameen Bank, "Banking for the Poor: Grameen Bank at a Glance," October 2010, www.grameen-info.org.

19. Grameen Bank, "Banking for the Poor."

20. David Stoez, Charles Guzzetta, and Mark Lusk, *International Development* (Boston: Allyn and Bacon, 1999); Grameen Bank, "Banking for the Poor."

21. Dugger, "Peace Prize to Pioneer of Loans."

22. World Bank, *World Development Indicators 2010,* www.worldbank.org; Inter-American Development Bank, "Countries Need to Ensure Regional Agreements Further Global Trade Liberalization," October 16, 2009, www.iadb.org.

23. "Profile: Association of Southeast Asian Nations," *BBC News,* June 14, 2010; "Southeast Asian Nations Talk of Economic Union," *Bloomberg News,* March 1, 2009; Neel Chowdhury, "Free Trade with China: ASEAN's Winners and Losers," *Time,* January 22, 2010.

24. Joanna Klonsky and Stephanie Hanson, "Backgrounder—Mercosur: South America's Fractious Trade Bloc," Council on Foreign Relations, August 20, 2009, www.cfr.org; "Mercosur Profile," *BBC News,* June 16, 2010.

25. Juliane von Reppert-Bismarck, "EU Trade Chief Touts Benefits of Mercosur Deal," *Reuters,* July 8, 2010.

26. David Ransom, "The Dictatorship of Debt," *New Internationalist* no. 312 (May 1999), www.oneworld.net; US National Debt Clock, accessed December 24, 2010, www .usdebtclock.org.

Chapter 9
Linking Concepts and Cases

1. D. E. Campbell, "A Saint for Lost Souls," *Foreign Policy* 179 (May–June 2010); Elisabeth Malkin, "NAFTA's Promise, Unfulfilled," *New York Times,* March 24, 2009; Association of American Chambers of Commerce in Latin America, "The North American Free Trade Agreement," www.aaccia.org.

2. Diana Villiers Negroponte, "Mexico: A Bad Case of the Blues," Brookings Institution, June 24, 2010, www.brookings.edu.

3. Central Intelligence Agency (CIA), *World Factbook 2010,* www.cia.gov; Diego Cevallos, "Crisis Drives Up Poverty Rate," *Inter-Press Service,* May 23, 2009.

4. Shannon O'Neil, "The Real War in Mexico," *Foreign Affairs* 88, no. 4 (July–August 2009); Organization for Economic Cooperation and Development (OECD), "Growing Unequal? Income Distribution and Poverty in OECD Countries," October 2008, www.oecd.org.

5. Campbell, "A Saint for Lost Souls."

6. International Monetary Fund (IMF), "World Economic Outlook Update: Global Recovery Advances but Remains Uneven," January 25, 2011, www.imf.org.

7. Malkin, "NAFTA's Promise, Unfulfilled"; Marla Dickerson, "A Free Market Man for Mexico," *Los Angeles Times,* July 16, 2006.

8. James C. McKinley, "Mexico's Besieged New Leader Faces Tough Challenges," *New York Times,* December 1, 2006; CIA, *World Factbook 2010.*

9. Adam Thompson, "Economy Poses First Test for Mexico's New Regime," *Financial Times* (London), September 6, 2006; CIA, *World Factbook 2010.*

10. Cynthia McClintock, *Revolutionary Movements in Latin America* (Washington, DC: US Institute of Peace, 1998).

11. Susan George, *The Debt Boomerang: How Third World Debt Harms Us All* (Boulder: Westview, 1992); McClintock, *Revolutionary Movements in Latin America.*

12. George, *The Debt Boomerang.*

13. Simon Romero, "Peru's Leader Uses Second Chance to Rewrite Legacy," *New York Times,* October 2, 2006; Robert Plummer, "Peru Still Wary of García's Past," *BBC News,* June 5, 2006.

14. IMF, "World Economic Outlook."

15. "Playing for Time," *The Economist,* July 18, 2009; "Peru: Free Traders," *The Economist,* July 1, 2006; Toni Johnson, "Peru's Mineral Wealth and Woes," Council on Foreign Relations, February 10, 2010, www. cfr.org.

16. World Bank, "Peru Brief," April 28, 2010, www.worldbank.org; Toni Johnson, "Peru's Mineral Wealth and Woes," Council on Foreign Relations, February 10, 2010, www .crf.org.

17. CIA, *World Factbook 2010.*

18. "Nigeria: Re-Opening Ajaokutu Steel Company," *Daily Independent* (Lagos), March 14, 2010, www.allafrica.com.

19. Anene Ejikeme, "The Oil Spills We Don't Hear About," *New York Times,* June 4, 2010.

20. US Energy Information Administration, "Nigeria: Oil," *Independent Statistics and Analysis,* July 2010, www.eia.gov.

21. Jean Herskovits, "Nigeria's Rigged Democracy," *Foreign Affairs* 86, no. 4 (July–August 2007).

22. "Nigeria and China Sign $23bn Deal for Three Refineries," *BBC News,* May 14, 2010.

23. John Campbell, "Opinion: Who's in Charge, China or Nigeria?" *Globalpost,* June 7, 2010, www.globalpost.com.

24. Jean Herskovits, "Politics in Nigeria Have 'Ground to a Halt,'" Council on Foreign Relations, March 25, 2009, www.cfr.org.

25. CIA, *World Factbook 2010;* Herskovits, "Politics in Nigeria Have 'Ground to a Halt.'"

26. "Nigeria's Economy: More Pain, Little Gain," *The Economist,* July 28, 2001.

27. CIA, *World Factbook 2010.*

28. International Monetary Fund, "Economic Outlook"; CIA, *World Factbook 2010.*

29. "Nigeria: The Next 10 Years," *Foreign Affairs* 88, no. 3 (May–June 2009).

30. Tony Hawkins, "End Game Lies in the Economy," *Financial Mail,* October 18, 2002; "From Breadbasket to Basket Case," *The Economist,* June 29, 2002.

31. Julius E. Nyang'oro and Timothy M. Shaw, "The African State in the Global Economic Context," in *The African State at a Critical Juncture: Between Disintegration and Reconfiguration,* eds. Julius E. Nyang'oro and Timothy M. Shaw (Boulder: Lynne Rienner, 1998); Robert I. Rotberg, "Africa's Mess, Mugabe's Mayhem," *Foreign Affairs* 79, no. 5 (September–October 2000).

32. Michael Wines, "Zimbabwe's Leaders Want to Delay Presidential Vote," *New York Times,* September 25, 2006; CIA, *World Factbook 2006.*

33. Greg Mills and Jeffrey Herbst, "Bring Zimbabwe In from the Cold," *New York Times,* May 28, 2009; Celia W. Dugger, "Zimbabwe Health Care, Paid with Peanuts," *New York Times,* December 19, 2010.

34. Angus Shaw, "Zimbabwe Government Wary of Annan Intervention in Political, Economic Stalemate," *Associated Press,* May 26, 2004; Celia W. Dugger, "Opposition Party to Join Zimbabwe's Government," *New York Times,* January 31, 2009.

35. Rachel L. Swarns, "Zimbabwe Starts Arresting White Farmers Defying Eviction," *New York Times,* August 17, 2002; "From Breadbasket to Basket Case," *The Economist.*

36. Daniel Pepper, "Zimbabwe's Army Takes Over Black Farms," *Christian Science Monitor,* June 5, 2006; "World," *Christian Science Monitor,* April 24, 2006.

37. Donald G. McNeil, Jr., "Zimbabwe: Report Shows Health Care System Declining After Years of Authoritarian Rule," *New York Times,* October 12, 2009; Mills and Herbst, "Bring Zimbabwe in from the Cold."

38. IMF, "World Economic Outlook"; Celia W. Dugger, "Zimbabwe: Economy Grows, but Future Is Uncertain," *New York Times,* May 25, 2010.

39. CIA, *World Factbook 2010;* Douglas Rogers, "Zimbabwe's Accidental Triumph," *New York Times,* April 14, 2010; Dugger, "Zimbabwe Health Care, Paid with Peanuts."

40. Dugger, "Zimbabwe: Economy Grows, but Future Is Uncertain."

41. Quoted in Robert F. Worth, "Iran's Plan to Phase Out Subsidies Brings Frenzied Debate," *New York Times,* December 2, 2009.

42. Anoushiravan Ehteshami, *After Khomeini: The Iranian Second Republic* (New York: Routledge, 1995).

43. Jahangir Amuzegar, "Iran's Economy in Turmoil," *International Economic Bulletin,* Carnegie Endowment for International Peace, March 2010. Amuzegar is a former minister of commerce and minister of finance who has represented Iran and other member states on the IMF's executive board.

44. "Islamic Banking: Forced Devotion," *The Economist,* February 17, 2001.

45. Robert F. Worth, "Iran's Plan to Phase Out Subsidies Brings Frenzied Debate," *New York Times,* December 2, 2009.

46. Amuzegar, "Iran's Economy in Turmoil."

47. See International Crisis Group, "Iran: Ahmadi-Nejad's Tumultuous Presidency," *Middle East Briefing* no. 21 (February 6, 2007), p. 8.

48. Michael R. Gordon, "Threats and Responses: The Allies: US Presses Turkey's Case on Europe and Cyprus," *New York Times,* December 3, 2002, p. 22.

49. Jonathan Head, "Keeping Turkey Focused on EU Challenge," *BBC News,* September 16, 2010.

50. Molly Moore, "IMF Grants Turkey $10 Billion to Stem Financial Crisis," *Washington Post,* December 6, 2000.

51. "Turkish Government's Decision to Drop Six Zeroes from Its Currency, the Turkish Lira," National Public Radio, *Day to Day,* May 5, 2005.

52. Quoted in Simon Cameron-Moore, "Turkey Referendum Win Boosts Erdogan for 2011 Election," *Reuters,* September 13, 2010.

53. Allan Sloan, "Let's Kill the Turkeys Before They Can Fly," *Newsweek,* December 4, 2006, p. 16.

54. Ross Terrill, "What If China Fails? The Case for Selective Failure," *Wilson Quarterly* (Autumn 2010), p. 54.

55. Frank Dikötter, *Mao's Great Famine: The History of China's Most Devastating Catastrophe, 1958–1962* (New York: Walker, 2010).

56. "Commuting Poverty," *The Economist,* March 18, 2006, p. 42.

57. Michael Bristow, "China Billionaires 'Second to US,'" *BBC News,* March 11, 2010.

58. Hana R. Alberts, "Why China Is an Incubator for Female Billionaires," *Forbes,* March 22, 2010, www.forbes.com.

59. The government continues to own a majority stake in the five major banks, and the Chinese Communist Party continues to appoint top leaders. See "Great Wall Street," *The Economist,* July 8, 2010.

60. David Barboza and Hiroko Tabuchi, "Labor Strife Signals Shift in China," *New York Times,* June 9, 2010.

61. David M. Lampton, "What If China Fails? We'd Better Hope It Doesn't!" *Wilson Quarterly* (Autumn 2010), p. 62.

62. Property developer Zhang Xin of SOHO China Limited, quoted in Bettina von Hase, "Zhang Xin and Pan Shiyi: Beijing's It-Couple," *The Times* (London), August 2, 2008.

63. William E. James, "Lessons from Development of the Indonesian Economy," *Education About Asia* 5, no. 1 (Spring 2000).

64. Andrew Higgins, "Some in Indonesia Praise, Seek to Replicate China's Fight Against the United States," *Washington Post,* March 29, 2010.

65. John Platt, "Indonesia's Palm Oil Economy Drives Human Fortunes—and Orangutan Misfortunes," *Scientific American,* December 2009.

66. Thomas Rumbaugh and Laura Lipscomb, "Indonesia's Economy: Strong with Room for Improvements," *IMF Survey Magazine,* September 17, 2010.

67. Ibid.

Chapter 10
From Ideas to Action: The Power of Civil Society

1. Richard Allen Greene, "Nearly 1 in 4 People Worldwide Is Muslim, Report Says," *CNN News,* October 7, 2009.

2. Sandra Mackey, *The Iranians: Persia, Islam, and the Soul of a Nation* (New York: Penguin, 1996).

3. Ibid.

4. Vali Nasr, "When the Shiites Rise," *Foreign Affairs* 85, no. 4 (July–August 2006), p. 59.

5. Mackey, *The Iranians.*

6. Quill Lawrence, "Brutality Against Women Stirs Fear in Afghanistan," August 20, 2010, www.npr.org.

7. David Martin, "The People's Church: The Global Evangelical Upsurge and Its Political Consequences," *Christianity Today,* January–February 2000.

8. Ibid.

9. Roger Eatwell, *Fascism: A History* (New York: Penguin, 1997).

10. Orville Schell, "Letter from China," *New Yorker,* July 1994, reprinted in *The China Reader: The Reform Era,* eds. Orville Schell and David Shambaugh (New York: Vintage, 1999).

11. Christopher Rohads and Loretta Chao, "Iran's Web Spying Aided by Western Technology," *Wall Street Journal,* June 22, 2009.

12. Brian Stelter and Brad Stone, "Web Pries Lid of Iranian Censorship," *New York Times,* June 22, 2009.

13. Ibid.

14. Lucie Morillon and Jean-François Julliard, "Enemies of the Internet: Countries Under Surveillance," Reporters Without Borders, March 12, 2010, www.rsf.org, p. 2.

15. "Antisocial Media," *The Economist,* August 25, 2010.

16. Richard Spencer, "Just Who Is the Glamorous Kitten Killer of Hangzhou?" *The Telegraph* (London), March 4, 2006.

17. Tom Downey, "China's Cyberposse," *New York Times,* March 3, 2010.

18. This definition is based on the classic perspective on political culture that was developed in the 1950s and 1960s. Its most common source is Sidney Verba, "Comparative Political Culture," in *Political Culture and Political Development,* eds. Sidney Verba and Lucian Pye (Princeton: Princeton University Press, 1965).

19. Gabriel A. Almond and Sidney Verba, eds., *Civic Culture: Political Attitudes and Democracy in Five Nations* (Princeton: Princeton University Press, 1963).

20. David J. Elkins and E. B. Simeon, "A Cause in Search of Its Effect, or What Does Political Culture Explain?" *Comparative Politics* (January 1979).

21. "World Takes Notice of Iran's Ahmadinejad," National Public Radio, *All Things Considered,* February 13, 2006.

22. Roberta Garner, *Contemporary Movements and Ideologies* (New York: McGraw Hill, 1996).

23. Benjamin R. Barber, *Jihad vs. McWorld* (New York: Times Books, 1995).

24. See Benjamin R. Barber, "Beyond Jihad vs. McWorld," *The Nation,* January 21, 2002.

25. Donald K. Emmerson, "Will Indonesia Survive?" *Foreign Affairs* 79, no. 3 (May–June 2000).

26. Célestin Monga, *The Anthropology of Anger: Civil Society and Democracy in Africa,* trans. Linda L. Fleck and Célestin Monga (Boulder: Lynne Rienner, 1996).

27. Martin Kramer, "Coming to Terms: Fundamentalists or Islamists?" *Middle East Quarterly* (Spring 2003), pp. 65–77.

28. Mohammed Ayoob, "Political Islam: Image and Reality," *World Policy Journal* (Fall 2004), p. 11.

29. "What Is Islamofascism?" National Public Radio, *Talk of the Nation,* August 31, 2006.

30. Larry Rohter, "As Pope Heads to Brazil, a Rival Theology Persists," *New York Times,* May 7, 2007.

31. Gustavo Gutiérrez, *A Theology of Liberation: History, Politics and Salvation* (Maryknoll, NY: Orbis, 1971). Other key events in the development of liberation theology included the 1968–1969 Second General Conference on Latin American Bishops, in Medellín, Colombia, which met to discuss the implications of Second Vatican Council (also known as Vatican II) for Latin America; 1967 publication of "A Letter to the Peoples of the Third World"; and the 1979 meeting of the Council of Latin American Bishops, in Puebla, Mexico.

32. While many of these ideas were and continue to be extremely popular at the grassroots level in many countries, the institutional Catholic Church has responded with harsh criticism. Boff, for example, was required to spend a year in "obedient silence" from 1985 to 1986 because of opposition from Rome toward some of his writings. He was eventually forced out of the priesthood for mixing politics and religion too much.

33. In recent years there have been many books and edited collections that focus on non-Western views of feminism. For a sampling, see Kumari Jayawardena, *Feminism and Nationalism in the Third World* (London: Zed, 1986); Guida West and Rhoda Lois Blumberg, eds., *Women and Social Protest* (New York: Oxford University Press, 1990); Jane Jaquette, ed., *The Women's Movement in Latin America: Participation and Democracy* (Boulder: Westview, 1994); Lesli Bethell, ed., *Ideas and Ideologies in Twentieth-Century Latin America* (Cambridge: Cambridge University Press, 1996).

34. Jaquette, *The Women's Movement in Latin America.*

35. Jane Jaquette, "Introduction: From Transition to Participation: Women's Movements and Democratic Politics," in Jaquette, *The Women's Movement in Latin America.*

36. Daniel Ottosson, "A World Survey of Laws Prohibiting Same Sex Activity Between Consenting Adults," International Lesbian, Gay, Bisexual, Trans, and Intersex Association, 2010, www.ilga.org, p. 4.

37. Dan Bilefsky, "Soul-Searching in Turkey After a Gay Man Is Killed," *New York Times,* November 26, 2009.

38. Interview with Jeff Sharlet, "Finding the Root of Anti-Gay Sentiment in Uganda," National Public Radio, *Fresh Air,* August 25, 2010; Jeffrey Gettleman, "Americans' Role Seen in Uganda Anti-Gay Push," *New York Times,* January 3, 2010.

39. Javier Corrales, "Gays in Latin America: Is the Closet Half Empty?" *Foreign Policy* (February 18, 2009).

40. David Agren, "Mexican States Ordered to Honor Gay Marriages," *New York Times,* August 10, 2010.

41. Tania Branigan, "Beijing's 'Happy Couples' Launch Campaign for Same-Sex Marriages," *The Guardian* (London), February 25, 2009.

42. Andrew Heywood, *Political Ideas and Concepts: An Introduction* (New York: St. Martin's, 1994).

43. Bager Moin, *Khomeini: Life of the Ayatollah* (New York: St. Martin's, 2000).

44. Heywood, *Political Ideas and Concepts.*

45. This definition is based on the pioneering work on this subject conducted by Sidney Verba, Victor H. Nie, and Jae-on Kim, *Participation and Political Equality: A Seven-Nation Comparison* (New York: Cambridge University Press, 1978).

46. "North Korea Reportedly Joins Facebook," National Public Radio, August 20, 2010.

47. Maurice Duverger, *Political Parties: Their Organization and Activity in the Modern State* (New York: Wiley, 1963).

48. Harold Meyerson, "Wal-Mart Loves Unions (in China)," *Washington Post,* December 1, 2004; "Wal-Mart Establishes First Trade Union in China," *Xinhua News Agency,* July 29, 2006.

49. "2010 Annual Survey of Trade Union Rights," International Trade Union Confederation, 2011, http://survey.ituc-csi.org.

50. International Labour Organization, "ILO Calls for Zero Tolerance of Violence Against Children in the Workplace," press release, November 20, 2006, www.ilo.org.

51. Sarah Bachman, "Underage Unions: Child Laborers Speak Up," *Mother Jones* (November–December 2000).

52. Sidney Tarrow, *Power in Movement: Social Movements and Contentious Politics* (New York: Cambridge University Press, 1998); William A. Gamson, "The Social Psychology of Collective Action," in *Frontiers in Social Movement Theory,* eds. Aldon D. Morris and Carol McClurg Mueller (New Haven: Yale University Press, 1992).

53. Reza Afshari, "A Historic Moment in Iran," *Human Rights Quarterly* 31, no. 4 (November 2009), p. 854.

54. Jon Leyne, "How Iran's Political Battle Is Fought in Cyberspace," *BBC News,* February 11, 2010.

55. Robert Dreyfuss, "The Nation: Iran's Elections: Ahmadinejad's Red Tide," National Public Radio, June 10, 2009.

56. Will Yong and Michael Slackman, "Across Iran, Anger Lies Behind Face of Calm," *New York Times,* June 11, 2010.

57. Maruja Barrig, "The Difficult Equilibrium Between Bread and Roses: Women's Organizations and Democracy in Peru," in Jaquette, *The Women's Movement in Latin America: Participation and Democracy.*

58. Ibid.

59. Monga, *The Anthropology of Anger.*

60. Damian Grammaticas, "China's Rising Nationalism Troubles West," *BBC News,* November 17, 2009.

61. Elaine Sciolino, "Iran's Well-Covered Women Remodel a Part That Shows," *New York Times,* September 26, 2000.

62. See Albert O. Hirschman, *Exit, Voice, and Loyalty; Responses to Decline in Firms, Organizations, and States* (Cambridge: Harvard University Press, 1970).

63. Douglas Frantz, "Turkish Women Who See Death As a Way Out," *New York Times,* November 3, 2000.

64. David Barboza, "After Suicides, Scrutiny of China's Grim Factories," *New York Times,* June 7, 2010.

65. Stephen Ellis, "Tuning In to Pavement Radio," *African Affairs* 88, no. 352 (July 1989).

66. Evidence Wa Ka Ngobeni, "Vigilante Group Sweeps Suburbs," *Daily Mail & Guardian* (Johannesburg), January 25, 2000; "Mapago a Mathamaga," n.d., www.mapogo.co.za (accessed March 24, 2011).

67. Leigh A. Payne, *Uncivil Movements: The Armed Right Wing and Democracy in Latin America* (Baltimore: Johns Hopkins University Press, 2000).

68. David Rieff, "The False Dawn of Civil Society," *The Nation,* February 22, 1999.

69. Alison Brysk, "Democratizing Civil Society in Latin America," *Journal of Democracy* 11, no. 3 (July 2000).

Chapter 11
Linking Concepts and Cases

1. Octavio Paz, "Latin America and Democracy," in *Democracy and Dictatorship in Latin America: A Special Publication Devoted Entirely to the Voice and Opinions of Writers from Latin America,* eds. Octavio Paz et al. (New York: Foundation for the Independent Study of Social Ideas, 1982).

2. Katherine E. Bliss, "Party Politics in Mexico's Midterm Elections," *Hemisphere Focus* (Center for Strategic and International Studies) 17, no. 3 (July 9, 2009).

3. James C. McKinley Jr., "Mexico Faces Its Own Red-Blue Standoff," *New York Times,* July 9, 2006.

4. Elisabeth Malkin, "Economic Decline Lifts the Prospects of a Vocal Populist," *New York Times,* February 4, 2009; Bliss, "Party Politics in Mexico's Midterm Elections."

5. Enrique Krauze, "An Anti-Incumbency Wave—in Mexico," *New York Times,* July 6, 2010.

6. McKinley, "Mexico Faces Its Own Red-Blue Standoff"; Wilson Center, "Mexico's Midterm Elections and the Future of Democracy," July 10, 2009, www.wilsoncenter.org.

7. Elisabeth Malkin, "In Mexican Vote, Nostalgia for Past Corruption," *New York Times,* July 6, 2009; Bliss, "Party Politics in Mexico's Midterm Elections."

8. Marc Lacey, "Disgruntled Mexicans Plan an Election Message to Politicians: We Prefer Nobody," *New York Times,* June 21, 2009; Malcolm Bleith, "Mexico's Blast from the Past," *Newsweek,* July 2, 2009.

9. "As You Were," *The Economist,* July 5, 2010; "Taking It to the Streets," *Houston Chronicle,* November 4, 2006.

10. Francisco Durand, "The New Right and Political Change in Peru," in *The Right and Democracy in Latin America,* eds. Douglas A. Chalmers, Maria do Carmo Campello de Souza, and Atilio A. Borón (New York: Praeger, 1992); Ernesto García Calderón, "Peru's Decade of Living Dangerously," *Journal of Democracy* 12, no. 2 (April 2001).

11. García Calderón, "Peru's Decade of Living Dangerously."

12. Alex Emery, "Peru's Farmers Fight Police over Southern Copper Mine," *Bloomberg Businessweek,* April 15, 2010; "Coca Growers Protest Disrupts Peru Power," *BBC News,* September 20, 2010.

13. Simon Romero, "As China Expands in Latin America, Tensions Fester at a Mining Venture in Peru," *New York Times,* August 15, 2010.

14. Kristina Aiello,"Peru's 'Cold War' Against Indigenous Peoples," North American Congress on Latin America, July 15, 2009, www.nacla.org.

15. Simon Romero, "Protesters Gird for Long Fight over Opening Peru's Amazon," *New York Times,* July 11, 2009.

16. Aiello, "Peru's 'Cold War' Against Indigenous Peoples."

17. Marisol de la Cadena, "Indigenous Cosmopolitics in the Andes," *Cultural Anthro-*

pology 25, no. 2 (May 2010); Gerardo Rénique, "Law of the Jungle in Peru: Indigenous Amazonian Uprising Against Neoliberalism," *Socialism and Democracy* 23, no. 3 (November 2009); Romero, "Protesters Gird for Long Fight."

18. "Blood in the Jungle," *The Economist,* June 13, 2009; Stephanie Boyd, "The Ticking Time Bomb," *New Internationalist* no. 427 (November 2009); "To the Barricades," *The Economist,* December 6, 2008.

19. de la Cadena, "Indigenous Cosmopolitics in the Andes"; Romero, "Protesters Gird for Long Fight."

20. Laura Fano Morrisey, "The Rise of Ethnic Politics: Indigenous Movements in the Andean Region," *Development* 52, no. 4 (2009); Rénique, "Law of the Jungle in Peru."

21. Funso Afolayan, "Nigeria: A Political Entity and a Society," in *Dilemmas of Democracy in Nigeria,* eds. Paul A. Beckett and Crawford Young (Rochester, NY: University of Rochester Press, 1997).

22. Stephanie Hanson, "Backgrounder: Nigeria's Creaky Political System," Council on Foreign Relations, April 12, 2007, www.cfr.org; "Nigeria: Investigations of Mass Killings in Nigeria," *IRIN News,* March 25, 2010.

23. Jean Herskovits, "Nigeria's Rigged Democracy," *Foreign Affairs* 86, no. 4 (July–August 2007).

24. John Campbell, "Flight 253 and Nigeria's Troubling Trends," Council on Foreign Relations, December 28, 2009, www.cfr.org; Adam Nossiter, "Killings Signal Violent Revival of Nigeria Sect," *New York Times,* October 19, 2010.

25. "The Candidates to Be Nigeria's Leader," *BBC News,* December 4, 2006.

26. "Profile: Umaru Yar'Adua," *BBC News,* December 17, 2006.

27. Ernest Aryeetey, "Can Nigeria Fail?" Brookings Institution, June 24, 2010, www.brookings.edu.

28. "Zimbabwe's Tighter Belts, and Shorter Tempers," *The Economist,* October 28, 2000.

29. Not all women are MDC supporters. Older, rural women with less formal education are some of ZANU-PF's staunchest supporters, and many of them fear the uncertainty that would come with a new government.

30. Douglas Rogers, "Zimbabwe's Accidental Triumph," *New York Times,* April 15, 2010.

31. Sam Moyo, "The Land Occupation Movement and Democratization in Zimbabwe: Contradictions of Neoliberalism," *Millennium* 30, no. 2 (2001).

32. Ibid.

33. Quoted in Greg Mills and Jeffrey Herbst, "Bring Zimbabwe in from the Cold," *New York Times,* May 28, 2009.

34. "Zimbabwe: Power-Sharing for Bankrupt Beginners," *Africa Confidential* 50, no. 3 (February 6, 2009).

35. "Still Adored," *The Economist,* December 19, 2009.

36. Mabasa Sasa, "No Imminent Elections," *New African* 493 (March 2010).

37. "World Takes Notice of Iran's Ahmadinejad," National Public Radio, *All Things Considered,* February 13, 2006.

38. "Future Perfect," *Newsweek,* November 18, 2009.

39. Azadeh Moaveni, in her book *Honeymoon in Tehran: Two Years of Love and Danger in Iran* (New York: Random, 2009), highlights this divide between religious militants and those preferring a more private interpretation of their faith.

40. Reza Afshari, "A Historic Moment in Iran," *Human Rights Quarterly* 31, no. 4 (November 2009), p. 840.

41. "The Clergy in Defence of Their Own," *The Economist,* May 12, 2001.

42. Frances Harrison, "Women Graduates Challenge Iran," *BBC News,* September 19, 2006.

43. Amir Daftari, "Iran Split over Female Soccer Fans," *CNN News,* May 1, 2006.

44. Azadeh Moaveni, "Will Iran's 'Marriage Crisis' Bring Down Ahmadinejad?" *Time,* June 9, 2009.

45. Ibid.

46. Jeffrey Gedmin, "Shirin Ebadi Prepares for the End," *Foreign Policy* (January 11, 2010).

47. "Turkey at a Crossroads: Worlds Merge in Turkey, Raising Identity Issues," *PBS Newshour,* October 8, 2008.

48. Quoted in Michael Thumann, "Turkey's Role Reversals," *Wilson Quarterly* (Summer 2010), p. 29.

49. Simon Cameron-Moore, "Turkey Referendum Win Boosts Erdogan for 2011 Election," *Reuters,* September 13, 2010.

50. Ece Toksabay and Ibon Villelabeitia, "In Quiet Revolution, Turkey Eases Headscarf Ban," *Reuters,* October 17, 2010.

51. Aygen Aytaç et al., *Human Development Report, Turkey 2008: Youth in Turkey* (New York: United Nations Development Programme, 2008).

52. Jonathan Head, "Turkish Kurdish War Reignites," *BBC News,* July 2, 2010.

53. "Turkey at a Crossroads," *PBS Newshour.*

54. Willy Lam, former China editor of the Hong Kong–based *South China Morning Post,* in Weiliang Nie, "Chinese Learn to Leap the 'Great Firewall,'" *BBC News,* March 19, 2010.

55. Chris Hogg, "Protest Not Unusual in China," *BBC News,* July 7, 2009.

56. Wu Jiao, "Religious Believers Thrice the Estimate," *China Daily,* February 7, 2007.

57. Fred Pearce, "As China's Pollution Toll Grows, Protesters and Media Push Back," *Yale Environment 360,* March 18, 2010.

58. "The Party, the People, and the Power of Cyber-Talk," *The Economist,* April 29, 2006, p. 27.

59. Edward Wong, "After a 10-Month Ban, Western China Is Online," *New York Times,* May 15, 2010.

60. David Barboza, "For Chinese, Web Is the Way to Entertainment," *New York Times,* April 19, 2010.

61. Didi Kirsten Tatlow, "Women Struggle for a Foothold in Chinese Politics," *New York Times,* June 24, 2010.

62. Jan Pierini, executive director of Beijing's PeopleLink, interviewed in Christina Larson, "China's Emerging Environmental Movement," *Yale Environment 360,* June 3, 2008.

63. Ibid.

64. Robert Cribb and Colin Brown, *Modern Indonesia: A History Since 1945* (New York: Longman, 1995).

65. Annette Clear, "Politics: From Endurance to Evolution," in *Indonesia: The Great Transition,* ed. John Bresnan (New York: Rowman and Littlefield, 2005), pp. 143–144.

66. Karishma Vaswani, "On Patrol with Aceh's Sharia Police," *BBC News,* February 2, 2010.

67. Karishma Vaswani, "Indonesian Church Row Raises Fears of Sectarian Conflict," *BBC News,* September 12, 2010.

68. Rachel Harvey, "A New Path for Troubled Papua?" *BBC News,* November 16, 2010.

Chapter 12
The Call to Arms: Violent Paths to Change

1. Jon Leyne, "Will Iran's Basij Stay Loyal?" *BBC News,* August 13, 2009.

2. Quoted in Jonathan Head, "Turkish Kurdish War Reignites," *BBC News,* July 2, 2010.

3. Walter Laqueur, *The New Terrorism: Fanaticism and the Arms of Mass Destruction* (New York: Oxford University Press, 1999).

4. Noam Chomsky, *Pirates and Emperors: International Terrorism in the Real World* (New York: Claremont, 1986).

5. For a concise summary of approaches to violence in the literature, see Jack A. Goldstone, ed., *Revolutions: Theoretical, Comparative, and Historical Studies,* 2nd ed. (New York: Harcourt Brace, 1994).

6. "Unrest in DR Congo After TP Mazembe Lose to Inter Milan," *BBC News,* December 18, 2010.

7. Arend Lijphart, *Democracy in Plural Societies: A Comparative Exploration* (New Haven: Yale University Press, 1977).

8. Charles Euchner, *Extraordinary Politics: How Protest and Dissent Are Changing American Democracy* (Boulder: Westview, 1996).

9. Michael Renner, "How to Abolish War," *The Humanist* (July–August 1999).

10. Daniel C. Diller, ed., *The Middle East,* 8th ed. (Washington, DC: Congressional Quarterly, 1994).

11. Ibid.

12. Kawe Qoraishy, "Iran's Kurdish Question," *Foreign Policy* (May 17, 2010).

13. Barbara Crossette, "Iraq Is Forcing Kurds from Their Homes, the UN Reports," *New York Times,* December 11, 2000.

14. Ranj Alaaldin, "Kurds Are Iraq's Kingmakers," *The Guardian* (London), October 18, 2010.

15. Yahya Sadowski, "Ethnic Conflict," *Foreign Policy* 111 (Summer 1998).

16. "Aceh's Sharia Court Opens," *BBC News,* March 4, 2003.

17. Tina Rosenberg, "A Guerrilla War Stoked by a Thirst for Cash," *New York Times,* December 27, 2001.

18. Cited in Gary J. Bass, "What Really Causes Civil War?" *New York Times Magazine,* August 13, 2006.

19. "Call to Help Colombia's Displaced," *BBC News,* July 16, 2009.

20. Christie Johnston, "Talking to Taiwan's New President," *Time,* August 11, 2008.

21. Toyin Falola, *The History of Nigeria* (Westport: Greenwood, 1999).

22. Eleanor O'Gorman, "Writing Women's Wars: Foucaldian Strategies of Engagement," in *Women, Culture, and International Relations,* eds. Vivienne Jabri and Eleanor O'Gorman (Boulder: Lynne Rienner, 1999).

23. The title of this figure comes from Eve Ensler, quoted in Bob Herbert, "The Invisible War," *New York Times,* February 21, 2009.

24. Nicolas Kristof, "The World Capital of Killing," *New York Times,* February 6, 2010; Lisa Shannon, "No, Sexual Violence Is Not Culture," *International Herald Tribune,* June 25, 2010.

25. Laqueur, *The New Terrorism.*

26. "The Accidental War," *The Economist,* July 22, 2006, p. 13.

27. "A Geographical Expression in Search of a State," *The Economist,* July 8, 2006.

28. Amy Caiazza, "Why Gender Matters in Understanding September 11: Women, Militarism, and Violence," *Institute for Women's Policy Research* no. 1908 (November 2001).

29. Amy Knight, "Female Terrorists in the Russian Socialist Revolutionary Party," *Russian Review* no. 38 (1979); Laqueur, *The New Terrorism.*

30. Christopher Dickey, "Women of Al Qaeda," *Newsweek,* December 12, 2005.

31. Adel Darwish, "From Boredom to Bombs: Two Female Terrorists," *WIN Magazine,* no. 20 (April 1999).

32. "China May Drop Death Penalty for Economic Crimes," *BBC News,* August 23, 2010.

33. "Iran Hangs Footballer's Mistress Shahla Jahed," *BBC News,* December 1, 2010.

34. Sita Ranchod-Nilsson, "'This, Too, Is a Way of Fighting': Rural Women's Participation in Zimbabwe's Liberation War," in *Women and Revolution in Africa, Asia, and the New World,* ed. Mary Ann Tétreault (Columbia: University of South Carolina Press, 1994).

35. The article that cited this figure noted that the distinction between armed civilian and regular soldier is blurred in many contexts, which may inflate the statistic. "The First Casualty: War and Its Victims," *The Economist,* August 25, 2001.

36. Mary Kaldor, *New and Old Wars: Organized Violence in a Global Era* (Stanford: Stanford University Press, 1999).

37. "Peace Deal Fails to End Darfur Violence," National Public Radio, *Morning Edition,* August 24, 2006.

38. "International Court Takes Case of Congo's Child Soldiers," National Public Radio, *Weekend All Things Considered,* October 29, 2006.

39. "Child Soldiers," National Public Radio, *Talk of the Nation,* February 16, 2005. See

also P. W. Singer, *Children at War* (New York: Pantheon, 2005).

40. Rachel Brett and Irma Specht, *Young Soldiers: Why They Choose to Fight* (Boulder: Lynne Rienner, 2004), pp. 9–36.

41. Coalition to Stop the Use of Child Soldiers, "Global Report on Child Soldiers 2001," www.child-soldiers.org; Juan Forero, "A Child's Vision of War: Boy Guerrillas in Colombia," *New York Times,* December 20, 2000; "Charity Decries Use of Children in War," *CNN World News,* October 31, 1996; "The Weapon That Changed the Face of War," National Public Radio, *Weekend Edition Sunday,* November 26, 2006.

42. "Uganda LRA Rebels on Massive Forced Recruitment Drive," *BBC News,* August 12, 2010.

43. Kenneth Walker, "UNICEF Works to Deprogram Children Who Have Been Kidnapped in Sierra Leone and Forced to Commit Murder for the Rebels," National Public Radio, *Morning Edition,* July 6, 2000; Coalition to Stop the Use of Child Soldiers, "Global Report on Child Soldiers 2001."

44. Seth Mydans, "Burmese Rebel Chief More Boy Than Warrior," *New York Times,* April 10, 2000; "Burmese Rebel Twins and Fourteen Followers Surrender in Thailand," *Associated Press,* January 17, 2001.

45. Rosenberg, "A Guerrilla War Stoked by a Thirst for Cash."

46. Isawa Elaigwu, "Nation-Building and Changing Political Structures," in *UNESCO General History of Africa: Africa Since 1935,* ed. Ali A. Mazrui (London: Heinemann, 1993).

47. Ergun Özbudun, *Contemporary Turkish Politics: Challenges to Democratic Consolidation* (Boulder: Lynne Rienner, 2000).

48. Marvine Howe, *Turkey Today: A Nation Divided over Islam's Revival* (Boulder: Westview, 2000).

49. Miguel Angel Centeno, *Democracy Within Reason: Technocratic Revolution in Mexico* (University Park: Pennsylvania State University Press, 1997).

50. Sorayya Shahri, "Women in Command: A Successful Experience in the National Liberation Army of Iran," in *Frontline Feminisms: Women, War, and Resistance,* eds. Marguerite R. Waller and Jennifer Rycenga (New York: Garland, 2000).

51. "DR Congo Women March Against Sexual Violence," *BBC News,* October 17, 2010.

52. John McBeth, "Bombs, the Army, and Suharto," *Far Eastern Economic Review* 164, no. 4 (February 1, 2001).

53. Ibid.

54. "In the Hands of the Militia," *The Economist,* September 16, 2000.

55. "American Use of South African Mercenaries As Bodyguards and Police Trainers in Iraq," National Public Radio, *Morning Edition,* February 15, 2005; "Questions About Mercenary Activities in Africa," National Public Radio, *All Things Considered,* March 17, 2004.

56. Frederick J. Hacker, *Crusaders, Criminals, Crazies: Terror and Terrorism in Our Time* (New York: Norton, 1976).

57. Rahul Bedi, "Mumbai Attacks: Indian Suit Against Google Earth over Image Use by Terrorists," *The Telegraph* (London), December 9, 2008.

58. Vikas Bajaj and Lydia Polgreen, "Suspect Stirs Mumbai Court by Confessing," *New York Times,* July 20, 2009.

59. Mike Crawley, "Somali Banking Under Scrutiny," *Christian Science Monitor,* November 28, 2001.

60. *The 9/11 Commission Report: Final Report on the National Commission on Terrorist Attacks Upon the United States* (New York: Norton, 2004), pp. 169–172.

61. Samuel Munzele Maimbo, "The Money Exchange Dealers of Kabul: A Study of the Hawala System in Afghanistan," Working Paper no. 13 (Washington, DC: World Bank, 2003), chap. 3.

62. Laqueur, *The New Terrorism.*

63. David Scott Palmer, "The Revolutionary Terrorism of Peru's Shining Path," in *Terrorism in Context,* ed. Martha Crenshaw (University Park: Pennsylvania State University Press, 1995).

64. John B. Bellinger III, a former US lawyer with the National Security Council and State Department, interviewed in Charlie Savage, "Obama Team Is Divided on Anti-Terror Tactics," *New York Times,* March 28, 2010.

65. Ray Takeyh, *Hidden Iran: Paradox and Power in the Islamic Republic* (New York: Holt, 2006), pp. 122–123.

66. Flynt Leverett, "Why Libya Gave up on the Bomb," *New York Times,* January 23, 2004, p. 23.

67. "A History of Chemical Weapons," National Public Radio, *Talk of the Nation,* May 8, 2006.

68. Organization for the Prohibition of Chemical Weapons, "Global Campaign to Destroy Chemical Weapons Passes 60 Percent Mark," press release, July 8, 2010.

69. Mao Zedong, "Report on an Investigation of the Peasant Movement in Hunan: March 1927," in *Selected Readings from the Works of Mao Tsetung* (Peking: Foreign Languages Press, 1971), p. 30.

70. See Goldstone, *Revolutions;* Theda Skocpol, *States and Social Revolution: A Comparative Analysis of France, Russia, and China* (New York: Cambridge University Press, 1979).

71. Elton L. Daniel, *The History of Iran* (Westport: Greenwood, 2001).

72. Ellen Kay Trimberger, "A Theory of Elite Revolutions," *Studies in Comparative International Development* 7 (1972). Trimberger also included the Meiji Restoration of 1868 as an example of this specific type of revolution.

73. Trimberger, "A Theory of Elite Revolutions." This point explicitly challenges the theories of Samuel Huntington and others who argued against the inclusion of mass mobilization because of its potentially destabilizing outcomes.

74. Margaret Randall, *Sandino's Daughters: Testimonies of Nicaraguan Women in Struggle* (New Brunswick, NJ: Rutgers University Press, 1995).

75. "North Korea Firing: Why Now?" *BBC News,* November 23, 2010.

76. Jack A. Goldstone, "The Outcomes of Revolutions," in Goldstone, *Revolutions.*

77. Jack A. Goldstone, "Revolutions in World History," in Goldstone, *Revolutions.*

78. Stéphane Courtois et al., *The Black Book of Communism: Crimes, Terror, and Repression,* ed. Mark Kramer, trans. Jonathan Murphy (Cambridge: Harvard University Press, 1999). In his study of the Great Leap Forward, Frank Dikötter estimates that this movement alone was responsible for at least 45 million deaths. See Frank Dikötter, *Mao's Great Famine: The History of China's Most Devastating Catastrophe, 1958–1962* (New York: Walker, 2010).

79. Donna M. Schlagheck, *International Terrorism: An Introduction to the Concepts and Actors* (Lexington, MA: Lexington Books, 1988).

80. Dariush Zahedi, *The Iranian Revolution Then and Now: Indicators of Regime Instability* (Boulder: Westview, 2000).

81. Robin Wright, "Iran's New Revolution," *Foreign Affairs* 79, no. 1 (January–February 2000).

82. Ibid.

83. Ibid.

Chapter 13
Linking Concepts and Cases

1. Shannon K. O'Neil, "Mexican-US Relations: What's Next?" *Americas Quarterly* (Council on Foreign Relations) (Spring 2010).

2. Michele Norris, "Tackling America's Drug Addiction," National Public Radio, *All Things Considered,* June 18, 2010; Enrique Krauze, "The Mexican Evolution," *New York Times,* March 24, 2009.

3. "Fifth Child Victim Killed in Mexico's Drug Violence," *Associated Press,* March 17, 2011.

4. Cited in "What Do You Want from Us?" *New York Times,* September 24, 2010.

5. Frank James, "Obama Rejects Hillary Clinton's Mexico-Colombia Comparison," National Public Radio, *The Two-Way,* September 9, 2010; Rory Carroll, "Hillary Clinton: Mexican Drug War Is Colombia-Style Insurgency," *The Guardian* (London), September 9, 2010.

6. Diana Villiers Negroponte, "Mexico: A Bad Case of the Blues," Brookings Institution, June 24, 2010, www.brookings.edu.

7. Shannon O'Neil, "The Real War in Mexico," *Foreign Affairs* 88, no. 4 (July–August 2008).

8. Randal C. Archibold, "Mexican Leader Pushes Police Overhaul," *New York Times,* October 7, 2010; Marc Lacey, "Mexican Democracy, Even Under Siege," *New York Times,* July 5, 2010.

9. Sam Quinones, "State of War," *Foreign Policy* (February 16, 2009); Transparency International, "Corruption Perceptions Index 2009" and "Corruption Perceptions Index 2010," www.transparency.org.

10. Archibold, "Mexican Leader Pushes Police Overhaul."

11. "UN Report Expresses Concern About Police Abuse in Mexico," *Associated Press,* November 11, 2006.

12. Randal C. Archibold, "A Proposal to Address Rights Abuse in Mexico," *New York Times,* November 20, 2010; Maureen Meyer, "Presidents Obama and Calderón Sit Down in a Context of Increasing Tensions Between the US and Mexico," Washington Office on Latin America, March 3, 2011, www.wola.org.

13. Archibold, "Mexican Leader Pushes Police Overhaul."

14. "Human Rights in Mexico: Untouchable?" *The Economist,* November 3, 2001; Kevin Sullivan and Mary Jordan, "Fox Takes Steps to End Army's Rights Abuses," *Washington Post,* November 11, 2001; Kevin Sullivan, "Memories of Massacre in Mexico," *Washington Post,* February 14, 2002.

15. The name "Shining Path" comes from one of Peru's most prominent authors, Jose Carlos Mariategui, who wrote, "Marxist-Leninism will open the shining path to revolution," "Shining Path," Britannica Online, 2011, www.britannica.com.

16. M. Elaine Mar, "Violence in Peru: Shining Path Women," *Harvard Magazine* (May–June 1996); Cynthia McClintock, *Revolutionary Movements in Latin America* (Washington, DC: US Institute of Peace, 1998).

17. Guzmán broke with China after Mao's death, considering Deng to be a traitor to the revolution. Shining Path preferred its isolation and sought no external support.

18. Carlos Ivan Degregori, "After the Fall of Abimael Guzmán: The Limits of Sendero Luminoso," in *The Peruvian Labyrinth,* eds. Maxwell A. Cameron and Philip Mauceri (University Park: Pennsylvania State University Press, 1997).

19. Peter Flindell Klaren, *Peru: Society and Nationhood in the Andes* (New York: Oxford University Press, 2000); Ramiro Escobar, "Rights-Peru: Reparations Near for Victims of Civil War," *Inter-Press Service,* May 2, 2006.

20. Klaren, *Peru.*

21. Human Rights Watch, "Peru: Torture and Political Persecution in Peru," December 1997, www.hrw.org; US Department of State, *Country Reports on Human Rights, 2000* (Washington, DC: US Government Printing Office, 2000); Escobar, "Rights-Peru: Reparations Near for Victims of Civil War."

22. Degregori, "After the Fall of Abimael Guzmán"; McClintock, *Revolutionary Movements in Latin America.*

23. William Aviles, "Despite Insurgency: Reducing Military Prerogatives in Colombia and Peru," *Latin American Politics and Society,* March 1, 2009.

24. "Fujimori Gets Lengthy Jail Term," *BBC News,* April 7, 2009.

25. Aviles, "Despite Insurgency"; Abraham Lama, "Military Reforms Key Feature of Transition to Democracy," *Inter-Press Service,* December 14, 2001; "Peru Congress Ratifies New Military-Civilian Judicial Panel," *Associated Press,* December 30, 2005.

26. Gregory Weeks, "A Preference for Deference: Reforming the Military's Intelligence Role in Argentina, Chile, and Peru," *Third World Quarterly* 29, no. 1 (February 2008); Human Rights Watch, "Peru: Amend Decrees for Prosecuting Military and Police Abuses," September 10, 2010, www.hrw.org; Lucy Komisar, "US Government Document Links García to 1980s Death Squad," *Inter-Press Service,* December 5, 2007.

27. Simon Romero, "Cocaine Trade Helps Rebels Reignite War in Peru," *New York Times,* March 17, 2009.

28. US Department of State, "2009 Country Reports on Terrorism: Peru," August 15, 2010, www.state.gov.

29. Aviles, "Despite Insurgency"; Romero, "Cocaine Trade Helps Rebels Reignite War in Peru."

30. Peter M. Lewis and Pearl T. Robinson, *Stabilizing Nigeria* (New York: Century Foundation, 1998).

31. Toyin Falola, *The History of Nigeria* (Westport: Greenwood, 1999).

32. Kent Hughes Butts and Steven Metz, *Armies and Democracy in the New Africa: Lessons from Nigeria and South Africa* (Carlisle Barracks, PA: Strategic Studies Institute, US Army War College, January 6, 1996); Falola, *The History of Nigeria;* Christina Lamb, "Life's So Unfair, Says General," *Sunday Telegraph* (London), February 28, 1999.

33. Falola, *The History of Nigeria.*

34. John Campbell, "Nigeria: More Presidential Turmoil," Council on Foreign Relations, February 24, 2010, www.cfr.org.

35. "Nigeria Bomb Toll Rises As Government Admits It Was Warned," *Reuters,* October 2, 2010; "Nigeria's MEND Militants Claim Oil Pipeline Attack," *BBC News,* November 23, 2010.

36. Robert Rotberg, "Nigeria: Elections and Continuing Challenges," Council on Foreign Relations, April 2007, www.cfr.org; Dino Mahtani, "Delta Militants Cause Oil Jitters," *Financial Times,* May 16, 2006.

37. Adam Nossiter, "Poverty Could Imperil the Amnesty in Niger Delta," *New York Times,* November 27, 2009; Alex Perry, "In Nigeria, an Ailing President and Peace Process," *Time,* December 21, 2009.

38. Ngwabi Bhebe and Terence Ranger, "Volume Introduction: Society in Zimbabwe's Liberation War," in *Society in Zimbabwe's Liberation War,* eds. Ngwabi Bhebe and Terence Ranger (Oxford: Currey, 1996).

39. From this point on ZANU became known as ZANU-PF, with "PF" indicating "Patriotic Front."

40. Dickson A. Mungazi, *Colonial Policy and Conflict in Zimbabwe* (New York: Crane Russak, 1992).

41. Richard P. Werbner, "In Memory: A Heritage of War in Southwestern Zimbabwe," in *Society in Zimbabwe's Liberation War,* eds. Ngwabi Bhebe and Terence Ranger (Oxford: Currey, 1996).

42. "Out in the Cold," *The Economist,* June 11, 2005.

43. Andrew Meldrun and Chris McGreal, "Mugabe Takes a Stride into Tyranny," *The Guardian* (London), January 10, 2002.

44. Celia W. Dugger, "Diamond Find Could Aid Zimbabwe, and Mugabe," *New York Times,* June 21, 2010; Celia W. Dugger, "Zimbabwe's Diamond Fields Enrich Ruling Party, Report Says," *New York Times,* June 26, 2009.

45. Dugger, "Diamond Find Could Aid Zimbabwe, and Mugabe"; Alan Cowell, "Group Allows Limited Sales of Zimbabwe's Diamonds," *New York Times,* July 16, 2010.

46. Jerrold D. Green, "Countermobilization in the Iranian Revolution," in *Revolutions: Theoretical, Comparative, and Historical Studies,* 2nd ed., ed. Jack A. Goldstone (New York: Harcourt Brace, 1994).

47. Mark J. Roberts, *Khomeini's Incorporation of the Iranian Military* (Washington, DC: Institute for National Strategic Studies, National Defense University, 1996).

48. Ibid.

49. Robert F. Worth, "Iran's President Praises Hezbollah," *New York Times,* October 14, 2010.

50. Nick Childs, "Iran Sanctions Cripple Aging Military," *BBC News,* July 28, 2010.

51. Walter Laqueur, *The New Terrorism: Fanaticism and the Arms of Mass Destruction* (New York: Oxford University Press, 1999).

52. Pew Research Center, "Turks Downbeat About Their Institutions," September 7, 2010, http://pewresearch.org.

53. Michael Thumann, "Turkey's Role Reversals," *Wilson Quarterly* (Summer 2010), p. 33.

54. Marc Champion, "Turkey Charges 11 More in Coup Plot," *Wall Street Journal,* February 26, 2010.

55. Sarah Rainsford, "'Deep State' Trial Polarizes Turkey," *BBC News,* October 23, 2008.

56. Stephen Kinzer, "Turkey Considers Scaling Back Military Challenge to Greece," *New York Times,* June 8, 2000.

57. "Seeking Out the PKK Gunmen in Iraq's Remote Mountains," *BBC News,* July 21, 2010.

58. Jonathan Head, "Turkish Kurdish War Reignites," *BBC News,* July 2, 2010.

59. Edward Cody, "Public Shaming of Prostitutes Misfires in China," *Washington Post,* December 9, 2006.

60. Mara Hvistendahl, "Hackers: The China Syndrome," *Popular Science,* April 23, 2009, www.popsci.com.

61. Siobhan Gorman, August Cole, and Yochi Dreazen, "Computer Spies Breach Fighter-Jet Project," *Wall Street Journal,* April 21, 2009.

62. Edward Wong, "Social Tensions Stoke School Attacks, China's Premier Says," *New York Times,* May 15, 2010.

63. Quoted in "Lone Madmen Without Guns," *The Economist,* May 12, 2010.

64. Sidney Jones, interviewed by John M. Glionna, "Bombings, Business, and the Future of Indonesia," *Los Angeles Times,* July 19, 2009.

65. Aubrey Belford, "Gunmen Storm Indonesian Police Station," *New York Times,* September 22, 2010.

66. Donald K. Emmerson, "Voting and Violence: Indonesia and East Timor in 1999," in *Indonesia Beyond Suharto,* ed. Donald K. Emmerson (Armonk, NY: Sharpe, 1999).

67. Ibid. This is the term Donald Emmerson, an election monitor with the Carter Center and a scholar of Indonesian politics, used to describe the situation.

68. "Indonesian Flashpoints: Papua," *BBC News,* October 22, 2010.

69. Ann Marie Murphy, "Indonesia and the World," in *Indonesia: The Great Transition,* ed. John Bresnan (New York: Rowman and Littlefield, 2005), p. 277.

Chapter 14
Ballots, Not Bullets: Seeking Democratic Change

1. Gilbert da Costa, "Nigerians Wonder: Could a Military Coup Help Us?" *Time,* January 31, 2010.

2. Octavio Paz, "Latin America and Democracy," in *Democracy and Dictatorship in Latin America: A Special Publication Devoted Entirely to the Voice and Opinions of Writers from Latin America,* eds. Octavio Paz et al. (New York: Foundation for the Independent Study of Social Ideas, 1982), p. 15.

3. Philippe C. Schmitter and Terry Lynn Karl, "What Democracy Is . . . and Is Not," in *The Global Resurgence of Democracy,* eds. Larry Diamond and Marc F. Plattner (Baltimore: Johns Hopkins University Press, 1993).

4. Ibid.

5. Ibid.; Juan J. Linz and Alfred Stepan, *Problems of Democratic Transition and Consolidation* (Baltimore: Johns Hopkins University Press, 1996); Larry Diamond, Juan J. Linz, and Seymour Martin Lipset, "Introduction: What Makes for Democracy?" in *Politics in Developing Countries: Comparing Experiences with Democracy,* eds. Diamond, Linz, and Lipset (Boulder: Lynne Rienner, 1995).

6. Schmitter and Karl, "What Democracy Is . . . and Is Not."

7. Freedom House, *Freedom in the World 2011,* www.freedomhouse.org.

8. Adebayo Adedeji, "Popular Participation, Democracy, and Development: Is There a Dialectical Linkage?" in *Nigeria: Renewal from the Roots? The Struggle for Democratic Development,* eds. Adebayo Adedeji et al. (London: Zed, 1997).

9. Freedom House, *Freedom in the World 2005* and *Freedom in the World 2010.*

10. Ibid., *Freedom in the World 2010.*

11. Doh Chull Shin and Jason Wells, "Is Democracy the Only Game in Town?" *Journal of Democracy* 16, no. 2 (April 14, 2005).

12. Larry Diamond, "Introduction: In Search of Consolidation," in *Consolidating Third Wave Democracies,* eds. Larry Diamond et al. (Baltimore: Johns Hopkins University Press,

1997); Diamond, Linz, and Lipset, "Introduction: What Makes for Democracy?"; Schmitter and Karl, "What Democracy Is . . . and Is Not"; Freedom House, *Freedom in the World 2011*.

13. Diamond, Linz, and Lipset, "Introduction: What Makes for Democracy?"

14. Shin and Wells, "Is Democracy the Only Game in Town?"; Gregory D. Schmidt, "Delegative Democracy in Peru? Fujimori's 1995 Landslide and the Prospects for 2000," *Journal of Inter-American Studies and World Affairs* 42, no. 1 (Spring 2000); Jeffrey Herbst, "Understanding Ambiguity During Democratization in Africa," in *Pathways to Democracy: The Political Economy of Democratic Transitions,* eds. James F. Hollifield and Calvin Jillson (New York: Routledge, 2000); Arch Puddington, "Freedom in the World 2011: The Authoritarian Challenge to Democracy," Freedom House, www.freedomhouse.org.

15. Larry Diamond, "Is the Third Wave Over?" *Journal of Democracy* 7, no. 3 (July 1996); Guillermo O'Donnell, "Delegative Democracy," *Journal of Democracy* 5, no. 1 (January 1994); Larry Diamond and Marc F. Plattner, "Introduction," in Diamond and Plattner, *The Global Resurgence of Democracy.*

16. O'Donnell, "Delegative Democracy." See also Kenneth M. Roberts, *Deepening Democracy? The Modern Left and Social Movements in Chile and Peru* (Stanford: Stanford University Press, 1998); Linz and Stepan, *Problems of Democratic Transition and Consolidation.*

17. Diamond and Plattner, "Introduction"; Linz and Stepan, *Problems of Democratic Transition and Consolidation.*

18. Freedom House, *Freedom in the World 2011.*

19. O'Donnell, "Delegative Democracy"; Merilee Grindle, *Challenging the State: Crisis and Innovation in Latin America and Africa* (Cambridge: Cambridge University Press, 1996).

20. Malaysia's Mahathir Mohammad was the strongest spokesperson for this exceptionalist view, which continues to be advocated by some third world leaders. Modern Chinese leaders, for example, argue that universal standards for human rights simply do not exist; rather, developed countries use these standards as a guise for meddling in the internal affairs of third world countries. Chinese leaders emphasize that differing levels of economic development and political conditions justify varying approaches toward rights and democracy.

21. Amartya Sen, "Democracy as a Universal Value," *Journal of Democracy* 10, no. 3 (July 1999).

22. Seymour Martin Lipset, *Political Man* (Garden City, NY: Doubleday, 1959); Linz and Stepan, *Problems of Democratic Transition and Consolidation.*

23. According to this view, popular with neoliberals, no democracy with a per capita income approaching that of South Korea or Taiwan has ever broken down, while (with some notable exceptions) new democracies in countries with per capita incomes of less than $1,000 have rarely lasted more than a few years.

24. Emmanuel Sivan, "Illusions of Change," *Journal of Democracy* 11, no. 3 (July 2000); Laith Kubba, "The Awakening of Civil Society," *Journal of Democracy* 11, no. 3 (July 2000).

25. Although this trend toward democracy may currently be the case, no condition is permanent. In a 1993 essay on the global resurgence of democracy, Samuel Huntington contends that the turbulence of the era may give rise to new ideologies with universalist aspirations. See Samuel P. Huntington, "Democracy's Third Wave," in Diamond and Plattner, *The Global Resurgence of Democracy.* An example would be Islamist movements, which reject liberal democracy's association with individualism and materialism. Or an economically advanced or militarily powerful country such as China or Russia may one day offer a successful and attractive alternative nondemocratic model of governance that struggling countries may find appealing.

26. Linz and Stepan, *Problems of Democratic Transition and Consolidation.*

27. Ibid.; Diamond, "Introduction: In Search of Consolidation."

28. Linz and Stepan, *Problems of Democratic Transition and Consolidation;* Diamond, "Introduction: In Search of Consolidation"; Schmitter and Karl, "What Democracy Is . . . and Is Not."

29. Linz and Stepan, *Problems of Democratic Transition and Consolidation;* Diamond, "Introduction: In Search of Consolidation"; "Democracy's Ten-Year Rut," *The Economist,* October 29, 2005.

30. Schmitter and Karl, "What Democracy Is . . . and Is Not."

31. Larry Diamond, "Three Paradoxes of Democracy," in Diamond and Plattner, *The Global Resurgence of Democracy,* p. 104.

32. Diamond and Plattner, "Introduction"; Diamond, "Introduction: In Search of Consolidation"; Linz and Stepan, *Problems of Democratic Transition and Consolidation.*

33. Jorge G. Castañeda, *Utopia Unarmed: The Latin American Left After the Cold War* (New York: Knopf, 1993).

34. Diamond, "Introduction: In Search of Consolidation"; Arturo Valenzuela, "External Actors in the Transitions to Democracy in Latin America," in *Pathways to Democracy: The Political Economy of Democratic Transitions,* eds. James F. Hollifield and Calvin Jillson (New York: Routledge, 2000).

35. "The Democratic Routine," *The Economist,* December 2, 2010; Kevin Casas-Zamora, "Latin America's Hour of Optimism: On the Results of Latinobarómetro 2010," Brookings Institution, December 16, 2010, www.brookings.edu.

36. Ibid.

37. Yun-han Chu and Min-hua Huang, "A Typological Analysis of Democratic Legitimacy," Global Barometer, Working Paper no. 48, 2009, www.globalbarometer.net; "Are Democratic Citizens Emerging in Africa? Evidence from the Afrobarometer," Afrobarometer, Briefing Paper no. 70, May 2009, www.afrobarometer.org.

38. Catherine Boone, "'Empirical Statehood' and Reconfigurations of Political Order," in *The African State at a Critical Juncture,* eds. Leonardo A. Villalon and Phillip A. Huxtable (Boulder: Lynne Rienner, 1998).

39. Juan J. Linz, "The Perils of Presidentialism," in Diamond and Plattner, *The Global Resurgence of Democracy.*

40. "Hints of a New Chapter," *The Economist,* November 14, 2009.

41. O'Donnell, "Delegative Democracy"; Grindle, *Challenging the State;* Scott Mainwaring, "Latin America's Imperiled Progress: The Surprising Resilience of Elected Governments," *Journal of Democracy* 10, no. 3 (July 2000).

42. O'Donnell, "Delegative Democracy."

43. Linz, "The Perils of Presidentialism."

44. Donald L. Horowitz, "Comparing Democratic Systems," in Diamond and Plattner, *The Global Resurgence of Democracy;* Linz, "The Perils of Presidentialism."

45. Arend Lijphart, *Patterns of Democracy: Government Forms and Performance in Thirty-six Countries* (New Haven: Yale University Press, 1999); Linz, "The Perils of Presidentialism"; Horowitz, "Comparing Democratic Systems."

46. Linz, "The Perils of Presidentialism."

47. Ibid.; Linz and Stepan, *Problems of Democratic Transition and Consolidation.*

48. Linz and Stepan, *Problems of Democratic Transition and Consolidation;* Diamond and Plattner, "Introduction"; Diamond, Linz, and Lipset, "Introduction: What Makes for Democracy?"; Horowitz, "Comparing Democratic Systems."

49. Linz and Stepan, *Problems of Democratic Transition and Consolidation.*

50. Ibid.

51. "Fiasco in Tabasco," *The Economist,* October 21, 2000.

52. Carter Center, "Final Report of the Carter Center Limited Assessment Mission to the March 2010 Villagers Committee Elections in Yunnan Province, China," May 2010, p. 4, www.cartercenter.org.

53. Dino Mahtani, "Nigeria on Alert as Census Takers Begin Mammoth Task," *Financial Times* (London), March 22, 2006.

54. "INEC to Display Voter Registration on Internet," *NBF Topics,* December 6, 2010.

55. Philip Rowan, "Democracy's Memorabilia," *Washington Post,* November 30, 2000.

56. Larry Rohter, "Chile Is Ready to Elect a President Like No Other," *New York Times,* January 15, 2006.

57. "Joining Forces: A Motley Political Alliance Scrambles the Presidential Race," *The Economist,* July 8, 2010; "Mexico's Calderón Proposes Major Political Reform," *Associated Press,* December 16, 2009.

58. O'Donnell, "Delegative Democracy"; Schmidt, "Delegative Democracy in Peru?"

59. "Q&A: Turkey's Constitutional Referendum," *BBC News*, September 12, 2010; Marc Champion and Joe Parkinson, "Turks Pass Constitutional Changes," *Wall Street Journal*, September 13, 2010.

60. Rafael Ruiz Harrell, "Building Trust with Mexico," *New York Times*, May 22, 2001; Diamond and Plattner, "Introduction"; Adedeji, "Popular Participation, Democracy, and Development."

61. Harrell, "Building Trust with Mexico"; Diamond and Plattner, "Introduction"; Adedeji, "Popular Participation, Democracy, and Development."

62. Linz and Stepan, *Problems of Democratic Transition and Consolidation*.

63. Patrick Guntensperger, "Yudhoyono Rides Anti-Corruption Wave," *Asia Times*, July 2, 2009; "Students, Workers Protest Yudhoyono, Corruption," *Agence France Press*, October 20, 2010.

64. Daniel Howden, "Anti-Corruption Advocate Returns from Exile," *The Independent* (London), June 7, 2010; Transparency International, "Corruption Perceptions Index 2010," www.transparency.org.

65. Salim Osman, "Yudhoyono's Twin Targets," *The Straits Times*, August 17, 2006.

66. Diamond and Plattner, "Introduction"; "Paying the Piper," *Foreign Policy* 154 (May–June 2006).

67. Olumide Taiwo, "Challenges and Possiblities for Progress in Nigeria," Brookings Institution, June 24, 2010, www.brookings.edu.

68. "RI Among the 10 Most Corrupt; House Worst Offender," *Jakarta Post*, June 4, 2009.

69. Larry Diamond, "The Uncivic Society and the Descent into Praetorianism," in Diamond, Linz, and Lipset, *Politics in Developing Countries*; Taiwo, "Challenges and Possiblities for Progress in Nigeria."

70. Transparency International, "Global Corruption Barometer 2009," www.transparency.org; Mike Sidwell, "Interview of the Month: Elizabeth Donnelly, Coordinator of Africa Programme, Chatham House," Transparency International, March 2008, www.transparency.org.

71. Guillermo O'Donnell, "Why the Rule of Law Matters," in *Assessing the Quality of Democracy*, eds. Larry Diamond and Leonardo Morlino (Baltimore: Johns Hopkins University Press, 2005).

72. Diego Cevallos, "Crime-Ridden City Where Anything Goes—and Frequently Does," *Inter-Press Service*, January 29, 2008.

73. Matthew Moffett, "Argentina's Crime Wave Becomes Election Issue," *Wall Street Journal*, May 28, 2009.

74. Ledgerhood Rennie, "Vigilantes Take on Liberian Gangs," *BBC News*, September 19, 2006.

75. "Ex-Crime Chief Arrested in Mexico," *BBC News*, November 21, 2008; Kareem Fahim, "Death in Police Encounter Stirs Call for Change in Egypt," *New York Times*, July 18, 2010.

76. Robert I. Rotberg, "Nigeria: Elections and Continuing Challenges," Council on Foreign Relations, April 2007, www.cfr.org; Diamond, Linz, and Lipset, "Introduction: What Makes for Democracy?"

77. "China Vows to Clean Up Judiciary After Conviction of Supreme Court Vice President," *Xinhua News Agency*, March 11, 2010.

78. Freedom House, *Freedom in the World 2010*.

79. European Commission, "Turkey 2010 Progress Report," working document, www.ec.europa.eu; Arch Puddington, "Erosion of Freedom Intensifies," in Freedom House, *Freedom in the World 2010*.

80. Robert Dahl, *Democracy and Its Critics* (New Haven: Yale University Press, 1989).

81. Howard J. Wiarda and Harvey F. Kline, *An Introduction to Latin American Politics and Development* (Boulder: Westview, 2001); Sonia E. Alvarez, *Engendering Democracy in Brazil: Women's Movements in Transition Politics* (Princeton: Princeton University Press, 1990); Diamond, "Three Paradoxes of Democracy."

82. Diamond, "The Uncivic Society."

83. Diamond, Linz, and Lipset, "Introduction: What Makes for Democracy?"; Diamond, "The Uncivic Society."

84. Freedom House, *Freedom in the World 2010*.

85. Alvarez, *Engendering Democracy in Brazil;* United Nations Development Fund for Women (UNIFEM), *Democratic Governance 2010*, www.unifem.org; United Nations Statistics Division, *The World's Women 2010: Trends and Statistics*, www.unstats.un.org.

86. United Nations, *The Millennium Development Goals Report 2010*, www.un.org; United Nations Statistics Division, *The World's Women 2010*.

87. Abraham Lama, "Women Lawmakers Unite Behind Gender Issues," *Inter-Press Service*, September 13, 2001; Jane S. Jaquette, "Regional Differences and Contrasting Views," *Journal of Democracy* 12, no. 3 (July 2001).

88. Ricardo Hausmann, Laura D. Tyson, and Saadia Zahidi, *The Global Gender Gap Report 2010*, World Economic Forum, www.weforum.org.

89. Hausmann, Tyson, and Zahidi, *The Global Gender Gap Report 2010;* Didi Kirsten Tatlow, "Women Struggle for a Foothold in Chinese Politics," *New York Times*, June 24, 2010.

90. Alvarez, *Engendering Democracy in Brazil;* UNIFEM, "Justice," in *Progress of the World's Women 2008/2009*, www.unifem.org.

91. UNIFEM, "Justice."

92. Hausmann, Tyson, and Zahidi, *The Global Gender Gap Report 2010;* Amnesty International, "Mexico-Amnesty International Report 2009," www.amnesty.org.

93. Gilbert da Costa, "Nigerians Wonder: Could a Military Coup Help Us?"; Richard Joseph, "Economic Transformation and Developmental Governance in Nigeria: The Promise of the Obama Era," Brookings Institution, June 24, 2010, www.brookings.edu.

94. Charles Fromm, "US Seeks to Resume Indonesian Training," *Asia Times*, March 6, 2010.

95. Linz and Stepan, *Problems of Democratic Transition and Consolidation*.

Chapter 15
Political Transitions: Real or Virtual?

1. Celia W. Dugger, "Opposition Party to Join Zimbabwe's Government," *New York Times*, January 31, 2009.

2. Quoted in Jon Miller, "Presidential Candidates in Peru Complain of Harassment from Police," National Public Radio, *Morning Edition*, December 21, 1999.

3. Larry Diamond and Marc F. Plattner, "Introduction," in *The Global Resurgence of Democracy*, eds. Diamond and Plattner (Baltimore: Johns Hopkins University Press, 1993).

4. Adam Nossiter, "Ensconced in the Presidency: With No Budging in Ivory Coast," *New York Times*, December 26, 2010.

5. Freedom House, *Freedom in the World 2010*, www.freedomhouse.org; "Egypt's Opposition Protests, Challenging Legislative Vote," *Associated Press*, December 12, 2010.

6. Lionel Beeher, "Q&A: Iran's Waning Human Rights," *New York Times*, August 10, 2006; Reporters Without Borders, "Press Freedom Index 2010," www.rsf.org.

7. Emmanuel Sivan, "Illusions of Change," *Journal of Democracy* 11, no. 3 (July 2000).

8. Abraham McLaughlin, "With Party Win, Mugabe's Grip on Zimbabwe Tightens," *Christian Science Monitor*, April 4, 2005; "Mugabe Signs in a Successor Law," *BBC News*, November 1, 2007.

9. Sivan, "Illusions of Change"; Laith Kubba, "The Awakening of Civil Society," *Journal of Democracy* 11, no. 3 (July 2000).

10. Merilee Grindle, *Challenging the State: Crisis and Innovation in Latin America and Africa* (Cambridge: Cambridge University Press, 1996); Catherine Boone, "'Empirical Statehood' and Reconfigurations of Political Order," in *The African State at a Critical Juncture*, eds. Leonardo A. Villalon and Phillip A. Huxtable (Boulder: Lynne Rienner, 1998); Larry Diamond, Juan J. Linz, and Seymour Martin Lipset, "Introduction: What Makes for Democracy?" in *Politics in Developing Countries: Comparing Experiences with Democracy*, eds. Diamond, Linz, and Lipset (Boulder: Lynne Rienner, 1995).

11. Boone, "'Empirical Statehood.'"

12. Grindle, *Challenging the State;* Leonardo A. Villalon, "The African State at the End

of the Twentieth Century: Parameters of the Critical Juncture," in Villalon and Huxtable, *The African State at a Critical Juncture.*

13. Barry Bearak, "Court Ends Terrorism Case Against Zimbabwean Activist," *New York Times,* September 28, 2009; Freedom House, *Freedom in the World 2010.*

14. Freedom House, *Freedom in the World 2010.*

15. Michael Slackman, "Upstart in Iran Election Campaigns As Champion of Poor," *New York Times,* June 23, 2005.

16. Edward Wong, "China Leader Makes Debut in Great Wall of Facebook," *New York Times,* May 28, 2008; "Despite Not Having to Face Elections, China's Communist Party Wants to Be Liked," *Reuters,* June 12, 2008; "Is 'Grandpa Wen' As Nice As He Seems?" *The Economist,* August 15, 2010.

17. "Egypt's Opposition Protests," *Associated Press;* Thanassis Cambanis, "Succession Gives Army a Stiff Test in Egypt," *New York Times,* September 12, 2010.

18. "Mugabe's Party Sweeps to Victory," *BBC News,* April 2, 2005.

19. Andrew J. Nathan, "Present at the Stagnation," *Foreign Affairs* 85, no. 4 (July–August 2006); Nadja Kostka, "Devastating Earthquake in China Reveals Weak Construction Standards in Sichuan," Transparency International, July 2008, www.transparency.org.

20. "Zimbabwe's Mugable, 86, to Party Amid Distress," *Sunday Nation,* February 27, 2010.

21. Douglas A. Chalmers, "Corporatism and Comparative Politics," *New Directions in Comparative Politics,* ed. Howard J. Wiarda (Boulder: Westview, 1985); Roy C. Macridis and Steven R. Burg, *Introduction to Comparative Politics* (New York: HarperCollins, 1991).

22. "Tommy Suharto Freed from Prison," *BBC News,* October 30, 2006.

23. James Risen, "US Identifies Vast Mineral Riches in Afghanistan," *New York Times,* June 13, 2010; United Nations Office on Drugs and Crime (UNODC), "Corruption Widespread in Afghanistan, UNODC Survey Says," January 19, 2010, www.unodc.org; Mark Landler, "Envoy Says Corruption Helps Taliban Win Recruits," *New York Times,* July 28, 2010.

24. Christopher Walker and Sanja Tatic, "Corruption's Drag on Democratic States," *Christian Science Monitor,* August 2, 2006; Transparency International, "Corruption Perceptions Index 2010," www.transparency.org.

25. Phillip A. Huxtable, "The African State Toward the Twenty-First Century: Legacies of the Critical Juncture," in Villalon and Huxtable, *The African State at a Critical Juncture.*

26. Boone, "'Empirical Statehood.'"

27. Grindle, *Challenging the State.*

28. Roger Cohen, "Yes, Democracy Is Imperfect, Even in Those Places That Never Heard of Chads," *New York Times,* November 30, 2000.

29. "Systematic Cleansing in Zimbabwe," *Christian Science Monitor,* June 23, 2005.

30. Michael Slackman and Nicholas Kulish, "Iran Continues to Focus on Outside Provocateurs, Now Blaming Germany," *New York Times,* January 27, 2010.

31. Lucien O. Chauvin, "García Win in Peru a Loss for Venezuela's Chávez," *Christian Science Monitor,* June 6, 2006.

32. "Report: Mugabe Calls Top US Official 'An Idiot,'" *Associated Press,* July 7, 2009.

33. Howard J. Wiarda and Harvey F. Kline, *An Introduction to Latin American Politics and Development* (Boulder: Westview, 2001).

34. Freedom House, *Freedom in the World 2010.*

35. Wiarda and Kline, *An Introduction to Latin American Politics and Development.*

36. Nathan, "Present at the Stagnation."

37. "Watch List: Four Countries in Big Trouble," *Foreign Policy* (July–August 2010); "Delayed Explosion," *The Economist,* November 21, 2009; Robert I. Rotberg, "Disorder in the Ranks," *Foreign Policy* (July–August 2009).

38. Stuart E. Eizenstat, John Edward Porter, and Jeremy M. Weinstein, "Rebuilding Weak States," *Foreign Affairs* 84, no. 1 (January–February 2005).

39. I. William Zartman, "Introduction: Posing the Problem of State Collapse," in *Collapsed States: The Disintegration and Restoration of Legitimate Authority,* ed. I. William Zartman (Boulder: Lynne Rienner, 1995).

40. Larry Diamond, "Is the Third Wave Over?" *Journal of Democracy* 7, no. 3 (July 1996); Guillermo O'Donnell, "Delegative Democracy," *Journal of Democracy* 5, no. 1 (January 1994); Diamond and Plattner, "Introduction."

41. Juan J. Linz and Alfred Stepan, *Problems of Democratic Transition and Consolidation: Southern Europe, South America, and Post-Communist Europe* (Baltimore: Johns Hopkins University Press, 1996).

42. Monte Palmer, *Comparative Politics: Political Economy, Political Culture, and Political Independence* (Itasca, IL: F. E. Peacock, 1997); Zartman, "Introduction: Posing the Problem of State Collapse."

43. Andrew J. Nathan, *China's Transition* (New York: Columbia University Press, 1997).

44. Bernd Debusmann, "Among Top US Fears: A Failed Mexican State," *New York Times,* January 9, 2009.

45. Ernest Aryeetey, "Can Nigeria Fail?" Brookings Institution, June 24, 2010, www.brookings.edu; "The Failed States Index 2010," *Foreign Policy,* n.d., www.foreignpolicy.com.

46. Diamond and Plattner, "Introduction."

47. Diamond, Linz, and Lipset, "Introduction: What Makes for Democracy?"; Villalon, "The African State at the End of the Twentieth Century"; Julius E. Nyang'oro and Timothy M. Shaw, "The African State in the Global Economic Context," in Villalon and Huxtable, *The African State at a Critical Juncture.*

Chapter 16
Linking Concepts and Cases

1. Daniel C. Levy and Kathleen Bruhn, "Mexico: Sustained Civilian Rule Without Democracy," in *Politics in Developing Countries: Comparing Experiences with Democracy,* eds. Larry Diamond, Juan J. Linz, and Seymour Martin Lipset (Boulder: Lynne Rienner, 1995).

2. Jorge G. Castañeda, "A Way to Peace in Mexico," *New York Times,* September 6, 2006.

3. Enrique Krauze, "Furthering Democracy in Mexico," *Foreign Affairs* 85, no. 1 (January–February 2006), pp. 54–65.

4. "Rising Violence, Fading Hopes," *The Economist,* July 10, 2010.

5. Luis Rubio and Jeffrey Davidow, "Mexico's Disputed Election," *Foreign Affairs* 85, no. 5 (September–October 2006); Marla Dickerson, "A Free Market Man for Mexico," *Los Angeles Times,* July 16, 2006; Elisabeth Malkin, "In Mexican Vote, Nostalgia for Past Corruption," *New York Times,* July 6, 2009.

6. Marc Lacey, "Mexican Democracy, Even Under Siege," *New York Times,* July 5, 2010.

7. Enrique Krauze, "An Anti-Incumbency Wave—in Mexico," *New York Times,* July 6, 2010.

8. "Peru's Presidential Election: The Known Against the Unknown," *The Economist,* June 3, 2006.

9. Washington Office on Latin America, "Deconstructing Democracy: Peru Under Alberto Fujimori," February 2000, www.wola.org.

10. Cynthia McClintock and Abraham Lowenthal, foreword, *The Peruvian Labyrinth: Polity, Society, Economy,* eds. Maxwell A. Cameron and Philip Mauceri (University Park: Pennsylvania State University Press, 1997).

11. David Scott Palmer, "Democracy and Its Discontents in Fujimori's Peru," *Current History,* February 2000; "Peru's Leader Tackles Crisis by Asking Ministers to Quit," *The Australian,* August 13, 2005.

12. Gonzalo Ruiz Tovar, "Toledo's Biggest Achievement Was Survival As Peru's Leader," *Deutsche Presse-Agentur,* July 27, 2006.

13. Ibid.

14. "A Murky Democratic Dawn in Post-Fujimori Peru," *The Economist,* April 7, 2001; David Gonzalez, "New Chance for Peru's Chief to Take Reins," *New York Times,* January 13, 2002; "Peru's New Government: Teething Troubles," *The Economist,* December 8, 2001; Steven Levitsky and Cynthia Sanborn, "A Hard Choice in Peru," *New York Times,* May 9, 2001; Ernesto García Calderón, "Peru's Decade of Living Dangerously," *Journal of Democracy* 12, no. 2 (April 2001).

15. Simon Romero, "Leading Again, Peru's President Still Unpopular," *New York Times,* August 27, 2010.

16. "Peru Politics: Presidential Field Widens," *The Economist,* November 10, 2010; Dan Collyns, "Why Peru's Traditional Political Parties Are Losing Ground," *BBC News,* October 27, 2010.

17. "Peru Politics: Presidential Field Widens," *The Economist,* November 10, 2010; Terry Wade and Marco Aquino, "Analysis: Peru Voters Shying Away from Adventure," *Reuters,* December 9, 2010; "Leading Peru Election Candidates Lose Ground," *Reuters,* March 13, 2011.

18. Larry Diamond, "The Uncivic Society and the Descent into Praetorianism," in Diamond, Linz, and Lipset, *Politics in Developing Countries.*

19. Craig Timberg, "Hope Tempered by Skepticism As Nigeria Faces Historic Vote," *Washington Post,* November 13, 2006.

20. Freedom House, *Freedom in the World 2005.*

21. Craig Timberg, "Support for Democracy Seen Falling in Africa," *Washington Post,* May 25, 2006.

22. "Nigerian Vice-President Vows to Pursue Presidential Quest," *BBC News,* November 13, 2006.

23. Jean Herskovits, "Nigeria's Rigged Democracy," *Foreign Affairs* 86, no. 4 (July–August 2007); Adam Nossiter, "Ruling Party in Nigeria Is Fractured by Infighting," *New York Times,* April 23, 2010.

24. Olumide Taiwo, "Challenges and Possibilities for Progress in Nigeria," Brookings Institution, June 24, 2010, www.brookings.edu; Richard Joseph and Alexandra Gillies, "Nigeria's Season of Uncertainty," *Current History,* May 2010; Gilbert da Costa, "Is Goodluck Jonathan the Answer to Nigeria's Woes?" *Time,* February 13, 2010.

25. Celia W. Dugger and Barry Bearak, "Mugabe Sworn to Sixth Term After Victory in One-Candidate Runoff," *New York Times,* June 20, 2008.

26. Celia W. Dugger, "Opposition Party to Join Zimbabwe's Government," *New York Times,* January 31, 2009.

27. "Zimbabwe: Power-Sharing for Bankrupt Beginners," *Africa Confidential* 50, no. 3 (February 6, 2009); Celia W. Dugger, "Rift Endangers Power-Sharing Deal in Zimbabwe," *New York Times,* October 10, 2010.

28. "Crime and Amnesty," *Africa Confidential* 50, no. 10 (May 15, 2009); Celia W. Dugger, "Fears Growing of an Iron Grip over Zimbabwe," *New York Times,* December 26, 2010.

29. "Opinion: Mugabe Prepares for Violent Campaign," *Globalpost,* November 13, 2010, www.globalpost.com; "Zimbabwe: AU Proposes Elections in 2013," *Zimbabwe Independent,* January 27, 2011.

30. Dugger, "Rift Endangers Power-Sharing Deal in Zimbabwe."

31. "Opinion: Mugabe Prepares for Violent Campaign," *Globalpost.*

32. "Shadows of Uncertainty," *The Economist,* June 10, 2006, p. 85. The article reviews Ali Gheissari and Vali Nasr's book *Democracy in Iran: History and the Quest for Liberty* (New York: Oxford, 2006).

33. Scott Peterson, "Iran Opens Door—a Little—to US," *Christian Science Monitor,* February 25, 2000.

34. Ali Alfoneh, "What If There Were Free Elections in Iran?" *National Review Online,* January 5, 2010, www.nationalreview.com.

35. Reza Afshari, "A Historic Moment in Iran," *Human Rights Quarterly* 31, no. 4 (November 2009), p. 843.

36. Mehrangiz Kar, "Reformist Islam Versus Radical Islam in Iran," Working Paper no. 4 (Washington, DC: Brookings Project on US Relations with the Islamic World, November 2010), p. 1.

37. Gheissari and Nasr, *Democracy in Iran,* pp. 147–148.

38. For discussion along these lines, see Michael Thumann, "Turkey's Role Reversals," *Wilson Quarterly* (Summer 2010), p. 33.

39. Carol Migdalovitz, "Turkey's 2007 Elections: Crisis of Identity and Power," *Congressional Research Service,* July 11, 2007, p. 5.

40. Simon Cameron-Moore, "Turkey Referendum Win Boosts Erdogan for 2011 Election," *Reuters,* September 13, 2010.

41. Michael Thumann, "Turkey's Role Reversals," *Wilson Quarterly* (Summer 2010), p. 33.

42. "China's Government Has Evolved, but Has Its Government?" *PBS Newshour*, December 10, 2010.

43. Quentin Sommerville, "Power Play Brings Down Shanghai Boss," *BBC News*, September 25, 2006.

44. "40 percent of All Business Bribes in Construction Sector: SPP," *Xinhua News Agency*, September 3, 2009.

45. Kevin J. O'Brien and Lianjiang Li, *Rightful Resistance in Rural China* (New York: Cambridge University Press, 2006).

46. Maria Yue Zhang and Bruce W. Stening, *China 2.0: The Transformation of an Emerging Superpower—and the New Opportunities* (Singapore: Wiley, 2010).

47. Prime Minister Wen Jiabao, interviewed by Fareed Zakaria on CNN's *Global Public Square*, October 3, 2010.

48. "Indonesia's Future: A Golden Opportunity," *The Economist*, September 10, 2009.

49. Philip Bowring, "Waking Up to Indonesia," *New York Times*, July 23, 2010.

50. Nelly van Doorn-Harder and R. Michael Feener, "Indonesia," in *Muslim Cultures Today: A Reference Guide*, ed. Kathryn M. Coughlin (Westport: Greenwood, 2006), p. 86.

51. Hannah Beech, "Indonesia Elections: A Win for Democracy," *Time*, July 8, 2009.

52. "Obituary: Ex-President Suharto of Indonesia," *BBC News*, January 27, 2008.

53. "Indonesia Fights Corruption with People Power," *BBC News*, November 6, 2009.

54. "SBY's Feet of Clay," *The Economist*, October 21, 2010.

55. Lucy Williamson, "Aceh Votes for Major Change," *BBC News*, December 12, 2006; "Aceh Frontrunner Praises Election," *BBC News*, December 12, 2006.

56. "Indonesia: Fraying at the Edges," *The Economist*, August 21, 1999, p. 33.

57. Christen Broecker, "Indonesia's Democracy Still on Shaky Ground," Human Rights Watch, May 19, 2010, www.hrw.org.

58. Endy M. Bayuni, "Commentary: SBY, the President Who Didn't Mess It Up," *Jakarta Post*, October 16, 2010, quoted in "SBY's Feet of Clay," *The Economist*.

Chapter 17
Sovereignty and the Role of International Organizations

1. This perspective is based largely on the views on "new regionalism" expressed by Sheila Page in her book *Regionalism Among Developing Countries* (New York: St. Martin's, 2000), pp. 5–6.

2. Michael Hirsh, "Calling All Regio-Cops: Peacekeeping's Hybrid Future," *Foreign Affairs* 79, no. 6 (November–December 2000).

3. Page, *Regionalism Among Developing Countries*.

4. Carol B. Thompson, "Beyond the Nation-State? Democracy in Regional Economic Context," in *Democracy and Socialism in Africa*, eds. Robin Cohen and Harry Goulbourne (Boulder: Westview, 1991).

5. Trade Law Centre for Southern Africa, "SADC's Free Trade Area Slow to Pick Up," January 12, 2010, www.tralac.org.

6. Page, *Regionalism Among Developing Countries*.

7. Mary Beth Sheridan, "For US and OAS, New Challenges to Latin American Democracy," *Washington Post*, July 6, 2009.

8. Paul Reynolds, "African Union Replaces Dictators' Club," *BBC News*, July 8, 2002.

9. Rob Watson, "What Makes a Good UN Secretary-General?" *BBC News*, October 2, 2006.

10. Because much of the world did not recognize the Communist Party's leadership of the People's Republic of China on the mainland, the "China seat" was occupied by the Nationalist Party, which operated from Taiwan after its loss to the Communist Party in 1949. The Taiwanese government of the Republic of China occupied this position until 1971, when the People's Republic first joined the United Nations.

11. Data compiled from http://globalpolicy.org/security-council/tables-and-charts-on-the-security-council-0-82/use-of-the-veto.html (accessed March 24, 2011). The total number

of vetoes cast by the current representative of the China seat in the United Nations, the People's Republic of China, is only five, with their first veto being cast in 1972. The sixth veto credited to the Chinese delegation was registered by the Republic of China (Taiwan).

12. "Thinking the UNthinkable," *The Economist,* November 13, 2010.

13. Ibid.

14. "Panel to Recommend Simplified UN," *BBC News,* November 8, 2006.

15. United Nations Department of Peacekeeping Operations, "Fact Sheet: United Nations Peacekeeping," January 2011, www.un.org.

16. Center on International Cooperation, *Annual Review of Global Peace Operations 2010* (Boulder: Lynne Rienner, 2010), p. 3.

17. Irwan Firdaus, "Three E. Timorese Sentenced in Deaths of Aid Workers," *Associated Press,* May 5, 2001.

18. US officials claim that Washington has paid in full, although UN officials contest this. See "UN Official: US Is $1.2 Billion in Arrears at UN," *Reuters,* October 14, 2010. Part of the challenge is found in "contested arrears"—monies that Washington disagrees it owes to the organization. Another reason why figures may be contradictory at times is that the PKO budget is often left out of the full UN budget, since missions are approved and financed on a case-by-case basis.

19. "Transcript: Can the UN Keep the Peace?" *PBS Now,* May 15, 2009.

20. "Haiti Cholera Investigation Announced by United Nations," *BBC News,* December 17, 2010.

21. Jeffrey Gettleman, "Frenzy of Rape in Congo Reveals UN Weakness," *New York Times,* October 3, 2010.

22. Ibid.

23. Ibid.

24. Francis Mading Deng, "State Collapse: : The Humanitarian Challenge to the UN," in *Collapsed States: The Disintegration and Restoration of Legitimate Authority,* ed. I. William Zartman (Boulder: Lynne Rienner, 1995).

25. Olivia Ward, "United Nations 'Army' Proposed," *Toronto Star,* June 15, 2006.

26. "Clinton to UN: Learn to Say No," *Miami Herald,* September 28, 1993. These statements, before the Rwandan genocide, were the basis for Presidential Directive no. 25, which was used to rationalize US inaction in Rwanda.

27. The number of Hutu killed during the civil war, genocide, and years that followed in Congo is less clear, with estimates varying between 10,000 and 100,000. Yet not all of these Hutu were killed by the Rwandan Patriotic Front (RPF) or the RPF-dominated Rwandan army; many moderate Hutu were singled out as traitors by the Hutu government and its supporters. Alan J. Kuperman, "Rwanda in Retrospect," *Foreign Affairs* 79, no. 1 (January–February 2000). See also Ian Martin, "Hard Choices After Genocide: Human Rights and Political Failures in Rwanda," in *Hard Choices: Moral Dilemmas in Humanitarian Intervention,* ed. Jonathan Moore (Lanham: Rowman and Littlefield, 1998).

28. William Shawcross, *Deliver Us from Evil* (New York: Simon and Schuster, 2000), cited in *The Economist,* May 13, 2000.

29. "Darfur Violence Becoming a Forgotten War," *CNN News,* December 10, 2009.

30. Elizabeth Dickinson, "Postcards from Hell: Images from the World's Most Failed States," *Foreign Policy* (July–August 2010).

31. Mary Kaldor, "Humanitarian Intervention: A Forum," *The Nation,* May 8, 2000. In this piece, Kaldor argues that "a genuine humanitarian intervention is much more like policing than warfighting or traditional peacekeeping." See also Mary Kaldor, *New and Old Wars: Organized Violence in a Global Era* (Stanford: Stanford University Press, 1999).

32. These two opposing views are expressed by Mahmood Mamdani in "Humanitarian Intervention: A Forum," *The Nation,* May 8, 2000.

33. Ibrahim A. Gambari, "The Role of Foreign Intervention in African Reconstruction," in Zartman, *Collapsed States.*

34. Karen A. Mingst and Margaret P. Karns, *The United Nations in the 21st Century,* 3rd ed. (Boulder: Westview, 2007).

35. Nitza Berkovitch, "The Emergence and Transformation of the International Women's Movement," in *Constructing World Culture: International Nongovernmental Organizations*

Since 1875, eds. John Boli and George M. Thomas (Stanford: Stanford University Press, 1999).

36. Waxhma Frogh, "CEDAW Ratification Would Be a Triumph for Afghan Women," *The Hill,* November 17, 2010. Frogh, an Afghani activist, provided testimony before the US Senate Judiciary subcommittee hearing on CEDAW ratification, stating, "The US failure to ratify CEDAW is of huge international significance."

37. Richard J. Goldstone, "Bringing War Criminals to Justice During an Ongoing War," in Moore, *Hard Choices.*

38. Martin, "Hard Choices After Genocide," p. 159.

39. "Accused Online: The Rwanda Genocide Trial," *The Economist,* February 10, 2001.

40. "Trial in Belgium Against Four Rwandans for War Crimes," National Public Radio, *Morning Edition,* April 30, 2001.

41. "War Crimes Tribunal in The Hague Establishes Sexual Enslavement As a Crime Against Humanity," National Public Radio, *All Things Considered,* February 22, 2001.

42. Craig Timberg, "Impunity on Trial in Africa," *Washington Post,* May 2, 2006.

43. Robert I. Rotberg and Dennis Thompson, eds., *Truth v. Justice: The Morality of Truth Commissions* (Princeton: Princeton University Press, 2000).

44. This is a dominant perspective expressed by many, although not all, of the contributors to the Rotberg and Thompson collection on truth commissions, *Truth v. Justice.* See also Priscilla B. Hayner, *Unspeakable Truths: Confronting State Terror and Atrocity* (New York: Routledge, 2001).

45. Colum Lynch, "UN Struggles to Prove Its Relevance," *Washington Post,* September 19, 2010.

46. Interview with Stewart M. Patrick, "Crisis of Relevance at the UN," Council on Foreign Relations, September 20, 2010, www.cfr.org (accessed March 24, 2011).

47. Lynch, "UN Struggles to Prove Its Relevance."

48. "When Is a Refugee Not a Refugee?" *The Economist,* March 3, 2001.

49. Martha Finnemore, "Rules of War and Wars of Rules: The International Red Cross and the Restraint of State Violence," in Boli and Thomas, *Constructing World Culture.*

50. Lucie Morillon and Jean-François Julliard, "Enemies of the Internet: Countries Under Surveillance," Reporters Without Borders, March 12, 2010, www.rsf.org, p. 2.

51. On the role of NGOs in the United Nations, see Karen A. Mingst and Margaret P. Karns, *The United Nations in the Post–Cold War Era* (Boulder: Westview, 1995), p. 77.

52. "When Is a Refugee Not a Refugee?" *The Economist.*

53. Helene Cooper, "Spielberg Drops Out As Adviser to Beijing Olympics in Dispute over Darfur Conflict," *New York Times,* February 13, 2008.

54. Courtney B. Smith, *Politics and Process at the United Nations: The Global Dance* (Boulder: Lynne Rienner, 2006), p. 278.

Chapter 18
Global Challenges—and Responses

1. "Maldives President: 'You Cannot Cut a Deal with Mother Nature,'" *BBC HardTalk,* December 6, 2010.

2. "Where There's Smoke," *The Economist,* October 28, 2010.

3. United Nations, "World Population to Exceed 9 Billion by 2050," press release, March 11, 2009, p. 1, www.un.org/esa/population.

4. Andrew C. Revkin, "The Climate Divide: Rich Nations Find It Easier to Adapt," *New York Times,* April 2, 2007. See also "Developing Countries and Global Warming: A Bad Climate for Development," *The Economist,* September 17, 2009.

5. "Indonesia Pledges Two-Year Deforestation Moratorium," *BBC News,* May 27, 2010.

6. "Owners of Ethos Trying to Provide Clean Drinking Water to People in the Third World Who Lack It," National Public Radio, *Day to Day,* January 18, 2005.

7. Integrated Regional Information Networks (United Nations), "Water Is Running Out: How Inevitable Are International Conflicts?" *World Press Review,* October 23, 2006.

8. Cited in Keith Bradsher, "China Fears Warming Effects of a Rising Consumer Class," *New York Times,* July 5, 2010.

9. Damian Kahya, "Global Warming Talks Just Hot Air?" *BBC News,* December 3, 2010.

10. John M. Broder, "Many Goals Remain Unmet in 5 Nations' Climate Deal," *New York Times,* December 18, 2009.

11. Mark Lynas, "How Do I Know China Wrecked the Copenhagen Deal? I Was in the Room," *The Guardian Online,* December 22, 2009, www.guardian.co.uk.

12. Achim Steiner, "Viewpoint: Cancún Can-Do," *BBC News,* December 21, 2010. Steiner is the executive director of the United Nations Environment Programme.

13. "The Cancún Climate-Change Conference: A Sort of Progress," *The Economist,* December 16, 2010.

14. Juliet Eilperin, "Experts Call for Protecting Sites in Asia to Ensure the Survival of the Tiger," *Washington Post,* September 14, 2010.

15. Sebastian Rotella, "Sharp Rise in Chinese Arrests at US Border," *Los Angeles Times,* October 5, 2009.

16. Sheldon Zhang and Ko-lin Chin, "Characteristics of Chinese Human Smugglers," US Department of Justice, Office of Justice Programs, August 2004, pp. 6–7, www.ncjrs.gov.

17. "Wahid Wanders While Borneo Burns," *The Economist,* March 3, 2001.

18. Office of the United Nations High Commissioner for Refugees, *The State of the World's Refugees 2006: Human Displacement in the New Millennium* (New York: Oxford University Press, 2006), pp. 65–66.

19. Merrill Smith, ed., "Warehousing Refugees: A Denial of Rights, a Waste of Humanity," in *World Refugee Survey 2004* (Washington, DC: US Committee for Refugees and Immigrants), www.uscrirefugees.org.

20. Doctors Without Borders, "Uprooted by Violence and Persecution, 33 Million People Worldwide Face Continued Insecurity and Precarious Living Conditions," press release, September 6, 2006, www.msf.org.

21. Merrill Smith, ed., *World Refugee Survey 2006,* p. 14, www.uscrirefugees.org.

22. United Nations Office on Drugs and Crime, "Human Trafficking FAQs," www.unodc.org.

23. M. P. Nunan, "Haiti Protects Its Border Against Post-Earthquake Child Trafficking," United Nations Children's Fund, October 15, 2010, www.unicef.org.

24. United Nations Commission on Sustainable Development, "Health and Sustainable Development: Report of the Secretary-General," World Summit on Social Development, April 30–May 2, 2001, p. 5, www.un.org/esa/dsd.

25. World Health Organization, "Ten Things You Need to Know About Pandemic Influenza," October 14, 2005, www.who.org.

26. Robert A. Guth, "Gates Rethinks His War on Polio," *Wall Street Journal,* April 23, 2010.

27. "Groups Take Aim at Tuberculosis," National Public Radio, *Morning Edition,* March 8, 2006.

28. "'Virtually Untreatable' TB Found," *BBC News,* September 6, 2006.

29. Cited in "Groups Take Aim at Tuberculosis," National Public Radio.

30. "HIV Epidemic 'Halted,' Says UN," *BBC News,* November 23, 2010.

31. "Unhappy Anniversary," *The Economist,* June 3, 2006, p. 24.

32. "AIDS 'Key Cause of Female Death,'" *BBC News,* March 3, 2010.

33. "Preventing Mother-to-Child Transmission of HIV," *Avert,* November 6, 2006, www.avert.org.

34. Nancy van Itallie, "Health," in *A Global Agenda: Issues Before the Fifty-fourth General Assembly of the United Nations,* eds. John Tessitore and Susan Woolfson (Lanham: Rowman and Littlefield, 1999). Van Itallie states that this revelation led to the first health-related resolution in the Security Council, sponsored by Richard Holbrooke, for "voluntary and confidential testing and counseling" of UN peacekeepers.

35. World Health Organization, "Diarrheal Disease," Fact Sheet no. 330, August 2009, www.who.org.

36. Celia W. Dugger, "Toilets Underused to Fight Disease, UN Study Finds," *New York Times,* November 10, 2006.

37. Duff Wilson, "Cigarette Giants in a Global Fight on Tighter Rules," *New York Times,* November 14, 2010, p. 6.

38. Ibid.

39. Ibid.

40. Geoffrey Cowley, "The Life of a Virus Hunter," *Newsweek,* May 15, 2006, p. 63.

41. Cited in Bill Saporito, "The Jeff Sachs Contradiction: Celebrity Economist," *Time,* March 14, 2005, p. 49.

42. Paul Bracken, "The Second Nuclear Age," *Foreign Affairs* 79, no. 1 (January–February 2000). See also Paul Bracken, *Fire in the East: The Rise of Asian Military Power and the Second Nuclear Age* (New York: HarperCollins, 1999).

43. Bracken, "The Second Nuclear Age."

44. Quoted in the presentation speech for the 2005 Nobel Peace Prize, delivered by Ole Danbolt Mjøs, chairman of the Norwegian Nobel Committee, December 10, 2005, http://nobelprize.org.

45. "Q&A: Iran Nuclear Issue," *BBC World News,* December 8, 2010.

46. John Pomfret, "Chinese Firms Bypass Sanctions on Iran, US Says," *Washington Post,* October 18, 2010.

47. Ibid.

48. Andres Oppenheimer, "Just What Latin America Needed—a New Arms Race," *Oppenheimer Report,* September 17, 2006; Sam Logan, "Russia's Race to Arm the Americas," *ISN Security Watch,* January 12, 2006, www.isn.ethz.ch.

49. See www.oneworld.org/guides/landmines.info.html.

50. For a detailed account of the ICBL treaty, see Maxwell A. Cameron, Robert J. Lawson, and Brian W. Tomlin, eds., *To Walk Without Fear: The Global Movement to Ban Landmines* (New York: Oxford University Press, 1998).

51. "Record Area Cleared of Landmines," *BBC News,* September 13, 2006.

52. "Controlling Deadly Trade," *Christian Science Monitor,* June 26, 1998.

53. Ibid.

Chapter 19
Linking Concepts and Cases

1. "Fox Announces 'More Dynamic' International Role for Mexico," *EFE News Service,* January 6, 2001.

2. Ginger Thompson, "Mexico and Peru Withdraw Ambassadors from Cuba," *New York Times,* May 3, 2004.

3. "Mexico: Stop the Climate Change Blame Game," *CBS News,* December 1, 2010; William Booth, "Mexico Seeks Leading Role in Climate Policy," *Washington Post,* November 28, 2010; Jo Tuckman, "Can Felipe Calderón Make Mexico a Leader in Combating Climate Change?" *The Guardian* (London), June 24, 2009; Jan Burck, Christoph Bals, and Verena Rossow, "Climate Change Performance Index 2010," *Germanwatch,* December 2009, www.germanwatch.org.

4. "ICJ Announces Date for Peru, Chile Rebuttals over Maritime Dispute," *Peruvian Times,* April 30, 2010.

5. G. Van Der Ree, "Chile's (Inter)National Identities: Framing the Relations with Bolivia and Peru," *Bulletin of Latin American Research* 29, no. 2 (2010).

6. Lucien Chauvin, "Peru Sees Shadowy Hand of Chávez, Everywhere," *Christian Science Monitor,* April 3, 2008.

7. Gabriel Marcella and Richard Downes, *Introduction to Security Cooperation in the Western Hemisphere: Resolving the Ecuador-Peru Conflict,* eds. Gabriel Marcella and Richard Downes (Boulder: Lynne Rienner, 1999); Monica Herz and João Pontes Nogueira, *Ecuador v. Peru: Peacemaking Amid Rivalry* (Boulder: Lynne Rienner, 2002); Ronald Bruce St. John, *The Foreign Policy of Peru* (Boulder: Lynne Rienner, 1992).

8. "Peru Slates 'Needless' Arms Spending in Latin America," *United Press International,* May 19, 2010, www.upi.com.

9. Okon Akiba, *Nigerian Foreign Policy Towards Africa: Continuity and Change* (New York: Peter Lang, 1998).

10. Jean Herskovits, "Nigeria's Rigged Democracy," *Foreign Affairs* 86, no. 4 (July–August 2007); Leonard H. Robinson Jr., "Clinton Visit Raises Hopes for Nigeria," *Chicago Sun-Times,* August 27, 2000.

11. Herskovits, "Nigeria's Rigged Democracy."

12. Richard Joseph and Alexandra Gillies, "Nigeria's Season of Uncertainty," *Current History,* May 2010; John Campbell, "Examining the US-Nigerian Relationship in a Time of Transition," US Senate Committee on Foreign Affairs, Subcommittee on African Affairs, February 23, 2010.

13. Andrew Meldrum and Jonathan Watts, "China Gives Zimbabwe Economic Lifeline," *The Guardian* (London), June 16, 2006.

14. Andrew Meldrum, "Africa Needs More Courage, Says Mugabe," *The Guardian* (London), February 21, 2006.

15. Greg Mills and Jeffrey Herbst, "Bring Zimbabwe in from the Cold," *New York Times,* May 28, 2009; "Zimbabwe's Mugabe in Diamond Export Threat," *BBC News,* February 17, 2010.

16. Christina Lamb, "Mugabe: Why Africa Applauds Him," *New Statesman,* August 7, 2006.

17. Celia W. Dugger, "Opposition Party to Join Zimbabwe's Government," *New York Times,* January 31, 2009; Dumisani Muleya, "Zimbabwe: Biti Sets Up Fund for 2011 Elections," *Zimbabwe Independent,* November 25, 2010.

18. "Africa to Press for End to Zimbabwe Sanctions," *New York Times,* September 7, 2009.

19. John Simpson, "Iran's Growing Regional Influence," *BBC News,* September 20, 2006.

20. Vali Nasr, *The Shia Revival: How Conflicts Within Islam Will Shape the Future* (New York: Norton, 2006), pp. 241–250.

21. "Economic Squeeze Made Iran Accept Peace," *United Press International,* July 19, 1995.

22. "Iraq: What Iran and Syria Want," *BBC News,* November 13, 2006.

23. Cited in Simpson, "Iran's Growing Regional Influence."

24. "All Still to Play For," *The Economist,* January 21, 2006, p. 46.

25. Quoted in Jay Solomon and Farnaz Fassihi, "Iran Rights Envoy Assails UN Censure," *Wall Street Journal,* November 19, 2010.

26. Quoted in Elaine Sciolino, "Iranian President Paints a Picture of Peace and Moderation," *New York Times,* September 22, 1998.

27. Louis Charbonneau, "UN Committee Slams Iran over Human Rights Record," *Reuters,* November 18, 2010.

28. Quoted in Jonathan Head, "Keeping Turkey Focused on EU Challenge," *BBC News,* September 16, 2010.

29. Heinz Kramer, *A Changing Turkey: The Challenge to Europe and the United States* (Washington, DC: Brookings Institution, 2000).

30. Ahmet Davutoglu, "Turkey's Zero-Problems Foreign Policy," *Foreign Policy* (May 20, 2010).

31. This argument was presented by the Turkish Minister of Foreign Affairs. See Davutoglu, "Turkey's Zero-Problems Foreign Policy."

32. Quoted in Blake Hounshell, "Mr. 'Zero Problems,'" *Foreign Policy: Top 100 Global Thinkers,* December 2010.

33. "Japan Defence Review Warns of China's Military Might," *BBC News,* December 17, 2010.

34. Sarah A Topol, "Q&A: Why China Has Become the Middle's East's Favorite Customer," *Christian Science Monitor,* July 13, 2010.

35. Tim Luard, "Buyers Line up for China's Arms," *BBC News,* June 16, 2006.

36. Ibid.

37. "Responsible China?" *Washington Post,* September 6, 2006.

38. J. Mohan Malik, "Security Council Reform: China Signals Its Veto," *World Policy Journal* (Spring 2005), pp. 20–21.

39. Quoted in "Indonesia's Place in the Global Jungle," *The Economist,* March 31, 2010.

40. Quoted in Marwaan Macan-Markar, "Indonesia: Saying No, Thank You, to IMF Loans," *Inter-Press Service,* November 26, 2008.

41. Ann Marie Murphy, "Indonesia and the World," in *Indonesia: The Great Transition,* ed. John Bresnan (Lanham: Rowman and Littlefield, 2005), p. 278.

42. Slobodan Lekic, "Suharto Avoids International Tribunal," *Associated Press,* March 28, 2006.

43. "Indonesia's Place in the Global Jungle," *The Economist.*

Chapter 20
Dealing with a Superpower: Views of the United States

1. "Thinking the UNthinkable," *The Economist,* November 13, 2010.

2. Fareed Zakaria, "The Rise of the Rest," *Newsweek,* May 3, 2008.

3. Moises Naim, "The Havana Obsession: Why All Eyes Are on a Bankrupt Island," *Newsweek,* June 12, 2009.

4. Quoted in Kim Ghattas, "US Gets Serious on Iran Sanctions," *BBC News,* August 3, 2010.

5. Karl E. Meyer, "America Unlimited: The Radical Sources of the Bush Doctrine," *World Policy Journal* (Spring 2004), p. 5; "The International Criminal Court: For Us or Against Us?" *The Economist,* November 22, 2003, p. 27.

6. "The Dangers of a Rising China," *The Economist,* December 2, 2010.

7. Quoted in Fareed Zakaria, *The Post-American World* (New York: Norton, 2008), p. 35.

8. Quoted in Waxhma Frogh, "CEDAW Ratification Would Be a Triumph for Afghan Women," *The Hill,* November 17, 2010. Afghanistan ratified CEDAW in 2003 and Qatar became the most recent state to ratify, in 2009.

9. Molly Moore and Peter Finn, "Around the Globe, Relief over US Vote," *Washington Post,* November 10, 2006.

10. "Obama More Popular Abroad Than at Home, Global Image of US Continues to Benefit," *Pew Global Attitudes Project,* June 17, 2010.

11. Quoted in Toby Harnden, "Barack Obama in Turkey: US 'Will Never Be at War with Islam,'" *The Telegraph* (London), April 6, 2009.

12. It has not been unusual for US presidents and other powerful members of their administrations to announce paradigms for US foreign policy. In the 1820s, James Monroe argued (in what later became known as the Monroe Doctrine) that the United States should limit European expansion into the Western Hemisphere, straining relations with Europe, and announced the United States as the "protector" of the Americas. The Truman Doctrine was used throughout the Cold War to contain totalitarian, namely communist, regimes. In the 1980s, Ronald Reagan challenged the legitimacy of nondemocratic, especially communist, regimes and proclaimed both the right and the responsibility of the United States to provide assistance to movements that challenge them. The Powell Doctrine (named for former chairman of the Joint Chiefs of Staff and former secretary of state Colin Powell) stated that US troops should enter battle only with decisive force and clear objectives (it was actually an idea promoted by Secretary of Defense Casper Weinberger).

13. "China Berates Bush for 'Axis of Evil,'" *Reuters World Report,* January 31, 2002; Jefferson Morley, "'Axis of Evil' Worries Friends and Foes Alike," *Washington Post,* February 1, 2002; Thomas E. Ricks, "European Security Leaders Alarmed by Bush's Stance: US Officials in Munich Stress Urgency of Anti-Terror Initiative," *Washington Post,* February 3, 2002; Thomas L. Friedman, "Crazier Than Thou," *New York Times,* February 13, 2002.

14. See Ray Takeyh, *Hidden Iran: Paradox and Power in the Islamic Republic* (New York: Holt, 2006), especially pp. 117–130.

15. Cited in Glen Kessler, "Clinton Declares 'New Moment' in US Foreign Policy in Speech," *Washington Post,* September 9, 2010.

16. Ahmet Davutoglu, "Turkey's Zero-Problems Foreign Policy," *Foreign Policy* (May 20, 2010).

17. See Zakaria, *The Post-American World,* especially chap. 15; James Fallows, *Postcards from Tomorrow Square* (New York: Vintage, 2008), especially chap. 7.

18. Zakaria, *Post-American World,* p. 1.

19. Fareed Zakaria, "Why Do They Hate Us? The Politics of Rage," *Newsweek,* October 15, 2001.

20. Richard Wike and Jacob Poushter, "Obama's Middle East Problem," *Pew Global Attitudes Project,* August 27, 2010.

21. "The Outlook for China," roundtable convened at the Brookings Institution, Washington, DC, March 18, 2010, p. 31.

22. Geoffrey Murray, *China: The Next Superpower—Dilemmas in Change and Continuity* (New York: St. Martin's, 1998).

23. Cited in Ross Terrill, "What If China Fails? The Case for Selective Failure," *Wilson Quarterly* (Autumn 2010), p. 56.

24. John Hudson, "Americans Think China Has the World's Largest Economy," *The Atlantic Wire,* December 10, 2010.

25. See the interesting exchange between Ross Terrill and David M. Lampton in the Autumn 2010 edition of *Wilson Quarterly.*

26. Jacques Martin, *When China Rules the World: The End of the Western World and the Birth of a New Global Order* (New York: Penguin, 2009), p. 428.

Chapter 21
Linking Concepts and Cases

1. Carlos Fuentes, *The Crystal Frontier* (New York: Farrar, Straus and Giroux, 1997), p. 266.

2. Roderic Ai Camp, *Politics in Mexico: The Decline of Authoritarianism* (New York: Oxford University Press, 1999).

3. Shannon O'Neil, "The Real War in Mexico," *Foreign Affairs* 88, no. 4 (July–August 2008); Elisabeth Malkin, "NAFTA's Promise, Unfulfilled," *New York Times,* March 24, 2009; Leonardo Martinez-Diaz, "Mexico's Economy: Preparing for a Tough Year," Brookings Institution, June 24, 2010, www.brookings.edu; D. E. Campbell, "A Saint for Lost Souls," *Foreign Policy* 179 (May–June 2010).

4. Camp, *Politics in Mexico;* Daniel C. Levy and Kathleen Bruhn, "Mexico: Sustained Civilian Rule Without Democracy," in *Politics in Developing Countries: Comparing Experiences with Democracy,* eds. Larry Diamond, Juan J. Linz, and Seymour Martin Lipset (Boulder: Lynne Rienner, 1995).

5. Quoted in Mary Jordan and Kevin Sullivan, "Mexico Steps into the Spotlight," *Washington Post,* January 31, 2001.

6. Michele Norris, "Tackling America's Drug Addiction," National Public Radio, *All Things Considered,* June 18, 2010.

7. Shannon K. O'Neill, "Welcome Move on Mexico's Drug Wars," Council on Foreign Relations, March 24, 2010, www.cfr.org; Ginger Thompson and Marc Lacey, "US and Mexico Revise Joint Anti-Drug Strategy," *New York Times,* March 23, 2010.

8. Marc Lacey and Ginger Thompson, "As Clinton Visits Mexico, Strains Show in Relations," *New York Times,* March 25, 2009.

9. Michael Hoefer, Nancy Rytina, and Bryan C. Baker, "Estimates of the Unauthorized Immigrant Population Residing in the US, January 2009," *Population Estimates,* US Department of Homeland Security, January 2010, www.dhs.gov.

10. Luis Rubio and Jeffrey Davidow, "Mexico's Disputed Election," *Foreign Affairs* 85, no. 5 (September–October 2006).

11. Jorge G. Castañeda, "A Promising Start for a Border Partnership," *Los Angeles Times,* February 14, 2001.

12. O'Neil, "The Real War in Mexico."

13. Gary Martin, "It's Not All Smiles As Leaders Meet," *San Antonio Express-News,* November 10, 2006.

14. Cynthia McClintock, quoted in "US Retreats on Peru Vote," *New York Times,* May 31, 2000.

15. "What Future for US-Backed Plan Colombia?" *BBC News,* June 12, 2010.

16. Cited in Dennis Jett, "Remember the Drug War?" *Washington Post,* January 13, 2002.

17. "Coca and Cocaine in the Andes," *The Economist,* March 16, 2006; United Nations Office on Drugs and Crime, "Divergent Coca Crop Cultivation Trends in the Andean Countries," June 22, 2010, www.unodc.org; "The Balloon Effect," *New York Times,* June 14, 2010; "Peru Overtakes Colombia as World's Leading Producer of Coca Leaf," *The Telegraph* (London), June 23, 2010.

18. Simon Romero, "Coca Production Makes a Comeback," *New York Times,* June 13, 2010.

19. Scott Wilson, "Peru Fears Reemergence of Violent Rebels," *Washington Post,* December 10, 2001; Jude Webber, "Critics Liken Bush's Tribunals to Peru's 'Faceless' Judges Trials," *Houston Chronicle,* November 18, 2001; Juan Forero, "Reeling from Blast, Peru Prepares for a Visit from Bush," *New York Times,* March 22, 2002.

20. "US Seeks Stronger Economic Ties with Nigeria," *AGOA News,* July 13, 2010, www.agoa.info.

21. Stephen Wright, *Nigeria: Struggle for Stability and Status* (Boulder: Westview, 1998).

22. US Department of State, "Background Note: Nigeria," November 1, 2010, www.state.gov.

23. Conn Hallinan, "Africa: No Butter, but Lots of Guns," *Foreign Policy in Focus,* Institute for Policy Studies, July 13, 2010, www.fpif.org; "US Seeks Stronger Economic Ties with Nigeria," *AGOA News.*

24. Jean Herskovitz, "Nigeria's Rigged Democracy," *Foreign Affairs* 86, no. 4 (July–August 2007); Hallinan, "Africa."

25. William D. Hartung and Frida Berrigan, "Militarization of US Policy, 2000–2005," *Synthesis/Regeneration* no. 39 (Winter 2006), www.greens.org.

26. "Nigeria Oil Rebels Say Mulling Obama's Truce Appeal," *Reuters,* May 4, 2008.

27. Michelle Gavin, "A Blow for Nigerian Democracy," Council on Foreign Relations, April 20, 2007, www.crf.org.

28. Quoted in Mike Nizza, "Mugabe Loses Honorary Degree from U Mass," *New York Times,* June 13, 2008.

29. "Iran and Zimbabwe 'Think Alike,' Says Mugabe," *Deutsche Presse-Agentur,* November 21, 2006.

30. "The Way Forward," *New African* (June 2005, special report), www.glob.co.zw.

31. "Obama Pledges Aid for Zimbabwe," *BBC News,* June 2, 2009; "What Now for US/Zimbabwe Relations," *BBC News,* July 7, 2009.

32. "Iraq: What Iran and Syria Want," *BBC News,* November 13, 2006.

33. Karim Sadjadpour, "The Sources of Soviet Iranian Conduct," *Foreign Policy* (November 2010).

34. John Simpson, "Iran's Growing Regional Influence," *BBC News,* September 20, 2006.

35. Ray Takeyh, *Hidden Iran: Paradox and Power in the Islamic Republic* (New York: Holt, 2006), pp. 117–118.

36. James A. Baker III and Lee H. Hamilton, cochairs, *The Iraq Study Group Report* (New York: Random, 2006), pp. 50–53. The group begins this section (which also discusses Syria) by stating, "Dealing with Iran and Syria is controversial. Nevertheless, it is our view that in diplomacy, a nation can and should engage its adversaries and enemies to try to resolve conflicts and differences. . . . Accordingly, the Support Group should actively engage Iran and Syria in its diplomatic dialogue, *without preconditions*" (p. 50, emphasis added).

37. Geoffrey Kemp, *Forever Enemies? American Policy and the Islamic Republic of Iran* (Washington, DC: Carnegie Endowment, 1994).

38. Hooman Peimani, *Iran and the United States: The Rise of the West Asian Regional Grouping* (Westport: Praeger, 1999).

39. Scott Peterson, "In Iran, 'Death to America' Is Back," *Christian Science Monitor,* February 12, 2002, p. 1.

40. Sabrina Tavernise and Michael Slackman, "Turkey Goes from Pliable Ally to Thorn for US," *New York Times,* June 9, 2010.

41. "The Awkward Partners," *The Economist,* September 30, 2006, p. 61.

42. Steven A. Cook, "How Do You Say 'Frenemy' in Turkish?" *Foreign Policy* (June 1, 2010).

43. Heinz Kramer, *A Changing Turkey: The Challenge to Europe and the United States* (Washington, DC: Brookings Institution, 2000).

44. "Turkey Wants Control in NATO Missile Shield-Erdogan," *Reuters,* November 16, 2010.

45. Owen Mathews, "Triumph of the Turks," *Newsweek,* November 28, 2009.

46. Soli Ozel, a professor of international relations at Bilgi University in Istanbul, quoted in Tavernise and Slackman, "Turkey Goes from Pliable Ally to Thorn for US," p. A1.

47. Steven A. Cook, *US-Turkey Relations and the War on Terrorism* (Washington, DC: Brookings Institution, 2001).

48. "US Hails Turkey's Mideast Diplomacy," *Turkish Daily News,* December 8, 2006.

49. Cook, "How Do You Say 'Frenemy' in Turkish?"

50. Humphrey Hawksley, "Chinese Influence in Brazil Worries US," *BBC News,* April 3, 2006.

51. "Aphorisms and Suspicions," *The Economist,* November 19, 2005, p. 23.

52. Senior Chinese Communist Party cadre Zhang Bijian launched the notion of China's "peaceful rise" in 2003, popularizing it in the West in a 2005 article in *Foreign Affairs.* See Elizabeth Economy, "The End of the 'Peaceful Rise'?" *Foreign Policy* (December 2010).

53. Michael Wines, "Behind Gusts of a Military Chill: A More Forceful China," *New York Times,* June 9, 2010.

54. "The Outlook for China," roundtable convened at the Brookings Institution, Washington, DC, March 18, 2010, p. 29.

55. Elizabeth Economy and Adam Segal, "Time to Defriend China," *Foreign Policy* (May 24, 2010).

56. US Department of State, "Indonesia-Military Assistance," Office of the Spokesman, January 4, 2006, www.state.gov.

57. "Iraq a Key Point of Difference During Visit," *Jakarta Post,* November 20, 2006.

58. "Indonesians Protest US President's Visit," National Public Radio, *Morning Edition,* November 20, 2006.

59. Quoted in Norimitsu Onishi, "In Jakarta Speech, Some Hear Cairo Redux," *New York Times,* November 10, 2010.

60. Richard Wike, "Indonesia: The Obama Effect," Pew Research Center, March 17, 2010, http://pewresearch.org.

61. Quoted in "Obama Trip to 'Muslim' Indonesia: Why Stereotypes Don't Work," *Christian Science Monitor,* November 9, 2010.

62. Ibid.

Chapter 22
Are We Living in a New Era?

1. Quoted in Mike William, "Slow-Burning Problems Could Singe US," *Montreal Gazette,* February 14, 2002.

2. Robert M. Gates, "Helping Others Defend Themselves: The Future of US Security Assistance," *Foreign Affairs* 89, no. 3 (May–June 2010).

3. Neil Patel, "Emergency to Efficiency," *Harvard Political Review,* December 5, 2010.

4. Madeleine K. Albright and Colin L. Powell, "Don't Forget About Foreign Aid," *Wall Street Journal,* May 5, 2009. Albright and Powell also state, "Stability and prosperity go hand in hand, and neither is possible in the presence of widespread and extreme poverty."

5. Joseph S. Nye Jr., "The Decline of America's Soft Power: Why Washington Should Worry," *Foreign Affairs* 83, no. 3 (May–June 2004), p. 17.

6. Joshua Kurlantzick, *Charm Offensive: How China's Soft Power Is Transforming the World* (New Haven: Yale University Press, 2007).

7. Carola McGiffert, ed., *Chinese Soft Power and Its Implications for the United States* (Washington, DC: Center for Strategic and International Studies, 2009), p. 126.

8. Quoted in "Viewpoints: The World Since 9/11," *BBC News,* September 8, 2006.

9. Howard LaFranchi, "Why World Leaders Smacked Down Obama at G20 Summit," *Christian Science Monitor,* November 12, 2010.

Selected Bibliography

Adedeji, Adebayo. "Popular Participation, Democracy, and Development: Is There a Dialectical Linkage?" In *Nigeria: Renewal from the Roots? The Struggle for Democratic Development,* edited by Adebayo Adedeji et al., 3–19. London: Zed, 1997.

Afolayan, Funso. "Nigeria: A Political Entity and a Society." In *Dilemmas of Democracy in Nigeria,* edited by Paul A. Beckett and Crawford Young, 45–62. Rochester, NY: University of Rochester Press, 1997.

———. "Women and Warfare in Yorubaland During the Nineteenth Century." In *Warfare and Diplomacy in Precolonial Nigeria,* edited by Toyin Falola and Robin Law, 78–86. Madison: University of Wisconsin–Madison Press, 1992.

Ai Camp, Roderic. *Politics in Mexico: The Decline of Authoritarianism.* New York: Oxford University Press, 1999.

Alexander, Jocelyn, JoAnn McGregor, and Terence Ranger. *Violence and Memory: One Hundred Years in the "Dark Forests" of Matabeleland.* London: Currey, 2000.

Almond, Gabriel A., and Sidney Verba, eds. *Civic Culture: Political Attitudes and Democracy in Five Nations.* Princeton: Princeton University Press, 1963.

Alvarez, Sonia E. *Engendering Democracy in Brazil: Women's Movements in Transition Politics.* Princeton: Princeton University Press, 1990.

Annan, Kofi. *Globalization and Governance.* Report issued to the Millennium Summit of the United Nations, 2000.

———. *We the Peoples: The Role of the United Nations in the Twenty-First Century.* Report issued to the UN General Assembly, Spring 2000.

Aydin, Zülküf. *The Political Economy of Turkey.* Ann Arbor, MI: Pluto, 2005.

Bakewell, Peter. *A History of Latin America.* Malden, MA: Blackwell, 1997.

Barber, Benjamin R. *Jihad vs. McWorld.* New York: Times Books, 1995.

Berkovitch, Nitza. "The Emergence and Transformation of the International Women's Movement." In *Constructing World Culture: International Nongovernmental Organizations Since 1875,* edited by John Boli and George M. Thomas, 116–121. Stanford: Stanford University Press, 1999.

Bethell, Leslie, ed. *Ideas and Ideologies in Twentieth-Century Latin America.* Cambridge: Cambridge University Press, 1996.

Bhebe, Ngwabi, and Terence Ranger. "Volume Introduction: Society in Zimbabwe's Liberation War." In *Society in Zimbabwe's Liberation War,* edited by Ngwabi Bhebe and Terence Ranger, 6–34. Oxford: Currey, 1996.

Bizzozero, Lincoln. "Uruguayan Foreign Policies in the 1990s: Continuities and Changes with a View to Recent Regionalisms." In *National Perspectives on the New Regionalism in the South,* vol. 3, edited by Björn Hettne, András Inotai, and Osvaldo Sunkel, 177–197. New York: St. Martin's, 2000.

Boahen, A. Adu. "Africa and the Colonial Challenge." In *UNESCO General History of Africa: Africa Under Colonial Domination, 1800–1935,* edited by A. Adu Boahen, 1–18. London: Heinemann, 1985.

———. "Colonialism in Africa: Its Impact and Significance." In *UNESCO General History of Africa: Africa Under Colonial Domination, 1800–1935,* edited by A. Adu Boahen, 782–809. London: Heinemann, 1985.

Bogle, Emory C. *The Modern Middle East: From Imperialism to Freedom, 1800–1958.* Upper Saddle River, NJ: Prentice Hall, 1996.

Boli, John, and George M. Thomas, eds. *Constructing World Culture: International Nongovernmental Organizations Since 1875.* Stanford: Stanford University Press, 1999.

Boone, Catherine. "'Empirical Statehood' and Reconfigurations of Political Order." In *The African State at a Critical Juncture,* edited by Leonardo A. Villalon and Phillip A. Huxtable, 129–142. Boulder: Lynne Rienner, 1998.

Bracken, Paul. *Fire in the East: The Rise of Asian Military Power and the Second Nuclear Age.* New York: HarperCollins, 1999.

Bresnan, John, ed. *Indonesia: The Great Transition.* New York: Rowman and Littlefield, 2005.

Burkholder, Mark A., and Lyman L. Johnson. *Colonial Latin America.* New York: Oxford University Press, 1998.

Castañeda, Jorge G. *Utopia Unarmed: The Latin American Left After the Cold War.* New York: Knopf, 1993.

Centeno, Miguel Angel. *Democracy Within Reason: Technocratic Revolution in Mexico.* University Park: Pennsylvania State University Press, 1997.

Chalmers, Douglas A. "Corporatism and Comparative Politics." In *New Directions in Comparative Politics,* edited by Howard J. Wiarda, 56–79. Boulder: Westview, 1985.

Chalmers, Douglas A., Maria do Carmo Campello de Souza, and Atilio A. Borón. *The Right and Democracy in Latin America.* New York: Praeger, 1992.

Chazan, Naomi, Peter Lewis, and Robert Mortimer. *Politics and Society in Contemporary Africa.* Boulder: Lynne Rienner, 1999.

Chomsky, Noam. *Pirates and Emperors: International Terrorism in the Real World.* New York: Claremont, 1986.

Clendinnen, Inga. *Aztecs: An Interpretation.* Cambridge: Cambridge University Press, 1995.

Cohn, Theodore H. *Global Political Economy: Theory and Practice.* New York: Longman, 2000.

Collis, Maurice. *Cortés and Montezuma.* New York: New Directions, 1999.

Cook, Steven A. *US-Turkey Relations and the War on Terrorism.* Washington, DC: Brookings Institution, 2001.

Cortright, David, and George Lopez. *The Sanctions Decade: Assessing UN Strategies in the 1990s.* Boulder: Lynne Rienner, 2000.

Coughlin, Kathryn M., ed. *Muslim Cultures Today: A Reference Guide.* Westport: Greenwood, 2006.

Courtois, Stéphane, et al. *The Black Book of Communism: Crimes, Terror, and Repression,* edited by Mark Kramer. Translated by Jonathan Murphy. Cambridge: Harvard University Press, 1999.

Crenshaw, Martha, ed. *Terrorism in Context.* University Park: Pennsylvania State University Press, 1995.

Cribb, Robert, and Colin Brown. *Modern Indonesia: A History Since 1945.* New York: Longman, 1995.

Crowder, Michael. *The Story of Nigeria.* London: Faber and Faber, 1978.

Dahl, Robert. *Democracy and Its Critics.* New Haven: Yale University Press, 1989.

Daniel, Elton L. *The History of Iran.* Westport: Greenwood, 2001.

Danopoulos, Constantine P., and Cynthia Watson, eds. *The Political Role of the Military: An International Handbook.* Westport: Greenwood, 1996.

Davidson, Basil. *Africa in History.* New York: Simon and Schuster, 1995.

Davidson, David M. "Negro Slave Control and Resistance in Colonial Mexico." In *People and Issues in Latin American History,* edited by Lewis Hanke and Jane M. Rausch, 200–206. New York: Markus Wiener, 1993.

de Waal, Victor. *The Politics of Reconciliation: Zimbabwe's First Decade.* Trenton, NJ: Africa World Press, 1990.

Degregori, Carlos Ivan. "After the Fall of Abimael Guzmán: The Limits of Sendero Luminoso." In *The Peruvian Labyrinth,* edited by Maxwell A. Cameron and Philip Mauceri, 179–191. University Park: Pennsylvania State University Press, 1997.

Deng, Francis Mading. "State Collapse: The Humanitarian Challenge to the UN." In *Collapsed States: The Disintegration and Restoration of Legitimate Authority,* edited by I. William Zartman, 207–219. Boulder: Lynne Rienner, 1995.

Diamond, Jared. *Guns, Germs, and Steel: The Fate of Human Societies.* New York: Norton, 1997.

Diamond, Larry. "Introduction: In Search of Consolidation." In *Consolidating Third Wave Democracies,* edited by Larry Diamond et al., xv–xlix. Baltimore: Johns Hopkins University Press, 1997.

———. "Introduction: What Makes for Democracy?" In *Politics in Developing Countries: Comparing Experiences with Democracy,* edited by Larry Diamond, Juan J. Linz, and Seymour Martin Lipset, 1–66. Boulder: Lynne Rienner, 1995.

———. "Three Paradoxes of Democracy." In *The Global Resurgence of Democracy,* edited by Larry Diamond and Marc F. Plattner, 95–107. Baltimore: Johns Hopkins University Press, 1993.

———. "The Uncivic Society and the Descent into Praetorianism." In *Politics in Developing Countries: Comparing Experiences with Democracy,* edited by Larry Diamond, Juan J. Linz, and Seymour Martin Lipset, 417–492. Boulder: Lynne Rienner, 1995.

Dikötter, Frank. *Mao's Great Famine: The History of China's Most Devastating Catastrophe, 1958–1962.* New York: Walker, 2010.

Diller, Daniel C., ed. *The Middle East.* 8th ed. Washington, DC: Congressional Quarterly, 1994.

Dimitrijevic, Vojin. "Human Rights and Peace." In *Human Rights: New Dimensions and Challenges,* edited by Janusz Symonides. Brookfield, VT: Ashgate, 1998.

Donnelly, Jack. *International Human Rights.* Boulder: Westview, 1998.

Durand, Francisco. "The New Right and Political Change in Peru." In *The Right and Democracy in Latin America,* edited by Douglas A. Chalmers, Maria do Carmo Campello de Souza, and Atilio A. Borón, 239–258. New York: Praeger, 1992.

Duverger, Maurice. *Political Parties: Their Organization and Activity in the Modern State.* New York: Wiley, 1963.

Eatwell, Roger. *Fascism: A History.* New York: Penguin, 1997.

Ehteshami, Anoushiravan. *After Khomeini: The Iranian Second Republic.* New York: Routledge, 1995.

Elaigwu, J. Isawa. "Nation-Building and Changing Political Structures." In *UNESCO General History of Africa: Africa Since 1935,* edited by Ali A. Mazrui, 435–467. London: Heinemann, 1993.

Ellis, Stephen. "Tuning In to Pavement Radio." *African Affairs* 88, no. 352 (1989): 321–330.

Emmerson, Donald K. *Indonesia Beyond Suharto: Policy, Economy, Society, Transition.* Armonk, NY: Sharpe, 1999.

———. "Voting and Violence: Indonesia and East Timor in 1999." In *Indonesia Beyond Suharto,* edited by Donald K. Emmerson, 354–357. Armonk, NY: Sharpe, 1999.

Esty, Daniel C. "Environmental Protection During the Transition to a Market Economy." In *Economies in Transition: Comparing Asia and Eastern Europe,* edited by Wing Thye Woo, Stephen Parker, and Jeffrey Sachs, 357–385. Cambridge: Massachusetts Institute of Technology Press, 1997.

Euchner, Charles. *Extraordinary Politics: How Protest and Dissent Are Changing American Democracy.* Boulder: Westview, 1996.

Evans, Tony. *Human Rights in the Global Political Economy: Critical Processes.* Boulder: Lynne Rienner, 2010.

Fallows, James. *Postcards from Tomorrow Square.* New York: Vintage, 2008.

Falola, Toyin. *The History of Nigeria.* Westport: Greenwood, 1999.

Falola, Toyin, and Robin Law, eds. *Warfare and Diplomacy in Precolonial Nigeria.* Madison: University of Wisconsin–Madison Press, 1992.

Farmer, Edward L., et al. *Comparative History of Civilizations in Asia*. Reading, MA: Addison-Wesley, 1977.

Ferguson, Niall. *Dead Aid: Why Aid Is Not Working and How There Is a Better Way for Africa*. Vancouver: Douglas and McIntyre, 2010.

Finnemore, Martha. "Rules of War and Wars of Rules: The International Red Cross and the Restraint of State Violence." In *Constructing World Culture: International Nongovernmental Organizations Since 1875*, edited by John Boli and George M. Thomas, 149–168. Stanford: Stanford University Press, 1999.

Frank, Andre Gunder. *Capitalism and Underdevelopment in Latin America*. New York: Monthly Review Press, 1967.

Friedman, Thomas L. *The Lexus and the Olive Tree*. New York: Farrar, Straus, and Giroux, 1999.

Fyle, Magbaily. *Introduction to the History of African Civilization*. Lanham, MD: University Press of America, 1999.

Galeano, Eduardo. *Open Veins of Latin America*. New York: Monthly Review Press, 1973.

Gamer, Robert E. *Understanding Contemporary China*. Boulder: Lynne Rienner, 1999.

Gamson, William A. "The Social Psychology of Collective Action." In *Frontiers in Social Movement Theory*, edited by Aldon D. Morris and Carol McClurg Mueller, 53–76. New Haven: Yale University Press, 1992.

Garner, Roberta. *Contemporary Movements and Ideologies*. New York: McGraw Hill, 1996.

Garrett, Laurie. *Betrayal of Trust: The Collapse of Global Public Health*. New York: Hyperion, 2000.

George, Susan. *The Debt Boomerang: How Third World Debt Harms Us All*. Boulder: Westview, 1992.

Gheissari, Ali, and Vali Nasr. *Democracy in Iran: History and the Quest for Liberty*. New York: Oxford University Press, 2006.

Gilley, Bruce. *China's Democratic Future: How It Will Happen and Where It Will Lead*. New York: Columbia University Press, 2004.

Goldstein, Joshua S. *International Relations*. 4th ed. New York: Longman, 2001.

Goldstone, Jack A. "The Outcome of Revolutions." In *Revolutions: Theoretical, Comparative, and Historical Studies*, 2nd ed., edited by Jack A. Goldstone, 194–195. New York: Harcourt Brace, 1994.

———. "Revolutions in World History." In *Revolutions: Theoretical, Comparative, and Historical Studies*, 2nd ed., edited by Jack A. Goldstone, 315–318. New York: Harcourt Brace, 1994.

Goldstone, Richard. "Bringing War Criminals to Justice During an Ongoing War." In *Hard Choices: Moral Dilemmas in Humanitarian Intervention*, edited by Jonathan Moore, 195–210. Lanham: Rowman and Littlefield, 1998.

Gould, Benina Berger. "Ritual as Resistance: Tibetan Women and Nonviolence." In *Frontline Feminisms: Women, War, and Resistance*, edited by Marguerite R. Waller and Jennifer Rycenga, 213–234. New York: Garland, 2000.

Graham, Richard. *Independence in Latin America*. New York: McGraw Hill, 1994.

Green, Jerrold D. "Countermobilization in the Iranian Revolution." In *Revolutions: Theoretical, Comparative, and Historical Studies*, 2nd ed., edited by Jack A. Goldstone, 136–146. New York: Harcourt Brace, 1994.

Grindle, Merilee. *Challenging the State: Crisis and Innovation in Latin America and Africa*. Cambridge: Cambridge University Press, 1996.

Gurtov, Mel. *Superpower on Crusade: The Bush Doctrine and US Foreign Policy*. Boulder: Lynne Rienner, 2006.

Hacker, Frederick J. *Crusaders, Criminals, Crazies: Terror and Terrorism in Our Time*. New York: Norton, 1976.

Hanke, Lewis, and Jane M. Rausch, eds. *People and Issues in Latin American History*. New York: Markus Wiener, 1993.

Hayner, Priscilla B. *Unspeakable Truths: Confronting State Terror and Atrocity*. New York: Routledge, 2001.

Heiner, Robert, ed. *Social Problems and Social Solutions: A Cross-Cultural Perspective*. Boston: Allyn and Bacon, 1999.

Hemming, John. *The Conquest of the Incas.* Boston: Houghton Mifflin Harcourt, 2003.

Heywood, Andrew. *Political Ideas and Concepts: An Introduction.* New York: St. Martin's, 1994.

Hirschman, Albert O. *Exit, Voice, and Loyalty: Responses to Decline in Firms, Organizations, and States.* Cambridge: Harvard University Press, 1970.

Hochschild, Adam. *King Leopold's Ghost.* Boston: Houghton Mifflin, 1998.

Hollifield, James F., and Calvin Jillson, eds. *Pathways to Democracy: The Political Economy of Democratic Transitions.* New York: Routledge, 2000.

Horowitz, Donald L. "Comparing Democratic Systems." In *The Global Resurgence of Democracy,* edited by Larry Diamond and Marc F. Plattner, 127–133. Baltimore: Johns Hopkins University Press, 1993.

Howard, Douglas A. *The History of Turkey.* Westport: Greenwood, 2001.

Howe, Marvine. *Turkey Today: A Nation Divided over Islam's Revival.* Boulder: Westview, 2000.

Huntington, Samuel P. "Democracy's Third Wave." In *The Global Resurgence of Democracy,* edited by Larry Diamond and Marc F. Plattner, 3–25. Baltimore: Johns Hopkins University Press, 1993.

Huxtable, Phillip A. "The African State Toward the Twenty-First Century: Legacies of the Critical Juncture." In *The African State at a Critical Juncture,* edited by Leonardo A. Villalon and Phillip A. Huxtable, 279–294. Boulder: Lynne Rienner, 1998.

Ignatieff, Michael. *Human Rights as Politics and Idolatry.* Princeton: Princeton University Press, 2001.

Inikori, J. E., and Stanley L. Engerman. *The Atlantic Slave Trade.* Durham, NC: Duke University Press, 1992.

Jaquette, Jane, ed. *The Women's Movement in Latin America: Participation and Democracy.* Boulder: Westview, 1994.

Jayawardena, Kumari. *Feminism and Nationalism in the Third World.* London: Zed, 1986.

Jianying, Huo. "A Recollection of the Splendor of the Tang Dynasty," *China Today* 50, no. 11 (November 2001).

Johnson, Paul. *The Civilization of Ancient Egypt.* New York: Harper Collins, 1999.

Joseph, Richard, and Alexandra Gillies, eds. *Smart Aid for African Development.* Boulder: Lynne Rienner, 2009.

Judt, Tony, and Denis Lacorne, eds. *With Us or Against Us: Studies in Global Anti-Americanism.* New York: Palgrave Macmillan, 2005.

July, Robert W. *A History of the African People.* Prospect Heights, IL: Waveland, 1992.

Kaldor, Mary. *New and Old Wars: Organized Violence in a Global Era.* Stanford: Stanford University Press, 1999.

Keen, Benjamin, and Keith Haynes. *A History of Latin America.* Boston: Houghton Mifflin, 2000.

Keightley, David N. *The Origins of Chinese Civilization.* Berkeley: University of California Press, 1983.

Kemp, Geoffrey. *Forever Enemies? American Policy and the Islamic Republic of Iran.* Washington, DC: Carnegie Endowment, 1994.

Kesselman, Mark, Joel Krieger, and William A. Joseph. *Introduction to Comparative Politics: Political Challenges and Changing Agendas.* Boston: Houghton Mifflin, 2000.

Kinsbruner, Jay. *Independence in Spanish America: Civil Wars, Revolutions, and Underdevelopment.* Albuquerque: University of New Mexico Press, 2000.

Klaren, Peter Flindell. *Peru: Society and Nationhood in the Andes.* New York: Oxford University Press, 2000.

Kohut, Andrew, and Bruce Stokes. *America Against the World: How We Are Different and Why We Are Disliked.* New York: Times Books, 2006.

Kramer, Heinz. *A Changing Turkey: The Challenge to Europe and the United States.* Washington, DC: Brookings Institution, 2000.

Kurlantzick, Joshua. *Charm Offensive: How China's Soft Power Is Transforming the World.* New Haven: Yale University Press, 2007.

Laqueur, Walter. *The New Terrorism: Fanaticism and the Arms of Mass Destruction.* New York: Oxford University Press, 1999.

Levy, Daniel C., and Kathleen Bruhn. "Mexico: Sustained Civilian Rule Without Democracy." In *Politics in Developing Countries: Comparing Experiences with Democracy,* edited by Larry Diamond, Juan J. Linz, and Seymour Martin Lipset, 171–217. Boulder: Lynne Rienner, 1995.

Lewis, Peter M., and Pearl T. Robinson. *Stabilizing Nigeria.* New York: Century Foundation, 1998.

Leys, Colin. *Underdevelopment in Kenya: The Political Economy of Neocolonialism, 1964–1971.* London: Heinemann, 1975.

Lijphart, Arend. *Democracy in Plural Societies: A Comparative Exploration.* New Haven: Yale University Press, 1977.

———. *Patterns of Democracy: Government Forms and Performance in Thirty-six Countries.* New Haven: Yale University Press, 1999.

Linz, Juan J., and Alfred Stepan. "The Perils of Presidentialism." In *The Global Resurgence of Democracy,* edited by Larry Diamond and Marc F. Plattner, 108–126. Baltimore: Johns Hopkins University Press, 1993.

———. *Problems of Democratic Transition and Consolidation.* Baltimore: Johns Hopkins University Press, 1996.

Lipset, Seymour Martin. *Political Man.* Garden City, NY: Doubleday, 1959.

Mackey, Sandra. *The Iranians: Persia, Islam, and the Soul of a Nation.* New York: Penguin, 1996.

———. *The Middle East.* 8th ed. Washington, DC: Congressional Quarterly, 1994.

Maier, Karl. *This House Has Fallen: Midnight in Nigeria.* New York: PublicAffairs, 2000.

Mamdani, Mahmood. *Citizen and Subject: Contemporary Africa and the Legacy of Late Colonialism.* Princeton: Princeton University Press, 1996.

Man, John. *The Great Wall.* Cambridge, MA: DaCapo Press, 2008.

Martin, Jacques, *When China Rules the World: The End of the Western World and the Birth of a New Global Order.* New York: Penguin, 2009.

Martin, Simon, and Nikolai Grube. *Chronicle of the Maya Kings and Queens: Deciphering the Dynasties of the Ancient Maya.* London: Thames and Hudson, 2000.

Mazrui, Ali A. *UNESCO General History of Africa: Africa Since 1935.* London: Heinemann, 1993.

McClintock, Cynthia. *Revolutionary Movements in Latin America.* Washington, DC: US Institute of Peace, 1998.

Meyer, Milton W. *Asia: A Concise History.* Lanham: Rowman and Littlefield, 1997.

Mingst, Karen A., and Margaret P. Karns. *The United Nations in the 21st Century.* 3rd ed. Boulder: Westview, 2007.

Minelli, Laura Laurencich. *The Inca World: The Development of Pre-Columbian Peru, A.D. 1000–1534.* Norman: University of Oklahoma Press, 2000.

Moaveni, Azadeh. *Honeymoon in Tehran: Two Years of Love and Danger in Iran.* New York: Random, 2009.

Moghadam, Valentine. *Gender and National Identity: Women and Politics in Muslim Societies.* London: Zed, 1994.

Moin, Bager. *Khomeini: Life of the Ayatollah.* New York: St. Martin's, 2000.

Monga, Célestin. *The Anthropology of Anger: Civil Society and Democracy in Africa.* Translated by Linda L. Fleck and Célestin Monga. Boulder: Lynne Rienner, 1996.

Morgan, David. *The Mongols.* Oxford: Wiley-Blackwell, 1990.

Morris, Stephen D. *Political Corruption in Mexico: The Impact of Democratization.* Boulder: Lynne Rienner, 2009.

Mungazi, Dickson A. *Colonial Policy and Conflict in Zimbabwe.* New York: Crane Russak, 1992.

Murphy, Ann Marie. "Indonesia and Globalization." In *East Asia and Globalization,* edited by Samuel S. Kim, 209–232. New York: Rowman and Littlefield, 2000.

Murray, Geoffrey. *China: The Next Superpower—Dilemmas in Change and Continuity.* New York: St. Martin's, 1998.

Nasr, Vali. *The Shia Revival: How Conflicts Within Islam Will Shape the Future.* New York: Norton, 2006.

Nathan, Andrew J. *China's Transition*. New York: Columbia University Press, 1997.

Needham, D. E., Elleck K. Mashingaidze, and Ngwabi Bhebe. *From Iron Age to Independence: A History of Central Africa*. London: Longman, 1985.

The 9/11 Commission Report: Final Report on the National Commission on Terrorist Attacks Upon the United States. New York: Norton, 2004.

Nyang'oro, Julius E., and Timothy M. Shaw. "The African State in the Global Economic Context." In *The African State at a Critical Juncture: Between Disintegration and Reconfiguration*, edited by Julius E. Nyang'oro and Timothy M. Shaw, 27–44. Boulder: Lynne Rienner, 1998.

Nye, Joseph, Jr., *Soft Power: The Means to Success in World Politics*. New York: PublicAffairs, 2004.

O'Brien, Kevin J., and Lianjiang Li. *Rightful Resistance in Rural China*. New York: Cambridge University Press, 2006.

O'Gorman, Eleanor. "Writing Women's Wars: Foucaldian Strategies of Engagement." In *Women, Culture, and International Relations*, edited by Vivienne Jabri and Eleanor O'Gorman, 91–116. Boulder: Lynne Rienner, 1999.

Oliver, Roland. *The African Experience*. Boulder: Westview, 1999.

Özbudun, Ergun. *Contemporary Turkish Politics: Challenges to Democratic Consolidation*. Boulder: Lynne Rienner, 2000.

Page, Sheila. *Regionalism Among Developing Countries*. New York: St. Martin's, 2000.

Palmer, David Scott. "The Revolutionary Terrorism of Peru's Shining Path." In *Terrorism in Context*, edited by Martha Crenshaw, 249–308. University Park: Pennsylvania State University Press, 1995.

Palmer, Monte. *Comparative Politics: Political Economy, Political Culture, and Political Independence*. Itasca, IL: F. E. Peacock, 1997.

Parrinder, E. G. "Divine Kingship in West Africa," *Numen* 3 (April 1956): 111–121.

Payne, Leigh A. *Uncivil Movements: The Armed Right Wing and Democracy in Latin America*. Baltimore: Johns Hopkins University Press, 2000.

Paz, Octavio. "Latin America and Democracy." In *Democracy and Dictatorship in Latin America: A Special Publication Devoted Entirely to the Voice and Opinions of Writers from Latin America*, edited by Octavio Paz et al., 5–17. New York: Foundation for the Independent Study of Social Ideas, 1982.

Peimani, Hooman. *Iran and the United States: The Rise of the West Asian Regional Grouping*. Westport: Praeger, 1999.

Pempel, T. J. "The Developmental Regime in a Changing World Economy." In *The Developmental State*, edited by Meredith Woo-Cumings, 137–181. Ithaca: Cornell University Press, 2001.

Phimister, Ian. *An Economic and Social History of Zimbabwe, 1890–1948*. London: Longman, 1988.

Pye, Lucian W. *China: An Introduction*. 3rd ed. Boston: Little, Brown, 1984.

Ranger, Terence. *Peasant Consciousness and Guerrilla War in Zimbabwe*. London: Currey, 1985.

Rittenberg, Libby. "Introduction: The Changing Fortunes of Turkey in the Post-Soviet World." In *The Political Economy of Turkey in the Post-Soviet Era: Going West and Looking East*, edited by Libby Rittenberg, 3–16. Westport: Praeger, 1998.

Roberts, Kenneth M. *Deepening Democracy? The Modern Left and Social Movements in Chile and Peru*. Stanford: Stanford University Press, 1998.

Roberts, Mark J. *Khomeini's Incorporation of the Iranian Military*. Washington, DC: Institute for National Strategic Studies, National Defense University, 1996.

Sachs, Jeffrey. *The End of Poverty: Economic Possibilities for Our Time*. New York: Penguin, 2006.

Sadri, Houman. "Iran." In *The Political Role of the Military: An International Handbook*, edited by Constantine P. Danopoulos and Cynthia Watson, 207–222. Westport: Greenwood, 1996.

Said, Edward W. *Reflections on Exile*. Cambridge: Harvard University Press, 2001.

Schelander, Björn, and Kirsten Brown. *Exploring Indonesia: Past and Present*. Honolulu: Center for Southeast Asian Studies, 2000.

Schell, Orville. "Letter from China." *New Yorker,* July 1994. Reprinted in *The China Reader: The Reform Era,* edited by Orville Schell and David Shambaugh, 246–256. New York: Vintage, 1999.

Schmitter, Philippe C., and Terry Lynn Karl. "What Democracy Is . . . and Is Not." In *The Global Resurgence of Democracy,* edited by Larry Diamond and Marc F. Plattner, 39–52. Baltimore: Johns Hopkins University Press, 1993.

Selcuk, Faruk. "A Brief Account of the Turkish Economy, 1987–1996." In *The Political Economy of Turkey in the Post-Soviet Era: Going West and Looking East,* edited by Libby Rittenberg, 17–36. Westport: Praeger, 1998.

Shafer, Robert Jones. *A History of Latin America.* Lexington, MA: Heath, 1978.

Shahri, Sorayya. "Women in Command: A Successful Experience in the National Liberation Army of Iran." In *Frontline Feminisms: Women, War, and Resistance,* edited by Marguerite R. Waller and Jennifer Rycenga, 185–192. New York: Garland, 2000.

Shawcross, William. *Deliver Us from Evil.* New York: Simon and Schuster, 2000.

Siapno, Jacqueline. "Gender, Nationalism, and the Ambiguity of Female Agency in Aceh, Indonesia, and East Timor." In *Frontline Feminisms: Women, War, and Resistance,* edited by Marguerite R. Waller and Jennifer Rycenga, 275–296. New York: Garland, 2000.

Singer, P. W. *Children at War.* New York: Pantheon, 2005.

Skidmore, Thomas E., and Peter H. Smith. *Modern Latin America.* New York: Oxford University Press, 1992.

Skocpol, Theda. *States and Social Revolution: A Comparative Analysis of France, Russia, and China.* New York: Cambridge University Press, 1979.

Smith, Courtney B. *Politics and Process at the United Nations: The Global Dance.* Boulder: Lynne Rienner, 2006.

Smith, Michael E. "Life in the Provinces of the Aztec Empire," *Scientific American,* Special Edition, 15, no. 1 (February 2005).

Soled, Debra E., ed. *China: A Nation in Transition.* Washington, DC: Congressional Quarterly, 1995.

Stiglitz, Joseph. E. *Globalization and Its Discontents.* New York: Norton, 2003.

Stoez, David, Charles Guzzetta, and Mark Lusk. *International Development.* Boston: Allyn and Bacon, 1999.

Sweig, Julia E. *Friendly Fire: Losing Friends and Making Enemies in the Anti-American Century.* New York: PublicAffairs, 2006.

Takeyh, Ray. *Hidden Iran: Paradox and Power in the Islamic Republic.* New York: Holt, 2006.

Tarrow, Sidney. *Power in Movement: Social Movements and Contentious Politics.* New York: Cambridge University Press, 1998.

Thompson, Carol B. "Beyond the Nation-State? Democracy in Regional Economic Context." In *Democracy and Socialism in Africa,* edited by Robin Cohen and Harry Goulbourne, 216–227. Boulder: Westview, 1991.

Tilly, Charles. "Reflections on the History of European Statemaking." In *The Formation of National States in Western Europe,* edited by Charles Tilly, 3–83. Princeton: Princeton University Press, 1975.

Ullman, Richard H. "Human Rights: Toward International Action." In *Enhancing Global Human Rights,* edited by Jorge I. Domínguez et al., 1–20. New York: McGraw Hill, 1979.

Valenzuela, Arturo. "External Actors in the Transitions to Democracy in Latin America." In *Pathways to Democracy: The Political Economy of Democratic Transitions,* edited by James F. Hollifield and Calvin Jillson, 116–129. New York: Routledge, 2000.

Verba, Sidney. "Comparative Political Culture." In *Political Culture and Political Development,* edited by Sidney Verba and Lucian Pye, 512–560. Princeton: Princeton University Press, 1965.

Verba, Sidney, Victor H. Nie, and Jae-on Kim. *Participation and Political Equality: A Seven-Nation Comparison.* New York: Cambridge University Press, 1978.

Villalon, Leonardo A. "The African State at the End of the Twentieth Century: Parameters of the Critical Juncture." *The African State at a Critical Juncture,* edited by Leonardo A. Villalon and Phillip A. Huxtable, 3–26. Boulder: Lynne Rienner, 1998.

Werbner, Richard P. "In Memory: A Heritage of War in Southwestern Zimbabwe." In *Society in Zimbabwe's Liberation War,* edited by Ngwabi Bhebe and Terence Ranger, 192–205. Oxford: Currey, 1996.

West, Guida, and Rhoda Lois Blumberg, eds. *Women and Social Protest.* New York: Oxford University Press, 1990.

Wiarda, Howard J., and Harvey F. Kline. *An Introduction to Latin American Politics and Development.* Boulder: Westview, 2001.

Wills, A. J. *An Introduction to the History of Central Africa: Zambia, Malawi, and Zimbabwe.* New York: Oxford University Press, 1985.

Wilson, Frank L. *Concepts and Issues in Comparative Politics: An Introduction to Comparative Analysis.* Upper Saddle River, NJ: Prentice Hall, 1996.

Woo, Wing Thye, Stephen Parker, and Jeffrey Sachs, eds. *Economies in Transition: Comparing Asia and Eastern Europe.* Cambridge: Massachusetts Institute of Technology Press, 1997.

Wright, David C. *The History of China.* Westport: Greenwood, 2001.

Wright, Stephen. *Nigeria: Struggle for Stability and Status.* Boulder: Westview, 1998.

Yu Kien-hong, Peter. "The Party and the Army in China: Figuring Out Their Relationship Once and for All." Working Paper no. 7. Singapore: East Asian Institute, 1998.

Zahedi, Dariush. *The Iranian Revolution Then and Now: Indicators of Regime Instability.* Boulder: Westview, 2000.

Zakaria, Fareed. *The Post-American World.* New York: Norton, 2008.

Zartman, I. William. "Introduction: Posing the Problem of State Collapse." In *Collapsed States: The Disintegration and Restoration of Legitimate Authority,* edited by I. William Zartman, 1–14. Boulder: Lynne Rienner, 1995.

Zedong, Mao. "Report on an Investigation of the Peasant Movement in Hunan: March 1927." In *Selected Readings from the Works of Mao Tsetung.* Peking: Foreign Languages Press, 1971.

Zhang, Maria Yue, and Bruce W. Stening. *China 2.0: The Transformation of an Emerging Superpower—and the New Opportunities.* Singapore: Wiley, 2010.

Index

Abacha, Sani, 81, 325, 354, 426
abertura, 308, 329, 332, 357
Abiola, Moshood, 8
abortion, 57, 75, 113, 157, 216, 294, 344, 387, 442
absolute poverty, xii, 111, 115
Abu Sayyaf Group, 256, 272
accountability, 304, 308, 310, 314, 317, 325, 338, 353, 358–359, 373; horizontal, 322–323; vertical, 323, 328
acephalous societies. *See* stateless societies
Acquired Immune Deficiency Syndrome (AIDS), 6, 15–16, 111, 158–159, 409, 411–412; medicines, xii, 131, 411–412, 468; orphans, 159; Zimbabwe, 108, 180, 455. *See also* Human Immunodeficiency Virus
African National Congress (ANC), 57–58
African Union (AU), 357, 373, 382–383, 418, 425–426
agrarian reform, 76, 165
aid, foreign, 132–133, 137, 142, 157, 163, 356, 454, 468
AIDS orphans, 159
Al-Qaida, 211, 256, 262, 272–278, 301
amnesty, 268, 291, 293, 334, 384, 390–391, 453
Amnesty International, 258, 393–394
anarchists, anarchism, 126, 198, 201–202
ANC. *See* African National Congress
Andean Community of Nations (CAN), 372, 423
Annan, Kofi, 103, 132, 377, 382, 436, 467
antifeminists, 215–216
antiglobalization movements, 222, 250

Arias, Oscar, 416, 418, 467
Armenian genocide, 91, 243, 256, 431, 459
ASEAN. *See* Association of Southeast Asian Nations
"Asian values" argument, 11–12, 309
aspiration gap, 252, 279, 294
assimilation, 50, 257
Association of Southeast Asian Nations (ASEAN), 169–170, 283, 371–372, 435–436
asylum, 235, 405–407
Atatürk, Mustafa Kemal, 91–92, 241–243, 279, 296, 431; military, 268, 279; model for Pahlavis, 87, 294; secularism, 359
Atlantic Charter, 59
austerity plan, 142–144, 147–148, 159, 173, 178, 223. *See also* extended credit facility; structural adjustment program
authoritarians, 62–63, 123, 169, 217, 226, 229, 281, 335–348; China, 94; colonialism, 52–53; democratization, 147, 304–329, 392; fascism, 200; Indonesia, 246–247, 364; Mexico, 73; military assistance, 142, 468; Nigeria, 81, 426; Peru, 77, 233, 352, 450; Turkey, 360
autogolpe, 77
avian influenza (bird flu), 410
"Axis of Evil," 444, 456–457
Aztecs, 31–38, 40, 44, 69–70

Babangida, Ibrahim, 84, 334
balance of payments, 134, 143–144
Bandung Conference, 98, 435. *See also* Non-Aligned Movement
Beijing Consensus, 147, 185–186, 188

Biafran War, 80, 259, 290, 396
bin Laden, Osama, 261, 273–274, 469
bioterrorism, biological weapons, 277, 441. *See also* weapons of mass destruction
bird flu (avian influenza), 410
blue rights, 11–12. *See also* civil and political rights
Boff, Leonardo, 514
Born Frees, 238
bourgeoisie, 198
Brasilia Consensus, 160
Bretton Woods Conference, 484, 496
British South Africa Company (BSAC), 46, 82
Buddhism, Buddhists, 12, 37, 39, 58, 96–97, 208
Buhari, Muhammadu, 334
Bush, George W., 212, 416, 441–442, 468; Indonesia, 462; Iran, 456–457; Mexico, 448; Nigeria, 453; Zimbabwe, 455
Bush Doctrine, 275, 444, 476

cadre parties, 220. *See also* political parties
Calderón, Felipe, 145, 175, 232, 322, 351, 422–423, 476, 448; war on drugs, 285–287, 351
caliph, caliphate, 37, 78, 90, 196
CAN. *See* Andean Community of Nations
capacity, capacity building, 257, 315, 323–324, 327, 342, 369, 379; East Timor, 385; Nigeria, 236, 354
Cárdenas, Lázaro, 72–73, 232, 269
caretaker governments, 98, 269
cartel, 121, 134, 164, 188; drug, 150, 233, 273, 285–286, 327, 418
cash crops, 47–48, 78, 120–122, 149
Catholic Church, 49, 71, 75, 195, 202, 212, 245, 397; liberation theology, 197, 212, 486, 514
caudillo, 62–63, 71, 269, 476
CCP. *See* Chinese Communist Party
CCT. *See* conditional cash transfer
CEDAW. *See* Convention on the Elimination of All Forms of Discrimination Against Women
Chapter VII (United Nations), 377, 379, 476
chemical weapons, 277, 457. *See also* weapons of mass destruction
Chiapas, 253, 270
child labor, 127–129, 131, 221, 386, 393, 409, 442
child soldiers, 264–266, 390, 442
Chimurenga, 83–84, 291
China, People's Republic of, 2, 22, 175, 292, 427; civil society, 204, 207–208,

215, 221, 223–225, 227–229, 244–246, 396; economy, 104–113, 119, 122–128, 135–138, 142–150, 160–163, 167, 169–170, 185–187, 372, 436, 476, 488, 508; environment, 14, 402, 405; history, 34–35, 44, 46, 48, 51, 92–96, 217, 244, 503; Indonesia, 436; international relations, 375, 377–379, 398, 402, 405–406, 414–417, 433–435, 439, 440–441, 446, 532, 541; Iran, 182, 430–431; Mexico, 24; Nigeria, 178; Peru, 287, 522; politics, 203, 217, 307–308, 313, 319, 327, 337, 339–340; relations with the United States, 459, 463, 468–469; violence, 251–252, 254, 256–263, 266–267, 270, 278, 283, 298–300; Zimbabwe, 292, 427, 453, 455
Chinamasa, Patrick, 239
Chinese Communist Party (CCP), 62, 95, 199, 217, 221, 244–245, 258, 260, 262; history, 298–299, 361
Chinese Empire, 34, 40–41, 94
Chirac, Jacques, 132
Çiller, Tansu, 92
CITES. *See* Convention on International Trade in Endangered Species
civic culture, civic culture study, 204–205, 231, 312, 490. *See also* political culture
civil and political rights, 11–12, 77, 123, 195, 213, 221–222, 237, 306–307, 309, 336, 348, 354, 376, 451
civil control over military, military professionalism, 268, 333–334, 486
civil society, 73, 193–229, 231, 233–234, 237, 239–240, 243, 246–247, 285, 302, 305–306, 318, 347–386, 393, 430, 476–477; China, 244–246; Indonesia, 246–248; Iran, 239–241; Mexico, 73, 231–233; Peru, 233–235, 352; Turkey, 241–244, 360; "uncivil society," 204, 228, 243; Zimbabwe, 237–239
cleavages, 63, 248, 251–252, 268, 296, 328–329, 344, 477
clientelism, 209, 485. *See also* patron-client relations
Clinton, Bill, 277, 382–383, 416, 441, 450–451, 458, 460
Clinton, Hillary, 286, 331, 444
Cold War, 134, 308, 336, 435, 458, 486, 488, 538; IGOs, 375, 377, 379, 391; post–Cold War era, 147, 191, 309–310, 340, 342, 372, 413–414, 467; proxy wars, 261, 292, 460
collective action, 221–222, 234, 251, 492–493
collective security, 375, 477

colonialism, 43–67; economic system, 46–48, 64–66; rationales, 45, 49–53; resistance, 55–59, 66
common market, 169–170, 371–372, 477
Common Market of the South (Mercosur, Mercosul), 170, 372, 423
Commonwealth, 425, 428, 436
communism, 76, 198–199, 246, 283, 292, 460
comparative advantage, 47, 119, 131, 477
comparative studies, 4–5, 477
comprador, 75, 127, 477
conditional cash transfer (CCT), 166, 174, 477–478
conditionality, 147, 161, 164, 166–167
Conference of Berlin, 45, 51
Conference on Disarmament, 416
conflict diamonds, conflict minerals, 260, 271
Confucius, Confucian cultures, 12, 92–94, 299
conquest, 27, 44, 49, 57, 66, 79, 87, 480; China, 93–94, 208; Mexico, 37, 70; precolonial, 31–32, 37, 40–41; Turkey, 89–90
consensus model, 316
conservatism, 176, 195, 198, 215, 485
consolidation, 311–312, 326, 333–334, 354, 363–364, 426, 478
Convention on International Trade in Endangered Species (CITES), 405
Convention on the Elimination of All Forms of Discrimination Against Women, (CEDAW), 387–388, 441–442, 534, 538
Convention on the Rights of the Child (CRC), 386–387
Convention Relating to the Status of Refugees, 407–408
convergence, 110–111
co-optation, 340–341, 355, 489
corruption, 191, 325–326, 331, 336, 340–342, 396, 475, 478, 495; China, 244, 341, 362; civil society, 223, 227–228; colonialism, 53; Indonesia, 188–189, 247, 325, 341, 363; Iran, 206; Mexico, 145, 233, 286, 327, 350; neoliberalism, 145, 147; Nigeria, 80, 236, 268, 325; Peru, 352–353; Zimbabwe, 180, 237
Cortés, Hernán, 32, 40, 70
Council of Guardians, 89, 203, 210, 358–359, 415
counterhegemonic, 163–164, 166
coup d'état, 63, 72, 268, 311–312, 314, 317, 331, 334, 345, 348, 426, 486; financial, 148; Honduras, 373, 423; Indonesia, 98,

435, 461; Iran, 87, 127, 268, 294, 457; Mexico, 72–73, 287; Nigeria, 80–81, 268, 289, 290, 333, 354; Peru, 75, 77, 280, 288–289, 343, 352; Turkey, 268, 280, 297, 359–360, 432; Zimbabwe, 293
crimes against humanity, 274, 369, 388–391, 426, 492
cultural imperialism, 49, 53
cultural relativism, 11, 216, 478
Cultural Revolution, 95, 143, 262, 280, 299, 478
customs union, 170, 371–372, 478

Dalai Lama, 208
Darfur, 256, 383–384, 391, 407; China, 398, 434; peacekeepers, 373, 379, 382, 384, 426; women, 264, 270
debt, 119–120, 132–139, 141–145, 148–149, 154, 186, 425, 494; Indonesia, 187–189; Mexico, 71, 173–174; Nigeria, 81, 136–137, 178–179; Peru, 76, 175–177; United States, 103, 134, 139, 171; Zimbabwe, 180
debt crisis, 134, 173, 372
debt relief, 135, 137–139, 141–143, 148–149, 164, 373, 435, 468, 483, 487; Iran, 456; Jubilee, 138, 166, 397; Nigeria, 178–179, 452; Peru, 176; Zimbabwe, 136
debt service, 65, 134–138, 142, 148
decolonization, 61, 376, 435
dedazo, 350
deepening of democracy, 311–312
default, 65, 134, 137, 168, 173–174, 176, 187
deficit, 41, 65, 76, 94, 117, 134, 142–144, 166, 461
deforestation, xi, 13, 154, 371, 402
delegative democracies, 307, 323, 335–336, 479
democracy, 61–62, 191, 303, 372–373, 475, 479; China, 223, 362; civil society, 228–229; colonialism, 53, 60; donor, 336; economic, 164; electoral, 306; Indonesia, 98, 212, 363–364, 462–463; Iran, 240, 358–359; Islamic, 211, 231–233, 336, 363; liberal, 306–308, 332, 341, 347, 351, 485, 525; low intensity, 338, 342–343; Mexico, 286, 326, 348, 350–351, 421, 449; Nigeria, 78–80, 178–179, 229, 235–237, 321, 333, 353–355, 425, 452–453; Peru, 75, 176, 234, 289, 351–353, 425, 450; political culture, 205; socialist, 337; structural adjustment, 147–148, 162; Turkey, 243, 268, 359–360; Zimbabwe, 83, 85, 356, 427, 429, 455

democracy dividend, 142, 178, 324, 479, 481
democratic institutionalization, 317–318, 352, 479
Democratic Republic of Congo: 62, 155, 157; child soldiers, 266; colonialism, 48, 57; economy, 106, 252; mercenaries, 271; Lord's Resistance Army, 274; rape, 270, 153; war, 260, 270, 346, 379–381, 391, 405–406, 533
democratic transitions, 191, 305–306, 311, 319–321, 324, 333, 335, 345, 479; Indonesia, 392; Mexico, 231, 321, 349; Nigeria, 290, 333, 452; Peru, 308; reverse waves, 313, 347–348, 351
Deng Xiaoping, 95, 185, 217, 281, 283, 299, 361, 522
deregulation, 10, 130, 141, 146–147
desertification, 13, 154
deterrence, 414, 416, 439, 479
devaluation, 144, 153, 174, 183, 227, 494
development, 64–65, 101, 103–139, 143, 147–162, 199, 468, 479; aid, 132–133; alternative approaches, 163–171, 255, 373–374, 476, 478, 494; China, 186, 245, 319; colonialism, 51, 67; disease, 16, 156, 158, 476, 478, 488, 494; environment, 12, 153–155, 157, 403–404; Indonesia, 187, 209; Iran, 294; Mexico, 174; multinational corporations, 125–126; Nigeria, 80, 178–179, 291, 354; Peru, 74–77, 235, 288, 450; political development, 61; refugees, 153, 155; social development, 386–387; sustainable, 164, 167, 373–374, 494; *ujamaa,* 199; uneven, 348, 468; women, 113–115; Zimbabwe, 180, 238, 420
devotee party, 220, 480. *See also* political parties
dictatorships, 308, 313, 321, 335, 340, 344, 495; Cold War, 339; Mexico, 73; modernization, 123; Nigeria, 81, 354; Turkey, 323; US support for, 63, 441; Zimbabwe, 357. *See also* authoritarians
Dirty War, 288
disintegration, 40, 74, 159, 346–347, 364, 426, 480
displaced persons, 394–395, 405, 407
divide and conquer, divide and rule, 40, 84, 63, 70, 74, 137, 480
Doctors Without Borders (Médecins sans Frontières, MSF), 395
donor, 132–139, 141, 147–148, 153, 166–169; democracy, 336; political reform, 335–348; Zimbabwe, 180, 356, 428

drug cartel, 150, 233, 273, 285–286, 327, 418
drugs, 8, 15, 41, 159, 258, 265, 273; Mexico, 285–287, 307, 327, 350–351, 448–449; Nigeria, 425, 452; Peru, 77, 289, 352, 449–451; Turkey, 459. *See also* narcotics
due process, 11, 391, 480
Dutch East India Company, 46–47, 97, 124

East Timor, 51, 364, 376, 379–380; elections, 271, 301, 385, 436; violence, 270–271, 300, 390, 392, 436
ECF. *See* extended credit facility
Economic Community of West African States (ECOWAS), 426–427
Economic Community of West African States Monitoring Group (ECOMOG), 426
economic liberalization, 115, 141, 160, 166, 480, 494; Mexico, 174; Peru, 234
economic reform, 143–149, 152, 156–160, 209, 348, 480, 485, 491; China, 167, 299; environment, 154; IMF riots, 146, 161, 223; Mexico, 173–175, 350; Nigeria, 81, 179; political reform, 309, 337. *See also* economic liberalization
economic sanctions, 84, 88, 377, 379–380, 430, 454, 476
economic, social, and cultural rights, 11–12, 495
ECOSOC. *See* United Nations Economic and Social Council
efficacy, 205, 218, 349, 362, 480
electoral democracies, 306
embargo, 183, 295, 379, 440, 454, 457, 462
emerging economies, 2, 14, 103, 111–112, 117, 123, 148, 160–161
empires, 27–29, 31–41, 44–47, 65–66, 278, 446, 480, 494; China, 93–94, 259; colonialism, 47–54, 56, 59–60; Iran, 85–88; Mexico, 69–70; Nigeria, 78; Peru, 74; Turkey, 89–91; United States, 439
encomienda, 70, 74
environment, 12–14, 108, 111, 122, 169, 156–157, 164, 309, 371, 479, 481, 483, 494; international organizations, 201, 203, 208, 222–223, 234, 246, 375, 396–397; Iran, 182; issues, 401–405; Mexico, 174, 423; multinational corporations, 127–131, 146, 167; Nigeria, 178, 290; Peru, 177; structural adjustment, 153–155; Turkey, 431
Erbakan, Necmettin, 92, 242, 249, 323, 361, 432, 458

Erdogan, Recep Tayyip, 184, 242–243, 249, 323, 361, 432, 458
ethnic cleansing, 12, 256, 269, 369
European Union (EU), 141, 405, 418, 484; integration, 169–170, 372–373; multinational corporations, 124; sanctions, 275, 295, 428, 454; Turkey, 184, 243, 263, 296, 323, 359, 374, 431, 440, 469, 481, 525
exceptionalist, 326, 440–441, 469
export promotion, 144, 153
extended credit facility (ECF), 142–143, 148, 161–162, 223, 481, 485. *See also* structural adjustment program
extraterritoriality, 94, 440, 481

fallacy of electoralism, 306, 481
famine, 48, 74, 180, 396, 403
fascism, 198, 200, 212, 341
fatwa, 283, 296, 358, 415, 481
female-headed households, 114–115
feminism, 198, 201, 209, 213–215, 237
feminization of poverty, 113–114
"fifth world" countries, 2
first generation rights, 11. *See also* civil and political rights
"first world" countries, 2, 32, 330, 408
formal sector, 113, 150–151, 481
founding elections, 320–321, 481
"fourth world" countries, 2
Four Tigers, 122, 481
Fox, Vicente, 232, 321–322, 350–351, 421–422, 448
Free trade area (free trade zone), 35, 169–170, 174, 371–372
Fujimori, Alberto, 77, 176, 233–234, 288–289, 343, 352–353
Fujimori, Keiko, 353
fundamentalism, religious, 88, 196–198

García, Alan Perez, 76–77, 176–177, 234–235, 288–289, 344, 352–353, 424–425, 451
GATT. *See* General Agreement on Tariffs and Trade
Gender Empowerment Measure (GEM), 330, 332
Gender-Related Development Index (GDI), 112–113
General Agreement on Tariffs and Trade (GATT), 116
General Assembly. *See* United Nations General Assembly
Geneva Conventions, 388–389, 440
genocide, 10, 256, 259, 270, 369, 373, 391; Armenia, 91, 243, 431, 459; Darfur, 383–384; Rwanda, 260, 381–383, 388–389, 396, 418
Ghana, 2, 55, 120, 148, 311, 377, 383, 410, 453; empire, 34–35, 37–38, 40
Global Alliance Against Traffic in Women, 394
globalization, 6, 8–10, 12, 159–160, 163–164, 171, 408; antiglobalization movements, 222, 250; children, 129, 159; colonialism, 66–67, 148; "deglobalization," 166, 169; disease, 156–159, 409; environment, 14, 153–155; identity, 207–208; integration, 167, 170; Mexico, 175, 232; migration, 149; multinational corporations, 126–132; neoliberals, 115–119, 124, 141; regionalism, 371; women, 151–152
global warming, 13–14, 131, 156, 403, 423. *See also* greenhouse effect
Golkar, 246–247, 363
Grameen Bank, 163, 168
grassroots-based movements, 57, 83, 164, 167–169, 226, 246, 394, 397, 403
Great Leap Forward, 163, 185
greenhouse effect, 13–14, 153, 397, 402–404, 423, 441
green rights, 12
growth, 31, 61, 103–131, 141–147, 163; China, 153, 185–187, 246; democratization, 310, 323–324, 341; environment, 13–14, 153–155, 157; Indonesia, 187–188; Iran, 182, 294; Mexico, 73, 174–175, 232; Nigeria, 179; Peru, 76, 176–177, 234, 353; Turkey, 183; Zimbabwe, 180–181
guerilla, 59, 76, 249, 257–260, 278; China, 299; Nigeria, 291; Peru, 75–76, 287–289, 352, 450–451; Turkey, 297; Zimbabwe, 84–85, 262, 264, 292
Guzmán Reynoso, Abimael, 262, 287–288, 298

Habibie, B. J., 98, 301, 385, 436
Hamas, 261, 275, 295, 310
hard states, 338, 344–346
HDI. *See* Human Development Index
hegemon, 40, 426; counterhegemonic, 163–164, 166; neoliberal, 171; United States, 211, 434, 455–456, 460
Highly Indebted Poor Country (HIPC), 138–139, 141
HIV. *See* Human Immunodeficiency Virus
horizontal accountability, 317, 322–323, 358; Turkey, 359. *See also* accountability

HRC. *See* Human Rights Commission
Hu Jintao, 95, 281, 299, 341, 361, 460
Humala, Ollanta, 353
Human Development Index (HDI), 104–106; Mexico, 174
Human Immunodeficiency Virus (HIV), 7, 15–16, 157–160, 411–413; Millennium Development Goals, 111, 131; Zimbabwe, 108, 180, 455. *See also* Acquired Immune Deficiency Syndrome
humanitarian intervention, 382–386, 394–395
human rights, 6–12; children, 129, 265; China, 398; democratization and, 313–314, 317, 332; Indonesia, 152–153, 300–302, 364, 461; Iran, 182, 240–241, 430; Mexico, 269–270, 327–329, 334, 416–418; Nigeria, 425–426, 452; Peru, 75, 235, 288–289, 352; refugees and migrants, 405–409; Turkey, 184, 263, 431, 459; United States, 440–442, 444, 450; women, 214, 224; Zimbabwe, 427–429
Human Rights Commission (UN), 379, 384, 442. *See also* Human Rights Council
Human Rights Council (UN), 379
human security, 108, 164–167
Hutu, 256, 260

ICBL. *See* International Campaign to Ban Landmines
ICC. *See* International Criminal Court
ICRC. *See* International Red Cross and Red Crescent Movement
ICTR. *See* International Criminal Tribunal for Rwanda
ICTY. *See* International Criminal Tribunal for the Former Yugoslavia
identity, 9, 27, 50, 58, 205–215, 256, 328, 344–347; civil society, 228; ideologies, 197, 200; Indonesia, 95–97, 246–248, 364, 463; Iran, 182, 196, 457; Kurds, 243, 255–256, 297–298, 458–459; LGBT, 215; Mexico, 447; multinational corporations, 124–125; Nigeria, 235–236; political parties, 200; religious, 196, 210–213, 374; social movements, 223–224; Turkey, 92, 184, 241, 243, 298
ideology, 8, 56, 194–205, 217, 310; China, 93–95, 208, 221, 244–245, 361; feminism, 213–216; Indonesia, 212, 248; Iran, 86–87, 240, 359; Islamism, 58, 211–212; liberation theology, 212, 213; Mexico, 232; Nigeria, 77–78, 252–253; Peru, 289; religion, 37, 58, 196; Turkey, 241–242, 296–298, 360–361

IFIs. *See* international financial institutions
IGOs. *See* international governmental organizations
IMF. *See* International Monetary Fund
imperialism, 45–53, 66, 82, 199
Inca, 32–44, 74–75, 233
Indonesia, Republic of: civil society, 209, 212, 246–248; economics, 147, 187–189; history, 47–48, 95–99, 207; international relations, 385, 390, 435–437; politics, 62–63, 341–343, 363–364; relations with the United States, 443–444, 461–463; violence, 152–153, 257, 271–272, 300–302, 334, 407–408
Indonesian Democratic Party–Struggle (PDI-P), 98. *See also* Sukarnoputri, Megawati
industrialization, 13, 47, 66, 122, 134, 209, 403; Iran, 182; Mexico, 209
infant industries, 66, 117, 123
informal sector, 150–151, 158
İnönü, Ismet, 92, 359
Institutional Revolutionary Party (PRI), 62, 210, 322; economic policies, 173; foreign policy, 421–422; transitional politics, 73, 231–233, 269, 349–351
integration, 167–169, 372–373; Peru, 423–424
interdependence, 8–16, 65–66
Intergovernmental Panel on Climate Change (IPCC), 13. *See also* United Nations, environment
International Campaign to Ban Landmines (ICBL), 417–418. *See also* Ottawa Treaty
International Court of Justice (ICJ), 88, 376, 391, 424
International Criminal Court (ICC), 274, 384, 390–391, 422, 441
International Criminal Tribunal for Rwanda, 388–389
International Criminal Tribunal for the Former Yugoslavia, 388
international financial institutions (IFIs), 65, 115, 118, 141–162; debt crises, 134–139; reform, 161–162; structuralist critique, 160–162; US policies, 456
international governmental organizations (IGOs), 116, 164, 370–393, 425; cooperation with NGOs, 417
International Monetary Fund (IMF), 116–124, 141–149, 164, 337, 370; debt crises, 134–139; environment, 153–155; IMF riot, 146, 161, 223; Indonesia, 189, 436; Mexico, 174–175, 423; Nigeria, 81, 178–179; Peru, 76–77, 176–177; reform,

161–162; Turkey, 183–184; Zimbabwe, 180. *See also* extended credit facility
International Red Cross and Red Crescent Movement (ICRC), 394–395, 397, 417
Internet, 8, 107, 203–204, 222, 229, 250; "antisocial" media, 204; China, 204, 245, 300, 396; Iran, 222, 239, 396; Mexico, 233; Nigeria, 320
intifada, 262
IPCC. *See* Intergovernmental Panel on Climate Change
Iran, Islamic Republic of: civil society, 196, 203, 210, 215, 222, 225, 227, 239–241, 396; economics, 181–183; history, 85–89; international relations, 343, 378–379, 408, 414–415, 429–431, 459–461; politics, 206, 307–308, 336–340, 357–359; relations with the United States, 275–276, 440–441, 444, 455–458; violence, 254–255, 261, 263, 293–296, 265–266, 268–270, 277–279, 282–283, 344
Iraq: economy, 142; history, 45, 51; international relations, 254, 265, 295, 379–380, 458; Islam, 196, 429; Kurds, 243, 255–256, 276–277, 298, 432, 459; relations with the United States, 132, 440–445, 457–459, 469
irredentist wars, 51, 207, 424
Islam, 37, 58, 430, 443; history, 196; identity, 208, 210, 256, 457; Indonesia, 96–98, 187, 209, 247–248, 257, 301, 363, 462–463; Iran, 85–89, 181–183, 225–227, 239–241, 279, 282–283, 294–296, 357–359; Islamic Jihad, 261; Islamism, 197, 211–212, 275, 310, 336; Kurds, 225, 255; Nigeria, 77–78, 236, 259; relations with the United States, 443–445, 456, 459; Turkey, 89–92, 241–244, 268, 297, 360; violence, 254, 261, 272–273; women, 214–215
Israel, 52; regional relations, 261, 374, 380, 414, 429, 458; relations with Palestinians, 265, 275, 445–456; relations with the United States, 132, 445–446
Israeli-Palestinian conflict, 52, 262, 265, 275, 445

Jiang Zemin, 95, 217, 281, 299, 361
jihad, 58, 78, 211; Islamic Jihad, 261; *Jihad v. McWorld,* 208
Jonathan, Goodluck, 290–291, 333, 426–427, 355
Juárez, Benito, 71, 195
Jubilee 2000, Jubilee USA Network, 137–139, 166, 397

Justice and Development Party (AKP), 211, 242, 323, 360, 432

Kashmir, 253–254, 273
Kemalism, 92
Khamenei, Ayatollah Ali Hussein, 89, 225, 239–241, 358–359, 415, 430, 456
Khatami, Ayatollah Mohammed, 89, 225, 241, 357, 429
Khomeini, Ayatollah Ruhollah Musavi, 269, 357; revolutionary, 88–89, 182, 216, 279, 282, 294–295, 456; theocracy, 240, 296; war with Iraq, 429
KMT. *See* Nationalist Party
Koran. *See* Quran
Kurdistan Workers Party (PKK), 243, 262, 276, 283, 296–298, 432, 459
Kurds, 51, 255, 432, 459; Iraq, 256, 277, 384; Turkey, 243, 297–298, 458
Kyoto Protocol, 403–404

Laissez-faire economics, 115–116, 123, 185, 238. *See also* Washington Consensus
landmines, 229, 385, 416–417, 441. *See also* International Campaign to Ban Landmines; Ottawa Treaty
land reform. *See* agrarian reform
League of Nations, 45, 51–52, 88, 375–377
legitimacy, 216–218, 259, 338; China, 361–362; colonialism, 58–59; crises, 161, 309, 350; democratization, 311, 323–328, 333; Indonesia, 364; international organizations, 370, 380, 392, 419; Iran, 88, 222, 295; Mexico, 350–351; Nigeria, 355; Turkey, 360; Zimbabwe, 356
liberal democracy, 306–308, 332, 341, 351, 485, 525; alternatives to, 341, 347
liberalism, 57, 71–72, 194–195; Iran, 88, 240, 336; liberal feminism, 213; neoliberalism, 77, 101– 104, 119, 141, 162, 163, 171, 224, 310; Peru, 75–76
Liberation theology (1998), 212–213
Liu Xiaobo, 244
López Obrador, Andrés Manuel, 163, 232, 318, 350–351, 422
Lord's Resistance Army (LRA), 274, 391
low intensity democracy, 338, 342–343
LRA. *See* Lord's Resistance Army

Majles, 87–89
malaria, 15, 111, 156–158, 396, 409, 412–413
malnutrition, 159
Mandate of Heaven, 93–94, 216
mandatory system, 44–46, 52
Mandela, Nelson, 52, 57, 281, 411

Mao Zedong, 95, 185, 361; CCP leadership, 220, 298–299; influence abroad, 76–77, 199, 287–289; legacy, 217, 282–283, 361; revolution, 259–260, 278–279
maquiladoras, 112, 128, 174
Marcos, Subcomandante, 279
Marx, Karl, 198–199, 209; China, 185, 259; liberation theology, 212; Marxist Leninism, 58, 258, 261; Peru, 272, 287; Turkey, 297; US opposition, 372
May 4th Movement (China), 94, 244
Ma Ying-jeou, 258
Mbeki, Thabo, 281, 373, 429
media, 203–204, 218–219, 226–229, 318; "antisocial," 204; China, 186, 244–245; Indonesia, 247, 300–301, 364; Iran, 89; Nigeria, 354; social media, 9, 204; Turkey, 228–229, 396; Zimbabwe, 356–357. *See also* Internet; Reporters Without Borders
MEND. *See* Movement for the Emancipation of the Niger Delta
mercantilism, 46–47
Mercosur. *See* Common Market of the South
Mexico, United Mexican States: civil society, 209, 213–215, 231–233, 387; economics, 112, 134–136, 145–147, 175; history, 48, 56, 69–73, 195; international relations, 421–423; politics, 307, 318, 321, 349–351; relations with the United States, 406, 447–449; violence, 63, 201, 269, 280, 285–287, 326–327, 332
microidentities, 208. *See also* identity
migrant labor, 48, 105, 120, 158
migrants, migration, 8, 149–150, 158, 160, 201, 344; China, 208; human rights, 405–409; Indonesia, 248, 405; Mexico, 448–449; Turkey, 227; to the United States, 406; Zimbabwe, 83
militaries, 201, 203, 263–272, 279, 340, 345–346, 413–418; China, 94, 298–300, 361, 433–435; civilian control, 94, 298–300, 361, 433–435; colonialism, 35–37, 40, 43–47, 51–52, 61–64; contempt for human rights, 153, 225, 229; Indonesia, 98, 248, 300–302, 363–364, 385; Iran, 87, 294–295, 358; Mexico, 73, 287; Nigeria, 77, 81, 226, 235–236, 289, 353–354; paramilitaries, 254, 258–259; Peru, 74–77, 233, 252–253, 288–291; precolonial, 29; Turkey, 92, 210, 241–243, 296–297, 359–360, 374; United States, 439–441, 445, 448, 450–453, 457, 458, 462, 468; Zimbabwe, 82–84, 292–293

military rule, 61–62, 268–270, 278; Iran, 294; Nigeria, 81, 289, 354; opposition to, 214; Peru, 76, 233
militia, 249, 258, 260, 263, 269–271; Indonesia, 301, 334, 385, 390, 392, 408; Iran, 249, 344; Lord's Resistance Army, 274; Nigeria, 229, 291; Peru, 288; Sudan, 383, 391
Millennium Development Goals (MDGs). *See* United Nations Millennium Development Goals
missionaries, 49–50, 70, 79, 245
Mnangagwa, Emmerson, 239
MNCs. *See* multinational corporations
Moctezuma, 40, 70
modernization, 51, 72, 87, 92, 208, 283, 434
Mohammed (prophet), 196, 211
monocultural economies, 112, 119, 121, 178
Mossadeq, Mohammed, 67, 88, 294, 457
mother country, 43, 46, 49, 53, 55–56, 60–61, 84
Movement for Democratic Change (MDC), 344, 356–357, 428; economic changes, 181; mass action, 237–239; unions, 221; violence, 293
Movement for the Emancipation of the Niger Delta (MEND), 291, 453
MRTA. *See* Túpac Amaru Revolutionary Movement
MSF. *See* Doctors Without Borders (Médecins sans Frontières)
Mugabe, Robert, 292, 335; economic policy, 179–181, 293; international relations, 427–429; opposition to, 237–239; politics, 336, 339–341, 343–345, 355–357; populism, 206, 210; relations with the United States, 454–455; rise to power, 84–85
Mujuru, Joyce, 239
Multilateral Debt Relief Initiative (MDRI), 138, 487
multilateralism, 116–117, 189, 370–375, 398, 401–404, 419, 425–426, 430
multinational corporations (MNCs), 146; globalization, 9, 65; low-income countries, 118; Mexico, 174; neoliberal ideology, 115, 124–128; Nigeria, 178; opposition to, 129–130, 164–166
multinational states, 51, 253, 255, 328
Mutambara, Arthur, 356
mutual assured destruction, 64, 261, 414

NAFTA. *See* North American Free Trade Agreement
NAM. *See* Non-Aligned Movement